LEGEND OF THE FALL

An Evaluation of
William Branham and His Message

Peter M. Duyzer

2014

Independent Scholar's Press

Legend of the Fall
by Peter M. Duyzer

Copyright © Peter Duyzer 2014

No part of this book may be reproduced, or utilized in any form, or stored in a retrieval system, or transmitted in any form or by any means - electronic, mechanical, photocopy, recording, or any other – except for brief quotations, without the prior permission of the publisher.

Published by Independent Scholars Press, CanBooks, Canada

Unless otherwise noted, Scripture quotations are from the King James Version Bible.

The author has striven to ensure the accuracy of Internet addresses at the time of writing, however the author cannot guarantee these urls will not contain errors, nor that these urls will not change, or disappear.

Library and Archives Canada
Duyzer, Peter M.

LEGEND OF THE FALL An Evaluation of William Branham and His Message

ISBN   978-1-927581-15-5
1. Apologetics. 2. Christianity and other religions.

Front cover artwork "Dragon's Hearts" by Myriam Catrin, used with permission
Front cover design: Lee Weeks

Dedication

Dedicated to Mieke, the wife of my youth and my faithful companion for over fifty years. Without her patience and sacrifice this book could not have been written. She endured many lonely nights, while I was in my office at my computer, or in libraries, doing research.

Legend of the Fall

Few people have investigated and analyzed the life and teachings of William Marrion Branham in greater detail than Peter Duyzer. Coming from within Branham's movement, itself, Duyzer demonstrates a unique understanding of both the man and his message. By all accounts Branham was both a fascinating and captivating religious figure of the twentieth century. His claims to be a prophet, a healer, and one who could disclose personal information of others, including diagnoses of their medical conditions, wowed many and earned him a very faithful following today. What are we to make of astounding claims and alleged activities like these? In this book, Duyzer has done the work that few others are either able or willing to do. As a trained theologian himself, he has looked deeply into Branham's sermons and unveiled the teachings embedded there, giving necessary comparisons with biblical teaching. He has also provided some background on the man himself, making this a comprehensive resource. Whether you are a follower, a critic, or simply a neutral observer, this book is a must read for anyone wanting to understand William Branham, his message, or even his life story.

Paul Chamberlain
Associate Professor of Apologetics & Philosophy
Director, Institute of Christian Apologetics,
Trinity Western University (ACTS division)

William Marrion Branham was one of the most interesting figures of popular religion during the twentieth century. As an influential healing evangelist of post-WWII America, he captivated crowds with his humble demeanor. Yet, the latter part of his life was marked by controversial doctrine and a loss of popularity among the Pentecostal masses. The Branham story remains fascinating because his doctrinal teachings endure as the "Message," and followers today believe Branham to be the prophet of the end-time. In this book, Peter Duyzer, after painstaking and thorough research into Branham's voluminous sermons (which serve as sacred writings to his followers) provides a thorough examination of Branham's doctrine. Readers who are interested in Branham's message, apologetics, the popularity of "new religious movements," and/or the popularity of "end-time" religious groups, will want to read Duyzer's analysis.

Doug Weaver
Professor of Religion
Baylor University

There is one name that represents the signs and wonders and healing movement more than any other in our modern history -- that is William Branham. He has become the source of inspiration and a ministry model for many today, yet much of his life and teachings are veiled. Peter Duyzer's book is unique, because of Peter's former background being part of the "message" believers. His research is thorough, as he takes us behind this veil and presents pertinent information not found anywhere else on this master of supernatural stories. Branham's claim to be the last days prophet to the church and his illness diagnoses are challenged and refuted. With much documentation and insight Peter shows the internal contradictions in his sermons, and spiritual experiences that are in opposition to the Bible. I highly recommend the book Legend of the Fall to anyone interested in learning about William Branham and modern church history.

Mike Oppenheimer
Director of Let Us Reason Ministries

Thirty-two years ago I was a follower of William Branham's "Message". My pastor back then had criticized a booklet which dared to suggest that if William Branham wasn't lying about having seen seven angels while hunting Javelina in the Arizona desert, then he was hunting out of season. That claim troubled me greatly. I checked it out for myself, and within 2 months I became a former follower of the Message. Little did I know that the man who wrote the booklet that would change the direction of my life would one day become my good friend and fellow servant of the Lord, Peter Duyzer. Peter's diligent research has led to the publication of his book, The Legend of the Fall, which I believe is the most comprehensive examination of the life and teachings of William Branham available. I highly recommend it not only to those who want to know more about William Branham and his teachings, but to those who still follow his Message. I guarantee that regardless of how much you know about William Branham, you will be surprised at the amount of relevant information you didn't know after reading this book.

John Kennah, Owner of :
William Branham and His Message Website
Host of Message of William Branham Support Forum

Peter Duyzer's book, "Legend of the Fall" changed my life. If you have ever heard the name William Marrion Branham, you need to read this book. It will set you free. *Reba Gould, Former Follower, Tucson, AZ*

I began to search on the Internet and came across Peter Duyzer's book, "Legend of the Fall". In this book the lies in William Branham Life Story and in his message are exposed one by one, until nothing is left to hold on to. It was a revelation! *Peter Coen, Belgium*

Years of research and vast numbers of references make "Legend of the Fall" the most authoritative book available to date regarding the ministry and false doctrines of William Branham. It is impossible to consider the preponderance of evidence and come away without a new view of Branham's legacy. *Jennifer Collins, Former Follower, Jeffersonville, IN*

Mr. Duyzer's research is a treasure for people currently or formerly involved with the ministry of William Branham. He knows it from the inside out. *Former Follower, Jeffersonville, Indiana*

With all of the information now available regarding William Branham's ministry, it is exciting to finally have a concise and well referenced work that brings all of the facts together in one place. I would highly recommend "Legend of the Fall" to all fellow students of Truth. *Emily Arndt, Missionary serving with Christian Veterinary Mission in Uganda, East Africa*

"'Legend of the Fall' is a goldmine of well-referenced facts. This book isn't just opinion: its the cold hard truth about William Branham's life." *Jeremy Bergen, Editor, Believethesign.com*

My grandfather was William Branham's associate, the current pastor of Branham's home church of Jeffersonville…Legend of the Fall was fundamental in my realization that the myths we believed were in error…[and did] not line up with recorded history, government documents, or even different versions of the stories Branham told as he travelled from town to town. The book was painful, each line tearing away threads of fiction that were woven around the worship that had molded each of us…Ultimately, this book was the reason behind my decision to help extricate those worshipping this man, who deceived the masses. Without its gentle approach to difficult truths, the magical spell cast by fictional heart-warming stories could not be broken. Thanks to Legend of the Fall, lives are being changed around the globe. *John Collins, Author and Webmaster, Seek Ye The Truth*

Table of Contents

Dedication		i
Endorsments		ii
Abbreviations		vii
Acknowledgments		ix
Foreword		xi
Introduction		xiii
Preface		xv
Chapter One	My Story	1
Chapter Two	Who Was William Branham?	7
Chapter Three	William Branham, A Man Sent From God?	23
Chapter Four	Wm. Branham's Claims of Poverty	39
Chapter Five	Wm. Branham's Non-Religious Background	56
Chapter Six	Wm. Branham's Angelic Commissions 1- 3	84
	No. One -In his mother's womb	
	No. Two -At his Birth	
	No. Three- At Seven Years old	
Chapter Seven	Wm. Branham's Angelic Commissions 4-6	96
	No. Four - At Fourteen years old	
	No. Five - In the hospital in 1932	
	No. Six –At the Ohio River	
Chapter Eight	Wm. Branham's Angelic Commissions 7-9	113
	No. Seven - In his Yard in 1944	
	No. Eight - In his Cabin in 1946	
	No. Nine -In Houston, TX, in 1950	
Chapter Nine	Wm. Branham's Angelic Commissions 10	125
	No. Ten - In Arizona in 1963	
Chapter Ten	Types of healing	140
Chapter Eleven	Healing in the Scriptures	151
Chapter Twelve	A Gift of divine healing	155
Chapter Thirteen	Healing Ministry of Wm. Branham	164
Chapter Fourteen	Wm. Branham's Healing Cases Examined	185
Chapter Fifteen	Major Prophetic Claims Examined	201
Chapter Sixteen	Holy Scripture and the Perfections of God	213
Chapter Seventeen	The Person of God	223
Chapter Eighteen	The Person of Christ	250
Chapter Nineteen	The Person of the Holy Spirit	266
Chapter Twenty	Creation of Man	273
Chapter Twenty-One	The Fall (Serpent's Seed)	288
Chapter Twenty-Two	The Fall – Hermeneutic	303
Chapter Twenty-Thre	Salvation	309
Chapter Twenty-Four	Summary Chapter	319
Bibliography		326

ABBREVIATIONS

AH	AuthorHouse
AP	Abingdon Press
APH	Augsburg Publishing House
BA	Baker Academic
BBH	Baker Book House Co
BHP	Broadman and Holman Publishers
CFN	Christ for the Nations
COJLDS	Church of Jesus Christ and the Latter-Day Saints
CART	Canada Apologetics Research Team
CP	Crown Publishers
CPH	Concordia Publishing House
DNP	Deseret News Press
EMC	Eastern Mennonite College
EPC	Eerdmans Publishing Co.
FHRC	Fleming H. Revell Co.
FHW	Fitzhenry and Whiteside
GAU	George Allen and Unwin
GP	Greenwood Press
GR	Gale Research
HC	Harper Collins
HHP	Harvest House Publishers.
HP	Hendrickson Publishers.
HR	Harper & Row.
HrldP	Herald Press.
HuP	Humanities Press
IUP	Indiana University Press
IVP	Intervarsity Press
JCC	James Clarke & Co
Jeff.	Jeffersonville
KCP	Kenneth Copeland Publications
MCMP	MacMillan Press
MPHU	Magnes Press, Hebrew University
MP	Moody Press.
MPC	Miller Publishing Co.
MSG	Message
MUP	Mercer U. Press

OUP	Oxford University Press
PB	Penguin Books
PBP	Particular Baptist Press
PP	Pandora Press
RKP	Routledge & Kegan Paul
SWP	Spoken Word Publications
TTB	Tucson Tabernacle Books
TTC	T. & T. Clark
VH	Voice of Healing
VMI	Vineyard Ministries International
WBEA	William Branham Evangelistic Assoc.
WBP	William Branham Publishing
WCL	William Carey Library
WMB	William Marrion Branham
WT	Int'l Bible Students Association Watch Tower Bible and Tract Association
WTM	Western Tract Mission
YUP	Yale University Press
ZPH	Zondervan Publishing House

ACKNOWLEDGMENTS

First I must state my utter regret, and deep repentance, not only for being involved, but also for deluding and attracting many people into this NRM (New Religious Movement), called "The Message."

I suppose that I am, in some respects, a product of all the people that have influenced my life. This book was not written in a vacuum, but was shaped through my reading, studies, and sermons I have heard in the past. I am thankful to my late father, who read the Scriptures to us at every meal of every day from earliest memory, until I left home. This deposited in me a wealth of Scriptural information, which has acted as a kind of filter throughout my life. This filter, subconsciously, seems to pick up on "stuff" that is not Scriptural. While I may not react to certain things immediately, but ponder things in my heart, eventually the time arrives when I have to act upon things. During my "Message" years, certain people continued to counsel me in love, regarding Wm. Branham and his Message. Thanks to people like Chet and Opal McGriff, a couple who spent their lives preaching the Gospel, as itinerant evangelists. Chet, who up until his mid-nineties and his death, never without tears, pled with people to embrace the Saviour. Thanks to Bill Badke, Librarian at Trinity Western University, for his assistance in locating many books. I must thank all my professors at ACTS Seminary, who shaped my thinking in many areas, especially Dr. Larry Perkins, whose input was very valuable. I also want to thank Dr. C. Douglas Weaver, for the work he did on Wm. Branham, but also for steering me to John J. Kennah. John has been very helpful in providing me with needful information and has become a very dear friend.

I must give a special thanks to my good friend Ray Chaffee who was with me back in 1977 during the early stages of research for this book. I also need to thank Joe Haynes, who made possible the early electronic version of this book, as well as my website, www.wmbranham.net. Since my research, especially in the last while, many people have come out of the Message of Wm. Branham, people that have taken up the torch, so to speak. I would be remiss if I did not thank all the posters and co-moderators on the forum, "*Examining The Message of William Branham*" hosted by John Kennah, for all the input, correction and love shown to me. For privacy reasons they must remain anonymous. Many have become friends, with whom I trust to have a continued relationship. Most of these forum posters know me as "Tsur," (meaning Rock) a name conferred on me by my esteemed Jewish Hebrew teachers, while studying Hebrew in Vancouver, BC. I must also thank John Collins of *http://www.seekyethetruth.com*

whose grandfather is the Pastor of Branham Tabernacle, in Jeffersonville, IN. John's work is also impacting many people around the world. Thank you to Rod Bergen, at www.believethesign.com, who finally escaped the clutches of Wm. Branham's message, is a man I always respected, even while he remained in the Msg until quite recently. A big thanks to Joe and Anna Grace Barone whose website *searchingforvindication.com* has done great and honest research into the claims of Wm. Branham. These sources have discovered much needed information which I have incorporated, at the eleventh hour, into my book. Please avail yourselves of these invaluable "new" resources. Thank you, Myriam Catrin, for giving us permission to use your art "Dragon's Hearts" for our front cover. To my publisher and editor - Thank you for all your help and for your patience. Also a big thank you to my good friend Lee Weeks, for his design of the front cover. Last, but not least, I want to thank my friend, teacher, mentor and former pastor, Dr. Vern Middleton, who has been like a father to me (not because of his age). I am sure there are scores of people I've not mentioned, you know who you are. God bless you all.

FOREWORD

Peter Duyzer's book, "*Legend Of The Fall*" is a timely document exposing the heretical teachings of William Branham. Most books on cults or new religious movements have ignored the Branham movement. Others who have written about William Branham have tended to classify his movement as fringe Christianity. Duyzer has corrected this pattern by a thorough investigation of the sermons, and statements of Branham. Duyzer's research, in effect, has provided us with a "systematic theology" of William Branham's beliefs and teachings. It is obvious from the contents of this book that Branhamism is more than a group of misguided Charismatics with a few points of theology gone awry.

Duyzer has demonstrated that Branham's theology was shaped by many factors, besides the Bible. Mormonism, Free Masonry, numerology, astrology and psychic concepts all shaped his thinking. Historically many of these cultic and occultic forces have tended to draw from one another, much the same way elements within the New Age Movement are being shaped by the general presuppositions of others today. The prophetic pronouncements of Branham were hardly "words from the Lord" as most turned out to be false and had to be re-interpreted to save face.

The influence of his prophecies did not cease with Branham's demise but continues on in other movements. A well-known seminary studied Branham's healing techniques shown on a Branham healing film, in an effort to understand how the Holy Spirit produced healing power. Even Branham's claim that healing power was evident by the trembling of the hands became a pattern for healing ministry among certain students.

Peter Duyzer writes from the perspective of one who was intimately involved in this movement. This factor adds a dimension of passion and conviction to his statements, and also lends credibility to his research, as he knew the people, and the places where resources could be found.

Although Branham has been characterized as being humble and a very simple man, it becomes evident through Duyzer's research that in the last ten years of his life he progressively moved to being an egocentric, narcissistic, self-centred individual where even Scriptures were interpreted as placing him centre stage. Branham's grave is marked by a stone pyramid, which places him among the who's who of Christian history.

Branhamism is a heresy with a very dangerous potential. The Branham web page continuously propagates the main features of his teachings. The material has been translated into several languages such as Spanish and Korean. The Branham movement has gone into a 'stabilizing mode'. The Branham churches have shifted to a defensive mode. Their church conferences emphasize 'ministering stability in trembling times.' They will have to do a lot of fence mending in the face of this publication by Peter Duyzer.

Vern Middleton, Ph. D.
Professor Emeritus of Missiology and Church
Northwest Baptist Seminary
at ACTS Seminary at
Trinity Western University
Langley, BC, Canada

INTRODUCTION

This book has been a work in progress ever since my wife and I came out of, what is called, the *Message of William Marrion Branham*, or *The Message*, or *Msg*, back in late 1978. The reason we left is found in the Chapter called *My Story*. The initial research commenced without helps, just some Msg books and tapes, which had to be personally transcribed. In 1978 this author produced several pamphlets on an old stencil machine. Later, the need for more research, as well as the honing of his writing skills, became clear. I returned to school and I graduated with a MA in Modern Apologetics and Cross-cultural Studies.

Especially for the past few years, some sincere followers of Wm. Branham have reacted against writings by people denying, or questioning Branham's claims. These followers have created websites to defend and to establish Branham's claims. However, a number of them have found Wm. Branham's claims to be unfounded. In fact, some of them have now openly rejected these claims as false and fabricated. In turn, many, including leaders, have now left that movement. Why, in the first place, would anyone, especially well educated people, fall into such error? The Apostle Paul writes, "because spiritual things are spiritually discerned." (1 Cor 2: 14). That is why, as seen already in Acts 8: 9-10, spiritual deception is very powerful:

But there was a certain man, called Simon, which beforetime in the same city used sorcery, and bewitched the people of Samaria, giving out that himself was some great one: To whom they all gave heed, from the least to the greatest, saying, This man is the great power of God.

My intended audience is those wanting to gain in-depth information about WMB that mostly consists of original research. This is intended to be an apologetics handbook. The chapters may contain some informational overlap, for which I ask my readers' indulgence. Though I do not find delight in exposing error, expose it I must. For this I do not apologize. Rather, my great desire would be that Message believers would read this book and become convinced of the need to only believe the Word of God as written in God's Bible. My prayer is that they consequently come to a place where they serve Christ alone.

Throughout this book I use "the author" rather than my name or personal pronoun.

Soli Deo Gloria,
Peter M. Duyzer
2014

About the Author

Peter M. Duyzer holds a Master's degree (MACS) with a double major in Modern Apologetics and Cross-cultural Studies, from ACTS Seminary, in Langley, BC, Canada. He has been in pastoral ministry in British Columbia and overseas. Peter is married to Anna Maria (Mieke), and together they have six children and eight grandchildren. They reside in Langley, British Columbia.

PREFACE

This book is written with the view of establishing to what extent William Branham's "Legend of the Fall" and its resultant teaching, is supported by Biblical Revelation. The Fall of mankind, as shown in Genesis, reveals foundational teachings regarding our Creator and his creation. If the foundation of any kind of structure is faulty, the building *will* fail. This book deals with what is commonly called *The Message* of William M. Branham, (hereafter, Msg or WMB). WMB taught the Fall of mankind did not consist of the literal eating of the fruit of the Tree of the Knowledge of Good and Evil. Rather, it was caused by the Serpent, an upright being, having intercourse with Eve and producing Cain, the Son of Satan. Eve afterwards brought forth Abel, resulting from her later relationship with Adam. WMB called his teaching Serpent's Seed.[1] There exists considerable debate regarding an exact definition of *The Message*. To date no WMB follower has been able to define it; hence the many factions within its ranks. Serpent's Seed is not an isolated sub-doctrine, but is the linchpin of all WMB taught.[2] Serpent's Seed affected his view of the Godhead, creation, the Fall, salvation, etc. In general, within evangelical Christianity, the doctrine of the Fall of mankind is seen as an event in which Eve partakes of the fruit of the Tree of the Knowledge of Good and Evil. Through her act of disobedience, in which Adam collaborated, subsequently, the whole human race was plunged into death. This is understood either in a historical or a figurative understanding, with the same underlying assumption, that it was Adam and Eve's disobedience that caused death.

WMB raised particular challenges to the doctrine of the Fall of Mankind by introducing an allegorical/mystical interpretation. He referred to it as the Mystery of the Serpent's Seed.[3] Out of WMB's 1,177+ recorded messages his teaching about the Serpent's Seed is found in over one hundred of them. He started this teaching in and around 1953 and continued to teach it until his death in December 1965.

Besides the hundreds of sermons that have been transcribed and published there are also two very important WMB books that deal with the Serpent's Seed. One is *An Exposition Of The Seven Church Ages* (referred to as the Church Age book) and the other is *The Revelation Of The Seven Seals* commonly called the Seven Seals book. The *Seven Seals* comprises a compilation of all his sermons on the topic of the seven seals. It was actually printed prior to the *Church Age* book, which incorporated the seven seals mystery teachings, including WMB's Serpent's Seed. Other publications exist regarding WMB's life and teaching, either pro or con. Some are simply biographical, or historical. There do not appear to be any that deal in real depth with WMB's overall theology and praxis. There are also a number of Internet sites, again either pro or con. All audio and audio transcribed messages of WMB are under public domain.

Notes:

[1] This particular Serpent's Seed teaching is WMB's own version, variants of Serpent's Seed are held by others.

[2] If one is not a believer in any Restoration movement, then WMB, as Elijah the Restorer, would no longer be relevant. Subsequently all his teaching would be redundant.

[3] WMB AT, *The Breach between the Seven Church Ages and the Seven Seals*, Mar. 17, 1963, Jeff., IN, "Now, but it is a Book, a mysterious Book. It's a Book of Redemption. (We'll get into that in a little while.) And now, we know that this Book of Redemption will not be thoroughly understood —it's probed at through six church ages, but at the end, when the seventh angel begins to sound his mystery, he winds up all of the loose ends that these fellows probed at, and the mysteries comes down from God as the Word of God and reveals the entire revelation of God. Then the godhead and everything else is settled. All the mysteries: serpent's seed and whatever more is to be revealed"

Chapter One
My Story

    The following chapter tells my particular story. As a babe in Christ, I did not have very much understanding. This was despite the fact of having been reared in a home where the Bible was read at every meal. Throughout my life I wondered why life in Bible times was so different from today. Already as a very young boy, I had lots of questions about God, election, damnation, hell, heaven, angels, miracles, and I could never get any satisfactory answers. I had an encounter with God, as a young child, in Sunday School and remember growing up with a sense of God's presence in my life. During my teenage years, I fell into a lot of sin and rebellion, and I lived a life for self, until I was in my late twenties. After God had shown me that He had sent His Son for me also, I remember the first thing I did was contact "Auntie Phyllis," my Sunday School teacher, then residing in Australia, to tell her God had saved me.

    My wife and I were married and had two children, when we were *love-bombed* into a *Jesus People* group in 1972. Until coming into contact with this kind of 'Jesus People,' group, we had never experienced friendship, or love, like we did there. It was the closest thing, in our minds, to the early church. We had all things in common, went daily from house to house in fellowship, prayer, etc. We saw things that we did not deem orthodox, but we loved these people, and those issues we thought, could be dealt with later. It wasn't very long after, that we were in, lock, stock, and barrel. The more we got involved, the more concerned we became about what is called "The Message," rather than lost souls. My wife and I, desperately wanting to live lives pleasing to God, even started sleeping in separate bedrooms, to crucify our flesh. Our marriage, in my opinion was, like many others, on the brink of collapse, directly attributable to this "Message." My wife was plugged into Msg tapes 24/7, trying to capture that ever elusive, "Rapturing faith," which WMB said, was found within messages such as *The Absolute*, Dec. 30, 1962, AM, Jeff., IN:

I believe she's ready to strike that final climax yonder to bring forth a faith that'll rapture the Church into glory (It's the truth.), and She's laying in the Messages. We're really at the end time.

Emotionally, it seemed, she had left me and had "married" the Message of Wm. Branham.

Ed Byskal, the leader of the group, was one of the closest friends I had ever had. He was the one who had, along with some others, been instrumental in my wife and I coming to Christ. Eddie was not in full-time ministry at that time, but owned a business in the city. He preached when the opportunity was presented. This group, Cloverdale Bible Way, held services on Tuesday and Friday nights, as well as on Sunday afternoons. This was done so the services would not interfere with those of other churches which Ed encouraged us to attend, and we did. Sunday mornings and evenings, most of us 'Jesus People,' attended elsewhere. The original emphasis of CBW was on getting sinners saved from their sin, and into the kingdom of God. The congregation (mostly young people) spent all of their free time out on the streets, witnessing for Christ. A serious drug problem existed in town, and some kids died of drug related causes. God was doing a real work, and we were up all hours of the night, ministering to those seeking deliverance.

The meetings were held in a house, and the youth of the town, would, only out of necessity, walk down our street, but only on the opposite side. Rumor had it that, when a person walked directly past the house, something would happen to them, and they would collapse. Some *Jesus-Freak*, supposedly, would then come out of the house and drag the person inside. While they were unconscious, something would be done to their heads. When they came to they'd be *Jesus-Freaks* too. The only times they would voluntarily come would be when they were hurting, perhaps a friend had overdosed and died, or their boyfriend or girlfriend, had left them. When the movie "Rosemary's Baby" was shown in a local theater, many came to the house into the wee hours of the morning, to seek deliverance, claiming they were demon-possessed. Hitch-Hikers were dropped off at the house by locals, who promised them that they would be fed, housed, and cared for, which was true. My wife and I had several young people living with us on a permanent basis, while others came as they had need. There was also a residence where young women could come and stay. It was very powerful, and many young people came to the Lord, and were delivered from all kinds of habits and addictions, and became responsible citizens. Later, when the Bible Way House became too small, the adjacent property was bought and a beautiful rustic log building was erected on the site.

CHAPTER ONE

In 1973, in part 3 of a series on "Contemporary Religion," a Mr. Dennis McGann stated,

> Mr. Ed Byskal, thirty-eight and father of three daughters is, like most others involved in the Jesus Revolution, totally dedicated to the cause. He accepts his position as 'pastor' although having no formal academic background...The Cloverdale Bible Way group meets at least once each week and youth dominates the small congregation. 'I can't pinpoint where and when it happened, but God's spirit just broke loose on the youth of the world today', Mr. Byskal stated, 'out of this movement all hues and shades and various Christian houses have risen.' In an attempt to explain why the Jesus Revolution seems to fill its rank with youth, the ... pastor said, 'I'm a parent, but I feel there's a sad failure on the side of the parents to teach their children the spiritual code that this country was built on.' He considers the parents' position more than a failure but 'a complete breakdown of spiritual responsibility'...The lateness of the hour spurs Mr. Byskal on with his spiritual work...The same impetus propels the group members to 'witness' whenever they can and the same lateness pushes the big-city, downtown street-ministers to collar as many passers-by as their fingers can grasp." [Sadly, the name of Publisher, the publishing date, and the page number has become misplaced. Attempts to locate Mr. Dennis McGann have been unsuccessful, to date. – PMD].

Our leader, Ed Byskal, made the occasional reference to taped messages by a man called William Branham, and we were given access to those tapes. To us WMB was, initially, another preacher, although, to other people, he clearly was more. In 1972 I was invited by someone to go to a Camp-Meeting in Northern Saskatchewan. I went while my wife stayed home with the children. There were a lot of American "WMB pastors" present. I became quite fearful, because a number of these pastors had WMB's picture with a "halo" on their belt buckles. They also seemed to preach about WMB a lot. There were even songs about WMB. There was also one real ambiguous song, some lines of which went like,

> *Some called him a prophet, some call him God*
> *Some called him a fortune teller, or Beelzebub*

The lines were ambiguous to me, because it was not clear in my mind, if they were singing about Jesus, or about WMB. Several men from the USA actually said that WMB was the Lord, something which was answered by WMB in his message, *Questions And Answers # 1*, Aug. 23, 1964, AM, Jeff., IN,

Why does people call me Messiah?...Well, one fellow out there showed me the other day, he had a little thing and he was go--carrying on, wanted all the people to be baptized in my name. That'd make me a antichrist. But I'm not for those things, and all you people know that. But you see...That only identifies the Message true.

At that time I knew I should leave that camp meeting. I did not believe Ed Byskal believed in that kind of idolatry, called the *Deity Doctrine*, by insiders.

The leaders there, in the main, did not have a lot of respect for Ed Byskal, because he, according to them, had not "fully" come into WMB's message. Ed's hair was too long, and he and his wife and children were said to be too worldly. I got into a big argument defending my friend. Part of me wanted to stay at the camp meeting, and part of me wanted to leave. I prayed about it and I made a 'deal' with the Lord. I told the Lord that I was going to go fishing in the lake, which was actually teeming with fish. My 'deal' with the Lord was that if I caught a fish, then I would know that God wanted me to stay. If I didn't catch any, I should go home. I fished for a while off the bank. This was unsuccessful, so I walked knee-deep into the water, and cast my line for a time. That didn't work, so I went in up to my waist, again without success. I finally ended up with literally just my head and arms sticking above the water and still casting for fish. I realized that I was practicing desperate measures. I capitulated and went home, together with another person, who since that time became a Message pastor.

More people started following WMB's taped messages, made available by Ed. Not long thereafter, Ed's daughters were in serious relationships with WMB followers. It was then, in my opinion, that Ed decided to fully embrace WMB's message. He had been with WMB in meetings and on hunts with him. Ed is mentioned in WMB's sermons and he soon rocketed into prominence.

Not long after, the man who, during the early days of our experience, would come to our house and pray with us; the man who would spend time to allay our doubts and fears, had now become a man who told me I was demon possessed. Why? I questioned the teachings of the "prophet," because I compared what I heard with the Scriptures. I was told to have blasphemed the Holy Ghost, when I chose the Bible over the teaching of WMB. The agony of soul my wife and I went through, as we contemplated the consequences of that judgment, was incredible. I thought I had become insane, because I couldn't find anyone within WMB circles to agree with me. In God's sovereign plan, He removed us from the local area. Seemingly, we

CHAPTER ONE

became more involved in the Message as I was "called" to pastor a Message church. However, we also were removed from Ed's influence. In seeking God for guidance to lead the flock for which I now had become responsible, I found Biblical answers to a lot of my questions.

On a trip to Tucson, AZ, at Christmas time of 1976, we got to visit Salt Lake City, and toured all the LDS sites. We were *blown-away* by the apparent similarities between Mormonism and "Branhamism." Clearly, looking back, we can see the hand of God guiding us. When we arrived in Tucson at Christmas time, we saw many things happening in the lives of followers of WMB's "Message," that were clearly not in line with the Word of God.

We decided to go home earlier than we had intended. We left Tucson just before New year's Eve. We brought Valerie Branham, the wife of WMB's younger son Joseph, and her young son Isaac, back with us to British Columbia and they stayed with us for a while. Valerie told us she had left Joseph over the Branham family believing Wm. Branham was the Christ. We had met Joseph a number of times at Pearry Green's place in Tucson, AZ. I had already personally met Mrs. Meda Broy Branham, Rebekah Branham Smith, Rebekah's husband George and Billy Paul, WMB's elder son.

In November of 1977, I received a phone call from a pastor of a small church I ministered to once a month. He told me that his congregation had decided to embrace WMB's message. This came at a time when my wife and I were contemplating to leave the message, because we kept coming across many discrepancies that we could not reconcile with Scripture. I asked this pastor to come and visit us for the weekend. That weekend turned into three weeks, during which we prayed and studied WMB's claims. Countless phone calls were made to people who were mentioned as witnesses of certain events by WMB. Our findings, based upon extensive research, made it very clear that we had to leave the message. We wept many tears of repentance and shame, which turned into a wonderful time of refreshing from the Lord. We then wept many tears of gratitude to such a gracious God; a God who had shown Himself so long suffering and patient during our wanderings from Him and His Word. My wife and I moved out of the area and I wrote four pamphlets:

1. Mystery Cloud, an Exposé on Wm. Branham,"
2. The Fable, Wm. Branham's doctrine of the Serpent Seed…disputed.
3. SAINT or AIN'T, Branham's "halo" examined.
4. 1977? The Return of Christ-The End of the World

Since then God has brought others to us asking us for information regarding WMB's teaching. We prayerfully, sought the Lord for guidance on how to deal with this in a spirit of humility and love. After thirty plus years of being away from Branham's teaching, we were absolutely shocked by our new research.

This book will look at the Branham movement from the perspective of a NRM, a New Religious Movement, which claims to be Christian; indeed it claims to be that "Old Time Religion." No one joins a NRM, nor do they believe they are in one. They join because they believe it has more truth, more love, more power, than traditional expressions of Christianity.

Chapter Two
Who was William M. Branham?

"**William Marrion Branham** was one of the most influential Bible ministers of our time. He was considered by many to be the **initiator** of the healing and charismatic revival that began in 1947, and from his ministry there sprang a myriad of other ministers who became internationally known"[1] [Bolding theirs - PMD]. "For twenty years, and before millions of people, William Branham demonstrated the Gift of Discernment and the Word of Knowledge (knowing the secrets of a person's heart) with an unerring accuracy that had never before been seen, and has never since been duplicated. His healing ministry was legendary, yet in the opinion of many, he wasted the great gift that God had given him by trying to preach. Few church leaders were able to see past his lack of education and recognize the purpose of the gift, which was not to attract attention to the man, but to the Word that was being restored. The promise of Matthew 17:11was being fulfilled: "And Jesus answered and said unto them, Elias truly shall first come, and restore all things." There was a reason why God chose William Branham to be His Voice to this generation. He was a man who was not shaped to a theological conformity or influenced by denominational barriers, therefore he did not hesitate to point people away from all man-made creeds and traditions, and back to the original Word, just as it was taught by the apostolic fathers. He had no ambitions or agendas of his own, choosing instead to remain a humble servant of God, never aspiring to a lavish lifestyle or promoting himself above others. He lived his life in total surrender to the leadership of the Holy Ghost. The profound anointing that surrounded his ministry, and the extraordinary demonstrations of the supernatural that occurred throughout his lifetime clearly identified him as a God-ordained prophet."[2] Full Gospel Men's Voice said, "In Bible Days, there were men of God who were Prophets and Seers. But in all the Sacred Records, none of these had a greater ministry than that of William Branham, a Prophet and Seer of God…"[3] WMB's campaign manager, Gordon

Lindsay[4] in collaboration with WMB, wrote,

> The story of the life of William Branham is so out of this world and beyond the ordinary that were there not available a host of infallible proofs which document and attest its authenticity, one might well be excused for considering it far-fetched and incredible. But the facts are so generally known, and of such a nature that they can be so easily verified by any sincere investigator, that they must stand as God's witness to His willingness and purpose to reveal Himself again to men as he once did in the days of the prophets and the apostles. The story of this prophet's life -- for he is a prophet, though we infrequently use the term -- indeed witnesses to the fact that Bible days are here again.[6]

It must be said for clarification that Christ For The Nations Bible College (Canada) was founded 20 years ago. Neither Mrs. Gordon (Freda) Lindsay, nor CFNI (Canada) has connections with the ministry of William Branham, nor with any of his followers, neither with Branham's fringe teachings.[7]

Evangelist T.L. Osborne stated,

> God came down here to show us how it would work...He walked here in a human body, a Godman--Whom we call Jesus...Some are going to think that I am sacrilegious or off doctrinally (and it doesn't really matter), but God came again in human flesh and said, "Apparently I must show them again...Once again they must know what God is like." And He stepped down and sent a little man, a prophet, but more than a prophet this time, a Jesus-man this time!...So, He sent forth a particular human vessel...Here comes Brother Branham along...GOD IN THE FLESH, again crossing our paths...I SAW JESUS THAT NIGHT IN A HUMAN FORM THAT THEY CALLED WILLIAM BRANHAM!...William Branham came our way as the prophet of God and showed us in the twentieth century precisely the same things that were shown us in the Gospels...We have walked with God in our day. He came and walked the shores of Galilee, but He also came to the streets of Phoenix, Portland, Oregon; Tulsa, Oklahoma; and across this nation. I saw it. And when I saw it once, I knew what it meant. This was the Word in flesh.[8] (Emphasis VOGR - PMD)

In 1990, Paul Cain, an early WMB associate, declared WMB to be, "the greatest prophet in the 20th century."[9] As an aside, ... Paul Cain, [V]anished from the scene for more that 25 years, in or around 1965, the year WMB died. Paul re-emerged in 1986 to begin a new phase of supernatural healing and prophetic ministry.[10] In 2005, Cain admitted, "I have struggled with homosexuality for an extended period of time."[11] Yet, in 2008, an unrepentant Cain appeared on the stage with Todd Bentley, in Lakeland Florida, and he publicly stated, "I've been a celibate all my life."[12] Todd Bentley, in speaking to Paul Cain, said this of WMB, "Paul, I knew you were with William Branham. I know…you did meetings…with the greatest healing evangelist of the 40s and 50s."[13] Paul Cain announced in his prayer that he met the New Breed,[14] a new movement which WMB called, "Super Seed." WMB said that Jesus came, that He might redeem the super seed of Abraham's race.[15]

WMB "birthed" many fringe movements, including but not limited to, the Manifested Sons of God,[16] Order of the Latter Rain,[17] the Shepherding Movement,[18] the Word-Faith Movement,[19] the Feast of Tabernacles teaching, [20] the New Breed and the Third Wave, movement.[21]

John Wimber (1934-1997)[22] of the Vineyard Church and C. Peter Wagner (1930 -) of the Third Wave, worked together, at Fuller Seminary. For five years they taught a course, which incorporated WMB's healing methods and theology. Fuller seminary apparently terminated the course due to controversies. Many, if not all, of the Televangelists are products of WMB, who called them his children.[23]

WMB claimed to be born of non-Christian parents of Roman Catholic Irish-Cherokee descent, (See WMB's Family Tree at the end of this chapter). He was the first of ten children born to Charles Branham[24] and Ella Harvey. According to Lee Vayle, Charles changed his name from Branam to Branham,[25] though WMB much later told Vayle that this name change had a spiritual meaning.[26] Allegedly, at age eighteen Charles married fourteen year old Ella. She gave birth to William a year later.[27] WMB noted that in the early days of Kentucky no birth records were kept.[28] People did marry very young in that culture, with the consequence that WMB would have been raised by an immature mother and father. Hence, WMB would not have received any foundation for life, or for religion. He also encouraged his followers to marry young and many do.

WMB grew up in abject poverty according to his many *Life Stories*.[29] His father Charles, a drunkard, brawler, knife-fighter, logger and bootlegger, owned several stills.[30] WMB said he observed unspeakable things around the stills, things that included drunkenness and young women "carrying on" with married men.[31] He mentioned similar house parties hosted by his parents.[32] In his sermons he typically railed on women and whiskey, yet never on the men. WMB hated women and said, "They were not worth a good clean bullet to kill them with."[33]

There was never enough to eat and he had no proper shoes,[34] nor proper clothing, even in winter, he said.[35] He was called a corn cracker[36] by the boys around and sissy by his best girlfriend[37] and even by his own father.[38] Charles was not around in William's formative years and not a lot afterwards either. William stated he had to quit school at fourteen to support his mother and siblings. Throughout his school years WMB cried a lot, because his classmates ridiculed him due to his appearance. As a 15 or 16 year old he was often crying because of rejection. WMB's family and also his doctor, believed he suffered from hysteria.[39]

WMB's parents did not attend church according to WMB,[40] but he did mention a number of religious ceremonies, like Corn Dances at a Cherokee reservation, where he observed speaking in tongues, prophecy, interpretation, automatic writing, etc.[41] He referred to these experiences throughout his life. His father Charles was very superstitious,[42] and WMB believed the Zodiac influenced people's lives[43] and doubtless, so did Irish folklore and magic. WMB, by his own account, grew up in a home of hillbilly superstition.[44] From very young he had auditory and visionary delusions, that scared him, and of which he wanted to rid himself.[45] By WMB's own admission he received his theology from nature, because God was in nature. Folklore and Magic claim nature as their source, as do New Thought, Scientific Christianity and Meta-Physics, etc., of which there exists much evidence in WMB's messages. A number of these associations teach a form of Serpent's Seed, a pivotal WMB tenet, of which more will be said. WMB had, within his immediate following, many people from various backgrounds. According to Mrs. Freda Lindsay, Branham had some erratic ideas, he was,

> A man easily influenced…unscrupulous men, in order to gain their own ends, would flatter him. [46]

WMB claimed the gift of second sight[47] and he was not alone in making this claim. Paul Cain was a man with similar gifting, including an angelic commission. Cain was much respected in the "Third Wave" movement. He used to take meetings for WMB, when the latter could not fulfill his obligations. WMB encouraged people to attend Cain's services as a continuation of his own.[48] After WMB's ascendancy in the healing revival, which started in 1947, many others entered the field. Each came with their own particular gifting and niche.[49]

Although WMB was born in the hills of Kentucky in the early 1900s, he grew up in Indiana and he lived there for most of his life. In his late teens and twenties he experienced the Roaring Twenties, the years of flappers, the Charleston, bathtub gin, petting parties, and the Stutz Bearcat. These were the days where America withdrew from the world and went into an orgy of self-indulgence.[50] These were the, "times where Mammon reigned and God was converted into a businessman.[51]

This stark contrast with WMB's poverty might have been the cause of his turning to preaching to make a living, as Jim "Jonestown" Jones alleged, [WMB] said, it's the way to make a living…Billy Branham …said you can't preach the truth about that Bible, he said…preach reincarnation, you cannot preach the truth about the Bible, you will be in trouble.' I said, 'I choose to…preach the truth.' He said, 'well, I'll be around, while you will be in trouble.' Well, I'm still here…[52] Jones was well acquainted with WMB. Jones invited WMB to come and preach at the, "Nation Wide Ministers Convention, Special Speaker William Branham Date June 11-15,

CHAPTER TWO

1956, Indianapolis, Indiana, location Cadle Tabernacle.[53] This is confirmed in the book, Raven, which states Jones,

> Organized a mammoth religious convention to take place June 11 through June 15, 1956, in a cavernous Indianapolis hall called the Cadle Tabernacle. To draw the crowds, Jim needed a headliner, and so he arranged to share the pulpit with Rev. William Branham, a healing evangelist and religious author as highly revered by some as Oral Roberts or Billy Graham...Some eleven thousand Christians attended opening day of the convention to see Branham and twenty-five-year-old Jim Jones.[54]

There is internal evidence that WMB did indeed speak at that convention, though all evidence that Jim Jones was involved, was carefully edited out by WMB's people.[55]

It was an age where everything was called NEW. "We were a new country in a new world, a new people, and we have seen such curiosities as a New Freedom, a New Nationalism, a New Deal, a new Frontier...a New Left, a New Right... Manufacturers of well-established products feel constrained every few years to advertise them as "new, improved," or "with ingredient X-17.[56] "New gadgets might be one thing, but a New Woman was quite another. (What after all, was wrong with the old one?)"[57]

By the early 1920s it seemed that every social ill in America could be attributed to the "flapper"----The notorious character type who bobbed her hair, smoked cigarettes, drank gin, sported short skirts, and passed her evenings in steamy jazz clubs where she danced in a shockingly immodest fashion with a revolting cast of male suitors.[58]

This promiscuous Flapper, "out and about[59] with their bobbed hair,[60] short skirts, make-up, cigarettes and bathtub gin,[61] evidently absolutely enraged[62] an already woman-hating WMB.[63] For WMB, as a young man, it was evidently fine for him to dress very fashionable in a natty suit, with beautifully quaffed curly hair and a carefully shaped "Errol Flynn" pencil moustache.[64] He spoke of being poor, but he had a brand new automobile in 1926.[65]

The Depression[66] hit in 1929 and lasted throughout the 1930s. Many people lost all they had and many committed suicide. "Unemployment reached a high of 25% in 1933, and hovered between 15% and 20% for the remainder of the 1930s. Small, rural towns were hardest hit, as were unskilled workers and minorities. Abject poverty quickly appeared. Children started receiving inadequate nutrition and healthcare, and starvation became an everyday occurrence. The unemployed were usually evicted from their homes and left to wander around homeless or to live in poorly constructed shelters made of any trash material that could be found. Many were so ashamed of their new lowered status that they committed suicide.

The suicide rate in the U.S. rose 30% between 1928 and 1932."[67] Poverty is difficult to describe and it is even more difficult to classify. Suffice it to say that life indeed was tough for most people. "The National Recovery Association (NRA) attempted to revive industry by raising wages, reducing work hours and reining in unbridled competition."[68] Some church people did not take any help the government provided through the NRA, because of their belief that taking help was the Mark of the Beast.[69] There was a marked increase in alcohol consumption as well as betting on horses and WMB admitted to doing the latter himself.[70]

WMB, like a lot of people of that day, spoke against women in the work force.[71] Jobs were scarce and women were seen to be depriving men of opportunities. Employers, Government agencies, labor unions and employers conspired against women entering the workforce,[72] yet there were many "women's" jobs that men refused to do, such as domestic help, or tailoring.

WMB claimed he was converted in September of 1928.[73] He said he was ordained as a local exhorter[74] that same year[75] by a Dr. Roy E. Davis, in the Missionary Baptist Church.[76] This church was actually called the First Pentecostal Baptist Church of Jeffersonville, IN.[77] Six months after his conversion he said he received the gift of healing, through the medium of a "great light" and a voice which told him,

> To preach and to pray for the sick and He would heal them regardless of what disease they had.[78]

In 1934 WMB attended a Oneness Pentecostal Convention in Mishawaka, Indiana.[79] and he felt called to go with the "Jesus Only" to spread the message of healing.[80] WMB's stated his angelic commission took place on May 7, 1946, where he was given two gifts for healing of the sick.[81] In 1947 the healing revival swept North America and the world, spearheaded by WMB.[82]

How was it possible that this apparently humble, unassuming, uneducated hillbilly and "Kentucky-Corn cracker" (per WMB's own account), became such a prominent person in the healing revival movement? Was it his great eloquence? No, by WMB's own confession he could hardly put a sentence together and his grammar was horrific. Was it because of his deep understanding of God's Word, the Bible? No, he showed an obvious lack of a proper hermeneutic, and exegesis. His poor command of the English language hindered him from understanding English Scripture, in particular the King James Version. In reality, his messages were few, but very often repeated.[83] Even though the message titles changed, the content was often quite similar. What catapulted WMB into the limelight? His followers would say that it was because he was God's man with a message for the hour. It would be more accurate to say that his early success was the result of the support of men like Gordon Lindsay, Ern Baxter,[84] and F.F. Bosworth.[85] WMB had quickly realized

CHAPTER TWO 13

that, to be successful, he had to get successful managers to organize his campaigns. Therefore, in 1947, he recruited these men. All three had been major figures in their own Revival meetings. F.F. (Daddy) Bosworth had been heavily involved with (Elijah) John Alexander Dowie[86] who had connections with Charles Fox Parham,[87] the founder of American Pentecostalism. Bosworth had known the most renowned healing ministries of the 20th century, including Smith-Wigglesworth. Also involved with Dowie were Gordon Lindsay's parents. Charles Fox Parham[88] preached in John G. Lake's church in Portland, Oregon, where Gordon Lindsay attended. John. G. Lake[89] was a disciple of Dowie.[90] Gordon Lindsay became a convert to Christianity at that time,[91] through Charles F. Parham,[92] who, already in the early 1900s, baptized in Jesus' Name.[93]

Lindsay was contacted by a Rev. Jack Moore from Shreveport, LA, and together they visited WMB's services in Sacramento, CA, sometime in late 1947. Gordon Lindsay became WMB's manager because he, due to his,

> Wide contacts in full gospel circles, would be the logical one to manage Branham's meetings.[94]

Lindsay and Baxter were indispensable to the success of WMB.[95] Due to WMB's occult leanings they only allowed him to bring a testimony. Baxter and Lindsay would preach,[96] after which WMB held a healing service.[97]

By the late 1950s the Healing Revival was over. Many evangelists began 'teaching ministries' in order to ride the wave of the emerging Charismatic movement. Ern Baxter left WMB's ministry and the reasons he gave are very sobering.[98] WMB fired his managers one by one and started his own healing campaigns. WMB expressed that he found it difficult to do the meetings on his own and would ask his audiences for their indulgence.[99] WMB, against the advice of friends and colleagues, decided to teach and preach. He, consequently lost his previously larger audiences.

Following WMB's death in 1965, a resurgence of his teaching ministry occurred when WMB's family and his close associates started tape and book ministries. This was duplicated by many, world-wide. WMB's messages have now been translated into more than 100 languages and spread throughout as many countries. All WMB's messages can be accessed through any Internet search engine. This proliferation of WMB's message transcripts has spawned numerous books, encyclopedia entries and websites. In 1950, Gordon Lindsay wrote, *William Branham, A Man Sent From God*. Julius Stadsklev, wrote, *A Prophet Visits South Africa*, no earlier than 1952."[100] According to WMB, Stadsklev's book was much better than Lindsay's book.[101] Pearry Green wrote, *Acts of the Prophet*, and Lee Vayle produced *Twentieth Century Prophet*. None of these books mention WMB's controversial teachings. One early book was written by Carl Dyck.[102] Dyck says, "Branham taught that sin came as a result of Eve having sex with a serpent before Adam had relations with her…"[103] The Dictionary of Pentecostal and Charismatic Movements states,[O]ther teachings placed him on the fringe of orthodoxy. His doctrine of the "serpent's seed" taught that Eve's sin involved sexual relations with the serpent. Some humans are descended from the serpent's seed and are destined for hell, which is not eternal, however, the seed of God, i.e., those who receive Branham's teaching, are predestined to become the bride of Christ.[104] Charles Lippy states that, "Branham began teaching doctrines that made him increasingly controversial: denial of an eternal hell, acceptance of divorce, doctrine of the serpent's seed."[105]

Notes - Chapter Two

[1] Cloverdale Bibleway Church, "*Who was William Branham,*" http://www.bibleway.org/home.do#path=/missions, (accessed April 07 2007).

[2] Voice of God Recordings, Inc., "*Life and Ministry of William Branham,*" http://www.branham.org/Branham&LoadPageDetail=WilliamBranham.htm (accessed April 07 2007).

[3] *Full Gospel Men's Voice*, Issue Feb. 1961 (Now known as Full Gospel Businessmen's Fellowship International, or FGBFI).

[4] Gordon Lindsay (1924–1973) was a healing evangelist. Lindsay became WMB's campaign manager in 1947 and in 1948 he began the magazine The Voice of Healing, upon urging from WMB to document his campaigns. Gordon and Freda Lindsay also founded Christ For The Nations Institute in 1970, and Freda is still at the helm of that operation.

[5] Rebekah Branham Smith, in "*Only Believe*" Vol. 4, Issue 11, 6, "The biography by Gordon Lindsay, "William Branham, A Man Sent From God" [was]…written in collaboration with William Branham, a distinction in authorship which was agreeable to both the subject and the writer. William Branham highly recommended the book and offered it for sale in the healing campaigns and from his home office."

[6] Gordon Lindsay, "*William Branham, A Man Sent From God*" (Jeffersonville, IN: Wm. Branham Publications, 1950, 216 pp.), 9.

[7] Ken Deeks, Academic Dean and Instructor, Christ For The Nations, Surrey, BC, Canada, in a phone interview by the author, March 14, 2008.

[8] T.L. Osborne, in *Address,* in Wm. Branham's Memorial Service, (Tucson: SWP, 1966), 22-37.

[9] Equipping the Saints Magazine, (Anaheim: VMI, Vol. 4, No.4/Fall 1990), 9.

[10] Paul Cain, July19, 2012, www.paulcain.org/sandbox/newsite/pagesaboutpaul.html

[11] J. Lee Grady, "*Prophetic Minister Paul Cain Issues Public Apology for Immoral Lifestyle,*" Charisma, February 28, 2005, http://www.charismamag. com/component/content/article/154-j15/peoplee vents/people-and-events/ 1514-prophetic-minister-paul-cain-issues-public-apo logy-for-immoral-lifestyle-

[12] "Paul Cain and Todd Bentley Pt. 1, " Youtube video, 2:49 [n.d.], June 17, 2008, posted by Elmoziffle, http://www.youtube.com/watch?v=o25jTVb5Bj8

[13] "Cain and Bentley Pt. 2, " Youtube video, 7:54 [n.d.], June 17, 2008, posted by Elmoziffle, http://www.youtube.com/watch?v=oR6JraFDtLk

CHAPTER TWO

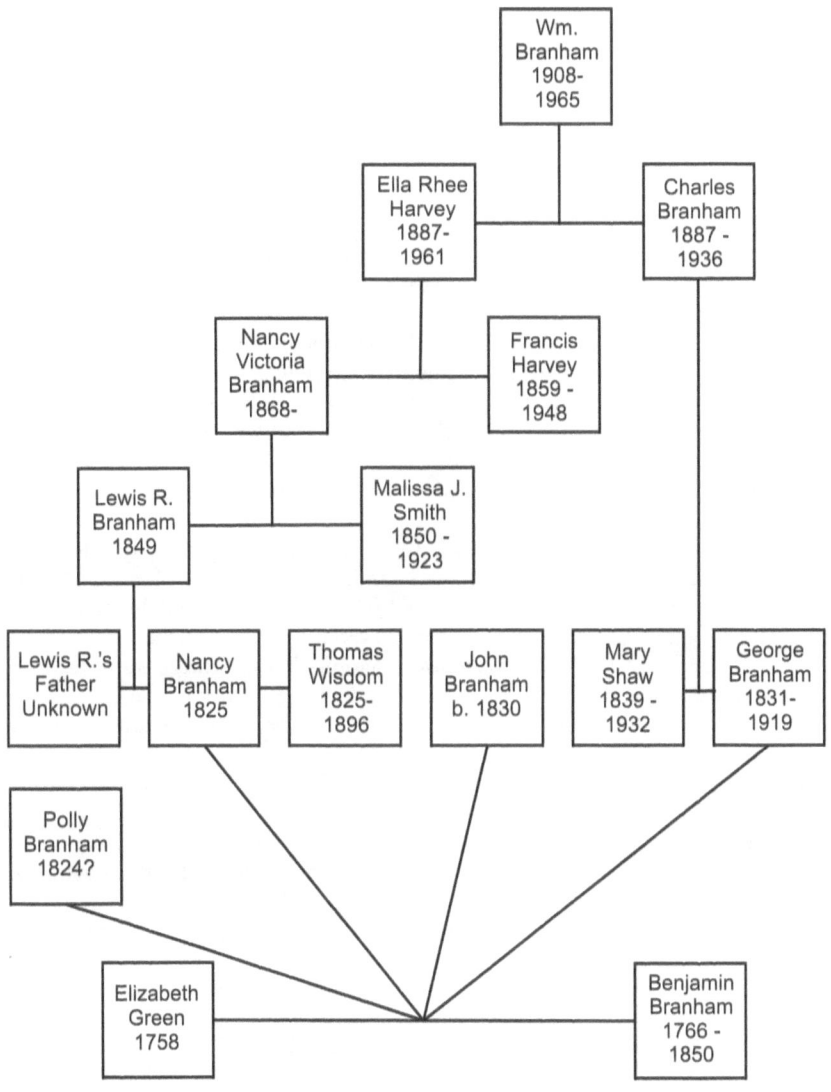

Wm. Branham's Family Tree

WMB's great-grandmother (Malissa Jane Smith Branham) on his mother's side was a full blooded Cherokee. WMB was therefore only 1/8th Cherokee. WMB' great-grandfather, on his father's side, was Ben Branham, who was his great-great-great grandfather on his mother's side. WMB was related to his mother through her Branham ancestry. Nancy Branham bore Lewis Riley Branham out of Wedlock. She later married Thomas L. Wisdom. Nancy's brother George. W. Branham was WMB's grandfather. Nancy had a sister called Polly and another brother called John.

¹⁴ Paul Cain and Todd Bentley Pt. 2, Paul Cain appeared with the (later) disgraced Todd Bentley and prayed, "[I] have met the New Breed uh absolutely met the New Breed. And when you uh brought uh Todd uh Bentley and I together, the angel of the Lord said, "You've found what you're looking for."

¹⁵ WMB, *Super Sign*, Jul. 24, 1962, South Gate, CA. See also: WMB, *Spoken Word Is The Original Seed*, Mar. 18, 1962, Jeff., IN, "These last days, true church Bride comes to the Headstone, will be the super church, a super race…"

¹⁶ John Robert Stevens (1919 - 1983), well-known as a disciple of WMB, founded the Manifested Sons of God Movement. Though it fell into disrepute, its most ardent disciples, under guise, still successfully promote this teaching in churches.

¹⁷ George Warnock, secretary to WMB's campaign manager Ern Baxter, got involved with the Latter Rain movement in 1949. Latter Rain's impetus came from WMB's meetings in Vancouver, B.C, in late 1947, where he met with the founders. It was condemned by some churches as a heresy in the 1950s, but has resurfaced in the last few years. George Warnock resides in Cranbrook, BC, and is known to this author.

¹⁸ The Shepherding Movement consisted of Don Basham, Derek Prince, Charles Simpson, Bob Mumford and Ern Baxter. This movement was also condemned as a heresy, but still flourishes under different names.

¹⁹ WMB, *Faith Without Works Is Dead*, Aug. 22, 1950, Cleveland, OH, "That's how you're saved is by faith…You just believe it. Act upon it as though it was." See also: Messiah, Jan. 17, 1961, Shreveport, LA, "Man, he is a god, he was made to be a god, his purpose here on earth was to be a god, to have a dominion over everything in the earth…"

²⁰ George Warnock, *The Feast of Tabernacles* (Cranbrook, BC: George Warnock, 1951), 14-20. The Feast of Tabernacles has as its premises that the history of the church age is foreseen in the Feasts of Israel starting with Passover, Pentecost. George Warnock was with the Latter Rain Movement back in North Battleford. The leaders of the Latter Rain, visited WMB when he was holding a campaign in Vancouver, BC, in 1947. After they returned home the revival started.

²¹ The Third Wave is a movement that emphasizes the Holy Spirit, spiritual warfare, power encounters, destruction of strongholds, etc., and has found many adherents within, and without, Pentecostal circles.

²² Vern Middleton, Ph. D., in an interview with this author, April 8, 2008. In the summer of 1983, Vern and his wife Helen attended the MC 510 Course led by Peter Wagner, Professor of Church Growth at Fuller Theological Seminary School of World Missions.. During his 28-year tenure at Fuller, he has taught students from nearly every country in the world. Wagner assisted by Wimber, commenced a course called MC 510, *Healing Ministry and Church Growth*. In the syllabus on page 60, it mentions William Branham's ministry. Video clips of WMB's healing and exorcism ministry were shown and studied. Anyone at all familiar with WMB's ministry will certainly recognize his influence on Peter Wagner's ministry.

²³ WMB, *Do You Now Believe?* Nov. 06, 1953, Owensboro, KY, "I feel like they're my children. Many of them are much older…yet, I feel like they're my children." All the following were mentioned by WMB: Gordon Lindsay, Jack Moore, F.F. Bosworth, Ern Baxter, Raymond T. Richey, Paul Cain, O.L. Jaggers, Kenneth Hagin, Velmer Gardner, Clifton Erickson, A.C. Valdez Jr., Tommy Hicks, little David Walker, David duPlessis, Morris Cerullo, A.A. Allen, Oral Roberts, William Freeman, William Hagen, David Nunn, Dale Hanson, Rex Humbard, Franklin Hall, and Demas Shekarian of Full Gospel Businessmen's fame.

²⁴ WMB, *Life Story*, Apr. 19, 1959, Los Angeles, CA, "And my father almost killed the

man, so he had to run and leave Kentucky and come…to Indiana…he was gone for almost a year, he could not come back, because the law was looking for him. And then when we'd heard from him by letter, signed by another name, but that he'd told mother how it would be that she'd hear from him…"

[25] Lee Vayle, *Twentieth Century Prophet: The Messenger To The Laodicaen Church Age*, (Jeffersonville, IN: Spoken Word Publications, 1965, 73pp), 68. "The original family name of this man is Branam. His father decided for some reason to add an H to the name; making it Branham."

[26] WMB, *Audio Letter To Lee Vayle*, May 1964, Tucson, AZ, ""Now, and another thing. If you'll notice, G-r-a-h-a-m is six letters. A-b-r-a-h-a-m is seven letters, and so is B-r-a-h-a-m seven letters. Now, if you're going to make that in conclusion, it might be a good thing…I believe I've already told you about referring to G-r-a-h-a-m being six letters, which means man, or world. B-r-a-h-a-m is seven, which is perfected, perfection…The message never went to Billy Graham's group. It went to the elected group, the group that is elected." [Note: WMB audibly spelled out, "B-r-a-h-a-m," (6 letters) and said it was seven – PMD].

[27] *Life Story*, LA, "Daddy was eighteen years old; mama was fifteen when I was born, just children."

[28] WMB, Abraham (*Jehovah-Jireh* #3), Aug. 03, 1960, Yakima, WA, "I said, 'Well, Bill, you're fifty years old.' Best I know, I was born in Kentucky where they don't have a birth records. And you know what my birth mark is, birth record in Kentucky? The year the old stump blowed away up over on the hill. And that's all they knowed. They say, 'When was that child born?' 'Tomato picking time.' 'What tomato picking time? When was this one born?' 'Corn cutting time.' 'What corn cutting time?' Now, that was the birth record up in the mountains of Kentucky. So I don't know how old I am, but anyhow, I'm ever bit of that [fifty years old in 1960 – PMD]…That's what my mother told me, and I think she'd be pretty close to right."

[29] WMB's *Life Story*, Little Rock, AR, February 1950; *My Life Story*, August 20, 1950, Aft., Cleveland, OH; *Life Story*, Phoenix, AZ, April 15, 1951, Af.; *Life Story*, July 22, 1951, Aft., Toledo, OH; *Life Story*, July 20, 1952, Aft., Hammond, IN; *Life Story*, November 8, 1953, Aft., Owensboro, KY; (*Life Story*, (*Why I'm Praying For The Sick*) March 14, 1954, Columbus, OH; *Life Story*, June 26, 1955, Aft., Zurich, SW; *Life Story*, April 19, 1959, Aft., Los Angeles, CA.

[30] *Life Story*, Phoenix, AZ

[31] *Life Story*, Hammond, "[I]f there ever was a woman hater, I was one of them. My, I seen how they come when my daddy run that bootleg place. And I'd see women come there, young women, with somebody else's husband. And the way they would carry on." See also: Life Story, Cleveland, "I was around, watched my father drinking and hung around those places, and maybe I'd be around, and I'd see how women come out and living untrue."

[32] WMB, *Communion*, Dec. 12, 1965, Tucson, AZ, "Pop and mom…they were sinners; there was no Christianity in our homes at all. And, oh, my, drinking, and parties, and carrying on; it made me sick. I'd take my--my lantern and my dog and go to the woods to stay all night. In the wintertime I'd hunt till the party was over, maybe daylight in the morning. Come home, wouldn't be over, I've laid on top of a shed and sleep, waiting for daylight to break."

[33] *Life Story*, LA, "But I can remember when my father's still up there running, I had to be out there with water and stuff, see young ladies that wasn't over seventeen, eighteen years old, up there with men my age now, drunk. And they'd have to sober them up and give them black coffee, to get home to cook their husband's supper…This was my remark

then, "They're not worth a good clean bullet to kill them with it." That's right. And I hated women. That's right. And I just have to watch every move now, to keep from still thinking the same thing."

[34] *Life Story*, Toledo, , "[T]oes sticking out of our shoes like turtle heads"

[35] WMB, *Here We Have No Continuing City*, Feb. 1950, Little Rock, AR, "I remember I didn't have any shirt to wear that winter."

[36] WMB, *You Must Be Born Again*, Dec. 31, 1961, Jeff., IN, "I was here in Indiana, born in Kentucky, so I was a corn cracker to these kids over here." See also: Life Story, Hammond, IN, "I, being the only Kentuckian among them, I sure had a hard way to go; I mean I did. They just teased me all the time about being a corn cracker."

[37] *Life Story*, Toledo.

[38] *Life Story*, Phoenix, "My daddy said, "No, I raised one sissy.""

[39] *Life Story*, LA, "And I was just hysterically. She called the doctor, and the doctor said, "Well, he's just nervous; that's all." So she put me to bed. And I never, from that day to this, ever passed by that tree again. I was scared. I'd go down the other side of the garden, because I thought there was a man up in that tree and He was talking to me, great deep voice that spoke."

[40] WMB, *A Trial*, Apr. 05, 1964, Louisville, MS, "My people formerly were Catholic…I never was in a church in my life…Mother and father both was Irish, and so they just married out of the church, and we had no religion."

[41] WMB, *God Being Misunderstood*, Jul. 23, 1961, PM, Jeff., IN, "I had an experience to one time going into a witch camp with Indians. They're devil-dancers…and do the corn dance, and speak in tongues and interpret it, and tell exactly the truth what's setting amongst the people. And seen a witch take a…pencil and lay it down, and see that pencil rise up and write in unknown tongues, and interpret it, and tell the people exactly what was going on out through there."

[42] WMB, *Questions And Answers #3*, Aug. 30, 1964, AM, Jeff., IN, "Papa used to say, 'I can't plant them potatoes at this time, because the moon isn't right. You can't plant them potatoes, Billy.' And I said, 'I'm not planting them in the moon; I'm planting them here in the ground.' Said, 'All right, smart aleck, go on. You get a few bumps on your head and you'll learn something.' I did. I did. I tell you: take a board and lay it down out there on the grass in the dark of the moon and watch what happens. That grass will die right now. Lay it on the light of the moon; you can let it lay there a week; it won't hurt it a bit…You plant something that spreads out on top of the earth. In the dark of the moon watch it go right down and make it like a radish or turnip will. You plant it back the other way and watch it spread out on top of the earth. "

[43] WMB, *Q & A #3*, Aug. 30, 1964, "You are John Doe; you were born in a certain month, and you were borned under a certain star…and that has something to do with you…The first thing, I went to that person and found their birthplace, and what sign that they were born under, and could tell what their birth was. Which way it set in their natural nature sets them in a certain line. "

[44] WMB, *Early Spiritual Experiences*, Jul. 13, 1952, Aft., Hammond, IN, "You know how superstitious the mountain people is…" See also: *The Mighty Conqueror*, Aug. 8, 1957, Edmonton, AB, CAD, "You may call me really superstitious after this, but that type of spirit hangs around those places, that's exactly right…If you go into a place of amusement, you find that type of spirit there. You go into a place of gambling, you find that type of spirit…" *Spirit Of Truth*, Jan. 18, 1963, Phoenix, AZ, "I'm scared of a cat. And so, I just don't like that superstitious feeling you get around them. And so, we don't have them around the house

...and I believe the cat can realize that I'm afraid of him. So my father was afraid of cats."

⁴⁵ *Early Spiritual Experiences*, "'But I'm tired of this. I can't live a prisoner.' I said, 'Everybody's telling me...that I'm a Devil, and so forth like that, by that, and me trying to live a Christian life...I read the Bible, I cried...no light in there so I had to close up the word...And I started praying; I said, 'God, please. I'm a Christian, I love you, you know I love you. You know in my heart, and you know me better than I know myself, I love you, and I'm told by the clergymen, and the so forth, that the Devil, a spirit's moving around me, and Lord, I don't want to have that around me, you know I don't. You know I love you, and I believe you with all my heart, so why do you let my life be plagued like this? Why would you do it? Why don't you set me free of that so I can go preach and feel free of that?' And on like that, and I was begging to Him. I was long about two or three o'clock in the morning; I was praying, and crying, and begging."

⁴⁶ Mrs. Gordon Lindsay, *My Diary Secrets*, (Dallas, TX: CFN, 6th ed., 1989, 289 pp.), 87.

⁴⁷ WMB, E*arly Spiritual Experiences*, Jul 13, 1952, Aft., "Before I was a Christian, confessing Jesus Christ as my personal Saviour, that gift was there just the same. When I was a sinner, an alien, far from the commonwealth of God, that gift was there just the same, saw visions just the same way...Gifts and callings are without repentance."

⁴⁸ WMB, *Expectations*, May 7, 1951, Los Angeles, CA, "Brother Paul [Cain] is to come in...Thursday night in this very tabernacle here. And we pray that God will give Brother Paul a very wonderful meeting here with hundreds of souls saved and many healings, and fill with His Spirit and goodness, getting ready for the coming of the Lord." See: *Believe Ye That I Can Do This?* May 9, 1951, Los Angeles, CA, " Paul Cain, is going to continue the revival on, beginning tomorrow night at the regular time, I guess, of seven-thirty."

⁴⁹ For more in-depth information see David Edwin Harrell, Jr., *All Things Are Possible*, (Bloomington, IN: IUP, 1975).

⁵⁰ Robert S. McElvaine, *The Great Depression*, (Fitzhenry and Whiteside, Ltd., Toronto, 1984, 402pp.), 13.

⁵¹ Ibid., "In the number one best-seller of 1925 and 1926, *The Man Nobody Knows*, advertising executive Bruce Barton related how Jesus 'had picked up twelve men from the bottom ranks of business and forged them into an organization that conquered the world.' Christ was 'the founder of modern business.'" 16.

⁵² Fielding M. McGhee, III, "*Jonestown Audiotape Primary Project*" : Transcripts, Tape Number : Q612, *The Jonestown Institute*. November 22, 2006, http://jonestown.sdsu.edu/AboutJonestown/Tapes/Tapes/TapeTranscripts/Q612.html

⁵³ Rev. James W. Jones, "*The Open Door*," April 1956, March 9, 2012, jonestown.sdsu.edu/AboutJonestown/PrimarySources/theopendoor_text.html

⁵⁴ Tim Reitman with John Jacobs, The Raven, *The Untold Story of Rev. Jim Jones and his People* (New York, NY: E.P Dutton, 622 pp., 1982), 50, 51.

⁵⁵ WMB's first and last convention messages were 56-0611 *Hear Ye Him* and 56-0615 *An Exodus*, resp. In *An Exodus*, Jim Jones is the person introducing WMB, though Jones' name is edited out.

⁵⁶ McElvaine, 18.

⁵⁷ Ibid., 19.

⁵⁸ Joshua Zeitz, *Flapper: A Madcap Story of Sex, Style, Celebrity, and the Women Who Made America Modern*, (Crown Publishers: New York, NY, 2006, 352pp.), 5-6.

⁵⁹ WMB, *Painted-Face Jezebel*, Oct. 05, 1956, Chicago, IL, "Sister dear, God made you for one place, the kitchen. When you get out of there, you're out of His will...She never

was made for office work. And it's caused more disgrace and divorces and things. You ought to be in the kitchen cooking your husband a pie for supper or something. Exactly right."

⁶⁰ Marion Meade, *Bobbed Hair and Bathtub Gin*, (New York, NY: Doubleday, 2004, 340 pp.), 91. "When Jane walked out of the salon, her head was shorn "just like a boy."

⁶¹ Bootleg Gin or homemade concoctions.

⁶² WMB, *Q & A on Genesis*, Jul. 29, 1953, Jeff., IN, "Women was the Devil's instrument in the beginning…She'll send more preachers to hell than all the bootleg joints there is in the world. Let a little flapper with a cigarette in the corner of her mouth, and her hair all cuticured up like that, and great big long eyelashes that blink up-and-down, brother, a little kind of nice-looking physique on her, watch what she'll do."

⁶³ *Life Story*, Hammond, "[I]f there ever was a woman hater, I was one…"

⁶⁴ William Branham Legacy., "*WMB with Moustache*," January 12, 2006, http://wmb1.com/de/~diego/images/t/ori/wbfamily/05wbf_young_moustache01.jpg

⁶⁵ WMB, *Lamb's Book Of Life*, Jun 3, 1956, Jeff., IN, "Mama, you remember when I had that little old T-model Ford, the little old '26 model? How I'd polish that thing. I was just a kid about sixteen, seventeen years old. And I was a sinner then…"

⁶⁶ John Steinbeck, *The Grapes of Wrath* (Penguin Books: New York, NY, 1976), is a historical novel that describes the depression in some detail.

⁶⁷ Northern Indiana Center for History (1920-1940), "Indiana Through Change," November 10, 2005, http://centerforhistory.org/learn-history/indiana-history/indiana-through-change-1920-1940.

⁶⁸ Ibid.,

⁶⁹ WMB, *Seal Of Antichrist*, Mar. 11, 1955, Los Angeles, CA, "All the religious people began to say, 'That is the mark of the beast. Don't receive it; my, that's horrible. Ever who joins the NRA, is sure to receive the mark of the beast.' Well, we found out, that wasn't so."

⁷⁰ ____, *Law Or Grace*, Oct. 06, 1954, Jeff., IN, "I once was lost, (out yonder, horse racing and everything else, on Sunday)."

⁷¹ ____, *Jehovah-Jireh*, Mar. 12, 1961, Richmond, VA, "That's what the ruin of our nation today, is women trying to take men's jobs."

⁷² Barbara Sinclair Deckard, *The Women's Movement: Political, Socioeconomic and Psychological Issues*. Third Edition (New York: Harper & Row, 1983), 293.

⁷³ WMB, *Believest Thou This?* Sep. 06, 1953, AM., Chicago, IL.

⁷⁴ ____, *Believest Thou This?* Jul. 16, 1950, Minneapolis, MN, "When I was first ordained as a Baptist preacher…And they just had a local exhorter license, just for the state of Indiana that I could preach, and marry, or bury, or baptize."

⁷⁵ WMB, *Thirsting For Life*, Mar. 04, 1960, Phoenix, AZ, "[T]hirty-two years since 1928, across the nation, around the world…" See also: *Just Once More, Lord*, Dec. 01, 1963, PM, Shreveport, LA, "I'm going to try to. I've tried it for the last thirty-five years, 1928 since I've been in the ministry…"

⁷⁶ Wm. Branham, *Footprints on the Sands of Time, An Autobiography of William Marrion Branham*, Vol. 1 (Jeff., IN.: Spoken Word Publications, 1975), 30., "And so, there was a minister, the one that ordained me in the Missionary Baptist church, Doctor Roy Davis… the Missionary Baptist church at Jeffersonville."

⁷⁷ C. Douglas Weaver, *The Healer-Prophet, William Marrion Branham*, (Macon: MUP, 1987), 33.

⁷⁸ Lindsay, 42.

⁷⁹ Apostolic Friends Forum, "Pentecostal History- September," June 6, 2012, http://

www.apostolicfriendsforum.com/index.php/t-26307.html; Third General Assembly of the Pentecostal Assemblies of Jesus Christ held in Mishawaka, Indiana, 17-23 September 1934.

[80] *Life Story,* LA.

[81] Pearry Green, *The Acts of the Prophet,* (Tucson, AZ: TTB, n. d., 207 pp.), 65-74.

[82] David Edwin Harrell, Jr., 25., "THE HEALING REVIVAL THAT ERUPTED IN 1947 thrust into positions of world-wide Prominence...the two giants of the healing revival, William Branham and Oral Roberts. Most of the participants of the revival looked upon Branham as its initiator. Out of his massive union meetings in 1947 spread reports of hundreds of miracles and marvels."

[83] This is a list of only some of WMB's 1,177 messages that have been recorded: *Led by the Spirit.* - 5x; *Believest Thou This?* – 7x; *Do you now believe?* – 6x; *Life Story* – 9x; *Expectations* – 9x; *At Thy Word* – 7x; *Shew us the Father* – 12x; *Jesus Christ, the same yesterday, today, and forever* – 22x; *Jehovah-Jireh* – 23x; *Blind Bartimaeus* – 23x; *Queen of Sheba* – 13x; *The Falling Apart of the World* – 4x.

[84] Ern Baxter (1914 – 1993) was born in Saskatoon, CAD and died in San Diego, CA. He began his ministry at 17 years of age, and was active until his death. – PMD.

[85] David Edwin Harrell, Jr., *All Things,* 4, 5. "F.F. Bosworth of Zion. His family had moved there while he was a youth and he served as a band director at Dowie's church...Then after World War I, he began conducting revivals. His reputation grew rapidly."

[86] *History and Times of the Kingdom,* "Elijah the Restorer," Reginald Parker, Richard Sweet, Editors, September 4, 2002, http://www.fwselijah.com/dowie.htm

[87] Nils Bloch-Hoell, *The Pentecostal Movement,* (New York, Humanities Press, 1964, 256pp.), 19. "In the autumn of 1900 a Bible school, called *Bethel College,* was opened in Topeka, Kansas...The leader of Bethel was an evangelist by the name of Charles F. Parham. H.J. Stolee speaks of him as 'a man of unsavory reputation...His morals and ethics were such that the civil authorities of more than one state had charges preferred against him. Stolee's severe words seem to cast rather unfavourable aspersions on the early Pentecostal Movement. But it has been confirmed from various sources that Parham's character was hardly blameless, and there is an insinuation in the fact that the later Pentecostal historians keep silent about him...Stolee's assertion is confirmed by O.L. Haavik, who relates that E.N. Bell, chairman of the General Council of the Assemblies of God, in the Pentecostal Evangel of Jan. 1922 wrote about the leader of the Pentecostal work in Houston, Texas, in the pioneer time (undoubtedly Parham) that he 'suddenly fell in disrepute'.

[88] James Gordon Lindsay. "Ephemera of James Gordon Lindsay – Collection 121." *Billy Graham Center. Archives,* available from http://www.wheaton.edu/bgc/archives/GUIDES/121.htm; (accessed March 14, 2008). "James Gordon Lindsay was born in Zion City, Illinois, in 1906. His parents were disciples of Alexander Dowie, the father of healing revivalism in America. After the family moved to Portland, Oregon, the young boy was influenced by John G. Lake and converted by Charles G. (*sic*) Parham. At the age of eighteen he began his ministry as a traveling evangelist conducting meetings in Assembly of God churches and other Pentecostal groups."

[89] Kenneth Copeland, *John G. Lake, His Life, His Sermons, His Boldness of Faith,* (Fort Worth, TX: Kenneth Copeland Publications, 1994, 548pp.), xii and xv. "John Graham Lake...born—March 18, 1870...in Ontario, Canada...xv. Though Lake had been born a sickly child in the 19th century, he now stood boldly at the threshold of the 20th century as a lightning rod stretched between heaven and earth, just waiting to be struck by the very 'lightning of God', as he later called it. And with each release of God's power that eventually charged his life, Lake in turn electrified the modern world."

⁹⁰ Ibid., 217, 218. Kenneth Copeland quoting John. G. Lake, writes, "Personally, I received my ministry in the gospel of healing through John Alexander Dowie, a man whom I have loved with all my soul. And though later in life he became broken in mind and committed many foolish things, so that discredit was brought upon his work…have gone to his grave since I have returned to this land, and as I have thought over that wonderful life, I have prayed in the silence of the night time, 'Lord God endue me with the Spirit of God in the measure that you did that life.'"

⁹¹ James Gordon Lindsay. *Billy Graham Center.*

⁹² Robert M. Anderson, *Vision of the Disinherited: The Making of American Pentecostalism* (New York: Oxford University Press, 1979), 140. Parham baptized in Jesus' Name as early as 1902.

⁹³ Water Baptism, The Old Landmark, Celebrating Our Pentecostal Heritage, available from http://oldlandmark.wordpress.com/glossary-of-pentecostal-history/ (accessed May 29, 2010)

⁹⁴ Mrs. Gordon Lindsay.

⁹⁵ Harrell, *All Things*, 32.

⁹⁶ *Faith in the Son of God*, "Jul. 15, 1952, Hammond, IN, "Brother Baxter and them does the preaching; I pray for the sick."

⁹⁷ Ern Baxter, *New Wine Magazine*, Dec. 1978, 56. "When he [Branham] would speak, especially in those early days, he would say some things that were terribly provocative. To me, (they were) unnecessarily so. So when we talked together, we agreed that apart from his giving testimonies and relating his life story, I would do all the speaking and he would do all the ministry to the sick." ; Mrs. Gordon Lindsay, 87-89., "Branham had some erratic ideas. In fact, at first some of his opinions…bordered on the occult."

⁹⁸ *A Tribute to Ern Baxter*, Dan Bowen, in *Life on Wings*, November 3, 2011, http://ern-baxter.blogspot.ca/2006_03_01_archive.html. "I [Ern Baxter-PMD] travelled with William Branham and he was probably the most gifted of all the healers. His supernatural gift was absolutely astounding and astonishing and 100% accurate within its boundaries. But William Branham always fancied himself as being some kind of a Bible teacher, and he left a bad legacy of error…I left the Branham ministry in disillusionment, questioning everything to do with the supernatural. Undoubtedly I had seen the supernatural and <u>it was real</u>, but I had at the same time seen uncorrected sin, corruption and un-sound doctrine. It seemed like a modern replay of Corinthianism…I had also seen gross irregularites in the midst of these impressive charismatic events." [Note: Underlining and Emphasis theirs-PMD].

⁹⁹ WMB, *At Thy Will*, Jun. 08, 1953, PM, Connersville, IN, "I have for some time been trying my best to operate the meetings myself…without my manager and them. There's no one here but my little son and I…So you bear with me a little while."

¹⁰⁰ WMB's South Africa campaign, held at the end of 1951, is thoroughly documented throughout Stadsklev's book, *A Prophet Visits South Africa.*

¹⁰¹ WMB, *Infallible Proof Of His Resurrection*, Jan 14, 1957, Sturgis, MI.

¹⁰² Carl Dyck, WILLIAM BRANHAM, *The Man and His Message*, (Saskatoon, SK: Western Tract Mission, Inc. 1984, 65 pp.), 40.

¹⁰³ Ibid., 40, 41.

¹⁰⁴ Stanley M. Burgess, Gary B. McGee, editors, Patrick H. Alexander, assoc. ed., *Dictionary of Pentecostal and Charismatic Movements*, (Grand Rapids, MI: ZPH, 1988, 914 pp.).

¹⁰⁵ Lippy, Charles H., ed. *Twentieth Century Shapers of American Popular Religion*, (New York: Greenwood Press, 1989. xxv + 494 pp.), 45.

Chapter Three
WILLAM BRANHAM
A MAN SENT FROM GOD?

Cloverdale Bible Way, a WMB Message church located in Cloverdale, British Columbia, Canada, claims the following regarding WMB:

> One Historian of that movement stated that William Branham was *"a prophet to our generation"*, and a Pentecostal Historian wrote, *"Branham filled the largest stadiums and meeting halls in the world."* The Full Gospel Men's Voice, (now, Full Gospel Businessmen's Fellowship International), in its February 1961 issue, wrote: "*In Bible Days, there were men of God who were Prophets and Seers. But in all the Sacred Records, none of these had a greater ministry than that of William Branham, a Prophet and Seer of God, whose photograph appears on the front cover of this issue of Full Gospel Men's Voice. Branham has been used by God, in the Name of Jesus, to raise the dead!*" From 1947 until the time of his passing in 1965, the powerful ministry of William Branham was well known and considered unparalleled in the history of gospel meetings. The impact of the supernatural ministry of this one man was felt not only in North America, but also around the world.[1] (Note:: Italics are used instead of original blue Hi-lite - PMD).

The above mentioned historian is David Edwin Harrell, Jr.[2] Harrell's book, as with any historian's account, is not an endorsement of anything that occurred. The statements are misleading, to say the least. To re-iterate the above quote, "One Historian of that movement **STATED THAT** William Branham was *"a prophet to* OUR *generation."* However, this was **NOT** what Harrell wrote. He actually stated, "William Branham became a prophet to a generation,"[3] which by no means is an endorsement of WMB, nor of his message. (Emphasis and italics ours - PMD) The next statement, *"Branham filled* *the largest stadiums and meeting halls in the world."* (Italics ours - PMD) is also misleading. This historian was Walter Hollenweger and he said,

> *Branham filled the largest stadiums and meeting halls in the world. He was reported in the newspapers, sometimes favorably, often critically, and in fact in most cases unfavourably*...by contrast to what he [WMB] claimed, only a small percentage of those who sought healing were in fact healed...As a matter of fact, 'The convincing miracles of God, the true evidence of his Spirit and power were absent.'[4] (Italics ours-PMD).

WMB's followers also publish other endorsements, such as the one below:

> The story of the life of William Branham is so out of this world and beyond the ordinary that were there not available a host of infallible proofs which document and attest its authenticity, one might well be excused for considering it far-fetched and incredible. But the facts are so generally known, and of such a nature that they can be so easily verified by any sincere investigator, that they must stand as God's witness to His willingness and purpose to reveal Himself again to men as he once did in the days of the prophets and the apostles. The story of this prophet's life -- for he is a prophet, though we infrequently use the term -- indeed witnesses to the fact that Bible days are here again.[5]

Pro-WMB websites often quote "testimonials" from well-known people. Frequently these testimonials are out of context and they are often re-quotes from other sources. This gives the appearance that these sources endorse WMB. It is always advised to check the original references.

A Calendar of Events

Following is a chronological list of significant dates in WMB's history. They have been compiled from WMB's messages, but also from official records. There is much confusion regarding many dates compiled from WMB's messages. E.G., WMB stated, there were no birth records kept back then in Kentucky and that might be true, in some instances. WMB claimed his birthday was April 6, 1909.[6] This date was told him by a fortune teller,[7] with serious ramifications. Below is a chronology of important dates in the life and history of WMB:

1885 Frank William Broy, WMB's 2nd father in law's, birth year.
1887 Charles Branham* was born on Jan. 2, according to 1920 USA Census.[8]

CHAPTER THREE

Charles is listed as 33 years old. Hence Charles was born in 1887. This birth date is confirmed by Charles' 1917 Military Registration Card, see 1917. Charles is listed as 30 years old and his birthdate as 1887. The 1906 marriage date is also confirmed by the *Find a Grave* database.[9] *The 1910 US Federal Census Records have Charles' name as Charley Brainon. Ella, or Ella Rhea, (Ellie R) Harvey, WMB's mother, born June,[10] from the 1900 USA Census, the earliest record available. The actual date was June 24, 1887, according to *Find A Grave*.

Emma *Hooper* Broy. WMB's 2nd mother in law, born Aug. 31, 1887.

- **1889** Charles A. (Alton) Brumback, WMB's father in law, born on Dec. 12.[11] Brumback appears to be Charles' official family name.
- **1894** Hazel Elizabeth *Scott* Brumback, WMB's mother in law, born.[12]
- **1906** Charles Branhan (Charles C. Branham) weds Ellie R. Harvey.[13]
- **1907** WMB's birth year according to 1910 US Federal Census Records.
- **1908** WMB's birth year? WMB swore on his Marriage License that he was born April 8, 1908. This document was signed and sealed by Ms. Lisbeth Borgmann and dated Feb. 07, 2011.[14] This document shows William M. Branham's birth date to be April 8, 1908. Copy at end of chapter. Date confirmed by the USA Population Census (1 Jan, 1920).[15]
- **1909** WMB's birth year? A Fortune teller told WMB he was born on April 6, which date he adopted,[16] as can be seen on his Marriage Certificate of 1941., See copy at end of chapter. This date contradicts his 1941 Marriage Licence 1908, which birth date he swore to under oath.[17]
- **1910** Winferd Branhan (Winford, or Wintey),[18] WMB's next sibling, was born May 12. WMB called him Edward or Humpy.
  WMB claimed being shot in his leg this year.[19]
- **1911** Move to Indiana.[20] WMB's "vision" of moving to New Albany, IN.[21]
- **1912** Melvin F. Branham, WMB's 2nd sibling was born May 12.
  Charles A. Brumbach and Hazel Elizabeth Scott married June 18.
- **1913** Amelia Hope Brumbach was born on Saturday, July 16.[22]
- **1914** Edgar Lee Branham, birth of WMB's third sibling on June 12.
- **1916** Jessie F. (Jesse) Branham, WMB's fourth sibling, was born on July 3.
- **1917** USA declares war on Germany. Europe was at war since 1914.
  Charles Branham's 1917 Military Registration Card, dated June 5, lists: Age: 30; DOB: Jan. 2, 1887.[23] He lists the number of dependents under 12 as five, including Jessie, not yet born until July 3, 1917.
- **1919** WMB's second wife, Meda Marie Broy, was born on April 26.[24]

1920 Charles R. Branham, WMB's fifth sibling, was born.
1921 Henry Levi Branham, WMB's sixth sibling, was born April 4.
1923 Howard E. Branham, WMB's seventh sibling, born May 23.
1925 WMB bought a 1926 Ford,[25] which he showed his grandmother.[26]
1926 WMB claimed to be a professional boxer. He claimed he fought fifteen bouts undefeated?[27] Golden Gloves Awards did not start until 1928.
1928 WMB in Arizona?[28] WMB claimed to be converted at age 20, in Sep.?[29] However, WMB was not converted until 2 years after his brother Edward died in 1929, and subsequent to his own illness.
James Donald (Donnie) Branham, WMB's 8th sibling brother born.
1929 Edward M. (Winferd/Winford/Wintey) Branham, WMB's first sibling, died of rheumatic heart failure on June 20, 1929, at 19 years old.[30]
WMB returned to Jeffersonville for his brother Edward's funeral.
WMB's ninth and youngest sibling, Dolores R. Branham, was born on May 12.
George Rogers Clark Memorial Bridge built.
1930 WMB often stated he preached since 1930.[31] WMB ordained?[32]
1931 WMB's wrote down his seven end-time visions?[33]
WMB started working at the Gas Plant 2 yrs, after his brother died.
WMB, at 22 years old, dated Hope?[34]
1932 WMB's read out loud from his seven end-time visions and mentioned this date.[35] WMB claimed to have ordained[36] by Dr. Roy E. Davis,[37] in Dec., 1932,[38] in the *First Pentecostal Baptist Church* of Jeffersonville, IN.[39] There are no records of WMB ever being a Missionary Baptist.
WMB said he was a "Holy Ghost" preacher.[40]
1933 A voice spoke to WMB during a baptismal in the Ohio River, stating, *"As John the Baptist was sent to forerun the first coming of the Lord, so are you sent to forerun His second coming."*[41] No Records exist, not even in the Winnipeg Free Press as Lee Vayle alleged.
Branham Tabernacle built (Dedicated?). There are no Records.
WMB was still with Roy E. Davis in the Pentecostal Tabernacle.
WMB's seven end-time visions.[42] Accounts changed over time.
1934 WMB married Amelia Hope Brumback (b. July 16, 1913 – d. July 22, 1937) on Friday June 22.[43] Hope was 21 years old and WMB was 26. WMB attended a "Jesus Only" convention in Mishawaka, IN,[44] Sep. 17-23,[45] two months after his wedding. He claimed to be 23 yrs old.[46] When registering he listed he was an evangelist[47] and did not as yet have a church by the end of September 1934.[48]

CHAPTER THREE

1935 WMB's son William (Billy) Paul Branham was born on Sept. 13.[49]
WMB's brother Charles was killed, on Aug. 5, at 15 yrs. old.[50]
WMB becomes pastor of Branham Tabernacle,[51] which is confirmed by Rebekah Branham Smith.[52]

1936 Charles, WMB's father, died at 52 yrs. old, on Nov. 30?[53] Contradiction, Charles was born Jan., 1887, thus he died at 49 yrs old.
Daughter Sharon Rose Branham, born Oct. 27.
Hope gets pneumonia prior to Christmas.

1937 WMB's wife Hope died of Tuberculosis, July 22, 1937.
Daughter Sharon Rose died July 26, of Tubercular Meningitis.[54]

1939 September 1, WW II breaks out in Europe.

1941 WMB's angelic commission. USA entered WWII, in December.
WMB married Meda Broy, on Oct. 23.[55]
WMB was making $27/wk.[56]
WMB's anointing returned. WMB's two-week revival concluded with a baptismal service at Totten's Ford, near Milltown, IN.[57]

1944 WMB's angelic commission. He received forgiveness in 1944 for the mistake he made in 1934 (his disobedience; his refusal to go with the "Jesus Only" people to spread the message of healing).[58] He received a double portion of His healing power, just like in all the other references to his gift.

1945 WMB's angelic commission.[59] WMB published, *"I was Not Disobedient To The Heavenly Vision."*[60] Neither VOGR, nor Spoken Word Publications, acknowledge the years of 1944 and 1945 for the occurrence. Why? It appears to conflict with WMB's Angelic Commission claim of 1946.[61]
WWII ends September 2.

1946 WMB's angelic commission said to have occurred on May 7, 1946. The angel conferred two gifts that would facilitate the healing of the sick.
Rebekah Branham was born Mar. 21.[62]

1947 WMB campaign entered Canada. Gordon Lindsay was added to the team in March.[63] Ern Baxter came on board in the Fall, in Vancouver, B.C.
UN approves the partition to create a Jewish and Arab state Nov. 29.

1948 May 14, Israel became a nation. (WMB stated it coincided with his angelic commission.)
WMB left field with a breakdown, returned 8 months later.[64]

1949 WMB asked Gordon Lindsay to rejoin him in his campaigns.[65]

1951 Sarah Branham was born March 19.

1953 WMB started to teach Serpent's Seed.[66]

1954 WMB rejected the Trinity, Triune Baptism, and Creeds, as Pagan, WMB's campaign mgr, Ern Baxter, leaves the WMB's Team.[67]

1955 WMB ran into difficulties with the IRS.[68] He owed $390K (reduced to $40K) in back taxes, which WMB never repaid. At WMB's death, $3M+ plus stocks & bonds was found in his vault.[69] A recalculation makes $3M (1965 USD) equivalent to 21M (2010 USD).

Joseph Branham was born May 19.

1958 The Healing Revival, which started in 1947, is deemed to be over.

1960 WMB preached on the Seven Church Ages in December.

1961 Ella (Ellie) Harvey Branham died Oct. 27, at 70 years old.[70] Ella was born in 1887 and she would therefore have been 74 years old at death.[71]

1963 Mystery Cloud in AZ. A constellation of angels opening the Seven Seals, instructed WMB to preach the Seven Seals, in Jeff., IN.

1965 WMB hurt in car crash. Succumbs to his injuries on Christmas Eve.

1966 WMB was buried at Easter.

1981 Meda Broy Branham, died on May 11.

The subsequent 2 pages are of the Book and Internet versions of, *"William Branham, A Man Sent From God."* Rebekah Smith, reaffirmed Lindsay wrote it in close collaboration with, and endorsed and sold by, WMB.[72] The Internet text was drastically changed.[73] Lindsay did not write it, he died on Apr. 1, 1973. Lindsay, stated the publishing date was 1951,[74] the book itself lists the date as 1950. The last two pages contain copies of WMB's marriage licenses.

CHAPTER THREE

William Branham, A Man Sent From God, by Gordon Lindsay in collaboration with Wm. Branham

William Branham, A Man Sent From God, by Gordon Lindsay in collaboration with Wm. Branham Substantially modified from the original Paperback version with the same title, published in 1950

Actual Book Version

It was breaking dawn on a beautiful April morning in the year 1909 in the hill country of Kentucky not far from the place where Abraham Lincoln was born almost exactly one hundred years before. In a humble cabin the light began to creep through the window over a crude small bed, when a baby's voice was heard, Two little hands of a five-pound infant were stroking the cheeks of its fifteen year old mother. Standing near the bed, was the young father, Charles Branham, with his arms folded in the bib of his new overalls, dressed up a bit, for mountain folks, for this special occasion. As the day dawned, the birds had already begun their singing, and it seemed to the father that the morning star shone a bit brighter. The little one cried again as its tiny head brushed against his mother's face. "We'll call his name William," said the father, as he gazed happily down on his newborn son. "That will be well said the mother, "for then he will go by the name of Billy." Little did the mother know that the hands of this little child, that were touching her cheeks would be used of Almighty God for delivering His people from sickness and bondage. No one in that part of the country would ever have thought that this little humble-born mountain baby would carry the message of the Gospel all over the world

Of all the mountain folk, the Branham family was the poorest of the poor. However, God's ways are past finding out! How could these people have believed it if someone would have told them that God, through those hands would cause demons to go out, the blind

Internet Version

Not unlike some of the Bible prophets, the birth of William Branham was marked by the Presence of the Supernatural. He was born on April 6th, 1909. The first child of **Charles and Ella Branham**. It was a beautiful morning in the hill country of **Kentucky**. In a humble log cabin the voice of a baby was heard. The parents of tis child were delighted over the birth of their first son. But **even from birth** he would be a peculiar child. On this morning **God Himself** would confirm that this child was His choice. The young mother and father **watched in astonishment** as the Pillar o Fire came into the little cabin, moved across the room and stopped directly over the sleeping child. Little did the mother know that this little five pound infant would be **used of Almighty God to deliver His people** from sickness and bondage. God would use him to carry the Gospel all over the world. No wonder, the neighbors, who gathered to see the new born baby, spoke of a strange feeling of awe in the room. No doubt it was caused **by the Presence of the Angel**, who would later speak to him, and guide him through his life and ministry.

Of all the mountain folk, the Branham's were the **poorest of the poor**. God's ways are past finding out. In the years to come **God would use this child** to cast out **demons**, bring sight to **the blind** - physically and spiritually, cause **the deaf** to hear, **cancers** to vanish, and **thousands** to go out, the blind to see, the deaf to hear, cancers to vanish to go out, the blind to see, and thousands upon thousands to fall prostrate at altars I tears of repentance? Nor could they have believed that airplanes crossing the continent at high speed would fly the sick to him. Or that trains and buses loaded with sick would be brought to him for deliverance. That they would come from the East and the West, the North and the South, to hear him tell the story of Jesus Christ the Saviour in his simple, humble way. As the neighbours gathered in to see the new born babe, there seemed to be, so it is told, a strange feeling of awe in the room. Who can say that it was not the presence of the angel who, under the direction of God, has guided William Branham in many of the events of his life, and who later was to speak to him in person? It was just two weeks later that the father and mother carried their baby down the creek to the Lone Star meeting house— a little old fashioned Missionary Baptist Church made of logs and clapboard shingles, with a dirt floor and seats made of boards lying across blocks of wood. It was little William Branham's first visit to a church!

hear, **cancers** to vanish, and **thousands upon thousands to fall prostrate at altars in tears of repentance.** TThey would come by plane, boat, busse, and automobile, to bring the sick to him. They would come from all over the world to hear him tell the story of Jesus in his **simple, humble way**. It was just two weeks after his birth that the father and mother took baby William down the creek to the old fashioned, Lone Star Missionary Baptist Church. It was here that the Pastor took William in his arms and dedicated him to the Lord. Little did that Pastor realize that this child would be used so mightily of the Lord to pull down the strong holds of Satan in the Twentieth Century. [Emphases theirs – P.M.D.]

Available from http://www.williambranhamhomepage.org/mansent2.htm; **Internet;** Accessed 01 April, 2002.

CHAPTER THREE 31

Here WMB swore his birth date was April 08, 1908. On the back of this form it is signed and sealed by: Lisbeth A. Borgmann, Clerk of Allen Circuit Court and ex-officio Clerk of Allen Superior Court, Allen County, Indiana. Pages 1. Attest: This instrument is a true and complete copy of the record on file in this office. (Clerk's signature and date Feb. 07, 2011). US Federal Census Records show that WMB was born in 1907. This is a serious discrepancy.

Here WMB swore that his birth date was April 6, 1909. We have two sworn statements with conflicting birth dates. It would be safe to state that the 1941 document reflects the date the fortune teller gave WMB. This is perjury and this discredits WMB and his claims.

Notes - Chapter Three

[1] Cloverdale Bible Way. To high-light some discrepancies this was re-quoted.

[2] David Edwin Harrell Jr., *All Things Are Possible*.

[3] Ibid., 25.

[4] Walter J. Hollenweger, *The Pentecostals*, (Peabody: Hendrickson Publishers, 1988), 354, 355.

[5] Lindsay, 9.

[6] *Life Story*, (*Why I Am Praying For The Sick*) Columbus, "At five o'clock in the morning, when I was born, there was a light, we have the picture of it, circled in the room and hung over the bed where I was standing."

[7] WMB, *How The Angel Came To Me, And His Commission*, Jan. 17, 1955, Chicago, IL, "So there was a little old fortune teller."

[8] United States Federal Census," [database on-line], Ancestry.com (http://ancestry.com: accessed 23 February, 2011) entry for Charles Branham, derived from Roll: *T625_425*; Page: *11A*; Enumeration District: *5*; Image: *60*, database (Year 1920, Census Place: Jeffersonville, Clark, Indiana, 2010).

[9] Find A Grave, "Charles C. Branham and Ella R. Harvey," accessed January 02, 2010, http://www.findagrave.com/cgi-bin/fg.cgi?page=gr&GRid=73486882 .

[10] "United States Federal Census," [database on-line], Ancestry.com (http://ancestry.com: accessed 23 February, 2011) entry for Ellie R. Harvey, or Ella R. Harvey, derived from: Roll T623_ 506; Page 18B; Enumeration District: 4, (Year 1900, Census Place: Gradyville, Adair, Kentucky).

[11] "Military Records," [database on-line], Ancestry.com (http://ancestry.com: accessed 23 February, 2011) entry for Charles Alton Brumbach, derived from: US World War II Draft Registration Cards 1942, U747, database (year 1942, Jeffersonville, Clark, Indiana, 1917).

[12] USA 1920 Population Census.

[13] Find A Grave, "Charles C. Branham and Ella R. Harvey," accessed January 02, 2010, http://www.findagrave.com/cgi-bin/fg.cgi?page=gr&GRid=73486882 . See also *Testimony of a True Witness*, Nov. 05, 1961, Jeff., IN, "And the lady turned around to bow to me, just before...And I'd walked up in the pulpit then to preach. And just as she held her head down, and I turned around like this, to her. And when I raised my head up, and she raised her head up facing me, it was mama. And she looked at me and smiled. She was young, real young. And a great thundering voice shook the place, and words came forth and said, 'Do not worry about her, she's like she was in 1906,' 'And when

the vision left me, I looked to see what 1906 was. That was the year she was a bride to my father." See also: WMB, *Spirit of Truth*, Jan. 18, 1963, Phoenix, AZ, "So I went and got the old family record. You know what she was in 1906? My father's bride. That's the year she was married ...Someone from somewhere sent me a nickel. I got it here in my pocket, 1906."; WMB, *Meanest Man I Know*, Jan. 27, 1962, Phoenix, AZ., "And when she raised up, it was mother, beautiful, young. Just then, like over here, a thunder and a lightning and a roar, and a Voice said, "Do not worry about her no more. She's like she was in 1906." I went away and looked in the old family Bible to find out what happened in 1906, and that was the year that she was a bride to my father."; Azusa Street Revival 1906.

[14] Ms. Lisbeth Borgmann, Clerk of Allen Circuit Court and ex-officio Clerk of Allen Superior Court, Allen County, Indiana, sent an officially signed and authorized copy of this certificate to the author, Feb. 7, 2011. This reveals that WMB perjured himself when he, in his own handwriting, listed his birth date to be April 6, 1909, on his Marriage Certificate of October 23, 1941, when he married Meda Broy.

[15] WMB's birth date, available from 1920; Census Place: *Jeffersonville, Clark, Indiana*; Roll: T625-425; Page: *11A; Ancestry.com. Unites States Federal Census* [data base on-line]. Provo, UT, USA: Ancestry.com Operations Inc, 2010. Images reproduced by FamilySearch. (Accessed February 23, 2011). WMB is listed as 12 years old, thus he was born in 1908.

[16] WMB, *How The Angel Came To Me And His Commission*, Jan. 17, 1955, Chicago, IL, "And she [Astrologist = Astrologer = Magi = Fortuneteller - PMD] said, 'You were born on April the 6th, 1909, at five o'clock in the morning.'"

[17] Barbara Thatcher Haas, Clerk of the Courts, Jeffersonville, IN, sent an officially signed and certified copy of this certificate to this author, January 18, 2011. This reveals that WMB perjured himself when he, in his own handwriting, listed his birth date to be April 6, 1909, on this Marriage Certificate of October 23, 1941.

[18] Winferd (AKA Edward, or Humpy) Branham, Accessed 23 February, 2011. [Author's note: The USA census records of 1930 do not show this sibling. Winferd (Edward) died in 1929, prior to the 1930 Census. See year 1929.

[19] WMB, *Being Led Of The Holy Spirit*, Feb. 19, 1956, Minneapolis, MN, "And I remember a preacher shooting at some birds and seventh shot hit me in the leg. I sure remember that...We come to Indiana when I was three years old. So you can imagine. That was about a year later, so I couldn't have been over two years old at the time when it first happened."

[20] Here's one of WMB's typical "after the fact," or "rearview mirror" prophecies. He already lived in New Albany when he "prophesied" he'd move there.

[21] *Life Story*, LA, "And when I was about... suppose be near three years old...And I heard a bird, and it was singing up in a tree. And I looked up to that tree and the bird flew away, and, when it did, a Voice

spoke to me. Now, I know you think I could not think and remember that. But the Lord God Who's Judge, the earth and the heavens and all there is, knows that I'm telling the truth. That bird, when it flew away, a Voice came from where the bird was in the tree, like a wind caught in the bush, and It said, 'You'll live near a city called New Albany.' And I've lived, from the time I was three years old until this time, within three miles of New Albany, Indiana."

[22] Author's note: Hope was born on July 16, 1913 and died on July 22, 1937, six days after she turned twenty-four. – PMD.

[23] C. Branham's 1917 Military Registration, available from http://search.library.com/ Browse/view.aspx?dbid=6482&path=Indiana.Clark+County,OB.38O, (Accessed February 22, 2011).

[24] WMB *Confirmation And Evidence,* Jun. 21, 1962, PM, South Gate, CA, "Well, I love my wife so, and to see her forty-three years old." WMB said he was 53 in 1962, Meda was 43. Thus Meda Marie Broy was born in 1919.; "[B]aby girl was born into the Broy family in the little town of Utica, Indiana...Twenty-two years later, Meda would become the bride of William Marrion Branham." Meda Marie Broy was born on April 26, 1919,

[25] *Lamb's Book Of Life,* "Mama, you remember when I had that little old T-model Ford, the little old '26 model?"

[26] WMB, *Abraham,* Yakima, Aug. 03, 1960, Yakima, WA, "'26 Chevrolet.'"

[27] ----------, *Faith Without Works Is Dead,* "I won 15 straight professional fights."

[28] ----------, *Resurrection Of Lazarus,* Jul. 29, 1951, Aft., Erie, PA, "One day I decided I'd go out west. And I run off from home and went out to Arizona. I landed out there just in time of a rodeo...I was about eighteen years old."

[29] High Lights in the Life of William Marrion Branham, "His conversion," April 01, 2002, http://www.williambranhamhomepage.org/bblife.htm.

[30] Kevin Freund. Clark Co. Health Dept." Email message to author, February 24, 2011, "Mr. Duyzer— The only name we have in our records for that time period, is Edward M. Branham, date of death 6-20-29, cause of death, rheumatic heart failure."

[31] WMB, *Blind Bartimaeus,* Jan. 24, 1961, Beaumont, TX, "I'm fifty-one years old, and I've been in the ministry thirty-one years."

[32] *Be Certain Of God,* Cleveland, "'Thirty years.' since 1929. See also: WMB, *As The Eagle Stirreth,* Apr. 03, 1960, Tulsa, OK, "Thirty years…" since 1929."

[33] ----------, *Jezebel Religion,* Mar. 19, 1961, Middleton, OH, "I seen it, thirty--1931. Seven things happened. I got it right on paper here with me, wrote it in 1931. How that I said, 'This President, Franklin D. Roosevelt, he will cause all the world, help do it, send the world to war.'"

[34] Wm. Branham, *Footprints,* 29.

[35] WMB, *Faith Once Delivered To The Saints,* May 01, 1955, PM, Chicago, IL, "Now, it's written on old paper, laying at the house today, dated way back in 1933--'32 or '33...Now, remember that;

keep it in mind. That was in 1932, or something like that." See also: *Condemnation By Representation (Hybrid Religion)*, Nov. 13, 1960, Jeff., IN., "I'd like to read something to you.1932: (Listen to this.)...I was getting ready to go on my way to church this morning, it came to pass that I fell into a vision... (Now remember, this is twenty-eight years ago.)" [1960 - 28 = 1932. On the audio recording 12 :26 minutes in, WMB reads the date out, "1932."

[36] *Believest Thou This?* Minneapolis, "I was first ordained as a Baptist preacher…a local exhorter license, just for the state of Indiana that I could preach, and marry, or bury, or baptize."

[37] *"Footprints."*

[38] http://www.biblebelievers.org

[39] Weaver. 33.

[40] WMB, *Shepherd Of The Sheepfold*, Apr 03, 1956, Chicago, IL, "One time in New Albany, Indiana, when our late President Roosevelt was coming down to make a speech, and he came down by the train, and they stopped down at the river…And two or three of us preachers, little, what we call Holy Ghost preachers..." [Note: Pres. Roosevelt had a whistle-stop in New Albany during his campaign tour of October 28-29 1932. – PMD].

[41] Green. 47.

[42] *Faith Once Delivered To The Saints,* Chicago.

[43] William Branham Home Page, "Marries Hope Brumbach," April 01, 2002, http://williambranhamhomepage.org/lhope.htm.

[44] WMB, *Here We Have No Continuing City*, Feb, 1950, Little Rock, AR, "Just before Billy was born, we had saved enough money, till I was, wanted to take a little time off…And on the road back, coming back, I seen a sign, great crowds of people everywhere when I passed through Mishawaka. I thought, "What are those people." And I went over there…There's a conference going on here. The Pentecostal people are having a conference. The- P. A. of J. C. This organization later became known as the UPCI.

[45] *Life Story*, LA. See also Third General Assembly of the Pentecostal Assemblies of Jesus Christ held in Mishawaka, Indiana.

[46] *Life Story*, Hammond, "I was…twenty-three years old then."

[47] *Life Story*, Jul 22, 1951, Aft., Toledo, OH, "I said, 'Billy Branham, evangelist, Jeffersonville, Indiana,'"

[48] *Life Story*, Apr 15, 1951, Aft., Phoenix, AZ, "And we was married …Along during that time, I'd just been ordained to be a minister. I didn't have no church as yet but we was just preaching around wherever I could in tent meetings and so forth."

[49] Birth of Billy P. Branham. http://www.biblebelievers.org

[50] Kevin Freund. Clark Co. Health Dept., Email to author, Feb. 24, 2011 states, "Mr.

CHAPTER THREE

Duyzer- Charles Branham died 8/5/1935, he is recorded as a 16yr old, single, white male with a cause of death as auto accident."

[51] 1935 Jeffersonville City Directory- Wm. Branham is listed as pastor of the Pentecostal Tabernacle.

[52] *Only Believe* Vol.2 No.2, Rebekah Branham Smith, *The Testimony Of Hattie Wright Mosier, Hattie - She said the right thing*

[53] C. Branham dies, available from http://www.biblebelievers.org/bblife.htm;(Accessed 31 January, 2006).

[54] WMB stated this was a direct result of his disobedience to God, for not going with the "Jesus Only" people. He later had a dream, or vision, of Hope, in which she made him promise to join the "Jesus Only" people, and to re-marry.

[55] Marries Meda Broy, available from www.williambranhamhomepage.org/lmeda.htm (Accessed October 20, 2008). "But God also had words of comfort for the young preacher. The words were direct and specific: 'You go get that Meda Broy and you marry her on October 23rd.'"

[56] *Early Spiritual Experiences*, "Making my twenty-seven a week."

[57] *Believers News*, April 1998. This ended 5 years of spiritual agony for WMB, according to *Believers News*, April 1998. This is confirmed by Gordon Lindsay in, "*William Branham A Man Sent From God,*" 50, 51.

[58] William Branham, *I was Not Disobedient To The Heavenly Vision*, (Jeffersonville, IN: William Branham Evangelistic Association: Jeffersonville, IN, 1945). This booklet is out of print, but an electronic version exists. Its accuracy is attested by typical electronic spelling errors of certain letters.

[59] WMB, *Angel Of God*, Nov. 02, 1947, Phoenix, AZ, "A little over two years ago.." Note: Referring to his angelic commission taking place two years prior, or in 1945.

[60] Internal evidence shows the booklet deals with events that occurred in 1944 and 1945. E.G., it lists departure and meeting dates. These meetings also occurred while gas rations were in effect until Aug. 15, 1945.

[61] *Voice of God Recordings* (VOGR) is run by Joseph Branham and *Spoken Word Publications* is headed up by Billy Paul Branham.

[62] Green.

[63] Gordon Lindsay added to Branham team, available from, http://www.wheatonedu/bgc/archives/GUIDES/121.htm, (Accessed March 13, 2002).

[64] WMB, *Do You Now Believe?* Dec. 06, 1953, PM, West Palm Beach, FL, "I was off the field for eight months."

[65] Gordon Lindsay, "*The Story of the Great Restoration Revival, No. IV*," in *World Wide Revival*, June 1958. 18.

[66] WMB, *Israel And The Church # 4*, Mar. 28, 1953, Jeff., IN.

⁶⁷ WMB, *Expectation, (Sons Led By The Spirit)*, Dec. 6, 1954, Binghamton, NY, "Mr. Baxter has resigned, he went into…some business that he couldn't take care of these campaigns." Note: This is the first time WMB mentioned Ern Baxter leaving.

⁶⁸ *The Angel of the Lord Visits William Branham!* As quoted in Harrell, 39-40. "'Branham's difficulties became more complicated in 1956 when the Internal Revenue Service filed a tax evasion suit against him."

⁶⁹ Sarah Branham de Corado, letter to followers of WMB's msg, accessed 31 May, 2011, http://wmb1.com/portico/modules.php?name=News&file=article&sid=15.

⁷⁰ Find A Grave.

⁷¹ Indiana State Board Of Health, Division of Vital Records, Medical Certificate of Death. Cause of death: Cerebral Thrombosis, Arteriosclerosis, Diabetes Myelitis, etc. Ella's Birthdate is listed as June 24, 1891. This is contradicted by earlier noted Government records. WMB provided the information and, based on other fraudulent information he provided, this date is suspect.

⁷² Rebekah Branham Smith, in *"Only Believe"* Vol. 4, Issue 11, p. 6, "The biography by Gordon Lindsay, *"William Branham, A Man Sent From God"* [was]…written in collaboration with William Branham, a distinction in authorship which was agreeable to both the subject and the writer. William Branham highly recommended the book and offered it for sale in the healing campaigns and from his home office."

⁷³ William Branham Home Page, *"William Branham, A Man Sent From God.,"* April 01, 2002, http://www.williambranhamhomepage.org/mansent2.htm

⁷⁴ Gordon Lindsay, "Sketches from the Ministry of William Branham," in *Voice of Healing*, February 1966, Vol. XVIII, No. 11, Gordon Lindsay, editor, (Dallas, TX: Voice of Healing).

Chapter Four
POVERTY CLAIMS EXAMINED

Can WMB's claims of poverty be established by his messages?

WMB was a born story teller and he was able to move multitudes with his tales of poverty. "At the height of his ministry, his halting tales of personal hardship generated a magical empathy with his audiences."[1] Julius Stadsklev said,

> William Branham was born on a farm near Berksville (sic), Kentucky...No one is sure of the exact date because no birth records were kept in Kentucky in those days...His early life was marked by tragedy, poverty and misunderstanding. Some of the most vivid memories of William Branham's youth are pertaining to the poverty in which they were forced to live. His father worked for a wealthy farmer for seventy-five cents a day...Saturday was the most important day around the Branham household. It was the day they would hitch Kootsie, the old mule, up to the lumber wagon and Mr. and Mrs. Branham and all the little Branhams would get into the wagon and take off for town. They would obtain their weekly supply of groceries and the grocery man always gave them a sack of peppermint candy for the five children.[2]

"Of all the mountain folk, the Branham family was the poorest of the poor..."[3] "I remember how dad had to work to pay the bills. It's no disgrace to be poor. But it is hard sometimes.'"[4] WMB said he was born in Little Renox Creek [Little Rennick's Creek - PMD], just a few miles from Burkesville, Kentucky.[5] This was the site of the earliest oil well in North America. WMB related that he was born in a little two room cabin, which had a loft. Three years after his birth the family moved to Utica, Indiana.[6] A year later they moved to New Albany, near Jeffersonville, IN. WMB said he did not know his birth date,

> I laid there a few moments, and I said, 'Well, Bill, you're fifty years old.' Best I know, I was born in Kentucky where they don't have a birth records. And you know what my birth mark is, birth record in Kentucky? The year the old stump blowed away up over on the hill. And that's all they knowed. They say, 'When was that child born?' 'Tomato picking time.' 'What tomato picking time? When was this one born?' 'Corn cutting

time.' 'What corn cutting time?' Now, that was the birth record up in the mountains of Kentucky. So I don't know how old I am, but anyhow, I'm ever bit of that [fifty years old – PMD]…That's what my mother told me, and I think she'd be pretty close to right.⁷

However, beginning with his sermon, *Show Us The father And It Sufficeth Us*, of Aug. 19, 1950 to the sermon, *A Trial*, of Apr. 27, 1964, Tucson, AZ, WMB always maintained that his birth date was April 6, 1909. WMB received this birth date from what he called, "a fortune teller, Magi (sic), stargazer, astrologer, astrologist or astronomer."⁸ This fortune teller said,

You were born on April the 6th, 1909, at five o'clock in the morning.⁹

As stated earlier, WMB's marriage license states he was born on Feb. 8, 1908.

WMB was the eldest of ten children, nine boys and one girl.¹⁰ He mentioned that his brother Edward, nicknamed "Humpy" was eleven months younger than he.¹¹ However, the earlier stated 1920 US Census records lists him as born in 1910, thus two years WMB's junior. WMB and Edward were the only ones born in Kentucky, the rest were all born in Indiana. Winferd Branhan died on June 02, 1929 under the name Edward M. Branham.¹² The next siblings were, Melvin F. (1912), Edgar Lee [Doc] (1914), Jessie F. (1917), Charles R. (1920), Henry L. (1922), Howard E. (1925), James Donald [Donny] (1928), Delores (1929). WMB actually stated in a number of messages that there were no more than three Branham children in that little two room cabin back in Little Renox Creek,¹³ yet there were only two. The stories of up to ten children living up in the loft of that Kentucky cabin appear to be a complete fabrication.¹⁴ WMB placing himself as the sole breadwinner in that context is misleading, to say the very least, but it makes for a great tale.

One thing needs to be understood, poverty is relative and the Branham family would not have been any worse off than any other folks in Little Renox Creek. Anyone with relatives dating back to that era, or later, will have heard similar stories. First, the living standard of the early 1920s would have seemed utter poverty to anyone in the 1950s, or in the times when WMB related this in his often repeated *Life Story*. Second, Charles worked as a logger.¹⁵ At that time the nearby town of Burkesville (Cumberland County Seat) was a booming river port, which would have had a variety of support industries. On the one hand, one would think that would have enabled anybody to generate enough money to support a family of three children. On the other hand, Charles was a drunkard and a brawler who almost knifed a guy to death, according to WMB. After Charles fled from the law things, could have become difficult, if he failed to support his wife and family. Charles fled to Indiana¹⁶ and allegedly changed his name from Branam to Branham.¹⁷ The following is stated by Lee Vayle, "The original family name of this

CHAPTER FOUR   41

man is Branam. His father decided for some reason to add an "h" to the name; making it Branham."[18]

Vayle goes on to explain the spiritual significance and compares it to the name change of Abram to Abraham. Both Branham and Abraham have seven letters (though Branam has six and Abram only five letters). However, the 1920 US Federal Census shows Branhan. Edward (Humpy) and Charles R. appear to have retained the name Branhan.[19]

The Branham family moved from Burkesville, KY, to Utica, IN, and they lived there about a year.[20] Afterwards they moved to New Albany, IN,[21] which is about 8 miles from Jeffersonville where Charles Branham had a farm.[22] WMB's father was hired to break horses[23] by a Mr. O. H. Wathen, who lived on the Utica Pike. Wathen owned the R. E. Wathen Distillery in Louisville KY.[24] Charles got hurt and became a chauffeur for Mr. Wathen.[25] One would think that Charles Branham, being a private chauffeur, would have a well enough paying job to support a family. Besides his day job Charles had the farm and grew corn,[26] likely for making whiskey,[27] because he owned up to three moonshine stills.[28] Even though WMB said his father was a heavy drinker, there is no way Charles could have consumed all he made, thus he must have sold it. No record exists of his father ever getting caught and thus it stands to reason that he must have made some money.

> "The American economy appeared to be in such a healthy state that, in 1928, Herbert Hoover, the man who was soon to become President of the United States, was able to claim that: 'We in America are nearer to the financial triumph over poverty than ever before in the history of our land.'"[29]

Indeed, Indiana, as a State, was prosperous too and boomed during the Roaring Twenties up until the Hungry Thirties. Yet, WMB throughout his life speaks only about the extreme poverty he experienced during that period. With all of WMB's poverty they still had a farm with horses,[30] a milk cow,[31] a mule,[32] and a wagon[33] as well as money with which to go grocery shopping. That Charles was able to pay cash for their groceries[34] indicates they were not as destitute as WMB made it sound. Charles, or the grocer, got them a bag of candy every week,[35] so they were not in dire straits. They celebrated Christmas and hung stockings on the wall in which they did receive toys, etc.[36] When WMB was 8 or 10 years old, his father would give him a dime, of which he spent a Nickel on "Schimpff Red-hots" and ice cream cones. The other Nickel he spent on going to the Movies.[37] Yes, according to WMB, his father drank, but whiskey cost 60 cents a quart to buy, cheaper if made at home. In 1912 a 16 oz. loaf of bread cost 4-1/2 cents, butter cost 39 cents and large skinned hams, 18 cents. Hamburger steak was $2.00 for twelve 17 oz. cans. Tennis shoes were 98 cents. WMB always spoke about their extreme poverty, living on cornbread and black-eyed peas and bacon grease three times a day.[38] WMB listed that his "poverty" diet consisted of beans, bread, potatoes and meat, three times a day.[39] Here is a menu of foods he ate:

- Breakfast - Corn bread, hominy grits and brown sugar molasses. [40]
- Lunch - Cornbread, beans, greens, popcorn and molasses.[41]
- Supper - Mulligan Stew, an Irish stew that contained beef, barley, onions, potatoes, carrots, beans, black-eyed peas, and meal. Out in rural areas other meats were added such a raccoon, opossum, rabbit, squirrel, pork or any kind of bird. It was eaten with cornbread on the side and a glass of chilled buttermilk.[42]

WMB stated he loved the food, especially Mulligan stew. One can still order it in Southern restaurants today. Cornbread and gravy does not sound the healthiest by today's standards, but it sticks to your ribs and is better than going hungry. He spoke about being so poor that they had to go barefoot. In the wintertime they wore tennis shoes with holes where the toes were, yet in other places he told of having white socks and brand new shoes.[43] Since WMB's mother was of Cherokee, blood she could easily have made the children moccasins. WMB certainly knew what moccasins were.[44] Back in 1953 WMB spoke of sixteen year old Arkansas girls coming barefoot to the meetings, brush off their feet and put on their stockings and shoes they were carrying.[45] Roads were not paved and they were very dusty. This is thirty+ years after he experienced it. Barefoot was considered normal then until one's arrival. It appears that WMB fabricated, or embellished, his *Life Stories* in order to illicit strong emotional responses in his hearers.

WMB's reports of extreme poverty do not jibe with reality. Compared with claims of others of that time this becomes abundantly clear. Below are some biographical details of a Mr. James Arthur Hamilton's life of about the same era:

> After my parents moved to the farm, Hillary and Walter were born. Then, on Nov. 27, 1893, is where I came into the picture. I was there in the old log house that day but really I don't remember it. I well remember the first real money I worked for. I helped a neighbor for a day and a half work in the hay harvest for 50¢ per day, and I had the sum of 75¢ to do with as I pleased. After I had grown up, many a day I worked for $1 per day. The first real tragedy in our house was on Sept 12, 1912 when our mother died of a heart attack. After that, it was still nice to go home, but it was never the same. After Mother died, I decided to go West and work for a while. I worked in Kansas in the wheat harvest. Got $9 per day, which was a lot of money then. After the harvest was

CHAPTER FOUR 43

over, I worked 18 months for a rancher-farmer for $25 per month. I saved enough money to come home and buy me a team of horses and farmed for one year but didn't make any money that year, so I decided to try something else. I tried for a job in a state mental hospital. I went to Richmond, Ind. at the salary of $22 per month. I started to work there on Nov. 2, 1916...Signed: James Arthur Hamilton.[46]

In 1916, Hamilton starts a job at $22 per month, or 85 cents a day. WMB's father making 75 cents a day was therefore not a poverty wage at all, as WMB claimed. WMB often stated that he only had a grade seven education. The reason given was that he had to go to work to provide for his nine siblings, due to his father's illness.[47] WMB claimed he worked for the Pennsylvania Railroad, while still in school, loading boxcars.[48] At fourteen he trapped and fished six days a week for a living.[49] The following account seems eerily close to WMB's story and concerns a trapper who disappeared in 1905:

Ziba Scott...lived off the land for he could earn more than the prevailing wage of one-dollar-a-day and his noon meal by hunting, trapping, fishing and digging ginseng roots which was used for medicinal purposes and sold for as much as fifteen dollars a pound when dried. He also supplied several restaurants and hotels in Scranton with trout, bear and venison...On July 3, 1867 Ziba Scott had married 15-year-old Elsie Louisa Purdy and they set up housekeeping... During the winter season, Ziba ran trap lines throughout the area, so many that he had a route for each day of the week. He trapped fox, skunk, weasels, bears, wild cats,, raccoons, mink, otter, muskrats—the hides of which he sold in Scranton to fur dealers... They ate rabbits, woodchuck, grouse, squirrels, deer, bear--anything edible that the woods provided. Their vegetables came from the luxurient garden beside their home which Elsie tended with the help of her brood. These were supplemented with wild strawberries, raspberries, blackberries, and huckleberries--and in the springtime, dandelions, milkweeds, cowslips, lamb's quarter and other "greens" were added to their diet. The members of the family would often find a bee tree which they would mark by carving their initials on it--the custom in those days of "finder's keepers." Again this brought a profit by selling the honey, for a bee tree would often yield several gallons.[50]

WMB's father's illness was drunkenness[51] and he was no longer able to hold a job. His alcoholism finally killed him, WMB said.[52] However, as he was so prone to do, WMB told different stories; in one place he said a doctor actually killed his dad by an overdose of Strychnine.[53] In another story his dad died of a heart attack.[54]

When WMB was around 16 to 18 years old, he worked for a Chris Meisner,[55] or Misner,[56] hauling groceries and he was able to purchase a 1926 car. He spoke about bringing the car to show his grandmother, and stated it to be a 1926, Model T Ford.[57] In another place he said it was a '26 Chevrolet,[58] which was probably a slip of the tongue on WMB's part, since he appeared to have preferred Fords. This car, brand new, would have cost around $290.00.[59] The interest rates for 1926 hovered around 5% or more.[60] In order to buy a car over a bank term of three years, WMB would have had to pay $8.69 a month. Chris probably paid him around 15 cents an hour. When he was twenty years old, he made $0.20/Hr.[61] In a typical 50-hour week at $0.15/Hr; he would have made $7.50 a week, or $32.50/month. This kind of payment of 27% of his income would seem extravagant. However, WMB did trap and fish and made a living.[62] He said he kept himself in school clothes by hunting and trapping.[63]

WMB said he ran away from home[64] when he was nineteen years old.[65] Some have him riding with a Mr. Francisco[66] to Arizona in a "spool top" Model T Ford. WMB said he drove to Arizona and it took him 16 days to cover the 1800 miles to Phoenix. The roads were what he called "rock roads" and he felt he was making good time.[67] Was this the brand new '26 Ford spoken of earlier? Where, in his poverty, did WMB get a brand new auto? Where did he get the money for food, gas and lodgings? What about him being the sole breadwinner of his nine siblings? What about WMB's mother having a boarding house? "A great group of men boarded there, and the big, long table set."[68]

There are very serious questions regarding his alleged poverty. Even a photograph of a young William Branham does not give the impression of poverty. He looked like a river boat gambler with his Errol Flynn style pencil mustache, his carefully coiffed hair and his natty suit, shirt and tie. He does not appear poor, he rather looks like a man at home in the places he later severely condemned: the gaming parlors on the river boats, the horse races, the casinos, and the boxing emporiums, etc.

> He changed my soul from the things of the world unto the things of God, from horse races, and gambling, and adultery, and lying, and stealing. He changed my soul, changed my thoughts; and then my thoughts become so real till they become words in my lips; and they materialize, and now I am a Christian. It made me a different person.[69]

WMB even stated,

> When I was a sinner boy, out yonder astraddle of a horse, trying to see who could ride a bucking horse the longest, or roping calves or something. You were on the corner preaching gospel; I was running horse races.[70]

CHAPTER FOUR

What sort of people hang out in boxing venues around the ring? WMB did. He said, "I was a sinner boy, around horse races…or around the boxing ring somewhere.[71] Besides any officials and boxers, it would probably be gamblers, which WMB confessed to have been.[72] He often claimed he was a boxer, which no one has ever been able to ascertain. WMB stated he was trained by Six Second Smith,[73] however this was a fictional character in a 1923 movie.[74] New evidence suggests that there was a Louisville, KY boxer, who adopted the name Six Second Smith. See: http://searchingforvindication.com/2013/03/14/Six-Second-Smith/. Sports and travel to boxing venues is a luxury, which poor people cannot afford. If he ever had a boxing "career" it was prior to him being a preacher.[75] He said he had long shaggy hair, not likely as a preacher back then.[76]

WMB stated he went to Arizona when he was about sixteen or seventeen, but most often he said he was eighteen or nineteen years old.[77] He also stated that he went to Arizona in 1926.[78] Gordon Lindsay, in the earliest publication of WMB's stories in 1950, written in collaboration with WMB, made it a "September morning in the year 1927."[79] WMB, according to Green, "came west to Phoenix, Arizona, in 1927, at the age of nineteen.[80] Stadsklev wrote, "So when he was nineteen he decided that he would go out west…"[81] WMB also claimed that he was 21 years old at that time,[82] but that date must be discounted.

In 1929, WMB returned home from Arizona to attend his brother's funeral. As per WMB's 1908 birth date, this made WMB 21 years old. After his return he said he started working for the Public Service Company of Indiana[83] for $14 a week, as he later told Hope's father.[84] Elsewhere WMB stated he made 20 cents an hour.[85] Fourteen dollars a week, or $60/month, or $720/year was a good laborer's wage.[86] WMB's future father in law Charlie Brumbach made up to $600 a month according to WMB.[87] A railroad union organizer making ten times a laborer's wage seems outrageous and incredible. Yet, WMB received his future in-laws' blessing even though he only made a laborer's wage. WMB lived at home and his mother ran a boarding house.

Two years into his employment, or around 1931, he said he was poisoned by gas and almost died.[88] The earliest account of his illness is found in Lindsay's book, where WMB stated, "I was overcome with gas, and for weeks I suffered from it." Both Stadsklev's account, as well as Green's book, would seem to have been borrowed from the same source. Lee Vayle's book written in 1965, radically departs from the original accounts and states,

> The tragic news of his brother's death soon brought him home. The sorrow of death and the pressure of his strange life caused a nervous debility to set in. His body became weakened, Appendicitis set in. An operation became imperative. While under the anesthetic he felt his life slip away, and for some time his lifeless body lay upon the operating table while the doctor worked frantically to restore his heartbeat.[89]

WMB, from very young, suffered from hysteria. After his illness he started out to find God, he said, of which more details will be discussed in a later chapter. Later he met his future wife, Hope. After he married Hope, he established a home of his own. He paid $4.00/mo. for rent,[90] less than 10% of his wage. WMB scrounged up various pieces of furniture. WMB said he was happy.[91]

WMB said he had a brand new 1933 Ford,[92] in which he drove Hope to church. It was the self-same car which he drove to the Jesus Only convention in Mishawaka, in 1934.[93] He said he had dedicated this car when he was the pastor of a Baptist church in Jeffersonville. WMB made payments on the car[94] and again, this was no indication of poverty in his life. Though a pastor, WMB said he continued to work as a lineman and a game warden. He later stated he never drew a salary as a pastor for the seventeen years he was there.[95] Throughout his career, however, people gave him love offerings which, combined with two jobs' wages, make his poverty claim unlikely.

WMB even saved up enough money to go on a fishing vacation. Again, this is an indication that he was not as financially desperate as he made it out to be. It is interesting to note that, as stated above, WMB, after his vacation, drove this selfsame 1933 Ford to the 1934 *Jesus Only Convention* in Mishawaka, Indiana.

In truth, there is no doubt that WMB had his share of hardships, though not necessarily those of a financial kind. WMB's sibling Charles died at 15 years old in 1935.[96] The year 1936 saw the death of WMB's father Charles. The next year WMB lost his wife and young daughter. He did record they had financial difficulties from the time they married until his wife and daughter died in 1937. WMB might have had doctors' and hospital bills in 1937. That could certainly impact a person's finances. Yet, he still had his guns, and his wife had saved enough money to put a down payment on yet another rifle.[97] He was quite upset when they re-possessed his favorite chair.[98]

Can WMB's claims of poverty be established from his messages? Poverty, of course, is a relative term. In comparison to other people, he was not poor. In fact, he appeared to have been much better off than most. There is no supporting evidence found for WMB's claims of poverty.

Notes - Chapter Four

[1] Harrell, 29.

[2] Stadsklev, 1, 2, 5.

[3] Lindsay, 28.

[4] Ibid., 33.

[5] *Life Story*, Cleveland, "I was borned in a little log cabin, way in the mountains of Kentucky, Cumberland County, near a little creek called Renox.

[6] *Life Story*, Toledo, "My father left Kentucky in his early days, at about twenty years old , I suppose; I was about three years old. And he moved to Indiana. We lived up on the Utica pike, just above Jeffersonville, going northeast of Jeffersonville. I had my schooling

CHAPTER FOUR

there on the Utica Pike School..." See also: *Being Led*, "We come to Indiana when I was three years old."

7 *Abraham (Jehovah-Jireh # 3)*, "April the fifth, or April sixth, 1909" See also: WMB, *Exhortation On Divine Healing*, May 01, 1951, Los Angeles, CA, "The year the old snag blew away upon the hill, that's the year that I was born. My brother was born at tomato picking time, if you know when that was...that was the count..."

8 *How The Angel Came To Me*, "...an astrologist, stargazer they call them."

9 Ibid.

10 *Life Story*, Cleveland, "My mother's the mother of ten children, nine boys and a girl. I was the oldest of the family."

11 *Life Story*, Los Angeles, "Eleven months difference between me and my next brother." This cannot be true, because, the 1930 US Federal Census reveals Winferd was 2 years and one month younger and he was born in Kentucky. This makes WMB about 4 years old when he had an "after the fact" prophecy regarding moving to Indiana, while he already lived there.

12 USA 1930 census. This record does not show this sibling. Edward (b. May 12, 1910), because he died on June 20, 1929, of rheumatic heart failure.

13 *Life Story*, Hammond, "I remember...First little old home we lived in was a log house. There was about three or four of us little Branhams out there. We didn't even have a floor, just the dirt."

14 *Life Story*, LA, "I was born in a little mountain cabin, way up in the mountains of Kentucky. They had one room that we lived in, no rug on the floor, not even wood on the floor, it was just simply a bare floor...nine of us [boys], and one little girl..."

15 *Early Spiritual Experiences*. "Now, I'm told by my mother and my father...Now, my dad was a logger in the woods."

16 Ibid., "My father was a long way from being a religious person. He was a typical mountain boy that drank constantly, all the time. And he had gotten in some trouble in a fight, and there had been two or three men almost killed as they fighting, shooting, and cutting one another with knives, at some kind of a party up in the mountains ...And it really must have been a terrible fight, because they, from all the way down to Burkesville, many miles away, they sent a sheriff up after Dad, horseback...there was a great knife fight ... my father almost killed the man, so he had to run and leave Kentucky and come across the river to Indiana."

17 *Early Spiritual Experiences*. "And he had a brother that lived, at the time, in Louisville Kentucky...And so he came to find his older brother, and while he was gone for almost a year. He could not come back, because the law was looking for him. And then when we had heard from him by letter, signed by another name, but that he had told mother how it would be that she'd hear from him."

18 Lee Vayle, 68.

[19] Charles R. Branham, available from http://www.findagrave.com/ (Accessed June 05, 2012).

[20] Lindsay, 30.

[21] *Life Story*, LA, "And I've lived, from the time I was three years old until this time, within three miles of New Albany, Indiana." See also: *Darkest Hour, Then Jesus Comes Along*, Nov. 14, 1955, San Fernando, CA, "And spent my life near New Albany…that's where I've lived for about forty years."

[22] Stadsklev. See also: WMB, *The Resurrection*, Dec. 05, 1953, West Palm Beach, FL, "I remember I used to want to be like him. I remember one time when he used have a little old farm we worked on."

[23] WMB, *A Trial*, Apr. 27, 1964, Tucson, AZ, "Three years later, we come to Indiana, and papa got a job. He was a rider, breaking horses for the ranchers and farmers, and so forth. He come out there to break some hackney ponies, for a--a rich man named O. H. Wathen, lives on the Utica Pike. He's a great owner of the Colonels, and also the R. E. Wathen Distillery, and all them in Louisville, and O. H. and R.E. And daddy was breaking saddle horses for him. And then he got hurt, and he went to being a private chauffeur for him."

[24] *Early Spiritual Experiences*, "I've been raised within four miles of New Albany, Indiana. The next appearing that I knew of It, I was about seven years old. I'd entered school. In them days the kiddies didn't go to school till they was about seven. I'd just entered school, and I loved fishing, and I wanted to go fishing. And I went out in the back of the pond, the old ice pond, dad worked for a millionaire then as a chauffeur."

[25] *Trial*, Tucson.

[26] WMB, *Show Us The Father*, May 21, 1961, Dawson Creek, BC, CAD, "I remember one time, daddy and I…we was plowing corn. And I was just a little boy and my horse just begin to snort so, back in Indiana on the farm."

[27] The Business Journals, "Growing Corn for Whiskey," available from http://www.bizjournals.com/louisville/stories/2007/05/07/story2.html?jst=s_cn_hl, (Accessed November 19, 2008). "When frontiersmen found they couldn't grow familiar crops from the east, they grew native corn, converting the surplus into storable, easily transportable whiskey, Morris said. When these frontier people got together, they raced horses and drank whiskey."

[28] *Life Story*, LA, "Later we moved to Indiana and Father went to work for a man, Mr. Wathen, a rich man. He owns the Wathen Distilleries. And he owned a great shares; he's a multimillionaire, and the Louisville Colonels, and--and baseball, and so forth. And then we lived near there. And Dad being a poor man, yet he could not do without his drinking, so he--he went to making whiskey in a--in a still. And then it worked a hardship on me because I was the oldest of the children. I had to come and pack water to this still, to keep those coils cool while they were making the whiskey. Then he got to selling it, and then he got two or three of those stills. Now, that's the part I don't like to tell, but it's the truth."

[29] Spartacus Educational, "American economy - Herbert Hoover," available from http://

www.spartacus.schoolnet.co.uk/USAprosperity.htm (Accessed November 29, 2008).

[30] WMB, *God's Provided Way*, May 13, 1953, Jonesboro, AR, "We was plowing corn, June, July… And when I was pulling my horses around…"

[31] *Resurrection*, West Palm Beach, "When I'd get in, I'd come in a little early and water my horse first. Poor daddy, he'd go plumb till dark, and had to milk the old cow."

[32] *Life Story*, Cleveland, "And I remember we'd set there and eat. I've eaten many places since then, but, oh, brother and sister, if I could only go back to that one more time (That's right,), to those old times back there, and all the loved ones. How we'd gather around there. And I remember when they moved from there to another place. And how dad used to take us down to town on Saturday night. That was a big night. They had a little old Jersey wagon, drove a little mule." In another account WMB related that the mule and wagon weren't theirs.

[33] WMB, *From That Time*, Jul. 13, 1962, Spokane, WA, "I can just barely remember as a little boy about five years old, when the First World War broke out. I know my father came up the road driving two horses in a spring wagon, and he had a sack of beans and some flour (he'd been to the grocery) setting on the seat."

[34] *Life Story*, Toledo, "Dad was a strictly an Irishman; every penny it didn't take to pay the grocery bill, he drank with the rest of it."

[35] *Life Story*, Cleveland, "Notice, and I remember when he would come in, and we'd go to town on Saturday night. We'd all get in a little old Jersey wagon, go to town, pay the grocery bill…And I remember when they'd pay their grocery bill, pop would get a sack full of candy for a treat. And he'd bring it out. That was for us boys. "

[36] WMB, *Christianity Versus Idolatry, or Christianity Versus Paganism*, Dec. 17, 1961, Jeff., IN, "I remember when we was little kids, they would get out and cut down an old cedar bush somewhere, and mom would pop some corn and string it around it. That's about all there was on the tree. But them little, old, ragged socks was hung up there just as… And, oh, and maybe she'd get a--maybe one little sack of candy, and--them little hard candy, and two or three to me, and two or three to Humpy, and two or three to this--just little pieces of candy. And we'd keep that all day long, sucking on that, you know. And wrap it up in a little piece of paper and put it in our pocket. And if we got an old cap pistol, or a little horn to blow, it was a great thing; it thrilled us."

[37] WMB, *Look Away To Jesus*, Dec. 29, 1963, PM, Jeff., IN.

[38] ____, *Thy Loving Kindness*, Feb. 02, 1958, Chattanooga, TN, "When I was a little boy I was raised up here in Kentucky. We were very poor. Black eyed peas and corn bread was all we had three times a day. And mama used to get down from the old store, country store, bacon rind. And she'd render them out to make the grease for the corn bread."

[39] ____, *From That Time*, Jul. 16, 1960, Klamath Falls, OR, "See, we eat food till we get

to a certain age. When I was sixteen...Let science answer this from me: I eat the same food when I was sixteen years old, I eat now: beans, bread, potatoes, meat. And every time I eat, I renew my life...Then I got stronger, bigger all the time. And when I got about twenty-two (you also), I still eat the same food, and getting older and weaker all the time, putting new life in my body."

[40] *Life Story*, Toledo, "They had some brown sugar in a box, and made molasses for breakfast. Did you ever eat brown sugar molasses?"

[41] *Life Story*, Cleveland, "I remember going to school. We kids, we couldn't take our dinner like other children...Their mothers would bake bread; they'd make sandwiches, you know, and put stuff between them. But we couldn't afford that kind of bread. I had a little half of gallon syrup bucket. And we'd take a little jar in there, and had greens in one. The other one had, maybe, beans or whatever we had left over: a piece of corn bread laying there and two spoons." See also: WMB, *Show Us The Father And It Suffices*, Aug. 19, 1950, Cleveland, OH, "I was walking down the school road...and a little old molasses bucket with corn bread and molasses to eat."

[42] *No Continuing City*. See also: *Life Story*, Toledo, "Hickory smoked ham and sorghum molasses...I tell you, marvelous."

[43] WMB, *Questions And Answers #4*, Aug. 30, 1964, PM, Jeff., IN, "I went down there to school, and I didn't have no clothes to wear, and my hair hanging down my neck. And pop--mom took pop's old coat that he was married in, and cut it up and made me a pair of pants to wear to school my first time...And she dressed me with a pair of white stockings on and a pair of tennis shoes."

[44] ____, *Show Us The Father And It'll Satisfy (Seeing God In Nature)*, Apr. 22, 1956, Spindale, NC, "And up there on the mountain I was going along, not so much to hunt the elk and things, my, no. Just to get to myself, out of the meeting, here alone, get the rifle in your hand, a pair of moccasins on, take off, hike thirty-five, forty miles a day, through the snow cliffs."

[45] ____, *God's Provided Way*, Jun. 13, 1953, Connersville, IN, "I've seen young ladies sixteen years old, come into the meeting...See them come packing their shoes and stockings under their arm. And then get down there and brush off their shoe--feet, and put on their stockings and shoes, and go on in the church. Have to make that one pair last a long time."

[46] Frank W. Hamilton, *My Life and Times*, Yesterdays of Hamilton County, IL available from http://www.carolyar.com/Illinois/Family/ArthurHamilton.htm. (Accessed December 03, 2008).

[47] WMB, *Who Hath Believed Our Report?* Jul. 19, 1951, Toledo, OH, "You know in my talk that I'm uneducated. I was raised in a big family of ten children. I got not even a grammar school education. Seventh grade was as far as I got in school. I had to go to work, take care of nine children. My father wasn't very healthy, died young, and I had to work."

[48] ____, WMB, *A Paradox*, Apr. 18, 1964, Brkfst., Tampa, FL, "I remember in school...working in a section gang." See also: WMB, *What Is The Holy Ghost*, Dec. 16, 1959, Jeff., IN, "I

used to work on the railroad…And we would go *down* to load a car. My brother, Doc, standing back there helps--loads cars."; WMB, *Adoption #4,* May 22, 1960, PM, Jeffersonville, IN, "I used to work for the Pennsylvania Railroad."' WMB, *Hearing, Receiving And Acting,* Jun. 07, 1960, Chautauqua, OH, "I used to work for the Pennsylvania Railroad."; WMB, *Mark Of The Beast And The Seal Of God #2,* Feb. 17, 1961, Long Beach, CA, "I used to work on the railroad."; WMB, *Have I Not Sent Thee,* Jan. 24, 1962, Phoenix, AZ, "I used to work on the railroad."; *Breach,* "I used to work for the railroad company."

[49] WMB, *Questions And Answers # 2,* Aug. 23, 1964, PM, Jeff., IN, "I got them traps set up there around Wathen's, up above that.' I'd leave every morning about 2 o'clock with a lantern to run these traps, then get back in time to go to school. I'd catch a rabbit; I got fifteen cents out of it. I'd get a box of shells out of that, and maybe that kill three or four rabbits. What we didn't have to make some biscuits and rabbits, why, and gravy for supper, I'd sell the other, and maybe get enough to get some bread, or some meal, or some flour to make gravy with…I'd set trout lines on the river; go down, and get them fish, and sell them for ten cents a pound."

[50] Ziba Scott, Family Tree Maker, *Ancestors of Merritt Scott,* available from, http://webcache.googleusercontent.com/search?q=cache:5G8bpRnh1woJ:familytreemaker.genealogy.com/users/h/e/n/Cynthia-L-E3Henning/PDFGENE3.pdf+1923+trapper+prices, (accessed December 05, 2008).

[51] *Life Story*, Los Angeles, "My father was a long way from being a religious person. He was a typical mountain boy that drank constantly, all the time…Dad being a poor man, yet he could not do without his drinking, so he went to making whiskey in a still…Then he got to selling it, and then he got two or three of those stills."

[52] *Life Story*, Cleveland, "My father'd drink very, very heavy. Irish and he just… Fact, it's what killed him."

[53] *No Continuing City*, "First thing, I lost my daddy. I run over to the house to see him, picked him up in my arms like that, he looked up at me like that, he smiled. A doctor had give him a dose of medicine that killed him. One overdose of strychnine for his heart, and it killed him. 'Course, there's nothing said about that. The undertaker covers up the doctor's mistakes sometimes. Nothing I got against doctors, but I say there's nothing said about that."

[54] WMB, *Is Your Life Worthy Of The Gospel,* Jun. 30, 1963, PM, Jeff., IN, "And my father, dying in my arms, and me talking to God as a healer. And my own father in a heart attack, laid his head in my arm, and me praying for him; and see him turn those eyes and look at me, and falled off, to go to meet God."

[55] ____, *The Flashing Red Light Of His Coming,* Jun. 23, 1963, PM, Jeff., IN, "I remember a man I worked for, Chris Meisner, up here on the corner." There is a Chris Meisner (b.1856 d. 1941) buried in Walnut Ridge Cemetery Jeffersonville, Clark County Indiana.

⁵⁶ WMB, *Who Is This?* May 10, 1959, PM, Jeff., IN, "It don't seem like it's been no time since I was hauling groceries for Chris Misner, about…sixteen, eighteen years old."

⁵⁷ *Lamb's Book Of Life*, "Mama, you remember when I had that little old T-model Ford, the little old '26 model? How I'd polish that thing. I was just a kid about sixteen, seventeen years old. And I was a sinner then…Sunday afternoon, I'd polish that little old Ford till it looked like the paint would almost come off of it."

⁵⁸ *Jehovah-Jireh #3, (Abraham)*, …little '26 Chevrolet."

⁵⁹ Ford Motorcar, 1926, available from www.wiley.com/legacy/products/subjects/business/forbes/ford.html, (accessed June 07, 2003).

⁶⁰ Interest Rates for 1926, available from http: //bases/www.rber.org/data macrohistory/rectdata/13/m13031.dat, (accessed June 07, 2003).

⁶¹ *Life Story*, Los Angeles, "Making twenty cents an hour, to marry his daughter."

⁶² *Q & A # 2*, Aug. 23, 1964.

⁶³ WMB, *Having Conferences (Conference With God)*, Jun. 08, 1960, Chautauqua, IN, "Years ago, I used to have an old hunting dog; his name was Fritz. And he was half Airdale and half Newfoundland; he was a great big dog. And he used to go with me everywhere when I'd go hunting, and the best old thing I ever had. He'd lay with me, and he put me in school clothes from hunting, treeing opossums and skunks, and what more I trapped. And so, he just kept me in school clothes… I was just about sixteen, seventeen years old…And about a year after that, I was saved."

⁶⁴ WMB lied to his mother and ran off to Arizona. *The Ministry Of Christ*, Jun. 07, 1953, Aft., Connersville, IN, "When I was about nineteen I told mother I was going up here in Indiana to Boy Scout Reservation, Green's Mill to camp. I run off and went out west, went to Arizona."

⁶⁵ Other messages give different ages, anywhere from 17 yrs old through to 19. *Ministry Of Christ*, "When I was about nineteen…I run off and went out west, went to Arizona."

⁶⁶ Wm. Branham goes to AZ. SOMETHING HUNGERING IN MY HEART, available from: http://www.williambranhamhomepage.org/lwest.htm (Accessed July 15, 2011).

⁶⁷ WMB, *A Super Sign*, Jul. 08, 1962, Grass Valley, CA, "Why, these cars that we got today, couldn't run over these highways we used to have. My first trip west, it taken me sixteen days to go from Jeffersonville to Phoenix, Arizona, eighteen hundred miles. But, my, the most of--it was 1926, they had nothing but just old rock roads. I was a little boy setting there, holding this spool-top Ford; I thought I was making good time." Note: 1926-1908 = 18 Thus WMB was 18 years old. - PMD].

⁶⁸ *How The Angel Come To Me And My Commission.* See also: WMB, *Expectations*, Apr. 05, 1950, New York, NY.

⁶⁹ WMB, *The Word Became Flesh, India Trip Report*, Oct. 03, 1954, AM, Jeff., IN.

⁷⁰ ___, *Zacchaeus*, May 17, 1958, Brkfst., Bangor, ME.

CHAPTER FOUR

71 WMB, *Message To The Laodicean Church*, Jun. 09, 1958, Dallas TX.

72 *Word Became Flesh*.

73 WMB, *Wisdom Versus Faith*, Apr. 01, 1962, Jeff., IN, "And I used to box. And there was a fellow named, here in the city, a poor fellow, drinks very bad now; one of his boys is on the police force, Smith, George Smith; they called him Six-second' Smith. He went to training me for boxing when we had, 'fore the Golden Gloves started."

74 Six Second Smith, Issued March 18, 1923, Directed by Malcolm St. Clair, starring George O'Hara and Leach Cross, accessed January 7, 2013. www.imdb.com/title/tt0783806/combined

75 WMB, *The Conflict Between God And Satan*, May, 31, 1962, Clarksville, IN, "I was fighting my fifteenth professional fight down here at Evansville, Indiana, and Howard McLain...And Howard was a welterweight, and I was a bantam weight, and I was fighting Billy Frick from Huntington, West Virginia. And Howard said to me, he said, "You know what, Bill?" I said, "What?" Said, "You look like a little Baptist preacher."...I said, "Now, wait a minute, Howard. Now, you laugh when you say that. Me, about *that* high, but I was ready to climb right on him. I wanted nothing to do with no preacher." [Note: No records exist that Welterweight Howard McLain, a real boxer from 1926-1929, ever fought in Evansville. Billy Frick was a Featherweight from Evansville, IN. There exists no record that Frick ever fought WMB, or anyone from Jeffersonville, IN., during his 1931-1934 boxing career. – PMD]. McLain's and Frick's careers did not overlap.

76 ____, *The Supernatural (Spiritual Atmosphere)*, Jan 29, 1956, Owensboro, KY, "I used to be a pugilist as you know, fight. I won fifteen professional fights (not bragging, I'm ashamed of it.)...And I had my picture there, when I was in my very best, muscles over me and black shaggy hair hanging around my neck...My little girl come in and seen my picture setting in the room; she said, "Daddy, you don't look like you used to."

77 *Ministry Of Christ*, "When I was about nineteen...I run off and went out west, went to Arizona."

78 *Super Sign*, Grass Valley.

79 Lindsay. 36.

80 Green, 42.

81 Stadsklev, 8.

82 WMB, *Hebrews Chapter Seven # 1*, Sep. 15, 1957, PM, Jeff., IN, "I used to be as a fighter, pugilist...I was strong and big. About twenty-one years old, I was, and one day I had a battle with *this*, *that*, and the *other*. I couldn't make out whether I wanted to be a fighter, or whether I wanted to be a trapper, or hunter, what I want to be."

83 When J. N. Shannahan replaced Samuel Insull as chairman of the company in 1931, the utility changed its name to the Public Service Company of Indiana; the following year, it merged with the Indiana Electric Corporation, available from http://www.fundinguniverse.com/company-histories/PSI-RESOURCES-Company-History.html; (accessed December 05, 2008).

84 *Life Story*, Hammond, "I said, 'I can't make her a living like you will, certainly not, Charlie, you make five hundred dollars a month and I'm making about fourteen dollars a week.'"

85 *Life Story*, Cleveland, "I said, 'Charlie, look,' I said, 'I can't make her a living the way you do.' I said, 'I--I--I'm only making twenty cents an hour.' I said, '...But Charlie, I love her with all my heart, and I'll work as hard as I can to make her a living.'"

86 Old Alimony Case Summaries, 12. THOMPSON v. THOMPSON, 226 U.S. 551 (1913): A quote from the case states: "The supreme court of the District, upon final hearing, held the Virginia divorce to be invalid, and made a decree awarding to the wife custody of an infant child born to the parties during the pendency of the proceedings, and requiring the husband to pay to the wife $75 per month for the maintenance of herself and the child, to forthwith pay to her the sum of $500 for counsel fees, and also to pay the costs of suit to be taxed." $500 was a year's labor for an average worker back then. $75 is more than the average worker made in a month back then." Available from http:// www.restoreliberty.com/oldalimony.htm, (accessed December 05, 2008).

87 *No Continuing City*, "Her father, during the time of the depression that that was, he made about six hundred dollars a month. He was a brotherhood organizer on the Pennsylvania Railroad. I made twenty cents a hour digging ditches."

88 WMB, *From That Time*, Mar. 31, 1960, Tulsa, OK, "One time, I myself, laying on a hospital bed...laying there dying...And the doctor said, "There's no way for him to live," and I heard it. And they pulled the curtain around me. Then I heard a sound coming through, like noise coming like leaves a blowing. I thought, 'This is it.' 'God, I can't offer you my life like this, like an old rose with the petals falling off.' I said, 'Sir, I don't know how to pray, but I've been told that You're a great Doctor, above all the doctors. If You'll just let me live, I'll never be ashamed of You no more. I'll scream it from housetop, from street corner...' And from that hour, I begin to live and I've lived ever since. And today, after thirty-nine years? I'm glad to be standing behind the pulpit tonight." [Note: This fits age 14 when he had his hunting accident. - PMD].

89 Vayle, 36.

90 *No Continuing City*, "We got married. We didn't have nothing to start housekeeping on. Only thing we had...I tell you what we had: A little old place where I rented; my rent cost me four dollars a month."

91 Ibid.

92 WMB, *Teaching On Moses*, May 13, 1956, Jeff., IN, "In 1933. I just got a 1933 Ford, and I dedicated it that morning to the Lord."

93 *Life Story*, Toledo, "I remember, it was that Ford that I visit Brother John Ryan for the first time in Dowagiac, Michigan; you remember this story, Brother Ryan." On his way back, WMB stopped at Mishawaka.

94 *Life Story*, Owensboro, "...right after the boy was born, I took my first vacation. We

saved up enough money till I had, I believe, around six, eight, ten dollars saved up, besides the car payment. And I went up to Michigan to visit an old friend of mine that I'd met, by the name of John Ryan..."

[95] WMB, *The Queen Of The South,* Jun. 20, 1958, Greenville, SC, "I worked seventeen years as game warden and for a electrician, as a public service company, and pastored the Baptist Tabernacle at Jeffersonville..."

[96] *Life Story*, Toledo, "Now, I never forget; trouble started when...My father took sick, died on my arm just a little bit after that. My brother was riding on the side of a car, fifteen years old."

[97] *My Life Story*, LA, "She [Hope]said, 'Please promise me.' Said, 'One thing I want to tell you.' Said, 'You remember that rifle?' I'm just crazy about guns. And she said, 'You wanted to buy that rifle that day and you didn't have enough money to make the down payment.'"

[98] *Life Story*, Hammond, "One time when I'd preached. I worked all day and preach every night. And I'd come in, and I wanted a place to rest. And I got an old Morris chair. I paid fifteen dollars for it. And I paid a dollar down and a dollar every other week. And I got five or six dollars paid, and I couldn't make the payments."

Chapter Five

NON-RELIGIOUSBACKGROUND EXAMINED

Can WMB's claim of not having a religious background
be supported by his own messages?

WMB was, and is, regarded as a prophet[1] by many and he is seen as the one who spearheaded the Great Healing Revival of the 1940s and 1950s.[2] These are substantial claims. It is imperative one engages the Scriptural warrant and, "Test the spirits to see whether they are from God, for many false prophets have gone out into the world" (ESV 1 Jn. 4: 1).

This chapter will examine to see if WMB's claim of not having a religious background can be supported by his own message. Nothing is known about WMB's background, outside of what he himself related. Much of what he said about his early life he claimed he heard from his parents. There are 1,177 plus, WMB's messages available,[3] and a number of books written by people from within WMB's following. Most sources outside of WMB's movement, have received their information, either directly from his followers, or from his family members, or from material written by them. This makes it hard to find objectivity. This Chapter will not be anecdotal, but will rely mostly on what WMB's messages state. In other words, this is a serious attempt to apply original research to WMB's messages with the aim of bringing objectivity.

WMB stated he was of Irish Roman Catholic ancestry and his forebears had come from Dublin, Ireland.[4] WMB noted several times that he was raised in a Baptist church.[5] He said he was rocked in a Baptist cradle[6] and also stated that he was dedicated on, or about, the eighth day, in a Baptist church.[7] This church was referred to by WMB by several names, the Southern Baptist Church, Missionary Baptist Church, Opossum Kingdom Baptist Church, and Lone Star Meeting House. WMB's mother, Ella Harvey Branham, spoke about worshiping there when she was a girl.[8] Ella Harvey was from Paris, Texas,[9] WMB said. Ella (AKA Ellie) allegedly came with Charles Branham to Renox Creek, Kentucky, as a fourteen year old bride.[10] In another place WMB stated that Ella was born in Green Briar Ridge, Kentucky.[11] Ella was actually born in Breeding, KY, about 14 miles from Burkesville, where WMB's grandfather had built a church.[12] There are a number of occasions where WMB himself confirmed that they did worship in a

CHAPTER FIVE 57

church way down in Kentucky.[13] This, of course, completely contradicts his claim that his parents, though Roman Catholic, never attended church.[14] Knowing this, it now actually makes sense that his parents took him to a Baptist Church for his dedication. If his parents *were* Roman Catholic, they would have known the RCC doctrine that states, "*In case of necessity, anyone, even a non-baptized person, with the required intention, can baptize, by using the Trinitarian baptismal formula.*"[15] If there were no priests in the area,[16] his own father could have sprinkled him by the authority of the Roman Catholic Church.

It is known that "Burkesville became a busy river port during the latter part of the nineteenth century, serving a large area at a time when water transportation was the only feasible way to move large quantities of goods in and out of the territory."[17] That being so, Burkesville, as the Seat of Cumberland County, presumably had at least a Roman Catholic church, though WMB was adamant there were not.[18] WMB's parents went to a Missionary Baptist church to dedicate William. This would indicate they had at least some kind of relationship with that church, which WMB allowed.[19] It's difficult to envision a lively Missionary Baptist church, such as described by WMB, agreeing to dedicate a child to God without any commitment by its parents to raise it in the fear of God. William is not at all a Roman Catholic Irish name.

As a fourteen year old boy, WMB appeared to have been serious in regards to honoring the Lord's Day.[20] Why would he do that if he did not know anything about Christianity? WMB said he played baseball for a Methodist church league,[21] which makes his claim of not knowing anything about Christianity even more difficult to believe. WMB's father had the Ten Commandments up on the wall at their house.[22]

A preacher shot WMB in his leg with birdshot, when he was only two years old.[23] Was it a Baptist preacher, or was he a Methodist, since WMB did not say, priest? What was a preacher doing at their house? He also said that, at about fourteen years old, he had a serious hunting accident. He said he almost lost his legs after he got shot by a shotgun.[24] He said that he was dying[25] and had a vision of hell and he prayed to God,[26] but there was no God there. Here it is seen that, even though WMB claimed he knew nothing about God, his prayer showed otherwise,

> I said, 'O God, if You'll let me out of here, I--I--I'll never be ashamed of You again. I'll never be ashamed. God, please give me a chance.'[27]

For WMB to say that he'd never be ashamed of God AGAIN would indicate there had previously been an incident of sorts where he had been ashamed of the Lord. In his second vision he saw himself standing in the West and felt the glory of God come off a golden cross and into his chest.[28] As stated in the last chapter, WMB said that while he was dying and his heart was only beating seventeen times a minute, he prayed and he was converted to Christ.²⁹ This had occurred thirty-nine years prior, he said, or in 1921, which would have made WMB 13 years old, as he also confirmed in another place:

> One time, I myself, laying on a hospital bed...A little nurse standing there, and <u>my heart only beating seventeen times to the minute: a block of anesthetic had went to my heart from an operation from a spinal block.</u> And the doctor said, "There's no way for him to live," and I heard it. And they pulled the curtain around me. Then I heard a sound coming through, like noise coming like leaves a blowing. I thought, "This is it." "God, I can't offer you my life like this, like an old rose with the petals falling off." I said, "Sir, I don't know how to pray, but I've been told that You're a great Doctor, above all the doctors. If You'll just let me live, I'll never be ashamed of You no more. I'll scream it from housetop, from street corner..." And from that hour, I begin to live and I've lived ever since. And today, after thirty-nine years?, I'm glad to be standing behind the pulpit tonight to say, "Jesus Christ is the same yesterday, today, and forever," because one day I met God.³⁰ [Underline mine – PMD].

WMB was 13 years old when this occurred. 1960 – 39yrs = 1921; 1921 – 1908 = 13. Based on his age, it must be concluded that this had to be the operation after his hunting accident. WMB mentioned, "my heart only beating seventeen times to the minute: a block of anesthetic had went to my heart from an operation from a spinal block," This is interesting because WMB's claim of his heartbeat of 17x/min., was later repeated regarding an operation performed at the Jewish Hospital in Louisville, KY, while he was employed by the Indiana Service Co.³¹ Later, in that same message WMB said:

> I was operated on, when I was shot, when I was a little boy. And when I come, from under the first anesthetic, I thought I was in torment, going down. The ether had me out. And I had been gone out for eight hours, I think. They was worrying about getting me around to myself again. They had a great operation, with no penicillin. Blood; both legs almost shot off, with a shotgun. A little boy friend let his gun go off. Then about seven months later, I took another anesthetic. And when I come from under that anesthetic, I thought I was standing out on the western prairies. And a great golden cross in the sky, and the glory of God shining down off of it. Me standing there like *this*."³²

This, obviously was about his hunting accident and this is confirmed by yet another quote:

> Now in this time, as I had this vision, and thinking that I--I had passed from this

CHAPTER FIVE

> life into torment. And seven months later, here at the <u>Clark County Memorial Hospital,</u> I had the second operation. And at that time, when I come out, I thought I was standing out in the West. I had another vision. And there was a great golden cross in the skies, and the Glory of the Lord flowing off of that cross. And I stood with my hands out like *this*, and that Glory was falling into my chest…The vision left me. My father was setting there looking at me, when the vision came…All people that's knowed me all these years, knows I've always wanted to go West.[33] Underline mine – PMD.

And "Go West" he later did, of which more will be said. WMB stated in the above quote that he was operated on in Clark County Memorial Hospital. Based on that information, this operation, by default, had to have been due to his hunting accident. WMB's operation, while employed by the Indiana Service Co., was performed in Louisville, KY:

> Many of you people right here in this building tonight from right around the home places here, that would've been dead in their grave if it hadn't been for Jesus Christ. And I am one of them. That's right. I'd have went years ago right here in the <u>Jewish hospital when a doctor of this city</u>, one of the famous doctors of this city, give me three minutes to live. And I'm here by the grace of God. Then when He let me live, I gave my heart to Him and been screaming from the housetop ever since.[34] Underline mine – PMD.

This issue regarding the similarities of what WMB said about the two different operations will be discussed a bit later in this chapter. WMB did relate how he started to seek and find God. He stated he went from church to church, but he found them all contrary to the Word.[35]

> I said, "Mother, when I was just a little boy, I knew there was a God, because I had seen His Person in different forms." And I said, "…Being in our family, and we lived by the side of Mr. Wathen up there on the Utica Pike, and we knowed nothing about church. They were Catholic." And I said, "I begin to studying. Now, as the Catholic church says that God gave His great power to His church…I studied that. Then I begin to find out there's almost nine hundred different organized bodies of believers…Mama, I could not base any faith. Because the Catholic church says one thing. The Lutheran church says "It's this a way." The Methodist church said, "No, they're both wrong. It's this way." The Baptist church says it's some other way. And nine hundred different beliefs, I could base no faith on that. But I said, "What I did, mama, I went back and read the Bible."[36]

In the above quote WMB clearly stated that he went to study God's Word while he and his family lived at Utica Pike, next door to the Wathen's home. WMB stated that he, "Knowed of God when I was a little boy...I wanted to find out about who God was, and my people didn't go to church."[37] He looked at various church affiliations and came to the conclusion that the churches were all wrong. He said he was glad God got a hold of him before any church did.[38] How could WMB, a young teenage boy, without any supposed Scriptural knowledge, determine which was correct and which was contrary? This sounds suspiciously like the testimony of the Mormonism founder, Joseph Smith, who said:

> I retired to the woods to make the attempt...I kneeled down....I saw a pillar of light exactly over my head...I asked...which of all the sects was right...I was answered that...they were all wrong...I was an obscure boy, only between fourteen and fifteen years of age.[39]

Not much is known about WMB's life in his mid-teen years, except he had a desire to go west.[40] Later, WMB, prompted by an astronomer, his name for a fortuneteller, did go west.[41] He remembered that, "One day as a little boy, about eighteen years old, running from the Lord. I went out west...There was something hungering in my heart. Oh, I tell you. I went down to the Baptist preacher; he said, 'Stand up and just say, Jesus is the Son of God; we'll put your name on the book.' That didn't satisfy me...The Seventh-day Adventists, [I] went to see him, a fine man, Brother Barker, lovely brother; he said, 'Billy, come and accept the Lord's sabbath.'...And I thought, 'Oh, my, that just still don't do it.'"[42] In another place WMB stated that he studied with the SDA and determined they were wrong.[43] This is problematic, because WMB used that same argument after he was hurt at the Public Service Company of Indiana, of which more below. While out West he worked at a ranch and he said he was confronted with the Gospel more than once, yet he walked away.[44] In fact, he actually prayed and said, "Sir, I don't know Who You are, but don't punish me until I can find the real thing."[45] Later he received notice that his brother Edward had died.

WMB returned to Jeffersonville for his brother Edward's funeral. Afterwards, he stayed and went to work for the Public Service Company of Indiana at New Albany, where he worked for seventeen years and where he got hurt.[46] Seventeen years would bring the date to about 1947, which fits the start of his healing campaigns. WMB said that prior to getting hurt, he received word that a co-worker had fallen ill and had been prayed for. He said, as a sinner, hearing that, struck his heart.[47] WMB said that occurred about 23 year prior to 1960, thus in 1931. This is what he related to Gordon Lindsay regarding getting hurt:

> About two years later, while testing meters in the meter shop at the Gas Works in New Albany, I was overcome with gas....I suffered with acid stomach caused by the effects of the gas...I was taken to specialists in Louisville, Kentucky. They

finally said it was my appendix and said I had to have an operation...I agreed to have it done, but insisted that they use a local anesthetic so that I could watch the operation.[48]

The location of the hospital was Louisville, KY, which WMB's own messages confirm. Would a surgeon agree to do an appendectomy under local anesthetic? Possibly. Back in the day, more people died under spinal anesthesia compared to today. A side effect was, and is, cardiac arrest. It appears that the epidural WMB underwent at 14 years of age had severe side effects and almost caused his death. It is quite likely that WMB opted for a local anesthetic, though it is doubtful he was allowed to watch.

In none of his other messages did WMB mention gas poisoning, nor did he refer to an operation, in this context. All that exists is his own account to Gordon Lindsay, with which Julius Stadsklev's and Pearry Green's accounts agree. Lee Vayle is the only dissenting voice here and he states the following about WMB,

> The sorrow of death and the pressure of his strange life caused a nervous debility to set in. His body became weakened. Appendicitis set in. An operation became imperative.[49]

Vayle wrote his book much later than the aforementioned authors and he was very close to WMB. Why did he not mention the gas poisoning? Vectren (Formerly the Public Service Company of Indiana), told this author over the phone,[50] that it was it was not the gas that poisoned people. Rather, it was the by-products from turning coke into gas that were poisonous. These poisons were not present in the meters that WMB allegedly tested. It would appear that Vayle was correct in not attributing gas poison to WMB's testing of gas meters. It was WMB's "nervous debility," another word for a recurring mental breakdown which WMB experienced in roughly seven year cycles. This appears to have been of of them. Some side effect of this mental illness are headshakes and hysterical blindness. Vayle continues and states that while under the anesthetic WMB felt his life slip away...During that time he saw visions of heaven and hades. He cried to God and promised that if God spared his life, he would seek Him and serve Him."[51] WMB stated, "'Well, this is death coming to take me.' Oh my soul was to meet God; I tried to pray but I could not."[52] WMB said he heard a voice that said, "'I called you and you would not go.' The words were repeated the third time. Then I said, 'Lord, if that is you, let me go back again to earth and I will preach your Gospel from the housetops and street corners. I'll tell everyone about it!' When this vision passed, I found that I felt better...After a few days I was allowed to return home, but I was still sick and was forced to wear glasses because of astigmatism. My head shook when I looked at anything for a moment."[53]

According to Gordon Lindsay, WMB felt himself getting weaker and weaker after the operation and he said he was not ready to meet his God."⁵⁴ Why WMB would call God *his* God is an interesting question. Was it because his experience at around 14 years old did not actually bring him to a place of repentance and faith? He continually said he was not a Christian. WMB had asked a minister from the First Baptist church to be with him during his operation and this minister prayed for him. Why would WMB ask for a Baptist minister when he believed all churches were wrong? Gordon Lindsay records WMB stating that he tried to find a church that held altar calls, but could not find one.⁵⁵ Where did he learn about altar calls, if he knew nothing about them? WMB stated in 1954, that altar calls were not an apostolic practice.⁵⁶

After WMB's release from hospital, WMB started out in search of God. He decided to write a letter to Jesus and tack it to a tree, so that when Jesus passed by He could read it.

> Knowing that I was a sinner, I couldn't even find a church that made an altar call. I went from one to the other. No one made an altar call; no one invited…I wanted to hear the Bible, the Word. You know how I first got saved? I might stop here to tell you. The first thing, I got me a pencil and paper, and went out, and was going to write a letter to Jesus. I'd been a woodsman all my life, game warden for years, lived in the woods, trapped and hunted all my life. And I knowed that He was the God of the forest, 'cause I could see Him out there, His nature, the way He made it. I was going to write me a letter and tack up on a tree in the woods, that when He come by, He could read it. I didn't know how to get saved.⁵⁷

When looking more closely at what WMB said in this quote, it is seen that he made a reference in this context to being a game warden for years. While it might be true that he was a game warden, he certainly wasn't one from the age of 14 up until sometime after the flood of 1937. Therefore, not when he was testing gas meters in, and around, 1931. There are no records of WMB hunting and trapping, after his return from Arizona. It is therefore safe to state that WMB's experience only fits the time around his mid-teens. That means that he started seeking for God sometime *after* his leg operation.

> I promised that when I was dying on the bed. And He let me… When the doctor done give me up, my heart was only beating seventeen times to the minute. And you know how slow that was. He said, "He's dying," and I heard it. Told my daddy, and pulled the curtains around me. And there in that room, that hour, I seen a big J's come all over that curtains around me like that. I heard that nurse crying, said, "There's nothing but a kid, see, and here he's going." <u>Spinal anesthetic had leaked through and got into in my heart.</u> See? It was only beating seventeen times a minute. When I got home, I had to prove that, that I--I loved God. And I--I got down there on that ground.⁵⁸ [Note: Underline mine – PMD].

As shown above, the incident with the spinal anesthetic proves it was the operation

CHAPTER FIVE 63

after WMB getting shot. When the rest of the quote is examined, it must be done in the same context of WMB being shot,

> I said, "I don't know how to pray." And I'd bite on my thumbnail. I thought, "Maybe...I seen pictures. I'll fold my hands like *this*, put my fingers together." I said, "Dear Sir, I would like to speak with You." I'd listen. I said, "I don't hear You." I said, "I folded my hands wrong. Maybe I ought to do it like *this*." I put my... I said, "Dear Sir, I... Jesus Christ, I would like to speak to You." I said, "Sir, I don't hear You. Answer me. I've heard other people say, 'God talked to me.' Now I want to talk this over with You. I promised You I would do it. I want to talk it over. Will You please come and speak to me, Sir?" Thought, "No, I ain't holding my hands right, or He would say something." I didn't know how to do it. Never prayed in my life.[59]

If this story were true, one would think these thoughts were those of a 14 year old, which would fit the time he got shot. To attribute this to, even a naïve person in his early twenties, would appear inconceivable.

> Didn't know what to do; this little old shed...I thought, "According to the Scriptures, as I've heard it read, He was a Man. And if He was a Man, He understands as a Man." Right. "And then I don't know whether You hear me." Devil said, "Why, you done sinned away your day of grace. There's no more. See, you been so mean, till He won't forgive you." I said, "I don't believe that. I just can't believe it. I believe He would talk to me." I said, "Sir, I don't know if I make a mistake, if I ain't got my hands folded right, or whatever it is, You--You forgive me for it. But I want to talk to You." I said, "I'm the lowest rascal in the world." I said, "I, I've done all these things, and--and I run from You, and all," went on talking like that.[60]

Where was WMB when this all took place? In a shed, he said, in the above quote. This is a crucial part in WMB's story that will be addressed in more detail later in this chapter. WMB continued his story:

> And the first thing you know, while I was talking, across the room come a little light, and went over on the side of the wall, and formed a cross of light, that light, and begin to talk with a language. I never, never heard of such a thing as speaking in tongues; never had even read the Bible; I was looking for James 5:14 in Genesis. I was looking up there, and I seen that light, and it was talking some kind of a language. Then it went away. "Sir," I said, "I don't know nothing about this Christian life." I said, "If that was You talking to me, I can't understand Your language, Sir...And if You can't speak my language, see, and I don't understand Yours, but...if You'll just come back there again, that'll be a sign between me and You, that You forgive me." There it was again.[61]

WMB said that spinal anesthetic had leaked through, and got into in his heart, whereas in 1931 it was an Appendicitis operation where WMB had refused anesthetic. That again, suggests it occurred when he was 14 years old. WMB said that it happened thirty five years prior 1961, which would bring the date to 1926.[62] This date is a bit problematic, yet it occurred *before* he left for Arizona in 1927. WMB often made mistakes in dates, so it could still fit the timespan after the hunting accident, anywhere from where WMB was 12,[63] through 15 years old.[64]

WMB said he knelt down in a shed,[65] where he saw a light in the form of a cross. He heard a voice that spoke in tongues and he felt his sins were forgiven him,

> And right there come a light across the room, in a cross form, and ever what was on it was speaking in tongues. I said, "I don't understand your voice, sir, your language. If you can't speak English, and I don't understand your language; if you'll just come back and speak again, it'll be a sign that you've accepted me.' And there it was again."[66]

However, not even a hint of such a thing is found in Scripture. When God spoke to anyone in Scripture, He always spoke in a human language, never in tongues. The Lord, nowhere in the NT nor in church history, appeared in the form of a cross of light, out of which he spoke in tongues *without* interpretation. God cannot violate his own law; tongues must be interpreted. Paul the Apostle experienced a light on his way to Damascus. He heard, *and* he understood, the voice that addressed him by name. It must be concluded that, whatever it was that WMB experienced, nothing like that experience is found in scripture. That ought to be a sobering thing. Yet, WMB stated clearly that he was saved there, his sins were forgiven him through this experience.

At this point it is important to return to the earlier mentioned shed where WMB's conversion occurred. A conversion experience, at least within the Christian context, is the event where a person receives new life. For a grown-up, this would be a momentous occasion; something not likely forgotten. WMB mentioned the locale of where this occurred, many times. He said it happened in a shed,[67] a coal shed,[68] a shed with a car wreck,[69] a coal shed garage with a car in/on the side,[70] or a garage.[71] Out of charity, these places will all be considered as the same building. WMB is emphatic that this was the place where he found God; this is where he got saved. This is what he said later,

> No man has a right to preach the Gospel; no person has the right to call themselves a Christian, until they can go back to a certain time in their life, where they could come on that sacred sands at the backside of the desert, where they know that they have met God…I want you to get this, and don't you never let it pass from you. But if a man's ever stood on that sacred sands at the backside of the desert, when he meets God face to face, there's not enough devils in all hell could take that away from him. He knows he met

God. He knows he had an experience; he talked to God. Regardless, of what the opposition is, he can say, "From that time, something changed in me."[72]

This would be a fitting end of WMB's long search. He had a troubled youth and ended up accidentally shot. He said he called out to God and promised Him he would live for Him. He received a vision in which the glory of God fell into his heart and he looked for a place to pray. He entered a shed and had an out of this world experience, which, he said, indicated to him that his sins were forgiven and he received salvation. He then went to search for a church and couldn't find one. For some reason, WMB decided he needed to go "Out West" and he hitched a ride to Arizona. The story moves from here to where WMB returned from Arizona to attend his brother's funeral. After the funeral, WMB went to work and he became ill and had an operation. After his operation, WMB set out to find God and this is what he said occurred,

> In a bunch of little, so-called holy-rollers one night, I found what I wanted…In a bunch of illiterate, uneducated, poorly dressed people, Negroes, to begin with, out yonder in a little old converted saloon on the floor…when that old darkie looked in my face, and said, "Have you received the Holy Ghost since you believed?" Oh, it was something that I wanted. I didn't expect to find it amongst those people, but they had what I needed.[73]

WMB said he found what he wanted, while he was on the floor of this converted saloon, full of black people. He said that was a problem for him as a Southerner,

> <u>In a little old saloon that had been used as a church</u> where some colored people was preaching the Gospel…And all the white girls that I'd went with, oh, not all of them, four or five standing there said, "Billy, you're not going in there?" I said, "Yes, I've got to go." Said, "Don't never ask me for another date." It didn't make any difference. I met God, and from that time I've been changed. Can point back to that time, I was changed.[74] [Note: Underlining mine-PMD].

As an aside, WMB was born in Kentucky, which is considered a Southern State. He was, however, raised in Indiana from around 4 years old. Indiana is not considered a Southern State. Earlier, WMB said that, when a person:

> Meets God face to face, there's not enough devils in all hell could take that away from him. He knows he met God. He knows he had an experience; he talked to God. Regardless, of what the opposition is, he can say, "From that time, something changed in me."[75]

The above quote being true, what happened to WMB when he was 14 years old? The conclusion that WMB was not saved, at fourteen years of age, is shared by Lindsay, Stadsklev and Green.[76] These authors only allot a few lines to the hunting accident and the operation and Vayle does not even mention it. Yet, they all received the information for their books from WMB himself. It can only be concluded that, contrary to WMB's claim, he was not converted in this shed, because the shed experience is tied to his operation at around the age of 12 through 15. That being so, his second experience had to be the one that occurred in the little black church meeting, in a converted saloon.

Gordon Lindsay writes that WMB, while in the hospital after his return from Arizona, heard a voice that said,

> I called and you would not go," The words were repeated the third time. Then I said, "Lord, if that is you, let me go back again to earth and I will preach your Gospel from the house tops and street corners. I'll tell everyone about it!" When this vision had passed, I found that I felt better.[77]

Lindsay continues, and he has WMB seeking for God and him ending up in the shed, with WMB experiencing the light in the form of a cross, etc. As mentioned, this is a repeat performance from age fourteen and must be discounted. Julius Stadsklev followed Lindsay's lead and thus this too must be discounted. Green, who wrote so much later, allows the shed account at this juncture, but it might be significant that he wrote:

> On another occasion, as he knelt in a woodshed to pray, a light came in and formed a cross.

Though Green posits this event sometime prior to WMB's preaching career, the phrase, "On another occasion," could indicate some uncertainty on the part of the author regarding the time this event occurred? This makes sense, because any serious student of WMBs messages knows that this experience could not have occurred until WMB started courting a young woman called Hope Brumbach.

Sometime in 1933, WMB started dating Hope Brumbach. He spelled it out, "B-R-U-M-B-A-C-H."[78] This date is established by WMB's claim that he had a brand new 1933 Ford[79] in which he drove Hope to church. He said he had dedicated this 1933 Ford when they were having services in the orphan's home, prior to the cornerstone being laid.[80] WMB was making payments on it after he was married. It was a new Ford and not a piece of junk, or half backslid as WMB always made it out to be.[81] Later, his future father in law, Charlie Brumbach, complimented him on his nice Ford.[82] WMB said he dated Hope for a year or something (or in June '33)[83] or, as late as about five months (or in January '34),[84] before they were married on June 22, 1934, in Fort Wayne, IN.[85] WMB first met her as he was high-diving out of a tree.[86] Hope started him going to church.[87] In fact, she made him attend church with her,[88] during which time he said he was converted.[89]

CHAPTER FIVE 67

> While I was going with her I had come to Christ and had found Him as my Saviour, and was studying in the ministry, the Baptist church.[90]

However, WMB contradicted this and said he met his future wife Hope *after* Roy E. Davis ordained him as an exhorter in the Baptist church.[91] Gordon Lindsay, Julius Stadsklev and Pearry Green, all followed suit in this matter and they deny everything WMB said on tape regarding this.[92] WMB was acquainted with Hope, prior to the Tabernacle being built. WMB even mentioned a photo where he, Hope, George DeArk and his wife were on a photo together, for the laying of the cornerstone.[93] One would think that sharing a photo together would indicate more than a casual acquaintance, but WMB said he did not know that Hope was even there.[94]

Subsequent to WMB meeting Hope, he never alluded to either falling ill, or that he had to have an operation. Therefore, it would be safe to say he met Hope after he was fully recovered. WMB said he believed in Divine Healing, though where he had heard about this is not known. He wanted to be healed of his astigmatism.[95] WMB went to his *own* Baptist Church and after being anointed with oil by his *own* pastor, which oil WMB himself had bought and prayed over already,[96] he stated he was healed.[97] WMB continued to confess that he was healed from his ailment, contrary to what he was experiencing (Positive Confession). He went home to his parents who did not know what to do when WMB asked to pray for the meal.[98] Not long after, his father threw him out of the house, he said[99] and he left while still ill. This illness may have been gastritis,[100] because later, in the early 1950s, he went to the Mayo clinic and they diagnosed it as a chronic condition.[101] His expulsion from his home could not have been permanent, because he speaks about living with his parents until he was married.[102]

About six months, or a year,[103] after WMB's conversion he was ordained as an exhorter.[104] He could not even read the Scriptures.[105] He said (jokingly?) he did not even know the books of the Bible and he looked for James 5:14 in the Book of Genesis. His claim that he was ordained as an exhorter in the Baptist church within one year of becoming a member appears to be a bit of a stretch because, scripturally, he would have been considered a novice. Yet, WMB did not know the books of the Bible, nor understand Scripture. He had Hope read the Scriptures as he preached[106] and was practically illiterate, he said.[107] WMB said he stayed with the Bible, but it is difficult to know what exactly he meant. WMB took Nature to be his real Bible,[108] which was where he went to find God.[109] In fact, WMB went to nature first, his first Bible. After that he brought it back to the Word of God (written Bible) to make sense out of it.[110] WMB had three Bibles, the Universe (Zodiac, or Nature), the Pyramid and the one written for intellectuals.[111] He referred to nature as his Bible[112] that led him to know God. He said good old Mother Nature would not lead one astray:

I was noticing, as for my first Bible I ever knew was grand old mother nature. If you'll just follow that, you won't be too far off the road, watching nature, how it works. It was that, that led me to God, knowing that there was a God...watching nature.[113]

The earlier mentioned conversion stories of WMB and his claim of receiving the Holy Spirit within a year after, evidenced by speaking in tongues, prove problematic. Elsewhere he stated that he did not speak in tongues[114] until he was a pastor in Milltown, prior to marrying Meda Broy,[115] on Oct. 23, 1941. WMB said in another account that he first saw Pentecost and tongues at Mishawaka,[116] in 1934. WMB's claim that he was baptized into the name of Jesus Christ by a Baptist pastor called Roy Davis does not appear to be truthful.[117] The Missionary Baptist Church only baptizes in the Trinitarian mode of Matt. 28. However, WMB claimed that they made an exception with him, yet until 1934 he had never heard of Baptism in Jesus' Name. Another issue that needs to be raised here is that there are records of a pastor called Roy E. Davis in the Pentecostal Holiness Church in Louisville, KY, in the year 1929.[118] That there were two different pastors with the exact same name and initial, within the same vicinity, would appear to be too much of a coincidence. The church, interestingly enough, was known as the First Pentecostal Baptist Church of Jeffersonville,[119] with Roy E. Davis as pastor, burned to the ground. WMB stated that Rev. Davis went back to Texas. WMB took over from there and the church first met in tent:

> And the Missionary Baptist Church burned down, which I was assistant pastor, at the time. And Mr. Davis come back to Texas...And so, while he was gone, I started to take over the congregation. Got a tent, and I begin to preach in the city...[120]

It appears that WMB did make a distinction between Roy E. Davis' church and his own.[121] When Roy E. Davis went back to Texas, it seems the congregation disbanded.[122] Afterwards, WMB and his followers rented a facility for two, or three years, to hold Sunday services.[123]

There is yet another puzzle that needs that needs to be resolved. This is the time lapse between the year in which WMB professed to have been converted and the year in which the Branham Tabernacle was built. WMB, and his following, insist that the Tabernacle was built in 1933. Why is that important? Throughout his ministry, certain things were sealed by, "Thus saith the Lord." One of these things was an angelic commission, which allegedly occurred in June of 1933, during WMB's first Baptismal service in the Ohio River. The events are all linked to this pivotal year of 1933.

WMB held services in a tent in June 1933.[124] Those professing faith were baptized in the Ohio River, at the foot of Spring Street, in Jeffersonville, Indiana.[125] The decision to build a Tabernacle was the direct result of the numbers of people being baptized. After the tent services were discontinued, as stated above, WMB's followers met in a rented hall for two, or three years. This means the Tabernacle would have to have been constructed in either 1935, or 1936. How could the corners stone have been laid and the building dedicated in March and September of 1933, respectively?[126] WMB said he was 20, or 25 years, old.[127] WMB being 25 years old would make the date 1933, which would fit. He also claimed he was 21, or 22 years old and not as yet married.[128] It was long before he was married, he said.[129] The ages of, 20, 21, or 22 years old do not add up, when his 1908 birth date is taken.

WMB's marriage to Hope occurred in June of 1934. The baptismal service is claimed to have happened in June of 1933, only a year earlier. WMB said he saw Hope, at that very baptismal service, holding a camera. How could he see her as he was baptized two or three years prior[130] to their marriage? Would that not put the baptism service in either 1931, or 1932?

After their marriage in June of 1934, WMB still had no church of his own.[131] That being true, how could the Branham Tabernacle have been finished and dedicated in September of 1933?

About three months after his wedding, WMB took a fishing trip to Paw Paw Lake, Michigan,[132] while at the same time he went to see a John Ryan in Dowagiac, Indiana. WMB had met John Ryan at the School of the Prophets, which was founded by William Sowders in Louisville, Kentucky, just across the bridge from Jeffersonville, Indiana.

> I met an old man…by the name of John Ryan… The old fellow with long beard and hair…I thought he was from Benton Harbor up here, at the House of David…they had a place in Louisville. I was trying to find them people, and they called it the School of the Prophets. So I thought I'd go over and see what that was…And there's where I met this old man, he invited me to come up to his place. I went up for a vacation.[133]

For a man who had no religious background, WMB knew an awful lot about people on the Christian fringe, groups that hold views that are unorthodox, and/or heretical. He mentioned Benton Harbor, Michigan, the home of the House of David cult, with its founder Benjamin Purnell.[134] "King Ben" Purnell was a British Israelite and believed he was the Seventh Messenger. He also wrote a book called the Seven Church Ages.[135] WMB said that the House of David people had a place in Louisville, Kentucky, called the House of the Prophets, with its founder William Sowders.[136] WMB never acknowledged William Sowders in his messages, yet it appears he was well acquainted with him.[137] WMB mentioned that while there, a John Ryan prayed and prophesied over him in tongues, which WMB said, was the first time he had ever heard tongues.[138] John Ryan invited WMB to visit him in Dowagiac, Michigan, a town about 25 miles (40 Kms) from Benton Harbor, MI, to go on a fishing vacation. For WMB, a recently married poor man, this would appear to be extravagant and irresponsible. After all, a round trip from Jeffersonville to Paw Paw Lake, without side trips to Benton Harbor and Dowagiac, is about 600 miles (about 1000 KMs). What made that lake so special to travel that far? However, if the real purpose was the Jesus Only Convention, it is possible that an exception could be made for a truth finding mission, (Fishing trip?), or for "pastoral" reasons. Remember, WMB was without a church at this time.

WMB did take the trip. On his way home he attended the "Jesus Only" convention in Mishawaka, IN, in 1934.[139] There he became convinced that God had called him to go with this new revelation and people. He spoke to his mother-in-law about it, WMB changed his mind and did not go. A series of mishaps befell him and WMB said he was being judged by God for his disobedience. WMB blamed his mother-in-law,[140] Hazel Brumbach. It would seem WMB was re-baptized[141] in the Name of Jesus,[142] at this "Jesus Only" convention.[143] Could this building in Mishawaka have been the converted saloon spoken of earlier? WMB spoke about six white ex-girlfriends that warned him not to enter. The 300+ miles distance would discount that. Consequent to his visit to this converted saloon church WMB claimed to have been baptized in the Holy Spirit and to have spoken in tongues.[144] This he alluded to when he got back home from Mishawaka and shared his experience with Hope.[145]

> I was coming down from Michigan, and I met a church group. They called them the Pentecostals. I had become a minister of the Baptist church. But I heard these people; they were happy, and they were rejoicing. And I wondered why they were so happy. I'd never heard of that kind of religion…I hurried home to my wife. And when she come to meet me, I told her about these happy people. She said, 'Oh, Billy, I would like to have that experience.' Said, 'What do they call it?' And I said, 'They said it was the baptism of the Holy Spirit.' I said, 'Let us go find Jesus like that.' So we did, and we both received the blessing…[146]

There is no evidence Hope ever did get re-baptized and she would have died a Trinitarian. If true, Hope's case might have been the reason why WMB, in his early ministry, softened his stance on people who were "ignorantly and wrongly baptized" into the "formula" of Matt. 28:18,[147] rather than the Acts 2: 38 passage championed by the Oneness people. WMB allowed that, because they were baptized in ignorance. WMB, otherwise, insisted on baptism in the name of the Lord Jesus Christ, to the tune of damnation if not obeyed.[148]

Can WMB's claim of not having a religious background be supported by his own messages? WMB's mother was a Methodist,[149] and his grandfather built a Methodist church. His parents dedicated him in a Baptist church. WMB said he

CHAPTER FIVE

was born and raised a Baptist. WMB played on a Methodist ball team and kept Sunday holy. As a youngster he visited many churches and determined they were all wrong. WMB was very religious and believed in mother Nature. He said that he had found God in Nature. WMB's claim of not having a religious background cannot be supported by his own messages.

Notes - Chapter Five

1. *A Ministry of William Branham.*

2. Harrell, 25.

3. WMB Sermons, available from http://branham.or/MessageSearch.htm, (Accessed April 13, 2010) and a number of other sources.

4. WMB, *We Would See Jesus*, Jul. 27, 1962, Victoria, BC, "I come from a Catholic background, being an Irishman. My people before me (not father and mother, but the next generation) come from Dublin, Ireland, and were...Catholic."

5. *Life Story*, Columbus, "Now, of course, you know I was brought up and raised in the Baptist church and was a Baptist minister." See also: *Discerning The Body Of The Lord*, Aug. 12, 1959, Chautauqua, OH, "I was raised in a Baptist church and ordained a Missionary Baptist preacher."

6. WMB, *God Commissioning Moses*, Jun. 03, 1953, Connersville, IN, "I was rocked in a Baptist cradle; I know what Baptist doctrine is." See also: *Jehovah-Jireh*, Richmond, VA, "Now, I was rocked in a Baptist cradle; I know what they believe."

7. ____, *Jesus Christ The Same Yesterday, Today And Forever*, Jun. 03, 1955, Macon, GA, "My people before me, Catholic. And my father and mother didn't attend church at all. I never was in a church house since the day I was...Well, I suppose about eight days old or ten when my mother take me up to old Southern Baptist Church up there for Sunday school. And I was dedicated to the Lord."

8. *Life Story*, Phoenix, AZ, "Well, now, when I started out to hold the meetings then, I was going to go to hold them. And I went and told my mother. She said, 'Well, God bless you, honey.' She said, 'Years ago down in Kentucky at the old Lone Star meeting house, we used to hear the people shout like that long time ago, and had that kind of a demonstration.'"

9. *Believest Thou This*, Minneapolis, "My father...was borned in the state of Kentucky. My mother's from Oklahoma, and moved down into Texas, just above Paris."

10. *Early Spiritual Experiences*, "My mother and father were married when my mother was fourteen years old and my dad was eighteen years old. I was born when mama was fifteen years old: just a child having a child, that was all."

[11] WMB, *Accepting God's Provided Way*, Jan. 15, 1963, Phoenix, AZ, "I was born on what they call Little Renox down there. My grandpa lived on Big Renox that empties into Bombshell. Bombshell Creek comes right down to Little Renox and runs out down by the Casey's Fork, and runs right on into the Cumberland River. Now, that's just across Green Briar Ridge. That's where my mother was born, up on Green Briar Ridge."

[12] ____, *The Unfailing Realities Of The Living God*, Jun. 26, 1960, Jeff., IN, "It's Breeding, Kentucky…a little church that my grandfather built, a little Methodist church that I preached in twenty-five, thirty years ago."

[13] *Life Story*, Cleveland, "Way down in Kentucky there's a old Missionary Baptist Church, we used to sing the song, 'Room, room, yes, there is room. There's room at the fountain for me.' Did you ever hear of it? It's a little old song, and that's what it is."

[14] *Early Spiritual Experiences*, "My people back before me were Catholic. I'm Irish on both sides…My people, not my mother and father, because they'd gotten away from the church."

[15] Catechism of the Catholic Church. Part Two; Section Two; Chapter One; Article One, THE SACRAMENT OF BAPTISM 1284. available from http://www.vatican.va/archive/ccc_css/archive/catechism/p2s2c1a1.htm, "In case of necessity, any person can baptize provided that he have the intention of doing that which the Church does and provided that he pours water on the candidate's head while saying: "I baptize you in the name of the Father, and of the Son, and of the Holy Spirit." (Accessed November 17, 2008).

[16] WMB, *Lamb and Dove*, Aug. 05, 1960, Yakima, WA, "My people before me were Catholic. And so there was no Catholic churches up there, and so they taken me over to a little Baptist church. And there I made my first visit to a church."

[17] Burkesville, "Area History," available from http://www.burkesville.com/html/area_history.html, (Accessed November 17, 2008).

[18] *Life Story*, LA, "Back there in the mountains there was not even a Catholic church."

[19] WMB, *We Would See Jesus*, Jul. 04, 1962, Grass Valley, CA, "And there'd been a little Baptist back somewhere in our generation…"

[20] ____, *Q & A # 2*, Aug. 23, 1964, "Now, you say, "Brother Branham, you hunt. Didn't you ever hunt on Sunday?" Let me tell you something…I believe we should honor that resurrection as a memorial…If you honor any day, honor that resurrection…I was about fourteen years old; I was trapping for a living…I'd set trout lines on the river; go down, and get them fish, and sell them for ten cents a pound…But look, a many a night have I went out in that river at 11 o'clock and shake every piece of bait off that line. If I couldn't catch enough in six days, I didn't want the one come on the seventh. I've stood there in the rain…"

[21] ____, *What Hearest Thou, Elijah*, Jun. 09, 1959, Chicago, IL, "When I was seventeen years old, I was a pretty active little fellow. I played shortstop, and I was playing for the Methodist church on a church league."

CHAPTER FIVE

²² Gordon Lindsay, 33.

²³ *Being Led Of The Holy Spirit*, "And I remember a preacher shooting at some birds and seventh shot hit me in the leg. I sure remember that…We come to Indiana when I was three years old…That was about a year later, so I couldn't have been over two years old at the time when it first happened."

²⁴ *Q & A # 3*, I had an operation for…when I was shot that time; I had to go to the hospital…And I was just only about fourteen years old, and I'd been shot…them shot legs, pretty near both of them blowed off like that…"

²⁵ *From That Time*, Tulsa.

²⁶ WMB, *Things That Are To Be*, Dec. 05, 1965, Rialto, CA, "As a little boy, I had been shot, and I was laying, dying in a hospital. And I had always knowed there was God. I remember the first prayer I ever tried to pray…I've never told this before. I just feel I'll tell it right now. I was shot, laying there, dying in a field. And the only plea that I could have to God, I said, 'You know, Lord, I never did commit adultery.' As a little, young boy about fifteen years old, I tried to live right. And I said, 'I've lived clean.' And that's all I could say. That's all the merit that I could offer Him."

²⁷ Ibid., "I said, 'O God, if You'll let me out of here, I'll never be ashamed of You again. I'll never be ashamed. God, please give me a chance.'"

²⁸ WMB, *Souls That Are In Prison Now*, Nov. 10, 1963, AM, "And I was out hunting with a boy, Jim Poole, a lovely kid…We're about six months apart, in age. And Jimmy let his gun go off, and it shot me through both legs, real close to me, with a shotgun. I was taken to the hospital…And seven months later, here at the Clark County Memorial Hospital, I had the second operation. And at that time, when I come out, I thought I was standing out in the West. I had another vision. And there was a great golden cross in the skies, and the Glory of the Lord flowing off of that cross. And I stood with my hands out like *this*, and that Glory was falling into my chest…The vision left me."

²⁹ *From That Time*, Tulsa.

³⁰ Ibid.

³¹ WMB, *The Resurrection Of Lazarus*, Nov 22, 1953, Evansville, IN, "I was laying yonder in the hospital, the doctor told me I had three more minutes to live, in Louisville, Kentucky, in the Jewish hospital."; *Redemption In Completeness*, Mar 03, 1954, Louisville, KY, "Twenty-three years ago in the Jewish Hospital, Dr. Morris Fletcher give me three hours; one of your best surgeons here in the city, give me three hours to live. I'm living tonight." Note: 1954 – 23 = 1931. This fits with the incident at the Service Co. – PMD

³² ____, *Is This The Sign Of The End, Sir?* Dec, 30, 1962, PM., Jeff., IN.

³³ ____, *Souls That Are In Prison Now*, Nov 10, 1963, AM, Jeff., IN.

³⁴ ____, *Sirs, We Would See Jesus*, Mar 28, 1954, Louisville, KY.

³⁵ ____, *Path Of Life*, Jun. 21, 1962, Brkfst., South Gate CA, "Then I went to the

church, but they said, 'This is the church,' and it was contrary to the Word. I went from church to church and I found out it was so contrary. So I stayed with the Word."

36 *Testimony Of A True Witness,*

37 WMB, *We Would See Jesus*, Victoria, BC, "[I] Knowed of God when I was a little boy...I wanted to find out about Who God was, and my people didn't go to church. So I asked the priest about God, and he said, 'God is in His church. There's where God dwells. You have to belong to His church.'...I played in a German neighborhood where I was raised...these boys were all Lutheran...they said...their church was the church. Then I come to find out there was another church called Baptist, Presbyterian, Anglican. Oh, my. Well, which one of them churches is He in? That's what I wondered. Where is He at? If this one's right, this one's got to be wrong, 'cause they're contrary one to another. Now, which one of them churches is God in? I set down and started reading the Bible, watching nature."

38 WMB, *An Absolute*, Shreveport, Dec. 01, 1963, AM, "One is tied to an organization, dogmas. But a *Christian* means 'Christ-like.' And only way you can be Christ-like is for Christ the Word to be in you. That's the ultimate. Yeah. I seen this before I was converted, and I'm glad God got a hold of me before the church did. A fine Baptist minister, Brother Naylor, he's in Glory today, he come down, he talked to me. And, oh, there's many people that talked to me when I was trying to find God. The Seventh - day Adventist preacher wanted me to join up with them, and so forth. But I seen that if I was going to be a Christian, I--I couldn't say, 'Now I am a Seventh - day Adventist.' Now, that's all right. 'I'm a Baptist.' It's all right, see, but I had to have something a little more sure than that. I couldn't trust, because each one was wavering. I thought, 'There is somebody somewhere, you have to have something that's true, somewhere.'"

39 Joseph Smith, *Doctrine And Covenants of the Church of Jesus Christ of Latter Day Saints/ Pearl of Great Price*, (Salt Lake City: Church of Jesus Christ of Latter Day Saints, 1982), Joseph Smith – History1: 14-23.

40 WMB, *Is This The Sign Of The End, Sir?* Dec. 30, 1962, PM, Jeff., IN, "I was a little boy and them visions would come upon me. And I would see them and tell my parents the things that was going to happen. They thought I was just nervous. You say, "Was that before your conversion?" Yes. Now, along the road, and when I was a little boy, my longing was...I was dissatisfied in the country I lived in. I long, somehow, to go West. And I was operated on, when I was shot, when I was a little boy."

41 *Souls That Are In Prison Now*, "All people that's knowed me all these years, knows I've always wanted to go West. You know how it is. It's always been something to the West. But because an astronomer told me one time, the same thing, that I should go west...The stars, when they cross their cycles and so forth, I was born under that sign, and I'd never be a success in the East; I'd have to go West."

42 WMB, *Sardisean Church Age*, Dec. 09, 1960, Jeff., IN.

43 ____, *Q & A*, on Genesis, Jul 29, 1953, Jeff., IN, "That was my first study, was Seventh-day Advent."

CHAPTER FIVE

[44] *Sardisean*, "About three weeks after that, I went down into the city, ...I heard a little noise down the street there, and went down there. And there was an old boy converted out of them bucking stalls out there, pot marks all over his face, and the tears running down his cheeks there, playing a guitar, singing: Glory to His Name! Oh, my. The tears running down his face, he stopped and said, 'Brother, you don't know what it is unless you receive this wonderful Christ;: Glory to His Name! And I pulled that big hat down and away I went."

[45] WMB, *Identified With Christ*, Dec. 20, 1959, PM, Jeff., IN,

[46] _____, *Earnestly Contending For The Faith*, Apr 04, 1954, AM, Louisville, KY, "Before my conversion we worked together at the public service...Before I got hurt at the public service company..."

[47] *Earnestly Contending For The Faith*, "'...he was very sick, and you know what? They had the preacher out there to pray for him.' But something, as a sinner boy, struck in my heart."

[48] Gordon Lindsay. 39, 40.

[49] Vayle. 36.

[50] Mark Miller in phone conversation with author, 12: 45 PM, Jun 13, 2012.

[51] Vayle. 36, 37.

[52] Ibid.

[53] Ibid., 41.

[54] Ibid., 40.

[55] Gordon Lindsay. 41.

[56] WMB, *Jubilee Year*, Oct 03, 1954, PM, Jeff., IN, "It ain't necessary that you come to the altar to become a Christian. They never had it during the Bible days...They never made a altar call...in the apostolic age. There's no altar calls."

[57] _____, *Redeemer, Redemption*, Nov. 19, 1955, San Fernando, CA.

[58] _____, *Victory Day*, Apr 21, 1963, Sierra Vista, AZ.

[59] Ibid.

[60] Ibid.

[61] Ibid.

[62] WMB, *Abraham's Covenant Confirmed*, Mar. 18, 1961, Middletown, OH, "He changed this wicked, cruel, Irish heart of mine, laying there on the bed, with just three minutes to live, by the specialist. My heart only beating seventeen times to the minute, but Jehovah Jireh came on the scene. And that's been about thirty-five years ago, when I had three minutes to live. But Jehovah Jireh provided me life. Why shouldn't I spend it, then, for Him?...I promised you there on that hospital bed that I'd never be ashamed of You, that I'd stand for Your Word, I'd scream it from the housetop, street corner... and for thirty-one years I have screamed it Lord."

[63] WMB, *Believing God*, Feb 24, 1952, Jeff, IN, And the only thing that kept me

from being saved when I was twelve years old, because a spirit hung over me, a devil, saying, "Wait a little while longer."

⁶⁴ *Things That Are To Be.*

⁶⁵ WMB, *Power Of Decision*, Oct. 07, 1955, Chicago, IL, "Why, I remember the night I was back in the--when I first got saved, went back in a little old shed." See also: *Victory Day*, Apr. 21, 1963, Sierra Vista, AZ, "I remember down there, that about ten o'clock one night, or when I was down there in that little old garage."

⁶⁶ *Look*, Apr. 28, 1963, Phoenix, AZ.

⁶⁷ WMB, *The Power Of Decision*, Oct. 7, 1955, Chicago, IL, "Why, I remember the night I was back in the--when I first got saved, went back in a little old <u>shed</u>."

⁶⁸ ____, *God Keeps His Word*, Apr. 7, 1957, AM, Jeffersonville, IN, "…yonder in that little old <u>coal shed</u> in the back of the building."

⁶⁹ ____, Dec 30, 1962, Jeff, IN, "I went out in the shed and knelt down, water, wet. Little, old car setting there, wrecked up."

⁷⁰ ____, *Jesus Christ, The Same Yesterday, Today, And Forever*, Sep 22, 1957, Jeff., IN, "I was saved in a coal shed, garage (where my car was setting in the side), on an old grass sack, and wet to my hips from there, praying."

⁷¹ *Victory Day*, "I remember down there, that about ten o'clock one night, or when I was down there in that little old <u>garage</u>."

⁷² WMB, *From That Time*, Mar 02, 1960, Phoenix, AZ.

⁷³ ____, *Without Money Or Without Price*, Aug. 02, 1959, Jeff., IN.

⁷⁴ *From That Time*.

⁷⁵ Ibid.

⁷⁶ Lindsay. "At the age of fourteen he was seriously wounded while hunting and had to spend seven months in hospital. God dealt with him but he still did not take heed. 36.; Stadsklev, "At the age of fourteen he was out hunting and had an accident which caused him to be hospitalized for seven months…God dealt with him during these months while he was in hospital, even though he all this time he rejected and refused to listen to God. 7.; Green. "Brother Branham almost died for the second time [Note: First time occurred when he was a baby-PMD] at the age of fourteen. Accidently shot…Yet he resisted the call of God upon his life…" 41, 42.

⁷⁷ Lindsay. 41.

⁷⁸ *Life Story*, LA.

⁷⁹ WMB, *Teaching On Moses*, May 13, 1956, Jeff., IN, "In 1933. I just got a 1933 Ford, and I dedicated it that morning to the Lord."

⁸⁰ ____, *Teaching On Moses*, May 13, 1956, Jeff. IN, "In 1933, when we were having services down…over here on Meigs Avenue. In 1933. I just got a 1933 Ford, and I dedicated it that morning to the Lord."

CHAPTER FIVE

81 WMB, *Here We Have No Continuing City*, Feb, 1950, Little Rock, AR.

82 Gordon Lindsay. 46

83 *Life Story*, Phoenix. "And she started me going to church."; *Life Story*, Toledo, "And she asked me to go to church with her, and I did. I kept going with her a long time…I'd been going with her for about a year and something,"

84 Julius Stadsklev. 12-13. "After about five months of courtship, William decided that he would have to ask her if she wanted to marry him."

85 *Life Story*, Toledo.

86 *Life Story*, Phoenix. "So, one day I happened to be out making a high-dive somewhere, out of a tree. And a car drove up, and a young lady stepped out…She happened to be a Christian girl, my little boy's mother."

87 Ibid., "And she started me going to church."

88 *Life Story*, Owensboro, "I finally found a girl that didn't drink and smoke…She was everything that a lady could be. I went with her. She was out of a good family…I'd go with her to church; that's where she'd taken me, to church."

89 *Life Story*, Zurich. "I met a lovely girl…notice a moment; I want you to get this part of it. I then become a Christian. Going with a girl, after while we got married."

90 *Life Story*, Hammond, IN.

91 *Visions Of William Branham*, Sep. 30, 1960, Jeff., IN, "Well, I remember after I was ordained in the church, the Baptist church, by Dr. Roy Davis, here at Watts Street in Jeffersonville…Later, I got acquainted with this young girl and went with her."

92 *Man Sent.* 43-44; *Acts Of The Prophet.* 64; *Prophet Visits South Africa.* 12.

93 On this special day, he and his wife-to-be, Hope, and special friend, George DeArk and his wife, posed for a photo, then everyone gathered for a group picture. http://www.bridemessage.org/lilypond.htm.

94 WMB, Q & A #4, Aug. 30, 1964, PM, Jeff., IN, "I was looking at the pictures when we laid the cornerstone . I looked upon the picture and seen Hope and I before we were married. I didn't even know that."

95 Astigmatism is a very common vision problem, which can be corrected by eyeglasses. Why WMB's head shook due to this operation has not been made clear at this point in the story, though this will be addressed later.

96 *Hearing, Receiving And Acting,* "I wore great big thick glasses. My head shook all the time with astigmatism. I was only just a boy like, but I believed Divine healing. Why? I heard it. I recognized it was God's promise…I went to my own Baptist church…I said, 'I'm sick.' 'What's the matter with you.' I said, "My eyes is bad. I can't hardly see. Take these glasses off, and they'd have to lead me around: astigmatism…' And I went down and got me some oil, and prayed over it…and handed it to him. He anointed me with oil like that. I said, 'Hallelujah.' Here I went."

97 *Hearing, Receiving And Acting,* "Doctor said if I eat one mouthful of solid food, it

would kill me. Said my stomach was nothing but one big, bloody ulcer. And I went home, and pop was sitting there. And we had some corn bread and beans and you know how poor people live...And I said (we never had a blessing asked at the table), and I said, 'Will you all bow your heads just a minute?' And I know dad looked at me, and mother looked at me strange. I said, 'God, I don't know how to pray, but somehow another, I believe you. I believe that you healed me. I've been anointed. And I'm taking your Word.'"

[98] WMB, *Believing God*, Feb. 24, 1952, Jeff., IN, "There'd never been a prayer said at our table. I remember dad setting on the corner there. I said, 'Can we pray?' Mom looked over and started to cry. Pop didn't know what to do."

[99] *Hearing, Receiving And Acting*, "My own father put me out of the house. I had my clothes in a paper sack. He said, 'You can't act like that around here'...so I took off."

[100] Gastritis, "Causes," available from: http://www.mayoclinic.com/health/gastritis, (accessed December 20, 2008).For many people, though, chronic gastritis causes no signs or symptoms at all. Causes: Severe stress due to major surgery, traumatic injury, burns or severe infections can cause acute gastritis.

[101] WMB, *On The Wings Of A Snow White Dove*, Nov 28, 1965, PM, Shreveport, LA, "Wife and I, and Becky back there...Sarah was a little, bitty fellow. I had just entered my healing ministry...I went through the clinic. Mayo Brothers, the next day, examined me... He said, "Well, you'll never get over it."

[102] ____, *Present Stage Of My Ministry*, Sep 08, 1962, Jeff. IN, "It's been about thirty-two years ago [1930-PMD], that when the Lord Jesus, within a hundred and fifty yards of where I'm present standing now, here in Jeffersonville at Eighth and Penn Street, the morning when I laid the cornerstone on this tabernacle...It was before I was married. I was living with my father and mother."

[103] ____, *Eagle Stirring Her Nest*, May, 1958, N. England Area, "When I was twenty-one years old, a man told me to look for James 5:14 in the Bible, and I was looking in Genesis to find it: twenty-one years old. And at twenty-two years old I was an ordained Baptist minister in Missionary Baptist Church."

[104] ____, *The Seed Is Not Heir With The Shuck*, Feb 18, 1965, Jeff., IN, "I was just young in the Lord then, about six months I had been preaching ....Just about six months after that, I had my first baptism down here on the river, when the Light came down right here at Spring Street."

[105] ____, *Pillar Of Fire*, May 09, 1953, Jonesboro, AR, "When I was a young Baptist preacher baptizing my first converts...And my education was so poor, till my girlfriend read the Bible while I preached...It's not much better tonight."

[106] WMB, ____, *Revelation Chapter Five # 2*, Jun. 18, 1961, Jeff., IN, "When I first started preaching about thirty years ago, I had to have my girlfriend set and read the Bible. I couldn't even read it, without much education. Sister Wilson, you ought to remember that

when Hope used to read the Bible to me back there, set and read it, and I'd say, 'Hear what it said, do just what it says. That's all I know to tell you.' ...She'd say, "God so loved the world He gave His only begotten Son." I'd say, "How many believes it? Read next, honey." "Gave His only begotten Son, whosoever believeth on Him has Eternal Life." I said, "How many believe it? You hear what it said." I couldn't read it myself."

[107] WMB, *Faith In The Son Of God*, Hammond, IN, "Now, some of my theological teaching, views on the Bible, it might be wrong. I can't say. I'm not a student by a long ways. I'm very illiterate, uneducated, grammar school education; that's not to my desire, but I couldn't have it. We was raised in a poor family of ten children, sickly father that died when he was just a young man. The burden was on me, the oldest one in the family."

[108] ____, *As The Eagle Stirreth*, Tulsa, "My first Bible was nature. If you'll just watch the way nature works, you can find God."

[109] ____, *Queen Of Sheba*, Jan. 19, 1961, PM, Beaumont, TX, "I find God in the woods. God, I hear him call in the coyote and the wolf, hear Him bugle in the deer. Why, sure. I hear him scream in the eagle, see Him in the sunset. Everywhere around is God. Get out in nature."

[110] WMB, *Harvest Time*, Dec. 12, 1964, Phoenix, AZ, "God, God the great Creator, let's try to speak on the form of nature, pick Him up in nature first, to bring it back to the Word."

[111] *Adoption # 4*, "God wrote three Bibles. One of them was the Zodiac in the skies. That's the first Bible...Then the next Bible was written, was in stone, called pyramid. God wrote in the pyramids...The third was wrote on paper, the Bible, for the great, smart intellectual world to come."

[112] WMB, *Let Us See God*, Nov. 29, 1959, San Jose, CA, "I found God in nature. That was my first Bible, was God in His nature, in His universe."

[113] ____, *God's Provided Approach To Divine Fellowship*, Jun. 30, 1960, Tulsa, OK, "I was noticing, as for my first Bible I ever knew was grand old mother nature. If you'll just follow that, you won't be too far off the road, watching nature, how it works. It was that, that led me to God, knowing that there was a God... watching nature."

[114] ____, *Questions And Answers*, Jan. 12, 1961, Jeff., IN, "I received the baptism of the Holy Ghost back in my shed. And about a year later, or something like that, I spoke in tongues. And about a year or two after that, I was preaching again in a church...Milltown Baptist church...And just as I stopped preaching, something just had me all carried away and said several words, four or five, or six words in unknown tongues."

[115] ____, *Questions And Answers On The Holy Ghost*, Dec. 19, 1959, Jeff., IN, "He give a vision of seeing these fish strung up, said, 'This is your Milltown church.' And four or five of them flopped off; and I said, 'Who's that?' Said, 'One of them is Guy Spencer and his wife. The other one is another Spencer there, and theirs.' And told the different ones, what would flop off. I told them; I said, 'Don't none of you eat.'...It was before we was married;

and she went home to stay all night with Sister Spencer...And he--and he went down there, and Opal said, to Meda, she said, 'Now, Meda, I believe Brother Bill.'"

[116] WMB, *Corinthians, Book of Correction,* Apr. 14, 1957, Jeff., IN, "That's when I first seen Pentecost, and it was at Mishawaka, Indiana...I'd never heard speaking in tongues and things like that before."

[117] ____, *Laodicean Church Age,* Dec. 11, 1960, PM, Jeff., IN, "Oh, I'm glad, so thankful that...around twenty-eight years ago, I felt that knock on my heart... And I received the Pentecostal blessing, received the Holy Ghost. Was baptized in the Name of Jesus Christ for the remission of sins, the only time I ever was baptized in my life, once a Baptist preacher baptized me. I said, 'I want to be baptized in the Name of the Lord Jesus Christ.' Dr. Roy E. Davis baptized me in the Name of the Lord Jesus Christ when I was just a boy."

[118] Roy E. Davis (Pentecostal Holiness Church); Louisville, KY; 1929, p.9, available from http://www.ptc.dcs.edu/teacherpages/tthrasher/listings/Ta.htm, (Accessed June 09, 2012).

[119] Wm. Branham, available from http://www.findagrave.com/cgi-bin/fg.cgi?page=gr&GSsr=281&GScid-84894&GRid=73469206&, (Accessed June 05, 2012).

[120] *Taking Sides With Jesus,* Jun 01, 1962, Jeff., IN, "And started off, over here in a tent, just across the street. And I remember when Brother Roy Davis, down there, and his church burnt down. "

[121] *Life Story,* Owensboro, "[M]y church thought I was a fanatic. They still do. Not my church body at Jeffersonville, no, no, I mean the Baptist church that I belonged to."

[122] WMB, *Taking Sides With Jesus,* Jun 01, 1962, Jeff., IN, "'That bunch of people was just like scattered sheep without a shepherd, had no place to go... He said, "Billy, if you wanting to start a church," he said, "I want you to know that we're behind you in anything we can do to help you."'

[123] Cornerstone, available from http://www.williambranhamhomepage.org/lcstone.htm#lilypond, (Accessed June 05), 2012. "During the first two or three years of his ministry in Jeffersonville, Brother Branham was holding Sunday morning services in a rented hall."

[124] *Taking Sides,* "Now, when I laid that cornerstone there that morning, I never felt that I'd ever be a pastor. It wasn't in my callings, at the beginning. And my first call was to be on the field of evangelism...And started off, over here in a tent, just across the street."

[125] WMB, *The Seed Is Not Heir With The Shuck,* Feb 18, 1965, Jeff., IN, "I was just young in the Lord then, about six months I had been preaching....Just about six months after that, I had my first baptism down here on the river, when the Light came down right here at Spring Street...And there is where the Angel of the Lord appeared in public, first, and at two o'clock, one afternoon."

[126] Lily Pond, The construction of the little Tabernacle was completed in September of 1933.

[127] WMB, *Exhortation On Divine Healing,*, May 01, 1951, Los Angeles, CA., "I never was in church I was a young man, about twenty years old, twenty-five." Note: WMB, at 20 years old, would make the date 1928, which was too early. He was still in Arizona. His age being 25 years old would certainly fit the 1933 date.

CHAPTER FIVE 81

[128] WMB, *God Hiding Himself In Simplicity Then Revealing Himself In The Same*, Mar. 17, 1963, Jeff., IN, "When we started at the first dedication of the church, I was just a young man and maybe twenty-one, twenty-two years old when we laid the cornerstone. It was before I was even married."

[129] *God Keeps His Word*, Jeff. IN, "It well brings to my memory what's wrote there in that cornerstone on that morning when we...laid the cornerstone. When the Lord woke me up, not knowing what visions was in those days. I'm looking at the chimney on top of the house, five feet or more from where I was sitting when the vision taken place twenty three years ago in 1933. Be about twenty four years ago, I suppose. I'm looking at the chimney right now. It was long before I was ever married. I was single at home. We were just building this church, and we was laying the cornerstone that morning, when the Lord gave me the vision."

[130] WMB, *A Court Trial*, Apr 12, 1964, Birmingham, AL, "And as I laid him into the water, I come up, I heard something going, "Whooosh!"...I heard a Voice say, "Look up!" [153] I thought, "What is that? Billy here, his mother, two or three years before we was married, she was standing there. I seen her face, white. She had a camera in her hand."

[131] *Life Story*, Phoenix, "And we was married ...I'd just been ordained to be a--a minister. I didn't have no church as yet but we was just preaching around wherever I could in tent meetings and so forth. And I went to work."

[132] *My Life Story*, LA, "And I remember one day I had saved up my money and I was going to take a little vacation, going up to a place, the Paw Paw Lake, to fish. And on my road back...And I thought, "That sounds strange, 'Jesus Only.'" And I begin noticing those signs...And I followed some of them down, and they come to a great big church....And I come to find out there were two great churches, one of them called a P.A. of J.C., and the P.A. of W...I think they're...called the United Pentecostal church."

[133] WMB, *How The Angel Came To Me And His Commission*, Jan 17, 1955, I met an old man...by the name of John Ryan . And I met him at a place... The old fellow with long beard and hair, and he may be here. I thought he was from Benton Harbor up here, at the House of David... they had a place in Louisville. I was trying to find them people, and they called it the School of the Prophets. So I thought I'd go over and see what that was...And there's where I met this old man, he invited me to come up to his place. I went up for a vacation."

[134] King Ben, founder of the House of David, available from Rearview Mirror: http://www.marycityofdavid.org updated April 17, 2000), (Accessed April 22, 2002).

[135] Recommended works: Clare E. Adkin, *Brother Benjamin a history of the Israelite House of David* (Berrien Springs, MI: Andrews University Press 1990); Robert S. Fogarty, *The Righteous Remnant: The House of David* (Kent, OH: Kent State University Press, January 3, 1989, 195 pp.)

[136] William H. Wallender, *Why the Holy Spirit Was Poured Out in 1900: An Insight for the People of God*, (Bloomington, IN: AH, 272 pp). This book lists incidents which occurred prior to WMB's ministry, that are strikingly similar to WMB's life and ministry.

¹³⁷ Wanda Mason, "Wiliam Sowders & William Branham, Similarities in Doctrine," available from http://www.gospelassemblyfree.com/facts/sowdersbranhamprint.htm, (accessed July 07, 2003).

¹³⁸ *The Faith That Was Once Delivered To The Saints*, May 01, 1955, Chicago, IL, "Many years ago, I was in Louisville one day. Setting in a meeting, an old gray-headed man raised up, come over and laid his hands upon me, not knowing me, begin to speak in tongues. I guess it's been close to twenty years ago. Was strange to me; I'd never heard such. He said, "You're just a boy now, but someday God is going to use you." That was Brother Ryan."

¹³⁹ Third General Assembly of the Pentecostal Assemblies of Jesus Christ held in Mishawaka, Indiana.

¹⁴⁰ *Here We Have No Continuing City*, "Well, I went and had to tell her mother. And that didn't work so good. She said, 'William.' She said,..'I don't want my daughter drug out among that bunch of trash.'" *Life Story*, Cleveland, "And the wife started crying. Well now, I couldn't stand that, so I told her; I said, 'Well, we'll wait and go later.' Now, there's where I made my mistake. And brother, sister, from right then my trouble started. The first thing, you know, my church begin to drop off. My brother was killed, having his neck broke in the street...My sister-in-law died a few days after that. My father died in my arms. Everything begin to go wrong. Then the '37 Flood came on..." [Note: WMB's wife Hope and baby Sharon Rose died – PMD].

¹⁴¹ The word *re-baptized* is used here, however, it must be understood that in WMB's thinking it would not be seen as re-baptized, but baptized, because he only considered baptism according to Acts 2: 38 to be legitimate. In other words, WMB considered his Spirit baptism, which only follows baptism in the name of the Lord Jesus Christ, as baptism and therefore would boldly state he was only baptized once.

¹⁴² *How The Angel Came To Me*, "And they was referring all the time to Acts, Acts 2:4, Acts 2:38, Acts 10:49, all that. I thought, "Say, that's Scripture! I just never seen it like that before." But, oh, my heart was burning, thought, 'This is wonderful!'"

¹⁴³ WMB, *Without Money Or Without Price*, Aug. 02, 1959, Jeff., IN, "In a bunch of little, so-called holy-rollers one night, I found what I wanted, that money could not buy. In a bunch of illiterate, un-educated, poorly dressed people, Negroes, to begin with, out yonder in a little old converted saloon on the floor, I found a price, a jewel, when that old darkie looked in my face, and said, "Have you received the Holy Ghost since you believed?" Oh, it was something that I wanted. I didn't expect to find it amongst those people, but they had what I needed."

¹⁴⁴ ____, *The Unwelcomed Christ*, Sep. 11, 1955, Jeff., IN, "I went up to...this brother, and I said, 'I hear that you belong to the Assemblies of God, a minister.' He said, 'I am.' He said, 'What are you?' I said, 'I'm a Baptist.' And he said, 'Well, have you received the Holy Ghost?' I said, 'Yes.' I said, 'I received the Holy Ghost?' He said, 'You speak in tongues?' I said, 'Yeah. Yeah, I spoke in tongues.' He said, 'Brother, you've got It. Hallelujah. Praise the Lord.

CHAPTER FIVE

That's It.' I said, 'Yeah,' I said, 'I received the Holy Ghost, and spoke in tongues, and for the evidence of it.'...He said, 'Oh, you'll come out of that old, stiff, formal Baptist church, then. Hallelujah.' And he spoke in tongues a few times. I said, 'Yeah, I received the Holy Ghost, was baptized in Jesus Christ's Name...He said, 'You what?' And I said, 'I received the Holy Ghost, and was baptized in Jesus Christ's Name. 'He said, 'You don't get the Holy Ghost like that.' I said, 'You told me a little too late.' I said, 'I done done it.'"

[145] *Life Story*, Phoenix, "During that time, we'd both received the Holy Ghost." [NoteL Right after WMB's return from Mishawaka, IN – PMD]..

[146] *Life Story*, Zurich.

[147] WMB, *Q & A*, Oct. 15, 1961, AM, Jeff., IN, "I believe if a man was baptized wrong ignorantly, not knowing that he was baptized wrong...Now, I can't say this Scripturally...I believe that God would overlook that and save him anyhow..."

[148] ____, *Q & A,*, May 15, 1954, Jeff., IN, "Now, you say, '...I was baptized in the name of the Father, Son, and Holy Ghost. I got the baptism of the Holy Ghost.' I don't doubt your word...I believe God give them the Holy Ghost up there before they was baptized at all; but... Now, you know what to do...And if you refuse to walk in light when light's brought forth, you turn to darkness."

[149] ____, *His Unfailing Words Of Promise*, Jan. 20, 1964, Phoenix, AZ, "Now, when I come to Christ, I knowed I had to have a foundation somewhere, to stand on. I was ordained in the Missionary Baptist church. Then when I seen the doctrine of the Missionary Baptist church was so contrary to the Scripture, then I could not place, base my hopes upon the doctrine of the Missionary Baptist church. Then I thought I would go over to my mother's church, she was Methodist."

Chapter Six
ANGELIC COMMISSIONS 1 - 3

Can WMB's claims of his many angelic encounters
and/or commissions be substantiated
by his own messages, or by reality?

Some of the earliest books about WMB already made much of an angelic commission occurring on May 7, 1946. In 1950, Gordon Lindsay, in collaboration with WMB,[1] wrote the book, *William Branham, A Man Sent From God.*[2] Lindsay has the angelic commission occurring on May 7, 1946. Both Julius Stadsklev's in *A Prophet Visits South Africa,*[3] and Pearry Green in *The Acts of the Prophet*[4] use that date, which originated with WMB.

WMB tied his 1946 angelic commission to Israel becoming a nation on that day.[5] However, Israel did *not* become a nation on May 7, 1946, but on May 14, 1948.[6] According to WMB, Israel also became a nation on May 6, 1946;[7] on May 6, 1947,[8] and on May 7, 1947.[9] How could he forget such a momentous event? This seriously calls WMB's identity, as God's messenger to the world, into question.

These angelic encounters, and/or, commission claims appear to be on a seven year cycle, though the hard dates are not easy to discern due to all the conflicting data. His angelic visitations happened prior to birth,[10] at birth,[11] in 1915, at seven years of age,[12] in 1920 at twelve years of age,[13] in 1923 at 14 or 15 years of age,[14] in 1930,[15] in 1931,[16] in 1932,[17] in 1933,[18] in 1936,[19] in 1944,[20] on May 6, 1946,[21] on May 7, 1946,[22] or on May 6, 1947,[23] in 1950 in Houston, TX, and finally in 1963, in Arizona. Seemingly coincidental with his many visitations, there exists a disturbing parallel seven year phenomenon of mental depression in the life of WMB. WMB himself alluded to this, just before he died.[24]

WMB inferred his call to be like that of Moses,[25] Joshua,[26] John the Baptist,[27] Elijah[28] and finally, the Seventh Angel of the Revelation.[29] Did any of the above biblical persons have numerous commissions? Not one, Jonah excepted. A single, one time, angelic commission would already be an event of biblical proportions. Why would WMB claim these occurred many times in his life? According to Ronald Kydd, WMB was very insecure:

> At times he felt that everyone, even his own church, Branham Tabernacle, was turning against him. He was convinced that he held a special relationship with God, but he could give indications that occasionally he was very insecure in it. A sermon he preached on August 12, 1959, is full of imploring questions: "Here is the showdown. Do you [congregation] believe I've told you the Truth?...You sitting there in front. You believe me to be God's prophet?...You believe I have God's message? Do you believe that I am telling you the Truth?"[30]

Ronald Kydd appears to be correct in his assessment. WMB's insecurity meant that he constantly had to find something re-enforcing and re-establishing, that he indeed was that messenger of God sent to the nations. To some, it might appear a redundant exercise to even enter into any kind of detail regarding these claims. However, due to the fact that these commissions were touchstones in ministry for WMB and his followers, they will be examined in some detail. This chapter will show the first three out of ten of WMB's visitation claims.

WMB's First Angelic Visitation

WMB stated that prophets were called from their mother's womb.[31] His his first visitation occurred, "By a vision that God gave me, when I was a little baby in my mother's womb.[32] WMB stated, "We all know that John the Baptist was...a Holy Ghost man? He was born from his mother's womb full of the Holy Ghost. But it was an Angel that came down and announced his birth..."[33] All WMB knew about his own early life was supplied by non-Christian, drunken, party going,[34] superstitious mountain people.[35] His angelic commission occurring by vision to WMB before birth is simply frivolous and should not be taken seriously.

WMB's Second Angelic Visitation

The second angelic visitation happened as a light, star, halo, angel, or a supernatural being, hung over his crib. Again, all WMB knew was what his mother told him,[36] which he then later relayed to others. At WMB's birth, states Stadsklev,

> Dawn was just breaking over the fields, sending a few rays of light into the room. With this light came a small circular halo about a foot in diameter which shown (sic) with brightness above the bed where the mother and baby lay.[37]

Gordon Lindsay in collaboration with WMB wrote,

> It was breaking dawn on a beautiful April morning in the year 1909...In a humble cabin the light began to creep through the window over a small crude bed, when

a baby's voice was heard…As the day dawned, the birds had already begun their singing and it seemed to the father that the morning star shone a little brighter.[38]

The above quote does not recount anything special. Enter Pearry Green,

> On April 6, 1909, a fifteen year old Kentucky mother gave birth to a baby boy… and on the day that he was born there was a strange aura, a Presence, in the rustic little log cabin. A light came whirling in through the window and hung over the crib. No wonder the people said, "What manner of child shall this be."[39]

Lee Vayle said,

> William Marrion Branham was born…April 6, 1909…in a most humble log cabin…For two days after his birth his fifteen year old mother, eighteen year old father, and visitors saw hanging over his crib, a white hazy light that had come in through the window, and stood over his head at birth. No one understood the significance of it, and no one, therefore, put any stock in it relative to his future life.[40]

WMB recalled his mother and father told him that a light, the size of a pillow, came and circled down on the bed.[41] This account quickly changed to the light being a Pillar of Fire[42] and the Angel of the Lord.[43] Of the many times WMB referred to a midwife being present, he only once said she was his grandmother.[44] This light came down and settled upon mother and baby.[45] Ironically, that same kind of combination of a "Madonna" and child, with light radiating from the child's head, was something that WMB strongly condemned in his *Exposition of the Seven Church Ages*.[46] WMB said the mountain people were very superstitious.[47] WMB stated that at 5:00 AM it was still dark when the light came in.[48] However, the U.S. Naval Observatory lists that, "Complete darkness…ends sometime prior to the beginning of morning civil twilight."[49] In April, it is, typically about 26 minutes before Daylight, which on April 6, 1909, occurred in Burkesville, KY, at 5: 21 AM.[50] At Twilight, normal daylight activities can be pursued. This would mean that Twilight occurred at about 4: 55 AM. Taking WMB's time of birth to be 5:00 AM would mean that is was already light out. For WMB's factual birthdate of March 8, 1908, Sunrise occurred at 05:18 AM[51] and Twilight would have been 4:52 AM. If it was still dark out, as WMB alleged, would his father open the solid wooden little hinged window? WMB said this was done so the people could see the little child. This would confirm the U.S. Naval Observatory's notation that it was already light at 4: 52 AM, thus 8 minutes before WMB's 5:00 AM birth happened allegedly occurred.

Stadsklev and Lindsay have light coming into the cabin. WMB had accounts, regarding the time lapse between his birth and the light appearing, anywhere from mere minutes to a

CHAPTER SIX

half hour after.[52] It would take some time between WMB being born, washed, dressed, etc., and put in his mother's arms. A half hour later it would be 5: 30 AM and fully day light. At which time, instead of a pillar of fire, it should have been a column of cloud, which WMB also affirmed.[53] For those that would introduce a Daylight Savings Time (DST) argument, there was no such thing until 1918. DST was later abolished, only to be re-enacted during WWII.[54] WMB's actual birth date was April 8, 1908, but the 3 minute time difference is insignificant. Can WMB's claim of an angelic encounter and commissions at birth be established by his own messages? No, there are too many contradictions! All WMB knew about his birth was what he was told. This claim of an angelic encounter at birth is also frivolous and must be rejected.

WMB's Third Angelic Visitation

WMB's third angelic visitation occurred at age seven, when he was carrying water to one of his father's moonshine stills,

> One day when he was but seven years of age, as he was carrying water for his father, he was startled to hear the sound of wind in the leaves of the tree under which he was resting for a moment. He looked up, but there was no physical movement. As he started to leave, the sound came again, but this time it was louder. Looking up he saw a whirlwind in the tree, and out of the whirlwind there came an audible voice saying, "Don't ever smoke, or drink, or defile your body in any way, for there is a work for you to do when you are older." <u>He was naturally frightened</u> and ran screaming into the house. Somehow <u>he was unable to tell his mother</u> the experience, so she concluded that William was a very nervous boy and needed rest.[55] (Underline ours – PMD). [WMB]...found himself passing underneath a poplar tree...a whirlwind stirred a section of the tree about the size of a barrel and a voice spoke from it saying, "Never smoke, drink, nor defile your body, for when you are older there is a work for you to do," He couldn't understand the mysterious event; it had frightened him, and he ran to his mother. She thought he had been snake bitten, then she thought he may have been in nervous shock, so she put him to bed and called the doctor.[56]

Stadsklev does not differ much in his account,

> <u>He was just scared</u> and did not tell her about the wind blowing through the leaves <u>nor did he tell her about the voice</u>. His mother put him to bed thinking he was suffering from a nervous shock. Whenever possible <u>he would avoid that tree</u>, choosing rather to detour around the other side of the garden.[57] (Underlining mine – PMD).

Lindsay quotes WMB:

> [T]hinking I was suffering from nervous shock. <u>I never did go by that tree anymore.</u> I would detour down the other side of the garden to avoid it. [58] As a matter of fact WMB was so scared he never in his life went back there. (Underlining mine – PMD).

"I believe that the angel of God was in that tree, and in later years I was to meet him face to face and talk with him,"[59] said WMB. Why did his mother think he had a nervous shock?[60] If no man was discovered,[61] it would make sense that he was put to bed. The doctor diagnosed WMB to be a neurotic.[62] WMB confessed he was a neurotic all his life; it was a seven year cycle of mental oppression.[63] WMB had a mental breakdown in 1948 and he left the field for eight months.[64] This angel told WMB he must never drink. WMB said he never lived an immoral life and he never drank.[65] Yet, communion wine must be alcoholic said WMB,[66] and thus he violated his "Nazarite" vow,[67] as well as his angel's command. WMB touched dead bodies, cut his hair and shaved, contrary to the requirements of a Nazarite. WMB did not have a Nazarite vow!

WMB interpreted, "Never defile your body in any way," to mean running around with women. Though he said he went out with the opposite sex, he despised women "They're not worth a good clean bullet to kill them with it," he said.[68] He never said anything negative about men in that context and he actually surrounded himself with homosexual men. Paul Cain was a homosexual as previously stated. WMB's "tape boys," Leo Mercier and Gene Goad, were gay, according to Lee Vayle, "I believe it was about 1956 and no later, that...God told Bro. Branham to hire them; two homosexuals."[69] WMB's manager, Baron Fraery Von Blomberg too, was a homosexual, according to Vayle:

> Faery Von Blomberg-even the name is typical-Fairy? Not trying to be facetious, but look at it. It's absolutely true. That was his name, and he was an avowed homosexual..."[70] [Note: Blomberg's name was Fraerie. Vayle's comment was not necessary – PMD].

Can the 3rd commission be substantiated? The third commission was only later given significance by WMB. There are also contradictions in his story, which make these claims invalid and they must, therefore, be rejected.

Notes - Chapter Six

[1] Rebekah Branham Smith, in *Only Believe* Vol. 4, Issue 11, p. 6, "The biography by Gordon Lindsay, *'William Branham, A Man Sent From God'* [was] written in collaboration with William Branham, a distinction in authorship which was agreeable to both the subject and the writer. William Branham highly recommended the book and offered it for sale in

CHAPTER SIX 89

the healing campaigns and from his home office."

² Lindsay, 76.

³ Stadsklev, 37.

⁴ Green, 66.

⁵ WMB, *Adoption # 1*, May 15, 1960, PM, Jeff., IN, "May the seventh, 1946, the night the angel of the Lord appeared to me up there…"

⁶ The UN approved the Partition to create a Jewish and Arab state on Nov. 29, 1947.

⁷ _____, *Manifestation of Thy Resurrection to the People of this Day*, Aug. 09, 1954, PM, Los Angeles, CA, "The very day that Israel was declared a nation again…the angel of the Lord sent me out to pray for the sick…May the 6th, 1946."

⁸ _____, *Great Coming Revival And The Outpouring Of The Holy Spirit*, Jul. 18, 1954, Aft., "The very day the angel of the Lord called me out, May the 6th, 1947, and issued the gift to pray for the sick, was the very same day that Israel become a nation."

⁹ _____, *Handwriting On The Wall*, Sep. 02, 1956, Jeff., IN, "[A]nd 1947 on May the seventh, they were once more recognized among the nations of the world for the first time for twenty-five hundred years, the Jews were."

¹⁰ _____, *Who Has Believed Our Report*, Jul. 20, 1952, PM, Hammond, IN, "It's by a vision that God gave me, when I was a little baby in my mother's womb."

¹¹ _____, Jan. 27, 1957, PM, Lima, OH, "[T]he angel who spoke to me and sent me here, said, 'Get the people to believe you, and be sincere when you pray.' I said, 'They won't believe me. 'He said, 'By this they will believe you. This was given at birth, when just a little baby boy.'"

¹² *Life Story*, Cleveland, "I remember…how the angel of the Lord …told me never to smoke or to drink or defile my body in any way, that there'd be a work for me to do when I got older: appeared to me in that bush, and how they have misunderstood it."

¹³ *Believing God*, "I want you to come here that I might fulfill my commission. I'm under obligation to my Lord. And my claims, as a divine angel appeared to me at my birth, and commissioned me at twelve years old, and sent me out here a few years ago, and said these things."

¹⁴ *Things That Are To Be*, "As a little boy, I had been shot, and I was laying, dying in a hospital. And I had always knowed there was God. I remember the first prayer I ever tried to pray…I've never told this before. I just feel I'll tell it right now. I was shot, laying there, dying in a field. And the only plea that I could have to God, I said, 'You know, Lord, I never did commit adultery.' As a little, young boy about fifteen years old, I tried to live right. And I said, 'I've lived clean.' And that's all I could say. That's all the merit that I could offer Him…I said, "O God, if You'll let me out of here, I'll never be ashamed of You again. I'll never be ashamed. God, please give me a chance.'" [Note: WMB listed this as happening when he either 14 or 15 years old – PMD].

¹⁵ WMB, *Testimony Upon The Sea*, Jul. 26, 1962, Port Alberni, BC, CAD, "I want to ask you, do you believe? See that picture over there, that pillar of fire that's on the picture? You seen it. Now, I've seen that since I was a little boy, it's all down through the records. The first time that was ever taken, the Canadian newspaper packed it thirty-one years ago, across the whole province of Canada, all the provinces, the Dominion of Canada. Said, 'A mystic light appears over a minister while baptizing in the river.' That was in 1930, at the foot of Spring Street at Jeffersonville, Indiana."

¹⁶ WMB, *What Was The Holy Ghost Given For?* Dec. 17, 1959, Jeff., IN, "I was a little old boy preacher about twenty-two years old…Here comes that big light hanging right yonder, come moving down over me and said, 'As John the Baptist was sent to forerun the first coming of Christ, you'll have a message that'll forerun the second coming of Christ.'" [Note: This occurred at 22 years old, which would make that 1908 + 22 = 1930 - PMD]. See WMB, *Q & A*, May 15, 1954, "Just the same thing He said when I baptized…twenty-three years ago, right on the Ohio River that light, angel, come right down to where we was at, and said, 'As John the Baptist was sent for a forerunner of the first coming of Jesus Christ, your Message will bring the second coming of Jesus Christ.'" [Note: This occurred 23 years prior, or in 1931 – PMD].

¹⁷ _____, *Is This The Sign Of The End Sir?* Dec. 30, 1962, PM, Jeff., IN, "And I suppose, besides my wife, there's people here tonight from thirty years ago that was standing close when that come down…Is there anybody in the audience now that was there when the angel of the Lord, that come down on the river." WMB stated this occurred 30 years prior which would make that 1962 - 30 = 1932.

¹⁸ _____, *Watchman, What Of The Night?* Jul. 22, 1960, Lakeport, CA, "I can remember 1933…June the 16th at two o'clock in the afternoon…I was baptizing five hundred…at the foot of Spring Street at Jeffersonville, Indiana."

¹⁹ _____, *Questions And Answers (COD)*, May 27, 1962, Jeff., IN, "Then I think about the river in 1936…I was just a boy, and of baptizing my first baptism, when that angel of the Lord came down and stood over where I was at."

²⁰ William Branham, *I was Not Disobedient To The Heavenly Vision*, "Then one year ago, while I was standing in my yard the Spirit came to me again; I was told that God had forgiven me and that a double portion of the power to heal would be given me. In this book are some of the things He did on my first trip for Him."

²¹ *Angel and The Commission*, Aug. 21, 1950, Cleveland, OH, "Way back in the hills. I'd went back there when I started in after six days, of May 1946."

²² WMB, *Prayer Line*, Nov. 27, 1953, Palm Beach, FL, "About seven years ago, on May the 7th, 1946, Green's Mill, Indiana, there was an angel come into the room where I was at, a man walking."

²³ *Great Coming Revival*, "And a strange thing of that, that you might not know, the very day the angel of the Lord called me out, May the 6th, 1947, and issued the gift to pray for the sick, was the very same day that Israel become a nation for the first time for twenty-five hundred years."

24 *Wings Of A Snow White Dove*, "I've been a neurotic all my life. As a little boy there was something struck me, that scare me, about every seven years it would happen to me. Brother Jack remembers when I first started, come off the field for a year; something just happened… And you don't know what I've suffered; just mental oppression. Every seven years it's come, all my life. That's where I'm at now, seven eights…I was so distressed; I cried, I begged, I pleaded. And I remember when I finally thought I had enough money to go to Mayo's for an examination; they said, 'They'll find what your trouble is.'…I had just entered my healing ministry. And we took off to Mayo's."

25 *Angel And The Commission*, "He said, 'As the prophet Moses was given two signs to prove that he was sent from God, so will you be given two signs to do before the people.'"

26 WMB, *As I Was With Moses, So I Will Be With Thee*, Sep. 11, 1960, AM, Jeff., IN, "He said, 'As I was with Moses, so will I be with you,' and when that hand come down and pointed that very same Scripture…For a long time I've wondered, because I didn't know what the commission was. I've looked for something supernatural beyond that. God cannot get away from His commission. God give the commission; that's what it must remain."

27 *How The Angel Came To Me*, "As John the Baptist was sent for the forerunner of the first coming of Christ, you've got a…a message that will bring forth the forerunning of the Second Coming of Christ."

28 WMB, *Spiritual Food In Due Season*, Jul. 18, 1965, PM, Jeff., IN, "This prophet, Elijah, we know very little about him, but we know that he was God's servant, and the servant of God for that hour. And God has used his spirit that was upon Elijah…and supposed to come just to issue in the Gentile Bride, and come with a Moses to take the Jews home, that's right. Five times that God promises to use the spirit of Elijah, and already done it three times."

29 _____, *First Seal*, Mar. 18, 1963, Jeff., IN, "John begin to bawl them people out; and standing there, looked like they'd have knowed that was that spirit of Elijah…Now, he will not start another church age like Luther, and Wesley, and all the rest of them did. He won't start another church, because there is no more church ages to come, see? There won't be any more, so he must be against it… Notice now when he did, he's not going to start a denomination because the "Laodicea Church Age" is the last age, and the messenger of the seventh angel, which is the seventh messenger to the seventh church age, is the fellow that is going to reveal, by the Holy Spirit, all these mysterious things…"

30 Ronald Kydd, *Healing Through The Centuries: Models for Understanding*, (Peabody, MA: Hendrickson Publishing, Feb. 2010, 272 pp.), 170, 171.

31 WMB, *Gifts And Callings Are Without Repentance*, Mar. 1950, Carlsbad, NM, "God told Jeremiah, 'Before you were born from your mother's womb, I knew of you, and sanctified you, and ordained you a prophet over the nations…'"

32 *Who Has Believed Our Report*, "It's by a vision that God gave me, when I was a little baby in my mother's womb." See also: *Faith Is The Substance*, Apr. 12, 1947, Oakland, CA,

"I said, 'Now, look, there was an angel came down into the room and told me that way back, back 'fore I was born, was foreordained to have a gift of Divine healing.'"; *Message Of Grace*, Aug. 27, 1961, Jeff., IN, "A prophet is not a prophet if somebody lays hands on him and makes him a prophet. A prophet's born from his mother's womb as a prophet."

33 *Expectations*, Cleveland.

34 *Communion*, "I used to remember, as a little boy...Pop and mom, they're gone on now to their rest. And them days they were sinners, there was no Christianity in our homes at all. And, oh, my, drinking, and parties, and carrying on; it made me sick, I'd take my-my lantern and my dog and go to the woods, to stay all night. In the wintertime I'd hunt till the party was over, maybe daylight in the morning. Come home, wouldn't be over, I've laid on top of a shed and sleep, waiting for daylight to break."

35 *Early Spiritual Experiences*, "You know how superstitious the mountain people is..."

36 *Pillar Of Fire*, My mother told me when I was about three minutes old...A light, about so big around, come whirling in and went down on the bed where mother was holding me in her arms." See also: *Witnesses*, Mar. 03, 1954, Phoenix, AZ.

37 Stadsklev. 1.

38 Lindsay. 27.

39 Green. 39.

40 Vayle. 35.

41 *Early Spiritual Experiences*. "Now, I'm told by my mother and my father...In there was light come whirling through the window about the size of a pillow. And it circled around where I was, and went down on the bed. Several of the mountain people were standing there. They were crying."

42 WMB, *A Personal Experience With God (Faith)*, Jul. 24, 1954, Chicago, IL, "I challenge your faith, in the Name of the Lord Jesus, to believe, that the testimony that I give concerning the angel of the Lord. That when I was a baby, he, that Pillar of Fire, hung over the crib, the very minute I was born."

43 _____, *Israel And The Church # 5*, Mar. 29, 1953, Jeff., IN, "And that Pillar of Fire...And my own mother setting back there now, that fifteen years old when I was born, she opened up the little window, and the Angel of the Lord come in and stood there."

44 *My Life Story*, LA, "And I was born on April the 6th, 1909...And so, the morning that I was born, Mother said that they opened up the window. Now, we had no doctors, there was a midwife...And that midwife was my grandmother."

45 WMB, *Deep Calleth Unto The Deep*, Nov. 04, 1952, Owensboro, KY, "My mother was laying on a straw tick with a shuck pillow when the midwife... washed me and laid me on my mother's arm, she opened the window. It was about five o'clock in the morning for the first break of the day...she wanted to look at her child; and through that came the light. Everybody begin to cry."

46 William Branham, *Exposition of the Seven Church Ages*, (Dallas, TX: Voice of Healing,

CHAPTER SIX   93

1975, 381pp.), 185. "Since it was not necessary to worship the creator-father, it was only natural that worship swung to the 'Mother and Child' as the objects of adoration. In Egypt there was the same combination of mother and son called Isis and Osiris. In India it was Isi and Iswara. (Note the similarity of names even.) In Asia it was Cybele and Deoius. In Rome and in Greece it followed suit. And in China. Well, imagine the surprise of some Roman Catholic missionaries as they entered China and found there a Madonna and Child with rays of light emanating from the head of the babe. The image could well have been exchanged for one in the Vatican except for the difference of certain facial features."

⁴⁷ *Early Spiritual Experiences,* "That morning on April the 6th, when the midwife opened up the window, so the light could shine in to…let mama see what I looked like, and papa… In there was light come whirling through the window about the size of a pillow. And it circled around where I was, and went down on the bed. Several of the mountain people were standing there. They were crying… they didn't know what happened. 'Course, you know how superstitious the mountain people is, said, 'That young'n that was borned over yonder on the hill,' you know. 'There was a light appeared over yonder in a room. Wonder what kind of a young'n it'll be…You know how mountain people are."

⁴⁸ *Life Story,* LA, "Well, they had told…'This light came in.…Some of them said it must have been the sunlight reflecting on a mirror in the house. But there was no mirror… And the sun wasn't up, so it was too early, at five o'clock. And then, oh, they just passed it by." See also: *The Revelation That Was Given Me* "And the morning when I was born, so my mother tells me, she opened a little door, that didn't have glass…she opened it back, father did, so that she could see me …when I was--he put me in her arms. It was early in the morning about five o'clock. The sun had never come up yet, so when they opened up the window, a light in the form of … a bucket or a pillow, come in the window and stood over the little bed where I was born."

⁴⁹ Civil Twilight, Burkesville, Kentucky, April 6, 1909, available from http://aa.usno. navy.mil/cgi-bin/aa_rstablew.pl, (Accessed April 26, 2010).

⁵⁰ Rise and Set for the Sun for 1909, Burkesville, KY, Astronomical Applications Dept. U. S. Naval Observatory. Washington, DC 20392-5420, accessed April 26, 2010. http://aa.usno.navy.mil/cgi-bin/aa_rstablew.pl?FFX=1&type=0&st=KY&place=Burkesville&xxy=1909

⁵¹ Rise and Set for the Sun for 1908, Burkesville, KY, Astronomical Applica-tions Dept. U. S. Naval Observatory. Washington, DC 20392-5420, accessed April 26, 2010. http://aa.usno.navy.mil/cgi-bin/aa_rstablew.pl?FFX=1&type=0&st=KY&place=Burkesville&xxy=1908

⁵² WMB, *God Revealing Himself To His People*, Aug. 13, 1950, Aft., Cleveland, OH, "And they got the picture. They asked me what to do about it first, before the…Now, as soon as I looked at it, I said, 'That's it.' See? 'Fore I seen it…My mother was the first one to see it come in the room when I was a baby, about a half hour after I was born, maybe not so long."

⁵³ _____, *Is This The Time Of The End, Sir?* Dec. 30, 1962, PM, Jeff., IN, "Did you notice, here, this angel, he was clothed in a cloud. He was cloud by day."

54 Heidi G. Yacker Daylight Saving Time; Congressional Research Service Library of Congress, Reference Division, Number: : 98-99 C, February 9, 1998, available from http://www.webexhibits.org/daylightsaving/congressionalResearchService.html, (Accessed 26 April 26, 2010).

55 Lindsay.

56 Green. 40.

57 Stadsklev. 3.

58 *Life Story*, Owensboro, "I said, 'There's a man in that tree. And I heard him, what he told me.' And I said, 'I ain't going to never go by there.' And till this day, I have never been there. I'd go down the one behind the garden, going back to...I've never been there to this day, and from that time. And that was--been a long time ago." See also: *Life Story*, Zurich, "I said there's a man in that tree. They went down to look: nobody there. They called the doctor, and he said I was just nervous. I said, 'No, I seen, and I heard him speak.' And I never would go by that tree."; *Life Story*, Los Angeles, "And I never, from that day to this, ever passed by that tree again. I was scared. I'd go down the other side of the garden, because I thought there was a man up in that tree and he was talking to me, great deep voice that spoke."

59 Lindsay. 31.

60 WMB, *Twentieth Century Prophet*, Aug.1953, "Passing by there, there was a whirl of wind in the tree, what we call here a whirlwind. Why, it was nothing odd for that time of year in this part of the country. But it remained in the tree. It didn't leave. I stopped to see what it was. And a voice spoke from it, saying, "Do not never smoke, or drink, or defile your body in any way, for there'll be a work for you to do when you get older." Frightened? That's not a word for it. I ran home quickly, telling my mother that a man spoke to me out of a tree. Well, she thought I was nervous. She put me to bed." See also: *Revelation That Was Given To Me*, Feb. 10, 1960, San Juan, PR.

61 *Life Story*, Owensboro, "I said, 'There's a man in that tree. And I heard him, what he told me.' And I said, 'I ain't going to never go by there.'" See also: *Life Story*, Zurich, "I said there's a man in that tree. They went down to look: nobody there."; *Life Story*, LA, "Well, I told that to Mama, and--and she just laughed at me. And I was just hysterically."; *Revelation That Was Given To Me*, "I said, 'There's a man up in that tree.'...She went down around the tree, and looked all around to see if there was anybody there."

62 *Life Story*, Owensboro, "She put me to bed and went over to Wathan's and called the doctor. He said, "Oh, he's just nervous."; See also: *Experiences*, Mar. 02, 1948, Phoenix, AZ, "They thought I was just at a little nervous hysterical child."

63 *Wings Of A Snow White Dove*.

64 *Hidden Life*, Oct. 06, 1955, Aft., Chicago, IL, "I had my great breakdown or come off the field for about eight months."

65 *From That Time*, Klamath Falls, "When I was seven years old, the angel of the Lord met me as a whirlwind in that bush that day and said, "Don't never smoke, drink, or

defile your body." I never smoked in my life, never drank in my life…I know no woman but my wife. And so then, I didn't live immoral when I was a sinner."

[66] WMB, *Questions And Answers*, Jun. 28, 1959, PM, Jeff., IN, "I believe that it should be a holy unleavened bread…And I believe that the Blood should not be grape juice, but it should be wine."

[67] _____, *Jehovah-Jireh*, Feb. 09, 1961, Long Beach, CA, "I said, 'But, you see, I was born under a Nazarite birth. I wasn't supposed to smoke, chew, or drink anything.'" See also: *The Oncoming Storm*, Feb. 29, 1960, Phoenix, AZ, "And Doctor Guggenbuhl setting next to me, which provided me an interpreter. I said, '…I was borned under a Nazarite birth; I'm not supposed to drink.'"

[68] *Life Story*, Cleveland, "I was around, watched my father drinking and hung around those places…I'd see how women come out and living untrue." See also: *My Life Story*, LA, "But I can remember when my father's still up there running, I had to be out there with water and stuff, see young ladies that wasn't over seventeen, eighteen years old, up there with men my age now, drunk…This was my remark then, 'They're not worth a good clean bullet to kill them with it.' That's right. And I hated women. That's right. And I just have to watch every move now, to keep from still thinking the same thing."

[69] Lee Vayle, *Godhead 11*, July 1, 2000, available from http://www.messagedoctrine.com/LeeVayle/Godheadseries/Godhead11.htm, (Accessed January 05, 2009).

[70] _____, *Godhead 11*, "Count Faery Von Blomberg. Von Blomberg was the adopted son of…a Count and a Countess. And he was recognized as a Christian, evidently in Full Gospel Businessmen circles, but he was a homosexual. And he approached a young man who was a Christian Pentecostal preacher named Sigfried Encke. I know what I'm talking about, because I know Sigfried Encke; met him in Columbus… he amazingly told me his story, how that this man did everything he could to engage him in some illicit sexual affair."

Chapter Seven

ANGELIC COMMISSIONS 4 - 6

Can WMB's claims of his many angelic encounters
and/or commissions be substantiated
by his own messages?

WMB's Fourth Angelic Visitation

WMB claimed his next angelic commission occurred at about twelve, fourteen, or fifteen years old.[1] During a hunting accident he was shot in both legs and he was dying, he said. A vision occurred, "A great golden cross in the skies, and the glory of the Lord flowing off of that cross. And I stood with my hands out like *this*, and that glory was falling into my chest."[2] WMB states later that from that time on he lived for God.[3] Stadsklev wrote that WMB was in hospital for seven months.[4] By having the Glory of God fall into his chest he was commissioned, yet he was not converted to Christ?

One would think that such a huge event would be remembered more accurately. There is also no biblical, nor Church historical account of anything like this kind of encounter, or commission. There are also too many conflicts to reconcile with regarding his age, etc. Later, when he was in his twenties, he often spoke of not knowing anything about Christianity. Yet here he asked people to believe he was commissioned while he was in an "unconverted" state? WMB's claims of an angelic encounter and commission from age 12 to 15, cannot be established by his own messages.

WMB's Fifth Angelic Visitation

WMB returned home from Arizona to attend his brother's funeral. Afterwards, WMB said, he started working for the Public Service Company of Indiana. Julius Stadsklev's account is an echo of what Lindsay recorded. This same sentiment was shared by Lee Vayle.[5] Pearry Green adds:

> [A] light came in and formed a cross. It was then that something swept over him and he experienced an exquisite feeling he had never known before. He once told

me personally that it felt like rain was pelting down on his body, He knew then that God had baptized him with the Holy Ghost.[6]

WMB spoke of being saved in a shed, or garage, but he also said this occurred in a converted saloon. The question is, "Where was WMB converted and commissioned?" It must be said, however, that in WMB's theology, one can believe and be saved *potentially*. Being saved is just the first step in a three step process of justification, sanctification, and the Baptism of the Holy Spirit, upon which a person is truly saved.[7] Hope Branham, WMB's wife, exhorted him on her death bed to stay with the *Jesus Only* people because it was through their ministry that they had received the Holy Spirit.[8] Gordon Lindsay recorded that WMB was commissioned about six months after WMB's experience in the shed:

> One day about six months later God gave me the desire of my heart. He spoke to me in a great light telling me to preach and to pray for the sick and He would heal them regardless of what disease they had. I then started preaching and doing what He told me to do.[9]

Stadsklev's account is almost identical to Lindsay's:

> About six months later when he received the Baptism, God spoke to him telling him to preach the Word and pray for the sick.[10]

Green said,

> After a lapse of centuries, God had once again visited the people of this generation through a prophet. He had sent a prophet chosen from his mother's womb, and had ordained this man's life from childhood…[11]

WMB's commission was preceded by the, "Baptism of the Holy Spirit." WMB claimed he experienced this as rain pelting his body. Green recorded this as follows,

> Something swept over him and he experienced an exquisite feeling he had never known before…it felt like rain was pelting down on his body. He knew then that God had baptized him with the Holy Spirit.[12]

Lee Vayle wrote,

> One day while looking to God, it seemed as though rain fell upon his body---- literally pelting it, and sinking deep within him. He was completely, over flowingly filled with the Holy Ghost.[13]

John the Baptist said that Jesus was the One who would baptize believers, not with water as he did, but rather with the Holy Spirit and with fire (Matt. 3: 11). This was fulfilled at Pentecost (Acts 2: 4). Baptism with the Holy Spirit, as rain pelting the body with water, would appear to be more of a Paedo-Baptist metaphor, rather

than Baptism by immersion. When WMB baptized people, he would say, "Father, as I baptize him with water, You baptize him with the Holy Spirit." [14]
Where would WMB have come up with this "rain pelting down on his body?" Interestingly enough, this *is* found within Hinduism:

> Shankaracharya called this energy "spun". He too described its nature as being like divine water showering down upon him as he meditated in the ecstasy of devotion. [15]

This "divine water showering down," is what is termed the *Kundalini Awakening*. It is referred to as the 'mystical anointing' in Eastern mysticism. The person who receives this is called a 'yogi' and becomes the object of meditation by others, as the pathway to bliss. WMB insisted his message was that pathway to bliss, (*Rapture*). His experience appears to be very akin to the Yoga, or Gnostic, 'counterpart' of WMB's 'Baptism of the Holy Ghost.' Is that why WMB said a person could have the "Baptism of the Holy Ghost" and yet go to Hell?

> We merely think, "I got the baptism of the Holy Ghost, I'm going to heaven." That don't mean one thing that you're going to Heaven. No sir. You can have the baptism of the Holy Ghost every hour of your life, and still be lost and go to hell…It's a real genuine Holy Ghost, and you could still be a devil…The sun shines on the just and the unjust, and the rain falls on the just and the unjust, but by their fruit you shall know them."[16]

WMB's angel wore a turban.[17] WMB knew Sikhs wear turbans.[18] Among Sikhs turbans are worn as a religious symbol. As a religious symbol this would not be applicable to angels, because angels have no religion. It also contradicted his own philosophy. WMB spoke about how Jesus would not have been recognized due to dress, hair, beard or turban, because Jesus would have appeared like any other man.[19] Yet, WMB *did* say that Jesus appeared to him in a vision wearing a white garment, sporting a short beard.[20] A short beard contrary to Mosaic law? Not likely.

Can WMB's claim of this angelic encounter and commission while dying in the hospital be established by his messages? No! There are too many discrepancies regarding dates, theological errors and issues, that warrant a dismissal of WMB's claims of this angelic commission.

WMB's Sixth Angelic Visitation

The next highly mentioned angelic visitation occurred during WMB's first baptismal service in the Ohio River, in Jeffersonville. Gordon Lindsay recorded,

> It was at this time that a heavenly light appeared above him as he was about to

baptize the seventeenth person. This was witnessed by the vast congregation that stood looking on, by the banks of the Ohio River.[21]

Stadsklev, Green and Vayle state, respectively,

> At the baptismal service which followed the campaign, over 130 people were baptized in water. It was at this time that the heavenly light appeared above him as he was baptizing the seventeenth person. This light was witnessed by the large congregation that stood on the banks of the Ohio River and the newspaper carried an article pertaining to it."[22]

> It was on June 11, 1933, as Brother Branham was baptizing in the Ohio River at the foot of Spring Street in Jeffersonville, that a strange Light, like a star, suddenly came whirling down and hung over his head...Some ran for fear; others fell in worship. Many pondered the meaning of this remarkable occurrence. Just as with Saul, a Voice spoke from the Light. These were the words, 'As John the Baptist was sent to forerun the first coming of the Lord, so are you sent to forerun His second coming... he...carved it on the inside of the door of his new home in Tucson, 'As John the Baptist was sent to forerun the first coming of the Lord. So are you sent to forerun His second coming.'"[23]

> It was during June of 1933 that as he was baptizing the converts in the Ohio River that a most amazing and well documented phenomenon occurred. As he was baptizing the seventeenth person...there appeared a blazing whirling star out of heaven with the sound of a rushing wind audible to all, and it came and hovered over him. As many ran in fear, and other knelt in prayer, a voice spoke out of the pillar of fire to him and said, "As John the Baptist was the forerunner of the first coming of Christ, so your message is the forerunner of the second coming of Christ." Of course he alone heard the words though others heard the sound.[24]

The only difference between the first two accounts is the additional statement regarding the newspaper carrying an article pertaining to it.

WMB said, "As John the Baptist was sent to warn the people of the first coming of Christ, so is this Message to warn the people of the second coming."[25] Out of the many times WMB related this statement, there are only four accounts that spoke about *him* being sent. All the other accounts state that *his message* would forerun the second coming of Christ. These accounts of WMB relating that he was sent, appeared thirty plus years after the supposed event, or in the 1960s.[26] Though some accounts appear close to what WMB wrote on his door, none actually match. The problem is not so much that particular statement, the important question is, "When was the statement made and who made it?" Lindsay (as told by WMB) does not mention any voice, nor does Stadsklev, and these two are the very first written accounts. Green and Vayle, both of whom wrote in the 1970s, added the saying and that constitutes a serious credibility problem. Why was that saying not in the very first accounts? Was it because the voice did not happen and was added later? In 1955 WMB related an incident, which he re-iterated in 1963, of a message in tongues by one man and an interpretation by another man.[27] The message was basically, "As John the Baptist was sent...etc." The problem is that in 1965 WMB repeated the same incident, but now the person doing the interpretation is a woman well known to him.[28] This is typical with WMB. The earliest account on tape is found in 1952 and states, "As John the Baptist was sent to warn the people of the first coming of Christ, so is this Message to warn the people of the second coming."[29] This account is about 30 years after the fact and re-enforces the thought that indeed this saying might have been added to embellish WMB's message and person.

On June 11, 1933, at about 2 o' clock in the afternoon, a light supposedly came down over the Ohio River, with a roar. WMB said,

> I was baptizing at two o'clock in the afternoon, and right out of the brassy skies, where there hadn't been rain for weeks, here he come with a roar.[30]

Only WMB heard the voice. He intimated that only *he* saw a light (A star, pillar of fire, the angel of the Lord, Holy Spirit). WMB, to justify it, said that, "No one could see that light that was hanging over Paul." There are other accounts where others saw the light, but those accounts can be quite suspect. Even WMB himself mentioned people did not believe him. He said, "Later when I was telling the people about this light being a pillar of fire: no one wanted to believe it..."[31] WMB said he received his commission at the Ohio River,

> My mission, I believe, to the earth is...to forerun...the coming Word which is Christ.[32]

"When they stood there and witnessed that morning star coming down out of the heavens, circling around like that, said, 'As John the Baptist was sent...to forerun the first coming of Christ, your Message will forerun the second coming.'[33] Don't you know what the very first thing He said down there on the river? Don't you remember what He said? 'As John the Baptist was sent forth to forerun the first coming of Christ, your message...' It's the message that will forerun the second coming of Christ. That's what the Angel of the Lord said... I believe that I have the message of the day. I believe that this is the Light of the day, and I believe it's pointing to that time coming."[34]

Can WMB's claim of a 1933 angelic commission on the Ohio be established from his own messages? The following section endeavors to answer that question.

In 1951, WMB stated that his commission on the Ohio River took place at two o'clock in the evening, on June, 1939.[35] However, WMB said he was commissioned years before he married Hope on June 22, 1934.[36] This 1939 commission date must be discounted.

In 1954, WMB stated that his commission on the Ohio River took place twenty-three years prior to 1954, thus in 1931.[37] This would place WMB to a date before he fell ill, and thus before his alleged conversion experience. This date must be discounted.

In 1955, WMB stated that the Angelic commission took place when he was 20 or 22 years old. Based on WMB's birth date of 1908, the date of his commission would range from 1928 to 1930, though he also mentioned June 15, 1933.[38] The date of 1928 does not fit because, WMB was in Arizona until 1929. The 1930 date also is to be rejected because, as stated earlier he had not as yet fallen ill. Later in 1955 WMB again stated that the Angelic commission took place on about June 15, 1933.[39]

In 1959, WMB stated that the commission took place when he was 22 years old. WMB was born in 1908 making the date of his commission 1930.[40] As stated above, this date must be rejected.

In 1960, WMB stated the Angelic commission took place at two o'clock in the afternoon on June 16, 1933. "All the skies were brassy. The corn was all withered up; we hadn't had rain for three weeks or more. Oh, it was suffering, the crops was. And the sky was like brass."[41] It occurred in, "June, 1933…"[42] he said. Traditionally this is the accepted date held by WMB's followers.

In 1962, WMB stated his commission on the Ohio took place in, "1930, at the foot of Spring Street…" but in this message he also sated it to be 1932,[43] a date he re-iterated in yet another sermon.[44] Again he said it was 1932 and added the light was accompanied by a roar.[45] The 1929 date he confirmed twice elsewhere,[46] when he said he was 21. Of course, taking his 1909 birthday, he would be 21 in 1930. WMB also stated that the commission took place in 1936,[47] which date is impossible, because it would have occurred after WMB's marriage to Hope. WMB also stated in 1962 that the Angelic commission took place on about June 15, 1933.[48]

In 1963, WMB stated that his commission on the Ohio took place when he was about 21,[49] thus in 1929. As stated, WMB just returned from Arizona in 1929 for his brother's funeral. He also stated that at 2 o'clock, on June 15, in either 1929 or 1930, his commission on the Ohio took place. He was about 20, 21 or 23 years old, which would cover 1929 through 1932. He also said that he and Hope were not as yet married, but dating.[50] He said the angelic commission took place at, "about two o'clock in the afternoon…"[51]

In 1964, WMB stated the angelic commission took place in June 1933. However, he referred to it as occurring 2 or 3 years prior to his marriage to Hope. WMB married in 1934, thus either in 1931 or 1932.[52] WMB also said it was a hot day. Elsewhere, he stated that the angelic commission took place around the middle of June, or on June 16, or June 18, in 1933. Again he said, "It had been so hot, for weeks. Hadn't had no rain for two or three weeks, and the country was burning up, nearly…brassy skies."[53] Why was WMB's mention about it being hot and no rain for weeks so important? Perhaps it was because of the record high temperatures. If so, it is to be noted that in Indiana, "The driest year was 1934."[54] It was the worst drought in US history. WMB mentioned a roar, was it thunder? Was it starting to rain?

In 1965, WMB stated the commission took place 35 years prior, thus in 1930.[55] There are an overwhelming number of claims in WMB's messages for a 1930 date of the Baptismal service on the Ohio River. However, WMB stated he was converted after he had worked for the Public Utility Company for two years, thus sometime after 1932. Therefore, the years of 1929, 1930, 1931, 1936 and 1939 fall outside the required parameters, so those will not be considered. That appears to leave 1932, 1933, 1934 and 1935 as possibilities. As noted, the generally accepted angelic commission date on the Ohio River is 1933. This date breaks down as follows: WMB mentioned June 15 (4x), June 16 (2x) and June 18 (1x). The repeated numbers of a date (say, 4x) would *appear* to increase a perception of truth. However, if it is a repetition of an error, that argument loses its power.

Quite obviously WMB was not sure about the year, but he was also not certain of the day, except that it was a Sunday afternoon.[56] Gordon Lindsay records a baptismal service, but mentions no date and neither does Julius Stadsklev. Lee Vayle, states the baptismal occurred in June, but he omits any day or year. Pearry Green is the only one that gives a date, June 11, 1933,[57] which date WMB never discussed. WMB mentioned another date, Sunday, June 18, 1933; though he also said it was about June the 15th or "The middle of June."[58] Green's June 11, 1933 date must be rejected. One would think that such a momentous event would be remembered accurately. The Friday June 2, 1933 edition of the Jeffersonville Evening News listed the conversion of 14 people.

Lindsay states that WMB was 24 years old when the event took place.[59] This would make the date 1933, had WMB's birth date been 1909. Because WMB was born in 1908, the date would be 1932. It must be remembered that WMB collaborated with Lindsay, which means that only WMB fed him the information.

WMB's very first recorded mention of the Baptismal date was not until five years after the publication of Lindsay's book, in which WMB claimed he, in 1933, was 20 or 22 years old. This would make the date 1930 [1908+22 = 1930]. This causes an internal contradiction,[60] which invalidates his claim. The Baptismal service was followed by the building of a place of worship. Julius Stadsklev wrote,

> Within six months after his conversion, plans were being made for his first service. He began tent meetings in his home town of Jeffersonville...At the baptismal service which followed his campaign, over a hundred and thirty people were baptized in water. It was at that time that the heavenly light appeared above him...The people who had been saved in the Jeffersonville meeting decided to build a tabernacle, which is now known as the Branham Tabernacle.[61]

Gordon Lindsay, Pearry Green and Lee Vayle agree with Julius Stadsklev in their accounts, regarding the Branham Tabernacle being built subsequent to the Baptismal service. Lindsay records that in the Fall of the year of the baptism,

CHAPTER SEVEN 103

"The people of Jeffersonville who had attended his meeting built him a tabernacle, which to this day retains the name of Branham Tabernacle."[62] WMB said he wanted to have the name changed, though that never did happen.[63] Prior to the building of the Branham Tabernacle, the meetings were held in a tent.[64] WMB rented[65] a Masonic hall[66] to hold services for 2-3 years. WMB said he made up his mind[67] to build a church sometime after the angelic encounter on the Ohio River.[68] He then purchased some property and laid the cornerstone. WMB claimed that all the money he had to build the church was eighty cents.[69]

There are photographs of the Branham Tabernacle in circulation which would call WMB's claim of a congregation of three thousand into serious question. These photographs provide clues regarding the approximate size of the building. It would appear from WMB's message that he dedicated the cornerstone as he laid it.

> The morning when I dedicated and laid that cornerstone there as a young man... And when I did, owing thousands of dollars...You could take up an offering in a congregation of this size and get thirty or forty cents, and our obligation was somewhat a hundred and fifty, two hundred dollars a month.[70]

WMB did not mention a dedication service, just a dedicatory prayer. However, this could not be the year 1933, because he said that it was years before he married Hope in 1934. WMB's hall rental would have occurred after his initial tent ministry, after which the new converts were baptized in the Ohio River. WMB laid the cornerstone and the building, ostensibly, was completed in September 1933, "At a total cost of $2,000. The congregation had 10 years to pay off the mortgage."[71]

The actual dedication service is taken to have occurred in 1933. WMB "corroborated" this in 1963, dedication,

> The Tabernacle itself has been dedicated in 1933...it would be a--a very good thing for just a--a small service of dedication again... When we started at the first dedication of the church, I was just a young man...maybe twenty-one, twenty-two years old when we laid the cornerstone. It was before I was even married...it's just a rededication, because the real dedication happened thirty years ago... And we, as ministers, dedicate ourselves to the preaching of the Word, to be instant in season, out of season, reproving, rebuking with all long-suffering as it's written there in the cornerstone from thirty years ago.[72]

This cornerstone was laid in 1933,[73] WMB said. Yet he also said it was a few years prior to '34. Thus the alleged 1933 date for WMB's Baptismal service in the Ohio River cannot be supported. He claimed it was at this Baptismal service he was commissioned as the second forerunner of Christ, as John the Baptist had been the first. This claim has been recorded as having happened anywhere from 1929 through 1939. It is also very important to note that Lee Vayle,[74] who was called on for Newspaper verification,[75] did not record this at all in his book. WMB's claim of this commission occurring in 1933, at the Ohio River, contains too many contradictions. The date of building of his Tabernacle in 1933 can also not be substantiated and must be dismissed.

It needs to be remembered that WMB was the only source of information. His followers are not known for contradicting their prophet. This is often due to fear of questioning the prophet, which would be construed as blasphemy of the Holy Spirit, for which there is no repentance. WMB said that he was a servant of God, an anointed prophet, with the vindicated word of the hour. God's people must, through the Holy Spirit, follow the vindicated Word.

How does one know that he/she has the Holy Spirit? WMB said, "There's only one evidence of the Holy Spirit that I know of, and that is a genuine faith in the promised Word of the hour."[76] If one did not believe WMB's message, one blasphemed the Holy Spirit and one would be condemned forever. That is circular reasoning, making this argument invalid.

> There's a lot of people that say they're born again and can't understand the message of God, can't see the angel of the Lord. Their eyes are blinded, brother.[77]

The following pages show a parallel ministry to that of WMB.[78] It is the ministry of William Sowders, a man who had a church and a camp in Louisville, KY. WMB met Will Sowders during the 1930's; a man who had a similar upbringing and ministry. These similarities, also listed elsewhere, are sufficiently close to suggest to this author that WMB was influenced by them and that he actually adopted them as his own.[79] WMB visited Wm. Sowders' church and his School of the Prophets in Louisville, KY.[80]

WMB never once mentioned Sowders, though he knew him and adopted Wm. Sowders' method of asking people to write out questions and he would answer them from the pulpit.[81] Sowders had out-of-body experiences and visions.[82] "[T]he Lord revealed to him [Sowders] the truth of the 'Godhead.' He was lead by God to take the middle ground on these issues. Through the truth of the word of God he could reach out to both his 'Oneness' and 'Trinitarian' brethren. The 'Trinitarians' taught three persons in the Godhead. The 'Oneness' people taught there was only one personal Deity. Brother Sowders contended that there were not three, not one, but rather, two separate persons in the Godhead." WMB certainly made it plain that his truth was in the middle between Oneness and the Trinity.[83] It appears WMB was strongly influenced by Sowders.

Can WMB's claims of his many angelic encounters and/or commissions be substantiated by his own messages? The fourth of WMB's alleged angelic commissions which occurred after he was in hospital at age 14; the next one after his appendicitis operation while he worked for the Indiana Service Company, at around age 25 and

CHAPTER SEVEN

the sixth one that supposedly occurred at the baptismal service at the Ohio River in 1933, cannot be substantiated by his own messages. They must, therefore, be rejected.

WILLIAM SOWDERS & WILLIAM BRANHAM SIMILARITIES IN DOCTRINE; Disclaimer: This is according to documents that I have in my possession that were given to us by Lloyd Goodwin and my own recollections of the teachings from various Gospel Assembly Churches through the years. I got the information about William Branham from one of his follower's Websites. If I am wrong about William Sowders, please give me your input. I was told that Branham met Sowders in the 1930's so it is possible that he got some of his teachings from Will Sowders. My comparison is not an acceptance or a denial of the truth or non truth of these doctrines but just to see if they were direct NEW revelations as claimed or were taken from other's and claimed as original. In my opinion, it is not what a group believes or teaches that makes it a destructive cult but the amount of control and coerciveness that is used to hold people in bondage to man made systems. Sincerely, Wanda Mason. (See chart on the next page)

William Sowders (1879-1952)	William Branham (1909-1965)
The young man **William Sowders**, born to Charles and Florence Meeky Sowders in Louisville **Kentucky** on **September 13, 1879**, was called by God to bring together the Body of Christ in this day.	Those who loved him call him "**Brother Branham**." He was born in the hills of **Kentucky** in a crude log cabin. **April 6, 1906.** Those present witnessed a strange hazy light hovering over him, although it was before daylight.
Brother Sowders began by running from God. He had been **searching for something** which only God could give him. He became a **hunter** and a fisherman in the small town of Olmstead, Illinois. Olmstead is where the Lord would lead Bro. Sowders to find his **calling**.	For a time **he still resisted the call of God** on his life. At the age of fourteen he was seriously wounded while **hunting** and had to spend seven months in hospital. God dealt with him then, but still he did not take heed. Nevertheless the urgency of the **call** became more and more conscious to him.
From the banks of the beutiful Ohio River in southern Illinois the movement of the **Body of Jesus Christ** was to originate in the twentieth century. Brother Sowders **heard a voice thundering** over his head which said, Son I want you to preach MY GOSPEL! He later recalled that the voice was so loud it actually took the life out of his body and almost burst his eardrums, especially when the Lord voiced **my gospel!**	He was called to bring about the healing of the Mystical **Body of Christ** - which is His Church. Borther Branham was baptizing in the Ohio river and a strange Light, like a star suddenly came whirling down and hung over his head. **A voice spoke from the Light** and said these words, "As John the Baptist was sent to forerun the first Coming of the Lord, so are you sent to **forerun His second Coming**....
When he came to himself he looked up and a **golden light** was around him. He then felt strength coming back into his body and he rose to his feet. However, from that wonderful experience he started out from there to study **God's Gospel.**	He spoke to me in that **Great Light** telling me to **preach the Gospel**, pray for the sick and he would heal them regardless of what disease they had. Obedient to His Voice I went forth preaching and praying for the sick and the Lord has confirmed His Word with signs following.
The man with **the divine call of God**, gave up his own life, subjected his life to Jesus, and launched into ministry. These Pentecostal revival themes were receiving the Holy Ghost with the evidence of speaking in other toungues, divine healing, and the soon coming of Jesus Christ. In fact they were saying then, that Jesus could come any night! About nine months after conversion, in 1912, William Sowders recieved the **baptism of the Holy Chost** according to Acts 2:4 under the ministry of Bob Shelton and George Aubrey on the "Gospel Boat."	There was another reason **why God chose** William Branham for the **great task of calling His people to the unity of spirit**. The Lord knew that he would never attempt to start another organization of his own. This he could have done. But to such suggestion he never gave one moment of consideration. "I began to pray for the **Baptism of the Holy Ghost**. One day about six months later God gave me the desire of my heart. It was then that **something swept over me** and I experienced an exquisite feeling I had never known before.
The **oneness people** stressed using the ceremonial formula of baptizing **in the name of Jesus**. The trinitarians steadfastly uttered the words, Father Son and Holy Ghost. The Pentecostal churches split over these issues. Many of the early twentieth centuriy Pentecostal groups shattererd because of the friction and fury generated by the Godhead and water baptism issues. God the Father, whom he alleged was a Spirit (Being) Jesus the Son, a Heavenly Creature. **He agreed with the Oneness element that the Holy Ghost was not a person**, but rather the Spirit or essence of God	Though he embraced the "**Oneness**" formula for water baptism - **in the name of the Lord Jesus Christ**, William Branham's view of the Godhead is far from the "Unitarian" concept or the concept preached by the United Pentecostal Church. Yet, the teaching of "three persons" in the Godhead is so ingrained in the people that to question its validity is immediately called heresy and branded as a 'cult.' **The trinity and oneness doctrine are both in error**. The World of God reveals the revelation of the Lord Jesus Christ and every Christian must confess that Jesus is the Son of God (1 John 4:15)
He advanced beyond his fellow Ministers in revealed truth. God restored to him the many Doctrines of the early church which were lost during the falling away and the apostasy of the dark ages. He moved beyond the knowledge of the **Holy Ghost** and the **Second Coming of Christ**. Brother Sowders began to preach the truth as God gave him on **Hell, Babylon, the Body of Christ**, Charity, Water **Baptism** (more than & in Jesus name). In addition Eternal Judgment, the **number and qualifications to be part of Christ's Bride**, and the **Godhead**.	And God is making an "end" of the "**Fulness of the Gentiles**" (Spiritual) and the "**Times of the Gentiles**" (Political) - "**Fulness**" covering the period of the Seven Church Ages of Revelation chapters 2 and 3, will climax with an "Indictment" of the religious systems of man, followed by the **Rapture of the Bride of Christ**. The "Times" beginning with **Babylon** and Nebuchadnessar will conclude with the battle of Armageddon - the ultimate end of Gentile domination, control and influence over Israel.
Brother William Sowders was a **"specially-called" and a "specially-anointed" man of God**, a leader and a teacher of men, called and sustained by God to further the work of restoring God's church in the earth in these last days. Truly in every sense of the word, he was God's man for the hour. God will see that his work continues until the Body of Jesus Chist in its healing, reaches maturity and the **last remaining members that go to make up the Bride of Jesus Christ are made ready.**	We will also show the fullfilment of these prophecies in a **man whom God has mightily used in this age**, to deny it is to deny "manifested" Truth. God called the man! God vindicated the man! God used the man in a ministry of **restoration to restore and reveal His Word to His Sons and Daughters**. By no means does that Ministry add to the Bible- but rather the mysteries contained in Scripture are revealed and will ultimately **give Rapuring Faith to the Bride of the Lord Jesus Chrst in This Age.**

CHAPTER SEVEN

Notes - Chapter Seven

¹ WMB, *Believing God*, Feb 24, 1952, Jeff, IN, "And my claims, as a Divine Angel appeared to me at my birth, and commissioned me at twelve years old…"; *Q & A, #3*, Aug. 30, 1964, AM, Jeff., IN, "And I was just only about fourteen…and I'd been shot."; *Things That Are To Be*, I was shot…As a little, young boy about fifteen"

² *Souls That Are In Prison*, "And seven months later [After his first leg operation-PMD], here at the Clark County Memorial Hospital, I had the second operation. And at that time, when I come out, I thought I was standing out in the West. I had another vision. And there was a great golden cross in the skies, and the Glory of the Lord flowing off of that cross. And I stood with my hands out like *this*, and that Glory was falling into my chest…The vision left me…And I was just only about fourteen years old, and I'd been shot."

³ *From That Time*, Tulsa.

⁴ Stadsklev. 7.

⁵ Vayle. 37. "One day while looking for God, it seemed as though rain fell upon his body—literally pelting it, and sinking deep within him. He was completely, overwhelmingly filled with the Holy Ghost."

⁶ Green. 43.

⁷ *Q & A #3*. "Because your name is on the Book of Life (because it is in heaven, your name has been recognized), that still doesn't mean that you are saved. You're not converted, until you receive the Holy Ghost. Remember that. You're only potentially converted…" See also: WMB, *Why?* Jun. 22, 1962, PM, South Gate, CA, "I only got one step: that's repent, and next is to be baptized in the Name of Jesus Christ for the remission of your sins. Then the next thing God said, 'I'll give you the Holy Ghost.' That's the three steps that I know of to take."

⁸ *Life Story*, Hammond. "She said, 'You know, Bill, that religion that we been talking about since we received the Holy Ghost?' And I said, 'Yes.' She said, 'Don't never cease to preach that.' She said, 'Stay with that.'"

⁹ Lindsay. 42.

¹⁰ Stadsklev. 12.

¹¹ Green. 43.

¹² Ibid.

¹³ Vayle. 37.

¹⁴ WMB, *How The Angel Came To Me And His Commission*, Jan 17, 1955, Chicago, IL.

¹⁵ Christ and the Kundalini, available from http://www.sol.com.au/kor/8_01.htm (Accessed July 10, 2012).

¹⁶ *Leadership*, Dec. 07, 1965, Covina, CA.

¹⁷ WMB, *Why Are People So Tossed About?* Jan. 01, 1956, Jeff., IN, "The man which was talking behind me, walked around in front of me, dressed in Palestinian clothes and a turban on

his head. He had a white robe. He said, "Brother Branham, that's it." [Note: Why would he be called brother? – PMD].

[18] *Word Became Flesh*, "Sikhs, they wear a turban;"

[19] WMB, ____, *Investments*, Mar. 14, 1964, Beaumont, TX, "Remember, all the Eastern people dressed alike, turban and beard, so forth. You remember, Jesus walked with them, too, on the road to Emmaus, all day long, after His resurrection, and they didn't even know Him. He was dressed the same way."

[20] *How The Angel Came To Me*, "The vision I saw of the Lord Jesus, He was a little Man...And there, standing not over ten feet from me, stood a Man; white garment on, a little Fellow; had His arms folded like *this*; a beard, kind of short; hair down to His shoulders...And I said, 'Jesus.' And when He did, He looked around like *that*. That was all I remember, He just reached out His arms. There's not an artist in the world could paint His picture, the characters of His face. The best I've ever seen is that Hofmann's *Head of Christ at Thirty-Three*, I've got it on all literature and everything I use. That's because that looks just like it...or pretty near, as close as it could be."

[21] Lindsay. 43.

[22] Stadsklev. 12.

[23] Green. 46.

[24] Vayle. 37.

[25] WMB, *Do You Now Believe?* Aug. 17, 1952, PM, Battle Creek, MI, "I was baptizing on the river at Jeffersonville, when all the local newspapers packed it, two o'clock in the afternoon...here it come right down out of the heavens, right at two o'clock in the evening, June, or in the afternoon, rather, in June, about the middle of June, hung right over where I was, and a Voice from it, saying, 'As John the Baptist was sent to warn the people of the first coming of Christ, so is this Message to warn the people of the second coming.'"

[26] ____, *Q & A*, Jan. 12, 1961, "As John the Baptist was sent forth to forerun the first coming of Christ, you're sent with this message, will forerun the second coming of Christ." See also: *Absolute*, Jeffersonville; *Sign Of The End, Sir?*; WMB, *An Absolute*, Jan. 27, 1963, Phoenix, AZ; *Look Away To Jesus*; WMB, *Trying To Do God A Service Without It Being God's Will*, Nov. 27, 1965, Brkfst., Shreveport, LA.

[27] *How The Angel Came To Me*, "And one night...in a cathedral, San Antonio, Texas, walking out there, a little fellow sitting up here begin to speak in tongues like a shotgun firing, or a machine gun, rapidly. Way back, way back there, a fellow raised up and said, 'THUS SAITH THE LORD! The man that's walking to the platform is going forward with a ministry that was ordained of Almighty God. And as John the Baptist was sent as the first forerunner of the coming of Jesus Christ, so he packs a Message that will cause the Second Coming of the Lord Jesus Christ.'"

[28] WMB, *The Way Back*, Nov. 23, 1962, Shreveport, LA, "Sister Schrader, you're a

good woman. I love you, my sister. You was the one, me not knowing you, when I walked in and someone spoke in tongues, and you gave the interpretation, and said the very same thing that that light did, when it come down over me down there, when I first was a Baptist preacher. Said, 'As John the Baptist was sent forth to forerun the first coming of Christ, you're sent forth, and your message will forerun the second coming.'"

[29] WMB, *Do You Now Believe*, Aug. 17, 1952, PM, Battle Creek, MI.

[30] _____, *Is This The Time Of The End Sir?* Dec. 30, 1962, PM, Jeff., IN.

[31] _____, *Paul, a Prisoner*, Jul. 17, 1963, Jeff., IN.

[32] _____, *Spoken Word is the Original Seed*, Mar. 18, 1962, AM, Jeff., IN.

[33] _____, *Man Running From The Presence Of The Lord*, Feb. 17, 1965, Jeff., IN.

[34] _____, *Revelation Chapter Four #2*, Jan. 01, 1961, Jeff., IN.

[35] _____, *My Commission*, May 05, 1951, Los Angeles, CA.

[36] *A Court Trial*, "Billy here, his mother, two or three years before we was married, she was standing there…She had a camera in her hand…'Look up!' I heard it the second time…And when I looked, here come that same Pillar of Fire that led Israel through the wilderness. Thousands of eyes looking at it coming right down over where I was standing. And said, 'As John the Baptist was sent forth…'" See also: *Seventieth Week Of Daniel*, Aug. 06, 1961, Jeff., IN, "Just think, about--around thirty years ago when I laid the cornerstone that morning…I wasn't even married yet, just a young man…." [1931? - PMD]; *God Hiding Himself In Simplicity Then Revealing Himself In The Same*, Mar. 17, 1963, Jeff., IN, "I was just a young man and maybe twenty-one, twenty-two years old when we laid the cornerstone. It was before I was even married."[1930/1931 – PMD]; *Q & A #3*, Aug. 30, 1964, AM, "I was looking at the pictures when we laid the cornerstone. I looked upon the picture and seen Hope and I before we were married."; *Ashamed (Ashamed Of Him, or Africa Trip Report)*, Jul. 11, 1965, Jeff., IN, "As, that lays right here in the cornerstone of this tabernacle today, of thirty-three years ago." [1932 – PMD]; WMB, *Anointed Ones At The End Time*, Jul. 25, 1965, AM, Jeff., IN, "Dig up that cornerstone out here and read a piece of paper that's put in there, thirty-three years ago…" [1932 – PMD]; *Spiritual Food in Due Season*, "And, God in Heaven knows, that lays right there in the corner of that Tabernacle stone since 1933, wrote on a page of a Bible, laying right there."; *God Keeps His Word*, Jeff., IN, "The vision taken place twenty three years ago in 1933. Be about twenty four years ago, I suppose. I'm looking at the chimney right now. It was long before I was ever married. I was single at home. We were just building this church, and we was laying the cornerstone that morning."

[37] *Q & A*, May 15, 1954.

[38] WMB, *Healing Of Jairus' Daughter*, Feb. 27, 1955, PM, Phoenix, AZ.

[39] _____, *Approach To God*, Jan. 23, 1955, Aft., Chicago, IL.

[40] *What Was The Holy Ghost Given For?*

[41] *Watchman, What Of The Night?*

42 *God Being Misunderstood.*

43 *Testimony Upon The Sea.*

44 *Is This The Sign Of The End, Sir?*

45 *Testimony Upon The Sea.*

46 WMB, *Second Seal*, Mar. 19, 1963, Jeff., IN.

47 *Q & A*, May 27, 1962.

48 WMB, *Perseverant*, Jun. 23, 1962, South Gate, CA.

49 *Second Seal.*

50 WMB, *Go Awake Jesus*, Nov. 30, 1963, PM, Shreveport, LA.

51 *Look Away To Jesus.*

52 *A Court Trial.*

53 *A Trial*, Tucson.

54 Marion T. Jackson, *The Natural Heritage of Indiana* (Bloomington, IN: Indiana University Press, 1997, 482 pp.) 89.

55 *It Is The Rising Of The Sun.*

56 WMB, *Everlasting Life And How To Receive It*, Dec 31, 1954, Jeff., IN, "As a young minister, when my first revival come, I had it over here on the corner, where this housing project in a tent. I was baptizing a group down at the river that Sunday afternoon."

57 Green, 46.

58 *A Trial*, "And I had a baptismal service down on the river, on 1933, on the middle of June, about sixteenth or eighteenth of June."

59 Lindsay. 43.

60 *Healing Of Jairus' Daughter*, "My first revival, five hundred came to Jesus Christ out of a three thousand congregation when I was twenty--about twenty-two years old. I was baptizing them down at the end of Spring Street in Jeffersonville, Indiana, in the Ohio River, when ... nearly seven or eight thousand people standing on the bank, bear witness, that two o'clock in the evening, June, 1933, how that a Pillar of Fire come down out of heaven, and hung over where I was standing."

61 Stadsklev. 12.

62 Lindsay. 43.

63 WMB, Serpent's Seed, Sep 28, 1958, Jeff., IN, "You Tabernacle here, I told you we're going to change the name of this. It's not right for it to be " Branham Tabernacle." That's just a man. We're going to change the name of it, make it some other name. We'll get on that after while. I just want it to be a--a church of the living God."

64 *A Trial*, Tucson.

65 William Branham Home Page, "Laying the Cornerstone," available from http://www.williambranhamhomepage.org/lcstone.htm Accessed May 06, 2010).

66 WMB, *God Keeps His Word*, Jan. 20, 1957, PM, Jeff., IN, "[W]e was over here

at the little Masonic temple, where we were having the parsonage over here on the next, second street over, where I was having the meetings..." See also: WMB, *Why Are We Not A Denomination?* Sep. 27, 1958, Jeff., IN.

⁶⁷ Stadsklev. 12. See also Lindsay. 43.

⁶⁸ *Taking Sides With Jesus*, "So upon my heart I made a promise to God that we would stay here and build the Tabernacle. The morning we laid the cornerstone, He met me over there in a vision about 8:00 that morning, when I was setting there watching out across the sun coming up, just about this time of year. And he had told me, after he had met me down there on the river...When the angel of the Lord appeared in that light, and I seen it in a distance, It looked like a star, and it come right down over where I was, and them notable words was spoken. And so then, I purposed then to get a place for the people to worship in."

⁶⁹ *Q & A # 4*, "My Brother, Sister Wilson, I want…to ask you two something. Remember how we all started? Remember the old floor when it was all full of mud? Had old windows that shook. We had eighty cents to start it on."

⁷⁰ *God Hiding Himself In Simplicity*, Jeff., IN.

⁷¹ *Life Story*, Los Angeles, "We had ten-years loan to pay it, and was paid off less than two years."

⁷² *God Hiding Himself In Simplicity*.

⁷³ *Seventieth Week*, "Just think, about--around thirty years ago when I laid the cornerstone that morning...I wasn't even married yet, just a young man...." [1931? - PMD]. See also: *God Hiding Himself In Simplicity*, "When we laid the cornerstone. It was before I was even married." [1930/1931 – PMD]; *Q & A # 4*, "I was looking at the pictures when we laid the cornerstone. I looked upon the picture and seen Hope and I before we were married."; *God Keeps His Word*, Jeff., IN, "It was long before I was ever married. I was single at home. We were just building this church, and we was laying the cornerstone that morning..."

⁷⁴ WMB, *Doors In Door*, Feb 06, 1965, Flagstaff, AZ, "Now, does anyone in here know Doctor Lee Vayle?...He asked me, he said, 'Can I write a book, just my comments?' And I said, 'Well, it's all right, Brother Lee .'....And it's called *Twentieth-Century Prophet*."

⁷⁵ _____, *This Day This Scripture Is Fulfilled*, Feb 19, 1965, Jeff., "In 1933, the supernatural Light that fell down yonder on the river, that day when I was baptizing five hundred in the Name of Jesus Christ…What did it say, Jeffersonville? What was it at the foot of Spring Street there, when the *Courier Journal*, I believe it was the *Louisville Herald*, packed the article of it? It went plumb across the Associated Press, plumb into Canada. Doctor Lee Vayle cut it out of the paper, way up in Canada, in 1933."

⁷⁶ _____, *Events Made Clear By Prophecy*, Aug. 01, 1965, PM, Jeff., IN, "Listen, hear me. Have I ever told you anything in the Name of the Lord but what come to pass? Is that right? Everything has always been right…I'm here to manifest God's Word of the hour. I've told you the Truth, and God has testified that it is the Truth."

77 WMB, *Mary's Belief*, Jan 21, 1961, Beaumont, TX.

78 Wanda Mason.

79 William H. Wallender, in a telephone interview with the author, April 15, 2010.

80 *How The Angel Came To Me*, "Later from that, I met an old man that's here in the church maybe now, or he was here over to the church, by the name of John Ryan. And I met him at a place...The old fellow with long beard and hair, and he may be here. I thought he was from Benton Harbor up here, at the House of David. And they had a place in Louisville. I was trying to find them people, and they called it the School of the Prophets. So I thought I'd go over and see what that was. Well, I didn't see nobody rolling on the floor, but they had some strange doctrines."

81 Wallender.

82 Wayne Hamburger, *Yoke Of Bondage*, Chapter Eight, Wm. Sowders, available from, http://www.gospelassemblyfree.com/gac/yoke8.htm, (Accessed April 14, 2010).

83 WMB, *Water Baptism*, Jan. 19, 1961, Aft., Beaumont, TX, "I think you're both wrong, both oneness and trinity. Not to be different, but it's always the middle of the road…"

Chapter Eight

ANGELIC COMMISSIONS 7 - 9

Can WMB's angelic commissions be
substantiated by his messages?

WMB's Seventh Commission Claim

WMB stated his next angelic commission occurred on May 7, 1946. However, there was another downplayed visitation. This one occurred in 1944, where WMB received a double portion of the power to heal. WMB, in *Not Disobedient To The Heavenly Vision*,[1] wrote:

> I wrote a small book entitled, "Jesus Christ, The Same Yesterday, Today and Forever." In that book I explained how our Lord Jesus called me when I was a child and told me I was to work for Him when I grew up. He gave me the Gift of Healing to help call His people to Him. If you can't find that book write me. For over three years He performed mighty miracles. Then one day He called me to take the Gift and to evangelize for Him. Many of my dear friends begged me not to leave them and I stayed. Because of this, the Gift was taken from me for more than five years...Then one year ago, while I was standing in my yard the Spirit came to me again; I was told that God had forgiven me and that a double portion of the Power to heal would be given me.[2]

As shown, WMB equated the "Spirit," with the pillar of fire, a light, a star, or the angel of the Lord, etc. Hence, this 1944 visitation constituted another commission. The above quotation referred to WMB's 1934 meeting with the *Jesus Only* people in Mishawaka, IN. These people baptized him in Jesus' name and he received many invitations to preach. WMB promised he would, but he then caved in to his mother-in-law's pressure. She would not allow her daughter to be associated with this Holy Roller trash.[3] WMB explained, "One year ago (1945-1944=1 year), God had forgiven him" and he again received power to heal. For five years or more he did not have that power. This power had been in action for three years, or since around 1934. The concept of time was always a difficulty with WMB. This is manifested here because WMB stated that immediately after he refused to heed God's call he was severely disciplined by God. Yet, his father Charles, his brother, his wife Hope and his daughter Rose were all killed by God about three year later, for *his* disobedience.

Five years later, or in around 1941, or 1942, WMB started a healing campaign in Mill Town, Indiana. WMB was a sort of circuit riding preacher[4] and claimed several remarkable occurrences of healing. WMB said he received forgiveness and a double portion of the power to heal, in 1944. This contradicts the 1941 and 1942 dates. What healing power was used in these meetings, if WMB had not, as yet, received that gift?

WMB's booklet, *NOT DISOBEDIENT...* is now out of print. It is not likely to be reprinted for reasons that will become clear. As an aside, the expression, "a double portion" is found in 2 Kings 2: 9, where Elisha is asking for a double portion of the spirit that was upon Elijah. What Elisha was requesting was to be Elijah's heir, he was not asking for twice the spiritual power of Elijah.[5]

WMB's Eighth Commission Claim

This brings us to the most heralded commission of all, that of an angel visiting WMB in a secret place in the year 1946, as recorded by the earliest authors of WM'Bs story. As with all of WMB's claims, there are no other sources other than WMB himself. Hence all accounts are based on his. Here is how Gordon Lindsay recorded WMB telling the story,

> I must tell you of the angel and the coming of the Gift. <u>I shall never forget the time</u>, May 7, 1946...I was still working as a game warden. I had come home for lunch, and was just going around the house taking off my gun, when a very dear friend of mine Prod Wiseman, a brother to my piano player in the church approached me and asked me to go to Madison with him that afternoon...[6]

Prod Wiseman is not mentioned in any of WMB's messages. WMB elsewhere mentioned a Mr. Gibbs, brother to WMB's piano player, Gertie Gibbs.[7] Again, in another place WMB called the man, Roger Broy, his wife Meda *nee* Broy's brother.[8] These are irreconcilable differences, which makes these claims invalid. Lindsay continued,

> I told him that was impossible as I had to patrol, and while walking around the house under a Maple tree, it seemed that the whole top of the tree let loose. It seemed that something came down that tree like a great rushing wind...My wife came from the house frightened, and asked me what was wrong. Trying to get a hold of myself, I sat down and told her that after all these twenty odd years of being conscious of this strange feeling, the time had come when I had to find out what is was all about. The crisis had come! I told her and my child goodbye, and warned her that if I did not come back in a few days, perhaps I might never return. That afternoon I went to a secret place to pray and read the Bible.[9]

Note that WMB did *not* say, "I told *her* [Meda] and *our* child goodbye," nor did he say, "I told her and *our* children goodbye." No, WMB said, "*my* child," and that child can only be his son Billy Paul by his first wife Hope. WMB and Meda had *their* first child Rebekah on Mar. 21, 1946.[10] This is how this looks:

1. WMB left before daughter Rebekah was born on Mar. 21, '46
2. <u>WMB said he received his commission on May 7, 1946</u>
3. Internal contradiction-WMB's claim is invalid.

This contradiction, together with the earlier listed ones, disqualifies WMB's claim of an angelic commission on May 7, 1946. If it had at all occurred in May, it would have to have been 1945. This is only the beginning of this story. Below are listed a number of accounts of WMB's "1946" commission by the angel. The earliest account (1950) is by Gordon Lindsay, writing in collaboration with WMB. He records that WMB had gone to a secret place. He prayed until about 11 o'clock (The 11th hour, WMB said) while sitting on a chair. He saw a light flickering in the room with a window, he looked out but he did not see anyone. The light was spreading and he jumped up from the chair and saw a great ball of fire, suspended in air. He heard someone walking across the floor, which startled him because he knew no one would be coming. He saw the feet of a man who weighed about 200 pounds. This man wore a white robe. He was smooth faced with a dark complexion. He wore no beard and he had dark hair to his shoulders. He had a pleasant countenance.[11] The next account is by Julius Stadsklev and he simply records, "On May 7th, an Angel who had spoken to Brother Branham in an audible voice, at intervals from his childhood down to the present time, finally appeared to him."[12]

However, when looking at WMB's message transcripts, the following is seen: In 1945 WMB was in a room and he heard something, which he thought was an automobile turning a corner. He looked out the door and there was no car. Instead he saw a huge 200 pound, smooth faced, dark eyed man with an olive complexion;[13] a Mexican, Spanish, a dark complexion, walking barefoot on floor boards.[14] Why would an angel shave, but have long hair? The man was six foot tall.[15] WMB also stated that, "And one day I just come from patrol, and I walked into…<u>my place</u>, and I was praying that night about one o'clock, between one and three. And I noticed <u>in my room</u>, a light begin to spread across the floor. And I wondered where it come from. I looked up, and that same light that appears in the meeting…"[16] In another place he said, "And I took my Bible, little old Scofield Bible, about like that, and I put it under my arms, and I took off. And I went, and I read until nighttime. I got a cave I go into, and it'll be way back in the hills, but this is a little old log cabin where I used to trap…And in there in prayer, all at once, I seen a light a flickering. I looked around, I thought, 'Well, here, somebody's coming with a flashlight? Couldn't be a car coming back in here.'"[17] Sometime in August 1953,

WMB was filmed. In this movie he related that at age 37 (thus in 1945) he was praying in his room,

> The pillar of fire was hanging just above, and was throwing the light on the floor. I heard someone walking…he'd be about two hundred pounds of weight. He had dark hair to his shoulder, an olive complexion. He was bare-footed.[18]

He also stated that he was praying in an old cabin at an old fishing camp at Greens Mill.[19] Greens Mill, or Tunnel Mill,[20] is located near Charlestown.[21] WMB used these names interchangeably.

As an aside, when WMB ran off to Arizona, he told his mom he was going to *that* Boy Scout Camp.[22] WMB used to drive[23] the 16 miles to pray at this camp, where, he said, he'd been a Scoutmaster for years.[24] WMB said there was a little dilapidated cabin which had a wooden floor and old drum stove and a stool.

The man, which appeared to him at around 3 o'clock in the morning, was barefoot, had a deep voice and he was very pleasant.[25] While he sat there he heard a six feet tall, 200 pound man with a Mexican, Spanish, or Jewish complexion, walking across the floor and an emerald light circling around. The man spoke and WMB recognized it as the same voice that had spoken to him from a tree at age 7. In another place WMB stated he was in a room and he thought he saw a car's headlights.[26] In yet another place he related that he was going from his cabin to his cave the next day and he looked out the window and saw nothing. However, he then saw the light, the halo, the pillar of fire standing there, which was the angel of God. WMB said this voice was the same voice he heard throughout his life. Yet, *then* it had scared him so much he never ever went by that tree again.[27] As mentioned, the man appeared to him when he was in his fishing camp where a light came shining through a knothole.[28] WMB also related that both his cave and cabin were found by him and they were already furnished when he found them.[29]

Was it a house, a cave, or a cabin? Contrary to Pearry Green's account, WMB's own family states it was, "An old trapping cabin."[30] This author believes there is enough evidence to suggest that WMB never actually left his house. Regarding the cabin, it would appear that WMB referred to the Scoutmaster's cabin which he knew quite well. It was located near the "John Work House"[31]…and is situated on the edge of the Tunnel Mill Boy Scout Camp Reservation northeast of Charlestown…The Lincoln Heritage Council of the Boy Scouts of America acquired the house and surrounding property in 1928 for a camp, one of the nation's oldest Boy Scout camps…the Work House served for a time as the camp ranger's home…"

There are many caves and cabins in the area. The area is, allegedly, haunted by many spirits. The house was occupied all year around. The Scoutmaster's cabin was used only when there was a camp meeting being held. This cabin burned to the ground in the

CHAPTER EIGHT

1960s, and is no longer to be found.[32] WMB stated he used that cabin when the angel appeared to him,

> And I went to a little cabin. I was scout master of the Baptist troop at Jeffersonville for years. And up at the Boy Scout camp...I went there where I have a little cabin. And I went to pray. And while praying there that night, about, around two--between two and three in the morning...And I no more than had prayed my prayer, till I seen a Light come on the floor. I looked up, and above it was that whirl of light, still there again, whirling around... And walking right to me, not a vision, just as natural as I am, come a Man about two hundred pounds in weight. He had His arms folded. He was strong looking Man, had a peaceful looking face, and very calm; He had dark hair to His shoulders, smooth face. And he walked up to me and looked down kind of pathetically, said, "Do not fear."[33]

According to Dr. Gary D. Purlee,[34] WMB never was a Scoutmaster, certainly not of any Baptist troop from Jeffersonville, as he claimed. WMB could have used the cabin for one night or so, during non-camping times, and weeknights only. Pearry Green realized that the accounts of cabin and cave differed and he sought to reconcile them as follows:

> Now in the book, Man Sent From God, there is mention made (as Brother Branham himself often stated) that he was at the ranger's cabin at Green's Mill. [Note: WMB never once mentioned in any of his messages that he was in a ranger's cabin at Greens Mill. - PMD]. That cabin no longer stands; it has deteriorated and rotted to the ground. Brother Branham, speaking on his tape Life Story did not tell all the little details, as he told his wife and children, and as he told me personally; but where he went that night, though at the ranger's cabin, was in a little cave near the cabin. God, sometime or another in Brother Branham's younger life, had led him to a cave which he has spoken of often in his later tapes and where he said that no man could find it. The cave is furnished by nature as though for his very own use, for inside there is a round rock shaped like a table, a rock shaped like a chair, and also a place for a man to lie down and sleep. He put none of this there—it simply was there...Brother Branham told me that he was in the cave when the angel appeared to him. I hope that this is not a stumbling block to some who felt that, since Brother Branham said, "at the ranger's cabin," and because he mentions the word "floor," looking out the "window," that he must have been inside a cabin. Since no one has seen the cave, we don't know what it looks like, except from the description. But he told me that was in the cave when the angel appeared to him on May 1946... he said, "Brother Pearry, I don't say anything about it in public, because people don't understand what a prophet is." I am sure that he didn't mention the cave as often in his early ministry as he did later on because he didn't want to have to explain it to everybody.

What can be said about this? WMB's accounts are listed above. Yet Green wants people to disregard WMB's elaborate details about being in his own home, or in his place, or in his house, or in his study with doors and windows, or in his cabin, or in his cave? He wants people to ignore WMB hearing perceived automobile tire noises, seeing headlights, and seeing a man coming at 3:00 AM, etc.?

For WMB, a cave, "Doesn't altogether have to be a made cave, like the prophet hid in; but it can be a little cave in our memory; it can be a cave in our soul where we can move back, stop, and take inventory, look around, and then listen to see what we can hear."[35]

The angel that appeared to WMB

One of the problems with this angel's description is that it contradicted WMB's own argument stated earlier. He said rightly that, in Jesus' time, not only Jesus,[36] but men and angels dressed according to the culture in which they found themselves.[37] Why would Hebrews 13: 2 speak about entertaining angels unawares, if one could be spotted immediately? The long white robe *might* have worked in today's multi-cultural society. Why was the angel smooth-faced, but have long hair? Even the olive complexion and long hair would have worked, but why the barefoot part? If the person were walking on a rocky cave floor, how would he be heard? In 1946 it would be rare to see anyone dressed like that, unless he was a Swami. As stated, WMB's angel also wore a turban,

> The man which was talking behind me, walked around in front of me, dressed in Palestinian clothes and a turban on his head. He had a white robe. He said, "Brother Branham, that's it.[38]

The angel wore a turban, or, as WMB said, he wore a towel over his head.[39] Is it possible that WMB's religious thinking was influenced by the early Swamis and their teaching that came to the USA in the late 1800's? Their teaching era coincided with New Thought, Theosophy, Christian Science, Mental Healing, etc., with which WMB was very familiar.

What the angel's commission all entailed is actually redundant, because WMB did not have an angelic commission on May 7, 1946. However, this is what the angel purported told WMB,

> IF YOU WILL BE SINCERE, AND CAN GET THE PEOPLE TO BELIEVE YOU, NOTHING SHALL STAND BEFORE YOUR PRAYER, NOT EVEN CANCER. [Capitals theirs – PMD].[40]

This, of course, is problematic on a number of points. One, the angel did not say, "If you can get people to believe in God…" That became manifest later, when WMB said belief in God was not required. Second, the angel did not say, "If you can get the people to believe God can heal you." That would also be redundant, because people coming to a healing campaign would already believe that God can heal. Third, is there any Scriptural precedent for what the angel said? Only Christ ever asked people, "Believe ye that I am able to do this?" Luke relates how Paul, while preaching, perceived a man, crippled from birth had faith to be healed and he, "Said with a loud voice, 'Stand upright on thy feet.' And he leaped and walked."

Another problem, that of manipulating they key date of 1946 in WMB's ministry, earlier alluded to, must now be addressed. In Lindsay's book, *A Man sent from God*, it is seen that, after WMB received his angelic commission, he related the experience to his congregation in Jeffersonville. During this service he received a telegram from St Louis, MO. A Rev. Robert Daugherty wrote to ask WMB to come and pray for his daughter Betty[41] who was very ill.[42] This is mentioned in WMB's booklet, *Not Disobedient To The Heavenly Vision*, printed in 1945.[43] It occurred during the latter part of WWII. Gas rationing was not lifted until Aug. 19, 1945.[44] That is why WMB took the train to St. Louis to pray for Betty, who was about seven or eight years old then.[45] Three months later, after the gas rations were lifted, the Daugherty family showed up at WMB's door. Arrangements were made for WMB to come for a healing revival. WMB and his party drove to St. Louis by car and arrived on June 14, 1945.

The campaign is recorded and daily entries are made from June 14 through June 26. The year is 1945, because the dates and days of the week do not fit any other year. Had they happened in 1946, WMB would have mentioned his 1946 commission in his booklet, "I Was Not Disobedient" WMB could not have allowed these meetings in St. Louis of 1945 to have occurred prior to his alleged angelic commission of 1946. Coupled with the in-breaking of the Healing Revival in 1947, the angelic commission of 1946, had to stand. Thus, the St. Louis meeting dates had to change.

Objections might be brought, based on the fact that in Lindsay's *Man Sent From God*, Robert Daugherty states that the meetings occurred in 1946. How can this be reconciled? In the booklet called, "Jesus Christ, The Same Yesterday, Today and Forever," written by WMB there is an almost identical testimony by Robert Daugherty, except he says, "I will be glad to write to anyone in question of her [Betty's – PMD] healing, or any of the healings that took place during the revival which Bro. Branham held here in St. Louis in 1945."[46] WMB gave only Lindsay all the information for his book including the changed date. It appears WMB had met Mr. Daugherty prior to Betty's healing[47] at a "Jesus Only" camp meeting in Mishwaka, IN.[48]

Regarding angels, did WMB borrow details of Mohammed's, Joseph Smith's, or Paul Cain's angelic encounter? Cain often filled in for WMB when the latter could not fulfill his obligations.[49] Cain said of WMB that he was, "the greatest prophet in the 20th century."[50] WMB encouraged people to attend Cain's services as a continuation of his own.[51]

WMB's Ninth Commission Claim

The next angelic appearance occurred in 1950. He said a halo appeared above his head in the Civic Auditorium in Houston, Texas.

> Look, hanging in Washington, D.C. tonight, the picture of the Angel of the Lord. As George J. Lacy, the head of the FBI fingerprint and documents for the United States Government, examined it from Houston Texas and said, 'This is the only supernatural Being that was ever photographed in all the world.' He ought to know; he's the best that's in the world for it.[52]

> And if He made Himself known that He was dwelling amongst His people by doing these things...He could even have His picture taken, scientifically prove it...let the mechanical eye of the camera catch Him standing there, that same Pillar of Fire that is the same yesterday, today and forever (Hebrews 13:8) to show that it is scientific in every other way, scientifically, in the spiritual realm, and every way it would be vindicated, it's been vindicated.[53]

The reprinted document from George Lacy states that, "the light streak above the head in a halo position, was caused by light striking the negative"[54] and confirms the negative had not been 'doctored.' No one questions that a light struck the negative. The question is, "What was that light?" Lacy does not state it was a supernatural light, an angel, a pillar of fire, or the logos, as claimed by WMB. The accounts changed from, "I don't know what it is." to "the pillar of fire," to "the angel of the Lord," to, "the logos," etc. This author published a pamphlet back in 1978, expressing the opinion that the light was an overhead light way back behind WMB. Hence it appeared out of focus on the photograph, if one were taking a picture of WMB's face. This was confirmed at that time, as well as later, by experts in photography.[55]

The real issue is not complicated. This light was either a supernatural being, as WMB claimed, or it was an actual light in the background. There are no newspaper photos with this light over WMB's head. There *were* suspended ceiling lights. Lacy never worked for the FBI as WMB claimed.[56] This is no vindication by God at all. The light "above" WMB's head has too many questions associated with it to make it a supernatural being. As an aside, for those insisting that the light above WMB's head *was*, in fact, a halo, the problem just gets bigger.

In Eastern religions there is often a halo surrounding a 'mystic.' This halo is called a crown chakra.[57] Modern psychics also speak of this halo as an aura that surrounds people, by which they can tell things about that person. Roman Catholicism also portrayed saints with halos. For that reason followers of WMB are re-thinking the implications of "halo," and are referring to it as the pillar of fire. However, the biblical pillar of fire was seen by all Israel and frightened the entire Egyptian army. To identify a small "lick of fire" with this pillar of fire is without biblical foundation.

CHAPTER EIGHT 121

Can WMB's claims of his many angelic encounters and/or commissions be established as true, by his own messages? The seventh of WMB's alleged angelic commissions which occurred in 1944 and the eighth, the "big" one in his cave in 1946, as well as the ninth occurring as a "halo" in 1950, cannot be substantiated as true, by his own messages. That leaves only one more angelic commission to be examined in the next chapter.

Notes - Chapter Eight

[1] William Branham, *I was Not Disobedient To The Heavenly Vision*. This booklet is out of print, but electronic copies still exist. They are not available from Voice of God Recordings or Spoken Word Publications, both of which are owned and operated by WMB's family. This author has an original issue.

[2] Ibid.

[3] *Here We Have No Continuing City*. "Well, I went and had to tell her mother. And that didn't work so good. She said, 'William.' She said, 'She's your wife. You may take her if you want to.' But said, 'I don't want my daughter drug out among that bunch of trash.'"

[4] WMB, *Is There Anything Too hard For The Lord?* Mar. 28, 1960, Tulsa, OK, "And at that time, I'd just taken over on my circuit, the Milltown Baptist Church. Being a Baptist minister, well, I was a preaching the circuit…And the angel of the Lord had been doing some great things."

[5] In biblical terms, the firstborn son, or heir, would receive a double portion. This meant that when a father had four sons, the inheritance would be divided into five portions and the eldest would inherit 2/5ths, or a double portion, and his brothers 1/5th. WMB's angel did not know that?

[6] Lindsay. 76.

[7] *Early Spiritual Experiences*.

[8] *Angel And The Commission*.

[9] Lindsay. 76.

[10] Green. 60. "Sister Meda gave birth to a baby girl. The date was March 21, and the infant was named Rebekah."

[11] *Lindsay*. 76-79.

[12] Stadsklev. 37.

[13] *Angel Of God*, Phoenix.

[14] *Angel And The Commission*.

[15] *My Commission*.

[16] WMB, *Obey The Voice Of The Angel*, Jul. 13, '50, Minneapolis, MN.

[17] *Angel And The Commission*, Cleveland.

18 *Twentieth Century Prophet*.

[19] WMB, *Palmerworm, Cankerworm, Locust And Caterpillar*, Jun. 12, 1953, Connersville, IN; See also: *Abraham's Covenant Confirmed*.

[20] *How The Angel Came To Me.*

[21] WMB, *A Total Deliverance*, Jul. 12, 1959, Jeff., IN, "I went up to my cave up above Charlestown, where I've been going for years, and I got in there and I prayed all that day…"

[22] *Ministry Of Christ.* "When I was about nineteen I told mother I was going up here in Indiana to Boy Scout Reservation, Green's Mill to camp."

[23] WMB, *Reaction To An Action*, Aug, 10, 1959, Chautauqua, OH, "…I got in my car and went out to my little old cave where I go to pray."

[24] _____, *Manifestation Of The Spirit*, Jul. 17, 1951, "And I went to a little cabin. I was scout master of the Baptist troop at Jeffersonville for years. And up at the Boy Scout camp… I went there where I have a little cabin. And I went to pray. Sometimes I'd pray all night, and maybe a day and night."

[25] *How The Angel Came To Me.*

[26] *Angel Of God*, Phoenix. "A little over two years ago now, I was sitting in the room. I was reading my little Scofield Bible, and I heard something. First, I saw a Light. And I thought it was an automobile that turned the corner. But it turned, but it got brighter. And I looked out the door and there was no automobile." WMB said it occurred a little over two years earlier. That means that if it "happened" it had to be sometime in the Fall of 1945.

[27] *Early Spiritual Experiences.* "I was long about two or three o'clock in the morning; I was praying, and crying, and begging…I was standing looked out a window, went back. I thought, 'Well, it won't be long till daylight…' 'When daylight comes,' I said, 'I'm going to leave the cabin, and going up in them knobs and get back up in my cave…' I seen a light flash in the room…And I thought, 'Somebody must be coming.' And here on the floor was a big light, coming around. Right above it stood this halo, pillar of fire, moving along, and come walking through there came an angel of God. Not imagination, he was there. I looked at him, talked to him."

[28] *Trial*, Louisville, MS. "One night, at a little camp where I was fishing…About three o'clock one morning, I seen a light coming. I had just been reading the Bible. I thought it was somebody coming, shining it through a knothole, a lantern or something. It was way in the wilderness. And I thought somebody was coming up. The light was on the floor; It spread greater and greater. I heard of somebody walking…It was a man. He was barefooted. He had hair to his shoulders, and he had on a robe."

[29] *What Hearest Thou, Elijah?* . "Walked right in to that old cave all my furniture in there. I never put any of it in there. I just found the cave." See also: *How The Angel Came To Me.*

[30] Voice of God Recordings, "A visitation of an Angel," available from http://branham.org/content/AboutUs/williambranham_pg3.aspx, (Accessed May 10, 2010).

[31] Greg Sekula, e-mail to the author, December 15, 2010. Greg Sekula is the Director of the Southern Regional Office of the Indiana Landmarks Organization. Mr. Sekula graciously directed this author to Nathaniel Logsdon of Taylor & Rose, Historic Outfitters of Charlestown, IN.

[32] Telephone interview with Nathaniel Logsdon on 15 December, 2010. Mr. Logsdon is

restoring the John Workhouse. He is an Indiana historian and he is very knowledgeable about this area.

[33] *Manifestation Of The Spirit.*

[34] Gary D. Purlee, e-mail message to author, May 19, 2010. Gary D. Purlee is an Indiana Author, Historian and Scoutmaster, "I have not seen any information concerning his [WMB] being involved as a scoutmaster. I do know that he was very familiar with the Tunnel Mill area along 14 mile creek near the Scout Camp east of Charlestown, Indiana...I am probably the best source of Scouting information in the southern Indiana area."

[35] *What Hearest Thou, Elijah?*

[36] WMB, *Jesus Christ The Same Yesterday, Today, And Forever*, Jun. 27, 1963, Hot Springs, AR, "But now how would we look for Him? What kind of a person would we look for...We, we would look for somebody that's, well, perhaps with a long robe, and a beard on his face, and nail scars in his hand, and thorn prints on his--on his brow? If you would look for a person like that, any hypocrite could deceive you on that. That's right, impersonation. A man could paint scars on his hands, and he could even prick himself with thorns and make the scars, but any impersonator could do that."

[37] *We Would See Jesus,* Jun. 12, 1958, Dallas TX.

[38] *Why Are People So Tossed About.*

[39] WMB, *Do You Now Believe*, Mar. 07, 1954, PM, Phoenix, AZ, "There stood a man with a towel over his head...He was kind of dark complected, and his nose was kind of flat in the front...I thought he was one of the patients at the house. He just raised his eyes and said, 'Brother Branham, don't go overseas until September.' I looked...He was gone. He was vanished."

[40] Lee Vayle. 41.

[41] WMB, *But From The Beginning It Was Not So*, Oct. 02, 1958, Jeff., IN, "I suppose you said she'd be here tomorrow night, didn't you, Brother Robert, to testify? [Speaking about Robert Daugherty's daughter Betty- PMD] So now that's been some fourteen years ago, I guess, twelve--fourteen years ago--thirteen years ago..." 1958 – 13 = 1945.

[42] *Man Sent From God.* 81-91.

[43] WMB wrote, "It was in the month of March, 1945, one morning about 3:00 A.M. that our Lord Jesus Christ gave me a vision. This He has done many times and I most humbly praise Him for it... About three weeks from the time of the vision, I received a telegram from a minister in St. Louis, Mo., by the name of Rev. Robert Daugherty. He asked me to come at once because his little daughter, Betty, was dying...The following afternoon the Rev. Daugherty's father came to my house and told me that his son had called him by phone at Arnold, Ky., and asked him to bring me to St. Louis at once. That was on Sunday afternoon. That night after my church services at the Tabernacle, I met with Rev. Daugherty's father at the Seventh Street Railroad Station in Louisville, Ky. At 11:30 P.M. we caught the train to St. Louis, Mo. We arrived in St. Louis at 10:00 A.M. the next morning. ...About three months later, one afternoon while sitting on my front porch, a car stopped in front of my house and a sweet, little curly-haired, plump girl jumped out of the car. She ran up the walk and threw her little arms around my neck.

Yes, it was little Betty Daugherty!" [Next, a lady traveling with WMB is quoted in the booklet - PMD] "We left Jeffersonville in a car, on the beautiful morning of June 14, 1945, and drove to New Albany for Sister Gertrude Gibbs, then started for St. Louis, Mo...About 1:00 A.M. Tuesday morning, my husband and I took Bro. Bill to the bus station, where he departed for home."

[44] *What Did You Do In The War, Grandma?* Timeline of WWII (1939-1945), available from http://www.stg.brown.edu/projects/WWII_Women/NewTimeline.html#1945, (Accessed May 10, 2010). US Gas rations lifted on August 15, 1945.

[45] *As I Was With Moses*, "How old are you now, Betty? Twenty-two. She was about seven or eight?" [Note: In 1960, Betty was 22 years old. Therefore Betty was healed around 1945. – PMD]

[46] John Kennah, *Was Wm. Branham Really Commissioned by an Angel in 1946?* available from http://people.delphiforums.com/johnk63/evetns.htm, (Accessed May 09, 2010).

[47] *I was Not Disobedient*. "I had known the Daugherty family previous to this time but did not recognize the little girl due to her condition."

[48] *Identified Masterpiece Of God*, Dec. 05, 1964, Yuma, AZ, "When I first seen a Pentecostal minister, it was Rev. Robert Daugherty from St. Louis." WMB never met a Pentecostal until Mishawaka, therefore WMB met Daugherty at Mishawaka.

[49] *Expectations*, LA. "Brother Paul Cain is to come in this very tabernacle here."

[50] Paul Cain, as quoted in *"Equipping the Saints"*, (Anaheim: VMI, Vol. 4, No.4/Fall 1990), 9.

[51] WMB mentioned Paul Cain in ten of his meetings, he called him a friend.

[52] WMB, *This Day This Scripture Is Fulfilled*, Jan. 25, 1965, Phoenix, AZ.

[53] Gordon Lindsay, *God's 20th Century Barnabas*, (Dallas: Christ for the Nations), 260.

[54] *Footprints*. 9. Lacy: "I am of the opinion that the light streak appearing above the head in a halo position was caused by light striking the negative." [Note: This statement only says the original negative had not been tampered with; the 'halo' was caused by some light source striking the lens. – PMD].

[55] *"Pillar of Fire Photo*, 1950"; Message of Wm. Branham Support Forum, available from http://forums.delphiforums.com/kennah/messages?msg=2199.64. (Accessed February 08, 2007); Ibid. msg 2199.81.

[56] This author has in his possession a letter signed by Mr. Clarence M. Kelley Director of the FBI, dated Sep. 5, 1974, stating, "With respect to your enquiries, the FBI has no information it can furnish you relative to the photograph you enclosed. I can tell you, however, that George Lacey (sic) has never been employed by this Bureau." George J. Lacy worked for the local Sheriff's office, not the FBI.

[57] Rosemary Ellen Guiley, *Harper's Encyclopedia of Mystical & Paranormal Experience*, (New York: Harper Collins, 1991). "A Crown Chakra is seen as a halo above one's head in Eastern mysticism."

Chapter Nine
ANGELIC COMMISSION 10

Can WMB's claims of his many angelic encounters
and/or commissions be substantiated
by his own messages?

WMB's Tenth Commission Claim

The next event used by WMB, and which is continued to be used by his followers, is the much publicized story surrounding WMB's message series called *The Revelation of the Seven Seals*. On Feb. 28, 1963, a cloud was seen high in the skies over Arizona. At first no one knew what caused the cloud, though science later established it was caused by debris of a detonated rocket. Newspapers and magazines carried photographs regarding the cloud and *Life* magazine called it a Cloud of Mystery. WMB stated this cloud of Feb. 28, 1963 was actually a constellation of angels which picked him up while hunting Javalina. The angels commissioned him to reveal the mysteries of the Seven Seals. This claim cannot be substantiated. WMB was in Houston, TX, and he had no idea about any "mystery" cloud till after he preached his series. Here is how that looks:

1. Cloud of Feb. 28, 1963 consisted of 7 angels who picked WMB up while hunting
2. Javelina hunting season was from March 01 through March 10, 1963
3. WMB was in Houston Texas on March 04, 1963.
4. <u>WMB started hunting March 06, 1963, shot his Javelina on Mar. 07 and angels appeared Mar. 08</u>
5. Internal contradictions. WMB's claim is invalid.

As stated prior, this author published a series of four pamphlets regarding some of WMB's claims. One of which, *'Mystery Cloud' - Exposé on Wm. Branham,*[1] challenged the dates of WMB's hunting trip and the seven angels picking up WMB on Feb. 28, 1963. There has since been a "spiritualization" of sorts of these events, which will be examined first. WMB's daughter Rebekah Branham Smith, now deceased, stated in *Only Believe,*

> The May 17, 1963 issue of Life magazine contained an unusual photograph, and the first person to take notice of it was Brother Gene Norman. According to the article

accompanying the photo, science could find no explanation for an extraordinary cloud that had appeared over Arizona, and that intrigued him. The following Sunday, he showed the magazine to his friend, "Brother Branham, have you seen anything like this?" he asked. "I guess you noticed it is in the form of a pyramid," was the only reply he was to receive on that occasion, but a few days later, on Friday, June 1, Brother Branham acknowledged the significance of the photo, Speaking to a small group of people that had gathered in the home of Brother Tom Simpson, he explained, "I looked, and right there were those Angels, just as plain as they could be. I looked to see when it was, and it was about a day or two before, or a day or two after, I was up there." Several months later, in Sierra Vista, Arizona, he clarified the event even further by reminding his listeners that God always shows His major events first in the heavens. "Did you notice," he commented, "before the Seven Seals were revealed, the great mysterious Light showed forth in the heavens up there above Tucson, where we were?"²

WMB said that, "I looked to see when it was, and it was about a day or two before, or a day or two after, I was up there." In other words, WMB did not remember this momentous occasion and applied a two day either way tolerance? The statement Rebekah Branham referred to, as being told several months later by WMB in Sierra Vista, AZ, was actually spoken on Jan. 12, 1964. See below:

> Now, in the heavens above. Did you notice I'm looking on this, the--the Light on the picture there out of the Life Magazine, that the brother that lives here in this home has put on his wall, that triangle of Light...But did you notice before the Seven Seals was revealed, before the great mysterious Light showed forth in the heavens up here at above Tucson, Flagstaff, where we were? Brother Fred, two of the man that was... the two men was with me that morning. When, that had been told months and months ahead of time, would happen. Both Brother Fred Sothmann and Brother Gene Norman sitting here this morning, when it... was there when the blast went off, and not knowing these things would take place. And He sent me back, said that the time was at hand for these Seven Seals which held the seven mysteries of the entire Bible, was sealed in with these Seven Seals... But before He broke forth on those Seven Seals to reveal them, that He showed miraculous, He showed it first in the heavens. That day they took pictures all across southern United States and Mexico. There it hangs now in the Life Magazine, still a mystery to them. But He declares it in the heavens before He does it on earth. He always does that. He shows His signs in the heavens first.³

Smith continues, "The remarkable saga of Sunset was not yet completed. In 1964, a dozen men assembled." This gives the casual reader the impression that the aforementioned details occurred in 1963, reinforcing her statement that they happened only a few months

CHAPTER NINE 127

after the actual event, rather than 7+ months, and into a new year. WMB, a week later, reiterated that, "God always shows things in the heaven before He shows them on the earth."[4] WMB, until his death in 1965, stated that the angels met him during the Javalina hunt, and called on his two hunting companions, Fred Sothmann and Gene Norman, as witnesses,

> In there I watched it until that circle went up, started sweeping up, and they turned into like a mystic light, like a fog. ...I was running and running, trying to find Brother Fred and them. After while, about a half hour later, I could see him way down, waving his hands; and Brother Gene coming, waving. They knowed something had happened.[5]

Gene Norman, the man who was with WMB on the hunt, told this author and a friend, in a November 1978 telephone conversation, that he watched the "mystery" cloud from his front window and only saw a flat cloud. When asked if he had seen the cloud on the mountain he said he had not seen anything, the sky was clear, though in his story in *Only Believe* magazine he said he saw two wispy clouds.

> I had gone just a few steps when what sounded like a tremendous explosion stopped me dead in my tracks. I quickly looked around expecting to see a ball of fire, or at the very least a cloud of dust, but there was nothing. The air was still. I looked up into the sky but saw nothing more than a couple of long, wispy clouds. I stood there for a few moments, then continued to head in the direction that would eventually bring me to the pre-arranged meeting place the three of us had agreed on earlier. Brother Fred and I arrived a few minutes apart at the place where Brother Branham was waiting for us. The first thing he said to us was, "Did you hear that blast?" I told him, "I've never heard anything quite like that before, in town or out of town." And that was the only mention he made to us concerning the blast.[6]

Mr. Norman, in the phone conversation, made it clear that he was not hunting Javalina on Feb. 28, 1963. He also did not see anything while hunting up in the mountains. Norman did say he heard a tremendous explosion, which would not be a surprise because Tucson has a military Air Force base and breaking the sound barrier was not an unusual thing in the early 1960s. In, or around, 1963, this author personally experienced a sonic boom caused by a fighter jet so high up in the sky it was just a tiny glittering speck. Yet the blast rocked people on their heels and shattered some shop windows. Apparently no jet planes caused the cloud of Feb. 28, 1963, but a sonic boom would be a reasonable explanation, had there been a blast of some sort.

The other hunting companion was Fred Sothmann, who said he even saw the cloud rise up from WMB's location at Sunset Peak at the time."[7] Yet WMB said the opposite occurred, the cloud came down and he was standing right under it.[8] Dave Davies of the Arizona Republic[9] said,

> Fred H. Sothmann, a 52-year-old Canadian wheat farmer moved to Tucson in 1962 to be closer to the religious leader, was one of two persons who were with Mr. Branham that day the cloud appeared. Sothmann's account: "Reverend Branham and another brother, Gene Norman, and myself were well up in the mountains hunting javelina. I remember it was late in the afternoon, a clear warm day with not a cloud in the sky. The three of us were spread out in different directions, perhaps a half a mile apart from each other. Then all of a sudden I heard this tremendous blast like a jet plane breaking the sound barrier, only much louder. Many rocks began to roll down the mountain not too far from me. Instinctively I looked in the direction of Brother Branham, but couldn't actually see him because he was behind a knoll. But just above him I saw this strange circular-shaped cloud rise into the air. It was kind of small at first, but the higher it rose the bigger it became.

Davies records further that,

> "Startled by the blast and the tumbling rocks, Sothmann said he didn't grasp the significance of the cloud then." 'But when Brother Branham and I got together a few minutes later,' he said, 'he told me that seven angels appeared to him and had instructed him to go home (to Jeffersonville, Ind.) and reveal the meaning of the seven seals of Revelation (chapters 6 through 8).[sic]. 'That was all he said. Gene Norman joined us a little later and we started down the mountain toward our car. There was no point in looking for Javelina after that.'"

A fortune teller told WMB "Before God does anything in the earth, He always declares it in the heavens, and then on the earth."[10] WMB himself often related that occurrence in his messages and he also himself used that expression.[11] WMB's elder son, Billy Paul Branham, in the foreword to WMB's book, *The Exposition Of The Seven Seals*, says this about his father:

> The Word of the Lord has promised that He would send to the earth once again the spirit of Elijah in the form of that End Time messenger ... the Angel to the Seventh Church Age in these final closing days of time. We believe firmly that this promise was fulfilled in the vindicated ministry of our precious brother, William Marrion Branham. Throughout the life of this humble servant of the Lord, who so epitomized the Spirit of Christ, we find manifestations of God, which were so perfectly vindicated that they cannot be explained away by any natural reasoning. Of the hundreds of thousands of visions which the Lord gave to Brother Branham around the world, not one time has there ever occurred a vision which was not confirmed and attested to be the Word of the Lord. On December 30, 1962 at the Branham Tabernacle, Jeffersonville, Indiana, Brother Branham brought a message entitled *Sirs, Is This The Time?* [The Spoken Word Vol. II No.11] In this Message he told of a vision that instructed him to move to Tucson, Arizona with his family. This vision foretold a blast that would take place, the force of

which would shake the whole country. This vision was fulfilled on Feb. 28, 1963 when 40 miles northeast of Tucson, Brother Branham was caught up in a constellation of seven angels and was told to return to his church in Jeffersonville, Indiana, where the mysteries of the Seven Seals would be revealed to him.[12]

The above quotation by Billy Paul Branham states the event took place on Feb. 28, 1963 and all followers of WMB hold that date as sacred. John Kennah saw Pearry Green denouncing this author's booklet, *'Mystery Cloud' Exposé on Wm. Branham*, from the pulpit of Tucson Tabernacle. Afterwards Kennah decided to check it out or himself. He contacted all the major players in WMB's message and the re-casting started in earnest. This author is indebted to John Kennah for the following information he provided on his Forum:

> I looked to see when it was, and it was time, same, about day or two before, or day or two after I was up there."--*William Branham relaying his thoughts after having just seen the Cloud photo in* LIFE *magazine for the first time.*
>
> Anyone who has known the Message longer than 20 years knows that WMB claimed many times that the Cloud of February 28, 1963 was formed by 7 angels while he was hunting with his friends, Gene Norman and Fred Sothmann. Sothmann even granted an interview for the Arizona Republic in 1967 where he said he even saw the Cloud rise up from WMB's location at Sunset Peak at the time. Message tracts and publications abounded containing WMB's account that the Cloud was a supernatural event caused by 7 angels when they appeared to WMB while he hunted javelina with his two friends. There was no doubt in any Message believer's mind that this is what happened, including Billy Paul Branham who personally told me in 1991 that he wouldn't believe anything else. Now, however, almost no Message believer believes WMB's former account. Instead, the official stance by the largest organizations affiliating themselves with the Message is that the Cloud was formed in the sky over Flagstaff as a sign that WMB would be visited by 7 angels over Sunset Peak a week later. Rebekah Branham-Smith even wrote an article with the revised position in the June 1992 issue of *Only Believe* magazine. In 1993 Pearry Green revised his book, *Acts of the Prophet*, for the sole purpose of reflecting this new stance. What is the evidence that WMB's story should be reinterpreted, in spite of over 10 clear quotes where he specifically stated he was present at the time and location that the Cloud appeared? It is found in the single quotation that appears at the top of this post.
>
> The official stance that Message believers have taken--that WMB was not at Sunset at the time the photos of the Cloud was taken--hinges on this one quote. So here's the question: What does that quote even mean?--It was "about a day or two before, or a day or two after I was up there"? On it's own, it is nonsense. How could the Cloud have appeared either a day or two before or a day or two after but not on the day WMB was at Sunset? We now know that it actually appeared a week before, but what

did WMB mean? As we do when interpreting anything we hear or read, we must look at the context. So what was the context in which WMB said this? WMB was describing for his audience the first time he saw the Cloud in *LIFE* magazine when Gene Norman showed it to him. According to Norman, he showed the *LIFE* picture to WMB with no thought that it had anything to do with their trip to Sunset. WMB describes what happened: And Brother Norman, Norma's father here, told me, said, "Did you notice this?" [referring to the Cloud photo in *LIFE* magazine] And just as I looked, right there was them Angels just as plain as They could be, setting right there in that picture. See? I looked to see when it was, and it was time, same, about day or two before, or day or two after I was up there. I looked where it was at. "Northeast of Flagstaff, or Prescott, which is below Flagstaff." Well, that's just where we was at, see, just exactly. [emphasis - JK]

"Twenty-six miles high." Why, vapor can't go over--over four, four miles high, or five, moisture, any kind of fog or anything, you see. Planes fly at nineteen thousand. That's to get up above all the clouds, you see. And nineteen thousand is about four miles high. This is twenty-six miles high, and thirty miles across it, and in the shape of the pyramid, if you've looked at the picture.

And on the right-hand side, as I told you, I noticed, outstanding, that Angel. There He is, chest out, wings back, coming right in, just exactly the way it was. I never noticed it when They first... There been so many things. 63-0601 COME.FOLLOW.ME_ TUCSON.AZ SATURDAY.

Taken in context, it is clear WMB is putting 2 and 2 together. He was not making a definitive statement that the Cloud was there at the approximate time he was there but not actually on the same date. He is describing how he formulated in his mind that the Cloud he was looking at in the *LIFE* magazine was there at the very time he was at Sunset Peak hunting javelina! Of course, it is now history that WMB intended for his followers to believe that the Cloud was indeed formed while he was hunting with Gene Norman and Fred Sothmann. We never find him correcting anyone during his lifetime for believing that the Cloud in LIFE appeared to him at Sunset. However, it is now proven to be an irrefutable fact that this could not have taken place as WMB described, and so it is that Message believers have grasped to this one single quote taken out of context to reinterpret what WMB, Billy Paul and all his followers had believed for over 25 years. It wasn't until Peter Duyzer exposed the truth about the Cloud discrepancy in a booklet he wrote which I later discovered in 1989 (thanks to Pearry Green) that the truth became public knowledge among Message believers. The problem became, how does one change what the prophet said so many times?

And so it is that the only evidence that Message believers can offer to prove

CHAPTER NINE 131

that their prophet did not intentionally mislead his family, friends and followers is this one single quote taken out of context.[13]

This author wholeheartedly agrees with John Kennah that WMB knew of the discrepancy and tried to "put two and two together," to create a way out of this controversy. This is quite typical of WMB and is one of the reasons for the many factions within, what is called, the Message. WMB often contradicted himself, which makes it near to impossible to construct a "theology" of his message. This re-casting was not just done by Rebekah Branham Smith, but also by Pearry Green, pastor of Tucson Tabernacle in Tucson, AZ. John Kennah writes the following:

> In another Message forum, someone asked one of the forum moderators what changes were made in the revised edition of Pearry Green's book, *The Acts of the Prophet*, (Tucson Tabernacle, 1993). I thought that might be a question others may be interested in knowing the answer to. I searched both editions of the book and noted that the entire revised version remains exactly the same in content except for three sentences in chapter 11. This chapter is titled, "The Cloud." Pastor Green revised this chapter in order to reflect newly publicized information that indicated that William Branham was not at Sunset Mountain hunting javelina when the Cloud was formed on February 28, 1963. The changes he made in those 3 sentences removed every reference of the Cloud having been formed at the same time Wm. Branham was hunting. Below, I have provided the original sentences as they appear in Pastor Green's first edition, followed by the same sentence in the revised version. I underlined the change in the 2nd edition so it could be more easily seen:
>
> **1st Edition, page 103, par. 3:** "The date was February 28, 1963."
> **2nd Edition, page 103, par. 3:** "<u>It was the pig season of</u> 1963."
> **1st Ed., p. 104, par. 3:** "It was when these seven angels departed from Brother Branham's presence that they formed the mysterious, science-baffling cloud in the sky."
> **2nd Ed., p. 104, par. 3:** "<u>Seven days before these seven angels appeared to Brother Branham, there appeared</u> the mysterious, science-baffling cloud in the sky."
> **1st Ed., p. 106-107, par. 5:** "I have been told by a man whom I believe to be the prophet of God for this age, Brother William Branham, that seven angels came to him and revealed the mysteries of the seven seals of the book of Revelation, caught him up into their midst, and leaving him, formed this cloud."
> **2nd Ed., p. 106-107, par. 5:** "I have been told by a man whom I believe to be the prophet of God for this age, Brother William Branham, that seven angels came to him and revealed the mysteries of the seven seals of the book of Revelation, caught him up into their midst, and <u>instructed him to go back and preach the seven seals</u>."
> Those are the only changes I believe one will find in the entire revised edition of *The*

Acts of the Prophet, by Pearry Green. One might say that books often go through more than one printing. But the 2nd edition of this book states clearly on the back side of the title page, "1993 Revision (#2)". Three sentences that represent the revision of an entire book; indeed, that represent the revised history of the life of William Branham! BTW, the moderator told the questioner that his question was one that Pearry Green or a spokesman for Tucson Tabernacle would have to answer. How interesting.[14]

A Vision Of Five - No, Seven Angels?

In the foreword to *The Exposition Of The Seven Seals*, a vision is mentioned; WMB was allegedly taken up in a constellation of seven angels. He was told to return east, because the mysteries of the Seven Seals would be revealed to him. The vision occurred on Dec. 30, 1962,

> A constellation of...no less than five, and not more than seven...in the shape of a pyramid...I was caught up into this pyramid, of constellation.[15]

WMB stated, "Remember, I tell you in the name of the Lord, I have told you the truth!"[16] What is interesting is that it did not mention a previous account of the vision. In a sermon of just a week prior, or on Dec. 23, 1962, WMB stated,

> It looked like in a form of a pyramid -- like two on each side with one in the top, came five of the mightiest Angels I ever saw in my life...I'd been brought into this constellation of a pyramid of them; inside this constellation of Angels, of five...And they looked like one, two, three, four, and then one right at the top, making five.[17]

In this same message WMB wrestled with the vision, because he thought it might be a vision of his death. However, he reasoned that, "A death angel would be one, five would be grace...Oh! It's coming with my message."[18]

Ever since Dec. 30th, 1962, no mention is ever again made of the 5 angels, obviously, because they did not fit WMB's scheme. There is another interesting note to make here. All during the messages WMB preached from Mar. 17, through Mar. 24, 1963, and no mention is made of Feb. 28, 1963, in connection with the vision. On the morning of Mar. 17, 1963,[19] WMB briefly mentioned the vision, but he said nothing about it being fulfilled on Feb. 28, 1963. On the evening of Mar. 17, he spoke about yet another "vision." In this vision he found himself in Sabino Canyon, which was about 30 - 40 minutes drive from his house. He said it was, "A week, or ten days ago." [Note: That would make the date somewhere around Mar. 7, to Mar. 10 - PMD.] This is what he said,

> I am more or less inclined to believe it was a vision...I had my hands out saying, 'Lord, what does this blast mean, and what does these seven angels in a constellation of the pyramid, picking me up from off the ground and turning eastward-what does it mean?'[20]

WMB was speaking of his alleged vision, because the day before his message of the Seven Seals he, evidently, had not yet experienced being taken up in the cloud. On March 22, 1963,[21] he mentioned Sabino Canyon again. He had not referred to the "Seven Angel vision" since Mar. 17, 1963. However, on Mar. 24th, 1963, the vision is mentioned once again.[22] The number of angels is now seen to have been revised to "seven, three on a side with one on top":

> Remember the constellation of the vision of the Angels when I left here to go to Arizona? Do you remember, 'What time is it, Sirs?'...there was only one great burst of thunder, and seven angels appeared. Is that right?- one burst of thunder, seven angels appeared.[23]

> I was up way back into the mountains, nearly to Mexico, with two brethren that are sitting here...and a blast went off that almost, looked like, shook the mountains down...And did you notice that one angel, I said in there was a strange angel? They were in a constellation- three on a side and one on top... And the one right next to me here, counting from the left to the right, would have been the seventh Angel. He was brighter, meant more to me than the rest of them...he had his chest out like that, and was flying eastward. I said, 'It picked me up, lifted me up!' Do you remember that? Here it is! The one with the Seventh Seal-the thing that I wondered all my life."...I went up in Sabino Canyon...I said, 'Lord, what does this vision mean?...does it mean my dying?[24]

A Cloud Of Mystery?

WMB never referred to anything significant regarding Feb. 28, 1963. Not until June 1, 1963, did Gene Norman show him a copy of *Life*. This is what WMB said,

> When I come, one thing, was by a vision, that I was standing above Tucson up here when a blast went off. Well, Brother Fred was there when it went off. And they took that picture now, you know, in the sky. And I didn't think much about it, never noticed it. So it begin to impress me somehow, other day. And Brother Norman, Norma's father here, told me, said, "Did you notice this?" And just as I looked, right there was them Angels just as plain as They could be, setting right there in that picture. See? I looked to see when it was, and it was time, same, about day or two before, or day or two after I was up there. I looked where it was at. "Northeast of Flagstaff, or Prescott, which is below Flagstaff." Well, that's just where we was at, see, just exactly.[25]

On May 17, Life Magazine published an article on page 112, with the following heading, "AND A HIGH CLOUD RING OF MYSTERY...Hovering like a giant smoke ring, a great cloud appeared at sunset over Flagstaff, Arizona, last Feb. 28, and set off a continuing scientific mystery. Watchers struck by the cloud's odd shape and huge size, took pictures, like these four, at different times, and from widely scattered locations in the state."[26] The article features a 7"x10" color photo and three small black and white photos of a cloud. On March 1, 1963, an article in Tucson's paper, *The Arizona Daily Star*, mentions some "Rare Nacreous Clouds" that were seen on the evening of Feb. 28, 1963. This cloud appeared in the Arizona skies, after sunset, the particulars of which were listed in WEATHERWISE, quoting Dr. James McDonald of UA. Below is listed most of what Dr. McDonald found:

- Cloud appeared over Flagstaff, Arizona, at 18:40 MST at a calculated altitude of 43 +/- 1 km.
- At 1352 PST [or 3 hrs. and 48 minutes earlier] a Thor Booster Rocket was detonated at an altitude of 44 km, almost directly over Vandenberg AFB, California.
- Distance from Vandenberg to Flagstaff is approx. 510 miles. Cloud speed would have to be about 135 mph.
- Winds were from the west that day, as well as the following morning when the wind speeds were measured to be 127 mph at an altitude of approx. 43 km.

In this author's possession is a letter from Mr. Louis Batten, Director of the Institute of Atmospheric Physics of UA, in Tucson, AZ. He states that Dr. McDonald was convinced the cloud was caused by a high altitude rocket, launched from Vandenberg AFB, CA.[27] Here it is seen that WMB never spoke about any cloud over Arizona, until he was given a copy of Life Magazine. About two years later, on April 18, 1965, WMB said,

> I would like to call your attention this morning to a…picture that was taken by the camera of a vision that I had…form of a pyramid, seven Angels…thinking it was the end of my life…in Sabino canyon one morning like this, while in prayer,[28] there had been a sword placed in my hand…the Sword of the Lord…Later, the angels appeared as was prophesied[29]…Science took the picture…Life Magazine packed the pictures… And so there He spoke to me and said, "The Seven Seals will be opened …You remember, I was preaching when this vision came, upon the subject of the Book of the Revelations…Christ was standing with hair like wool, white …Well, if you turn the picture like this[30] and look…it's Christ. See His eyes looking here…the white wig of Supreme Deity and Judge…Can you see His eyes, nose, His mouth? Just turn the picture…the way it's supposed to be…Can you see it? He is Supreme Judge; there's none other but Him. And that is a perfect identification again, a vindication that this message is the truth…see the dark, His face, His beard, His eyes.[31]

How did Hoffman's, 'Head of Christ,' appear inside the cloud picture? Pearry Green, the pastor of Tucson Tabernacle in Tucson, visited Cloverdale Bible Way, in the mid 1970s. Green told this author personally at that occasion, that someone from his church inserted it.

CHAPTER NINE

A Javelina Hunt, During Which, Angels Appear?

Was WMB hunting and being picked up in this constellation of angels on Thursday, Feb. 28, 1963, in Arizona? No! WMB was in Houston, TX, on Monday night, March 4, 1963. He stated,

> Good evening to Houston...It's been many years since I've had the privilege of being here...I had arrangements made for something else another place...[32]

What were those other arrangements? By Branham's own admission it was the Javelina hunt. On July, 25, 1965 he said,

> I was going hunting with a friend...and someone called me...I had to go to Houston about his son, for he was going in the death-row and was going to be killed in a few days...(they) ...give me what they call an Oscar, or whatever you want to call it, for saving a life. Then we went back. I went up the mountain to hunt.[33]

WMB was hunting Javelina hogs. On the last page of this Chapter is a copy of the Arizona Game and Fish Department's Javelina hunt regulations.

This author testifies here that, upon hearing what WMB said on tape, he was in shock. He realized that what he had heard had serious consequences for WMB and for himself. He phoned the above listed department and personally spoke to Ms. Maria Rodriguez to ask if there were exceptions made to the regulations, or if perhaps someone could have had a special Javelina permit. According to Ms. Rodriguez, no special permits were granted that year. Javelina season was from March 1-10, 1963.[34] Maria sent a copy of the hunting regulations, which is found at the end of this chapter. This was a life changing discovery for this author.

WMB drove back from Houston to Tucson right after he preached, which brought him back to Tucson, in the afternoon of Wednesday, March 6, 1963. After all, it is about 1,100 miles (1,760 KMs). On the second day of his hunt, Thursday, March 7, 1963, WMB shot his hog, and on the third day, Friday, March 8, 1963, he claimed the angels appeared. This has now been confirmed by an article in *Only Believe*, Vol. 5, No. 1. As stated earlier, On March 17, he mentioned another "vision" he had in Sabino Canyon. He said the "vision" occurred a "week, or ten days ago." or around March 7, to March 10, which would fit the hunting dates. Again, as shown earlier, on March 24, 1963 the vision is once again mentioned:

> Notice, there's witnesses of three sitting here, that a week ago,(a little over a week ago) I was up way back into the mountains, nearly to Mexico...[35]

When the date of Feb. 28, 1963, is used, there are a number of serious problems. One, of course, is that WMB would've been hunting one day prior to open season, which would be poaching, a serious offence. WMB, as an ex-game warden and an avid outdoorsman, would not have poached. This is what WMB said on March 23, 1963, about poachers,

> There's some genuine men, but there's just one of a thousand that you can find. Shoot anything that they can see, anyway they want to, that's right-that's a murderer. That's right. He's heartless. He'll shoot out of season.[36]

WMB said the blast took place in the morning. Yet the actual cloud appeared in the evening. On June 23, 1963, WMB preached a message, in which he said,

> I had to go to Houston about getting that little boy saved from the electric chair. And then I went back and I went hunting up there with the brethren. And that morning, I was standing there picking ...burrs off of my trouser leg. And the blast did just exactly the way it is said ...and just above me was the Angels of the Lord that sent Message back, for me to come here to break these Seals...I didn't know at the time, that they were taking pictures of that...I didn't know they were taking a picture of it, 'cause immediately I hurried east.[37]

WMB left Tucson on March 13, to return to Jeffersonville. The cloud appeared over Flagstaff, which is about 260 miles NNW of Tucson. From where WMB was hunting, 40 miles NE of Tucson, which is 200+ miles away, the cloud appears quite flat. A photo of the cloud taken from about 160 SE from Flagstaff does not at all look like the picture in Life Magazine.

It is now agreed that on Feb. 28, 1963, WMB was not near the site where the constellation appeared. Now it is stated that WMB had his 'angelic' experience on Mar. 8, 1963, which flies in the face of what WMB himself always said. WMB always tied his experience to the cloud, but this cloud appeared on Feb. 28, 1963, not on Mar. 8, 1963. *Only Believe* now has WMB saying that the cloud appeared before the actual event. 'God always shows His major events first in the heavens.' That means the 'angels' did not, on Feb. 28, 1963, pick WMB up into the constellation. Thus, they did not then give him the revelation of the Seven Seals. WMB had his alleged Sabino Canyon experience and in this vision he cried out, unsuccessfully, to know the meaning of the vision of the angels.

That WMB had anticipated preaching on the Seven Seals is evident from his build up to the event, starting back in September of 1962[38] right through December of 1962. This is especially seen in his reaction to his vision of Dec. 12, 1962 where he exclaimed that the angels were coming with his message[39] and his subsequent direction to his son Billy Paul to start mailing out notices for a series of services on *'The Revelation Of The Seven Seals'* to be held at the Branham Tabernacle during the week of Mar. 17 – Mar. 24, 1963. On Mar. 13, 1963, WMB left to preach the Seven Seals. WMB made it clear that these revelations were "THUS SAITH THE LORD." and they thus vindicated his ministry. That makes it difficult for some to judge those revelations objectively by the Bible.

CHAPTER NINE

The above discussions regarding the cloud raise some real difficulties with this being the vindication to WMB's ministry. He had plans all along to come back to Jeffersonville to preach the Seals. During the series of messages the cloud of Feb. 28, 1963 was never mentioned as the occurrence of him being picked up by a constellation of angels. That came more than two months later, after he had learned about the "Cloud of Mystery." They neither establish him, nor his claims, as true. That means not a single one of his ten commissions can be substantiated, which constitutes a serious problem for WMB's ministry. If there is no messenger there is no message. However, it would appear that WMB's followers, even while acknowledging the physical impossibilities of his commission claim of 1963, still hold to the inspiration of his revelation.

See below a copy of the Arizona Game and Fish Department's Javelina hunt regulations for March 1 through March 10, 1963. This author personally spoke to Ms. Maria Rodriguez at the Arizona Game and Fish Department, and she said, "No exceptions were made to the regulations and no special permits were granted and

---

1963 JAVELINA. HUNT REGULATIONS
T-12, JAVELINA HUNT REGULATIONS ARIZONA GAME & FISH DEPARTMENT

SEASON: March 1 - March 10, 1963, inclusive
LEGAL ANIMAL: One javelina, any age, either sex.
BAG & POSSESSION LIMIT: One javelina, See Commission Order P-3b
OPEN AREA: Statewide, EXCEPT Three Bar. Santa Rita, Tucson Mountain. Robins
  Butte, and Arlington Wildlife Areas, and Game Management Unit 20,
  and posted portions of the Cibola and Topock Wildlife Areas.
A valid Class F or G licnese and valid javelina tag must be in possession of any
person hunting javelina.
FORT HUACHUCA MILITARY RESERVATION SPECIAL JAVELINA HUNT.
SEASON: March 1 - March 10, 1963, inclusive.
NUMBER OF PERMITS: 125
DESCRIPTION OF AREA:
  The Fort Huachuca Military Reservation lying within Game Management Unit 35.
  The Fort Huachuca Military Reservation shall be open only to hunting by properly
  licensed civilian and military personnel attached to Fort Huachuca.
  Hunters will be selected by drawing with the numbers of civilian and military
  hunters to be determined on the basis of the ratio of civilian to military applications.
  Aplication blanks will be available beginning January 28. 1963. at Fort Huachuca.
  Applications will be received at Fort Huachuca on or after January 28, 1963, and
  before noon on February 15. 1963, and quota for the hunt will be filled by public
  drawing at Fort Hucahuca in the presence of Arizona Game and Fish Department personnel on February 15, 1963. Permits will not be valid until countersigned by the
  commanding General, or his representative, at the time and place designated by him.
  All hunters must personally check into and out of the area through a checking
  station as designated by the Commanding General.

the regular Javalina season was from March 1 through March 10, 1963. That this is, in fact, a scanned document and can be verified by the spelling mistake of the word "license,"* which has been left as is. The original is in the author's possession. - PMD.

Notes - Chapter Nine

[1] Peter M. Duyzer, *'Mystery Cloud' - Exposé on Wm. Branham*, (Fort McMurray, AB, Canada: Peter M. Duyzer, 1980, 27 pp.)

[2] Rebekah Branham Smith, *The Road to Sunset*, in Only Believe, Vol. 5, No. 1, June 1992, (Tucson, AZ: Believers International Inc.).

[3] WMB, *Shalom*, Jan. 12, 1964, Sierra Vista, AZ.

[4] _____, *Shalom*, Jan. 19, 1964, Phoenix, AZ, "Well, now, we realize that God always shows things in the heaven before He shows them on the earth. Like the wise men followed the star, and so forth. A heavenly sign takes place, first, then the earthly vindicates the heavenly sign.

[5] _____, *Trying To Do God A Service*, Nov. 27, 1965, Brkfst., Shreveport, LA.

[6] Eugene Norman, *Bread Upon The Waters*, in Only Believe.

[7] Dave Davies, *The Cloud*, March 26, 1967 pull-out section in Arizona Republic newspaper.

[8] WMB, *Perseverant*, Aug. 02, 1963, Chicago, IL, "I didn't know it; but cameras from all over the country was taking the picture of That, as the white Cloud settled down, went on the Associated Press. I think even Chicago paper packed it, all around. Life magazine packed it....That...was it right there, just exactly the way it said it, standing right under it when it come down and formed."

[9] Davies.

[10] *How The Angel Came To Me*.

[11] WMB, *Hear Ye Him*, Jul. 11, 1962, Spokane, WA, "And before God does anything usually on the earth, He usually speaks of it out of heaven first."

[12] Wm. Branham, *Introduction*, in *The Revelation of The Seven Seals*, (Tucson: Spoken Word Publications, Dec. 1967, 597 pp.)

[13] John Kennah. Message of Wm. Branham Support Forum. *Issues & Events in WMB's Life*, available from http://forums.delphiforums.com/kennah/messages?msg=2132.502 , (accessed July 16, 2011).

[14] John Kennah, available from http://forums.delphiforums.com/kennah/messages?msg=2909.1 , (accessed July 16, 2011).

[15] *Is This The Time Of The End, Sir?* ,

[16] Ibid.

[17] WMB, *Reproach For The Cause Of The Word*, Dec. 12, 1962, Jeff., IN.

[18] Ibid.

CHAPTER NINE

19 *God Hiding Himself In Simplicity.*

20 WMB, *Breach Between The Seven Church Ages And The Seven Seals*, Mar. 17, 1963, PM, Jeff., IN.

21 _____, *Fifth Seal*, Mar. 22, 1963, Jeff., IN.

22 WMB, *Seventh Seal*, Mar. 24, 1963, PM, Jeff., IN.

23 On March 17, he said it was a week prior, or March 10, or March 7, if it was 10 days. The foreword says he was forty miles NE of Tucson, not nearly to Mexico.

24 *Seventh Seal.*

25 WMB, *Come Follow Me*, Jun 1, 1963, Tucson, AZ.

26 *LIFE* Magazine, May 17, 1963, Time Inc., 112. Printed with permission.

27 In a letter, dated November 30, 1977, by William G. Hoyt, Director of the Public Information Office of the University of Northern Arizona, and a Research Associate of The Lowell Observatory, he states," Dear Mr. Duyzer: I am sorry that I can add little to what you apparently already know…It is my impression that is was generally agreed that the cloud was an atmospheric distortion of a cloud produced by the launch of a missile at Vandenberg Air Force Base…but certainly at first some scientists thought it might be a very rare noctiluscent cloud, never before seen at such low latitudes." Another letter, dated Dec. 05, 1977, from Louis J. Batten, stating, "Dear Mr. Duyzer…Dr. McDonald had convinced himself that the cloud was caused by water released form a high altitude rocket launched from Vanderburgh (sic) Air Force Base. Such an explanation certainly was acceptable to most people who examined the scientific elements involved." Another letter from Louis J. Batten, Head – Department of Atmospheric Sciences, University of Arizona dated September 17, 1974, states, "In my conversations with Dr. McDonald during and after this period, I am convinced that he was convinced it was produced by the rocket released from Vandenberg."

28 WMB was asking God what the vision meant, did it mean his death, as Branham relates in other accounts?

29 At the time of the Sabino Canyon vision, the 'event' had not yet taken place.

30 The picture has to be turned 90 degrees from the way it appeared.

31 *It Is The Rising Of The Sun.*

32 WMB, *Absolute*, Mar. 04, 1963, Houston, TX. This is not the Absolute preached in Jeffersonville, Dec. 30, 1962.

33 _____, *What Is The Attraction On The Mountain?* Jul. 25, 1965, PM, Jeff., IN.

34 Late October 1978, this author spoke with Ms. Maria Rodriguez, of the Arizona Game and Fish Department. Ms. Rodriguez stated, "No special permits were issued and the regular Javalina season was from March 1 through March 10, 1963."

35 Mar. 08, 1963 would have made it about 2 weeks prior, Feb. 28, 1963 was a whole month prior. The foreword says he was 40 miles NE of Tucson, not nearly to Mexico.

36 WMB, *Sixth Seal*, Mar. 23, 1963, Jeff., IN.

37 _____, *Standing In The Gap*, Jun. 23, 1963, AM, Jeff., IN.

38 _____, *In His Presence*, Sep. 09, 1962, PM, Jeff., IN, "I want to take, the next time that we start, on the Seven Seals of Revelations."

39 *Reproach For The Cause Of The Word.*

Chapter Ten

TYPES OF HEALING

To what extent is William Branham's claim
of Divine healing supported by
Biblical Revelation?

Divine Healing, or Faith Healing

Both the terms Divine healing and Faith healing were employed by WMB.[1] Technically, Divine healing indicates that Divinity, or Deity, is involved in the process; Faith healing suggests faith is the operative word. As a matter of fact, WMB stated that faith healing did not require faith in God, it just required faith.[2] This kind of faith is called "Faith in faith." That this is the kind of faith WMB promoted is seen in his first recorded message called, *Faith Is The Substance*.[3] This title is, of course, a derivation of Hebrews 1: 1, "Now faith is the substance of things hoped for, the evidence of things not seen." As the NLT puts it:

> What is faith? It is the confident assurance that what we hope for is going to happen. It is the evidence of things we not yet see.

Faith is the sure hope that something "unseen," is real. Not the kind of hope, as used in everyday language, such as, "I sure hope so." That is more like wishful thinking. The Scriptures go on to illustrate what it meant for the saints of old. Verse 4: *By faith* Abel…; v.5. *By faith Enoch*…; v.7 *By faith* Noah…; v.8 *By faith* Abraham…, etc. They did not see it, but they believed it as if they had seen it.

WMB stated that faith is a revelation. What does Scripture mean by revelation? The Greek word for revelation is *apokalupsis*, meaning, *disclosure*. - appearing, coming, lighten, manifestation, be revealed, revelation. The Apostle John wrote *The Revelation of Jesus Christ*, and the apostles Paul and Peter, had apocalypses, or revelations.

> But I certify you, brethren, that the gospel which was preached of me is not after

man. 12 For I neither received it of man, neither was I taught it, but by the **revelation** of Jesus Christ." (Gal. 1: 11).

It is a walk by faith, not by sight (2 Cor. 5:7), and if faith is a revelation like a vision, it is something seen, and does not qualify as a substitute. Perhaps it would be helpful to determine what exactly WMB meant when he used the word *faith*.

> What is a…revelation? Jesus said, "Upon this rock I'll build My church, and the gates of hell can't prevail against it." Faith is a revelation, because faith has been revealed to you. Abel, by faith offered by revelation…to God a more excellent sacrifice than that of Cain.[4]

Faith, according to WMB

To return to the issue of faith, what, beside revelation, did WMB mean when he used the word *faith*? Here are some instances:

> Faith is the sixth sense, known to some people as you want to as mental telepathy or… or whatever you want or wish to call it, many of the call it names, but to me its faith.[5]
>
> Faith is an element, it's a sense. It's the sixth sense…[6]

For WMB, faith was a revelation, the sixth sense, or mental telepathy. WMB confirmed this by other statements he made regarding faith as a mental attitude,

> Your right mental attitude towards God's Divine promise will bring any promise to pass. Now, maybe you don't believe that. You say, "Well, my faith is weak." I wouldn't confess it, see? Don't let the devil know that. Always say, "I've got good faith. I believe God with all my heart."[7]

For WMB, faith is having the right mental attitude. Does this teaching accurately reflect Scripture? Below is reproduced an account of what WMB described as faith:

> If you have faith, I want to ask you and show you, rather, that...you do not have faith…Hanging in the room from a chandelier was a string, and on the end of that string was a little…bracelet…I said to the young lady; I said, "How far are you away from that bracelet?" She said, "Approximately fifteen feet."…I said, "Now, you tell me you've got faith to believe for all things." She said, "I have, sir."…"Now, you look right directly at that bracelet" and it hanging there in mid-air, "and you make that bracelet swing around and around in the room. Then you make it swing back and forth in the room, and then stop it, and I'll believe you have faith." She said, "Oh, brother Branham" said, "my, why ask me something like that?" I said, "I wanted to see if you had faith." I said, "Jesus said, 'All things are possible if you believe.'"[8]

There's not the slightest hint in Scripture of such a test of faith. WMB went on to address his audience regarding what he calls faith,

> Now, that's just pure faith, friends. Magicians use it many times to play pranks and so forth, burst glasses and things. It will, if you believe. But I'm trying to base your... thought on faith so you know what I'm talking of.[9]

What WMB called faith was/is actually Magic, and WMB went on to bring confusion to this child:

> Then she said, "Why, Brother Branham, no one could do that." I said, "Oh, yes, anyone can that believes." And she said, "Well, I don't believe that anyone could do that."[10]

This poor girl was asked by WMB to practice Magic. WMB continued to seduce that young girl's mind, just like Satan did to Eve.

> I said, "I thought you said you believed for all things." See how she was caught right there. I said, "You said you believed all things, I want you to prove it." And she said, "I don't believe there's anyone can do that; that's material, Brother Branham." She said, "Could you do it?" I said, "Yes, ma'am." And she said, "Well, could I see it done?" I said, "If you desire." And she said, "I desire."[11]

Mission accomplished, the young woman now was ready to get involved.

> Then of course, putting my mind on it, and having her to watch that and not me... Now, then of course, fastening my eyes to that bracelet, which you can yourself, if you won't doubt it in your heart, and it started moving around. And then it moved back and forth, around, crossways, and stopped it.[12]

WMB now gave away a trade secret. He had the girl focus away from him and on the bracelet and she was unaware of what WMB was doing. She knew something was not right and said, "that's spiritualism." She said, "There's no such a thing can be showed in the Bible of anything like that." WMB said that it was indeed in Scripture, and he quoted Jesus saying,

> If you'd say to this mountain, 'Be moved,' and doubt it not in your heart, by and by it would come to pass.'" "Now, if the faith the size of a mustard seed would move that mountain, how much more smaller faith would you have to have just to move that bracelet?"[13]

Just as Satan tempted Jesus with Scripture, we see WMB also using Scripture. In the above quote, WMB told the young girl that Jesus had that same kind of faith as demonstrated by Jesus cursing the fig tree. If there is one thing to be learned in the Christian experience, it is the importance to always check the Scriptures. Here is what Jesus actually said,

CHAPTER TEN

> Verily I say unto you, If ye have faith, and doubt not, ye shall not only do this which is done to the fig tree, but also if ye shall say unto this mountain, Be thou removed, and be thou cast into the sea; it shall be done. 22 And all things, **whatsoever ye shall ask in prayer**, believing, ye shall receive (Matt. 21: 22). [Note: Emphasis mine-PMD].
> And Jesus answering saith unto them, **Have faith in God.** 23 For verily I say unto you, That whosoever shall say unto this mountain, Be thou removed, and be thou cast into the sea; and shall not doubt in his heart, but shall believe that those things which he saith shall come to pass; he shall have whatsoever he saith" (Mk. 11: 23). [Note: Emphasis mine-PMD].

In Matthew's Gospel, Jesus said one must have faith, which, He said, means faith in God (Cf. Mark's Gospel). Then whatever one asks for, IN PRAYER, shall be received. The young lady asked WMB,

> Did God move that or did the devil move that? "I said, "Neither one moved that." She said, "Then how in the world did it move?" I said, "I moved it." She said, "Well, you're fifteen feet or better away from it." I said, "No, its my faith that moved it."...

WMB got her to a place where she could be influenced to believe, not in the power of God, nor in the power of Satan (at least not directly), but in human mind power. She capitulated and,

> She said, "Let me believe." And I took a hold of her hand then. There was a vibration pouring from that ruptured appendix, had prayer for her and it stopped immediately. I said, "God bless you, sister. Your faith now has saved you."[14]

WMB declared her saved.

The question here is not, *"Did that bracelet move?"* It is possible that the bracelet moved, although suggestion can play a big role in things of this nature. If it was not God, or any force of Satan, but WMB that "moved" it, did he employ trickery, or some kind of personal or magical power? If there is a choice to be made here, it would be safe to hold it to be trickery. Magicians employing this kind of trick *have* been "debunked." Following is another one of WMB's Magic claims:

> Faith is the only direct and positive sense, and it's the sixth sense...Here, in my pocket, I think there's an old Barlow knife I've carried for years. Now, I do not see that knife. I do not feel that knife. I do not taste that knife. I do not smell that knife. But I know that knife is in there. How do you know? Because I believe it's in there...faith will put it in there, if it's not there. That chokes you, I know. But...but that's true. If you believe, all things are possible. You're afraid to take God, friends. You're scared. Now, I might've left that knife laying on the dresser where I changed clothes awhile ago. But

just as sure if that knife is on the dresser right now, if I believe it with all my heart, it'll be in my pocket. That chokes you. But God is able to put it there if you believe it.[15]

WMB taught that healing power is within people and does not come from an outside source.[16] If this were true, why is there a need for a healer? Throughout his entire ministry WMB stated that no man can heal,[17] not even Jesus can heal,[18] but God alone. Then again he said faith alone is capable of healing.

Faith, in WMB's vocabulary, does not just mean faith in God. As stated, WMB's perception of faith included "Sixth sense," mental telepathy and mindreading. These were all expressions of the same thing and WMB said they were all employed by Jesus.[19] In fact, WMB stated that it does not matter what one calls it, as long as it produces what it is supposed to.[20] WMB believed that, "the end justifies the means." Whatever works healing, even if it is through an idol, *use it*, insinuated WMB. He acknowledged healing through differing means. WMB said he did not heal people,[21] how did they get healed? One could pretty well pick and choose from anything in WMB's messages, between nature,[22] mental powers,[23] psychic powers,[24] Christian Science,[25] faith in whatever,[26] the healing power within,[27] the angel at WMB's right side,[28] a sixth sense,[29] or Christ in the atonement.[30]

Are there any Biblical examples of the healing methods employed by the Divine/Faith healers of yesteryear, or today? The truth is there are none. WMB himself acknowledged he stood condemned, because he stated that there was no Apostolic tradition for the methods he employed.

> Now, here is my condemnation. Before Almighty God, Whom I stand before this night as a minister...I say it from the depths of my heart: I am condemned the way I use it. Now, that's right. One thing, I'm a harming the people, so many of them. And another thing, I'm not obeying what He told me to do. ... and as I take them one at a time as they come up here, begin to tell them, talk to them, and so forth like that, tell them all about their diseases... Never did one of the apostles do that. Never did Jesus do that. They did not do that. Yet the gift is here to do that.[31]

WMB nevertheless argued from outcome. This, of course, is fraught with danger. Just because something works does not mean that it is of God.

What is healing?

What happened in WMB's healing campaigns? In order to properly deal with the issue of WMB's faith healing, or divine healing, it is expedient to first establish what healing is. The following is one definition of healing:

> The act or process in which the normal structural and functional characteristics of

health are restored to diseased, dysfunctional, or damaged tissues, organs, or systems of the body.[32]

God created mankind with an immune system. When health is compromised, human bodies, do continuously heal themselves of common illnesses, such as colds, flues, infections and other illnesses. When a bone is broken, a doctor cannot heal it, he only sets it. Rest is often prescribed, because rest is a powerful assistant in healing. Pain is often the mechanism that tells a person to rest and be healed. However, today pain is usually treated with pain-killers and can actually be detrimental when rest is not taken.

Sometimes people experience a "spontaneous remission," of an illness, including cancer. This is not limited to Christians, but people, in all cultures and religions, experience this. One reads news articles of someone receiving their sight, after being blind; their hearing, after being deaf; walking after being paralyzed, etc. (None of these cases today consist of people who had no eyes to begin with; no hearing organs; no spinal cord). For whatever reason, these bodily functions never functioned, or ceased operation, perhaps the result of some past trauma, psycho-somatic illness,[33] or hysteria.[34] Other means, such as hypnosis, euphoria, placebos, kundalini, acupuncture, etc., can be successfully employed to reverse these situations. In other words, means outside of the direct realm of Scripture are employed in order to restore people to physical health. As earlier alluded to, there is also a form of healing called the placebo effect. People put their faith in something or someone, and they get healed. There are documented cases where tremendous healings have taken place. When a "patient" puts her faith in a cure or a healer, something triggers in her brain setting mechanisms in motion that facilitate the return to well-being. These are natural, not miraculous healings. Euphoria, or Hypnosis, can also produce healing. The Beatles demonstrated this in Australia, as well as in Britain:

> "I must say," Derek continued, "that working with the Beatles is an experience that I wouldn't have missed for the world. It's incredible, absolutely incredible! Here are these four boys from Liverpool. They're rude, they're profane, they're vulgar, and they've taken over the world. It's as if they've founded a new religion. They're completely anti-Christ. I mean, I'm anti-Christ as well, but they're so anti-Christ that they shock me, which isn't an easy thing. But I'm obsessed with them. Isn't everybody? I'm obsessed with their honesty. And the people who like them most are the people who should be outraged most. In Australia, for example, each time we'd arrive at an airport, it was as if De Gaulle had landed, or, better yet, the Messiah. The routes were lined solid with people. Cripples threw away their sticks. Sick people rushed up to the car as if a touch from one of the boys would make them well again. Old women stood watching with their grandchildren, and, as we'd pass by, I could see the look on their faces. It was as if some saviour had arrived and people were happy and relieved as if

things somehow were going to be better now."...The only thing left for them is to go on a healing tour.[35]

WMB's associate did not read the portion at the end of the article, which should have been inserted just between the sentence that states, "as if things somehow were going to be better now," and "The only thing left..." The missing portion is listed below.

> The telephone rang. It was a newspaper reporter asking for tickets to the Royal Premiere. "Utterly out of the question!" Derek exploded, trying to sound apologetic and reaching for a pack of cigarettes, "I'm sorry!" Putting a cigarette into his mouth and turning toward me, he said: "If I were a Beatle, this would be the ultimate. The Royal Premiere would be the ultimate---except for the Sermon on the Mount.[36]

The Mayor of Liverpool, the hometown of the Beatles, reported that healings took place in a hospital of sick children.

> The Beatles' next appearance was with the...Lord Mayor of Liverpool...Then the Lord Mayor made a speech. "I have here," he said, "a letter from the Orthopedic Hospital which says that when the children heard Beatle songs, they took a new lease on life and many were inspired to get up and walk for the first time." [37]

WMB attributed these healings by the Beatles to Satan, which, of course, in other places he contradicted. This is how this looks:

1. Satan cannot heal
2. <u>Satan *can* heal</u>
3. Internal contradiction. WMB's teaching is invalid.

Dyed in the wool followers of WMB, who hold Satan *cannot* heal, now have a problem. They have now made WMB either a false teacher, or a liar, or both.

During WMB's nervous breakdown in 1948, he experienced the "shakes," as well as "blindness."[38] He also previously had the shakes and blindness back in the early 1930s, and admitted to being a hysterical child.[39] Today the word "hysterical," has been replaced by "conversion disorder," where a person's psychological problems convert into physical symptoms. These symptoms can include hysterical deafness, blindness, and may cause jerks or shakes. This illness is not incurable.

Healing experiments have been performed where a "healer" was located in a chamber made of "one-way" glass. People were asked to focus on the unseen healer, or just simply pray. Several people claimed healing. The experiment was repeated with the chamber empty (no healer present), without telling the audience. Afterwards people claimed to have been healed. Who, or what, was doing the healing in this context?

CHAPTER TEN

To what extent is William Branham's claim of Divine Healing supported by Biblical revelation? Though he always claimed he was commissioned by an angel who gave him a gift of healing for the nations, WMB never claimed to heal. He taught that his gift was only there to encourage faith for healing. The problem is that WMB's angel never said that the gift was only to encourage people's faith. On the contrary, the angel said that NOTHING would be able to stand against WMB's prayer, not even cancer. WMB said, "Then one year ago, while I was standing in my yard the Spirit came to me again; I was told that God had forgiven me and that **a double portion of the Power to heal would be given me**."[40] (Emphasis mine – PMD). These are internal contradictions, which invalidate WMB's claim. Earlier it was mentioned that a "double portion" does not mean what people, including WMB, believe it means. Why would an angel use an expression that is not understood in this culture?

WMB's faith for healing did not require faith in God. In fact, it was faith in faith that affected healing. To no extent is William Branham's claim of Divine Healing supported by Biblical Revelation.

Notes - Chapter Ten

[1] WMB, *God Hath A Provided Way*, Jan. 08, 1956, Jeff., IN, "This healing, you must have faith. It's called faith healing."

[2] _____, *God Keeps His Word*, Jan. 15, 1957, Sturgis, MI, "Healing is not based upon your works, or your good deeds, or your experience of Christianity, and upon your salvation of your soul; healing…I've seen people come through the line was renowned saints, and go right off the platform sick yet. I've seen ill famed people walk through and be healed with blinded eyes and everything. See? It's based upon your--your faith, not upon your religion, not upon your experience. It's on faith."

[3] *Faith Is The Substance*, Oakland.

[4] WMB, *Invisible Union Of The Bride Of Christ*, Nov. 25, 1965, Shreveport, LA.

[5] *Faith Is The Substance*, Oakland, "Faith is the sixth sense, known to some …as mental telepathy or…whatever…wish to call it…but to me its faith…Faith is the only direct and positive sense, and it's the sixth sense."

[6] WMB, *Faith - Africa Trip Report*, Jul. 25, 1952, Zion, IL.

[7] _____, *Hour Is Come*, Apr. 15, 1951, PM, Phoenix, AZ, "Now, there was many things that Jesus Himself could not do because of unbelief. Is that right? Many things He could not do. We hate to think that, but He could not do it because of their unbelief. Now, the right mental attitude…All you along here, do you understand what I mean when I say, 'The right mental attitude?'…Your right mental attitude towards God's Divine promise will bring any promise to pass. Now, maybe you don't believe that. You say, 'Well, my faith is weak.' I wouldn't confess it, see? Don't let the devil know that. Always say, 'I've got good faith. I believe God with all my heart.'"

[8] *Faith Is The Substance*, Oakland.

[9] Ibid.

[10] Ibid.

[11] Ibid.

[12] Ibid.

[13] Ibid.

[14] Ibid.

[15] Ibid.

[16] WMB, *Uncertain Sound*, Dec. 18, 1960, Jeff., IN, "You know, now don't teach this, but did you know man in the beginning, when God made him, he didn't make him to be doctored. He had his own doctoring in him, he was equipped, he was…a unit of his own, see? Then healing does not come from any outside resource, it has to come from the inside…Healing only comes by the…the power that's within yourself to build back the…the tissue that's been torn from the place it's been taken out…and therefore, healing is in you…"

[17] *Expectation*, New York, "There's no man can heal, not even Jesus." See also: WMB, *Jehovah-Jireh # 1*, Apr. 02, 1964, Louisville, MS, "You just believe. You can't heal. I can't heal. There is no man can heal. God is the healer."

[18] WMB, *Jesus Christ, The Same Yesterday, Today And Forever*, Feb. 05, 1961, PM, Tucson, AZ, "Now, remember, Jesus, when the works was being done, Jesus did not heal anyone. He said, 'I cannot heal no one.' He said, 'It's not Me that doeth the works; it's My Father, and He dwelleth in Me.'" See also: *Jehovah-Jireh*, Aug. 17, 1955, Karlsruhe, DEU, "Look. That sounds strange, that Jesus could not heal unless you'd believe. When He went to His own country, the Bible said, 'Many mighty works He could not do, because of their unbelief.'" Note: Jesus chose not to heal, because of their unbelief. Jesus had power and authority over all things but, because of their unbelief, as Mattew declares, "He did not do many miracles there." (13: 58). Jesus chose not to do many miracles there. – PMD.

[19] *Faith Is The Substance*, "Faith is the sixth sense, known to some people as you want to as mental telepathy…or whatever you want or wish to call it, many of the call it names, but to me its faith." See also: *Jesus Christ The Same Yesterday, And Today, And Forever*, May 06, 1953, Jonesboro, AR, "Someone said the other day, said, 'Brother Branham, do you say Jesus was a mind-reader?' Sure. He perceived their thoughts. Call it whatever you want to."

[20] WMB, *Why Little Bethlehem?*, Dec. 14, 1963, Phoenix, AZ, "What we need today is a opening of the word that lives, and he's the same yesterday, today, and forever, he cannot fail. They can call it mental telepathy; they…they can say whatever they want to, or spiritualists, or a devil, as long as that word's flowing free and producing exactly what it said it would do…"

[21] WMB, *As I Was With Moses, So Will I Be With Thee,* "Now, I am not a healer, but I have a gift of healing. That was witnessed. It's been proved that that's the truth, see, way back, a long time ago."

[22] ____, *I Was Not Disobedient To The Heavenly Vision,* Zion, IL, "But nature has to do the healing, and nature is God. God is nature."

[23] *Hour Is Come,* "Your right mental attitude towards God's divine promise will bring any promise to pass." See also: *From That Time,* Phoenix, "A man getting up from a wheelchair, that could be mental healing. You know that. That could be mental healing."

[24] *Jesus Christ, The Same yesterday, Today, And Forever,* Tucson, "It's more of a challenge than to walk down to this woman in a wheelchair and say, 'Stand up and walk,' certainly. She could actually do that through psychic power, that's right, mental."

[25] Ibid., "Oh, isn't that a challenge? Think of that, it's more of a challenge than to walk down to this woman in a wheelchair and say, 'Stand up and walk,' certainly. She could actually do that through psychic power, that's right, mental. She could do it in Christian Science faith, it's been done."

[26] WMB, *Show Us The Father And It Will Satisfy Us,* Jun. 31, 1960, Yakima, WA, "About your witch that you've got in your neighborhood. I said…'Course those people get healed.' Because, I said, 'In Africa, I've seen them go to idols and get healed. In Las Alderaines they got a monument there of some dead woman, in a Catholic church. They go there and look at that dead woman, say a 'Hail Mary,' and get healed. Sure, because the people think they're approaching God through that, and God heals on the basis of faith, and wherever faith's met God's got to meet that requirement.'"

[27] WMB, *Power Of Transformation,* Oct. 31, 1965, AM, Prescott, AZ, "A healing comes from the inside, let that healing come from the spirit that's in you."

[28] *Expectation,* New York, "And may the angel of God, who's guided me through my life, fed me since I was born, be here tonight to heal the sick and afflicted."

[29] *Faith Is The Substance,* "Faith is the sixth sense, known to some people as you want to as mental telepathy or…or whatever you want or wish to call it, many of the call it names, but to me its faith."

[30] *Not Disobedient To The Heavenly Vision,* Zion, "And I do not see how that clergy could say and could preach the Gospel without including Divine healing in the atonement, because "He was wounded for our transgressions; and with His stripes we are healed."

[31] *Angel And The Commission.*

[32] Mosby's Medical Dictionary, 8th edition. © 2009, Elsevier.

[33] An illness, or symptoms, resulting from neurosis.

[34] Neurotic disorder, characterized by disturbances of sensory and motor functions.

[35] *Questions And Answers # 2,* Aug. 23, 1964, PM.

[36] Al Aronowitz, The Beatles, available from http://www.blaklistedjourna-List.com/column17.htm, (accessed 19 April 19, 2005).

[37] Ibid.

38 *Faith Without Works Is Dead*, "I'd just went ahead once walked around with a great big glasses on, just…Sometimes I just fell…Just had to lead me, I'd be so blind."

[39] *Experiences,* "They thought I was just at a little nervous hysterical child…" See also: *Life Story,* LA, "I was just hysterically. She called the doctor, and the doctor said, 'Well, he's just nervous; that's all.' So she put me to bed."

[40] *Not Disobedient.*

Chapter Eleven

HEALING IN SCRIPTURE

In Scripture, the concept of healing is found as early as Genesis, where God, in order to protect Abraham's wife Sarah, had made all the females in King Abimelech's household to be temporarily barren, and later He healed them (Gen. 20: 17-17). The next occasion is found in Gen. 43: 28 where Jacob is listed to be in good health. Of course, the moment humanity fell, pain, death and decay came upon the earth and consequently healing became manifest. God's people look to the Creator and Sustainer of the universe to provide that kind of care and cure. God Himself promised that He would be Israel's Healer, IF they would obey Him (Ex. 15: 26). Within the context of Israel in Egypt, the diseases that God inflicted upon the Egyptians would not be inflicted upon His own people, IF they would obey Him. The word "disease" is translated from the Hebrew word *Khalah* which can also be translated "To be afflicted, to be grieved, to be weak, to be infirm." The bodily afflictions experienced by the Egyptians were: bites of disease causing flies, boils and the death of their firstborn. The other plagues were upon their livestock, crops and their comfort. As an aside, this being true, is it justified to appropriate God's promise to Israel as universally applicable? Not in this author's opinion.

When looking at the actions of the magicians, Jannes and Jambres (2 Tim. 3: 8), it shows these two enemies of God could also bring afflictions upon people:

> There was blood throughout all the land of Egypt. 22 But the magicians of Egypt did the same by their secret arts. (Ex. 7: 21c, 22)
>
> [F]rogs came up and covered the land of Egypt. 7 But the magicians did the same by their secret arts and made frogs come up on the land of Egypt (Ex. 8: 6b, 7).

That the enemy of God can afflict is also demonstrated by Jesus when He said, "Ought not this woman, being a daughter of Abraham, whom Satan hath bound, lo, these eighteen years, be loosed from this bond on the Sabbath day?" (Lu. 13: 16). If these magicians could afflict the people, could they also withdraw (heal) these afflictions? Presumably, Satan could also have loosed, or changed the affliction, depending on his purposes.

Scripture reveals that sickness and sin came into the world as a result of our first parents' sin. The age long question for Christians has been the issue of the origin of evil, sin, destruction and disease. God cannot be the author of sin. If God is not the author of sin, who is? Scripture speaks about sin being introduced through the serpent, which is identified to be, "The Devil, and Satan, which deceiveth the whole world." (Rev. 12: 9b). The serpent, notwithstanding the fact that Adam and Eve were already made in the image of God, thus already godlike, suggested to Eve a shortcut to becoming like God. Any shortcut to becoming godlike, is like magic. The following is a definition of magic,

> Magic is usually defined subjectively rather than by any agreed-upon content. But there is a wide consensus as to what this content is. Most peoples in the world perform acts by which they intend to bring about certain events or conditions, whether in nature or among people, that they hold to be the consequences of those acts. If we use Western terms and assumptions, the cause and effect relationship between the act and the consequence is mystical, not scientifically validated. The acts typically comprise behavior such as manipulation of objects and recitation of verbal formulas or spells. In a given society magic may be performed by a specialist.[1]

Satan, whose design was, and continues to be, to thwart God's plan and destroy His creation, found and still finds, God turning his plans around to God's own glory. Even though mankind sinned and fell, God will save them through Eve's off-spring. Satan, through Pharaoh, plotted to destroy God's people by his ingenious plan to kill Joseph. With Joseph dead, and through means of a huge famine, he would kill Joseph's family. This would include Joseph's brother Judah, through whose line Messiah was promised. Was Satan successful in his design? No, Joseph was brought to a position of honor and, because of that, he saved God's people. Did Joseph's brothers sin and do evil? Yes, but Joseph said, "But as for you, ye thought evil against me; but God meant it unto good, to bring to pass, as it is this day, to save much people alive." (Gen. 20: 50).

Did God inspire Pharaoh to do this or did Satan? Satan planned it to destroy, but God used it for his purposes. This is also seen in 2 Sam. 24: 1, "Again the anger of the LORD was kindled against Israel, and he incited David against them, saying, 'Go, number Israel and Judah,'" and in 1 Chron. 21: 1 it says, "Then Satan stood against Israel and incited David to number Israel." Is there a contradiction? No, God allowed Satan to incite David, but God used it for his purposes. This sort of scenario is seen throughout Scripture. Some sickness and healing should probably be seen in this same kind of construct. Satan brings disease and even death, as Job experienced (Job 2: 6), but God uses it for His purposes.

We see Jesus, being full of compassion, feeding the hungry and healing the sick in His presence. (Matt. 9: 35, 36; 14: 14;15: 32 20: 34).

Jesus had compassion on the crowds and He did whatever was required to alleviate their suffering, because He said,

> For this purpose the Son of God was manifested, that he might destroy the works of the devil." (1Jn. 3: 8).

Jesus did not stop healing anyone who came to him, not even nine ungrateful lepers. Jesus never, not even for the person's own edification, asked, "Is there sin in your life?" No, Jesus simply healed, though He did sometimes say, "Go and sin no more!" As an aside, Jesus first forgave the woman caught in adultery and THEN told her, "Go and sin no more!" Jesus' disciples believed people suffered illnesses because someone had sinned, either the man or his parents. This sounds curiously of what today is called bad Karma. Jesus answered, "Neither hath this man sinned, nor his parents: but that the works of God should be made manifest in him." (Jn. 9: 3). Jesus even healed his enemies, as is seen in the restoration of Malchus' ear after Peter "accidently" cut it off. (Lu. 22:51). Surely he meant to lop off more than just an ear.

Yet, over against Satan causing lots of grief, the Flood was certainly caused by God. Satan is nowhere mentioned in the process. At the end, God will again cause destruction upon this earth. God inflicted leprosy upon Moses' hand and He also healed it (Ex. 4, 6, 7). God answered Moses complaint and, "...said unto him, "Who hath made man's mouth? or who maketh the dumb, or deaf, or the seeing, or the blind? have not I the LORD? (Ex. 4: 11). He also struck Miriam with leprosy and healed her. (Num. 12: 10-15). God sent his destroying angel and killed all Egypt's firstborn. (Ex. 11: 4-6). "Shall there be evil in a city, and the LORD hath not done it?" (Amos 6: 2b). Ananias and Sapphira were struck dead for lying to the Holy Spirit (Acts 5: 1-10). Paul called Elymas the sorcerer, a Jew whose name was Barjesus, a child of the devil and struck him blind. The man's name was Barjesus, which means son of Jesus. How ironic is that? How reminiscent of Matt. 7: 21-23. One can have the "right" name and do all the "right" things and still go into perdition.

There has been a long standing debate in the Church regarding the Charismata. Did the gifts, or did they not, extend beyond the apostolic era? Many books, pro and con, have been written on this topic. *This* book solely deals with the claims of WMB, who preached and claimed to practice divine healing in the Twentieth century. WMB's followers do believe divine healing is for today, and they are still propagating his message. This chapter is to examine to what extent WMB's Claim of Divine Healing is supported by Biblical Revelation.

The Great Commission

It must be said that neither Jesus, nor his Apostles ever *preached* Divine Healing. Neither were any of his disciples ever charged with that commission.

> And Jesus came and spake unto them, saying, All power is given unto me in heaven and in earth. 19 Go ye therefore, and teach all nations, baptizing them in the name of the Father, and of the Son, and of the Holy Ghost: 20 Teaching them to observe all things whatsoever I have commanded you: and, lo, I am with you always, even unto the end of the world. Amen (Matt. 28: 18-20; Cf, Mk 16: 15-18, Lu. 24: 47, Jn. 20: 21- 23, Acts 1: 8).

What is readily seen is that Christ commissioned his disciples to preach the Gospel to all nations (ethnics) and He would be with them until the end of the age. Scripture teaches and commands that the Gospel must be preached; people must repent, believe and be baptized; believers of this gospel will have signs FOLLOWING them. What is preaching the Gospel? Mark records,

> Now after that John was put in prison, Jesus came into Galilee, preaching the gospel of the kingdom of God, [15]And saying, The time is fulfilled, and the kingdom of God is at hand: repent ye, and believe the gospel. (Mark 1: 14- 15).

The Gospel is the in-breaking of God's reign on earth. It is the good news to ALL mankind that a Savior has come to bring an end to the enmity between God and man. Paul says,

> Moreover, brethren, I declare unto you the gospel which I preached unto you, which also ye have received, and wherein ye stand; [2] By which also ye are saved, if ye keep in memory what I preached unto you, unless ye have believed in vain.[3] For I delivered unto you first of all that which I also received, how that Christ died for our sins according to the scriptures;[4] And that he was buried, and that he rose again the third day according to the scriptures: (1 Cor. 15: 1-4)

The great mass healing revivals seen since the 1940s were typically not advertised as Gospel meetings, rather they were advertised as healing revivals. That reveals they are not following Christ's command to preach the Gospel. Yes, of course, the Gospel might be mentioned, but the main message is that of healing. This book's primary concern is WMB's ministry. Note; Many healing ministries, of yesterday and today, claim to have received WMB's mantle, and many, like WMB, use an Eagle as part of their logo.

Notes -Chapter Eleven

[1] John Middleton, ed. *Theories of Magic"* in *Encyclopedia of Religion* Vol. 9, (New York, NY: McMillan, 1987), 82.

Chapter Twelve

GIFT OF DIVINE HEALING

To what extent is William Branham's claim
of a Divine healing gift supported
by Biblical Revelation?

WMB claimed he was commissioned in 1946 by an angel sent from the presence of God. He stated he was given a gift of Divine Healing. Divine healing, as per WMB's definition, comprises ALL kinds of healing.[1] WMB claimed this Divine Healing gift was sent: For the people;[2] To the people;[3] To the people of the world;[4] To the people of the nations;[5] into parts of the world;[6] to the peoples of the world[6]

What is this "Divine gift of healing?" The answer lies in the larger question, "What are the gifts God has given to his people?" In 1 Cor. 12: 8-10,[8] Paul lists nine spiritual gifts. Below is a list, with scriptural references, which states that the following persons, among others, had these spiritual gifts:

1. Wisdom - Solomon (1Ki. 4: 29, 30, 34).
2. Knowledge - Peter (Acts 5: 1-11).
3. Faith – Abraham (Gal. 3: 14)
4. Healing - Jesus (Matt. 8: 16; 9: 35; 14: 14; Mk. 1: 34; 13; 4: 40; Lu. 9: 2).
   The Twelve (Matt. 10: 1, 8; Mk. 3: 15; Mk. 6: 7-13).
   The Seventy (Lu. 10: 1-20. Paul (Acts 28: 8).
5. Miracles- Stephen (Acts 6: 8). Philip (Acts 8: 5-7). Peter (Acts 5: 16). Barnabas (Acts 15: 12). Paul (Acts 19: 11).
6. Prophecy - Agabus (Acts 11: 27-29) The 4 daughters of Philip (Acts 21:8-10).
7. Discernment – Peter (Acts 8: 9-24).
8. Tongues – Upper Room people (Acts 2: 4). Paul (1 Cor. 14: 18).
9. Interpretation – Daniel (Dan. 2: 26-47; 4: 19-37).

As stated previously, the question here is not, "Healing gifts, do they, or do they not, exist today?" Rather, the question in the context of this chapter and book is, "Did the possessors of these gifts have the power and obligation to exercise these gifts?"

The Parable of the Talents answers that question. The ones that used the gifts were awarded and the one who did not was punished. Jesus allegedly sent "The angel of God" to WMB to bestow upon him a Divine Healing Gift. When someone receives a gift, it means it is theirs to have and to use. Peter received a gift of Divine Healing and thus he became a healer. Of course, Peter was not a healer, in and of, himself. God had endowed him as an Apostle, with gifts which included the gift of healing. WMB's motive in referring to Peter appears to be that this would make himself also a healer. He said,

> Oh, I hope you see it, friends, look. You see, it was God's gift. What now, I want to ask you, was it Peter done the healing?[9]

WMB understood this and *did* insinuate that it was Peter who did the healing. Peter exercised his gift in great confidence in Him who bestowed it. For WMB to make Peter's healing gift a *Divine* Healing Gift is redundant. By definition only God gives Divine gifts. Peter gave from what he was given unto the man at the Gate Beautiful, and Scripture says:

> Then Peter said, Silver and gold have I none; but such as I have give I thee: In the name of Jesus Christ of Nazareth rise up and walk (Acts 3: 6).

This man wanted alms, but Peter did not give them. This is what Peter would have sounded like, had he spoken in the manner of WMB:

> You believe with all your heart? I can't heal you. Laying here in this stretcher, cots. I can't heal you, but if God will reveal to me what's your trouble, will you accept it? You will?...If you want to believe Jesus Christ...I can't heal you, but you can't hide your life now. But if you will do as I tell you, as God's servant, you'll rise up from there in the Name of Jesus Christ, and go home. I know you think you can't walk, but you can.[10]

Peter did not say, "I have a divine gift of healing, but that won't heal you.[11] This divine gift of healing is only to build up your faith[12] because it is YOUR faith that heals you. No man, not even Jesus Himself could heal you."[13] There is no record of Peter praying about it! He simply gave what he had to an expectant man. The Apostle Paul also had the Gift of Healing. What did Paul do? Well, he healed people. Paul too, did not tell people he could not do it, he just healed them.

> And it came to pass, that the father of Publius lay sick of a fever and of a bloody flux: to whom Paul entered in, and prayed, and laid his hands on him, and healed him (Acts 28: 8).

WMB said healing was *not* his gift. What then was it that this angel conferred upon him? What was that double portion of the power to heal that would be given to him?[14] WMB said he was given a gift of healing for the nations. If healing was NOT his gift, what then was his gift? Here is a list he himself provided; Praying for the sick;[15] Gift of visions;[16] Gift of prophecy;[17] Gift of discernment;[18] Gift of revelation.[19]

We see in Scripture that Joshua was fully aware of *his* gifting and operated them confidently, which included commanding the sun to stand still. WMB acknowledged that to be true. He said that Joshua stood in the line of duty and made the sun stand still.[20] Why would WMB, standing in the line of healing, deny having the ability to heal if, as he alleged, he received the gift of healing? This is a contradiction which makes WMB's claim invalid.

1. WMB's denial of being a healer would deflect all consequences for any non-healings away from his person. He said, "I cannot heal you;" "only God heals;" "your faith heals,"[21] etc. If, on the other hand, a healing would occur, it would strengthen his position. In reality, to whom did WMB attribute healing?

    a. WMB said it was God alone who healed.[22] The problem here is WMB's concept of God. Who is God, in WMB's teaching? WMB taught that man is God and God is man.[23] This teaching is found in Mormonism[24] as well as in Eastern and New Age religions. In fact, WMB taught that God is in all.[25] This teaching is called Pantheistic Monism, which is popularly called, "All is One, One Is All, All is God." This teaching is contrary to Christianity. WMB taught a non-scriptural concept of God and this must be rejected. (Deu. 11: 28).

    b. WMB said it was the Holy Spirit.[26] If, as WMB taught, healing was in the Atonement, then it could not have been the Holy Spirit, because the Holy Spirit never died to purchase humankind's salvation. WMB's own teaching also contradicted that when he said that the Holy Spirit departed from Christ in the Garden of Gethsemane, so Christ could die as a man.[27] If Jesus was just a man when He died, there is no Kinsman Redeemer and all mankind is still in sin. This is heresy and must be rejected. Of course, WMB said that mankind was purchased by the Blood of God, quoting Acts 20: 28. In WMB's "theology" God has a body, just like a man and would presumably have blood.[28] However, WMB also made it clear that *Jesus* was the Blood of God, or the offspring of God.[29] Thus, WMB's claim that we are healed by the Holy Spirit is contradicted by his own teaching. Any internal contradiction makes the teaching invalid.

    c. WMB said it was the spirit within a person which performed the healing.[30] This is a dangerous teaching. WMB also said that this spirit within a person is an eternal spirit and makes one part of God.[31] This is heresy. God is without Potentiality, which means that God cannot change. If people, upon becoming Christians, become part of God, then God has changed. This is a very old heresy. WMB here taught another God.

d. WMB said it was the angel of God,[32] whose picture appeared as a halo-like over WMB's head and who did the healing.[33] This photo has been sufficiently dealt with elsewhere. WMB himself contradicted the angelic healing claim and said the Angel has nothing to do with the healing.[34] This contradiction, of course, makes WMB's claim invalid. Last, but not least, WMB believed, as in the above,[35] the angel that stirred the waters of Bethesda as being the same angel in his ministry.[36]

e. WMB also stated, referencing John 5: 18-21, that it was Jesus who healed, but not in and of Himself, it was the Father healing through Him.[37] The Scripture does not quite state what WMB alleged (Jn. 8: 26- 29). WMB missed the context and this opens up a whole new interpretation. He taught that Jesus was anointed with the Holy Spirit[38] which made Him God.[39] However, the anointing of Jesus did *not* make Him God. WMB's teaching subtly undermined the Person of Jesus and His Godhood.[40] WMB stated he himself also completely surrendered himself to God.[41] WMB thus became omnipotent,[42] which would have made him God, or a god.[43] Others, according to WMB surrendered completely and they were gods as well.[44] This teaching makes Jesus a kind of Avatar, or part of a succession of incarnations of a Deity. This then becomes something to which others can also aspire. This teaching too, is heresy.

2. WMB's denial of being a healer would make it appear that he was a man of simplicity and humility which, in turn, would enhance his credibility. WMB based his denial of being a healer upon a faulty understanding of Scripture. As shown earlier, Jesus did not become a god, or God, at his baptism in Jordan. Jesus was God in flesh. Contrary to WMB,[45] Jesus, as God, healed the sick, (Matt. 8: 7; Matt. 12: 13; Jn. 4:46-50), just like he forgave sin, in and of himself(Matt 9: 2-7) and judged in and of himself (John 5: 22). When Jesus bestowed gifts of healing(s) upon anyone, they had the power to heal in "Jesus Name," or by His authority (Acts 1: 8).

3. WMB's denials caused the insidious belief that WMB was more than a man. As was stated earlier, WMB made claims that inferred that man was a god; the prophet was god;[46] a fully surrendered man was omnipotent, etc.[47] This teaching[48] ultimately led to the belief that people, including his own wife and children, believed him to be Jesus Christ.[49] This author himself was told exactly that, by one of Branham's own family members. Oh, it supposedly upset WMB when he found out that some people really believed that he was the Lord.[50] He prayed and said, "What have I ever done, Lord,

to deserve this?⁵¹ He stated that people came and repented of this error. Yet WMB, until his death, continued to preach the same "ambiguity," *if* it was that. One of the strong ambiguities was WMB's parallel of Abraham's angelic visit. He'd speak about the angel (who was Christ, he said) revealing Sarah's thoughts in the tent behind him. WMB would turn his back to patients on the platform and tell them the "secrets of their hearts."⁵²

This author met people back in 1972, believing and preaching WMB was the Lord, and even baptizing in his name, or having been baptized in WMB's name.

To what extent is William Branham's claim of Divine healing supported by Biblical revelation? WMB said he never claimed to heal, his gift was only there to encourage faith for healing. His faith for healing did not require faith in God. In fact, it was faith in faith that affected healing. To no extent is William Branham's claim of Divine healing supported by Biblical revelation, nor by his own messages.

Notes - Chapter Twelve

1. *Infallible Proof Of The Resurrection*, "All healing is Divine healing."
2. *Faith Is The Substance*.
3. WMB, *At Thy Word, Lord*, Mar. 05, 1948, Phoenix, AZ.
4. *Gifts And Callings Are Without Repentance*.
5. *Obey The Voice Of The Angel*.
6. *Early Spiritual Experiences*.
7. WMB, *Get The People To Believe*, Jul. 17, 1952, Hammond, IN.
8. "For to one is given by the Spirit the word of wisdom; to another the word of knowledge by the same Spirit; 9 To another faith by the same Spirit; to another the gifts of healing by the same Spirit; 10 To another the working of miracles; to another prophecy; to another discerning of spirits; to another divers kinds of tongues; to another the interpretation of tongues." 1 Cor. 12: 8-10
9. *Faith Is The Substance*, Oakland
10. *Healing Of Jairus' Daughter*. See also: WMB, *Jairus And Divine Healing*, Feb. 16, 1954, Wood River, IL, "I could not heal you; you know that. I'm just a man, but your faith is what would heal you...If I, by the Holy Spirit, by a Divine gift, and the love of God can see what God would say something for you, then surely, it'd take all doubt away, and you'd believe with all your heart. Would you do it?"
11. WMB, *Show Us The Father*, Jun. 25, 1955, Zurich, SW, "Jesus said, before He went away, 'The same things that I do, that is what the Father shows Me, you'll do also.'...Now, I believe He's here with this people. And just as a Divine gift, it does not heal anyone; it only raises their faith to a place so you can accept your healing, the same thing as preaching the Word. But if Jesus will come here now and do the same things that He did when He was here

on earth, will it encourage you so that you can go home and know that He's raised from the dead?"

[12] *Ministry Explained*. "Now, remember, the signs does not heal; the signs raise faith to heal. But only through faith is it healed. Do you understand? See, see? Signs only works faith …Now, gifts and callings does not heal you. Gifts and callings stimulates faith… Faith is what heals you."

[13] *Blind Bartimaeus*, San Jose, "Jesus didn't heal people; He only healed as God showed Him to heal. How many knows that? Saint John 5:19. 'The Son can do nothing but what He sees the Father doing.'"

[14] *I Was Not Disobedient*.

[15] WMB, *The Children Of Israel*, Nov. 23, 1947, Phoenix, "My gift is to pray for the sick and the afflicted."

[16] WMB, *Jesus Christ The Same Yesterday, Today And Forever*, Jan. 16, 1955, PM, Chicago, IL, "My gift is seeing visions."

[17] WMB, *Hear Ye Him*, Jan. 26, 1958, Waterloo, IA, "But my gift is a prophetic gift."

[18] *Be Certain Of God*, Cleveland, "But my gift of God…He's given me a gift of discernment… And not one time has it ever failed. That has to be God."

[19] *God Revealing Himself To His People*. "But my gift of God is only to tell you what is wrong with you, and what you can do to be healed. Now, if I'll do that, will you believe with all your heart?"

[20] *Paradox*, Tampa, "Whatever God did, I don't know. But the sun stood still, the moon over Ajalon, because a man, a human being, a human being was in the line of duty. In the line of duty, he commanded the sun to stand still. And if we're Christians, we have to believe this to be the infallible Word of God, everywhere. He stopped the world, stopped the sun. Whatever He did, it stood still for twenty-four hours. I believe it."

[21] *God Hath A Provided Way*, "This healing, you must have faith. It's called faith healing."

[22] *As The Eagle Stirreth Up Her Nest*, Chautauqua, "Now, no one can heal. God is the Healer, and it's already did. It's just to prove your faith in God. It's called 'Faith healing,' your healing."

[23] *Messiah*, Shreveport, "When God made man in Genesis 1:26 it shows, if you're putting that Scripture down, Genesis 1:26, it shows that God made man to be a god to begin with. Man was made to be a god, a lesser god, he was made in the image and likeness of God. He had hands like God; he had feet like God, eyes, ears, and intelligence like God, his whole fibre, because he was a son of God…There's something about a man, he is a god, he was made to be a god, his purpose here on earth was to be a god, to have a dominion over everything in the earth. Oh, my. Now, don't let that stagger you, 'cause I got some

more Scriptures wrote down here, see?...He's fashioned like a god, he looks like God, sure was. That's the reason God was man, man was God."

[24] Joseph Smith Jr., *Teachings of the Prophet Joseph Smith*, ed. Joseph Fielding Smith, 4th ed. (Salt Lake City: The Deseret News Press, 1943) 345, 346. "God himself was once as we are now, and is an exalted man, and sits enthroned in yonder heavens."

[25] *Mary's Belief*, Jan. 21, 1961, Beaumont, "Do you know the very dirt that you're sitting on is the manifestation of the Word of God?...So the chair that you're setting on is the Word of God. This earth that the floor rests on is Word of God. All these things are from the dust of the earth, the Word of God. And you, yourself, are the Word of God. That's right. Then why can't that little heart in there begin to move all the doubt out of this thing here. Let it be."

[26] WMB, *Works That I Do Bear Witness Of Me*, Apr. 13, 1951, Phoenix, "And I know the Holy Spirit is here now to heal the people."

[27] *It Is The Rising Of The Sun*, "The Spirit left Him, in the Garden of Gethsemane. He had to die, a man."

[28] *Teaching On Moses*, "When God made man in Genesis 1:26 it shows, if you're putting that Scripture down, Genesis 1:26, it shows that God made man to be a god to begin with. Man was made to be a god, a lesser god, he was made in the image and likeness of God. He had hands like God, he had feet like God, eyes, ears, and intelligence like God, his whole fibre, because he was a son of God...Jesus referred to him as god."

[29] WMB, *Jesus Christ, The Same Yesterday, Today And Forever*, Aug. 10, 1952, PM, Chicago, IL, "And Jesus was the Blood of God."

[30] *Power Of Transformation*, "Let the Holy Spirit come upon any person that's truly got something down there to...a healing comes from the inside, let that healing come from the spirit that's in you."

[31] *Why Are We Not A Denomination?* "So if you're a part of God, the Spirit that's in you never had a beginning or it never will have an end, and you're eternal with the Spirit that's in you."

[32] *Expectation*, New York, "And may the angel of God...be here tonight to heal the sick and afflicted...the Spirit of God. He is the healer."

[33] *Ministry Explained*, "How many's ever seen the picture?...That's the One that does the healing. Not I myself; I'm just a channel. Like the pool of Bethesda, it--it wasn't the water that healed ; it was the angel on the water that done the healing. It's not man that heals; it's the Spirit of God on the man that does the healing."

[34] *Angel Of God*, Toledo, "And with His stripes we were healed ...It's in Christ and not in me, or not in the angel of God. This angel of God has nothing to do with the healing, only to vindicate what Almighty God has done for you, according to your faith. The angel does not heal; It only shows and sees visions."

[35] *Ministry Explained*.

³⁶ WMB, *Looking For Jesus*, Feb. 28, 1954, PM, Phoenix, AZ.

³⁷ _____, *Would See Jesus*, Dec. 05, 1954, Binghamton, NY, "[T]he Son can do nothing in Himself, but what He sees the Father doing.'...'The Father worketh and I worketh hitherto.' In other words, 'I can do nothing as the Son of God.'...said, 'I can do nothing.' He didn't claim to be a healer. Said, 'It isn't Me that does the work. It's My Father that dwelleth in Me; He doeth the works.' ...He said, 'I can do nothing except My Father shows...This may shock just a little. But Jesus Christ, the Son of God, never performed one miracle without first seeing a vision of it, or He told something wrong there. He said, 'The Son can do nothing in Himself, but what I see the Father doing.'" Note: Scripture has no record of Jesus having visions of his Father doing things and then Jesus copying what he saw. – PMD.

³⁸ *Sardisean Church Age*, "And Jesus was anointed with the Holy Ghost, went about doing good. Is that right?"

³⁹ WMB, *The Church And Its Condition*, Aug. 05, 1956, Jeff., IN, "And John said, 'I bare record, seeing the Spirit of God like a Dove coming down, and abiding on Him.' ... when God and Man became one. That's when heaven and earth embraced each other. Hallelujah. That's when God was made flesh...that's when God came down from the Spirit form and was made a Man and dwell among us. That's when all eternity embraced each other. That's when the human fallen race of Adam's people and Jehovah God and every angel come together, when God and man was made one on that great memorial day when John baptized Jesus."

⁴⁰ As another example, WMB always referred to sin as unbelief and connected that to Jesus saying, "Who can accuse me of unbelief? There at least appears to be an inference that Jesus, whatever he might or might not have done, he did not have unbelief. This, when applied to WMB, started an embryonic teaching that blossomed into the belief that WMB was the Lord.

⁴¹ WMB, *Testimony On The Sea*, Mar. 07, 1964, Dallas, TX, "I want you to know now that my heart is completely surrendered..."

⁴² WMB, *Patmos Vision (John's Patmos Vision)*, Dec. 04, 1960, PM, Jeff., IN, "Man is omnipotent. You don't believe that, but he is. A man that's fully surrendered to God is omnipotent."

⁴³ *What Is The Holy Ghost?* "I have completely surrendered every will and everything that I know of to the Lord."

⁴⁴ WMB, *Discernment Of Spirit*, Mar. 08, 1960, Phoenix, AZ, "Moses was a god. Joseph was a god. The prophets were gods. The Bible said they were. They were gods because it--they had completely surrendered themselves to the Spirit of God."

⁴⁵ *Looking For Jesus*, "Now, look. Now, He did not do the healing Himself then."

⁴⁶ WMB, *Revelation Of Jesus Christ*, Dec. 04, 1960, AM, Jeff., IN, "A prophet is the word. We know that. The word 'prophet' means 'a divine interpreter of the Word.' The

Divine Word is wrote, and the prophet has the Divine Spirit of God within him. And, you know, the prophet in the Old Testament was called 'god.'"

⁴⁷ WMB, *Led By The Spirit*, Apr. 07, 1959, Los Angeles, CA, "I have a gift. It's the gift of the Holy Spirit. Then let the Holy Spirit so enshroud us with His power, until I won't know what I'm saying, and I'll be able to be so surrendered to Him, that He will speak through my lips and tell you the secrets of your heart like He did when He was here on earth…"

⁴⁸ _____, *God's Gifts Always Find Their Places*, Dec. 22, 1963, Jeff., IN, "Now, the same as now, they reject identified Deity. Do you get it? They will certainly put their name on a church book and say, 'I'll try to live by this creed.' They'll take an oath by this. But when it comes to accepting Deity, and expressing back the same kind of a gift like they did… that you are identified by your gift, that you give your entire being to it, to identified Deity. Then you identify yourself with the Deity, by giving all you are, what you are, to Deity Himself."

⁴⁹ Raymond M. Jackson, letter to Billy Paul Branham, June 25, 1990, available from http://www.wmb1.com/portico/modules.php?name=News&file=article&sid=66, (Accessed June 03, 2010). "Now after almost 25 years since Bro. Branham's departure, you still cater to men who hold Bro. Branham as being Jesus Christ, Lord, or God. I well remember the Sunday that Bro. Branham preached on the "Bruised Serpent." How he condemned that spirit that wanted to make him Jesus Christ. Then that afternoon these men all came and parked in the driveway of his home and were suppose to have repented to him of that. Now almost 25 years later some still go on believing tat (sic). And you go along with that, plus a lot of other things that some men teach. Not one time have you reached out to touch them, or corrected them."

⁵⁰ WMB, *Revelation Chapter Five, #1*, Jun. 11, 1961, Jeff., IN, "…when it comes to be calling anointed Christ, or something, that was too much for me. So I just couldn't stand that… After leaving the meeting at Canada, I found out that way up in the Eskimos or the Indians up there, it had got among them…And I wondered; if it would've been some enemy of mine, it would been all right, but I would just have laughed at it and went on; but when it come to being precious brothers, precious sisters, then that's what hurt me."

⁵¹ Ibid.

⁵² WMB, *Mark Of The Beast And The Seal Of God # 1*, Feb. 16, 1961, Long Beach, CA, "The angel of the Lord set with his back turned…I hope you all get this. I am not the angel of the Lord; I'm William Branham. I'm your brother. But he was dwelling in human flesh then that he created himself and just disappeared. Do you believe that? Now, do you believe that was God? The Bible said it was God. Abraham said it was…my back turned, if I call her name, maybe she'd understand. Mrs. Hanson, stand up and receive your healing…Was those things true, lady? Are we strange to one another? If it is, wave your hand like this. Was all true, was it? Then the same angel of God that was setting there at Sodom and Gomorrah to give a sign to Abraham that the hour was drawing close for the burning of Sodom, is here tonight."

Chapter Thirteen

HEALING MINISTRY

To what extent is William Branham's ministry
of Divine healing supported by
Biblical revelation?

This chapter will focus primarily on the healing ministry of WMB. Within this context, the healings are attributed to faith. This faith was triggered, enhanced, or built up, by the "revelations" that WMB claimed came to him via his angel standing by him. Ronald Kydd lists a number of Modalities of healing, one of which he calls the Revelational Model. Kydd, under this model, discusses the ministry of WMB. This is what he says regarding WMB,

> However one assesses his work, it must be acknowledged that he did much to foster a very wide spread expectation that God could be counted on to heal miraculously. This led to an international healing movement in which thousands of people were caught up…A major inspiration for the ongoing ministry of healing evangelism was William Branham.[1]

This author agrees with Kydd's excellent summation of WMB's ministry and accomplishments, but he does so with a strong caveat. When Kydd says negatively, "However one assesses [WMB's] work," he acknowledges that not all was well in WMB's wonderland. Kydd then follows up with a very positive statement, "[I]t must be acknowledged that…" It appears that Kydd acknowledges the rest to be commendable, and here appears the problem. This is not to suggest that Kydd's statement is purposely ambiguous. No, Kydd's ambiguity is due only to the assumption that the "healing entity," spoken of in the context of WMB's ministry, is the God of Creation and Scripture. Christians, whether pro or anti Charismata, will not dispute that God heals. However, having been involved in WMB's message as a leader, and after 40 years of research, this author can unequivocally state that WMB did a lot to create a worldwide delusion that "God," (WMB's god) could be counted on to heal. Through WMB's constant claims of being commissioned by an angel of God; by his claims of having this angel on the platform with him; by his claims of this angel revealing people's conditions to him; by his claims that this angel would heal ALL their diseases, including Cancer, WMB was able to create an expectancy within the people that was, if nothing else, hypnotic. The masses believed it was God and, as Kydd states, "This led to an international healing movement in which thousands of people were caught up...A major inspiration for the ongoing ministry of healing evangelism was William Branham."

For WMB, the "entity" affecting the healing was FAITH, not God. WMB's god was not the Triune God of the Bible, whom he described as the, "three unclean spirits like frogs..." (Rev. 16: 13). WMB's god, among other things, was the god of nature, which god he served since young. WMB claimed he knew God from nature before he ever even read a page from Scripture.[2] He stated that he was glad that God got a hold of him before the church did.[3] This contradicts Scripture which states God's Church is the Pillar and Ground of Truth (1 Tim. 3: 15).

WMB did not attribute healing to Jesus, but to the healing power resident in man. WMB's healings were thus not miraculous at all. This healing power could be triggered by faith. This faith was not the faith described in Scripture, but a belief system, which he called a number of unscriptural things, listed in an earlier chapter. For WMB, faith was a quantifiable substance, of which one needed a certain amount to get results. He said that if people could not muster up enough faith for healing, how could they expect to be in the Rapture?[4] This is not a Scriptural example of faith. The ones Jesus raised from the death, Lazarus, the young man of Nain and Jairus' daughter, did not get raised from the dead by *their* faith at all. It was accomplished by a power not resident within *them*. The power that healed them from the ultimate sickness, that of death, was resident in Christ. James states the faith of the elders brought healing, not the faith of the recipient.

The above is this author's assessment of WMB's faith healing ministry. Yes, WMB's ministry did lead to an international movement, in which thousands of people were caught up. Millions of people are still caught up in WMB's movement, besides all the other healing and spin-off movements of today. Jesus said, "Ye shall know them by their fruits." (Matt. 7: 15-17). The test of time has shown the fruits of the healing revival. "How are the mighty fallen!" Time and space do not allow a listing of all the big names of that period which have fallen into error, sin and shame. Sad to say, these fruits have brought, and are continuing to bring, great reproach upon Christ and His Church.

Two Signs like Moses

WMB, as discussed, claimed to have been visited by an angel of God, who commissioned him to bring a healing gift to the nations.[5] It has already been established what kind of claim this constituted. Therefore, for those who have already concluded that WMB was not who he claimed to be, this exercise is really redundant. Many still follow WMB as a prophet, so his claims will be examined further. WMB, contrary to all his later claims, early on spoke only of having received one gift. This gift would help him discern diseases called germs[6] through vibrations in his hand.[7] In WMB's first message he mentioned that Moses himself was actually God's gift to Israel,[8] as was Elijah.[9] WMB strongly inferred that he, like Moses and Elijah, was God's gift to America[10] and the nations. He hoped that people would see that written between the lines.[11] WMB made a reference to his birth in this regard, which was not too subtle.[12] WMB believed he was that gift of divine healing to the world.

WMB never mentioned two signs until Apr. 05, 1950,[13] three years since the commencement of his 1947 healing campaigns. WMB's messages on Moses, apparently gave him the idea to appropriate two signs just like Moses. That is how he continued to present it. In 1954 he called them the two gifts,[14] or the two miracles.[15]

According to the biblical account in Ex. 4, the rod becoming a serpent was the first sign. It was performed in order to establish the identity of Moses as the servant of Yahweh. (Ex.4: 5). It signified Moses was the ambassador of God's Kingdom and as such he had dominion over Pharaoh's domain. Moses destroyed the serpents, which were representative of Egypt's gods. The magicians used trickery, not supernatural power to accomplish their rods turning into Cobras. One commentary states:

> **11. Then Pharaoh also called the wise men and the sorcerers,** etc.—His object in calling them was to ascertain whether this doing of Aaron's was really a work of divine power or merely a feat of magical art. The magicians of Egypt in modern times have long been celebrated adepts in charming serpents; and particularly by pressing the nape of the neck they throw them into a kind of catalepsy, which renders them stiff and immoveable - thus seeming to change them into a rod…Just the same trick was played off by their ancient predecessors, the most renowned of whom, Jannes and Jambres (II Tim. 3: 8), were called in on this occasion…
>
> **12. but Aaron's rod swallowed up their rods**—This was what they could not be prepared for, and the discomfiture appeared in the loss of their rods, which were probably real serpents.
>
> **14. Pharaoh's heart is hardened**—Whatever might have been his first

impressions, they were soon dispelled; and when he found his magicians making similar attempts, he concluded that Aaron's affair was a magical deception, the secret of which was not known to his wise men.[16]

The magicians were masters of trickery, though exposed by the power of God.

The second sign involved the hand of Moses turning leprous and then the hand became flesh again. (Ex.4: 5). It surely established Yahweh's power over all creation. Jannes and Jambres duplicated neither the first sign nor the second. The rejection of both these signs triggered the Ten Plagues upon the enemies of God.

WMB's first sign was a vibration in his hand,[17] which would tell him what kind of disease it was. This is in contrast with Moses' first sign, which was designed to establish supreme authority over magic. No one could copy it. In WMB's case this is not so. His "sign" was a diagnostic that others also possessed. Oral Roberts, of Cherokee blood, too used his hand to detect diseases. This kind of diagnostic is also seen among psychic healers, as well as among Native American healers, such as Apache, Cherokee and Navajo,

> There are many types of Navajo diagnosticians. One can go to a traditional hand trembler who diagnoses through personal connections with vibrations of natural forces. Hand tremblers use energies of certain stars as well as the energy and wisdom of the horny toad and thunder. The vibrations that come to the hand trembler in response to questioning lead to diagnosis of the cause and potential resolution of the patient's problem. [18]

WMB's Great-grandmother, Malissa Jane Smith Branham, was full blood Cherokee. He would go with her to the reservation and attend Snake Dances and Corn Dances and such. He observed the Witch-doctors first hand.[19] There is no mention of hand trembling in Scripture, and to be found outside of Scripture is a dangerous place to be. The fact that the phenomenon can be duplicated would suggest some kind of trick. This actually makes sense, because WMB, at first, had to guess before he finally figured out how this method worked.[20] This does not correspond with Moses' first gift, although, as Jamieson, Fausset, and Brown suggest, the magicians had time to practice their trick before performing it. Guessing is not a spiritual gift. Guessing also indicates that WMB occasionally guessed wrong. That is also not the Holy Spirit. It appears WMB's gift, unlike as Moses' gifts, came without instructions. The second sign WMB mentioned was that of knowing the secrets of a person's heart.[21] Again, this does not correspond to Moses' second sign.

> He said, "You'll be given two signs as the prophet Moses was given two signs, to get the people to believe you is the really the issue." He said, "One of them was detecting diseases just by holding the person's right hand in your left." He said, "Then if you'll be sincere, it shall come to pass that you'll tell the very

secrets of their hearts, and the things that they are doing wrong, to build the faith in the people to be in faith and to vindicate you that I, God will send it to you."[22]

WMB claimed this gift became operative in Regina, Saskatchewan, Canada, in 1949. This was what occurred, according to WMB:

> I said, "He told me, 'If you'll be sincere (See?), then it will come to pass that you'll tell the people the very secrets of their hearts, and the things that they have done in their life that's wrong, and so forth, if you'll be sincere with what I give.' Did I say that? How many remembers me saying that? Well, that has come to pass...Regina, Saskatchewan...about three months ago."[23]

There is no tape recording of what happened in Regina in 1949, WMB's word is all there is for this claim. WMB did start employing the "gift of discernment" in the 1950s. The gifts, according to WMB were the bait,[24] within which was contained the hook that brought faith to the people.[25]

The 1947 WMB healing campaigns did not produce healings in the magnitude claimed by WMB. Walter Hollenweger, the famed Pentecostal historian said,

> Branham filled the largest stadiums and meeting halls in the world. He was reported in the newspapers, sometimes favorably, often critically, and in fact in most cases unfavourably...by contrast to what he [WMB] claimed, only a small percentage of those who sought healing were in fact healed... As a matter of fact, 'The convincing miracles of God, the true evidence of his Spirit and power were absent.'[26]

Gift of Discernment

Many healers claim to employ the gift of knowledge, or discernment. WMB, before praying for the sick, often referred to the Scripture where Jesus "calls out" Nathanael and said,

> Behold an Israelite indeed, in whom is no guile! 48 Nathanael saith unto him, Whence knowest thou me? Jesus answered...Before that Philip called thee, when thou wast under the fig tree, I saw thee. 49 Nathanael answered and saith unto him, Rabbi, thou art the Son of God; thou art the King of Israel (Jn. 1: 47- 49).

The above is Scripture and is therefore true. Jesus had the gift of discernment and therefore he did discern. WMB too, claimed he had the gift of discernment, but did he employ this gift? A thing of note is that Jesus never explained what He was doing, He just did it. WMB spent much time speaking about how the religious leaders accused Jesus of casting out Satan by the power of Satan. Why would WMB refer so often to Jesus being called Beelzebub, a fortune teller, a witch? It appears that WMB worked hard to find acceptance. He tried hard to assuage people's fears by showing parallels between Jesus' ministry and his own. WMB stated he was not mindreading,[27] but perceiving thoughts; reading their hearts, or contacting their spirits, just like Jesus did.[28] On the other hand, WMB did say that the Holy Spirit, the Fortune teller,[29] and magicians also performed these kinds of things.[30] It is confusing because he often contradicted himself. This is how this looks:

- No spiritualist or telepathist preaches the Gospel[31]
- <u>The Devil impersonates everything God has</u>[32]
- Internal contradiction. Statement is invalid.

Consequently, in WMB's scheme there are three options regarding discernment,

- God reads minds
- Satan reads minds
- A Magician can employ "magic" and seemingly read minds

God reads minds.

How does God read our minds? Christians do experience that their hearts and minds are an open book to God.(Jer 20: 12a NLT; Heb. 4: 11- 13 NLT). It is normal for the Christian to experience God's correction. The Holy Spirit will guide into all truth by His Word, the Bible, and will expose falsehood in the lives of His people (Jn. 16: 13). After all, "All scripture is given by inspiration of God, and is profitable for doctrine, for reproof, for correction, for instruction in righteousness…" (2 Tim. 3: 16). A preacher will bring his sermon and, even unbeknownst to him, something he says might pierce someone's conscience and bring God's conviction, correction and repentance, etc. This also occurs through personal reading of the Bible. If a preacher can experience this, can others also? Yes, it is called spiritual discernment. Christians may have that gift. To sum up, God can discern hearts by various means, either directly, through his word, through Bible reading and through one of God's servants.

Satan reads minds.

WMB said that Satan could imitate most anything God does.[33] Surely that cannot include Satan knowing the thoughts of men in the way God does. In fact, he contradicted that himself.[34] If Satan does not read our minds, how does he know our hearts? Well, Satan knows the Scriptures, as is seen during the temptation of Jesus. Satan knows the heart of man is desperately wicked and is full of iniquity. (Jer. 17: 9; Matt 15: 17-20a). Any parent understands and knows when a child has done something wrong. They know what a child will do, before it actually does it. How? They know their child's heart and inclinations. This, coupled with the child's expressions and body language, allows a parent to even predict their actions. It's not magic at all, just observable patterns in a child. This is the same with professionals, psychics, magicians, or faith healers, they seemingly read minds. There is no scriptural example that shows Satan can read thoughts and minds. Scripture only reveals that God knows every evil thought, imagination, our vain thought of our heart, (Gen. 6:5; Ps. 94: 11; 1 Chron. 28: 9; Jer. 17: 10a; Lu. 6: 8).

Magicians seemingly read minds

In order to be a Magician, a Psychic, or a healer, a person must be well informed about people. These people are highly trained in being very observant. They look for clues that could give away information without the "patient" knowing it. Part of their repertoire would include, but would not be limited to, knowing:

- Most common names
- Most common diseases
- Most illness are located in abdomen and chest area
- Most accents, speech, dress, shoes, accessories, jewelry, societal status.
- Facial, lip, eyes, head, hand and foot movements, from the patient and surrounding people, which focuses on *them* for the next trick
- Older people typically have lost loved ones, have arthritis, bad eyesight, diabetes, and other age related illnesses

Cold Reading

The healer (H), calls a dark haired woman (DW), who speaks English with an Irish kind of accent. He will ask if they have never met previously. He will spend some time in chit-chat. It is designed to relax the person, which helps him to build rapport and trust. It also lowers her defenses and increases the chance of her inadvertently giving away clues. After the chat this could follow:

H: You're not from around here. Correct? (Based on her Irish accent)
DW: Yes.
H: I see water. (This is called fishing. The healer is asking questions and looking at the woman for acknowledgment by some visual clue).
DW: Yes.
H: I see lots of water.
DW: Yes.
H: It's a sea.
DW: Yes.
H: You live on an island
DW: Yes.
H: You live in Newfoundland
DW: Yes.
H: Your name is Ma...Mar...Margaret, is that right? (Fishing for Mary, Margaret)
DW: Yes.
H: You're here for yourself.
DW: Yes. (her hand automatically went to the affected area, her stomach)
H: I see a man dressed in white...it's a doctor...I see him talking with you.
DW: Yes.

CHAPTER THIRTEEN 171

H: He gives you a piece of paper…it's a prescription…a referral to a specialist.
DW: Yes.
H: He told you he wants to look into your stomach through a little tube. This is called an endoscopy and it scares you.
DW: Yes.
H: It's an ulcer, isn't it?
DW: Yes.
H: Yes, if I told you where you lived would you believe me that you are healed?
DW: Yes.
H: Margaret O'Halloran. Return to 10 Corrigann Street, Gander, NLD and be well.

The above scenario is fictitious. How did the healer know the information? Possibly through a technique called hot reading, shown below.

Hot Reading

Hot reading is a technique where crucial "patient" information is gathered by the healer's helpers who greet the patients when they arrive. They are very friendly and engage in seemingly innocuous conversation to help the patient feel relaxed. During the course of the conversation the following is gleaned: Name of the person(s), address, why they've come, some past history, description of; tall or short, skinny or fat, clean-shaven moustache, beard, glasses, hair, skin color, accents, ethnicity, clothing worn, i.e., a red polka dot dress, a black hat; religious affiliation, etc. It is noted where they are sitting in the audience. When the healer starts his performance, he could employ a number of the cold reading type questions during the staging part. There are two scenarios. One is used for when the patient is in the audience. The other is where healer and patient are on the platform, as shown below:

H: We are strangers to each other, correct?
DW: Yes.
H: You're not from around here. Correct? (Based on card information)
DW: Yes.
H: I see water. The healer knows Chicago is on a lake.
DW: Yes.
H: I see lots of water. (Lake Michigan)
DW: Yes.
H: I see you in a store… Saks fifth Avenue? (Prada shoes and Dior handbag)
DW: Yes.
H: You live in Chicago.
DW: Yes.
H: You're here for yourself.
DW: Yes. (her hand automatically went to the affected area, her stomach)

H: I see a man dressed in white…it's a doctor…I see him talking with you.
DW: Yes.

H: He gives you a piece of paper…it's a prescription and a referral to a specialist.
DW: Yes.

H: He told you he wants to look into your stomach through a little tube. This is called an endoscopy and it scares you.
DW: Yes.

H: It's an ulcer, isn't it?
DW: Yes.

H: Yes, if I told you where you lived would you believe me that you are healed from this?
DW: Yes.

H: Margaret O'Halloran. Return to 12335 Lakeshore Drive, Chicago, and be well.

When cards are used the healer will have the patients come up in sequence. He may have ten of the cards memorized. This system is called mnemonics. The patients must stay in sequence or the system does not work. The other scenario would be when the patient is in the audience:

H: I can't see her with my eyes, but there is a lady on the balcony, the corner seat of row 3. Will the lady in the red polka dot dress wearing the black hat please stand. (lady stands up).

H: We are strangers to each other, correct?
DW: Yes.

H: You're not from around here. Correct? (Based on info received from helper)
DW: Yes.

H: I see water. (The healer knows Chicago is on a lake).
DW: Yes.

H: I see lots of water and it is very windy there, you once lost your hat, is that right?
DW: Yes.

H: It's…You live in Chicago.
DW: Yes.

H: I see a man dressed in white…it's a doctor…I see him talking with you…
DW: Yes.

H: He gives you a piece of paper…it's a prescription and a referral to a specialist.
DW: Yes.

H: He told you he wants to look into your stomach through a little tube. This is called an endoscopy and it scares you.
DW: Yes.

H: If I told you where you lived would you believe you are healed from this ulcer?
DW: Yes.

H: You would? Okay Margaret O'Halloran. Return to 12335 Lakeshore Drive, Chicago, and be well. You won't need the test.

CHAPTER THIRTEEN

There is no doubt, by this time the healer has established his credentials and the audience is ready and willing to believe anything the healer says. The audience is convinced that the healer is a true psychic and can read their minds. The question is, "Which option was demonstrated during WMB's healing campaigns?"

- God reads minds – Possibly
- Satan reads minds – No, except in the sense of magic, see below.
- A Magician can employ "magic" and seemingly read minds.

A Typical WMB healing campaign

Staging

The following is a snapshot of what went on in a typical WMB campaign. Prayer cards have been handed out and WMB is on the platform. WMB takes some time making his patients feel at home. This is the staging period. WMB explained what is happening in the prayer line, "…standing here at the platform just now, as he walked up, I felt a welcome spirit. I said, 'You're a Christian believer.' Now, that's the same Spirit that said through our Master to Nathanael.[35]

> Talk about mental telepathy…My, it's the power of Jesus Christ in His promise by His Word, that He said He would do these things in the last days…He was called a spiritualist and a medium too (That is true), called Beelzebub. One time, there was a man came to Him by the name of Philip. And he got saved, and he went and got his brother Nathaniel.[36]

Again, "Nathanael looked at Him, said, 'When did You know me, Rabbi?' Said, 'Before Philip called you, when you were under the tree.'"[37] "Today, he'd probably said, 'Mental telepathy. A witch.' The Jews in them days called Jesus, because He could do that, and they said He was Beelzebub…the chief of the fortunetellers, the worst of all the devils. But He wasn't. He was the Lord Jesus, the same Jesus, the same God that was on the prophet."[38]

WMB, in creating the scenario for the prayer line, often brought up his background of being born in a small cabin in the hills of Kentucky, where his first angelic commission took place.

> Was born in a little mountain cabin in Kentucky, that light that you see on the picture, that the scientific research of the world has claimed it to be a supernatural Being, came in the room. It's been with me since I was a little boy, and it spoke to me.[39]

> Way back, back 'fore I was born, was foreordained to have a gift of Divine healing. And He came and told me in the room one night that God had sent the gift, and it was a gift of Divine healing for the people. And if I could get the people to believe me and would be sincere when I prayed, that nothing would stand before the prayer.[40]

> So, I tell the Truth. And if I spoke and said it was me, myself, I would be a liar…I speak

of Him and He is Truth. And He will testify it being true. If you people will pray and be sincere tonight, while the service is in session, if God will show me what's happened to you, I shall pronounce it...And I, as His servant, challenge each of you sick people tonight... There's a great many cards out here. We can only call a few to the platform, because under that anointing I only last so long.[41]

Now, someone might wonder when people come into the line, of knowing their diseases and their thoughts...I wouldn't know it but a few moments. If the angel of the Lord comes to me, it's God's gift.[42]

As seen above, WMB preps the people to understand that even though they have prayer cards, they might not be called. In Grassland, CA, he said that his son, Billy Paul Branham, handed out 500 prayer cards. He said that he would pray for *everyone*. However, no one was called out, there was no "word of knowledge" or "discernment, WMB just held a general prayer."[43] In Chicago, fifteen people were given cards but numbers 14 and 15 went missing. WMB prayed for only about 10 people with prayer cards and then he switched to the audience.[44] In Salem, OR, WMB said, "Do we have many prayer cards out? We got to make these...You know, we got to pray for them. Every person gets a prayer card gets prayed for."[45]

The use of Prayer Cards

In Port Alberni, British Columbia, Canada, WMB said,

My son, he came over a few moments ago, and he gives out prayer cards to pray for the sick. Usually we don't do that around the first night when it's going to be a big meeting, until we get everybody settled down till they understand...I believe Billy said he give out, how much? About fifty prayer cards?...and we've got two or three missing, but that'll be all right."[46]

However, it did not prove to be alright. Only 15 prayer cards were called and only two people were prayed for. This was a pattern which occurred often in WMB' healing campaigns. Whenever there was a mix-up with the cards, either he would not call people into a prayer line, or he would just pray for a few and switched to calling out people from the audience. Why? Because there was an inherent danger that WMB's credibility as a "seer" would have been, and indeed was, destroyed. Prayer cards, why were they needed? Why, if WMB's angel allegedly would go into the audience and call people out at random and divulge information regarding their name, address and illnesses? WMB stated they were used to increase people's faith.[47] In case of a baby, who cannot have faith, because it cannot understand what was said, WMB stated the mother's faith would be increased.[48] That raises issues.

CHAPTER THIRTEEN

Did that also mean that WMB was limited in his ability to pray for others who had certain limitations? Perhaps limitations that included mental conditions, catatonics, people in comas, dead people? There is proof that prayer cards were used because of the information written on them. The testimony of Rosella Griffith Martin[49] makes that quite clear. She received a prayer card from Billy Paul Branham, who asked her what was wrong with her. She told him she was an alcoholic, which he wrote on the card, she said.

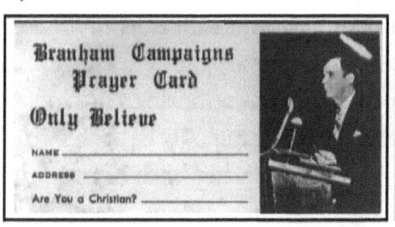

The above is a copy of the front of an actual *Branham Campaigns Prayer Card*. On the back it had a number and the patients would fill in their illnesses and particulars.[50] The back of *this* card was filled out by this author, because prayer cards would not be kept as records and are thus not available.

The Prayer Line

This is how a WMB prayer line appears to have worked. People came in and brought their previously handed out prayer cards, on which was recorded their personal information and their diseases.[51] Typically WMB's son, Billy Paul, would be in charge. There is strong evidence that WMB used mnemonics,[52] as demonstrated with the aforementioned Rosella Griffith Martin, whose card was filled out by Billy Paul Branham. How exactly this information was relayed to WMB is not yet clear, possibly Billy Paul used mnemonics, though other methods cannot ruled out. That it was not God bringing discernment mnemonics to WMB in the prayer lines is seen in the fact that WMB,

1. Kept the number of the prayer cards called, quite small, as discussed earlier.
2. Would not use cards when numbers were missing, or he'd stay shy of those missing.
3. Would get confused when cards got out of sync. He'd abandon the prayer line.
4. Would make many spelling mistakes with people's names, or other information. Simply human error, no angel or Holy Spirit was involved at all.
5. Would seldom use prayer cards in non-English settings due to the language barrier, except with English speaking patients.
6. WMB would often get stuck with pronouncing somewhat unusual names.

Some would have it that the discernment WMB employed, was through Occultism, or perhaps by Satanic discernment. As much as this would seem a reasonable solution, that would make it a "spiritual" discernment, which is not acceptable, because that would make Satan capable of discerning hearts. Some followers of WMB have expressed, to this author personally, that they would prefer Satanic discernment over a simple magic trick. However, WMB himself stated that Satan cannot discern people's hearts, nor can he read people's minds. It is always possible, of course, that Satan, or one of his minions, could have inspired the faith healer, in this case WMB, to employ magic tricks in order to "discern." Of course, as seen in Scripture, demons did discern Christ, or servants of Christ, though this is not under discussion here. It must be concluded there was no angel of God, nor a demon, that was with WMB on the platform. Therefore, it can only be a magic trick.

Even though WMB would always tell his subjects that they were strangers and had never met, he still could, or would, know *about* them. How? Somehow he read their cards. WMB did say that sometimes prayer cards were kept overnight to be prayed over for the next meeting. If he didn't know anything about them, why would he say, "Is this the person?"[53] Who else would they be? In the case of Ms. Rosella Griffith Martin, Billy Paul asked her what ailed her, he even wrote it on the prayer card. Besides Billy Paul, others also were involved in the process. WMB's managers, Leo Mercier, Gene Goad,[54] F.F. Bosworth,[55] Hall[56] and Ern Baxter,[57] et. al., also spoke with people and gave out prayer cards. Earlier it was explained that the greeters gathered information. Thus, even off the platform, and outside the prayer line, the healer would still use mnemonics as he turned to the audience and called people out,

> That woman setting right back there praying for her husband, red polka-dot dress on. If she'll believe with all of her heart, God will grant the request to her, if she'll just absolutely believe it. God bless you. I don't know the woman. She don't need no prayer card. Have you got one? You don't? You have a prayer card? You have one? Well, you don't have to use it. You don't have to come in the line. You just don't doubt…you can have what you said.[58]

WMB identified people as shown above, but sometimes confusion ensued:

> Your little friend setting there next to you, there, you believe me to be God's prophet? I mean the little lady in the back with the green dress on, setting next to the lady that…Raise up just a minute, lady. There's so many people believing. You right there, it's hanging over you. I thought it was on the little lady here with her hand reaching towards me. Stand up. He's wanting to tell you something, but I…There's so many people praying and such faith moving in the building. You're--you're real nervous for one thing. And you have trouble with your head, a head trouble. Isn't that right? And you, I see you writing or reading, isn't your name Amelia…?. Your address is number

CHAPTER THIRTEEN

> one Columbia Avenue, Hartsdale, New York. Your head trouble is finished, sister; your faith has healed you. Jesus Christ has made you whole.[59]

Since, according to WMB, the Holy Spirit revealed all the information to him, why would there be confusion? Why would this angel, whom WMB claimed was the Holy Spirit, or even Christ Himself, get confused in a meeting with a few hundred, or thousands, of people? If that were true, how can God be trusted to hear the millions of prayers that go up every nanosecond of every day, in every place on earth? It would follow that whatever was happening in the healing service was not of God at all. Since the Holy Spirit is not the author of confusion, and knows the name of any person, why did He not call the person's actual first name, instead of his initial B. as shown below?

> Sir, setting there with the prostate trouble…Is your name Mr. French? Isn't it? You… Yes, sir. Is that right? B. French, is that right? Raise up to your feet. I heard your name called by an Angel of God.[60]

This would be another indication that this was not the Holy Spirit, but simply a trick. The above is very revealing and important, information. This destroys WMB's credibility as a "seer" and exposes him for what he really was. If all healing comes from God, it would seem redundant to even judge anything regarding healing. If it is true, as WMB alleged, that God winks at people's ignorance and heals even through idols, what does that do to scriptures like Ex. 20: 3 and De. 5: 7?

Earlier, it was noted that WMB himself acknowledged there was no Apostolic tradition of the methods he employed.[61] If one is sick, let him call for the elders of the church, he said. This alone should be sufficient for all Christians everywhere to know that healing meetings with "discernment," and "angels" on the platform, are not an Apostolic tradition. Surely Paul, or the other Apostles, or Luke, the historian, would have mentioned any other method. Jesus sent his disciples out to preach the Gospel and to anoint for healing. WMB justified his actions by stating that even though something was not written in the Bible (Thus non-Scriptural), when WMB spoke it, it was to be accepted as true.[62] He defended it by saying that handkerchiefs were taken from Peter's body and that was nowhere else to be found in the Bible either.[63] There is a great need to be discerning. Followers of WMB would not for one moment believe any discernment to be genuine IF, or when, it happened outside of what is called "the message." That this was a difficult task WMB himself acknowledged:

> I remember when I was first converted and I begin to see the working of the Spirit and how that some could just impersonate the real genuine Holy Spirit into such a way…Why, it was just impossible to tell which was right and wrong hardly.[64]

As stated prior, according to WMB all the gifts of the Spirit can be impersonated.[65] If that is true, then good judgment must be shown when anyone claims to have gifts of prophecy, discernment, healing, etc. If one claims to be above scrutiny, there would appear to be even more reason to examine why someone would be beyond scrutiny.

Where would a person start in evaluating discernment? Besides Scripture and the Holy Spirit, one must employ what is called Ockam's Razor. William Ockam (1288 – 1348) was a philosopher who stated that when one is faced with a choice of two options, the simplest is typically correct. For example, if a magician produces an egg out of the air, a person is faced with a couple of choices. One, he created the egg out of nothing. Two, through sleight of hand, he created the illusion that he created it out of nothing. The second solution is the simplest and is therefore the most likely. How is Ockam's razor applied to the type of meeting as related above? First the two scenarios, or options, need to be established. One, cause is paranormal. Two, there is a natural explanation. Ockam's Razor would dictate the natural explanation to be the simplest, and, therefore, to be preferred. This argument is strengthened by the fact that, if the discernment were supernatural, the following things would not be required:

1. Prayer cards. They would be redundant. The supernatural agent would know who needed healing.
2. Place in prayer line. This would not be important. The supernatural agent would know, "who's who."
3. The prayer line. The line itself would not be important.
4. With God, or an angel of God, there will never be any mistakes, either in pronouncing, or knowing, the full name of any person, regardless of ethnicity. Neither would an angel ever have to spell any name of a street, city, state, or country. Angels also do not stutter, nor speak broken English, or use unfinished sentences, neither will the grammar be wrong.

If what is stated above is true, the implications of the discernment not being supernatural would, of course, be devastating to followers of truth. This is not necessarily true for "dyed in the wool" followers of WMB.

Who attends these meetings?

A large percentage of people attending healing meetings have psycho-somatic illnesses, according to the healers themselves. Throughout WMB's ministry he claimed that up to 80%[66] of his audience was nervous, or neurotic, a term now replaced by the word "hysteria," a form of mental illness. Then there are others with imaginary illnesses, and those under medical or psychiatric care. Their doctors know that, physically, there is nothing wrong with them. There are also people who have had a serious illness, like cancer, and live under the constant threat of a recurrence. When a healer tells them they have cancer, they are ready to believe him. Of course, when they do get another medical check-up and there is no cancer, they are convinced they were healed. When the healer pronounces someone healed, but there is no spontaneous observable result, he tells them to affirm their healing, as per instructions from the healer. The sad thing is they are not healed, and were never healed. Most die shortly after being pronounced healed.

What happens to all these people?

A typical healing service needs a momentum of expectation. Today, this is often done with music, or through singing certain songs, but the sure fire way is through miracles which must be of the kind that can be demonstrated. They are designed to increase people's faith to be healed. Here are the typical miracles employed by healers:

1. Opening the eyes of the blind
2. Opening the ears of the deaf
3. Making the lame walk

The patients selected do not have to be clued in to what is going on. The "healer" knows that blindness is not reserved for people who do not have eyes. Blindness is a condition that can be measured on a continuum from no sight to below normal sight. The healer already knows that the patient is legally blind. They will typically cover the blind person's eyes and cast out that spirit of blindness. Then they will hold up two fingers with their white shirt as a background and ask, "How many fingers do you see?" the answer is, of course, "two fingers."

The same goes for the deaf person. Again, deafness can be read from a continuum of hearing impaired to stone deaf. The healer will put his hands on the person's head while a finger from each hand covers the ear openings. The healer will ask the patient if he/she can hear what he is saying. They can't, of course, he's plugging their ears. He then will cast out a demon of deafness. Afterwards he will go behind the person and snap his fingers a few times and ask the person, "Can you hear this?" "Yes!" Also if the healer remains in front of the person he will, after casting out the demon, take his fingers out of the patient's ears and whisper something. Of course, they will hear.

The lame will walk. One of the most popular healings is lengthening someone's leg. They will have the patient sit down on a chair and have heir legs stretched out. The healer will pull the patient's shoe off by a couple of inches, so it appears to the audience that the far leg (hidden beyond the near leg) is longer. The healer prays and cast out a demon and slowly pushes the shoe back on. Both legs are now the same length and the atmosphere in the meetings is now hypnotic. People experience a feeling of euphoria and nothing seems impossible. Some people even get out of wheelchairs and claim healing. However, once the euphoria wears off, they "crash," and they are back to their old self. Some appear to get healed after time, just like they were promised. Often an illness just needs time to heal. Do people get healed spontaneously? Some do. No one should be amazed that when thousands of people are involved, the healer gets "lucky," and someone actually gets healed. It must also be acknowledged that God may smile upon people's ignorance and heal them. However, even when a genuine healing takes place, one might still not know what caused it. People will typically attribute healing to the last thing they tried.

To what extent is William Branham's ministry of Divine Healing supported by biblical revelation? WMB's healing campaigns, discernments, healing lines, prayer cards and his hot and cold reading, etc., are not found in Scripture. Jesus discouraged people from telling about being healed. WMB himself stated that what he did was wrong, but he continued because it worked. To no extent is William Branham's ministry of Divine Healing supported by biblical revelation.

Notes - Chapter Thirteen

1. Kydd. 180.
2. WM, *Choosing Of A Bride*, Apr. 29, 1965, PM, Los Angeles, CA, "Now, as we see that all of the natural thing is a type of the spiritual things, as we went through in our lesson this morning, as the sun and his nature. That was my first Bible. Before I ever read a page in the Bible, I knew God."
3. Ibid.
4. WMB, *Moses' Commission*, Jan. 10, 1950, Houston TX, "If you haven't got faith enough to believe for your sick body, how you going to have faith enough for the rapture?"
5. *Faith Is The Substance*, Oakland, "An angel came down into the room and told me that… back 'fore I was born, was foreordained to have a gift of Divine healing."
6. *Angel Of God*, "A cancer is a germ; a cataract is a germ; a tumor is a germ; tubercular is a germ… That's medical names, saying, 'cancer, cataract,' so forth like that. Jesus called them a devil."
7. *Moses' Commission*, "And said, 'That you might know, it'll come to pass that you'll take people by the right hand in your left.' And said, 'You'll feel the results of it, I call it vibrations, upon your hand. You'll become familiar with that. And you'll tell people all of their diseases, and what they've got in their body.'"
8. *Faith Is The Substance*, Oakland, "Moses was God's gift to Israel. You believe it?"
9. Ibid., "Elijah…was God's gift to Israel. You believe it?"
10. WMB, *Scriptural Signs Of The Time*, Apr. 10, 1964, Birmingham, AL, "But when He sends a sign and it's rejected, that generation goes into chaos. It always has. What if the people of America, tonight, would receive the sign of God in this last days?"
11. *Faith Is The Substance*, Oakland, "I hate to have to bring this out like this, friends, but I'm trusting you're getting between the lines of it."
12. Ibid. "There's…hundreds of thousands of precious saints of God suffering tonight. And they…cried for years for God to restore the gift of Divine healing to the church. And when God moved the orbits 37 years ago, and foreordained it and sent it, many hundreds of people are passing by without recognizing it, friends….God have mercy."
13. *Expectation*, New York, "He told me I'd be given two signs."

CHAPTER THIRTEEN

[14] WMB, *God's Provided Way Of Healing*, Jul. 19, 1954, Aft., Chicago, IL, "He said, 'There will be given to you…two gifts like was given unto Moses, and you'll perform these things. And by this, they will believe.'"

[15] _____, *Expectation*, Feb. 20, 1954, Wood River, IL, "He said, 'There'll be two signs given you, like was given to Moses to perform a miracle, two miracles.' And He said, 'By this they'll believe.'"

[16] Jamieson, Fausset and Brown, *Commentary Practical And Explanatory Of The Whole Bible*, (Grand Rapids, MI: Zondervan Publishing House, 1978, 1591 pp.).

[17] *How The Angel Came To Me*, "And He said, 'As the prophet Moses was given two gifts…' to vindicate his ministry…so are you given two gifts to vindicate your ministry." He said, "One of them will be that you'll take the person that you're praying for by the hand, with your left hand and their right," and said, "then just stand quiet, and there'll be a physical effect that'll happen on your body." And said, "Then you pray. And if it leaves, the disease is gone from the people. If it doesn't leave, just ask a blessing and walk away."

[18] Nancy C. Maryboy and David H, Begay, *Integral Health and Healing*, Ceremonial Healing, available from, http://media.noetic.org/uploads/files/s3_maryboybegay.pdf Accessed May 25, 2010).

[19] WMB, *Presuming*, Jun. 10, 1962, AM, Southern Pines, NC. "My mother…was a half Indian. I've been in the camps, and watched the witch doctors speak in tongues, and lay a pencil down, and it raise up and write in unknown tongues."

[20] *Moses' Commission*, "That was in operation. Not perfect, because I guessed at the diseases a whole lot. Because I didn't know how it felt. I'd feel a funny feeling; sometimes female trouble and cancer. I couldn't detect it…

[21] *Gifts And Callings Are Without Repentance.*

[22] WMB, *Gifts and Callings Are Without Repentance*, March, 1950, Carlsbad, NM.

[23] *Moses' Commission.*

[24] WMB, *Does God Ever Change His Mind About His Word?* Apr. 18, 1965, PM, Jeff., IN, "It's just the bait on the hook, you see. I show the signs of trying to show that God knows, in discernment, and knows the hearts of the people, and does these things. That's an evangelistic gift, just to stir the people."

[25] _____, *Ministry Explained*, Jul. 11, 1950, Minneapolis, MN, "God knows I know not what's wrong with you. But under the anointing, there's no one could come to this platform but what would be told just what was wrong with them, and what they…done in their life, maybe the cause of the sickness. Now, what that is for is to build the faith of the patient."

[26] Hollenweger. 354, 355.

[27] WMB, *At Thy Word*, Jul. 14, 1950, Minneapolis, MN, "I'm not reading your mind. But what you're thinking is, what am I going to tell *you.*"

[28] WMB, *Jesus Christ The Same Yesterday, And Today, And Forever*, Jonesboro, "Someone said the other day, said, 'Brother Branham, do you say Jesus was a mind-reader?' Sure. He perceived their thoughts. Call it whatever you want to."

[29] *Infallible Proof Of The Resurrection*, "What's the two words, what means the difference between mind reading or perceiving a thought?...It's both the same, but Jesus was using the power of God. The fortune-teller is of the devil."

[30] *Messiah*, Shreveport, "And now, if you can crack a glass of water because that you have a telepathy, a mental conception, and a certain power that you can put off by being a human being, a power of mental force that's unseen and unknown of only through that cycle...But that kind of a spirit--a human perverted, damned spirit, because you were fashioned in the image of God, what can you do when you let the God that fashions you come into you and control you? Amen. You can bring every promise of God to pass. Yes, sir. Every promise God promised will come to pass...Let God come in there, he can go back and bring the dead back."

[31] WMB, *God Is His Own Interpreter*, Feb. 05, 1964, Bakersfield, CA, "So that it'll get it out of your mind that I'm trying to say something to the woman, looking her in the face, or get all the things about telepathy or whatever you want to know. Anybody that knows about telepathy should have better sense than that...Did you ever see a telepathist preaching the Gospel? Did you ever see a spiritualist preaching the Gospel, doing signs and wonders, proclaiming Jesus Christ the same? No."

[32] *Manifestation Of Thy Resurrection*, "Jesus did not work through mental telepathy, as we call it today, but He read the people's mind. Do you believe that? The Scriptures said He did. He perceived their thoughts. Is that right? Well, what's perceiving a thought, perceiving what you're thinking of? Not these psychic readers out here, that's of the Devil. That's the Devil. Any fortune-tellers or psychic...But did you know the Devil impersonates everything that God has?... As Jannes and Jambres withstood Moses, so do these resist the truth."

[33] *Door Of The Door*, "Satan can impersonate most anything that God does." See also: WMB, *Debate On Tongues*, Aug. 07, 1960, Yakima, WA, "Satan can impersonate any of those gifts."

[34] WMB, *Seventh Seal*, Mar. 24, 1963, PM, Jeff., IN, "I'm planning on doing something, I know better than to tell anybody about it. Not that that person will tell it, but Satan will hear it. He can't get it in my heart there, as long as God's got it closed up with the Holy Spirit, so it's between me and God. He don't know nothing about it until you speak it, then he hears it."

[35] *My Commission*.

[36] WMB, *At Thy Word*, May 06, 1951, PM, Los Angeles, CA.

[37] *Manifestation Of The Spirit*.

[38] WMB, *Jesus On The Authority Of The Word*, Feb. 17, 1954, Wood River, IL.

39 WMB, *Church Of The Living God,* Jul. 27, 1951, Erie, PA.

40 *Faith Is The Substance,* Oakland.

41 *Church Of The Living God.*

42 *Gifts And Callings Are Without Repentance..*

43 *Super Sign,* Grass Valley," I'm going to call every person. Billy says there's five hundred prayer cards out in here. I'm going to pray for every one of them."

44 WMB, *Come And See,* Aug. 30, 1953, PM, Chicago, IL.

45 _____, *Behold, A Greater Than Solomon Is Here,* Jul. 21, 1962, Salem, OR.

46 *Sir, We Would See Jesus,* Port Alberni.

47 *Three Witnesses,* "Sir, you being a stranger to me, me, I knowing you not, and you knowing me not… there's perhaps something wrong with you. If there is, God can reveal that to me. And if He does, why…I know it would increase your faith."

48 *Led By The Spirit,* "How do you do? For you, or the baby? The Baby? Why, a little bitty tot; it couldn't understand anything that I'd say. What about you, as its mother? You believe that if God would let me know what's wrong with the baby, would it increase your faith?"

49 Rosella Griffith Martin, *Only Believe,* Vol. 6, No. 2, June 1993, 5. "After the service was dismissed, Billy Paul Branham, Brother William Branham's son came by with prayer cards for that evening's prayer line. He asked me if I wanted one, and I answered, "Yes." Then he asked me what was wrong and I said, "I'm an alcoholic." He wrote it on the card and handed it to me. The number on the card was J-27…That night Brother Branham's sermon was titled, 'Come, See A man'…After the preaching, Brother Branham began to call the prayer cards. He began with J-25, which meant that I was third in line. When I came before him, he immediately said that he saw me in darkness. He asked. 'Do you believe me to be God's prophet?' I replied, 'Yes, sir.' Then he questioned me, 'If God reveals to me what is the matter with you, and if Jesus heals you, will you serve Jesus the rest of your life?' Again I said, 'Yes, sir.' He looked at me and said, 'You're an alcoholic.'"

50 WMB, *Good Shepherd Of The Sheep,* Mar. 08, 1957, Phoenix, AZ, "Prayer card…On the back of it it's got a P, and on there it's got a number. We do that in order to keep people lined up; that's the only reason."

51 _____, *Believe Ye That I Am Able To Do This?* Aug. 20, 1950, PM, Cleveland, OH, "They bring the prayer cards up, and shuffle them out, hand them to each person and they write down their diseases."

52 _____, *Queen Of The South,* Feb. 08, 1958, South Bend, IN, "I like to preach to them about three nights and let them get their prayer cards and get them, hold them and wait and be in prayer and then start the healing service."

53 *Do You Now Believe?* Phoenix, "Is this the patient?" See also: WMB, *Deep Calleth To*

The Deep, Jun. 24, 1954, Washington, DC, "Is this the patient?"; *Who Is This?* Nov. 22, 1959, San Jose, CA, "…is this the patient? Is this one of the…All right. Lady, we don't know each other, but God knows us both…Your name is Benson, Beson, B-e-s-o-n."

54 WMB, *Hear Ye Him,* Sep. 30, 1956, Chicago, IL, "Now, the prayer cards will be given out at seven-thirty here at the auditorium. And Billy, and Brother Wood, and Gene, Leo, and them will all be here."

55 _____, *What Is The Works Of God,* Apr. 04, 1959, Los Angeles, CA, "Brother Bosworth told me that one time…He was giving out the cards for me."

56 *Hour Is Come,* "Brother Hall and them gets them the next day and prays for them all."

57 WMB, *Testimony,* Sep. 02, 1953, Chicago, IL, "Brother Baxter both was standing out to pick me up when we come in. I was late. He said he give out prayer cards B."

58 *Why?* South Gate.

59 *South Africa Testimony.*

60 WMB, *Presence Of The Lord Jesus,* Jun. 12, 1955, Macon, GA.

61 *Angel And The Commission,* Cleveland.

62 WMB, *Fourth Seal,* Mar. 21, 1963, Jeff., IN, "If it's not written in the Bible, God stands behind it anyhow, if it's God's Word. See? And then if it's outside of that, it's revealed to prophets."

63 _____, *Inner Veil,* Jan. 21, 1956, Sturgis, MI, "How about in Acts 19 when Paul taken handkerchiefs off of his body, and aprons, and sent it to the sick? What if somebody would say, 'Now, that's not written in the Bible.' But God did it anyhow."

64 *Corinthians, Book Of Correction.*

65 *Manifestation Of Thy Resurrection.*

66 *Pillar Of Fire,* "there's a least, right now in this building, eighty percent of what's setting here is nervous, afflicted with nervous trouble."

Chapter Fourteen
MAJOR HEALINGS EXAMINED

To what extent are William Branham's major
claims of healing supported by his
messages and by reality?

Healing of Congressman Upshaw

Probably the most publicized story of healing in WMB's ministry is that of Congressman William David Upshaw. Upshaw was born in Coweta County, GA, on 15 Oct. 1866 and died in Glendale, CA, on 21 Nov. 1952. Upshaw's healing took place on 08 Feb. 1951, though there is no recording of that meeting. His original testimony[1] can be found in *The Voice of Healing*.[2] Upshaw had been saved at age eighteen, just prior to a farm accident that left him crippled. He states he prayed for immediate healing but there was "too much Willie Upshaw" in that prayer. He sat under the ministries of Wm. Freeman, Oral Roberts and Wilbur Ogilvie. Without ceasing he prayed for the "appropriating" faith, but never seemed to be able to take a hold of it and walk, he said.

> I walked into that Branham-Baxter meeting in Calvary Temple, Los Angeles, in February, 1951,...on my crutches that had been my "buddies"...my helpful comrades for 59 of my 66 years as a cripple... 7 of those years having been spent in bed...We knew "Billy" Branham would be great but we were not prepared for Baxter, who is an imperative John the Baptist, preparing the way for Branham. I sat entranced, still praying for "appropriating faith," but holden somehow to that contact... and that contract with the Lord 60 odd years ago. Others were healed all around me. Then Brother Branham, exhausted, was carried from the platform. Angels were hovering near! I knew my blessed wife and her "prayer warriors" were wrapping me in prayer. I remembered how she said, "When you are trying to lead a sinner to accept Christ, you say: "Accept... confess Christ and step out- He will do the rest and bring the feeling.'" "It was the touchstone. Brother LeRoy Kopp, Calvary's Temple golden hearted pastor, came back to the pulpit and said: "Brother Branham says, 'THE CONGRESSMAN IS HEALED'." *My heart leaped.* I said in my battling soul, "Brother Branham

knows the mind of God....I will step out and accept the Lord as my healer. "I laid aside my crutches and started toward the startled LeRoy Kopp and my happy, shouting wife...and the bottom of Heaven fell out...My crutches are still on the Calvary temple pulpit, and I am "Happy on the way...Leaning on the Everlasting Arms." Praise God! William David Upshaw. Is it 2524, 24th Street, Santa Monica, Calif.

The above quote from Congressman Wm. D. Upshaw's Tract is abbreviated, but it contains all the essentials. There is, however, quite a difference between Upshaw's version and WMB's. Upshaw's testimony is not complicated. He prayed and his wife encouraged him to step out in faith, that was his *touchstone,* Upshaw said. WMB never prayed nor spoke with him. There was no mention of any vision WMB had regarding him. WMB was being carried out of the meeting when WMB told LeRoy Kopp to say, "*The Congressman is healed.*" Afterwards, LeRoy Kopp told Mr. Upshaw what WMB had told him to say. Hearing that, Wm. Upshaw stepped out in faith, and received his healing and walked without crutches. About six months later WMB stated that Upshaw was healed without being touched,[3] right after *The Voice of Healing* released Upshaw's testimony. Within days WMB's embellishments started. He added that the Holy Spirit came down and told him about Upshaw's condition and said he was healed.[4] The next day WMB added that Upshaw sat in meetings with Billy Sunday, Paul Rader and B. E. Rediger, whereas Upshaw mentioned a completely different trio.[5] On Wednesday, May 9, 1951, Wm. Upshaw said the following in WMB's service, "I'm eighty-four years young, speak three and four times a day, preach the Gospel of the Christ Who saved me, stood by me on bed seven years, and made me happy, and then took me off of the crutches that I have used for fifty-nine years and now, glory to God I'm walking."[6] In July, WMB related more of his "vision" of how he saw a young man fall.[7] Here is where WMB really started to add to the story:

> [Upshaw] said, 'Young man, how'd you ever know me?'...Said, 'I've been prayed for, since I was a little boy, but I always believed that God would heal me 'cause I took the right stand in the time of prohibition. I, when liquor was going to be brought in, I was called one of the dry bones.' He said, 'I lost the president of the United States because of my stand.' I said, 'That's a gallant thing, sir.' I said, 'May the Lord bless you.' I said, "All right, bring your first patient here, the first person who's to come up.' When it did, something happened to the lady, and it told her about it. And I turned, to look again. And I seen that Congressman with a pin-striped suit on, a red necktie, going down, bowing hisself like *this,* to the people, just walking right across the people. I said, 'Congressman, Jesus Christ has honored you. You're eighty-six years old now, but God has honored you'...I said, 'Look like He'd a healed you then, but He has healed now.' He said, 'Do you mean I'm healed now?' I said, 'THUS SAITH THE LORD.' I said, "Have you got a pin-striped suit?" He--he was wearing a dark suit, with a red tie. I said, 'You got a pin-striped

suit?' Said, 'Yes, sir, just bought one the other day.' I said, 'Rise up. Jesus Christ makes you whole.'[8]

WMB gave Upshaw an offering to send his testimony around the country.[9] Upshaw comments:

> Remember, I'm sending this folder to every congressman, and senator, the president, and his wife, and now sending this week to the king of England for whom he prayed, and Winston Churchill. And I'm going to send them to Joseph Stalin. God have mercy on his soul.[10]

On April 09, 1959, WMB stated Upshaw lived for many years afterwards, though he actually died within 21 months[11] of his healing, or on Nov. 21, 1952. What is one to think regarding an apparently wonderful testimony of God's grace, the healing of an eighty-four year old crippled man? There are no other records, except from WMB sources (including *TVH*, of which WMB was then Publisher), about the healing of Wm. Upshaw. As far as can be determined there are no medical certificates issued prior, or subsequent, to Upshaw's healing. Upshaw evidently believed he was healed because of his stand for prohibition. A stand, he said, that cost him the Presidency of the USA.

Today Paraplegics are being healed through Yoga, Kundalini, and by a "John of God," a medium in Brazil, who says, "I do not cure anybody. God heals, and in his infinite goodness permits the Entities to heal and console my brothers. I am merely an instrument in God's divine hands"[12] This is what WMB himself stated, "A man getting up from a wheelchair that could be mental healing."[13] He said a woman in a wheel chair could be healed through psychic power, or through Christian Science[14] WMB stated that hundreds of people who've been in wheel chairs for years could be told to, "Get up and walk," and they'd walk. All healed through the power of Mental Healing, or through Christian Science.[15] WMB shared a "secret," which his hearers were not to teach. He said that healing came from the inside of a person.[16] This certainly indicates that a person need not be a Christian in order to heal, something which WMB allowed.

What is puzzling is that WMB made healing a matter of predestination. He said that, "No matter how much faith you have, it'll never change the predestinated will of God. It's got to be by vision to see what happen."[17] This is not the time or place to discuss the theological issue of "predestination," but rather the place of it in WMB's "theology of healing." This comes from a man who said his angel promised that if he could get people to believe him, NOTHING would stand before him, not even cancer.[18] This from one who called himself a prophet, and always said and sang, "All things are possible, only believe." This from a man who said all healing comes from inside a person.[19] WMB's "predestination" in healing appears to be nothing but another ruse to deflect any failed cases away from his person.

Who, or what, then healed the Congressman? There is no question that something drastic occurred in the life of Wm. Upshaw. He was bedridden for seven years and on crutches for 59 years. In 1951, he suddenly was able to walk. What caused this dramatic change? WMB claimed to have been God's instrument in the healings of Congressman Upshaw and countless others. This claim was contradicted by WMB himself, because he said healing comes from the inside of a person and is triggered by faith. It did not matter faith in what, as long as it was faith, he said. WMB also stated man is absolutely a god and, "He could just speak, and everything obeyed him, because he was a god within himself."[20] One would think that predestination should not be an obstacle, because, for man, it would have included being a god. WMB believed that a fully surrendered man is omnipotent[21] and is deity.[22] According to WMB, people seeking healing did not have to be Christians because God only looks at faith, as a substance. WMB was a man who was not a Christian in the orthodox sense of the word. He taught the Trinity consisted of the three unclean spirits like frogs, of the Revelation.[23] He said if a man were born of God, they would receive his teaching.[24] This man taught that Jesus was a man who became God at his baptism and ceased to be God in Gethsemane. It would appear this man believed God allowed any means of healing, including the use of idols. Upshaw came to *this* man for healing and he received what he came for. Did God, the creator of the ends of the earth and the Father of the Lord Jesus heal him? Is it possible that God winked at Upshaw's ignorance and healed him? God's mercy is very great toward sinners. Is it possible that he received this apparent healing from the enemy of man's soul? Why would Satan heal? Was it to make WMB appear as Simon in Acts 8: 10, "To whom they all gave heed, from the least to the greatest, saying, This man is the great power of God?" To many people, WMB is the Word of God for this hour. WMB's teachings have spread worldwide. God is a jealous God, He will not share His glory with another.

Healing of Florence Nightingale Shirlaw

WMB got a lot of mileage out of the "miraculous" healing of a woman he referred to as Florence Nightingale. The woman's actual name was Florence Nightingale Shirlaw. The healing occurred during WMB's sight-seeing trip in London, England, en-route to his Scandinavian healing tour. Gordon Lindsay wrote, "Early in April, the party (which included besides Brother Branham, Rev. J. Ern Baxter, Rev. Jack Moore, Howard Branham and the writer) …prepared to leave for Europe. On April 6, 1950…the party….took off for London, England…the party landed on the following mid-morning at the Northolt Airport near London. Several days were spent in visiting historic buildings and shrines… The climax of the party's stay… was the visit to Wesley's chapel. While there we also saw the Wesley residence…"[25] This account was written in collaboration with WMB. Lindsay says the CLIMAX was the visit to Wesley's Chapel. Nothing is said about Ms. Shirlaw. WMB said he had simply prayed the Lord's Prayer.[26] Lindsay was not even in the room with WMB, according to Rev. Gwilam Francis.[27]

CHAPTER FOURTEEN 189

WMB was met by Rev. Francis.[28] at a London Airport on Good Friday, Arrangements were made for Easter Sunday, April 9, 1950, for the WMB party to meet with Miss Shirlaw. Francis relates,

> Brother Branham and myself visited Miss Florence Nightingale Shirlaw at her mother's home at 11, Clarendon Road, London W II...We were only four persons in the room that Sunday afternoon, Miss Shirlaw, her mother, Brother Branham and myself, and you [Gordon Lindsay] will probably recall that we were probably there for over an hour. When the atmosphere seemed to be charged with the presence and power of God, Brother Branham took Miss Shirlaw's hand, and offered a very short prayer, after which he requested her to eat. That is all that happened in that room...Miss Shirlaw's recovery took a few weeks, I was in constant touch with her during this period.[29]

Gwilam Francis wrote the above account (Published in TVH in 1954) because there were discrepancies in Julius Stadsklev's book, *William Branham, A Prophet Visits South Africa*, regarding what happened in London.[30] Stadsklev was not in the party, so he only related what he was told. Stadsklev called Miss Shirlaw, *Florence Nightingale*, as did WMB. This identifies WMB as the source for Stadsklev's 1952 story, which was a rather large, after the fact, embellishment by WMB. The basic facts, according to Rev. Francis, were that Miss Florence Nightingale Shirlaw resided in London with her mother. Francis did not make mention of her coming by plane from Durban, South Africa. WMB alluded to her being "in the field."[31] However, WMB also mentioned Wm. Upshaw being in the field,[32] so it might just be an expression he used. Francis stated that the discrepancies, "Do not in any way affect the miraculous healing of our sister, Miss Shirlaw." Someone found out that WMB would be at the London airport and Rev. Francis paged him. WMB made arrangements with Francis to meet with Miss Shirlaw on the coming Sunday at her mother's home in London.

Due to space and time restraints, the following is only a partial recount of WMB's story regarding Miss "Nightingale." WMB stated he received a request on, or about, Jan. 22, 1950,[33] from a Miss Florence Nightingale. WMB said it included a skeleton picture of her and she asked him to come and pray for her.[34] She supposedly even sent him airplane tickets[35] to fly to Durban, ZA.[36] WMB said she weighed anywhere from 27 pounds;[37] 30 or 40 lbs,[38] less than 35 lbs,[39] 37 lbs,[40] less than 60 lbs,[41] and 64 lbs.[42] If anything, the latter numbers of 60 lbs or so are probably still too low to be realistic.[43] WMB just prayed for her, he said.[44] Even though she apparently begged for help, nothing else was done.[45]

The reader must understand that there is no record of WMB mentioning a Miss Florence Nightingale [Shirlaw] in his messages until April 13, 1951; one whole year after her alleged request. WMB and his party landed and he was "paged" by a minister [G. Francis- PMD] asking me to come and pray for Miss Florence Nightingale. How she knew that he was there, he didn't know, he said.⁴⁶ WMB told him he would come and pray for her in a couple of days, because he wanted to go sight-seeing first.⁴⁷ Sightseeing he did,⁴⁸ even though Rev. Francis told WMB she was dying and might not last that long.⁴⁹ Lindsay never mentioned WMB praying for her. WMB said they were picked up by the minister on Sunday, to visit Miss Nightingale *at the minister's house*, by his church.⁵⁰ Many welcomed them, he said,⁵¹ including two nurses and several ministers and four of his managers.⁵² This contradicts what Francis stated regarding that Sunday,

> Brother Branham and myself visited Miss Florence Nightingale Shirlaw *at her mother's home* …We were only four persons in the room that Sunday afternoon.⁵³

WMB, in direct contradiction to Rev. Francis' account of only four people being in the room, said there were thirteen, a doctor, two nurses, two or three ministers, the [4] campaign managers and himself,⁵⁴ were in the room. G. Francis and Miss Shirlaw were there too. WMB even had Ern Baxter turn his head at the sight of Miss Shirlaw⁵⁵ and calls on him as a witness to what he said.⁵⁶ In contradiction to Rev. Francis, WMB prayed the Lord's Prayer, and his favorite bird, a white dove, showed up. The windows were open and it was a foggy day,⁵⁷ was that realistic for a dying person? When the dove flew onto the window sill, it hopped around and flew away, WMB said, "THUS SAITH THE LORD, you'll live and not die."⁵⁸ WMB affirmed this with the nearest thing to an oath, "My Bible is open before me. And our heavenly Father is near to listen to what I have to say."⁵⁹ Eight months after the event, WMB received a photo of a recovered Miss Shirlaw. And that is where the story started to gather momentum, or rather, embellishment.

WMB spent time in and around London until flying to Paris for a couple of days of seeing the sights there.⁶⁰ No word of seeing King George VI. These sights included a visit to Place Pigalle, the Paris Red Light District. It was called Pig Alley by US soldiers visiting this prostitution district during WW II. WMB said he had heard about its immorality and just had to go there and see it for himself. His verdict, "It's true!"⁶¹

To what extent is William Branham's Case of the healing of Miss Shirlaw supported by Scripture and by reality? Apart from the contradictory accounts, there is no evidence of any miraculous healing. WMB never touched or laid hands on her. After he prayed the Lord's Prayer, Florence did not immediately rise up. It would appear that a natural healing process took place, which took awhile.

Not All Were Healed

Pastor Pohl, a one-time enthusiastic, ardent supporter of WMB, personally related to this author that he became very disillusioned, when people died days after being pronounced healed by WMB. He said, "After Branham and his party were gone, many people returned to their original condition, or died."⁶² Pohl related that in Winnipeg, MB, Canada, 1947, the local newspaper did an investigative report on the healings that allegedly took place there in a WMB campaign. They found them **all** to be fraudulent.

CHAPTER FOURTEEN 191

The newspaper made a deal with an upset pastor by saying, "Find us one genuine healing and we will print a front page contraction."[63] They found none, yet WMB claimed 98% were healed.[64] As stated, Hollenweger confirms, "By contrast to what he [WMB] claimed, only a small percentage of those who sought healing were in fact healed."[65] The majority were NOT healed,[66] as a matter of fact, "The convincing miracles of God, the true evidence of his Spirit and power were notably absent."[67]

In 1947, in Phoenix, AZ, WMB laid out a healing challenge:

> If I come here to Phoenix in the name of a prophet, and I do not the things that a prophet does, then don't believe me...If the deaf don't hear, the dumb don't speak, the blind don't see, the cripples don't walk...then believe that THIS ANGEL THAT COME TO ME IS FALSE AND I'M FALSE WITH IT. But if it manifests itself here on the platform before you, you believe it and repent of your sins and disbelief, for the hour of His visitation is drawing near. That's right. For He only does those things to confirm His Word. [68] [Caps mine – PMD].

WMB basically said, "If healings do not take place, I AM A FALSE PROPHET AND MY ANGEL IS A DEMON. [Caps mine – PMD]. So, what transpired in this meeting? WMB focused on a particular deaf man and said:

> If that man comes in this prayer line this afternoon, and I get to touch him under this anointing that I have now, the man's ears will be perfectly opened. THUS SAITH THE LORD. [Caps theirs – PMD]. If that isn't right, then call me a false prophet. I could call him to the platform.[69]

Next WMB told his audience that the healing was not working that day:

> AND I HAVE NEVER IN ALL MY LIFE, TILL THIS AFTERNOON SEEN ANYTHING LAID BEFORE THE GIFT OF HEALING WITHOUT BEING HEALED.[70] [Caps mine – PMD].

WMB apologized to God in his closing prayer and said he was wrong: God, I've been wrong. I've done wrong since the very hour...forgive your servant.[71]

Really? WMB was wrong when he said he was wrong, he should have said, "I AM A FALSE PROPHET AND MY GUIDING ANGEL IS A DEMON." His managers should have shut down the meetings and left town.

King George VI not Healed

WMB claimed he prayed for King George VI, upon the king's personal request and he claimed that God healed him of multiple sclerosis.[73] However, King George never had Multiple-sclerosis. Rather he had Arteriosclerosis, or hardening of the arteries, due to heavy smoking. He received surgery for it on Mar. 12, 1949. WMB claimed the King also had stomach ulcers, which was common knowledge. It was the cause of George's discharge out of the Navy. WMB, contrary to his claims, never went to see King George to personally pray for him. Buckingham Palace has no record of his name.⁷⁴ In 1950, when in London for a sight-seeing tour, WMB said he was going to see if King George VI was in.⁷⁵ To think one could just drop by and say, "Hey, George, remember me, I'm here to pray for you!" Doctors removed King George VI's left lung on Feb. 23, 1951. He continued to deteriorate and died in his sleep on Feb.06, 1952.⁷⁶ He was buried on Feb. 15, 1952. Five months after the King's demise, or on Jul. 13, 1952⁷⁷ WMB continued to talk as if George VI was still alive, declaring him healed long after he had already died.

Donny Morton and Reader's Digest.

Another case where WMB's pronouncements of healing were not true, was Donny Morton. ⁷⁸ WMB pronounced him healed and a great deal of publicity was made of this. Reader's Digest⁷⁹ published an article detailing the whole affair. However, within a year, Donny died. Why was it that, as with King George, WMB never mentioned that Donny died within such a short time? Many, in fact, died within a very short period after being prayed for. In the Bible, we never encounter this phenomenon. When Jesus, or the Apostles, healed someone, they were healed instantaneously, although, of course, *eventually* all died.

A Boy Raised To Life In Finland?

Another, much more serious incident, is the case of a little Finnish boy who supposedly was raised from the dead. An eyewitness of the event in Finland, Pastor Vilho Soininen, describes it in *Man Sent From God,*

> A terrible accident occurred. A car ahead was unable to avoid striking two small boys, who ran out into the street in front of it, throwing one down on the sidewalk, and the other five yards away into a field. One unconscious boy was carried into a car just ahead of us and the other, Kari Holma, was lifted into our car and placed in the arms of Brother Branham and Miss Isaacson who were sitting in the back seat. Brothers Moore and Lindsay were in the front seat with me. As we hurried to the hospital, I asked through Miss Isaacson, the interpreter, how the boy was. Brother Branham, with his finger on the boy's pulse, answered that the boy seemed to be dead, since the pulse did not beat at all. Then Brother Branham placed his hand over the boy's heart and realized that it was not functioning. He further checked the boy's respiration and could detect no breath. Then he knelt down on the floor of the car and began to pray. And Brothers Lindsay and Moore prayed too, that the Lord would have mercy. As we neared the hospital, about five or six minutes later, I glanced back, and to my surprise, the boy opened his eyes. As we carried the boy into the hospital, he began to cry, and I realized that a miracle had taken

place....the boy, Kari, was dismissed from the hospital in just three days, and is feeling very well considering the circumstances.[80]

The other boy lay dying at the hospital, but he gradually improved over the following weeks. WMB told of a vision he had received two years prior, of the raising of a dead boy, which was now fulfilled. There are discrepancies, however. In WMB's vision, the car was lying wrecked across the road; apparently, it had struck some rocks. The little boy [There's only one in WMB's vision] had "the bones in his body broken." WMB recounted that he said,

> 'If that boy isn't on his feet in two minutes from now, I'm a false prophet, ride and run me out of Finland.' Certainly!...I said, 'Heavenly Father, across the sea yonder, two years ago, You said this little boy would lay here.' I said, 'Death, you can't hold him any longer, God has spoken! Come back, give him up!' And the little boy raised up and looked around like that. The people got to fainting and everything. There it is, wrote right there and signed by the mayor of the city, by a notary public.[81]

The eyewitness account of Vilho Soininen tells of one boy feeling very well, considering the circumstances. He was released after three days. Weeks later, the other boy was still lapsing into unconsciousness. Which one was the boy of the vision? Who was on his feet in two minutes, or WMB was a false prophet? This author spoke with Gordon Lindsay over the phone for verification, but all he said was, "No comment." It is interesting that Lindsay, perhaps conveniently, let pastor Soininen tell the story. There is an inordinate amount of subjectivity present in the account. No one beside WMB held the boy; he alone checked the boy's pulse; his heartbeat and breath; and pronounced him dead. If the child was dead, and his bones broken, why transport him? There are too many questions and embellishments. This story must be discounted.

Five Death Certificates

WMB claimed, "There was only three people raised from the dead by Jesus Christ, and we have on record, doctor's record, five."[82] Around 1973, Ed Byskal, together with this author, held meetings in Lima, Ohio. Billy Paul Branham, his sister Rebekah and Mrs. Meda Broy Branham, attended. This author asked Billy Paul to see the five death certificates. Billy Paul replied, "Well, Brother Peter, I lent them out to someone, and I can't remember who." Weaver told this author that he had asked a similar question of Billy Paul regarding the death-certificates, and received a similar response. How can such important documentation get lost? There were no certified copies made? The originals are all lost and people are just asked to believe all this?

To what extent are William Branham's major claims of healing supported by Scripture and by reality? The major cases of Congressman Upshaw, Florence Nightingale Shirlaw, King George VI, Donny Morton and the young boy from Finland, and others, can neither be supported by WMB's messages, nor by reality.

Notes - Chapter Fourteen

[1] This author has noticed a number of changes in some of WMB followers' accounts of Upshaw's testimony.

[2] Gordon Lindsay, *Voice Of Healing*, April-May, 1951, p. 2. CRIPPLED CONGRESS MAN WALKS From Branham Healing Service.

[3] WMB, *As I Was With Moses*, May 03, 1951, Los Angeles, CA, "And now, I'm very thankful that--that God is confirming that what I have...spoken to be the truth. Now, there's the brother that was in the meeting yesterday, a paralyzed man, today, a well man. I never touched him or nothing. He looked up here on the platform; he seen the Holy Spirit doing signs and wonders out there. He just said in his heart, no doubt, '...Why, Holy Spirit, You healed me too. So I'll just accept You.' And there it was. And that's happened...The congressman, Brother Upshaw here, who was crippled for sixty-six years. I never even touched the man in no way. I just stood here. I did see a vision of the man; that is true. And then he just accepted what I said. That was all. There he is; he's walking."

[4] *Expectations*, "I was thinking when I was talking to the Congressman this afternoon, when I met him, about when he'd been all these years on these crutches and crippled, and the times he'd been prayed for. But he had stood here, and he had seen what the Holy Spirit had said to everyone while revealing the hearts and the secrets of the hearts. And he seen that when He'd told people, no matter what was wrong with them, that they were healed, they got up and acted on it and was well. Then he thought, "Oh, if he could only tell me." And there the Holy Spirit fell down, told him his condition and all about it, and said he was healed. Up he got. He believed it. No matter what the ifs, how long he'd been crippled or what it was all about, God had done made the promise, and it was him to believe it."

[5] *Faith Is The Substance*, LA.

[6] WMB, *Testimony (Believe Ye That I Can Do This?)*, May 09, 1951, Los Angeles, CA.

[7] *Who Hath Believed Our Report?* Toledo, "Well, one night I walked into the building, and I seen a vision. All the wheelchairs was setting there. I looked, and I saw a young man in his teens, fall; he hurt himself. He fell on a hayrack or something. That's all I could say, knew of. I seen him in a high place, wore a strange looking collar, looked like the same man. Somebody was applauding to him. That's all I knew...Brother Baxter said, 'You know who that was you seen?' I said, 'No.' Said, 'Did you ever heard of Congressman Upshaw?' I said, 'No, sir.' Said, 'He's setting before you. That's him.' Then I looked, and I said, 'That's the guy. That's him setting there.'"

[8] *Court Trial*.

[9] *Testimony Believe Ye That I Can Do This?* LA, "And you know what this offering is for? He's not able to send this testimony around the country. He's...He can't do it. He's aged, and he has no income. This here offering is to help him send this to all the big men, rulers, and so forth of the nation."

CHAPTER FOURTEEN

[10] Ibid.

[11] WMB, *Mary's Belief*, Apr. 09, 1959, Los Angeles, CA, "Congressman just said, 'Something struck him that he knowed it was the truth.' I didn't know him. 'And if God was that close to him, he would accept it.' And out of the chair he went. And that did it. Lived for many years testifying, glorifying God. And with an immortal body tonight he's walking the streets of gold with the saints that's gone on before."

[12] John of God, available from http://www.johnofgod-healing.com/index.asp, (Accessed June 12, 2010).

[13] *From That Time*, Phoenix.

[14] *Turning Northward*, "Think of that, it's more of a challenge than to walk down to this woman in a wheelchair and say, 'Stand up and walk,' certainly. She could actually do that through psychic power, that's right, mental. She could do it in Christian Science faith, it's been done."

[15] *From That Time*, Phoenix, "A man getting up from a wheelchair, that could be mental healing…For we even know by doctor's records, that many times, hundreds of people, that's been in wheelchairs for years, get up and walk away and things like that. Sure. Mental healing. Christian Science has it."

[16] *Uncertain Sound*, "You know, now don't teach this, but did you know man in the beginning, when God made him, he didn't make him to be doctored. He had his own doctoring in him, he was equipped…Then healing does not come from any outside resource, it has to come from the inside… Healing only comes by…the power that's within yourself…healing is in you."

[17] *Who Hath Believed Our Report*, Toledo, "The Spirit of the Lord come into the audience and just sapped my strength. And just as I started to go down, my brother run to me to catch me. And I looked; I seen Congressman Upshaw. And he'd been in meetings ever since he was a lad when he first fell and hurt himself. He wanted to be healed then by God. He listened to Mr. Roberts; he'd been in Mr. Freeman's meetings, Mr. Ogilvie, and many of them had prayed for him. Friends, I've got something to say along them lines after a bit. No matter how much faith you have, it'll never change the predestinated will of God. It's got to be by vision to see what happens. And as it started out, I seen him in a brown suit going down the street, tipping his hat to people like that. I said, "Congressman Upshaw is healed in the Name of the Lord."

[18] WMB, *AT Thy Word*, Sep. 28, 1951, New York, NY, "If God can heal one person here with cancer, He can heal every one of you with cancer. And He has healed every one of you that's got cancer. The only thing you have to do is just accept it."

[19] *Power Of Transformation*, "Let the Holy Spirit come upon any person that's truly got something down there to…a healing comes from the inside, let that healing come from the spirit that's in you."

[20] *Uncertain Sound*, Jeff., IN, "Man in the beginning, when he was made, a man is a god. He's absolutely a god, for he was made in the image of God, being a son of God, and then he's an heir of all that God is…He could just speak, and everything obeyed him, because he was a--a god within himself."

21 *Patmos Vision.*

22 *Resurrection Of Lazarus*, Erie, PA.

23 Rev. 16: 13 And I saw three unclean spirits like frogs come out of the mouth of the dragon, and out of the mouth of the beast, and out of the mouth of the false prophet.

24 *Anointed Ones*, "Notice Revelation 16:13 to 14, between the Sixth and Seventh Vial, "'Three unclean spirits like frogs' (did you notice that?) went out of the mouth of someone." A trinity of spirits! Now denominational brother, set still just a minute. Don't get up and walk out of the room, back out there on this radio, telephone hook-up. Don't turn your tape recorder off. Set still just a minute, and listen. You're born of God, you will…Where was trinitarianism born at? Remember, 'three unclean spirits,' individual spirits. Are you getting it? Notice, they look back to the Nicaea Council where the trinity doctrine was born at, not in the Bible. There's no such a thing. They look back to the Nicaea Council at Nicaea, Rome, where the trinity was born at."

25 Lindsay, 208.

26 WMB, *The Principles Of Divine Healing*, Sep. 23, 1951, Jeff., IN.

27 Gwilam I. Francis, in *The Voice Of Healing*, Nov. 1954, 6.

28 Ibid.

29 Ibid.

30 Ibid.

31 *Works That I Do Bear Witness Of Me.*

32 *At Thy Word*, New York.

33 *Church Of The Living God*, "I was in Houston the night the picture was taken back there, of the Angel of the Lord. Two days before the picture was taken, Dr. Bosworth came in, said, 'Looky here, Brother Branham.' He had a picture of the…granddaughter of the late Florence Nightingale." WMB refers to the "halo" photograph taken in Houston, TX, on 24 Jan. 1950.

34 *Early Spiritual Experiences*, "The day after that [after the "halo" picture was taken in Houston, TX, PMD] Brother Bosworth come showed me a skeleton picture. Said, "Brother Branham, Florence Nightingale is calling from Durban, South Africa, come pray for her."

35 Ibid., "I was in Houston the night the picture was taken back there, of the Angel of the Lord. Two days before the picture was taken, Dr. Bosworth came in, said, 'Looky here, Brother Branham.' He had a picture of the…granddaughter of the late Florence Nightingale, the noted nurse of England. Her great-great-granddaughter, I believe it was. She was in South Africa, and had a malignant growth over the…of the stomach. They had her holding up there, when she wasn't nothing but bones, just eat her up. They stood her up like this, she's almost six foot tall; tall, thin, blond-haired woman. She's standing like that, and her arms about that big around; I believe she weighed forty pounds, or thirty-five pounds, or something. And through her body, here, she had a small clout around her. And when he showed me that… And she was begging. She'd sent a airplane ticket, for me to fly to Africa from there, right quick."

CHAPTER FOURTEEN

[36] WMB, *Expectations*, May 07, 1953, Jonesboro, AR, "I remember when Florence Nightingale…I was in Houston when I got her picture…sent many letters and three or four airplane tickets to fly to Durban, South Africa: nothing but a skeleton. Cancer on the duodenum of the stomach…She'd cried and begged. And I committed it to the Lord, and said, 'Lord, if You'll just heal her, I will go down there someday.'"

[37] WMB, *Jesus Christ, The Same Yesterday, Today And Forever*, Aug. 06, 1955, Campbellsville, KY, "Here not long ago when I was in England to praying for the notable Florence Nightingale, who's picture's in the book that you received tonight. And dying with cancer weighing twenty seven pounds, I believe it was, when she was healed"

[38] _____, WMB, *What Think Ye Of Christ*, Dec. 13, 1953, AM, Chicago, IL.

[39] _____, *I Perceive That Thou Art A Prophet*, Jun. 14, 1953, PM, Connersville, IN.

[40] _____, *Jesus Christ, The Same Yesterday, Today And Forever*, Oct. 27, 1952, Edmonton, AB, CAD.

[41] _____, WMB, *God's Provided Way*, May 16, 1961, AM, Grande Prairie, AB.

[42] _____, WMB, *Expectations*, May 08, 1958, Burlington, VT.

[43] Skeleton weight in a 160 pound woman is approx. 20 Lbs. Weight of skin about 12% of body weight, or 20 Lbs. Total organ weight is approx. 15 Lbs. That adds up to 53 Lbs, not counting the weight of blood, muscle, flesh and water. Total weight of Miss Shirlaw would probably have been around 75 Lbs minimum, if indeed a woman of her size could still be alive at that point.

[44] "'Brother Bosworth, I can't go, the way things are now. I can't do it.' I said, 'Let's pray.' We knelt down on the floor, he and I, my little girl, and my wife, and we knelt in the floor, and prayed. And I said, 'God, if You'll heal this Miss. Nightingale, then that'll be sign for me to go to Africa, 'cause, I've always wanted to go down there to that, them people and take this to them.' And I said, 'If You'll heal her.' I forgot about it. Weeks passed, six or eight weeks."

[45] *Expectations*, Jonesboro, "She'd cried and begged. And I committed it to the Lord, and said, 'Lord, if You'll just heal her, I will go down there someday.'"

[46] *Who Hath Believed Our Report*, Toledo.

[47] *Church Of The Living God*, "I told him, I said, 'You take her on to your home. I want to go down there to Buckingham Palace. And then you call me, and I will be at the Piccadilly Hotel.' Brother Baxter and I fixed it up with him. We went on to the hotel."

[48] *Expectations*, Jonesboro, "I told that Anglican minister, I said, 'Take her to your parsonage. I'm going down to Westminster Abbey. And after that, I'm going over to Buckingham Palace. I will be to see you.' And I didn't get to see her till the next morning." WMB saw her two days later.

[49] *Who Hath Believed Our Report*, Toledo, "And when Brother Baxter and I, and all of us arrived in London…and they paged me…I was wondering if it was the king's call to come to the Buckingham Palace, or what it was, immediately. But what it was, the page was to go over…There was a

lady had just flown in front of me from Africa, and they couldn't hardly get her out of the plane: Miss Florence Nightingale. How she knowed I was to be there, I don't know yet. And I told this minister, I said, 'Take her somewhere, and I'll see you in a day or so.' We wanted to go down to the palace. So he said, 'If she lives that long.' Said, 'Brother Branham, she's dying.'"

⁵⁰ Ibid., "So they got her down to the place, and that day when Brother Baxter and I, and Brother Lindsay, and Brother Moore, the managers, we went down to the place. The minister came and got us, and we went up to the place to pray for the woman. When I walked in that room, friends, I--I--I can't tell you how I felt. There laid a skeleton a breathing."

⁵¹ *Church Of The Living God*, "And on the second day, after we'd went to the palace, and up to John Wesley's place, and so forth, we came back down the Westminster Abbey. Then we went into the hotel. And this minister, English minister, called, with his little cab. And we went down to his house, and it's kindly foggy that morning. We went up... had a lovely place, and his big church. We went upstairs. And there were many of them to welcome us."

⁵² *Principles Of Divine Healing*, "I was taken up to a lovely home where two nurses was waiting on this Mrs. Nightingale. And when I went in, there was several ministers there. Four of my managers went with me."

⁵³ Gwilam I.

⁵⁴ *Do You Now Believe*, Owensboro, "And in the room set her doctor, two nurses, two or three ministers when the campaign manager--managers and myself walked in. And I walked over; they had a white sheet laying over her."

⁵⁵ *Who Hath Believed Our Report*, Toledo.

⁵⁶ Ibid.

⁵⁷ *Principles Of Divine Healing*, "And usually, England is foggy, about--an island like. And the window was up. And I'll never forget this experience. I knelt down to pray...Those ministers all gathered around. And I started praying. I said, 'Our Father, Who art in heaven, hallowed be Thy Name...' and just as I said that, a little turtledove flew in the window and begin to walk up and down the cell--sill of the window, going, 'Coo, Coo, Coo.' And all the time I was praying, he walked back and forth, up and down the sill of the window. Then when I said, 'Amen,' the little fellow spread his wings and flew away. Those ministers raised up and said, 'Did you notice?' And before I could say anything, the Spirit of the Lord came and told her that she'd be well."

⁵⁸ *Church Of The Living God*.

⁵⁹ Ibid.

⁶⁰ *Man Sent From God*, 208.

⁶¹ WMB, *Baptism Of The Holy Spirit*, Sep. 28, 1958, AM, Jeff., IN, "When they told me that Pigalle in Paris was such a ill-famed place, how did I know; I was never there. But I went down there to find out if it was right or not. I took two or three more ministers and went down there to those womens and things that stripped on them streets and things.

It's the truth." See also: WMB, *Conflict Between God And Satan,* "I'd heard different people tell me about, especially down in France, down in the place called Pigalle, and how that the people was so immoral...I went down in Pigalle, the first night, me and three more ministers. Brother, what a surprise we got...some of the prettiest girls I ever seen in my life was there: appealing. Certainly. Sin is appealing and attractive."

⁶² See also: Carl Dyck, *WILLIAM BRANHAM, The Man and His Message,* (Saskatoon: Western Tract Mission), 14.

⁶³ Interview of Pastor Alfred Pohl, by David Cloud, in *'O TIMOTHY'* magazine, Feb. 21, 1990.

⁶⁴ WMB, *Children In The Wilderness,* Nov. 23, 1947, Phoenix, AZ, "The highest percent was at Winnipeg, Canada. Ninety-eight percent of what was prayed for was healed. Ninety-eight percent...my secretary called me...he said, 'Brother Branham, I believe it's going to be one hundred percent from the way the testimonies are coming in.'"

⁶⁵ Hollenweger. 355.

⁶⁶ Ibid., 356.

⁶⁷ Ibid., 355.

⁶⁸ *Angel Of God,* Phoenix, AZ.

⁶⁹ Ibid.

⁷⁰ Ibid.

⁷¹ Ibid.

⁷³ WMB, *Jesus At The Door,* May 29, 1958, New Haven, CT. See also: *Paradox,* Tampa.; *Doors In Door,* Feb. 06, 1965, Flagstaff, AZ.; *At Thy Word,* Los Angeles, *Take The Rod And Gather The People,* Aug. 27, 1950, PM, Cleveland, OH.; *Faith Is The Substance,* LA. "I have a photostatic copy of King George's thanks for my prayer and things when he was healed of multiple sclerosis. And other great men across the nation in fulfillment."; *Who Hath Believed Our Report?* Toledo, "My first shock was when King George of England sent me a cablegram, come pray for him to be healed of his multiple sclerosis, which God did heal him."; *Early Spiritual Experiences,* . "I've got a letter right here now, and a cablegram from King George of England who is suffered multiple sclerosis... And he sent two cablegrams already for me to come pray for him, over there, and I said, 'King George of England, the highest king, the biggest, greatest king on earth today.' And I said, 'God told me, that angel that sent from him, said, I'd be praying for kings and great men."; *I Perceive You Are A Prophet,* Jun. 14, 1953 PM, Connersville, IN.; "King George of England called to be prayed for with multiple sclerosis...Here's a man sitting here, with the letter in his hand from King George of England, who called me come from pray him with multiple sclerosis. And the king was healed."; *Testimony,* Nov. 29, 1953, PM, West Palm Beach, FL, "King George of England sent word to me. I have his statements and have his letters of his fields and every...To come pray for him of multiple sclerosis, and so I couldn't go up that time. So I just wired back and told the king that I would pray for him here, that God would hear here just the same as he would over there. And so, then another telegram come

through and wanted me to come on over immediately. Later when I went to England, over there, to see him, and the Lord healed him."

[74] Buckingham Palace, "Buckingham Palace Fact," No. 36," available from http://www.londonforfun.com/info-for-Buckingham-palace.htm , (Accessed June 15, 2010).

[75] *Early Spiritual Experiences*, "I was going to go down to see if the King George would--being in."

[76] Ronald Allison and Sarah Riddell, *The Royal Encyclopedia*, (London: MacMillan Press, 1991), 224.

[77] *Early Spiritual Experiences*.

[78] WMB, WMB, *Be Not Afraid, It Is I*, Mar. 05, 1960, Phoenix, AZ., "Many of you, about three years ago in *Reader's Digest*, read the article of the miracle of Donny Morton, when I was...in California. How the Lord, after Mayo's, and John Hopkins, and all of them had turned that little twisted up baby down, the power of God unfolded that child and made him well. And Mayo's called for an interview for it, wanted to know what happened. Sure. *Reader's Digest* wrote it up. What happened to little Donny, that little Canadian boy? All hopes was gone after Mayo and John Hopkins said the child cannot be healed...I seen him walking off the platform with that little twisted baby. I said, 'Let him alone, Billy. Bring him on up here.' And when the father, trembling, brought the little fellow, and his head sideways, his big eyes cast back in his head, shaking his hands, twisted down, his little legs drawed up behind him, I said, 'Sir, if I could heal your baby, I'd do it...This little baby's name is Donny Morton.' The father begin to shake, and he said, 'That's true.' I said, 'Do you believe?' And he started screaming, he said, 'With all my heart.' He went right straight from that meeting that night and bought Donny his first pair of shoes, and he wore them the next day."

[79] Alma Edwards Smith, *Reader's Digest*, Condensed from Chatelaine. Vol. 61, Nov. 1952, pp. 29-35.

[80] Lindsay. 210-211.

[81] *Absolute*, Dec. 30, 1962.

[82] *Is This The Sign Of The End, Sir?* "Remember, there's only about three people raised from the dead by Jesus Christ, and we have on record, doctor's record, five."

Chapter Fifteen

MAJOR PROPHETIC CLAIMS EXAMINED

To what extent are William Branham's
prophetic claims supported by
his own messages and reality?

William Branham's '1933' Series Of Seven Visions

There are many claims regarding WMB's prowess as prophet, especially in regard to a series of seven visions he claimed he had. These visions contained all sorts of predictions regarding world events that would take place by 1977. WMB claimed the '1933' visions appeared in 1930, or 1931, "I got it right on paper here with me, wrote it in 1931,"[1] or in 1932.[2] The most telling one is where he read out loud from his prophecy paper and stated it was dated 1932.[3] The 1932 date, since he read it out loud from what he had written, must supersede all others. That is very troubling, because WMB had the seven visions and the Commission on the river, occur in the same year 1933. However, as shown earlier, the best fitting date for the Ohio River commission (discounting the probability of the commission being a fabrication), would be 1934. WMB's visions took place after the Baptism and commission; after WMB's tent ministry; after they rented a building for about 2-3 years. If WMB fabricated the dates, why would anyone believe the vision, since, over time they were updated.[4]

Mussolini and Ethiopia

WMB's claims of the accuracy of his vision of Mussolini and his demise, after the invasion of Ethiopia, leave a lot to be desired. Indications of 'backward looking' answers are already evident in the fact that Ethiopia was called Abyssinia until after WWII. The rightful heir, Emperor Haile Selassie, was exiled to Britain after Benito Mussolini entered Abyssinia, during the invasion of 1935 – 1936. Haile Selassie was restored to the throne by British forces in 1941.[5] Mussolini (1883 – 1945) was not rising to power in 1933 as a "new" dictator. He had been in power since 1922, and he died in 1945.

The president which now is, President Franklin D. Roosevelt...Now remember, this is twenty-eight years ago, will cause the whole world to go to war; and the new dictator of Italy, Mussolini, shall make his first invasion towards Ethiopia, and he will take Ethiopia; but that'll be his last. He shall come to his end. [6]

Ethiopia (Abyssinia) was not his last invasion, as WMB prophesied:

Said, "This new dictator, Mussolini, will take his first step toward Ethiopia, and Ethiopia will fall at his feet." It did. It said, "That'll be his last. He will end in disgrace."[7]

How that Mussolini would go towards Ethiopia, his first invasion, and would take it; that'd be the end; he'd die off after that.[8]

How that Mussolini would make his first invasion to Ethiopia, and he would take it, but he'd come to a disgraceful end.[9]

Abyssinia was Mussolini's first, but not his last, invasion. He next "invaded" Spain, Albania, Africa, Greece, and Yugoslavia, contrary to WMB's vision. In 1961 WMB spiced up some of the supposed 1933 prophecies, and included the details of Mussolini's disgraceful death. WMB made it sound as if Mussolini died shortly after the 1935 invasion of 'Ethiopia,' which execution did not take place until 1945.

I said, "The dictator that's now arising in Italy (which is Mussolini), he will come into power, and he will go to Ethiopia; and Ethiopia will fall at his steps."...But I said, "He'll come to a shameful end," and he did. Him and the woman he run with was turned upside down and hung on a rope in the street with their feet up, their clothes hanging down. All right, that come to pass.[10]

Mussolini and his mistress, Claretta Petacci, were shot and killed. They were dropped on the street and urinated upon. They were hung upside down with others. Claretta's skirt was tied in place with a rope, it was not hanging over her head as, WMB "prophesied."

The Siegfried Line?

WMB supposedly predicted a great American defeat at the Siegfried Line in Germany, but he also confused it with the Maginot Line in France. He said that he predicted the building of this great concrete wall eleven years before construction. The French Maginot Line, was built from 1930 to 1935 and the German Siegfried Line was built in 1938. There is no verification documentation. This is what he prophesied,

How the Siegfried Line would be built, and how that the Americans would take a beating there, and they never would admit it till just about two years ago, and they got the German pictures of the siege there...lost their whole army almost right there...[11]

CHAPTER FIFTEEN

And eleven years beforehand, it said that we'd go to war with Germany, and Germany would be fortified behind concrete, the Maginot Line. It happened just that way.[12]

The Three 'Isms'

WMB 'predicted' three "isms' Communism, Fascism and Nazism. He stated that these three "isms" would all end up into Communism and that Communism would burn the Vatican. He equated Fascism with Rome. WMB stressed the importance of Russia (Communism), "Watch Russia" he repeatedly stated.

> And how that then the three isms, Nazism, Fascism, and Communism, would all wind up in Communism. **And how many in here remembers me just keep having you stand, and say it over like that, "Watch Russia. Watch Russia, the king of the north. Watch Russia, king of the north. Watch Russia, king of the north?"** How many has heard me just say this, wave that over, over? The old-timers, you see, back in the early part of the church. Just stand there and wave it over and over, "**Watch Russia, the king of the north.** See, what he would do, for all those isms will heap up into Russia."[13] [Emphasis mine – PMD].
>
> How these great isms would rise up and all fall back into Communism; Hitlerism, and Mussolini, and Nazism, and so forth, would all fall back into Communism.[14]
>
> I said, "And there's three isms, the Nazi, and the Fascism, and Communism." I said..."**Keep your eyes on Communism**; it'll all head up in there."[15] (Emphasis ours – PMD).
>
> I wasn't against Germany; it was the Nazism. I wasn't against the Italians; it was against the Fascism. And remember, I made another prediction in that time…just a prediction, and many of you old-timers remember it. I said, "There's three isms" trying to take a hold of the world today…[16]

WMB stated a number of times that the three 'isms' would end up in Communism, "Watch the King of the North" he emphatically declared.

> **Now, I just had you all to repeat it over: "Keep your eyes on Russia." You remember that? "Keep your eyes on Russia. She'll all wind up in Communism.** And then it'll all wind up finally in Catholicism. Remember, it'll all wind up in Catholicism in the end time. That's exactly right. That's at the battle of Armageddon, right over in here when Christ comes Himself.[17] (Emphasis mine – PMD).

In WMB's, *Revelation of the Seven Seals*, he did a 180° turn and stated:

> **It just makes me sick at my stomach to hear so many preachers hollering about Communism**, and they don't even know what they're crowing about. That's right. **Communism ain't nothing.** It's a tool in the hand of God...[18] (Emphasis mine– PMD).
>
> **Don't you never watch Communism.** It's nothing but a tool playing in the hands of God...[19] (Emphasis mine – PMD).

These are serious contradictions which make this prophecy invalid. It seems strange that WMB's source of revelation did not worry about Islam at all, there is not even a hint of it.

The "Egg-Shaped" Car of the Future

A lot of 'mileage' is still being made of this 'prediction' of an egg-shaped car capable of travelling down the highway without the benefit of a steering wheel. Today, vehicles are capable of traveling driver-less. There is, as yet, no egg-shaped car without a steering wheel traveling down any highway. Our safety laws will not allow it and people would, in today's technological age, not be playing checkers in the back of a car. Is it possible that something like that will be in the future? Not likely, because our technology has already surpassed what WMB "prophesied." That being true, where is that car that WMB spoke about? This is what WMB said:

- "They'll look like an egg...And that's the way they'll be just before the rapture.[20];
- Automobiles, just before the coming of the Lord, will be in the shape of an egg."... That was in 1932, or something like that...[21];
- "Cars would keep getting more like a egg, until the last days they'd be just in the shape of an egg...those cars will not be run by a steering wheel"[22];
- It will be controlled by some other power;[23]
- They can control it right from their headquarters."[24]
- Automobiles looking like an egg going down the street. There's cars go down highways with some kind of a control they don't have to guide it. I seen American family playing checkers in the back of a car. They've got the car right now, if they just had the highways to put it on. The little **Volkswagen**'s the perfect egg, just exactly...Could you imagine in 1933 what the cars looked like to now?[25]

It's interesting that the Volkswagen 'Bug' has re-appeared, but it still does not look like an egg and it does not have a 'glassed over top.' It also is not a car that is big enough to seat four people in the back playing checkers or cards. It does still have a steering wheel and this is 2014, about 37 years after the world was supposed to end in 1977 (see following page). This car was to appear just before the Rapture in 1977 and the total annihilation of the USA, another prophecy gone awry.

1977 - Destruction of the USA

WMB predicted that by 1977 the USA would be destroyed by atomic bombs. It did not happen. By 1977 the Rapture should have taken place and the End of the world should have been ushered in. There is not a Msg believer dating back to that year that did not believe this to be true. This prophecy is now "explained" by the occurrence of the 'Parousia,' a later teaching, that states that the Lord has actually returned in the form of the Message of William Branham, reminiscent of the way J.W.'s, and others, have dealt with failed prophecies.

> Then I saw the United States as one smoldering, burnt-over place. It will be near the end." Then I've got in parenthesis ("I predict that this will take place") Now remember, that's what the Lord showed, but (" I predict this will take place before 1977")...then the bomb comes that explodes her...[26]

> I predicted then...this that was THUS SAITH THE LORD... I seen, looked like just a-burning; rocks, blowed out; stumps and the whole United States just looked bare, laying like that, as far as I could see where I was standing.[27] (Emphasis theirs, PMD).

1977 - The Rapture, the Millennium, the Coming of the Lord

WMB predicted the destruction of America, The Rapture, The Millennium, and the coming of the Lord to be by 1977. WMB erroneously distinguished between predict and prophesy. WMB stated that his visions are infallible; they can't fail, thus establishing 'predict' and 'prophesy' to be the same. WMB, in referring to the same 'prophecy,' used prophecy and predict interchangeably.[28]

> From the time God made the promise to Abraham...to the time of Christ being rejected in A.D. 33, by the Jews...the power of God was with the Jews exactly 1954 years. God dealt with the Jews 1954 years.....we have exactly (listen!) seventeen years left, and we will have the same span of time given to us as God dealing with us in the power of the Holy Spirit since A.D. 33 until 1977, the same span of time of 1954 years. [Math problem: 33 + 1954 = 1987, PMD.]...in 1977 will be the seventieth Jubilee...Jubilee means the going up, the release...Don't miss it. It'll be the Jubilee of the going up of the Gentile Bride and the return of Christ to the Jews, when they go out of bondage...I predicted that there be some great tragedy happen to the United States before or by the year of 1977...I saw this United States burning like a smolder - rocks had been blowed up. And it was burning like a heap of fire in logs or something

that just set it afire; and I looked as far as I could see and she had been blown up...I never said the Lord told me that...I'll predict that the time - I don't know why I'm saying it - but I predict that that'll happen between right now, 1933, and 1977. And not knowing it, God knows my heart, I never knew until yesterday, that 1977 is the Jubilee...Don't misunderstand me now, and say, " Brother Branham said Jesus will come in 1977." I never said no such thing. Jesus may come today. But I have predicted that between '33 and '77 something would take place, that these things that I seen come to pass in the vision would take place. And five of them has already took place.[29]

As a servant of God who has had multitudes of visions, of which NONE has ever failed, let me predict (I did not say prophesy, but predict) that this age will end around 1977. If you will pardon a personal note here, I base this prediction on seven major continuous visions that came to me one Sunday morning in June, 1933. The Lord Jesus spoke to me and said that the coming of the Lord was drawing nigh, but that before He came, seven major events would transpire...The last and seventh vision was wherein I heard a most terrible explosion. As I turned to look I saw nothing but debris, craters, and smoke all over the land of America. Based on these seven visions, along with the rapid changes which have swept the world in these last fifty years, I PREDICT (I do not prophesy) that these visions will all have come to pass by 1977. And though many may feel that this is an irresponsible statement in view of the fact that Jesus said that 'no man knoweth the day nor the hour,' I still maintain this prediction after thirty years because Jesus did NOT say no man could know the year, month or week in which His coming was to be completed. So I repeat, I sincerely believe and maintain as a private student of the Word. along with Divine inspiration that 1977 ought to terminate the world systems and usher in the millennium.[30] (Emphasis mine, PMD)

And at 1906 the Laodicean Church Age set in, and I don't know when it'll end, but I predict it'll be done by 1977. I predict, not the Lord told me, but I predict it according to a vision that was showed me some years ago, that five of those things has (out of the seven) - has already taken place.[31] (Emphasis mine, PMD)

We know that an atomic bomb's got our name wrote on it...[32]

We believe, before the atomic powers ever blow this earth to pieces, the church will be gone...the bombs are hanging in the hangers, tonight.[33]

There's a rocket hanging yonder. Several of them. Cobalt bombs and everything else...And there'll be a destruction by fire like there was by water.[34]

A Woman Ruling the USA

WMB predicted the rise of a woman that would rule the United States. He vacillated

CHAPTER FIFTEEN

between a woman president, the Roman Catholic Church, and a Roman Catholic president in his interpretation. Looking back one can always make something fit. It is not surprising to see that for WMB, giving women the right to vote, was America's downfall.

- I predict that a woman will be president before we're annihilated. I said that in 1933 by a vision.[35]
- I predicted that women would keep demoralizing and the nation would keep falling...America would be ruled by a woman. Mark it and see if it's not right. A woman will take the place of a President or something, of great, some high power in America.[36]
- I've already predicted in 1933, a woman would rule this nation before the chaos, by the annihilation. See her face on the money.[37]
- There'll be a great woman rise up, 'cause America is a woman's nation... A great woman will rise up and be president, or something like that in the nation.[38]
- How many remembers that vision here in the church? Said that how that even Kennedy would be elected in this last election. How that women would be permitted to vote.[39]

The prophecy changed from a 'powerful woman' (In parentheses - Possibly Roman Catholic Church?) to the Roman Catholic Church; to the Roman Catholic President John Fitzgerald Kennedy, (1917- 1963), the 35th president of the United States (1961-1963). This was easy to predict, especially after the election took place in the fall of 1960 and the last mentioned WMB quote was from December of 1960. Throughout every mention of this 'prophecy,' WMB said it was "Thus saith the Lord" and it all had to take place before the bombs fell prior to 1977. Today, in 2014, the USA is still the most powerful nation on the planet. During WMB's early career there was a Roman Catholic candidate for the presidency, named Alfred E. Smith. He was defeated by Hoover. There is no doubt that WMB was terribly biased against him, because of his stand on Rum and Roman Catholicism.

> After serving as sheriff of New York County for several years beginning in 1915, Smith was elected governor of New York in 1918. He lost the election of 1920 in the Republican landslide of that year, but was reelected governor in 1922 and served three more terms...In 1924 he unsuccessfully sought the Democratic nomination for president...Al Smith finally secured the Democratic presidential nomination in 1928...Smith was the first major-party Presidential candidate of the Roman Catholic faith...Hoover defeated Smith by a significant margin in the 1928 Election. Part of Smith's especially poor showing can be attributed to anti-Catholic bias (Smith was accused of standing for 'rum, Romanism, and rebellion'), anti-New York City bias, and Smith's own bad campaigning... Smith was the first major-party Presidential candidate of the Roman Catholic faith.[40]

Because Smith was the first major RC presidential candidate in 1928, or prior to 1933, it is no wonder that WMB would "prophesy" about America being run by Roman Catholicism. Of course, there have since been elections of new Popes, but as yet no Rapture of the Church, nor the destruction of North America.

> I believe, one of these glorious days, when this united confederation of church goes together, and the new pope is brought out of the United States and put over there according to prophecy, then they'll form an image like unto the beast. And I tell you, the true Church of God will be drove together. The real, true believers out of Methodist, Baptist, Presbyterian, Pentecostal, Nazarene, Pilgrim Holiness, whatever they'll be, will go together and cemented by the love of God, that'll make the Body of the Lord Jesus Christ, all the believers. And agnostics and shallow-minded will be cast to one side; they'll go right on into the confederation of churches.[41]

When one looks carefully at the above quote it is seen that WMB made two statements about things that had to take place prior to the Image of the Beast being formed. WMB said in 1954, "When this united confederation of church goes together, and the new Pope is brought out of the United States and put over there according to prophecy, then they'll form an image like unto the beast." There has not as yet been an election of a Pope from the USA. Therefore the confederation of churches that was supposed to get together cannot be the WCC, because that was formed in 1948. Thus, the next thing that did NOT happen was the formation of the Image of the Beast, which, according to WMB is denominationalism.[42] Denominationalism has been around since the Reformation of the 1500s, so that prophecy too will have to be discounted.

WMB named certain denominations, some of which came into being after 1906 (Azusa Street Revival), and out of those the TRUE CHURCH OF GOD, or the Bride of Christ would be formed. Message believers hold that they are the only true church. There are hundreds of message churches all over the world, but they consist of many factions. In fact, WMB said that message churches would denominate. Some churches, in order to avoid being a denomination, call themselves an association, or fellowship of churches. This might seem to be a solution but, in actuality, it is often only a case of semantics. Anyone, in any kind of association, would have to agree to a common belief system. Those outside that agreed upon distinction, fall outside the circle, and are not welcome. The truth is that the Church (Roman Catholic, Protestant, or other) was based upon the synagogue, which was highly organized. This, of course, makes total sense when one considers the synagogue was based upon Temple worship, which was highly organized by God Himself. Even the nation of Israel was instituted and organized by God. Everything God does is highly organized. One look at His creation should be enough to convince anyone.

Just prior to the election of Pope Benedict XVI in 2005, there was a lot of speculation by WMB followers, that an American successor would be elected according to WMB's prophecy. That did not happen and WMB's followers had to re-write their interpretations. Pope Benedict XVI resigned in Feb., 2013 and now there is Pope Francis I. Argentinian, Cardinal Jorge Mario Bergoglio, was elected on March 13, 2013. WMB has not as yet been vindicated, as a prophet in this case. However, there is always the next U.S. Presidential election that could fulfill this elastic prophecy.

No follower of WMB has ever seen the piece of "yellow" paper on which WMB purportedly recorded his seven visions. Some have repeatedly asked his son Billy Paul to produce it, without results. Another thing that has never been re-produced is a copy of the fly-leaf of WMB's Bible, on which WMB said he had recorded his prophecies and his visions. A friend's relatives who have seen it, said it was illegible and incomprehensible.

There exist divisions among WMB's following regarding his prophecies. Some hold all things have been fulfilled, some are still waiting for the fulfillment. Some unfulfilled prophecies are: the Tent vision; the brown bear he would shoot; his claim to, "ride this trail again"; an American Pope before the Rapture (1977?); his message, "The Trail of the Serpent."

Destruction of California

Another famous WMB prediction was that of the destruction of California. Of course, many, including Edgar Cayce, have predicted that Los Angeles will slide into the Ocean. There have been predictions, from scientists to psychics, that this will happen. Here are some of the things that WMB prophesied,

- In a few days a great earthquake's going to strike on the West. And it won't stop. California, Los Angeles will sink. It's going down. It'll slide right into the ocean. And two days after that, the Alaskan earthquake shook Alaska...[43] [WMB said this on Nov. 26, 1965, one month before his death. Emphasis ours, P.M.D.]
- I said, "Judgment will strike the West Coast." Two days after that Alaska almost sunk. Remember, that same God said that, said Los Angeles is doomed. And she's finished. I don't know when; I can't tell you...that same Spirit of God that said all these things and done all these things, It said there, "Oh city, Capernaum, who called yourself by the name of the angels, Los Angeles. How you've exalted yourself into Heaven...if the mighty works had been done in Sodom that'd been done in you, it'd stood today. But your hour is come." You watch and see. If it ain't, I'm a false prophet...[44] [Emphasis ours, P.M.D.]

WMB supposedly predicted that prior to the quake that shook Alaska in 1964. He did not say Alaska, but "West Coast." The term "West Coast" specifically denotes the states Washington, Oregon and California. When Americans say they are moving to the West Coast, nobody understands them to say "Alaska."⁴⁵ WMB repeatedly spoke about the sin of Los Angeles, and how its judgment was coming, so why Alaska? Again, this prophecy failed to come to pass. Los Angeles did not sink, or slide into the ocean.

Sharks Down-Town Los Angeles

WMB's son Billy Paul *is* an old man now, he turned 78 years old on Sep. 13, 2013. WMB already called himself old when he was 48.⁴⁶ WMB told Billy Paul on Sept. 11, 1965,

> Billy...I may not be here, but you won't be an old man until sharks will swim right where we are standing [Downtown Los Angeles - PMD]⁴⁷

WMB's followers now realize that the above prophecy is a problem and they are "spiritualizing" it by saying Billy Paul will see it when he has a glorified body. Or he won't be *considered* an old man UNTIL the sharks are swimming in LA..

To what extent are William Branham's Prophetic Claims supported by Scripture and by reality? Prophecies in Scripture came to pass and prophecies of doom left room for repentance on the people's part. No biblical prophecies were "after the fact." WMB's major prophecies did not come to pass, they had already happened before they were predicted. WMB's prophetic claims are clearly not supported by Scripture, neither by reality.

Notes - Chapter Fifteen

1. *Jezebel Religion*, "There'll come a worship of a woman in the United States, and that'll be Mary. I seen it, 30--1931. Seven things happened. I got it right on paper here with me, wrote it in 1931."

2. *Faith Once Delivered*, Chicago, "That was in 1932, or something like that."

3. *Condemnation By Representation*, "I'd like to read something to you.1932: -Listen to this- getting ready to go on my way to church this morning, it came to pass that I fell into a vision...while I was in this vision I seen some dreadful things take place. I speak this in the Name of the Lord...I got, Thus saith the Lord."

4. Ibid., "I'd like to read you a prophecy...By the way, Mr. Mercier and many of them are going to take some of these old prophecies and dig them out, and revise them a little, or bring them up to date, and put them in papers."

5. Ethiopian History, "The Italo-Ethiopean Wars," available from http://www.selamta.net/history.htm, (Accessed November 17, 2010).

6. *Condemnation by Representation*.

7. WMB, *Conference*, Nov. 25, 1960, Shreveport, LA.

8. _____ ,*Ephesian Church Age*, Dec. 05, 1960, Jeff., IN.

9. *Laodicean Church Age,.*
10. *Seventieth Week.*
11. _____, *Questions And Answers # 1*, Aug. 23, 1964.
12. *Ephesian Church Age.*
13. *Laodicean Church Age.*
14. *Ephesian Church Age.*
15. *Thyatirean Church Age.*
16. *Daniel's Seventieth Week.*
17. Ibid. See also: *Thyatirean Church Age*, "As I started to Sunday school I fell into a trance… And I seen this President Roosevelt leading the world to a world war: predicted. I said, "And there's three isms: the Nazi, and the Fascism, and Communism." How many in here remembers? I said, 'Keep your eyes on Communism; it'll all head up in there.'"
18. *First Seal.*
19. *Fourth Seal.*
20. _____, *Israel And The Church # 3*, Mar. 27, 1953, Jeff., IN.
21. *Faith Once Delivered to the Saints*, Chicago.
22. *Why are we not a Denomination?*
23. *Condemnation by Representation.*
24. *Q & A # 1*, Aug. 23, 1964, AM.
25. _____, *Voice of the Sign*, Mar. 21, 1964, PM, Denham Springs, LA.
26. *Condemnation By Representation.*
27. *Thyatirean Church Age.*
28. WMB, *Painted Face Jezebel*, Oct. 05, 1956, Chicago, IL, "I predict that before the coming of the Lord that a woman will be a great ruler in the United States."
29. *Seventieth Week.*
30. WMB, *Church Age Book*. 321, 322.
31. *Ephesian Church Age.*
32. Wm. Branham, *The Breach*, Mar. 17, 1963, PM, Jeff., IN.
33. *Thyatirean Church Age.*
34. WMB, *Serpent's Seed*, Sep. 28, 1958, Jeff., IN.
35. _____, *God's Covenant With Abraham*, Apr. 28, 1956, Charlotte, NC.
36. *Teaching on Moses.*
37. WMB, *Thirsting For Life*, May 12, 1958, Everett, MA.
38. _____, *By Faith, Moses*, Jul. 20, 1958, Jeff., IN.
39. *Ephesian Church*. See: *From that Time*, Klamath Falls, "In 1933…'Thus saith the Lord!' there will be a woman rule before the end time. She'll either be President, Vice-President, or it'll be

the Catholic church as a woman. I've seen her. A great woman, the nation bowed to her. It'll be one before the end time. 'Thus saith the Lord!' Write it down…you young people. See if it happens. If it isn't, I'm a false prophet."

[40] Eleanor Roosevelt Papers Project, "Alfred E. Smith," available from http://www.gwu.edu/~erpapers/teachinger/glossary/smith-al.cfm, (Accessed October 14, 2004).

[41] WMB, *Acts of the Holy Spirit,* Dec. 19, 1954, PM, Jeff., IN.

[42] _____ , *Q & A,* May 15, 1954, "We find out that the mark of the beast…had to come out of Rome…It can't come out of no other country but Rome. There's where it's seated; that's where it's placed…Something was made… a image unto this beast, which was Luther-ism, Methodist-ism, Baptist-ism, Pentecostalism, Holines-ism; all them isms formed up into an organization and made an image just like the beast…And the beast was the Vatican City, the Catholic hierarchy… Then the Protestant church come out of the Catholic church, and organized themselves a little power. That is a image. The Protestant denominational churches is the image of the beast, because it's denominated just exactly like Catholicism is. And God never did order His Church to be organized in any age, but has always bitterly condemned it."

[43] WMB, *Works is Faith Expressed*, Nov. 26, 1965, Shreveport, LA.

[44] *Rapture*.

[45] West Coast, "The western seaboard of the United States from Washington to California," available from http://www.elook.org/dictionary/west-coast.html; (Accessed 03 May, 2005).

[46] WMB, *Sirs, We Would See Jesus*, May 16, 1957, Saskatoon, SK, CAD.

[47] Green. 119.

Chapter Sixteen

HOLY SCRIPTURE AND THE PERFECTIONS OF GOD

To what extent can WMB's teaching on the
Holy Scriptures and God's Perfections be
supported by the Scriptures?

This particular chapter will examine to what extent WMB's teachings on the Holy Scriptures and the Godhead can be supported by the Scriptures. Throughout WMB's messages it is evident that WMB did not have a systematic theology. Many things he said in one place he contradicted in others.

Holy Scripture

WMB stated that the Bible *is* God's infallible Word,

> I don't know how you feel about it, but to me the Bible is the infallible Word of God. And I believe that God has watched over His Word that there's not one punctuation out of place.[1]

WMB said he *believed* the Bible to be the infallible Word of God:

> Now, I believe that God can do anything that He desires to do, because He's God. But I like for it to just come out of the Bible, then I know I'm right. I believe the Bible to be the infallible Word of God. I do not believe it should be added to or taken from.[2]

At first blush, the above statements appear to be very orthodox declarations on WMB's part. However, the reader needs to know that WMB believed in a variety of Bibles, as stated earlier. Not different translations, but completely different things he called "Bible." Old mother Nature, the Zodiac, the Great Pyramid, and the written Word. WMB was not alone in this Pyramid teaching. WMB was strongly influenced by Charles Taze Russell, Franklin Hall, Clarence Larkin, British-Israelism, Freemasonry, etc. The Bible was written in between the lines,[3] said WMB, in order to confuse the learned people. This is, of course, contrary to Scripture. Paul says, "Our letters have been straightforward, and there is nothing written between the lines and nothing you can't understand. I hope someday you will fully understand us…" (2 Cor. 1: 13 NLT).

WMB contradicted the Word of God. This is how this looks.

1. WMB - The Bible is written between the lines
2. Paul – There is nothing written between the lines
3. An irreconcilable difference – WMB's teaching is invalid.

WMB himself said, "All it takes is just one word changed and that little leaven then leavens the whole lump. He that offends in one point of the law is guilty of all. Eve just changed one word. That will do it."[4] WMB, almost superstitiously, said he would never change one word,[5] but yet he would change its meaning. This is seen in his understanding of God being infallible. When WMB used the word "infallible," he meant that if God did something one way once, he had to do it that way again,[6] or else he would not be God.[7] That, of course, is not a correct understanding. God once destroyed Jericho by Israel marching around it and, "the walls came tumbling down." God is NOT obligated to use the same method today, as WMB advocated. God's Word is infallible which, simply stated, means that it is correct in the truth it conveys.

For WMB, besides the written Word of God, there was also the Spoken Word, which was inspired.[8] This "Spoken Word" represented the words that he, WMB, allegedly spoke to his generation. For this reason his businesses were/are called *Spoken Word Publication* and *Voice of God Recordings*. The following makes it clear Scripture contains all mankind needs for life and for godliness (2 Pe.1: 2-4):

> The Holy Scripture is the only sufficient, certain, and infallible rule of all saving knowledge, faith, and obedience, although the light of nature, and the works of creation and providence do so far manifest the goodness, wisdom, and power of God, as to leave men inexcusable; yet are they not sufficient to give that knowledge of God and his will which is necessary unto salvation…All of which are given by the inspiration of God, to be the rule of faith and life.[9]

The Perfections (Attributes) of God

WMB, throughout his messages, used the term attributes (perfections) to describe God. Is what WMB taught compatible with Scripture?

God is eternal, with which WMB would have agreed, as can be seen below:

> We believe that God is eternal. And anything that has a beginning has an end. But God had no beginning; so therefore, He has no end. And the world was made by Him, because He is the Creator. He made it out of things He had not to make with, just His spoken Word, it come into existence.[10] God alone has eternal Life. The Bible said so. God alone has eternal Life.[11]

CHAPTER SIXTEEN

In the above quotation, WMB appears to be orthodox regarding the attribute of the eternality of God. God *is* eternal, but WMB stated also that God was not always God. The word, "God" denoted, "object of worship."[12] God is a Nordic word. The original language of the Scripture did not use "God," that word was *Elohiym*, which does not mean "self-existing" as WMB asserted. Also, contrary to WMB, God is not lonely, nor in need of fellowship, neither lacking anything. WMB averred that for God to be God, he had to become an object of worship. God demands our worship, but He is not dependent upon His Creation. According to WMB, God wanted to be our healer, our savior, our shepherd, but could not, because He had not created us yet. More is said under "Potentiality." He also stated he believed God is infinite, omnipotent, omnipresent, and omniscient.[13]

God's Infiniteness

For WMB, God's infiniteness meant at least two things. One, because every decision God makes is perfect, He cannot change it. He must stay with His first decision.[14] Not that this is untrue, but that is not what Infiniteness means. Two, God knows every Gnat on earth, including every time the gnat its eyes doth bat."[15] Again, this is not what the word infiniteness means. Infiniteness, as applied to God, means that He is without measure, infinitely, indefinably great.

> If God is infinite, and perfect…If He cannot make a mistake, then the way God acted in the beginning when a crisis arose, He's got to act the same way when the same crisis arise, or He acted wrong when He acted back there…Then if God said something He's got to stay with that, in order to be God.[16]

The Self-Sufficiency of God

WMB described God with the terms of Self-sufficient, as can be seen below:

> But you know, God does things to suit Himself. He don't have to ask anybody about it. He's the self-sufficient One. See? He don't have to ask nobody.[17] He abides alone. He's Elohiym, the self-sufficient one.[18]

There is, at surface, no argument with the above. However, for WMB to say something in one place was one thing, but if he negated in another place, there is a problem. That is exactly what is found throughout most, if not all, of his other messages.

> He came down 'cause He wanted to be worshipped.[19] The word 'god' means 'an object of worship.' God wanted to be worshipped, so He had to project something that would worship Him. Jesus said to the woman at the well, "God is a Spirit. And they that worship Him must worship Him in Spirit and in Truth."[20] The Fatherhood…When God dwelt alone, holy, His Laws, His righteousness

makes Him holy. He wanted to be in man, He wanted to worship with man. He wanted man to worship Him, He had to come to man.[21]

WMB differentiated between The Eternal, before He became God, or an object of worship after He became God. There is not space here to elaborate, any reading of WMB's messages will show what he asserted of God's Self-Sufficiency. His teaching on this issue is quite deficient.

The Sovereignty of God

God is sovereign,[22] which means He is autonomous and free from external control. Thus, He does not have to act in the same predictable way as WMB taught.[23] However, if God had to act in the same predictable way in order to be Sovereign, then Our Lord and the Apostle Paul would not have had to pray three times without results (2 Cor. 12: 8; Mat. 26: 39 – 44). In the wilderness, God said, "Look and live" (Num. 21: 8), but Hezekiah destroyed that brazen serpent (2 Ki. 18: 4). This kind of teaching that God must always act in the same way is presumptuous. Presumption is a grave error that is strongly condemned in Scripture. It is also a great condemnation of WMB's followers, who, after WMB's death on Christmas Eve, 1965, prayed and expected WMB to rise. They delayed his burial until Easter of 1966. Some followers still expect him to rise, and finish his ministry. These people only followed what WMB taught them about God's "sovereignty."[24] Of course, rebuttals were published which stated the reason for the delay was Mrs. Meda Branham. She was still recuperating from the accident.[25] WMB's followers still meet every Easter, expecting him to rise and continue his ministry.

The Omnipresence and Omniscience of God

For WMB, God is only omnipresent, or everywhere present, by virtue of the fact that He knows all things.[26] WMB stated God is not like the air, but dwells in a certain place.[27] Scripture states that God *does* fill all heaven and earth (Jer. 23: 23). WMB said that, "if God were like the air, he'd be a myth, and not God."[28] This is what it looks like:

1. God is not like the air, or the atmosphere
2. God is just like the air. He fills all the universe.[29]
3. This is an internal contradiction, making the teaching invalid.

Omniscience in WMB's teaching meant "all knowing," but his use of it is puzzling because he made it the reason for God's omnipresence: "By being omniscient, knowing all things, He can be omnipresent."[30]

The Immutability (Unchangeable-ness) of God

According to WMB God is unchanging, but this needs to be brought into context. WMB meant that God was forever bound to do something the same way, an issue which was addressed earlier.

God is unchangeable. Malachi 3 said, 'I am God, and I change not.' God's first way of doing anything, that's God's ever way of doing anything.[31] Being infinite...He cannot change... God is perfect, and His first decision is...He cannot change it anymore, because it's perfect, 'cause God would not do any-thing unless it was perfect.[32]

This reflects the mechanistic god of Deism, or of Magic. WMB's view of God is actually more complex. He stated that God DID change. WMB described how God dwelt alone, as the eternal, but "[T]hen God being made material, tangible"... "a little white light, like a mystic light, like a halo," God become "bodilized," and formed into "the Logos," "The Word of God," and "the Son of God."[33] WMB's definition of the immutability of God is that God does not change His mind; His program; His method; His healing promise. In reality, God has changed his program, He no longer requires circumcision to become part of God's kingdom; God no longer requires animal sacrifices; God no longer requires worship in Jerusalem. He wants to be worshipped in Spirit and in Truth. WMB said that God doesn't change, he did not understand that meant that God, the great I AM is who He is, was, and is to come. "For I am the LORD, I change not; therefore ye sons of Jacob are not consumed" (Mal. 3: 6, Cf. Ex. 34: 6, 7).

God is without Potentiality (Change)

An acorn is potentially an oak tree. This expresses 'a progressive change' takes place in the life within the acorn until it comes to full fruition as a majestic oak. In WMB's theology, there is a progression of being, in God.

> The first creation was God himself; then out of God came the Logos, which was the Son of God; then out of the Logos, which was the word...came forth the...man.[34]

First of all, WMB stated here that God was created. That concept is foreign to Christian orthodoxy. Elsewhere he did say that God was not created,[35] so if that is not a contradiction, it certainly is confusion. As stated, WMB said that God is a great eternal, but before the beginning, He was not even God.[36] Scripture says,

> Before the mountains were brought forth, or ever thou hadst formed the earth and the world, even from everlasting to everlasting, thou art God (Ps. 90: 2).

Secondly, WMB indicated that God changed from a singular god to a plurality of gods, because man is God[37] and a part of God.[38] Man is eternal, he was created a god, said WMB. When man receives the message of the hour it shows he is eternal,[39] because he is one with the Word and therefore he, in eternity, was in God.[40] This is polytheism, a strange belief system for a man who stated that the Trinity was Tri-theism[41] and was a doctrine of devils.[42] Some of his followers now claim godhood.

God is Indivisible

Orthodox Christianity states that God is indivisible and has no parts. Therefore, there is no room for Tri-theism, for that would mean three gods. There is also no room for Christians being a part of God, because that would constitute polytheism. In 1953, WMB had the same sentiment, "You can't separate God and put Him in parts. God is one, and we can't make parts out of God."[43] Only a year later he contradicted and invalidated his own message by saying,

> Therefore, a man being borned again, his spirit has been changed, and he becomes a part of God; insomuch that he is a son of God. And he's just as eternal as God is eternal, because he's a part of God, by his birth, spiritual birth."[44]

To what extent can WMB's teaching on the Holy Scriptures and His Perfections be supported by the Scriptures? WMB said he believed the Bible, but his Bible was NOT the Scripture of the New and Old Testaments. To no extent can WMB's teaching on the Holy Scriptures and God's Perfections be supported by the Scriptures.

Notes - Chapter Sixteen

[1] *Spoken Word #1.*

[2] WMB, *Jesus Christ, The Same Yesterday, Today And Forever,* Jul. 18, 1962, Salem, OR.

[3] WMB, *Water Baptism,* Jan. 20, 1960, Beaumont, TX.

[4] *Church Age Book.* 123.

[5] WMB, *God Projecting His Love,* Aug. 06, 1957, Edmonton, AB, CAD, "If I had the power, I would in no wise change it. If I would be offered all the money in the world, and to be the king of the universe, and a million years to reign in health, I still wouldn't change one word of that text. Because it's God's Word, and it can never change."

[6] _____, *Jesus Christ, The Same, Yesterday, Today And Forever*, Jan. 18, 1961, Beaumont TX, "Remember, when you read the Word of God, as we Protestants believe it to be the infallible Word of God...Then when God is ever called on the scene to act and has to make a decision, the way God acts on that case He has to act on every case thereafter the same. "

[7] _____, *Infallibility Of God's Word*, Apr. 04, 1956, Chicago, IL, "He asks that requirement, 'If you can believe you can be healed.' And then He turns back over here and this man said, 'Lord, You know my heart, I believe You,' and won't do it, He couldn't be God and do that. He has to act the same way He did here, or He did wrong here. Then if He done wrong, He's not God. So there you are. He isn't infallible. Then He's just like we would be. Have to say, 'Well, I acted that way,

but I made a mistake there.' 'But I won't make the mistake over here. 'See, God can't do that and be God. He has to be God forever. See? He has to be the same forever. He has to act the same way every time. And He does do it. And I've seen it proven over, and over, and over again that I know He does."

⁸ *At Thy Word*, New York, "He has a prophetic gift that He sent into to His church in these last days to stimulate the faith of the people. Then if He should speak through me, that would be secondarily, but it would be His Word just the same. Now, to doubt this written Word would be sin, and to doubt His spoken Word would be sin."

⁹ 1689 Baptist Confession. 1.1

¹⁰ WMB, *Faith Once Delivered*, Jun. 10, 1957, Indianapolis, IN.

¹¹ _____, *Hebrews Chapter Six # 2*, Sep. 8, 1957, PM, Jeff., IN.

¹² _____, *Who Is This?* Oct. 4, 1959, AM, Clarksville, IN, "The word 'God' means 'an object of worship.'"

¹³ _____, *Jesus Christ The Same Yesterday, And Today, And Forever*, Mar. 23, 1958, Middletown, OH, "God is all powerful, omnipotent, omnipresent, omniscient, knows all things, can be anywhere anytime."

¹⁴ WMB, *God's Provided Way*, May 16, 1961, AM, Grande Prairie, AB, CAD, "God being infinite, He cannot make another decision about it. He's got to stay with His first decision, because every decision's perfect."

¹⁵ _____, *Jesus Christ, The Same Yesterday, Today And Forever*, May 16, 1961, Aft., Grande Prairie, AB, CAD, "Before there was a world, He knew we'd be assembled here this afternoon if He's infinite. He knowed what you're thinking about in your heart, before the world ever started. He knew what you'd be thinking about at this moment. He knowed every gnat would be on the earth, every time it would bat its eyes. That's what infinite means."

¹⁶ *Law Having A Shadow*.

¹⁷ WMB, *Greater Than Solomon Is Here*, Jul. 25, 1962, Port Alberni, BC, CAD.

¹⁸ _____, *God's Provided Way For This Day*, Feb. 06, 1964, PM, Bakersfield, CA.

¹⁹ _____, *Hear His Voice*, Oct. 05, 1958, AM, Jeff., IN.

²⁰ *Who Is This?* Clarksville.

²¹ _____, *Palmerworm, Locust, Cankerworm, Caterpillar*, Aug. 23, 1959, Jeff., IN.

²² Merriam-Webster Definition: Sovereignty = supreme power, freedom from external control; autonomous (self-rule).

²³ *Manifestation Of The Spirit*, "And now, Divine healing is based on His Word. And we know that God is sovereign. People think that God can just do anything He wants to do. God cannot do anything. God is obligated to His Word. God cannot lie. The Bible says He can't. So there's one thing that God can't do. And when God says anything, and makes a promise, God can't take that promise back, because He's God, and He's sovereign, and He can't go back on that promise."

[24] *Hebrews Chapter Four*, "If God healed the sick in the Old Testament, He has got to do it in the New Testament and today, or He did wrong when He healed them back there. He's got to act the same, every time. And He will do it, when the same faith meets the condition. The fault is in us, not in God. If God ever raised the dead, He is obligated to do it again."

[25] Green. 183.

[26] WMB, *Fellowship*, Jun. 11, 1960, Brkfst., Middletown, OH, "Now, we find out in the Old Testament, that God had…one meeting place. The only place He would meet with His people was in one place, the Tabernacle. And that was under the shed blood…the only placed He can meet with us today… God's just not like…the air. If He would, you would never have to seek the Holy Ghost: it would be in you, 'cause He'd filled all space and things. God's omnipresent, sure, by being omniscient, knowing all things. But God has a dwelling place, because He is a Being."

[27] _____, *Dedication Of Building, To The Lord*, Jul. 08, 1959, Cleveland, TN, "I would like to make this statement: That it is known among most of us, and especially among scholars, that God is omnipresent. Well, I believe, in a measure, that God is omnipresent. God is omnipresent, Him being omniscient makes Him omnipresent. If God is omnipresent just like the atmosphere, then He is a myth. But God is a Person. Therefore He has to have a certain place that He dwells. And He is omnipresent by being omniscient. Therefore if He is everywhere, because being omniscient, He knows everything. Therefore if He knows everything, He knows what's going on at every place. But God Himself dwells in a certain place."

[28] Ibid., "If God is omnipresent just like the atmosphere, then He is a myth."

[29] *Resurrection Of Lazarus*, Erie.

[30] *Calling Jesus On The Scene*, "Now, in Spirit, He was God. Jesus said, in Saint John 3, 'When, the Son of man which now is in Heaven, yet standing here on earth, when the Son of man which now is in Heaven. 'How would you answer that? He said He was in Heaven then, and here He was standing on earth. Oh, my! You see, that, He had to be God, omnipresent. See? Sure, He is present everywhere. He knows every thought. By being omniscient, knowing all things, He can be omnipresent."

[31] WMB, *The Feast Of The Trumpets*, Jul. 19, 1964, AM, Jeff., IN.

[32] _____, *To Take On The Whole Armor Of God*, Jul. 01, 1962, Santa Maria, CA.

[33] _____, *When Their Eyes Were Opened, They Knew Him*, Mar. 12, 1964, Beaumont, TX, "He is the eternal One. And then, these things that's happening now are only the attributes of God's thinking. At first it has to be a thought and then a word…When a thought expressed is a word. And then it's spoken, it has to happen. And the whole thing is God unfolding Himself in His attributes. And then God being made material, tangible, that we can talk to, speak with in His whole church body, and everything…Therefore, your name was in His thinking. That's how you have eternal life. You can't have it no other way. If you got eternal life you always was."

[34] *Q & A On Genesis*. See also: WMB, *Five Definite Identifications Of The True Church*

CHAPTER SIXTEEN 221

Of The Living God, Sep. 11, 1960, PM, Jeff., IN, "He wasn't God then…he was God, but there wasn't nothing else, no worship. So 'god' is 'an object of worship,' and there's nothing to worship him…The first thing he created was angels to worship him, then he become God."

[35] WMB, *Smyrnean Church Age*, Dec. 06, 1960, Jeff., IN, "But God was not created; He was always God."

[36] ____, *Marriage And Divorce*, Feb. 21, 1965, AM, Jeff., IN, "What is God? God is a great eternal. At the beginning, way back before there was a beginning, He wasn't even God. Did you know that? A god's an object of worship, and there wasn't nothing to worship Him; He lived alone."

[37] *Messiah*. "There's something about a man, he is a god, he was made to be a god, his purpose here on earth was to be a god, to have a dominion over everything in the earth…He's fashioned like a god, he looks like God, sure was. That's the reason **God was man, man was God.** And this is his off springs, man…The man, what is he? He's got a hand like God, got eyes like God, got ears like God, got a body like God, he was fashioned after God, he was given an earth and a dominion." [Emphasis mine – PMD]

[38] WMB, *Show Us The Father And It'll Satisfy*, Spindale, NC, "Do you know what? The Bible said you're gods because you're a part of God; you're sons and daughters of God. When your theology is left, all of your mental things here is not looking at anything else but the Word of God, and the Holy Ghost comes down here to bear witness, you are a part of God." See also: *The Falling Apart Of The World*, Dec. 16, 1962, Jeff., IN, "Christ is the King of kings and Lord of lords, the anointed Messiah. The believer holds to that Word. God and His Word is One. I and my word are one. You and your word are one. Then don't lean, use your own thoughts; use His thought, then you're a part of God because His Word and you became the same."

[39] *Invisible Union*, "The anointed Word of God being vindicated before any man that's born to be a son of God, with the predestinated germ into him for this hour, he'll see God's Message as sure as there's a God in Heaven…Why? It was put in there by predestination. You were foreordained to a son of God. You were in God before the foundation of the world… you are a part of that Word, by predestination. Because, look, the God is the Word. You believe it?…He always was the Word. 'In the beginning was the Word.' And if the Word was God, then you were in God. The Word, the part that you're to play, was in God before the foundation of the world. He seen you. He knew you. He predestinated you to it."

[40] *Why Are We Not A Denomination?* "You, you're in a time space, and the only thing that's eternal is something that had no beginning or no end. Anything eternal never had a beginning, or it never will have an end. See? So if you're a part of God, the Spirit that's in you never had a beginning or it never will have an end, and you're eternal with the Spirit that's in you."

[41] WMB, *Mark Of The Beast*, May 13, 1954, Jeff., IN, "Martin Luther come out with catechism, a whole lot of things. He come out with a baptism; he come out giving a triune,

Trinitarian baptism which was never taught in the Bible, never taught in the Bible. There never was anybody ever baptized in a Tri- theist baptism in the Bible."

⁴² *Anointed Ones*, "Revelation 16:13-14, between the Sixth and Seventh Vial, three unclean spirits like frogs…A Trinity of spirits… A Trinity of frogs…Remember, three unclean spirits, individual spirits…Notice, in the trinity of frogs came out of an old Trinity, give birth to a new Trinity, their mother. What'd it come out of? A Trinity, the dragon…the beast, and the false prophet, a Trinity."

⁴³ WMB, *Jehovah-Jireh,* Jun. 12, 1957, Indianapolis, IN.

⁴⁴ _____, *Handwriting On The Wall,* Jan. 08, 1958, Chicago, IL.

Chapter Seventeen

THE PERSON OF GOD

Can WMB's teachings on the
Person of God be supported
by the Scriptures?

The Person of God

When speaking about the Word of God, it is assumed there is a God to speak those words. This God has revealed Himself to mankind. Often people use the phrase, "God has revealed Himself in two books, *general revelation* and *special revelation*." Psalm 19: 1 states," The heavens declare the glory of God; and the firmament sheweth his handywork." Paul, in Rom. 1: 20, says, "For the invisible things of him from the creation of the world are clearly seen, being understood by the things that are made, even his eternal power and Godhead; so that they are without excuse." It is understood from creation that there is a Creator, which is called general revelation. Does this creation communicate to mankind that this Creator is a God who saves? Salvation is only discovered through God's written revelation, which is the only Bible God ever inspired men to write. It is clear from Scripture that the knowledge God wants people to have regarding Him comes from knowing His written Word, the Bible. This knowledge, found in the Old and New Testaments, reveals to mankind how to act toward God and fellow man. The OT law and the Law of Christ are really only different in motivation. Murder, theft, adultery, or any other sin, is still a violation against another person created in the image of God, and thus against God. David's sin, recorded in Psalms 51, was ultimately, against God. Can knowledge about God be gained in peering at a flower for thirty minutes? WMB contended that one could, as can be seen below:

> And now, today we are trying to educate people to…the scientific approach to God, and you can't do that. God is known not by science, but by faith we know God. And I'd say this, that…a man can set down and look at a bunch of flowers, a bouquet, and study that thirty minutes sincerely with all of his heart, and know more about God than he did if he…had all the degrees that a Bible school could give him.[1]

There is a need to understand who God is and why He came in Christ, and what He did. Does nature, the Zodiac, a flower, or a mountain, do a better job than God's eternal Word, the Bible, in teaching us who God is? Does creation tell us how God sent His one and only Son to die for miserable sinners? Of course, creation can make one aware that there must be someone "out there" responsible for all these magnificently created things. However, these are insufficient, in and of themselves, to reveal who God is. For that, His Word, the Bible, is needed. That is not to say that there are not things humans can know about God. Timothy George says, "Even apart from channels of special revelation, it is evident from Scripture that fallen human beings can and do know many true things about God on the basis of general revelation, in both the conscience within and the cosmos without."[2] George goes on to say, "On the basis of God's general revelation, there is this primordial awareness that God is and that, indeed, God is one."[3] This chapter is focused on determining to what extent WMB's teachings on the Person of God can be supported by the Scriptures.

WMB and the Trinity

WMB said he was ordained as an exhorter in a Missionary Baptist Church. These churches were, and are, Trinitarian. In the early days of his ministry WMB stated he was a Trinitarian,[4] but it does not take long to discover that WMB's concept of the Trinity fell outside of Orthodoxy. WMB seemingly professed to believe in the Trinity doctrine up until 1953,[5] where he appeared to do a complete flip on his teaching of the Trinity.[6] In 1954, in his home church in Jeffersonville, WMB clearly showed he rejected the Trinity teaching as false.[7] However, away from home WMB continued to teach the Trinity doctrine, for a while at least.[8] Evidently, WMB did not know which Person was which, because he did call Jesus the third Person of the Trinity.[9] Yet he often did refer to the Holy Spirit as the third Person.[10] WMB modified his views from an Orthodox Trinitarian view to a Modalistic view, where he stated that God is a Trinity of offices,[11] much like a three-foot rule, where the first "twelve inches" is the Father, the second "twelve inches" represents the Son, and the third "twelve inches" represents the Holy Spirit.[12] Unbeknownst to WMB, he contradicted his own "explanation" when he catalogued each twelve inches to be a unit. Properly understood, the first 12 inches, though equal in length to the second 12 inches, is not the second 12 inches, neither is the second 12 inches, though equal in length, the same as the third 12 inches. All three 12 inch lengths make up the three foot rule. It is rather more of a crude "explanation" of the Trinity. God could never be explained as a mathematical formula. However, this "three foot rule" teaching WMB had already contradicted in August, 1953, when he attributed it to the Oneness people, when he declared, "It's a three foot rule that you let out."[13]

One of WMB's views of God was linear and one-dimensional. Yet he contrasted that elsewhere with a two-dimensional view of God when he spoke of God as represented by a triangle.[14] WMB contradicted himself later when he stated that the symbol of the triangle was Rome's symbol.[15] Strangely, he denied the "Oneness position" of the analogy of a finger[16] with three joints and three bones, which is no different from his "three foot rule." One cannot both, *have* and *not* have, a three foot rule and triangle. Not only did WMB hold to a one-dimensional view of God (3 Ft. rule), and a two-dimensional view (Triangle), but WMB also held a three-dimensional view of God. WMB stated God lived in a three-room house[17] which, with its kitchen, living room and bedroom, is yet one house. Pushing this analogy further, the kitchen is *not* the bedroom, and *neither* is the living room the kitchen, etc. Again, this actually would serve as a simple explanation of the Trinity, rather than of the Oneness position. The Creeds added the measures of the same essence, substance, co-equal, yet distinct, etc., for their view of God. With WMB's analogy of a three-room house, these same distinctions cannot be applied. These three views of God make it clear that WMB really had no consistent concept of the Godhead. This is how this looks:

1. God is like a 3 Ft. rule - One dimensional
2. God is a like triangle – Two dimensional
3. <u>God is a like a three-room house - Three dimensional</u>
4. Internal inconsistency, WMB's teaching on the godhead is invalid.

WMB was ignorant of the development of the Trinity doctrine, and its purpose. He became increasingly more intolerant of that view to the point of blasphemy:

> You say, "The blessed holy trinity." Find me the word "trinity" anywhere in the pages of God's Bible...It's not in God's holy Writings. And the "Father, Son, and Holy Ghost" is hatched out of hell; there's no such a thing as three Gods.[18]

> A trinity of spirits...A trinity of frogs...Remember, three unclean spirits, individual spirits...Are you getting it?...They look back to the Nicaea Council at Nicaea, Rome, where the trinity was born at. Notice where they come from... the trinity of frogs came out of an old trinity, give birth to a new trinity, their mother.[19]

WMB accused orthodox Christians of being Tri-Theistic, worshipping three gods.[20] He does appears to have received that from the Oneness people he met in 1936. Warren Chastain employs the following "explanation" of the Trinity: because God is infinite (∞), Christ is infinite, and the Holy Spirit is infinite, the formula looks like, $\infty \times \infty \times \infty = \infty$. Chastain states this is not an adequate explanation, because God is more than a kind of mathematical oneness, but more an organic oneness of life and personality,

> We do not worship the number "one" written large; we need to personally know a Father who relates to man. Although the Trinity is unique so that every

illustration drawn from nature has shortcomings, we can suggest that in God's creation as one rises from the lower forms of life to the higher we encounter a progression away from simple oneness to a complexity of unity. Each man is one, but he is more complex than a one-celled bacterium. Is it glorifying to God to proclaim Him to have a simple mathematical oneness akin to a germ? If the oneness of man involves spiritual aspects as well as physical, surely the oneness of God is not diminished by seeing complexity within that oneness. The mind of man makes a complex one God a possibility; the heart of man makes it a necessity...[21]

God is obviously more complex than we can ever imagine, or think. God created the universe, all the creatures, and all the systems that control all creation. Shall puny little man now comprehend God? Shall man, who cannot even understand "his" universe, or "his" space-time continuum, now attempt to understand God? In order for people to find God, they must start with His self revelation, the Scriptures. God is ONE. Scripture warns not to make any likeness of God.(Ex. 20: 1; Isa. 46: 9).

God said, "I am the Lord..." and not, "We are the Lord..." So, it is within that frame work of Mono-theism people need to find their understanding of God. It is also clear that humans can only comprehend those things within a limited human understanding. Philip Yancey states that man can communicate with a lower being to some extent, but not fully. Imagine trying to explain to your dog what a computer is. Try to explain that to a wood tick. That is a very limited comparison of God communicating to man.[22] Yet, humans may know whatever God has revealed of Himself through His Word, and ultimately through His Son, Jesus.[23]

Though WMB claimed Jesus was neither Jew, nor Gentile (There exists no other human flesh on earth), Jesus was nevertheless human flesh.[24] This claim of Jesus having human flesh was later contradicted, when WMB said that Jesus' blood was God's blood.[25] Science has shown that blood determines the species. In WMB's scheme, therefore, it would logically follow that Jesus' flesh could not have been human flesh, but flesh of God; especially since WMB also said that Jesus took nothing from Mary.[26] He went on to state that the Father is God, the Son is God and the Spirit is God, three manifestations of the One God. WMB also taught the Father is a Spirit[27] and has a body.[28] The Son also has a body and a Spirit and, "the Holy Spirit is a person."[29]This can only mean that, in WMB's theology, contrary to what he said and believed, there are unmistakably signs of three persons, or a Trinity of Persons, in his explanations of the Godhead.

Through a Glass Darkly

The OT revealed One God but, as stated before, there were indications that this Unity was, somehow, a Plurality. This was not a new thing, as is seen in Apocryphal and Rabbinical writings. Indications; shadows; something seen "in a glass darkly," were

CHAPTER SEVENTEEN 227

evident, and in the NT we see staunch Jewish men, like Matthew, Mark, John, Peter, James and Paul, speaking about Jesus being equal with God, without concluding that there was more than one God. These same men attributed personhood to the Holy Spirit, without compromising their Mono-theistic beliefs in the One God. John and Paul could, respectively, write things like,

> Now have they both seen and hated both me and my Father. 25 But this cometh to pass, that the word might be fulfilled that is written in their law, They hated me without a cause. 26 But when the Comforter is come, whom I will send unto you from the Father, even the Spirit of truth, which proceedeth from the Father, he shall testify of me (Jn. 15: 25-26).

> 5 And now, Father, glorify me in your presence with the glory I had with you before the world began. 6 "I have revealed you to those whom you gave me out of the world. They were yours; you gave them to me and they have obeyed your word. 7 Now they know that everything you have given me comes from you. 8 For I gave them the words you gave me and they accepted them. They knew with certainty that I came from you, and they believed that you sent me (Jn. 17: 5-8).

> Though he (Christ Jesus) was God, he did not demand and cling to his rights as God. He made himself nothing; he took the humble position of a slave and appeared in human form. And in human form he obediently humbled himself even further by dying a criminal's death on a cross (Phil. 2: 5).

The Church, since Pre-Niceae, has held to a Trinitarian view of God. The Reformers too held the same view. Martin Luther, disliked the word Trinity, but explains that God is only One; but there are three Persons: Father, Son, and Holy Ghost.[30] In his answer to "Who is the only true God?" Luther answers, "The only true God is the *Triune God*; Father, Son, and Holy Ghost, three distinct Persons in one divine Being, or Essence. (The Holy Trinity).[31] John Calvin also did not like to use the word Trinity, precisely because the word was not in Scripture, but it is abundantly clear from his writings that he was in full support of the doctrine of the Trinity. He said,

> Where names have not been invented rashly, we must beware lest we become chargeable with arrogance and rashness in rejecting them. I wish, indeed, that such names were buried, provided all would concur in the belief that the Father, Son, and Spirit, are one God, and yet that the Son is not the Father, nor the Sprit the Son, but that each has his peculiar subsistence.[32]

Calvin, if one reads him without preconceptions, does a wonderful job of explaining the Trinity. He quotes Heb. 1: 3, where Scripture states very clearly that Christ is "the express image of his person." Scripture designates God as a person, and Christ as the express image of that person. Christ was a person, so there are at least two persons in the Godhead in that one verse alone:

> *The three "Persons" in God.* But there is another special mark by which he designates himself, for the purpose of giving a more intimate knowledge of his nature. While he proclaims his unity, he distinctly sets it before us as existing in three persons. These we must hold, unless the bare and empty name of Deity merely is to flutter in our brain without any genuine knowledge. Moreover, lest any one should dream of a threefold God, or think that the simple essence is divided by the three Persons, we must here seek a brief and easy definition which may effectually guard us from error. But as some strongly inveigh against the term Person as being merely of human inventions let us first consider how far they have any ground for doing so. When the Apostle calls the Son of God "the express image of his person," (Heb. 1: 3,) he undoubtedly does assign to the Father some subsistence in which he differs from the Son. For to hold with some interpreters that the term is equivalent to essence, (as if Christ represented the substance of the Father like the impression of a seal upon wax,) were not only harsh but absurd.[33]

Michael Durrant[34] makes the observation that if, as even Calvin suggests, the Father is different from the Son in his subsistence, one cannot have the ability to count. It is impossible to count anything if what one is counting is unknown. Durrant says that when one asks how many are there in God, it needs to be qualified by inserting some descriptor. How many apples are there in that bowl? How many men are there in the room? Obviously one cannot ask, "How many gods are there?" without being Tri-theists. Augustine's question, "Three what?" can thus not be asked, if "they" consist of three different entities. Durrant makes an important observation when he says that Augustine makes it clear that whatever one says of God does not come from empirical observation. Rather, it comes from assumptions that God is opposite to man.

Augustine warns that one will not just get a false "picture" of God, but an impossible one. It is agreed that from our paradigm as human beings, living in space-time, it would be impossible to put the "Being" of God in a formula, and get it right. That said, it does not mean that the word Trinity cannot be used. Creeds, or any extra-Biblical literature, though important, must always subordinate to the Scriptures. The councils who developed the creeds, stated everything the Scriptures said regarding God the Father, Christ the Son, and the Holy Spirit, without explanation of how exactly this works. The Trinity doctrine was brought into being to combat the heresies of Arianism, Monarchianism, Sabellianism, Modalism, et. al.

CHAPTER SEVENTEEN

Calvin understood the arguments brought forth by opponents of the usage of the word person, and Trinity. He agreed that certain words used in theology are not expressly stated in Scripture, but he did not believe this disqualifies their use to explain a difficult concept. As long as the concept is found within the bounds of Scripture:

> If they call it a foreign term, because it cannot be pointed out in Scripture in so many syllables, they certainly impose an unjust law - a law which would condemn every interpretation of Scripture that is not composed of other words of Scripture. But if by foreign they mean that which, after being idly devised, is superstitiously defended, - which tends more to strife than edification, - which is used either out of place, or with no benefit which offends pious ears by its harshness, and leads them away from the simplicity of God's Word, I embrace their soberness with all my heart. For I think we are bound to speak of God as reverently as we are bound to think of him. As our own thoughts respecting him are foolish, so our own language respecting him is absurd. Still, however, some medium must be observed. The unerring standard both of thinking and speaking must be derived from the Scriptures: by it all the thoughts of ours minds, and the words of our mouths, should be tested. But in regard to those parts of Scripture which, to our capacities, are dark and intricate, what forbids us to explain them in clearer terms - terms, however, kept in reverent and faithful subordination to Scripture truth, used sparingly and modestly, and not without occasion? Of this we are not without many examples. When it has been proved that the Church was impelled, by the strongest necessity, to use the words Trinity and Person, will not he who still inveighs against novelty of terms be deservedly suspected of taking offence at the light of truth, and of having no other ground for his invective, than that the truth is made plain and transparent?[35]

John Calvin stated that it was necessary for the church to use terms like Trinity and Person, to root out heresies and to unmask false teachers. This is clear in the deceptive teaching of Arius, who publicly stated Christ was God, and the Son of God, because he could not deny that was what Scripture states. However, he also taught that Christ was created, and had a beginning. This is also exactly how WMB operated. WMB could not deny that Scripture taught that Jesus had a Father, but he also taught that Jesus and His Father were the same person:

> Jesus couldn't have been His Own Father...If He's one like your finger's one, then what? Then He was His own daddy. How could He have been? That's wrong, He had a Father, Jesus did.[36]

> He was the Father; He was Son; He was Holy Ghost. You try to make three Gods, friend; it's wrong; it's error.[37]

The church, in order to expose Arius' error, added that Christ was eternal and consubstantial with the Father. That Christ is a Person is beyond dispute. WMB declared that God is a person, and the Holy Spirit is a Person,

> God is a Person. Therefore He has to have a certain place that He dwells.[38]

> Christian Science says the Holy Ghost is a thought. And the Bible said, "He, the Holy Ghost." And He is a personal pronoun; it's a Person, not a thought; it's a Person. Absolutely.[39]

There is no argument with WMB when he says that all three are persons. There is also no argument in WMB regarding God being three, as we can see below:

> God dwells in three. God is perfected in three."[40]

WMB also spoke of the "Three in One," but made it clear it could not have been three people,[41] and of course, that is agreed. As stated, Augustine also wrestled with this concept of "three what?" Countless heresies sprung up, already in apostolic times. It was because of these heresies that the orthodox position was developed. It would be wrong and arrogant to just dismiss the arguments brought forth in this context. It was not a decision the church Fathers came to lightly.

There is a strong debate in this Post-Modern era that the teaching of the Trinity is no longer relevant, and there is a return to a more Modalistic view of the Godhead. There are others who seek to "relativize" the concept of the Trinity in light of our space age and Quantum Physics. That is simply a return to an Eastern adaptation of the Christ principle, which has occurred and can occur where and whenever "God," decides. In Thor Hall's thinking, man must not be so naïve as to think that this planet earth and Jesus are the center of everything in this universe:

> I would propose the following formula as a working hypothesis: (1) that the contemporary Christian view of God as the divine Spirit active in the universe—i.e., as the creative force at work universally, as the redemptive presence incarnate where there is need, and as the indwelling spirit wherever there is spirituality; (2) that the symbol of this new Trinity not be the triangle, but a sphere, coterminous with the universe and penetrated by a dynamic dimension which energizes the whole, actualizes itself in the particular, and inspires everything and every one who is possessed of spirituality; and (3) that to relate this view to classical trinitarian thought, one can simply say that "God the Father" is here in the universal divine Spirit; "God the Son" or "Christ" the historical actualization—incarnation—of divine Spirit; and "God the Holy Spirit" the personal interiorization—indwelling—of divine Spirit."[42]

This seems to be another re-statement of a Modalistic view of God and appears to

CHAPTER SEVENTEEN

be based on conjecture and presumption that there is other life outside our Universe. While that may, or may not, be true, is not the point here. This is what is known, "Christ came to earth to save sinners."[43] Scripture does not reveal any other saving work of Christ outside this Universe and man can only say with what Moses said,

> The secret things belong unto the LORD our God: but those things which are revealed belong unto us."(Deu. 29: 29a)

When Jesus said, "The meek shall inherit the earth," (Matt. 5: 5), he did not mean meek Extra-terrestrials would qualify."When Scripture is read without knowing the Trinitarian "controversy," there does not appear to be any real issue with the "person" of God. It is clear that readers, when they read, "the Father," they understand that God the creator is meant. It is understood that this God is One God.

Also, when reading about Jesus, the reader knows He is the Son of God. It is also clear that the religious leaders of Jesus' day understood Jesus claim to be equal with God. The reader too, will realize that only God could do the things Jesus did. He had power over nature, disease, death, and He forgave sins, something only God can do.

The person of the Holy Spirit, when read without pre-conceived notions, is also not seen as the introduction of another God. Thus, there should be no problem.

However, it is not likely that any person will have lived in total isolation. That is where the problem comes in, because one will come across the term "Trinity" regarding the person of God. Upon inquiry, they will either be told that, the doctrine of the Trinity is a mystery and to be accepted as such, or the Trinity doctrine is wrong, and to be rejected. The other issue is that if people express questions, regarding either side of the debate, they will likely get sincere, but wrong explanations. So, how does one respond to that? First, as indicated earlier, the controversy must be seen in its proper context. Second, man cannot speak scientifically about God. God cannot be examined, or empirically observed (Jn. 1: 18). Therefore, all that can be known of God, His Son Jesus declared. Jesus spoke of God as Father, or as a "person" apart from himself (Cf., Mt. 6: 9). Jesus also referred to the Holy Spirit as God being distinct from Himself,

> And I will ask the Father, and he will give you another Advocate, to be with you forever. 17 This is the Spirit of truth, whom the world cannot receive, because it neither sees him nor knows him. You know him, because he abides with you, and he will be in you...26 But the Advocate, the Holy Spirit, whom the Father will send in my name, will teach you everything, and remind you of all that I have said to you (Jn. 14: 16, 17, 26).

> When the Advocate comes, whom I will send to you from the Father, the Spirit of truth who comes from the Father, he will testify on my behalf (Jn. 15: 26).

> Nevertheless I tell you the truth: it is to your advantage that I go away, for if I do not go away, the Advocate will not come to you; but if I go, I will send him to you (Jn. 16: 7).

Therefore, based on all the above, it is seen that the Father is God, the Son is God, and the Holy Spirit is God. These "Three" interacted with each other as is seen in Jesus' baptism, for example, as well as in the Book of Revelation. Scripture does not reveal the "mechanics" of how this works. However, for reasons of simplicity, apologetics and confession of what one believed regarding God, the Trinity formula was developed. Thus, there is no reason to abandon the doctrine of the Trinity as expressed in the Creeds, nor is there a reason to adopt a Modalistic position. Further debate regarding the Trinity doctrine is always encouraged. Not in the light of Darwinian space age technology, but in the light of Scripture which must remain the sole authority in faith and practice.

WMB said that God is *a* Spirit, echoing the KJV (mis)translation of John 4: 24. However, the original manuscript reads, "God is Spirit," not God is *a* Spirit.[44] From this mistranslation sprung up a whole different development of God making man in His own image.[45] Jesus, who is fully God and fully man, even according to WMB, only became God at His baptism[46] and ceased to be God in Gethsemane,[47] WMB said. The Spirit left Jesus so he could die as a man, a sinner,[48] though they were not His sins He carried.[49] However, as shown above, Jesus could not have been a man, according to WMB's theology, where He was both God in flesh and in Spirit (Docetism). If Jesus was God's flesh and blood,[50] and not human, and the Spirit of God left him, which one of the Offices died on the cross? Humans are not saved by the death of an office; but by the death of the man Jesus, who was God. WMB's Oneness, or Modalistic view of God, is not adequate in bringing a better understanding than does the Trinity, regarding the Person of God.

WMB and Heterodoxy

The reality is that WMB's description of God as being three offices in One Person is not the only one view he held of the Godhead. It gets rather complex and reflects the early Gnostic understanding of God. There is no single source to which one can point in order to determine where WMB would have gotten these ideas.[51] However, his messages are riddled with all sorts of references that a discerning reader will understand to come from heterodox sources. These include, but are not limited to, Freemasonry, Gnosticism, Hermeticism, K.K.K, Mormonism, Seventh Day Adventism,[52] British-Israelism, Eastern Mysticism, Kundalini, Jehovah's Witnesses, Jesus-Only Pentecostalism, Christian Science, Native Indian lore, Shamanism, Irish folklore, Kentucky mountain magic, New Thought, Meta-Physicism, Theosophy, E. W. Kenyon, Franklin Hall, et. al.

WMB's belief system includes that of a Great Fountain of Spirit(s)[53] from which seven spirits emanated.[54] These spirits, in turn, created the Logos.[55] This is the Gnostic concept of the Pleroma, the Fullness, or the Divine Being, from which aeons, or spiritual powers or spirits, emanate which, in turn, create the Demiurge, the great architect, or

CHAPTER SEVENTEEN

Creator.[56] WMB's use of the concepts, "Great Fountain of Spirits" and Architect, or Great Architect"[57] is found in Freemasonry, as well in Jehovah's Witness, and in SDA sources. WMB taught that in eternity, within that hierarchy of the Great Fountain of Spirit(s), or Spirits, are found the angels, and next is God.[58] WMB stated that the Holy Spirit came down past the angels to redeem sinners.[59] This hierarchy is, of course, not found anywhere in Scripture. Within Orthodoxy, the Holy Spirit, though active in convicting sinners, is not the Redeemer of the human race; that is the work of Christ. This great Fountain of Spirit(s), spoken of earlier, consisted of seven spirits[60] who went out and created the Logos.[61] Since Jesus *is* the Word, how then can the Word of God create the Word of God? This is another serious contradiction. The seven spirits[62] WMB described as being the seven colors of the rainbow.[63] WMB mentioned some colors, red for love and blue for fellowship,[64] or righteousness.[65] He also said these seven Spirits were the seven fruits of the Spirit.[66] Of course, Scripture lists nine (Gal. 5: 16) and it reads, the *fruit* of the Spirit, not *fruits*."

WMB stated that these seven spirits were poured into, what he termed, the Logos, a theophany.[67] God, as a Spirit could not go down and talk to man, WMB claimed, and therefore He would come as a man.[68] This, said WMB, God accomplished by forming a supernatural body, because He is not like the air but He needs a body to dwell in.[69] At this time it is necessary to point out that, amid all WMB's inconsistencies and contradictions, it appears that whom WMB called God, was NOT the Great Spirit. No, it was a created being,[70] the first bodily form of God,[71] because God is[72] and was a man,[73] with a body like a man.

This overarching spirit in WMB's theology also includes the pre-existent spirits of sons (and daughters) of God.[74] Christians have eternal life, declared WMB, because of their existence prior to the creation of the world, in eternity.[75] Originally the spirits of Christians were a part of the Great Fountain of Spirits and had to go down to earth.[76] Christians have their "theophanies", celestial bodies[77] waiting for them upon death[78] and they return to God[79] because they were created as supernatural beings[80] and they are part of God.[81]

This is all very problematic, because IF man is just as eternal as God, what differentiates them? WMB said that this ocean of God was poured in its fullness into Jesus, whereas man only has a cupful of ocean water, it would make him act, like God.[82] In other words, it is not the quantity of the Spirit that makes the difference. What differentiates Christ from a man if they both originate in eternity and are made "theophanies" which come to earth and return to Heaven?

This is Eastern mysticism.[83] WMB stated he existed before the creation of the world, in eternity.

> When God created me, William Branham, I was before the foundation of the world. He made my being, my spirit, I wasn't conscious of anything, as far as I know of, but... I was there.[84]

God created man in His own image, a spirit being,[85] a god,[86] before he created him from the dust,[87] said WMB. On the one hand he stated that man was created, yet he is as eternal as God; on the other hand, Jesus, though created, was not an eternal Son.[88] On the one hand, Jesus is less than man; on the other hand He is God the Father. On the one hand man is Christ, the Spirit man, who is the Son of God; on the other hand is Adam the Spirit man, who is the Son of God.[89] Can this be reconciled? No, because "God is not the author of confusion, but of peace, as in all churches of the saints" (1 Cor. 14: 33).

The first "man," that was created was God,[90] said WMB. This God, as previously noted, needed a body to dwell in, because He is not like the air, He had a body like a man. The second man,[91] WMB stated, was created a spirit being, which WMB called a "theophany."[92] The third man[93] was man created out of the dust of the earth (Adam) and in him was placed this, in eternity created, pre-existent theophany,[94] which became his soul. This "soul," from 1948 through 1964, he referred to as the nature of man's spirit.[95]

God created all these spirits and "theophanies" in eternity[96] and, as stated earlier that is why humans, presumably at least the "chosen ones," have eternal life. That is a problem. Regardless of where Orthodox theologians stand regarding election, pro, or con, it is agreed that not all people go to heaven. That being true, where are all the bad spirits "stored?" In WMB's system, upon birth, a spiritual body of nature,[97] or an angel spirit,[98] a little messenger,[99] a spirit of a worldly nature,[100] enters the baby.[101] It is impossible, of course, for there to be that many options, which makes it unscriptural. However, the larger issue by far is that this teaching is indicative of something sinister, which will be examined next.

WMB and Reincarnation

Reincarnation is the belief that after death, the soul/spirit of a person enters another body. WMB, in his Church Age Book, edited by Lee Vayle, stated, "You will want to know if I believe in the doctrine of preexistence. I don't believe in that Mormon doctrine of the preexistence of souls any more than I believe in reincarnation or the transmigration of souls."[102] That is what WMB said, cased closed, or is it? It does not take a Ph.D. in rocket science to discover that WMB never once used the word "transmigration," in any of his messages! It was added by Vayle. Neither is it rocket science to see WMB *did* believe in the Pre-existence of souls/spirits,[103] reminiscent of LDS teachings.[104]

How is this contradiction explained? WMB preached *The Seven Church Ages* in a series of messages from Dec. 04 through Dec. 11, 1960. He delivered a series of messages on the "Revelation of the Seven Seals" in 1963. Sometime after, the late Lee Vayle, a follower and close personal acquaintance of WMB,[105] edited the messages for a book version. WMB started calling him a scholar, or Dr. Vayle, in 1953,[106] although there is no record to be found of his alleged scholarship. There were many controversies regarding the editing of the book, even before WMB went off the scene. These recorded messages, as preached in Jeffersonville, were sent first to Ruth Sumner, of Tifton GA., who transcribed the tapes and typed the completed manuscript. On Oct. 14, 1962, she delivered the manuscript into the hands of WMB in Jeffersonville.[107] More than a year passed, before the manuscript was delivered to Anna Jean Moore Price, the daughter of WMB's supporter, Jack Moore.[108] For several reasons she was not able to do the editing, so it was passed to Lee Vayle.[109] According to Rebekah Branham Smith, numerous people were involved in the editing of the book, and each correction was personally viewed by WMB.[110] Lee Vayle was said to have been in constant communication with WMB regarding issues in the book.[111]

The book went to press with the *Voice of Healing*, in Dallas, Texas, which was originally a magazine started by WMB, and turned over to Gordon Lindsay.[112] WMB, about a month before his death stated the following:

> You all seen in my book, it'll all be drawn out in the *Seven Church Ages*, which He told me. Which I stand by as a witness to God to be judged at the day of judgment for it. It come from God, not from my thinking.[113]

There were many rumors regarding the book, prior to printing and well into the 1970s. Some of these issues personally confronted this author. The major concern was the actual authorship, was it WMB, or Lee Vayle?[114] According to Smith, WMB became aware of these issues and halted the printing for a while.[115] About two weeks before his death, WMB issued a cheque for the release of the book to print,[116] indicating his approval of the contents. Smith, in her article, makes it clear that she believed her father to be the author of the book, although she acknowledges that controversies still exist.[117]

As asked prior, is the case closed regarding WMB believing in reincarnation? This needs to be looked at in some detail. Most religions that promote reincarnation believe the spirit enters the same species, although the Kausitaki Upanishad states that, "He is reborn here either as a worm, or as a butterfly, or as a fish, or as a bird, or as a lion, or as a serpent, or as a tiger, or as a person, or as some other being in this or in that condition, according to his works, according to his knowledge"[118] This type of reincarnation,[119] was abhorred by WMB. However, it is to be noted that he disagreed only with the concept of reincarnation or transmigration to a different species.[120] In other words, did WMB believe a person can be reincarnated as another person, and not an animal, or an insect, like some Pagans do? WMB did speak about Judas and Jesus being re-incarnated.[121] In fact, he said that Jesus Christ was reincarnated in His Church in this last day, and let out that, "This is me that's concerned in here."[122] WMB was very careful and spoke mostly about Christ being reincarnated in His Church, but at the same time he speaks about Jesus Christ being reincarnated in flesh doing signs and wonders.[123] The only person that would have appeared to have qualified for this in WMB's church would have been WMB. No one else made any of the claims WMB made. The spirit WMB spoke about was on him[124] and in him,[125] allegedly working miracles, signs and wonders, just like Jesus did.[126] WMB stated clearly that if the spirit of Beethoven lived in him, he would be Beethoven;[127] if the spirit of John Dillinger lived in him he would be Dillinger,[128] and again, if the spirit of Fidel Castro dwelt in him, he would be Castro.[129] If the spirit of Shakespeare lived in a man, that man would be Shakespeare.[130] It was shown previously that all of the alleged works WMB performed, they were sadly lacking, or even devoid of, truth and substance. That being true, what was that spirit on and in WMB, which performed all these things? WMB went on,

> And if Jesus Christ is in me, his works I'll do, because it's him. And didn't he say that same thing would take place, see?[131]

WMB was careful not to spell it out, though some followers, as stated prior, including his direct family, did believe he was the Lord. They are still waiting for his return.

Throughout his messages WMB is seen emphasizing the fact that it was not him, but the Spirit of Christ, Christ, the angel of God, the Pillar of Fire, etc., who did the works. In so much, that one would say in the style of Shakespeare, "Methinks he doth protest too much." In Col. 2: 18, Paul warns the Church regarding false humility,

> Let no man beguile you of your reward in a voluntary humility and worshipping of angels, intruding into those things which he hath not seen, vainly puffed up by his fleshly mind.

Amongst followers and ex-followers, the jury is still out on whether WMB understood the implications and ramifications of his "reincarnation" teaching. This author believes that WMB, though neither neatly nor systematically, *did* believe in a form of reincarnation. He often said that a spirit never dies but it stays on the earth,[132] and enters another person at birth. Was WMB real clear on how exactly this happened? WMB was never real clear on anything, especially in his doctrine of man. He did say man is eternal,[133] and existed in heaven.[134] WMB failed to give a satisfactory Scriptural explanation of how man could be eternal, and yet become a sinner in need of a Savior. Sin, according to WMB, started in Heaven,[135] and when Lucifer was thrown out of heaven two thirds of the angels came with him and these angels became humans.[136] When these humans died their spirits entered new born babies, because Satan takes his man but never his spirit of the earth. One third of the angels, or pre-existent human spirits,[137] stayed true and those spirits enter new born babies as well. Elsewhere, WMB stated that the dead saints and sinners still walk the earth, being judged for their deeds done in the body.[138]

CHAPTER SEVENTEEN

WMB believed that humankind possessed an eternal seed that was placed in people from eternity. When God's light would strike it, it would spring to life.[139] That is reminiscent of the "Spark within," teaching,[140] which is found within Eastern Mysticism and New Age doctrine. This divine spark assists people to find their way back to God.[141] Nowhere in Scripture is there a hint of God depositing seed in pre-existing human spirits, in order to illuminate this seed after they have come to earth. This is not the way God ordained to manifest them to be the sons of God. Instead, God ordained that faith was to come through hearing the Word of God, which is the Seed that would be sown in people's hearts (Matt. 13: 19). There is no teaching in Scripture that Christians are God's seed. Rather, they *become* Abraham's seed or off-spring, through faith in Christ and become heirs of the Promise (Gal. 3: 29). The order is important here. Paul says, "And if ye be Christ's, then are ye Abraham's seed, and heirs according to the promise." He does not say, "If ye be Abraham's seed then are ye Christ's..." This is clearly demonstrated in Christ's encounter and dialogue with the Jewish leaders, they were Abraham's seed, but they hated Jesus enough to kill Him" (Jn. 8: 37, ff.).

According to WMB, Christians, both men and women, are predestined to eternal life, because of that divine seed resident in their pre-existent state with God. What WMB did not think about is that Adam and Eve, the first man and woman, were created male and female, which WMB interpreted to mean "androgynous." If these pre-existent beings are androgynous, how are they separated today? How does a baby girl get her spirit? Is this not a death-blow to WMB's doctrine of the Serpent's Seed, the linchpin of his message?

His mission, WMB said, was to correct all the errors that had crept into the church over the millennia and lead God's people back to God.[142] Throughout his messages, WMB continued to show that his understanding of the Biblical God was far removed from what the church has held from the very beginning right throughout the ages.

To what extent can WMB's teachings on the Person of God be supported by the Scriptures? WMB's "explanation" of the Godhead, as one dimensional, two dimensional, and three dimensional, is contradictory and thus invalid. His teaching on God being an androgynous being is not found in Scripture. God is neither male nor female. Adam too, was not androgynous, as WMB taught. God was also not *created*, as WMB alleged, neither did God become God.. Man was never part of God and never will be part of God, God cannot change. God is not an overarching spirit like the Gnostic concept of the Pleroma and the demiurge. WMB's taught his own ideas of reincarnation and they must be dismissed. To no extent can WMB's teachings on the Person of God be supported by the Scriptures.

Notes - Chapter Seventeen

[1] WMB, *God Hiding Himself In Simplicity*, Apr. 12, 1963, Albuquerque, NM; See also: *As The Eagle Stirreth*, Tulsa, "My first Bible was nature. If you'll just watch the way nature works, you can find God."

[2] Timothy George, *GOD, the Holy Trinity, Reflections of Christian Faith and Practice*, Ed. Timothy George, (Grand Rapids, MI: Baker Academic, 2006, 175 pp.), 120.

[3] Ibid.

[4] *At Thy Word*, LA, "See, you believe in God; you believe in the Son, believe in the Holy Ghost; that's the Trinity. We believe in that."

[5] WMB, *Testimony Of Jesus Christ*, Aug. 29, 1953, Chicago, IL, "The Trinity, not three gods, but three persons in one God."

[6] One of WMB's reasons for rejecting the Trinity was that that the word "Trinity" was not in the Bible, which no Trinitarian would deny. However, just because a word is not found in Scripture, does not mean that the word is invalid.. The word "Bible" is not in the Bible and WMB used it 12,938 times in his messages, which would make it an average of eleven times per message. The phrase "Baptism of the Holy Ghost" is not found in the Bible, WMB used it 1,237 times. The phrase "Baptism of the Holy Spirit" is not found in the Bible, WMB used it 506 times. The term Church Age is not in the Bible, he used 1166 times. The word "predestination" is not in the KJV Bible, WMB used it 104 times. His argument is not valid. More will be said about this later.

[7] WMB, *Q & A*, May 15, 1954, Jeff., IN, "Now, in the first place, not one place in the Bible was Trinity ever mentioned. You find it and show it to me. There's no such a thing. It's Catholic error, and you Protestants bow to it."

[8] ____, *Gifts*, Dec. 07, 1956, Brooklyn, NY, "Anyone that knows God, and knows His Bible, know that those three are One. Not three gods, one God, manifested in three persons." See also: *Resurrection Of Lazarus*, "May the Holy Spirit, the third Person of the Trinity, come in now."

[9] *South Africa Testimony*, "Now, tonight Jesus Christ has risen from the dead, and is living right here among us in Spirit form, called the Holy Spirit, the Holy Spirit of God, which is Jesus Christ, the third Person of the Trinity."

[10] WMB, *Our Hope Is In God*, Sep. 29, 1951, New York, NY, "He said, 'This is My Beloved Son…setting at the right-hand of God the Father, making intercessions now for we who've accepted the Holy Spirit, the third Person of the Trinity."

[11] ____, *Hebrews Chapter One*, Aug. 21, 1957, Jeff., IN, "Who is this great guy, this great fellow Christ? Here: God in Father, Son, and Holy Spirit is not as the trinity…But it's not a trinity of people. It's a trinity of office of one God."

[12] *Deep Calleth Unto The Deep*, "And that makes God like a three foot rule. The first twelve inches God, the Father; second twelve inches God, the Son; third twelve inches God, the Holy

CHAPTER SEVENTEEN

Spirit. That's the reason we was commanded to baptize in the Name of Father, Son, Holy Ghost. But it's the same God, not three Gods, which, that'd be heathen...But it's our God, one God."

[13] *The Testimony Of Jesus Christ.*

[14] *God's Provided Approach,* "Father, Son, and Holy Ghost. Everything is in a three. And a three is a triangle."

[15] *Church Age Book.* 184, "Now how was this trinity expressed? It was expressed by an equilateral triangle even as it is expressed in Rome today. Strange, the Hebrews did not have such a concept."

[16] *Palmerworm, Locust, Cankerworm, Caterpillar,* "You Oneness brethren, many of you get off the wrong track when you try to think that God is one like your finger is one. He can't be His Own Father."

[17] *Fellowship,* "God lived in a three room house: it's Father, Son, and Holy Ghost." See also: WMB, *God's Provided Way Of Approach To Fellowship,* Jul. 09, 1960, Klamath Falls, OR, "God lived in a three room house."; *Basis Of Fellowship,* Feb. 14, 1961, Long Beach, CA, "God lived in a three room house: Father, Son, and Holy Spirit."

[18] *Palmerworm, Locust, Cankerworm, Caterpillar.*

[19] *Anointed Ones.*

[20] WMB, *I Will Restore,* Mar. 09, 1957, Brkfst., Phoenix, AZ, "They had one God, the Father, with a long beard. I seen the pictures right at the Vatican. They had another one, God, the Son, with a younger man and a little bird flying around like a dove, calling the Holy Ghost."

[21] Warren Chastain, *Muslim Stumbling blocks,* in *Perspectives on the World Christian Movement,* ed. Ralph D. Winter and Stephen C. Hawthorne, (Pasadena, CA: William Carey Library, 3rd Ed., July 2000).

[22] Philip Yancey, *Reaching for the Invisible God,* (Grand Rapids, MI: ZPH, 2000), 109.

[23] "The secret things belong unto the LORD our God: but those things which are revealed belong unto us and to our children for ever, that we may do all the words of this law" (Deut. 29: 29). "No man hath seen God at any time; the only begotten Son, which is in the bosom of the Father, he hath declared him" (Jn. 1: 18).

[24] WMB, *The Perfection,* Apr. 19, 1957, Jeff., IN, "But there came One from the portals of glory; none other, not a man, not a good man, neither a Jew nor a Gentile; He was nothing less than Almighty God hid in human flesh."

[25] _____, *Conferences,* Apr. 10, 1961, Bloomington, IL, "Listen, if that was the blood of a Jew or Gentile, we're all lost. That was the blood of God Himself. He wasn't no Jew nor Gentile: He was God manifested in the flesh."

[26] _____, *Super Sign,* Jun. 24, 1962, South Gate, CA, "God created the entire Being of Christ in the womb of Mary, and she was just a woman, an incubator, that bare this Son. Wasn't nothing of her."

27 *Deity Of Jesus Christ.* "God is a Spirit."

28 *Messiah.*

29 *Sirs, We Would See Jesus,* Tifton, "Not a thought now, the Holy Spirit is a Person."

30 Martin Luther, *Small Catechism*, (Saint Louis, MO: Concordia Publishing House, 1943), 32.

31 Ibid., 49-51.

32 John Calvin, *Institutes Of The Christian Religion*, Transl. Henry Beveridge, Vol. 1, (Grand Rapids, MI: Wm. B. Eerdmans Publishing Company, 1973), 110.

33 Ibid., 110.

34 Michael Durrant, *Theology and Intelligibility*, (London: Routledge & Kegan Paul, 1973), 145-196.

35 Calvin. 111.

36 WMB, *Lord, Show Us The Father And It Sufficeth Us*, Sep. 07, 1953, Aft., Chicago, IL.

37 *Questions And Answers*, May 15, 1954.

38 *Dedication Of Building.*

39 WMB, *Hebrews Chapter Six And Seven*, Sep. 15, 1957, AM, Jeff., IN.

40 *Dedication Of Building.*

41 WMB, *Hebrews Chapter Four*, Sep. 01, 1957, PM, Jeff., IN. See also: *Ephesian Church Age*, "The Trinitarian, the Triune people that believed in the trinity, which finally formed in the Catholic church, they went to complete Trinity, making God three people."

42 Thor Hall, *Evolution Of Christology*, (Nashville, TN: AP, 1982), 111-127.

43 Glory to God in the highest, and on earth peace, good will toward Men. (Lu. 2: 14). ; This [is] a faithful saying, and worthy of all acceptation, that Christ Jesus came into the world to save sinners; of whom I am chief. (1 Tim 1: 15).

44 The reader is encouraged to read the Translators' Preface to the King James Version 1611. In it the translators write about the need for updating this Translation.

45 WMB stated that God first created Adam as spirit and afterwards he created him from the earth, a very Gnostic idea that Irenaeus condemned in his *Against Heresies*. Paul contradicts that by writing, "The first man is of the earth, earthy; the second man is the Lord from heaven" (1 Cor. 15: 47). WMB's interpretation is not Scriptural.

46 *Church And Its Condition*, "And John said, 'I bare record, seeing the Spirit of God like a Dove coming down, and abiding on Him.'…That's when God and Man became one. That's when heaven and earth embraced each other. Hallelujah. That's when God was made flesh…that's when God came down from the Spirit form and was made a Man and dwell among us…when God and man was made one on that great memorial day when John baptized Jesus."

47 *It Is The Rising Of The Sun*, "The Spirit left Him, in the Garden of Gethsemane. He had to die, a man."

[48] WMB, *Unpardonable Sin*, Oct. 24, 1954, Jeff., IN, He took the sin of every man, every beast, every mortal, upon Himself, and died as a sinner, with your sins upon Him." Jesus did not die for the sins of animals because animals do not sin.

[49] *Demonology, Religious Realm*, "He died a sinner, knowing no sin, yet our sin was on Him."

[50] WMB, like many others, interpreted Acts 20: 28, to say that God shed His blood for the Church. This derives from the Vulgate translation, "Church of God." Better MSS read, "Church of the Lord."

[51] 1. WMB had no formal education beyond the 7th grade. This is not a slight against WMB, it is a simple fact. He already demonstrated difficulties in understanding the Bible. 2. He likely would not have had access to Hindu teaching, even though he was in India for a campaign. It seems more probable he received "bite-sized" pieces of these heterodox teachings through other media, such as listed in the text.

[52] The SDA is included only because of some of their teachings, which are not accepted within Evangelicalism. This author is acquainted with godly people within that denomination.

[53] WMB, *Hebrews Chapter Seven # 2*, Sep. 22, 1957, Jeff., IN, "God, in the beginning, was a great fountain of Spirit." See also: *Hebrews Chapter One*, "The Logos, and this great Fountain, this great Fountain of Spirit which had no beginning or no end; this great Spirit began to form, in the creation, and the Logos that went out from It was the Son of God. It was the only visible form that the Spirit had. And It was a theophany, which means a body, and the body was like a man."

[54] *Q & A on Genesis*, "I think that the people today that are possessed with this Spirit, or the spirit, [are] a part of these angelic beings, spirits which rotated off of God…"

[55] WMB, *Thirsting For Life*, Jun. 30, 1957, Chicago, IL, "And the Logos, which was the Son of God went out, created by these great fountains of purity, God, as those Spirits went out, and it created the Logos."

[56] The reader is encouraged to read Irenaeus' *Against Heresies* to more clearly see the connection between WMB and Gnosticism. This does not imply that WMB studied or knew firsthand the beliefs of Gnosticism. He more than likely adopted these teachings through secondary sources. Eg., Pleroma, in Gnosticism means Fountainhead, or Fullness, a word WMB used; Demiurge means architect, another word WMB used numerous times.

[57] Regular Grand Lodge of England, "Great Architect of the Universe," available from http://www.rgle.org.uk/RGLE_Tenet.htm, (accessed August 11, 2012).

[58] WMB, *God Perfecting His Church*, Dec. 04, 1954, Binghamton, NY, "There is a of heaven…The first is the Holy Spirit, above, for Christians. The next layer is Angels. And the next heavens is God. Holy Spirit, Angels and God… The Holy Spirit come a past Angels, come down to redeem sinners." The Holy Spirit did not redeem sinners, as WMB stated. Scripture says that Christ came into the world to save sinners. – PMD.

[59] *God Perfecting His Church*.

⁶⁰ *Q & A on Hebrews #2*, "And God was this great Spirit. We pictured Him like…the seven colors of the rainbow that covers…All those seven spirits (as we get in Revelations), they come out, was--made up God, was perfection."

⁶¹ *Thirsting For Life*, Chicago, "…those Spirits went out, and it created the Logos. And it was a body. It was in the form of what we are now, which is called in the clergy way of speaking it, a theophany. It's a body that doesn't have a spirit in it."

⁶² WMB used the term *Seven Spirits* found in Rev. 1: 4. The first part of this verse identifies the One who gives the blessing, "him which is, and which was, and which is to come" (Yahweh) with the God and Father of the Lord Jesus Christ (V. 6). The seven spirits John spoke of were not seated on the Throne of God, but were located before the throne. In Rev. 4: 2, John makes clear that there was only ONE sitting on the throne. The Lamb was in the midst of the throne (Rev. 7: 17), which echoes Jesus when He said He is in the bosom of the Father (Jn. 1: 18). It is clear that the Seven Spirits are not God the Father, but are understood to be the seven eyes of the LORD, which run to and fro through the whole earth (Zech. 4: 10; Rev. 5: 6). These spirits could be angels (Heb 1: 13-14), because in the Apocrypha we find reference to seven angels before the throne, "I am Raphael, one of the Seven Holy Angels which present the prayers of the saints, and which go in and out before the glory of the Holy One" (Tobit 12: 15). However, traditionally it is understood that the seven spirits refer to the sevenfold Spirit of God (Cf. Isa. 11: 2). If this is correct then, in this drama described by John, the following is seen: God the Father, Christ and the Sevenfold Spirit. In Scripture the number seven is understood to be the number of perfection.

⁶³ WMB, *Life*, May 12, 1958, Everett, MA, "That great Spirit, we would call it the--the colors of the rainbow, the best way I could illustrate it. One was the Spirit of love, the other one, the Spirit of righteousness, and so forth, the seven Spirits of God, that make up God." See also: *Life*, May 19, 1958, Bangor, ME, "There's only one type of Eternal Life, and that is God's Life. That was the great Spirit in the beginning, the seven Spirits of God like the seven rainbow colors."

⁶⁴ *Baptism Of The Holy Spirit*, "The first great Spirit of God which is love. God's like the great rainbow; we couldn't imagine what He looks like. But just say He looked like the rainbow in Spirit. The perfect Spirit of love, red; blue, the perfect Spirit of fellowship, just all perfect Spirits. And then they begin to condescending, coming down, and they come all the way down from…Agapao love to Phileo love, and on down to lust, and down to the lowest."

⁶⁵ *Life*, Everett.

⁶⁶ *Revelation Chapter Four # 2*, "The seven Spirits of God are the seven fruits of the Spirit that would reflect back in His people."

⁶⁷ *Q & A on Hebrews, # 2*, "It was a Theophany, that all this rainbow condescended into a Theophany. Moses saw It when it passed through the rock like that. He saw the back parts, said, "It looked like a man."

⁶⁸ WMB, *Jehovah-Jireh*, Aug. 10, 1957, Edmonton, AB, CAD, "He said, 'I'm going down to talk to Abraham, He might not understand Me. If I go as a man, he will know it.'"

⁶⁹ WMB, *We Would See Jesus,* May 16, 1957, Saskatoon, SK, CAD, "And then the Logos that went out of God in the beginning become what we would call a theophany, or a supernatural body. God is just not like the air but He's in a body."

⁷⁰ *Q & A on Genesis,* "The first creation was God himself; then out of God came the Logos, which was the Son of God; then out of the Logos, which was the word, 'In the beginning was the Word, and the Word was with God, and the Word was God. And the Word was made flesh and dwelt among us,' out of the Logos came forth the--the man."

⁷¹ *The Pillar Of Fire,* "The very beginning of nature of creation was God. And now, the Bible teaches us that the Logos went out of God, or I might say, all of the God becoming his first body form when the Logos went out of God."

⁷² WMB, *Q & A,* Oct. 15, 1961, AM, Jeff., IN, "God is a man. And there's only really one, and that is a man."

⁷³ *Why Are We Not A Denomination?* "God is a man, the Bible said He was a man. He is a man."

⁷⁴ WMB, *Hebrews Chapter Two #3,* Aug. 28, 1957, Jeff., IN, "And what God does is **off of God,** which is as eternal as God is. And man's just as eternal as his Creator, because he was made from eternity."

⁷⁵ _____, *Believer's Position In Christ,* Jan. 16, 1955, Aft., Chicago, IL, "Listen, you don't remember it, neither do I, but we was before the foundation of the world."

⁷⁶ _____, *Who Is This Melchisedec?* Feb. 21, 1965, PM, Jeff., IN, "You will never be the **Word** unless you was a thought at the beginning. That proves the predestination of God…You had to be in the thinking first. But you see, in order to stand temptation you had to bypass the theophany; you had to come down here in flesh to be tempted by sin." (Emphasis mine –PMD)

⁷⁷ _____, *Life,* Jun. 02, 1957, Jeff., IN, "If this earthly tabernacle is dissolved, we have a theophany to go into, a body celestial."

⁷⁸ _____, *The Entombment,* Apr. 20, 1957, Jeff., IN, "It takes death to develop the picture, to put us back in the theophany we come from."

⁷⁹ *Q & A on Genesis,* "Now, the first man, now, he made the first man in his image, and we're returning back to that image, that's right, to our first created image."

⁸⁰ *Early Spiritual Experiences,* "I believe that man's spirit was made before all the supernatural was made before the natural."

⁸¹ WMB, *As The Eagle Stirs Her Nest,* Jan. 22, 1961, Beaumont, TX, "We're sons of God, parts of Him…"

⁸² *Conference,* Shreveport, "Now, remember Jesus was God. We're not God. He had the Spirit without measure. The Fulness of the Godhead bodily dwelt in Him, but we have the Spirit by measure. Well, now if I took a spoonful of water out of the ocean, that would be comparison. You'd never miss it. Well, that's the Holy Spirit that's on me and on you…And Jesus had the whole ocean

was in Him, all of it. But if I took a spoonful of water out of the ocean, the same chemicals that's in the entire ocean is in that--that spoonful. Ever chemical in the ocean's in there. It's in the water. It's the same Spirit, but not as much of it; but It'll act the same way, 'cause He promised it."

[83] This could have come to WMB through either Freemasonry or Mormonism, both of which came from Freemasonry and both were influenced by Hinduism and Gnosticism.

[84] *Q & A on Genesis,* See also: *Believer's Position In Christ,* "Listen, you don't remember it, neither do I, but we was before the foundation of the world."

[85] WMB, *Show Us The Father And It'll Satisfy Us,* Jun. 10, 1953, Connersville, IN, "After he made a man in his own image, he made a supernatural being, yes, indeed, Genesis 1:28." See also: WMB, *I Will Restore,* Jun. 20, 1954, AM, Des Moines, IA, "Adam was a man like God, he was a spirit man."; *Turning Northward,* "Man was made to be a god, we know that …God had hands. God had feet, and so therefore a man was made like Him."

[86] *Uncertain Sound,* Jeffersonville, "Now, listen close, and think hard now before you pass your thought of this, man in the beginning, when he was made, a man is a god, he's absolutely a god, for he was made in the image of God, being a son of God, and then he's an heir of all that God is."

[87] *Pillar Of Fire,* "I believe that in the beginning God made man in his own image, and God is a spirit. And God made man spirit-man. Then he made him in the dust of the earth."

[88] *Q & A on Hebrews #2,* "The Catholic call it, 'the eternal sonship of God.'… Which as I have said before, the word doesn't even make sense. See, there cannot be an eternal son, because a son had to have a beginning. And so Jesus had a beginning; God had no beginning…but the Son that was with the Father in the beginning was the Logos that went out of God."

[89] *Cruelty Of Sin, And The Penalty That It Cost To Rid Sin From Our Lives,* "So then when God made his first man, he was a spirit man. He was something on the order of God, or the Son of God, the Logos, that was the first man."

[90] *Deity Of Jesus Christ,* "All right, so he made a man. God was Spirit; he had to be a spirit man made in his image. He put him here on the earth to lead the animal life and so forth …There's no man to till the soil, and He put him in five senses… He had blessed fellowship with his Father, speaking, and then, we're going to make this second man…The first man, you can't see him. God…The second man was a halo. And now He takes a third man and makes him like a little white cloud, coming over, we can see him. Holy Spirit coming down, and he's all man. That's the soul of man, eternal then."

[91] Ibid.

[92] WMB, *Q & A on Hebrews #3,* Oct. 06, 1957, Jeff., IN, "That's Genesis 1, where he created man in his own image, which was in the theophany, and in Genesis 2, he made man out of the dust of the earth, which was the human man that we have now."

CHAPTER SEVENTEEN

[93] *Deity Of Jesus Christ.*

[94] *Hebrews Chapter Two #3*, "But the difference between an animal and a man, God put a soul in a man, and he didn't put it in the animal, because the soul that was in the man, is that theophany."

[95] *Experiences*, "Your soul, that's the nature of the spirit of course."

[96] WMB, *Comforter*, Oct. 01, 1961, PM, Jeff., IN, "God has created a soul and created a spirit to be in that baby just as soon as it's born into this world"

[97] _____, *Adoption # 2*, May 18, 1960, Jeff., IN, "When a little baby drops from its mother, as in natural birth, its little body is a-twisting and legs a-jumping, and so forth, excuse the expression, you young women, but when it does, it's got life muscles a-jerking, but when it comes to the earth, the first thing, it catches its breath, and there is a spiritual body of nature to come into that baby right then …For when this earthly body is brought here, there is a spiritual body ready for it."

[98] *Things That Are To Be*, "There's a little angel spirit waiting to receive that natural body. Just as soon as it's born, the breath of life comes into it. And God breathes it in there, and it becomes a living soul. Now, just as this baby is being born, then the spiritual body is there to receive it."

[99] *Q & A # 4*, "That little angel, little spirit, a little messenger to this little tabernacle is ready to come forth into the world. And then, when this little angel comes into the body - That's a little angel of the earth, a spirit that's ordained of God to take this body - then that baby has to have a choice. It makes its decision. Then when this takes place, then you see the Angel of the Lord now comes in here which is a spiritual body, that eternal."

[100] *Q & A # 4.*

[101] *Comforter*, "It's just like a little baby…as soon as it's born, you don't see it, but there's a spirit and soul hanging near that mother to come into that baby just as soon as it's born."

[102] *Church Age Book.* 154.

[103] *Do You Now Believe?* Battle Creek, MI, "But your spirit, your soul was made up before the foundation of the world, when God made man in his image." See also: *Demonology, Physical Realm*, Connersville, "But your souls were made up before the foundation of the world when God created man in his own image, spirit of man; not a man in his own image, but man in his own image, see?; *Faith Of Abraham,* Nov. 18, 1955, San Fernando, CA, "And you begin with a soul before the world was ever formed, when God created man in his own image."

[104] This author was in Salt Lake City en-route to Tucson, AZ, for a New Year's Convention where many people were gathered for the Rapture to take place in 1977. While in Salt Lake, all the LDS centers were visited and many similarities were found regarding LDS doctrine and WMB's message. This was the beginning of the end of belief in WMB and his message, for this author.

[105] Rebekah Branham Smith, *Whose Book Is It?* in *Only Believe,* issue 11 (June 1991). "William Branham acknowledged authorship of only one major literary work during his lifetime: An Exposition Of The Seven Church Ages."

¹⁰⁶ *Look Away To Jesus*, "Brother Lee Vayle, of course, is a scholar and a Doctor of Divinity, that he really earned his degree."

¹⁰⁷ Rebekah Branham Smith, "Transcribing the 10 sermons from the seven-inch reel tapes on which they had been recorded, was a time-consuming task. Sister Ruth Sumner of Tifton, Georgia, volunteered her typing skills and on October 14, 1962, she delivered the completed manuscript to Brother Branham at the Tabernacle in Jeffersonville. A few moments later he stepped onto the platform and thanked her publicly for her efforts."

¹⁰⁸ Ibid., "Anna Jeanne Moore, and she was the daughter of Brother Jack Moore of Shreveport, Louisiana, a close friend and associate of Brother Branham."

¹⁰⁹ Ibid., "Brother and Sister Vayle rented a small apartment in Beaumont, Texas, and immediately began to work on an outline of the material in the manuscript. In the three years that had passed since 'The Seven Church Ages' were preached, several other essential messages had been delivered, including the series entitled, 'The Seven Seals.' Brother Branham wanted much of that material to be included in the book in order to make it as complete as possible. Therefore, a part of Brother Vayle's job was to reconstruct the original manuscript and bring it 'up to date.'"

¹¹⁰ Ibid., "Most corrections were done in pen, directly onto the page or on the reverse side of the paper, as Brother Branham dictated. He felt his handwriting was too difficult to read. Lengthy corrections were typed, then numbered to indicate where they were to be inserted."

¹¹¹ Ibid., "In addition, Brother Branham spent several hours recording on tape the answers to questions which Brother Vayle would ask in order to further clarify a point of the book."

¹¹² Ibid., "When the new manuscript was completed, it was sent to the large Voice of Healing print shop in Dallas, Texas, for the typesetting and printing of the hard-bound book…proof-reading was an arduous and time-consuming task…Five-thousand copies were produced at the time of the first printing. A dust cover had been designed and ordered, but the order was canceled at the last minute, leaving a very simple, dark blue book. The gold lettering on the spine proclaimed it to be *An Exposition Of The Seven Church Ages* by William Branham."

¹¹³ *Trying To Do God A Service*, Shreveport.

¹¹⁴ Rebekah Branham Smith, "For months before its release, rumors had been circulating that there were major errors in the book *An Exposition Of The Seven Church Ages*. The growing concern amongst the ministry was that perhaps this was Lee Vayle's book, and not Brother Branham's."

¹¹⁵ Ibid., "Brother Branham turned to Billy Paul and instructed that no more of the books were to be released until he'd had a chance to read through it himself and talk to Brother Vayle. 'Call Lee and tell him to meet me in Tucson in a week,' he said."

¹¹⁶ Ibid., "On December 12, Brother Lee Vayle met with Brother Branham…in Tucson, and together they went over the controversial portions of the book…Satisfied, that

CHAPTER SEVENTEEN

evening Brother Branham preached the message 'Communion,' at Tucson Tabernacle. After the service, in Brother Pearry Green's office, he wrote a check for the price of the printing and gave instructions that the two thousand copies of the book (that had already been delivered) were to be released. He autographed approximately 15 copies to be given to the ministry.

[117] Ibid., "There is no doubt in my mind that *An Exposition Of The Seven Church Ages* is William Branham's book. And knowing, first-hand, how hard he struggled to get it published, I cannot remain neutral on the subject of its authorship. If you haven't done so lately, I would encourage you to take another look at this very important, blue book."

[118] New Age Catholic Website, Scaria Thuruthiyil, "Reincarnation in Hinduism," available from http://www.spiritualwholeness.org/faqs/reincgen/hindrein.htm, (accessed October 25, 2010).

[119] *Sir, We Would See Jesus*, Port Alberni, "Now, think of it, they worship idols, animals, and some of them believe in reincarnation, that is, you die one thing, and come back another. It was the awfullest mess you ever seen."

[120] *Harvest Time*, "I find many over there, and around the world, they believe in reincarnation, that, they, that you die here as a man and you come back as a bird or an animal. See, that doesn't speak with nature."

[121] WMB, *Faith That Was Once Delivered To The Saints*, Nov. 29, 1953, Aft., West Palm Beach, FL, "Now, look, here was the son of perdition come from hell returning back to hell. Here was the Son of God coming from heaven, returning back to heaven: Perfectly Judas and Jesus the reincarnation. Judas and Jesus, both of them brothers: One was the pastor, the other one was the treasurer."

[122] *Souls That Are In Prison Now*, "The ministry of Jesus Christ reincarnated in his church in this last day...that's what many of us believe. I believe with you. I believe this. If I didn't believe it, I'd do something else about it, because after all, this is me that's concerned in here. And if the spirit of God be in you, you're concerned about the people."

[123] *Resurrection*, West Palm Beach, "I believe that same resurrected Jesus Christ manifests hisself here every night in power, and signs, and wonders...I believe that's Jesus Christ reincarnated in flesh in the human church here on earth a doing signs and wonders."

[124] *Perseverance*, Jeff., "His Spirit is on me." See also: *Condemnation by Representation*, "His Spirit on me."; *Jehovah Of Miracles*, Nov. 26, 1959, San Jose, CA, "The anointing of the Holy Spirit is on me..."

[125] WMB, *True Vine And The False Vine*, Jun. 07, 1955, Macon, GA, "The Holy Spirit is in me." See also: *The Unchangeable God Working In An Unexpectable Way*, Jan. 20, 1962, Phoenix, AZ, "His Spirit is in me."; *A Super Sign*, Jeff., "To me He's the super Sign. The Holy Ghost in me."

[126] *Is There Anything Too Hard For The Lord?* "Remember, Jesus Christ, the Son of God, said that same thing would repeat again: 'As it was in the days of Sodom, so shall it be in the coming of the Son of man,' that God would be working through human flesh, doing the same thing that He did then...You say, 'Oh, God doesn't send angels any more.' The Holy Spirit is that angel. The Holy Spirit is that Person." See also *Letting Off The Pressure*, May 18, 1962, Green Lake, WI.

[127] WMB, *He That Is In You*, Nov. 10, 1963, PM, Jeff., IN, "What if Beethoven lived in you? What if Beethoven lived in you? You know what you'd do? You would write songs like Beethoven, the great composer. You would write songs like Beethoven, because Beethoven would be your life. You would be a Beethoven, reincarnated, again."

[128] _____, *Token*, Nov. 28, 1963, PM, Shreveport, LA, "If the life of John Dillinger lived in me, I would be John Dillinger."

[129] *He That Is In You*, "If Castro was in me, I'd be a Castro."

[130] WMB, *Go, Wake Jesus*, Nov. 03, 1963, Tucson, AZ, "If I told you that Shakespeare lived in me. I'd be a poet…you could make up poems, because Shakespeare, the great writer, would be in you, and you would be Shakespeare."

[131] Ibid.

[132] *Faith In The Son Of God*, "The Devil takes his man, but never his spirit, he just… moves on gets another one."

[133] WMB, *Hebrews Chapter Five And Six, #1*, Sep. 08, 1957, AM, Jeff., IN, "You will never be an Angel. God made Angels, but God made man. And what God does is off of God, which is as eternal as God is. And man is just eternal as his Creator, because he was made from Eternity."

[134] _____, *Believer's Position In Christ*, Jan. 16, 1955, Aft., Chicago, IL, "Listen, you don't remember it, neither do I, but we was before the foundation of the world."

[135] _____, *That Day On Calvary*, Sep. 25, 1960, Jeff., IN, "And sin did not start on the earth. Sin started in heaven. Lucifer, the devil, was a condemned creature for his disobedience before he ever struck the earth. Sin began in heaven, where God put the angels and so forth upon the same basis that He put human beings on."

[136] *Q & A On Hebrews #3*, "Now, the souls that were in prison that repented not, were not Angelic beings that had--had been brought down in the form of Angels, but it was the spirits of those angelic beings that fell before the foundation of the world, back there when the war went on in heaven…Michael and the dragon fought and Lucifer. And Lucifer was cast out with all of his children, all of the angels that he had deceived, and those angels come to the earth and was subject then to become human."

[137] *Unfailing Realities*, "When we enter into God…We rest eternal; we got Eternal Life. The Holy Spirit gives you Rest….'Cause they were predestinated of God to search for Life. They was once the angels…who did not fall. Two-thirds of the angels of heaven fell; that's these evil spirits working amongst people, very religious."

[138] WMB, *Who Is This Melchisidec*, Feb. 21, 1965, PM, Jeff., IN.

[139] _____, *Why Cry, Speak*, Jul. 14, 1963, AM, Jeff., IN, "The seed of God is actually placed in us from the foundation of the world. And when that light first strikes that seed, It brings it to Life, but the light first has to come upon the seed."

[140] *Communion*, Tucson, "…I was born of Charles and Ella Branham. In their nature I was a sinner, I came to the world, a liar, and all the habits of the world laid right in me. But down in

there, too, was another Nature present, see, predestinated, was in there by God. In this same body, see, two natures in there...But down in there was a little speck of Life all the time."

[141] Ed Hinson and Ergun Caner, *The Popular Encyclopedia Of Apologetics, Surveying the Evidence for the Truth of Christianity,* (Eugene, OR: Harvest House Publishers, 2008, 562 pp.) 235, "Their teaching provided the information needed to illuminate the divine spark in humanity so that it can find its way back to the divine realm. Gnostic teaching was given in secret to the elect alone. In this way Gnosticism fostered a type of spiritual elitism and secrecy that created real divisions within the early Christian communities. At any rate, the Gnostics taught that with the appropriate knowledge, the Gnostic individual could leave this mundane physical life to return the divine spark back to God."

[142] *Church Age Book*, "The unchanging God with unchanging ways invariably sent His prophet in every age where the people had strayed from Divine order. With both the theologians and the people having departed from the Word, God always sent His servant to these people (but apart from the theologians) in order to correct false teaching and lead the people back to God."

Chapter Eighteen

THE PERSON OF CHRIST

To what extent can WMB's theology of the
Person of Christ be supported by his
messages, or by the Scriptures?

Virgin Birth

WMB believed that Jesus was conceived by the Holy Spirit in the womb of the Virgin Mary. At first blush that sounds right. However, what was actually meant by WMB falls outside of what is considered to be orthodox Christianity. WMB stated that Jesus was born of an egg and sperm that were created directly by God the Father and placed in Mary's womb.[1] It is necessary to pause here for a moment and contemplate what WMB in fact did, when he said this. The biblical account is clear regarding Jesus being the Seed of the Woman, with which WMB agreed.[2] Yet, in typical fashion, he also denied that a woman can have a seed,[3] or that Mary had a seed.[4] Jesus was also of the seed of Abraham, as well as of David's, seed. (Matt. 1: 1). Jesus Himself emphatically said he was the Son of Man, or *Ben Adam*, which primarily meant that he was of true human descent, which meaning was also held by Calvin.[5] This can be seen in passages, such as Ps. 8: 4, "What is man, that thou art mindful of him? and the son of man, that thou visitest him?" WMB shows this connection only once in all of his messages.[6]

As an aside, throughout his life, WMB taught that *Son of Man*[7] meant prophet, though that is not sustainable in light of Scripture.[8] WMB strongly associated this with his own ministry. WMB contradicted Ps. 8: 4 when he stated that Jesus was not born of Mary. Earlier, it would appear that WMB *did* believe that Mary was the mother of Jesus. He related the occasion when Elisabeth under inspiration of the Holy Spirit called Mary the mother of her Lord.[9] What does it mean for WMB that he gainsaid the Holy Spirit speaking through Elisabeth? When Peter contradicted Jesus, he was told, "Get thee behind me, Satan: thou art an offence unto me: for thou savourest not the things that be of God, but those that be of men" (Matt. 16: 23). Jesus addressed Peter in his unconverted state, whereas WMB claimed to be God's prophet when he did that. Scripture states Mary, "Brought forth her firstborn son." (Lu. 2: 7). When any woman brings forth a son, she is the mother. Again, WMB contradicted the

CHAPTER EIGHTEEN

Holy Spirit, which is blasphemy.[10] WMB himself said that the Holy Spirit cannot deny His own Word.[11] In quite a number of places WMB stated that Mary *was* the mother of Jesus.[12] Other references could be produced where WMB said that Mary *was not* Jesus' mother.[13] In WMB's book, which was edited by Lee Vayle, he wrote, "He created the very cells in the womb of Mary for that body. It was not enough for the Holy Spirit to simply give life to a human ovum supplied by Mary. That would have been sinful mankind producing a body."[14] This is an internal contradiction and this is what that looks like:

1. Mary *is* the Mother of Jesus
2. <u>Mary is *not* the Mother of Jesus</u>,[15]
3. Internal contradiction, WMB's teaching is invalid.

Consequences of WMB's teaching regarding Mary and the Person of Jesus:

I. If Mary is not the Mother of Jesus, then Jesus is also not the Seed of the Woman, nor is He Son of David, nor the Son of Abraham. Scripture, in Jesus' genealogy, lists that Jesus was born of Mary. No one can gainsay God's Word. Again, this constitutes a serious contradiction in WMB's message, which invalidates his teaching.

II. If Mary is not the mother of Jesus, then Jesus was neither Jew, *nor* Gentile, WMB concluded.[16] If that were true, then He was not a kinsman, nor a Kinsman Redeemer, as WMB also stated.[17] Hence, humankind would still be in sin. No need for Church age messengers, as per WMB.

III. If Mary is not the Mother of Jesus, then who is Jesus? WMB taught Jesus was a new creation.[18] If true, then Jesus was not from eternity and therefore He was not God. Hence, He is not the Savior of humanity, and all are lost. This is the Arian heresy of Jesus being a created being.

IV. If Mary is not the Mother of Jesus, but she was only, "An incubator, that hatched Jesus…,"[19] that would make it another Gnostic heresy revived. The horrible language employed by WMB, regarding one of the most sacred events in history, must be deemed unacceptable. WMB went as far as saying that not only could any woman have qualified for this, but that God could have hatched Jesus on a stump,[20] or simply used a puppy dog.[21] The aforementioned heresy that Jesus was born "out of" Mary was already denounced by Irenaeus in the 2nd Century.[22]

V. If a woman has nothing to do with the conception of a child, why does Scripture forbid a Jew to marry a foreign woman, and he had to put her away? Irenaeus wrote, "we may infer, that offspring is partly procreated by the seed of the mother. According to the common custom of nations, mothers are deemed progenitors, and with this the divine law agrees, which could have had no ground to forbid the marriage of the uncle with the niece, if there was no consanguinity between them. It would also be lawful for a brother and sister uterine to intermarry, when their fathers are different."[23] WMB agreed that Boaz was born of Rahab[24] and that Jesus came through her line. This invalidates his statement that nothing was contributed by the mother.[25] WMB was, Scripturally and biologically, incorrect when he said the child's blood is always that of its father.

VI. If the Virgin Mary did not conceive a Son, as prophesied by Isaiah, humanity would not have a savior. WMB stated that conception takes place by a sensation in the woman that allows the egg to drop. He was emphatic that Mary did not have these sensations because that would have meant that God had physical intercourse with her.[26] WMB's idea might have originated from his belief that God was a man[27] with hands and feet,[28] and presumably sexual organs. WMB said that on crucifixes Jesus always has a loincloth covering his lower body, whereas the Scripture states He was naked.[29] That can only mean that Jesus was a man. WMB stated that man was created in the image of God. He stated that God was both male and female, and that God, the Mother God, had breasts like a woman.[30] That would infer that God would have male organs as well, a term called Hermaphroditic, or Androgynous. What use would God have for male and female organs? WMB displayed an intimate knowledge of Freemasonry, which holds God is Hermaphroditic. WMB was also influenced by Mormonism. Mormonism is wrong and so was WMB, because God is Spirit, not man.

VII. If Mary is not the mother of Jesus, but simply an incubator "hatching" Jesus, then Christendom has learned nothing since its inception. Irenaeus battled the heresy of that Jesus was "born out of," and not "from" Mary. WMB said in some places that Jesus came "through" Mary, though it is doubtful that he purposely differentiated this from "of" or "from." However, his teaching made it unequivocally clear that he believed Jesus was born "out of" Mary.

VIII. Jesus being neither Jew nor Gentile, the only two peoples on earth, would make Jesus some kind of Avatar,[31] without connection to Scripture. Hence, there would be no salvation for humanity.

IX. If Jesus was not a Jew nor a Gentile, but simply God, the Son of God,[32] that would contradict WMB's official view of the godhead. He did say that Jesus could not be his own father,[33] yet he also said that Jesus *was* the Father.[34] This is contradicted by WMB's own, often used adage, that there is no such thing as a black white bird, or a drunk sober man.[35]

CHAPTER EIGHTEEN 253

X. If Jesus is God and is also the Son of God the Father, and everything must bring forth after its own kind,[36] WMB confirmed, then Jesus MUST be God, because Jesus was the Son of God.[37] This contradicts WMB's Modalistic view, because obviously there are at least two beings in WMB's godhead. Lee Vayle, one of WMB's most ardent supporters, does hold a duality view of God.

XI. Teaching Jesus was neither Jew nor Gentile, but only God (meaning Spirit), as per WMB,[38] constitutes the heresy called Docetism, which teaches that Jesus was Spirit only, not flesh. John says that people who do not believe Jesus came in the flesh are Antichrist (1 Jn. 4: 3; 2 Jn. 1: 7), which voids WMB's claim to be a Christian *and* a prophet.

XII. Teaching Jesus was neither Jew nor Gentile, but only God, brings another problem. Why would God incarnate Himself in Mary's womb, only to become God again later? Is this a kind of rebirth? WMB contended Jesus was only an anointed man,[39] because God descended on Him at His Baptism[40] and left Him prior to the Crucifixion.[41] This is a heresy called Cerinthianism,[42] already condemned by Irenaeus.

XIII. Teaching Jesus was neither Jew nor Gentile, but only God, which WMB taught, would make Jesus eternal. This is contradicted by WMB's claim that Jesus was NOT eternal.[43] If Jesus were not eternal, that would contradict WMB's teaching that man *was* eternal.[44] Jesus was a man, but He is *not* eternal? This is an irreconcilable contradiction.

XIV. If Jesus were a new creation,[45] He would not be human, because He would not share human DNA. If He did not have human DNA going back to Adam, He would only seem to be a man. This, again, is Docetism.[46]

XV. If Jesus were a new creation, that would mean he was not Pre-existent. This means He would not have appeared in the OT, of which WMB did speak.[47]

XVI. If Jesus is Pre-existent, which He is, why would Jesus have to be *created* in the womb of the Virgin Mary, as WMB taught?

XVII. If Jesus *was* pre-existent in WMB's theology, He is not pre-existent in a biblical way. WMB used the word "theophany," describing it to be a spiritless body that can be inhabited by God. It is the same kind of body awaiting Christians at death.[48] A spiritless body that God and man can step into, is that like some kind of cosmic pair of overalls a person dons?

XVIII. If Jesus, for WMB, is pre-existing, He is by definition, not a *new* creation. In WMB's theology, Jesus pre-existed as Michael the archangel,[49] something which Jehovah's Witnesses also teach. Within the context of Michael as archangel, WMB had Satan (Lucifer) as the original archangel of God.[50] Not only did he make Satan the original archangel, he made him God's right hand man and co-worker, partly equal with God.⁵¹ It would thus appear that Jesus (Michael) only by default became pre-eminent. The Bible states that Jesus did not take on the nature of angels. (Heb. 2: 16).

XIX.   If Jesus is pre-existing as Michael, WMB likely received that teaching from the Seventh Day Adventists, with whom he was involved, earlier in life.⁵² WMB's connection to Mormon teaching is reflected by his teaching on Michael and Lucifer being brothers. In fact, WMB came close to calling them twins.⁵³

XX.   If Jesus were a new creation that was created *ex-nihilo* (out of nothing), that again would prove there was no connection with Adam. Adam was created out of the earth, not ex-nihilo. Paul said that Jesus took on flesh (Rom. 1: 3; 9:5; Eph. 5: 30; 1 Tim. 3: 15; 1 Pe. 4: 1; 1 Jn. 4: 2, 3). As stated, those that deny it, are Antichrist (Ibid. 3). Because Jesus was of human flesh He calls the redeemed his brothers.

The above section regarding Mary and the birth of Jesus shows that WMB propagated ancient and more modern heresies. WMB's claim that he was sent to straighten out all the errors that had crept into the church throughout the ages cannot be substantiated.⁵⁴ As stated prior, Irenaeus was the disciple of Polycarp, who was a disciple of John. In apostolic days, truth was disseminated from teacher to disciple. Irenaeus was two steps removed from apostolic authority, which was actually why WMB selected him as the second Church messenger.⁵⁵

Jesus was a Jew, how else would he have been able to teach in the Synagogue and Temple courts? How is Christ the Seed of the Woman, if she had nothing to do with it? This is an internal contradiction which makes WMB's teaching invalid. Not only is it an internal contradiction, it is also heresy. WMB contradicted Scripture and thereby showed a lack of reverence toward God. WMB did not consider God's Word sacred and inviolable and thereby made himself guilty of blasphemy. This, in itself, should be sufficient to establish that WMB's teachings on the Person of Christ cannot be supported by the Scriptures. However, it is important to examine the details of WMB's position.

The issue at hand is the "problem" of how Jesus could be sinless and yet be part of sinful humanity. Already in the Early Church Irenaeus dealt with this:

> Those, therefore, who allege that He took nothing from the Virgin do greatly err, [since,] in order that they may cast away the inheritance of the flesh, they also reject the analogy [between Him and Adam]. For if the one [who sprang] from the earth had indeed formation and substance from both the hand and workmanship of God, but the other not from the hand and workmanship of God, then He who was made after the image and likeness of the former did not, in that case, preserve the analogy of man, and He must seem an inconsistent piece of work, not having wherewith He may show His wisdom. But this is to say, that He also appeared putatively as man when He was not man, and that

He was made man while taking nothing from man. For if He did not receive the substance of flesh from a human being, He neither was made man nor the Son of man; and if He was not made what we were, He did no great thing in what He suffered and endured.[56]

Irenaeus made it clear that Jesus had to be a descendent of man. He could not just appear to be a man, which is what Docetism taught. In fact, WMB said that Mary was just an incubator and had nothing to do with the process.[57] Why bother with using a human "incubator" at all? Why would God not just speak Jesus into existence as a fetus?

WMB's misconception goes back to his heretical understanding of Creation, the Fall of Adam and Eve, and God's commandment to "Be fruitful and multiply" (Gen. 1: 22, 28). WMB taught that prior to the Fall, Adam was to reproduce by speaking children into existence,[58] without intercourse with Eve.[59] Scripture reveals absolutely nothing of the kind. How can a woman and a man be one flesh without having sexual relations? It is not a new teaching, it is an ancient Gnostic tenet. WMB also stated flesh is evil and spirit is where it's at.[60] Why did God bless man and say, "Be fruitful, and multiply," just exactly as he had blessed other creatures and told them to multiply" (Gen. 2: 22, 28) if it were not a natural act of procreation? WMB taught the Gnostic position that intercourse was a perverted act, even within the bounds of marriage. He said he himself was, "…brought forth, yet through a sinful act that God permitted to be done, a perverted act by holy wedlock from my father and my mother."[61] WMB, strongly but wrongly, believed that a woman's egg would not descend without a sensation (meaning sexual arousal) and these sensations were evil.

> The Protestant more or less believes that it was the Mary produced the egg. If that be so, look what you make Jehovah God doing. The egg cannot be produced without a sensation. So you see, God made both egg and germ; he created both in the womb of Mary. And that man was not nothing but God himself made flesh and dwelled among us, Emmanuel.[62]

In other words, this could be taken to mean that if some kind of union takes place without a sensation, it is not a perversion? Obviously WMB had not thought this through, or he would have understood that a rape victim can get pregnant, even though the only sensations the woman would have, would be of revulsion, of pain, of degradation, etc.

Today "In - Vitro-Fertilization (IVF)"[63] is used. Thus, it is possible to become pregnant without a "sensation." Mice have been developed from eggs only, no male sperm involved, a feat that had until recently been impossible.[64] This teaching by WMB of sexual intercourse without "a sensation," is actually very ancient. Lucretius, a disciple of Epicurus (ca. 342 – 270 B.C.), stated there was no harm in sexual intercourse, provided it was divorced from passion."[65] Mormons hold that Mary's impregnation was natural. The Holy Spirit is God, and this God has a body like a man, with sexual organs, which WMB also allowed. This God overshadowed a virgin, and she became pregnant. What conclusion did WMB expect anyone to come to?

WMB's argument regarding the Virgin birth of Jesus might simply be taken to be WMB's ignorance of biological facts, as Mennonites now say about Menno Simons and his colleagues. Simons also believed that Mary was not involved in the process, except providing nourishment.[66] There are, however, differences between WMB and Menno Simons. During the Radical Reformation there did not exist the information that is readily available today. One would expect that, as a 20th century prophet, WMB would have had that knowledge. It is, in fact, more problematic, because with most, if not all, of WMB's teaching, there is a Gnostic root. This same affinity to heresy and Gnosticism is not seen in Menno Simons,[67] nor in his colleague Dirk Philips,[68] neither is it seen in their followers today. Today's Mennonite leaders acknowledge Menno was wrong.

The Gnostics were never satisfied with mystery and needed to have answers for everything. Therefore, this mystery of a virgin birth needed to be explained so people could understand. Because humans are sinful, it would not do to have Jesus born from a sinful woman. Therefore, a way had to be devised to take care of that problem. This was done by making Mary a kind of funnel through which the Christ could come into the world. Irenaeus said,

> Those, therefore, who allege that He took nothing from the Virgin do greatly err, [since,] in order that they may cast away the inheritance of the flesh, they also reject the analogy [between Him and Adam]. For if the one [who sprang] from the earth had indeed formation and substance from both the hand and workmanship of God, but the other not from the hand and workmanship of God, then He who was made after the image and likeness of the former did not, in that case, preserve the analogy of man, and He must seem an inconsistent piece of work, not having wherewith He may show His wisdom. But this is to say, that He also appeared putatively as man when He was not man, and that He was made man while taking nothing from man. For if He did not receive the substance of flesh from a human being, He neither was made man nor the Son of man; and if He was not made what we were, He did no great thing in what He suffered and endured. But every one will allow that we are [composed of] a body taken from the earth, and a soul receiving spirit from God. This, therefore, the Word of God was made, recapitulating in Himself His own handiwork; and on this account does He confess Himself the Son of man, and blesses "the meek, because they shall inherit the earth." (6) The Apostle Paul, moreover, in the Epistle to the Galatians, declares plainly, "God sent His Son, made of a woman."(7) And again, in his Epistle to the Romans, he says, "Concerning His Son, who was made of the seed of David according to the flesh, who was predestinated as the Son of God with power, according to the spirit of holiness, by the resurrection from the dead, Jesus Christ our Lord."(8)

Irenaeus showed he had a real grasp of the issues at hand and his judgement of heresy still stands and is applicable to WMB's teaching.

So, how did Jesus take on flesh and not be a partaker of the sinful nature? This has been an age long question and has been debated since early Church times. The RCC "solved" the problem by dogmatizing the immaculate conception of Mary in 1854 and, subsequently, her ascension, in 1950.[69] Time and space is lacking to expand on that here, except to ask the question how Mary, in her *Magnificat,* could sing about, "My spirit hath rejoiced in God my Saviour" (Lu. 1: 47) if she was without sin? It has already been discussed how Radical Reformers, Menno Simons and Dirk Philips, dealt with this issue, but how did Protestantism deal with it? Protestantism holds to Mary being involved in the process, yet Jesus was without sin. Jesus appeared, in the words of Matthew Henry,

> In the likeness of sinful flesh. Not sinful, for he was holy, harmless, undefiled; but in the likeness of that flesh which was sinful. He took upon him that nature which was corrupt, though perfectly abstracted from the corruptions of it. His being circumcised, redeemed, baptized with John's baptism, bespeaks the likeness of sinful flesh.[70]

It would seem that Jesus was *affected* by the Fall, he hungered, thirsted, grew weary, wept, was tempted, etc., yet without sin. Does this mean that Jesus, born of a sinful Virgin mother, inherited original sin? If Jesus inherited original sin, did that mean he inherited original guilt?[71] This author believes that "original sin" must be seen, not as inherited from mother and father, through the act of procreation, as per WMB and others, but rather through the act of allegiance to the human race. Adam represented the human race and because of his sin, we are sinners. As an example, people can hold a citizen of a country to be guilty of killing, when they personally have not killed anyone, simply because their government is held to be guilty. These are deep questions and it is not this author's intent to give definitive answers. He holds them as a mystery. Scripture is clear that Jesus had no sin. How exactly that happened is not explained and is therefore not within humanity's domain. If it is outside of what is revealed to mankind, then people can only speculate.

Pre-existence of Christ

In order to get some understanding of who God is, it is necessary to go to the source of the earliest revelation of God to man, in the teachings of Moses. The Scriptures state that Moses saw the form of God,

> He [The Lord] said, "Listen to my words: 'When a prophet of the LORD is among you, I reveal myself to him in visions, I speak to him in dreams. 7 But this is not true of my servant Moses; he is faithful in all my house. 8 With him I speak face to face, clearly and not in riddles; he sees the **form** of the LORD. Why then were you not afraid to speak against my servant Moses?'" 9 The anger of the LORD burned against them, and he left them. (NIV Num 12: 6 – 9).

The Scriptures also state that no one can see God and live (Ex. 24: 9 – 11; Ex. 33: 20). It is recorded in Genesis that Abraham also saw God, and he was called Yahweh, or "I AM." Is there a contradiction? Jesus stated in the NT that it was He (Jn. 8: 56 - 58). The religious leaders considered that blasphemy on Jesus' part, because He made Himself equal with God.[72] Of course, Jesus did say, "I AM" which was God's Name, indicating that Jesus was pre-existent as "I AM," as Moses wrote. Of which Stephen testified during his trial, when he referred to the Angel of the Lord. This Angel he identified as being in the burning bush, and whom Scripture identifies as *I Am*, or, *The Lord*.

> This Moses whom they refused, saying, Who made thee a ruler and a judge? the same did God send to be a ruler and a deliverer by the hand of the angel which appeared to him in the bush. 36 He brought them out, after that he had showed wonders and signs in the land of Egypt, and in the Red sea, and in the wilderness forty years. 37 This is that Moses, which said unto the children of Israel, A prophet shall the Lord your God raise up unto you of your brethren, like unto me; him shall ye hear. 38 This is he, that was in the church in the wilderness with the angel which spake to him in the mount Sinai, and with our fathers: who received the lively oracles to give unto us (Acts 7: 35 – 38).

Moses could not have seen God, "the invisible."[73] He must of necessity have seen God in the form of Christ, who is the only and express image of God, revealed to man. Moses, the one who said that God (Gen. 1: 1) was *Elohiym*, a Plurality in Unity, could not have conceived of more than one God, without violating the revelation of God, as shown in "Thou shalt have no other gods before me" (Ex. 20: 3; Deut. 5: 7). God spoke to him through a visible form, and not through dreams or visions, like with other prophets. There is therefore no contradiction. Moses met with the pre-existent Christ. This argument for the pre-existence of Christ also fulfills two of the criteria of the *Seven Tests of Truth*, the Test of Comprehensiveness, and the Test of Simplicity.[74] There is also Rabbinic tradition regarding the Messiah as a pre-existent incorporeal being. Linwood Urban relates that,

> Genesis Rabbah speaks of three things as having been created before the creation of the world. One of them is 'the name of the Messiah,' which in the context does not refer to a concept or idea of Messiah but to a real, though incorporeal being.[75]

The Apocryphal Book of Enoch mentions "the name of the Son of Man" and other Rabbinic sources make reference to a pre-existent Messiah-King.

> And there I saw One who had a head of days (age marked), And His head was white like wool, And with Him was another being whose countenance had the appearance of a man, And his face was full of graciousness, like one of the holy angels. 2 And I asked the angel who went with me and showed me all the hidden things, concerning that 3 Son of Man, who he was, and whence

CHAPTER EIGHTEEN 259

he was, (and) why he went with the Head of Days? And he answered and said unto me: This is the son of Man who hath righteousness, With whom dwelleth righteousness, And who revealeth all the treasures of that which is hidden."[76]

To what extent can WMB's theology of the Person of Christ be supported by his messages, or by the Scriptures? The importance, in the context of WMB's teaching, which is the focus of this book, is that the message of WMB is shown to be inconsistent, contradictory and based on Gnostic heresies. To no extent can WMB's theology of the Person of Christ be supported by his messages, or by the Scriptures.

Notes - Chapter Eighteen

[1] WMB, *Forsaking All*, Jan. 23, 1962, Tempe, AZ, "She was just an incubator that God used to bring the baby, 'cause if there was anything of that woman that belonged into that Boy...that woman... You understand. You adults know what I mean. There had to be some kind of a conception, some kind of a sperm come from that woman, to just... Then it was absolutely like a sexual act with Almighty God: could not be. God created the baby, both egg and blood. Both cell of woman and man, God created."

[2] *Revelation That Was Given To Me*, "From the garden of Eden, Jesus was the seed of the woman that was to crush the serpent's head."

[3] WMB, *Proving His Word*, Aug. 16, 1964, Jeff., IN, "Now, the woman doesn't have a seed."

[4] WMB, *Shalom*, Jan. 19, 1964, Phoenix, AZ, "There would have to be a sensation, even to be a seed of Mary. He wasn't even a seed from Mary."

[5] John Calvin, Institutes, Vol. One, "Wherefore, our Lord himself not contented with the name of man, frequently calls himself the Son of man, wishing to express more clearly that he was a man by true human descent." 409.

[6] WMB, *Presuming*, Jun. 10, 1962, Southern Pines, NC, "I'm just a man. All of us are just human beings. "What is man that Thou art mindful of him, or the son of man that thou would visit him?"

[7] _____, *Lean Not Unto Thine Own Understanding*, Jan. 20, 1965, Phoenix, AZ, "Now remember, 'Son of man' is a *prophet*. Jehovah called Ezekiel a 'son of man.'"

[8] *Trial*, Tampa, "*Son of man* means prophet." WMB erroneously interpreted *Son of Man* to mean prophet. This is like saying a horse is an animal and therefore an animal is a horse. The prophet was a son of man, or a man and not a god.

[9] *Believest Thou This?* Houston, "Little John begin to leap in his mother's womb for joy, and the Holy Spirit came upon Elisabeth. She said, 'Whence cometh the mother of my Lord? For as soon as your salutation came into my ears, my baby leaped in the womb for joy.'"

[10] Merriam Webster - Blasphemy: 1a : the act of insulting or showing contempt or lack of reverence for God. 1b : the act of claiming the attributes of deity. 2: irreverence toward something considered sacred or inviolable.

[11] WMB, *Why I'm Against Organized Religion*, Nov. 11, 1962, PM, Jeff., IN, "And when a man says he's got the Holy Ghost, and deny the Word of God and place It somewhere else, how can the Holy Ghost deny His Own Word?"

[12] *Israel And The Church # 3*, [I]f God made the <u>mother of Jesus Christ</u> go up there to receive the baptism of the Holy Ghost 'fore she could go to heaven, you'll never get there anything shorter than that." [Underline mine-PMD].

[13] *Oneness*, "He didn't have to say, 'Mary, you loan me a egg; I want to make a body so I can dwell in it.' God the Creator spoke, and she was a mother right then. She wasn't a mother; she was just a woman bearing His Seed. That's right. Remember, <u>she was not Jesus' mother</u>." [Note: Underline mine-PMD].

[14] William Marrion Branham, *An Exposition Of The Seven Church Ages*, (Tucson, AZ: Spoken Word Publications, no date, 381pp.), 336.

[15] *Forsaking All*, "Now, that was not her Son. You all know that. Jesus never one time called her mother…The Holy Ghost overshadowed her. That's the reason Jesus couldn't call her mother. He was no part of her, nothing."

[16] Ibid., "Jesus was neither Jew nor Gentile. He was God. That's right. God Himself created a body that He dwelt in; that was His Son, Jesus Christ. That holy virgin birth brought forth this human being, immaculate conception by the Holy Ghost. Woman had nothing to do with it, neither egg nor blood cell."

[17] WMB, *The Deity Of Christ*, Dec. 25, 1949, Jeff., IN, "Before God could be a Redeemer, He had to be, according to the law, a kinsman Redeemer. He had to be kinfolks to us."

[18] *Forsaking All*.

[19] *Oneness*, "He can't have a mother. Jesus was not even anything to Mary… She was an incubator that hatched Him."

[20] WMB, *And Thy Seed Shall Possess The Gate Of His Enemy*, Jan. 21, 1962, AM, Phoenix, AZ, "He could put it on a stump if He'd wanted to. Yes, sir. He could put it anywhere He wanted to…"

[21] *Oneness*, "You could tie a little pup down over the top of a--a bird egg, and it would hatch a bird, the pup would. It's the warmth of the body that hatched the egg. And that's the same way it is with Jesus. Mary was just the incubator."

[22] Irenaeus, *Against Heresies*, available from http://carm.org/irenaeus-heresies3-15-25 , (Accessed September 18, 2010). "Those, therefore, who allege that He took nothing from the Virgin do greatly err, [since,] in order that they may cast away the inheritance of the flesh, they also reject the analogy [between Him and Adam]. For if the one [who sprang] from the earth had indeed formation and substance from both the hand and workmanship of God, but the other not from the hand and workmanship of God, then He who was made after the image and likeness of the former did not, in that case, preserve the analogy of man, and He must seem an inconsistent piece of work, not having wherewith He may show

His wisdom. But this is to say, that He also appeared putatively as man when He was not man, and that He was made man while taking nothing from man. For if He did not receive the substance of flesh from a human being, He neither was made man nor the Son of man; and if He was not made what we were, He did no great thing in what He suffered and endured."

²³ Ibid.

²⁴ *As I Was With Moses, So I Will Be With Thee*, "This great harlot Rahab become a believer...After she was considered and brought into the faith, because of her belief in God, she was brought into Israelite faith, a proselyte. She courted a general in the army, of the Israelite army. Watch what God did for that woman...and they had a son; and this son, they called him Boaz. Out of Boaz, he married Ruth, from Ruth and Boaz come Jesse; out of Jesse come David; out of David come Jesus."

²⁵ WMB, *Deity Of Jesus Christ*, Dec. 25, 1949, Jeff., IN, "The baby is always the blood of its father, never of its mother."

²⁶ *Oneness*, "[T]he immaculate conception was that God overshadowed her and put a blood cell in there, but the egg come from the woman. If the egg come from the woman, there has to come a sensation to bring the egg through the tube to the womb. See what you do with God? You make Him in a sexual mess. God, Who created the blood cell, created the egg also.."

²⁷ *The Messiah*.

²⁸ WMB, *Why?* Jan. 28, 1961, Phoenix, AZ, "A man was made to be god, to be a god. Do you know that? He's in the image of God; he's a son of God; he's like Him. He was given a domain (Genesis 1:26), dominion over the whole earth. That's right. He ruled the earth. He ruled the animal kingdom, and all the other kingdoms--all but the Kingdom of God above. He was god; he was an amateur god. He was made in the image of God, made like God, had hands and feet like God. He was in the image of God." See also: *Entombment*, "God's got a body, and it looks like a man. Moses saw it, others saw it, and it looks like a man."

²⁹ _____, *Living, Dying, Buried, Rising, Coming,* Mar. 29, 1959, Sunrise, Jeff., IN, "There hanging, that precious life that knowed nothing but love and doing good, hung there between the heavens and earth, lifted up there, stripped naked, embarrassed... Think how you would be, stripped naked; you wouldn't know embarrassment to what God would hanging there. I know the crucifix has...something around Him, but they never did that; that's just put on because of the artist put it there. They stripped His clothes from Him."

³⁰ _____, *Abraham's Grace Covenant*, Mar. 17, 1961, Middletown, OH, "He said, 'I am El Shaddai. I am the breasted, mother God.'"

³¹ An Avatar is "one who descends" in Hinduism. Included among Avatars are Buddha, Krishna, Rama, Jesus.

³² *Forsaking All*.

³³ *Lord Show Us The Father*, Chicago, "Jesus couldn't have been His Own Father, and if God is a Man, then Jesus was born sexual desire and not virgin birth. That settles the whole thing.

You see? If He's one like your finger's one, then what? Then He was His Own daddy. How could He have been? That's wrong. He had a Father, Jesus did." [Note: This constitutes another problem because elsewhere WMB said the Godhead was like a three foot rule. – PMD].

34 *Who Is This Melchisedec?* "Mary wasn't His mother. That's the reason He called her woman, not mother. He had no father, for He was the Father, the Everlasting Father, the three in the One. He had no mother. Certainly not. He had no father, for He was the Father."

35 WMB, *Contending For The Faith*, Feb. 00, 1956, Georgetown, IN, "You never seen a man drunk and sober at the same time. You never seen a black white bird. There's no such a thing. And there's no right and wrong mixed together. It's either right or it's wrong."

36 *Church Age Book*, "The law of reproduction is that each specie brings forth after its own kind, even according to Genesis 1:11…" 171.

37 *Hebrews Chapter Seven # 1*, "…Melchisedec…He wasn't the Son of God. He was the God of the Son. He wasn't the Son of God, Melchisedec wasn't, but He was the Father of the Son of God."

38 *Forsaking All.*

39 *Spoken Word*, Christ' means 'the anointed One,' a Man that was anointed.

40 *Church And Its Condition*, . "And John said, 'I bare record, seeing the Spirit of God like a Dove coming down, and abiding on Him.' …That's when God and Man became one. That's when heaven and earth embraced each other. Hallelujah. That's when God was made flesh… that's when God came down from the Spirit form and was made a Man and dwell among us…when God and man was made one on that great memorial day when John baptized Jesus."

41 *Adoption # 2*, "In the Garden of Gethsemane, the anointing left Him, you know, He had to die as a sinner. He died a sinner, you know that; not His sins, but mine and yours." See also: *It Is The Rising Of The Sun*, "The Spirit left Him, in the Garden of Gethsemane. He had to die, a man."

42 J. Gresham Machen, *The Virgin Birth Of Christ*, (London: James Clarke & Co. Ltd., 1958, 415 pp.), 13. "[Cerinthus] supposed that after the baptism the Christ descended upon the man Jesus and enabled Him to proclaim the unknown Father and to work miracles, only to leave Him again before the crucifixion."

43 *Word Became Flesh*, Then in our Catholic thoughts of the Eternal sonship, there could not be. For if He was the Son of God, He had to have a beginning of time. He had to be borned off of to be a Son (is that right?), if He was the Son of God."

44 *Hebrews Chapter Five And Six, # 1*, "And man is just as Eternal as his Creator, because he was made from Eternity."

45 *Forsaking All*, "God created the baby, both egg and blood. Both cell of woman and man God created."

CHAPTER EIGHTEEN

[46] Merriam Webster, *Docetism*: *a belief opposed as heresy in early Christianity that Christ only seemed to have a human body and to suffer and die on the cross."*

[47] WMB, *Door To The Heart*, Mar. 16, 1958, PM, Harrisonburg, VA, "When the angel come to Abraham, Sarah was back in the tent. How many knows that? And the angel had his back turned to the tent. How many knows that? The Bible said so. And the angel, which was Christ... We know that was Christ."

[48] *Thirsting For Life*, Chicago, "And the Logos, which was the Son of God went out, created by these great fountains of purity, God, as those Spirits went out, and it created the Logos. And it was a body. It was in the form of what we are now, which is called in the clergy way of speaking it, a theophany. It's a body that doesn't have a spirit in it. It's a body that's waiting for you Christians. As soon as the life leaves this, you go into that body. When this earthly tabernacle be dissolved, we have one already waiting, a theophany. Now, when God was in theophany, which was Christ in the making, then that theophany become flesh and dwelled among us."

[49] *Beginning And Ending Of The Gentile Dispensation*, "'And at that time Michael shall stand, the great prince.' Michael was Christ, of course, Who fought the angelic wars in heaven with the devil. Satan and Michael fought together, or fought against each other, rather."

[50] WMB, *Q & A*, Jun. 28, 1959, "Satan was the original archangel of God."

[51] *Seal Of The Antichrist*, Mar. 11, 1955, Los Angeles, CA, "The right hand man of Almighty God was Lucifer, the son of the morning. The first, God granted him almost co-workers with Him; he was a co-worker, partly equal with Him; only Satan could not create. God is the only Creator, but Satan took something that God created and perverted it back into something else, evil."

[52] *Q & A on Genesis*, "That was my first study, was Seventh-Day Advent. That's right. Was Seventh-day Advent, what I studied first."

[53] *Q & A #3*, "Now, if you notice it's always been twins all along. There was... Cain and Abel were twins, and Esau and Jacob were twins. Jesus and Judas come out of the same tribe and in the same church. And the--even the Holy Spirit and the antichrist is to be twins, so close that would deceive the very elected if possible. Have you got it? All right."

[54] *Evening Messenger*, "And today the precious Holy Spirit and God's Word is a Messenger to the church, to straighten them out and to bring them back to the Word."

[55] *Ephesian Church Age*, "Irenaeus is who I know that was the angel of that day ... He was God's angel light, and he pulled the light on over after Polycarp had been crucified or murdered, assassinated, then Irenaeus was one of his students, and Polycarp was a student to Saint Paul--or Saint John. And then Irenaeus taken his place, and he brought the light."

[56] Irenaeus.

[57] *Paradox*, Phoenix, "The virgin birth was a paradox. I do not believe that Jesus was any part of Mary. That was not His mother. It was a woman that God used for that purpose, a incubator to bear His Child."

[58] *God Hiding Himself In Simplicity*, "[Man]... he's a son of God; he's an offspring from God. He's an inheritance of the earth. He can control nature. He can speak into existence. Why, he's a creator himself. He's an offspring of God."

[59] *Marriage And Divorce*, "Now the world is to be repopulated, not by the original creation of God, like in the beginning, not by the original creation, but by sex desire ...when she crossed that line and brought this sin, now the world is to be repopulated again, by sex, not by creation; by sex...That's the reason Jesus had to come through the woman, to bring it back to its original beginning again, without sex desire. He is virgin born. But, hallelujah, there will come a time where it won't be no more sex, but God shall call His children from the dust of the earth, back like they was in the original..."

[60] WMB, *Q & A*, Jun. 28, 1959, PM, "The body is the flesh that you look at that must rot. It was born by sexual desire of father and mother. It must rot. It's no good. Therefore in the new birth, in the resurrection when--when you're brought forth again in a new body, it'll be God's creative power that'll speak like He did to Adam and you'll come forth."

[61] ____, *Ye Must Be Born Again*, Jun. 19, 1958, Brkfst., Greenville, SC.

[62] ____, *Seed Shall Not Be Heir With The Shuck*, Apr. 29, 1965, Brkfst., Los Angeles

[63] IVF is a fertilization method where a man's sperm and a woman's egg are brought together in a laboratory setting to allow fertilization to occur and form an embryo. This embryo is then injected into the woman's uterus to allow it to grow into full childbirth.

[64] Vancouver Sun, Thursday, April 22, 2004, article entitled, *"Scientists Create Mice without male's sperm."* A 4.

[65] Bertrand Russell, *History of Western Philosophy*, (London: George Allen and Unwin Ltd., 1961), 253.

[66] Myron Augsburger, *Irvin B. Horst, Historian, Bibliophile, Churchman*, in *MENNO SIMONS: A REAPPRAISAL*, ed. Gerald R. Brunk, (Harrbonburg, VA: Eastern Mennonite College, 1992, 215 pp.), 34., "Menno believed that Jesus Christ was truly the Son of God and both divine and human he believed that Jesus received his full nature from the Father, and nothing from Mary except his physical body. This belief was based more on an inadequate understanding of biology than on a heretical theology... The debates surrounding Menno's teaching give abundant evidence of his sincere convictions about the divine-human nature of the Christ."

[67] Jacobus ten Doornkaat Koolman, *DIRK PHILIPS, Friend and Colleague of Menno Simons, 1504-1568*. Transl. William E. Keeney (Kitchener, ON: Pandora Press, 1998, 234 pp.), 34.

[68] Dirk Philips, *The Writings of Dirk Philips*, Translated and edited by Cornelius J. Dyck, William E. Keeney and Alvin J. Beachy, (Scottsdale, PA: Herald Press, 1992, 701 pp.). 633. "And that is my confession about the deity and incarnation, that Jesus Christ is true God and human being. God born out of God the eternal Father and became a pure, unspotted human being in time, conceived by the Holy Ghost and born out of Mary, the virgin, a Son of the Most High."

[69] Jaroslav Pelikan, *Mary Through the Centuries, Her Place in the History of Culture*, (New Haven, Conn: Yale University Press, 1996, 267 pp.). 205.

[70] Matthew Henry, *Whole Bible Commentary*.

[71] The author found the following a helpful book: Oliver D. Crisp, *Divinity and Humanity*, (Cambridge, UK: Cambridge University Press, 2007, 187 pp.).

[72] The Jewish leaders understood the significance of what Jesus was saying. He was not as yet fifty years old and yet he existed prior to Abraham?

[73] "Who is the image of the invisible God, the firstborn of every creature" (Col. 1: 15).; "Now unto the King eternal, immortal, invisible, the only wise God, be honour and glory forever and ever. Amen" (1 Tim. 1: 17); "By faith he forsook Egypt, not fearing the wrath of the king: for he endured, as seeing him who is invisible" (Heb. 11: 27).

[74] Paul D. Feinberg, Editor Steven B. Cowan, *Five Views on Apologetics*, (Grand Rapids, MI: Zondervan Publishing House, 2000). (*The Test of Comprehensiveness*. This criterion requires that we prefer theories or systems of belief that explain more evidence over those that might account for less. *The Test of Simplicity*. This test instructs to not multiply explanatory items unnecessarily.

[75] Linwood Urban, *A Short History Of Christian Thought*, (New York, NY: Oxford University Press, 1995) 23. Quoted from Athanasius, *The Incarnation*, chap. 1, sec. 11.

[76] *The Book Of Enoch*, Ch. XLVI, Head of Days and the Son of Man. Ibid, Ch. XLVIII, available from http://www.heaven.net.nz/writings/thebookofenoch.htm; (Accessed June 14, 2005). The Book of Enoch, The Fount of Righteousness: the Son of Man -the Stay of the Righteous: Judgement of the Kings and the Mighty. " 2. And at that hour that Son of Man was named. In the presence of the Lord of Spirits, And his name before the Head of Days. 3. Yea, before the sun and the signs were created, Before the stars of the heaven were made, His name was named before the Lord of Spirits. 4. He shall be a staff to the righteous whereon to stay themselves and not fall, And he shall be the light of the Gentiles, and the hope of those who are troubled of heart. 5. All who dwell on earth shall fall down and worship before him, And will praise and bless and celebrate with song the Lord of Spirits. 6. And for this reason hath he been chosen and hidden before Him, before the creation of the world and for evermore."

Chapter Nineteen

THE PERSON OF THE HOLY SPIRIT

To what extent can WMB's theology of the
Person of the Holy Spirit be supported
by the Scriptures?

Who, or What, is the Holy Spirit?

When WMB asked the question, "What is the Holy Spirit?" the answer he gave was, "It's Jesus Christ in Spirit form,"[1] or it is a, "Person, Jesus Christ, who is the Holy Spirit over us now."[2] Though WMB did acknowledge that the Spirit of God was a Person, and was addressed by a personal pronoun,[3] he most often referred to the Holy Spirit, or the Holy Ghost, as IT.[4]

In the earlier chapter on the Person of God, it has been clearly shown that WMB rejected the doctrine of the Trinity as established in the Nicene Creed. He, instead, embraced the Oneness, or Modalistic, view of God. It should, therefore, not be a surprise to the reader that WMB did not understand, nor believe, the orthodox doctrine of the Person of the Holy Spirit. A statement regarding the Person of the Holy Spirit, viewed in isolation from the rest of WMB's messages, would not always, at first sight, be recognized as unorthodox. What did WMB mean when he mentioned the Holy Spirit? He endeavored to explain it in one of his sermons and said, "Tonight I want to speak on the subject of: 'What is the Holy Ghost?' And tomorrow night I want to preach on: 'What Was it Given For?' And on Friday night... 'How Do I Get the Holy Ghost, and How Do I Know When I Have it?'"[5] WMB in his sermon, "What Is The Holy Ghost?" stated:

> What is the Holy Spirit?" What is it? And now, the reason I have taken these subject in line like this, you cannot come and receive the Holy Spirit, unless you know what it is. And you cannot receive it (if you know what it is), unless you believe it's given to you and it's for you. And then you cannot know whether you've got it or not, unless you know what results it brings. So if you know what it is, and who it's to, and what action it brings when it comes, then you'll know what you've got when you get it. See? That just would settle it.[6]

CHAPTER NINETEEN 267

That is clear enough, right? No, it is not clear enough! However, in *one* sense it is, because it reveals that WMB's "definition" has nothing to do with the Person per sé, but more with the actions the Holy Spirit performs. The following is what he said, in answer to, "What is the Holy Spirit?"

1. You cannot receive the Holy Spirit unless
2. You believe the Holy Spirit is given to *you* and then
3. You must receive the Holy Spirit and then
4. You will know the Holy Spirit by "its" actions

This makes it clear that WMB was not speaking about the *Person* of the Holy Spirit, but rather about the actions of the Holy Spirit in a human being. WMB's understanding of the Holy Spirit was that "it" was a spirit,[7] or the Spirit of Jesus Christ in the form of the Person of the Holy Spirit.[8] This spirit left the body of Jesus Christ sitting on His Father's throne,[9] never to return to earth,[10] and came to set up his throne on earth.[11] This throne is the human heart.[12] God dwells in man like He did in Jesus;[13] the Holy Ghost is God Himself in man.[14] He is deity dwelling in a man; "Tabernacling" Deity.[15] In fact, WMB said that people become an idol, or image, a representative, in which God dwells and through which He reconciles the world to Himself.[16] That is not in accordance to God's Word; that is a role reserved for Christ alone. WMB was asked the question, "If God is one personality, why, or how could He talk to Himself on Mount Transfiguration?"[17] He answered it by quoting Jesus in John 3: 13, "And no man hath ascended up to heaven, but he that came down from heaven, *even* the Son of man which is in heaven." Here Jesus is on the earth, while He also is in Heaven. He asked the person, "That Holy Ghost dwells within you, is that right? Do you talk to Him? Speak to Him? Pray to Him? All right, that's all I want... Thank you very much. Now, do you get it?" In other words, when people pray, they pray to the indwelling Christ. WMB contradicted Jesus Who said, "After this manner therefore pray ye: Our Father which art in heaven..." (Mat. 6: 9).

WMB stated the Holy Spirit was God Himself and was sent by God.[18] Which means that God (the Father) was the sender of God (the Holy Spirit). That would indicate two different entities or, in Trinitarian language, persons. This he unwittingly reinforced when he said that God is a Father, God is a Son and God is a Holy Spirit, with the Father and the Holy Ghost being the same Spirit.[19] That would leave God the Son[20] and God the Spirit, two beings. In other places WMB differentiated between God the Father and God the Holy Spirit. He stated that God the Father had nothing to do with the conception of Jesus, who was God. He was conceived by the Holy Spirit.[21] It is clear that this gets more confusing as one delves deeper into WMB's teaching because he did say that the Spirit is the Son of God.[22] How can the Son of God conceive Himself in Mary's womb? This teaching would translate into having the Son of God stand in the Jordan River and receive the anointing from the Son of God, while the Father, Whose name is Jesus,[23] speaks from heaven and says, "This is Me, Myself, in whom I am well pleased."[24] That is something that is not written in Scripture. WMB found that between the lines;[25] an expression he often used, because God hid things from the seminarians, but he revealed them to babes.[26] Paul said *nothing* was written between the lines.[27]

The Holy Spirit, according to WMB, dwelt in the hearts of men to replicate what Jesus did when He was here on earth. However, said WMB, the Holy Spirit is restricted because, even though the Holy Spirit was poured out in an anointing, it had to enter a person in order to operate.[28] This person had to be fully yielded to God[29] and when that occurred, it would no longer be the human but God operating through this person's lips and body,[30] out of control[31] and taken over by the Spirit.[32] That was how God and Christ became one, WMB said.[33] Apart from his error of Christ and God becoming one, the problem is, of course, that a Christian is commanded to not ever lose control, but exercise self control (Gal. 5: 23). Prophets must have control over their spirits, taught the Apostle Paul (1 Cor. 14: 32). Here WMB spoke against Apostolic authority. When WMB spoke about the anointing of the Holy Spirit, he equated that with a number of things such as, the Pillar of Fire in the wilderness;[34] the Angel that led the Hebrews to the Promised Land;[35] the Angel of the Lord;[36] the angel of God;[37] the angel of the covenant;[38] Christ, the Lord Himself.[39] No wonder that WMB ascribed deity to this angel and prayed to him as to God,[40] though he denied that he did.[41] WMB stated he did not worship that angel, but he said that he loved him,[42] and asked to be cleansed by the Blood of Jesus through that angel.[43] Not only that, but he spoke about people praying to an alleged photograph of that "angel" and receiving healing.[44]

WMB referred to the Holy Spirit as the Sixth Sense, which would never lead one astray, it cannot lie.[45] As shown earlier, WMB spoke "Thus saith the Lord," in cases of healing and yet people died; He spoke "Thus saith the Lord," yet the prophecies did not come to pass; the angel got people's names wrong in the prayer lines, etc. WMB's Holy Spirit was not what WMB claimed "it" was.

To what extent can WMB's theology of the Person of the Holy Spirit be supported by the Scriptures? Even though WMB said the Holy Spirit was a Person, he always seemed to speak about the Holy Spirit as a force or influence. To no extent can WMB's theology of the Person of the Holy Spirit be supported by Scripture.

Notes - Chapter Nineteen

[1] *Prophet Elisha,* Jul. 23, 1954, Chicago, IL, "What is the Holy Spirit? It's Jesus Christ in Spirit form."

[2] *Paradox,* Phoenix.

[3] WMB, *Abraham And His Seed After Him,* Apr. 16, 1961, Bloomington, IL, "You that don't believe the Holy Ghost as a Person, "he" is a personal pronoun."

[4] *What Is The Holy Ghost?*

[5] Ibid.

[6] Ibid.

⁷ *Q & A On The Holy Ghost*, "The Holy Ghost is a Spirit."

⁸ *Behold A Greater Than Solomon Is Here*, Salem, "The Holy Spirit Himself is here. Christ in the form of the Holy Ghost is here with us."

⁹ WMB, *Arrow Of God's Deliverance, Shot From A Bow*, Aug. 01, 1956, Shreveport, LA, "The Holy Ghost is none other but the Spirit of the Lord Jesus Christ, Who came down on the day of Pentecost to dwell with us, and in us, till the end of the world…Now, if He was Jesus that way yesterday, He's got to be Jesus that way today if He is the same. Now, the only thing is different then, He hasn't got a corporal body. His body is setting on the throne of God. That's not Jesus' throne He's setting on tonight. The Bible said, 'He's setting on His Father's throne.' Is that right? 'He that overcomes shall set with Me on My throne as I've overcome and set on My Father's throne. Now, His throne is on the earth. He's to be here with people."

¹⁰ WMB, *Former And Latter Rain*, Mar. 03, 1960, Phoenix, AZ, "But the Spirit of Jesus Christ is here, and you can be that man, or whoever He's chose to be that one, that He can work through…'cause the only lips He has is yours and mine. See, His body's at the right hand of God, will not return."

¹¹ ____, *Maniac Of Gadara*, Jul. 20, 1954, Aft., Chicago, IL, "The Holy Spirit is here now on earth, but Jesus Christ is setting at the right hand of the Majesty on high, above all Angels and Archangels and all, and has received a Name that all the family of heaven and earth is named after Him…That's our Lord Jesus Christ."

¹² ____, *Future Home Of The Heavenly Bridegroom And The Earthly Bride*, Aug. 02, 1964, Jeff., IN, "See, the heart has to be cleansed like that. Before God can come down in the person of the Holy Ghost, which is Christ coming down and dwell in the human heart."

¹³ *Q & A On The Holy Ghost*, "And we find out the Holy Ghost is Himself in you. God was above you in the Pillar of Fire with Moses. God was with you in Jesus Christ. Now God is in you in the Holy Ghost: no three gods, one God working in three offices."

¹⁴ Ibid., "The Holy Ghost is God Himself in you."

¹⁵ *Testimony Of A True Witness*, "The Holy Ghost is Deity, God tabernacled in men."

¹⁶ *Perseverance*, Jeff., IN, "The Holy Ghost is God coming down from heaven, a Spirit. You prostrate yourself before idols, trying to hypnotize a life into that. You are the idol; God brings His Spirit into you and you're His living representative. God's in you, reconciling the world to Himself."

¹⁷ *Q & A On The Seals*.

¹⁸ *Oneness*. "We're coming down to the end now. Watch. God sent the Holy Ghost, and the Holy Ghost is God Himself."

¹⁹ WMB, *Christ Is The Mystery Of God Revealed*, Jul. 28, 1963, Jeff., IN, "He was a Father, He was a Son, and He is the Holy Ghost. And the Father and the Holy Ghost is the same Spirit."

[20] *Souls In Prison Now,* "So the Holy Ghost is God, so was Jesus God."

[21] *Q & A On The Seals,* "That which is conceived in her has nothing to do with God the Father; it's the Holy Ghost. And now, we know that God was His Father…The Holy Ghost is God's Spirit, of course."

[22] *A Trial,* Tucson, "In the church age, He is called the Son of God. Now, anyone knows that God is a Spirit. Is that right? And the Holy Ghost is the Son of God."

[23] WMB, *God's Chosen Place Of Worship,* Feb. 20, 1965, Jeff., IN, "And now we find out that Jesus said, also, "I came in My Father's Name, and you received Me not." Then, the Name of the Father must be Jesus. That's right. The Name of the Father is Jesus, 'cause Jesus said so. "I carry My Father's Name. I come in My Father's Name, and you received Me not. Then, His Name was Jesus."

[24] Jn. 3: 12, "This is my beloved Son, in whom I am well pleased."

[25] WMB, *Unconditional Covenant,* Mar. 06, 1954, Phoenix, AZ, "Now, this is not written right in the Scripture, but read between the lines with me now."

[26] ____, *Queen Of Sheba,* Feb. 08, 1958, South Bend, IN, "You read the Bible not as a newspaper, not in some theological seminary interpretation of it, but as a love letter, the Bible said so… Jesus said, 'I thank Thee, Father, that thou hast hid it from the seminary students, the wise and imprudent, and revealed it to babes such as would learn.' It's hid from the eyes of smart and educated, it's revealed to babes such as will learn."

[27] 2 Cor. 1: 13, "Our letters have been straightforward, and there is nothing written between the lines and nothing you can't understand. I hope someday you will fully understand us."

[28] WMB, "*Questions And Answers,* Dec. 23, 1959, Jeff., IN, "The Holy Spirit… covers the earth but it is almost helpless until it gets into you and to me. God is depending on you and I…The earth is full of the Spirit of God, but it's poured out. But it cannot operate until It comes into us, we human beings, to operate." Note: God does not need us, but we have that privilege. – PMD.

[29] *Gifts And Callings Are Without Repentance,* "And a man is just a man until he's fully submitted to God, and then Deity dwells in that man, the Holy Spirit. Not the man, but God in the man does the work."

[30] WMB, *Hand Of The Lord Came Upon Him,* Apr. 03, 1954, Louisville, KY, "May this poor, unworthy man, just be so completely yielded to the Spirit of God, until the Holy Spirit will stand here and take the body, and the lips and speak with His own voice and a vindicate to this little audience tonight, that the Lord Jesus has rose from the dead, and is living among us tonight, proving this by signs and wonders of His life, doing the same things that He did when He was here on earth."

[31] *Trying To Do God A Service,* Shreveport, "A prophet's supposed to be the

CHAPTER NINETEEN

mouth of God speaking, not his own thinking...so completely yielded to God, he don't want to hurt nothing, but he has to say what God says, 'cause he has no control of It hisself."

[32] WMB, *Faith*, Apr. 27, 1956, "As I get myself completely yielded to the Holy Spirit, then He starts talking...He is using my voice, but it's not me. It's Him."

[33] *Identified Masterpiece*, "Just think, that, a person so yielded until identified Himself in there, in that body, and...Him and God became one. 'I and My Father are One. My Father dwelleth in Me. I do that always which pleases the Father.'"

[34] *Speak To This Mountain*, Brooklyn, "Now, if He's the same yesterday, today, and forever; if He is risen from the dead, sent back the Holy Spirit to be the Comforter, to do the works. The Holy Spirit is Christ. That was the Pillar of Fire that was in the wilderness with the children of Israel."

[35] *Expectation*, New York, "I claim that it's the same Pillar of Fire that led the children of Israel through the land of the wilderness to the promise. Was it a Pillar of Fire? Well, when the Holy Ghost, this angel of God, permitted his picture to be taken, that's exactly what it was, a Pillar of Fire, the same thing."

[36] WMB, *Angel Of The Lord*, Jul. 18, 1951, Toledo, OH, "And I believe the angel of the Lord is leading the church today, and it's the same Holy Spirit. And anyone knows the angel of the covenant was Christ."

[37] *Obey The Voice Of The Angel*, "It was the Angel of God that went before Moses. It was a Pillar of Fire at night and a cloud by day. And when you see the picture that we're going to show you, shortly, if we haven't. I believe you'll feel that it's the same Pillar of Fire that's leading the people today, the angel of God. Which we know the angel that led Moses was the angel of the covenant, which was Christ, the Son of God."

[38] *Early Spiritual Experiences*, "Jesus is here with us...How many believes that the pillar of fire, the pillar of fire that led the children of Israel was the angel of the Covenant? Let's see your hand. That was our Lord Jesus, is that right? It was Christ, the Anointed."

[39] *Sirs, We Would See Jesus*, Tifton, "The Holy Spirit is a Light. How many knows that? How many knows that the angel that led Moses through the wilderness was Christ, the angel of the covenant?"

[40] *Experiences*, "Therefore, angel of God, you who told me to go, and if I'd be sincere, the people would believe; there would be nothing stand before the prayer...O God, I plead. Oh, before you, I bow to ask you with all my heart, angel of God, you who came into the room that night, and told me these things." See also: WMB, *Angel Of God*, Mar. 04, 1948, Phoenix, AZ, "Angel of God, I do not see you, but I know that you are standing near. Please, thou knowest my heart, and know how I

love these people, stand by me tonight, and may not one go through without faith. And I know that your words have been true. I've took you at your word, for you said you were sent from God. I believed you, and you've stuck by me. You have confirmed the word with signs following. Now, again tonight, in this March the fifth, this Memorial night, may you stand now and heal everyone."

[41] *Angel Of God,* "Now, this is in no means, friends, an angel worship, it is not. I do not pray in the name of the angel, or even know his name."

[42] *Holy Ghost Given For?* "And that same angel of God is right here in this building tonight, oh, how I love him."

[43] *In His Presence,* "Father, I confess my sins. I want the angel of God to cleanse me from that by the Blood of Jesus."

[44] WMB, *Missionary Talk*, Mar. 30, 1958, Aft., Middletown, OH, "She went and got that picture, and set it down on the floor, and knelt down, and she said, 'Oh, angel of God, whose picture is on this paper, send Brother Branham to me, right quick.'"

[45] *Water Of Separation,* Jan. 21, 1955, Chicago, IL, "It's the sixth sense, the fourth dimension, or whatever you want to call it, to me, the Holy Spirit."; See also: *Super Sense*, Dec. 27, 1959, PM, Jeff., IN, "Now, the sixth sense cannot lie, it's a super sense, and that's what I want to speak about…And the super sense is the Holy Spirit, the faith of God that dwells in you. And if you'll let the five senses be yielded to the sixth sense, it'll guide you and bring all the other five senses under control of that super sense."

Chapter Twenty
CREATION OF MAN

To what extent is William Branham's account
of the Creation of Man supported
by Biblical Revelation?

WMB had his own creation account and he taught that God[1] first created the angels and then he became God, after which he created spirit "man."[2] WMB, up until 1965, the year of his death, taught that man was created first as a spirit being, [3] a god.[4] These spirit beings were either male or female,[5] according to WMB.[6] A spirit being could not tend a garden, so God made a body of earth in which God placed the spirit being.[7] The God who created mankind was a creation himself, who in turn created the Logos, which in turn created the man.[8] Later the woman was created from a rib of the man, and her pre-existent female spirit was placed in her. In essence this is what WMB's Gen. 1: 26-28 looks like when one includes what is "written between the lines,"[9] shown in italics:

> Let us make [*a spirit being*] in our image [*which is a spirit*], after our likeness [*Thus a spirit*]: and let them have dominion over the fish of the sea, and over the fowl of the air, and over the cattle, and over all the earth, and over every creeping thing that creepeth upon the earth. 27 So God created [*a spirit being*] in his own image [*a spirit*], in the image of God created he him; male [*spirit*] and female [*spirit*] created he them. 28 And God blessed them, and God said unto them, Be fruitful, and [*speak many more spirit beings into existence*], and replenish the earth, and subdue it: and have dominion over the fish of the sea, and over the fowl of the air, and over every living thing that moveth upon the earth. [*And then He said, "There's no man to till the soil." So He created man out of the dust of the earth. Now, He gave him a hand like a monkey and a foot like a bear. And He put this supernatural being which was called man, the third Person of the Trinity, Holy Spirit, into mankind and He made him in His own image*].[10]

WMB stated that Adam had an animal form.[11] He said, "I can see Adam standing... Let's take this way, see him standing like a tree. God had made him. He was dead as he could be, his toes, like the roots sticking in the ground. And God said, 'Let there be,' or breathed the breath of life into him, and he jumped, came to himself...Breathed the breath of life into him, he became a living soul."[12] WMB told his audience that Adam differed from the animals in that he did not have a spirit of nature, as they did. Adam had the Spirit of God and became an eternal being with God, even a god.[13] Scripture states that God breathed into Adam the breath of life, but it also says that all flesh had the breath of life. (Gen 7: 21-23). In other words, Adam was not different from all other creation because God's breath was in him. No, Adam was different because he was made in the image of God. God never said, "Let us make fish, fowl, cattle, animals, creeping things like serpents or snakes, and so forth, in our image and likeness."

Paul tells us that Adam was a living soul.[14] Therefore, this living soul, or person, did not reflect what God looked like, physically. People, no matter how deformed physically, are nevertheless made in the image of God. That alone should put to rest any ideas that God was a physical Being. WMB taught that God was *a* spirit and therefore man must have been *a* spirit being. However, as stated elsewhere, that was not correctly translated, but should read "God is spirit." It is problematic, because WMB elsewhere stated that God *was* a man. God could not be a man, because that would mean that God was created *before* Adam, from dirt that He Himself had made. It must be understood that this would not cause a real problem for WMB because he said, "God is all and in all."[15]

The above view, fits with WMB's Gnostic understanding of the Godhead. This very expression, "God is all and in all" is found in Hinduism, in Pantheism, but not within Christianity. Even though WMB asserted that God does not dwell in material things,[16] yet he said everything is a manifestation [or emanation] of God's Word, which is God. The earth, his pulpit, a chair, a platform, they all are manifestations, or emanations, of God.[17] He made it sound "Christian" but the concept is Pantheistic. What then does it mean that man was made in God's image? Since it cannot mean spirit, nor can it mean body, it must have to do with man's essence or attributes. Man possesses certain spiritual attributes in his being that he, in an imperfect way, shares with God; attributes (perfections) such as: mind, creativity, language, holiness, goodness, justice, truth and power and others. These are the things that separate man from the rest of Creation. Regarding Creation, this is what God actually said,

> Let us make man in our image, after our likeness: and let them have dominion over the fish of the sea, and over the fowl of the air, and over the cattle, and over all the earth, and over every creeping thing that creepeth upon the earth. 27 So God created man in his own image, in the image of God created he him; male and female created he them. 28 And God blessed them, and God said unto them, Be fruitful, and multiply, and replenish the earth, and subdue it: and have dominion over the fish of the sea, and over the fowl of the air, and over every living thing that moveth upon the earth. (Gen. 1: 26-28).

Verse 26 clearly states that God said,

CHAPTER TWENTY

Let us make man [adam] in our image, after our likeness...

The word "adam" means "red." This does not mean that God is red, nor does it mean that God created a red spirit being. It probably means Adam was created from red earth. God said that he would let man have dominion over all his creation. Nothing is said in the text that Adam was a god, amateur or otherwise. That is what WMB read back into the text, which is a method called Eisegesis, which is not a sound interpretive method. Verse 27 reads, "So God created man..." The word "So" actually is "And" and acts as a punctuation mark. The ancient texts did not have periods or commas, etc, so they devised other means to show the start of another sentence or thought. "In the image of God created He him (Adam)." Thus, Adam was the first created male human being. "Male and female created He THEM." The verse shows a shift in pronouns from "him" to "them." The KJV text uses a semicolon[18] to separate the creation of "the man," from the later creation of "woman" from Adam's rib. WMB claimed everything in Scripture, which for him was the KJV, was inspired,[19] and without error,[20] even in punctuation. That being true, it is clear there are two different things expressed. The first was the creation of man from dirt. The second was the creation of the woman from one of Adam's ribs. WMB contradicted Scripture by teaching Adam was of a dual[21] nature, male and female.

In a natural[22] way of reading, the biblical creation story states that God created the heavens and the earth, mankind as well as all else that is contained in this universe. God considered all He had made very good, or beautiful (Gen. 1: 31). God created Adam and Eve and blessed them and told them to be fruitful and multiply. He also told them to subdue the earth and for them to have dominion over creation. "Be fruitful and multiply" was God's command to all animal life, as it was to man. The evidence, to suggest that God is an androgynous being and that he created androgynous humankind, is lacking. It is, therefore, not a biblical teaching. If WMB's foundational understanding and teaching of the godhead is built on a faulty foundation, will his entire superstructure of teaching stand? If WMB's God is not the God of the book of Genesis, which God is he?

WMB's concept of the Creator God shows a capricious and devious god, incapable of keeping His own creation. WMB stated that Eve was specifically designed to fall. In order for God to escape the blame,[23] WMB accorded Satan semi-godhood,[24] incapable of creation, but able to design Eve as an evil being.[25] The words design and create are synonymous and cannot be attributed to Satan. WMB said everything produces after its own kind and therefore, so did God. Because Adam was God's son (Lu. 3: 38) Adam must produce another son of God. When Cain appeared, he could not have originated with God because he was evil, therefore Satan must be his originator. However, Adam had sexual relations with Eve *after* they had been expelled from Eden (Gen. 3: 24-4:1) and produced off-spring. So an evil Cain does not require a direct satanic sire, given the fallen condition of his parents, both of whom had disobeyed and defied God.

The task of establishing to what extent WMB's creation account is supported by biblical revelation is a daunting one, due to all the confusion. At this juncture it is important to remember that… "The creator God of Genesis shows himself throughout the Bible as a God who speaks. His word, as opposed to the silence of the mystics and the din of pagan worship, is a word in the proper sense, an orderly discourse…For thus says the LORD, who created the heavens (he is God!), who formed the earth and made it (he established it; he did not create it empty, he formed it to be inhabited!): 'I am the LORD, and there is no other. 19 I did not speak in secret, in a land of darkness; I did not say to the offspring of Jacob, "Seek me in vain." I the LORD speak the truth; I declare what is right.'"[26] (Isa. 45: 18f.).

"Let us." (Vv. 26-27) is a difficult part of Scripture to understand. It is understood by John J. Davis as the "royal we." [27] Dr. Cassuto, Professor at the Hebrew University, concluded that it is the plural exhortation, as in 'Let us go!' or 'Let us rise up!'…and the like."[28] The Reformers took it as an "intra-Trinity dialogue" which however can only be understood as a canonical reading, since the intended first audience would not have understood this sense.[29] *"In our image…"* This, "Conveys here that humans have the highest position in the created order. As God's representative on earth, humans were invested by God with authority to subdue the earth and rule over the animals."[30] The Reformers tended to speak about God's image in terms of righteousness, holiness and transferable attributes, (perfections) which would not contradict the previous statement.

WMB's teaching showed a God revealing Himself as androgynous and making man androgynous. John Skinner says,

> The persistent idea that man as first created was bi-sexual and the sexes separated afterwards…is far from the thought of this passage.[31]

Though perhaps supported by some theologians, it cannot be supported by the text, or the context, at all. Though God and his actions are described in anthropomorphic terms, this does not mean that they physically represent His person or actions. God is a community of "persons," Father, Son and Holy Spirit. He created mankind to be a community, man and wife, with the command to procreate and enlarge this community.

The charge by WMB that Eve was a by-product, must now be addressed. This author must confess that the more he contemplated the words of Genesis, the more awestruck he became by its careful design and detail. WMB, as a self-proclaimed prophet, showed absolutely no insight into God's divine plan and purpose. He treated it rather flippantly and seemed only concerned about his own spurious insights. When God told Adam to name all the animals, a lot of thought was put into that process by the man. He named them for what they were. After all the animals were named, no companion was found for Adam. God had personally formed all these animals in the Garden. Now he caused a deep sleep to come upon Adam and built a woman out of the rib He took out of Adam. As Leopold says,

> It would not have been seemly to use *yatsar* 'to mold,' a verb applicable in the case of clay, not of flesh. 'Build' somehow applies to the fashioning of a structure of some importance; it involves constructive effort. Both of these factors are in evidence in the creation of woman. When God brings her unto man, this act of his is the institution of marriage and stamps marriage as a divinely willed and approved state.[32]

When Adam awakes he sees a female version of himself. He says in effect, "*this one* shall be called woman. I called that an elephant, that a giraffe and that a monkey, but *this* I call woman!"

WMB made Satan to be Eve's designer, but that would make him like God, because the designer is the creator. When God built Eve from one of Adam's ribs, there is no mention of a serpent being present. In fact, there is no serpent or snake mentioned at all in Gen. 1 and Gen. 2, but only in Gen. 3. There is no space or time allotted for anything WMB alleged, regarding Satan fashioning Eve, during this time of Eve's creation by God. However, God had already said that all He created, made, formed, moulded and built, was very beautiful. What was left to be done?

WMB's argument of a serpent having intercourse with Eve and producing Cain (Serpent's Seed) cannot be substantiated by Scripture. The simple fact is that Adam did not know Eve until after they had been expelled from the Garden. WMB's followers point out that the words, "jealousy; one husband; chaste virgin; Satan beguiled Eve; subtilty and corrupted," all indicate the sin was sexual because some of these words were also used in their interpretation of Gen. 3.

This for them confirms Serpent's Seed, but does it? At this point it is prudent to take a look at 2 Cor. 11: 1-4:

> Would to God ye could bear with me a little in my folly: and indeed bear with me. 2 For I am jealous over you with godly jealousy: for I have espoused you to one husband, that I may present you as a chaste virgin to Christ. 3 But I fear, lest by any means, as the serpent beguiled Eve through his subtilty, so your minds should be corrupted from the simplicity that is in Christ. 4 For if he that cometh preacheth another Jesus, whom we have not preached, or if ye receive another spirit, which ye have not received, or another gospel, which ye have not accepted, ye might well bear with him.

WMB's followers appear to go further than WMB himself (as research has shown so far) when they interpret these verses as follows: *Paul refers here to Gen. 3. In which chapter he is exhorting the Corinthians to bear (as in having children) with him, because he has espoused them to Christ as a chaste virgin. He warned them not to be impregnated by Satan, as was Eve.* However, Genesis Three says nothing of the kind and neither does 2 Cor. 11: 1-4. Paul makes reference to Eve's mind being deceived by Satan. He is afraid that other teachers would come, which would beguile them too. Paul exhorts them to bear with him, to put up with him, in his folly, since they also put up with false teachers.

WMB mentioned Jesus calling the religious Jewish leaders vipers and serpents (Matt. 23: 23) as support for his Serpent's Seed teaching. Jesus did speak of them being of their father the Devil[33] who was a deceiver and a murderer from the beginning (Jn. 8: 44). However, in the same chapter Jesus also said they did have Abraham as physical ancestor (37, 56), which indicates Jesus meant they were spiritual off-spring of Satan.

In WMB's Serpent's Seed teaching, God is mentioned, as well as Lucifer and Satan. Nothing is said of Christ because, according to WMB, He did not exist as God yet. Christ Jesus became God at his baptism in the Jordan[34] and ceased to be God in the Garden of Gethsemane.[35] WMB made reference to Jesus being in heaven as Michael, warring with Satan[36] whom elsewhere he called Lucifer.[37] Lucifer, as God's co-worker[38] appears to have had a position in heaven superior to Michael (Christ), though Michael did defeat him, as WMB's story goes. There is no space to develop this here. Suffice it to say that without the mention, even in embryonic form, of Father, Son and Holy Spirit, WMB's concept of God is certainly not orthodox. It appears somewhat like the Mormon concepts of God.[39] WMB was earlier connected with Mormonism, though he left it.[40] God is a man, according to WMB,[41] and had flesh and bones, hands and feet,[42] but man is also a god,[43] or God.[44] According to Mormonism, "…God himself was once as we are now, and is an exalted man, and sits enthroned in yonder heavens."[45] Mormonism has duality of persons, the Father and the Son, appearing to Joseph Smith, in his first encounter with God.[46] In Mormonism the Holy Spirit is not a person but a Mind.[47] In WMB's view we have seen that he did have duality in his concept of male/female, or Father/Mother nature of God.

On one hand WMB was emphatic that God was a man, but on the other hand, he stated that God said, "I am El Shaddai. I am the breasted, mother God"[48] and actually called God, the Mother of Abraham.[49] The question is, "Who is this God with the two breasts?"[50] If God is a man, as WMB so vehemently asserted, why does He or She have two breasts?[51] WMB stated that God has one breast for salvation and another breast for healing. WMB showed a lack of sound lexical principles by stating that *El Shaddai* is the plural form of *shad*,[52] (Heb.-breast).

> God appeared to him in the Name of Almighty God. The 'Almighty' there comes from the Hebrew word of the 'El Shaddai' which means the bosom or breast of a

woman. May they come in through Christ just now, come to the breast of the El Shaddai, which was wounded for our transgressions. And then in return tonight, lay their head over on the bosom of the Mother God. The only One that could give us birth rightly is God, our Mother, and our Father.[53]

It appears that WMB relied on questionable sources in relation to El Shaddai and also mentioned Scofield's Bible (Notes).[54] There are few commentaries that deal in depth with Gen. 49: 25. Some, if they mention anything regarding El Shaddai, make no reference to breasts, except in "the blessings from above and below."

The interpretation of Shaddai as a god with breasts originates with Canaanite fertility religions being assimilated into Yahweh. Its outcome is an androgynous monotheism. "These interpretations of Shaddai [God with breasts], however, are farfetched, and as such the explanation of El Shadday based on them is untenable,"[55] though some scholars are awaiting additional information.[56] Some suggest that El Shaddai means "God of the udder," to be understood in the context of blessing. God did promise a land overflowing with milk and honey. This should not be understood to mean, "the Udder God." There exists no proof in Scripture that God is two-breasted. God is always "Our Father," and never "Our Mother." The only Mother the Christian has is, "Jerusalem which is above is free, which is the mother of us all," (Gal. 4:26).

God's law decreed that all created things must produce after its own kind, but WMB did not consider that God exists *outside* the created order. WMB saw God as an androgynous being, which created Adam as androgynous. Adam, in turn, must bring forth after his kind, which is an androgynous being. The Fall occurred, but ultimately all mankind will be restored to an androgynous state, which WMB allegedly saw beyond the Curtain of Time.[57] It was Jesus' job, according to WMB, to bring back the original seed again.[58] WMB saw redemption in Jesus restoring mankind back to their pre-Fall, and presumably androgynous, condition. Yet, Jesus Himself was *not* androgynous, according to WMB.[59] This is an irreconcilable inconsistency, because Jesus, if he were to be like His Father, should have had breasts.

WMB taught man was a god from creation.[60] WMB never once spoke about a woman becoming a god(dess?), except in the negative sense of a sex goddess. He even claimed himself to have attained creative powers.[61] The problem with man was due to the woman's transgression in the garden. Man, being a god, is superior to woman and when man sins it is the woman's fault, just like it was in the Garden. Strong examples of that are found in WMB's statements like,

> Did you know Jesus Christ said, "Whosoever looketh upon a woman to lust after her, hath committed adultery with her already in his heart." Does anybody know that?...And if you dress yourself sexy like, no matter how modest you think it is, and go out on the street, and some old sinner looks at you to lust

after you, at the judgment bar you'll be guilty of committing adultery with that man when he answers for it. Why is it? **It was you was the one done it. You presented yourself that way, so you are the guilty one.** And you, no matter how virtuous and pure you've lived, you'll be guilty before God of committing adultery with a sinner, just the same as you'd went through the act. Jesus said so.[62] (Emphasis mine – PMD)

Jesus said that a *man* looking at a woman to lust after her, has committed adultery with her in his heart. Who committed adultery? The man, Jesus said! Jesus did not mention the woman. WMB, as typical, changed Jesus' words to make the woman guilty for tempting the man, even if unwittingly. WMB said men are wired that way and can't help themselves; boys will be boys, after all.[63] When men lust after women who are decently and modestly dressed, the woman is still guilty, said WMB.[64] This horrific misogynous attitude is seen in many of WMB's messages.

Every time that a funeral goes down the street, a woman caused it. Every time a baby screamed out, a woman caused it...Every gray hair, a woman caused it...Everything that's wrong, a woman caused it."[65] "Every sin that ever was on the earth was caused by a woman."[66] "There's nothing designed in all creation that can stoop as low as a woman can...designed alone for filth and unclean living."[67] "Put the woman back in the kitchen where she belongs and everything will be all right."[68] "Your kind was the cause of all sin."[69] WMB also blamed women as the cause of 94 % of all car accidents.[70]

WMB taught the Serpent's Seed until his death. WMB's legacy lives on and his following after his death is far greater than anytime during his lifetime.

To what extent can William Branham's account of the Creation of Man be supported by Biblical Revelation? WMB's account of creation is a re-write of an early church heresy, already condemned by Irenaeus in his *Against Heresies*:

But their mother (Sophia) cunningly devised a scheme to seduce Eve and Adam, by means of the serpent, to transgress the command of Ialdabaoth. Eve listened to this as if it had proceeded from a son of God, and yielded an easy belief. She also persuaded Adam to eat of the tree regarding which God had said that they should not eat of it. They then declare that, on their thus eating, they attained to the knowledge of that power which is above all, and departed from those who had created them. When Prunicus perceived that the powers were thus baffled by their own creature, she greatly rejoiced, and again cried out, that since the father was incorruptible, he (Ialdabaoth) who formerly called himself the father was a liar; and that, while Anthropos and the first woman (the Spirit) existed previously, this one (Eve) sinned by committing adultery.[71]

CHAPTER TWENTY

Can WMB's account of the Creation of Man be supported by Biblical Revelation? Certainly not. It is what Paul refers to as a Jewish fable. To no extent can William Branham's account of the Creation of Man be supported by Biblical Revelation.

Notes - Chapter Twenty

[1] For WMB, God here means the overarching Fountain of Spirits, see the chapter on the Person of God.

[2] *Five Definite Identifications*, "So the first thing He created...Now, some of you want to know about my Genesis story; God said, 'Let us make man.' The first thing He created was angels to worship Him, then He become God. Then when He said, 'Let us make man after our image,' what kind of a man did He make? Spirit man; then when He made that man, He give him control. Then He made man out of the dust of the earth; then he fell."

[3] *Resurrection Of Lazarus*, Erie, PA, "Then he had to make a man in his own image. John 4 says that God is a Spirit. And he had to make a spirit man." See also: *Seed Shall Not Be Heir With The Shuck*, "Adam was spirit to begin with...Man was created in God's image, God is a Spirit, so he's a spirit man."

[4] *Uncertain Sound*, "Now, listen close... a man is a god, he's absolutely a god, for he was made in the image of God, being a son of God, and then he's an heir of all that God is."

[5] *Q & A On Genesis*, "So He knew He was going to have some women, so He just made their spirit right there. The Bible said He would in 1, Genesis 1:26, "He created he him, man in a prefigure, male and female."...In a prefigure He made the woman and the man before they was ever formed out of the dust of the earth. And then God made the man, not in His Own image. This body's not in the image of God; this body's in the image of beasts."

[6] Ibid., "And then God taken from his side a piece of him, a rib, and made a woman. Now, where did He get the spirit, woman?...Genesis 1:26, He said, 'Let us make man in our own image, after our own likeness, created He them man, male and female.' He made the burly spirit for the man; He made the tender, little, delicate, feminish spirit for the woman."

[7] *Deity Of Jesus Christ*, "And God in the beginning made his first man. He made him out of spirit, and spirit is the invisible part of man that you don't see. Now, God made man in his own image...God made man in his own image. "And God is a Spirit," says the Bible, and the first man that was made had the government over all the creation...He led the creation, he led the animals, but there was no man to till the soil, so God made man out of dust of the earth...he put this immortal spirit that never dies into this man, and he become more than a brute, he became a man...This is the body of flesh that he's just living in, like a house, it's going back to the dust of the earth, but the spirit is immortal, it comes from God. That's the image of God, God is a spirit."

[8] *Q & A On Genesis*, "The first creation was God Himself; then out of God came the Logos, which was the Son of God; then out of the Logos, which was the Word...out of the Logos came forth the man."

⁹ *Unconditional Covenant*, "Now, this is not written right in the Scripture, but read between the lines with me now."

¹⁰ *Show Us The Father*, Connersville, "And then He said, 'There's no man to till the soil.' So He created man out of the dust of the earth. Now, He might've give him a hand like a monkey and a foot like a bear…And He put this supernatural being which was called man, the third Person of the Trinity, Holy Spirit, into mankind (That's exactly right.), that man and He made him in His own image."

¹¹ *Oneness*, Jeff. IN, "See, nothing has a soul but man. God put… He's an animal form (That's true.), but He put a soul on him. That's what made him different from the animals. He knowed right from wrong when his soul come on him…The highest form of animal life is a human being."

¹² *Q & A On Genesis*.

¹³ *Blasphemous Names*. "I want to ask you something. If he was a man, what kind of a breath was he breathing before that God breathed this breath of life into him?…But what God did, He breathed the breath of Eternal Life, then he become a living soul, a soul that can't die…breathed the breath of Eternal Life into his nostrils. And he became an eternal soul, 'cause God breathed (not what nature done, but what God did)--breathed the breath of life into his nostrils, and he become a living soul…But God specially, upon Adam, breathed the breath of Eternal Life, and he become an eternal person with God. He had power like God: he was a amateur god. He was god of the earth, not God of heaven now, god of the earth. And someday the sons of God will again become gods. Jesus said so: 'Is not it written in your law, 'Ye are gods?'"

¹⁴ "And so it is written, 'The first man Adam was made a living soul; the last Adam was made a quickening spirit.'" (1 Cor. 15: 45).

¹⁵ *Seeking After Jesus*, May 31, 1953, Connersville, IN.

¹⁶ *Faith Is The Substance*, Oakland, "God is not in material things. God is in men."

¹⁷ *Testimony Of Jesus Christ*, "This is the Word of God made manifest. This pulpit, this wood, just everything in here, everything that the eye sees was made manifest because God spoke it into existence."

¹⁸ WMB, *Divine Healing*, Dec. 19, 1954, AM, Jeff., IN, "And as far as believing the Word's inspired, I believe that every iota in that Bible is inspired."

¹⁹ _____, *Thirst*, Sep. 19, 1965, Tucson, AZ, "Anything that's--that's in this Bible is inspired, whether it's history, whether it's songs, whatever it is. It's inspired."

²⁰ _____, *Expectation*, Feb. 07, 1961, Long Beach, CA, "This Bible cannot make an error." See also: *Events Made Clear By Prophecy*, "The the Bible, no man could write, no one in the space of sixteen hundred years, by forty different writers, could write, and not one error be in it."

²¹ *Corinthians Book of Correction*, "Now, in the beginning they were one. God, when He made man, He made him a dual person, both male and female."

[22] By "natural" is meant a normal way of reading the text, without looking for mystical insights.

[23] *Marriage and Divorce,* "Now, watch His great program unfold, as we go on through here now, just as perfect as perfect can be. I didn't know this till the other day. Why didn't He make her [Eve] like that in the beginning, like the rest of His females? Because it would be unbecoming to Him. He is the Fountain of all purity. That's the reason He had to let Satan get a hold of her, what he done in the perversion. Such a creature would be, would not be becoming to Him."

[24] *Seal of The Antichrist,* "The right hand man of Almighty God was Lucifer, the son of the morning. The first, God granted him almost co-workers with Him; he was a co-worker, partly equal with Him; only Satan could not create."

[25] *Marriage and Divorce,* "Now, there is nothing can stoop like her, and she is designed so that she can be deceiving. And Satan is really working on her today, in these last days, because he is her designer. I can prove that now. To go right back at the beginning, who started to work on her, Adam or Satan, God, God or Satan? See, that's her designer. It's her chief weapon to throw man to her filth, being a pretty woman, she can sway a man any way she wants to. Brother, it ain't the bootleg joint down here that gets the man; it's the pretty woman walking down the street, twisting herself, half dressed. That's what takes...That's the deceiver right there. And she is deadly with it, absolutely deadly. You may question me about Satan being her designer, but that's the truth. Satan designed her. He still does it."

[26] Henri Blocher, *IN THE BEGINNING, The opening chapters of Genesis*, Translated by David, G. Preston, (Downers Grove, IL: Intervarsity Press, 1984), 73.

[27] John J. Davis, *Paradise to Prison,* (Grand Rapids, MI: Baker Book House Co., 1975), 80.

[28] U. Cassuto, *A Commentary on the Book of Genesis,* (Jerusalem: The Magnes Press, Hebrew University), 55.

[29] Kenneth A. Mathews, *The New American Commentary, Genesis 1-11: 26,* General Editor E. Ray Clendenen., (Nashville, TN: Broadman and Holman Publishers, 1995).

[30] John E. Hartley, *New International Biblical Commentary, Genesis,* (Peabody, MA: Hendrickson Publishers, Inc., 2000), 48.

[31] John Skinner, *Genesis, 2nd Ed.,* (Edinburgh: T. & T. Clark, 1969), 33.

[32] H.C. Leupold, *Exposition of Genesis,* Vol. I Chapters 1-19, (Grand Rapids, MI: Baker Book House Company, 1975).

[33] D.A. Carson, *The Gospel According to John,* (Grand Rapids, MI: Wm. B. Eerdmans Publishing Company, 1991, 715 pp.), 353. "Precisely because this kind of Sonship is predicated on kinship of behaviour and values, it is not surprising that Jesus' opponents want to carry out their father's designs." See also:

John Gill, *An Exposition of the Gospel According to John,* (Springfield, MO: Particular Baptist Press, 2003 edition, 742 pp.) 290. "Not of his substance but by imitation and example; and as being under his authority and influence, his instructions and directions, and ready to follow after him and obey his commands; the word *your* is rightly supplied..." See also:

R.C.H. Lenski, *The Interpretation of St. John's Gospel*, Minneapolis, MN, "There are children of God, but you unbelieving Jews, are the devil's children. Of course, the devil did not create these Jews while God created those people who are his children by faith. The fact that moral and spiritual relationship is referred to the clause with *kai* places beyond question."

34 *Church And Its Condition*, "And John said, 'I bare record, seeing the Spirit of God like a Dove coming down, and abiding on Him.'...That's when God and Man became one. That's when heaven and earth embraced each other. Hallelujah. That's when God was made flesh... that's when God came down from the Spirit form and was made a Man and dwell among us... when God and man was made one on that great memorial day when John baptized Jesus."

35 *Adoption # 2*, "In the Garden of Gethsemane, the anointing left Him, you know, He had to die as a sinner. He died a sinner, you know that; not His sins, but mine and yours." See also: *It Is The Rising Of The Sun*, "The Spirit left Him, in the Garden of Gethsemane. He had to die, a man."

36 *Beginning And Ending Of The Gentile Dispensation*, "And at that time Michael shall stand, the great prince." Michael was Christ, of course, Who fought the angelic wars in heaven with the devil. Satan and Michael fought together, or fought against each other, rather."

37 *Seal Of The Antichrist*, "Did you know that in heaven, that the devil was God's right hand man in the beginning, that Lucifer, the son of the morning, was given power?... In his pride went over in the north, and set up a kingdom, and fought against Michael and his Angels..."

38 *God's Covenant With Abraham*.

39 Joseph Smith Jr., *Teachings of the Prophet Joseph Smith*, ed. Joseph Fielding Smith, 4th ed. (Salt Lake City: The Deseret News Press, 1943), 345, 346.

40 WMB, *Faithful Abraham*, Apr. 24, 1959, Aft., San Jose, CA, "Joseph Smith met an angel. I wouldn't doubt that a bit. But when he got off the Bible, that's when I left it. See, right there when he leaves the Bible." See also: *Conferences*, Bloomington, "People seeing angels and so forth...Joseph Smith seen one. I different with Joseph Smith because it was not Scriptural, but I don't say the man never saw an angel. I'm not to dispute the man's word. There's been many angels, and so forth, saw."; *Spoken Word*, "Joseph Smith...you killed him up here in Illinois: shot him without a cause, because he had something a little different." WMB, *The Sixth Seal*, Mar. 23, 1963, Jeff., IN, "Some of the finest people I--you would want to meet would be in the Mormon people, very fine type of people; and then their--their prophet, Joseph Smith, that the Methodist people killed here in Illinois, on their journey over...that fine man."

41 *Entombment*, "God's got a body, and it looks like a man. Moses saw it, others saw it, and it looks like a man."

42 *The Messiah*.

⁴³ *Uncertain Sound,* "Man in the beginning, when he was made, a man is a god. He is absolutely a god, for he was made in the image of God, being a son of God, and then he's an heir of all that God is. And man was given a domain, and the domain was the earth. You have power over the fishes, over the fowls of the air, and over everything. He could just speak, and everything obeyed him, because he was a god within himself: not universal God...but he was a ruler in his domain."

⁴⁴ *Jehovah-Jireh,* Charlotte, VA, "When God became man, so man became God; we're sons and daughters of God ."

⁴⁵ Joseph Smith Jr. 345, 346.

⁴⁶ Joseph Smith, *Joseph Smith's History, Doctrines and Covenants of the Church of Jesus Christ and the Latter-Day Saints, and The Pearl of Great Price,* (Salt Lake City, Utah: The Church of Jesus Christ and the Latter-Day Saints, 1982) 49. "I saw two Personages...standing above me in the air. One of them spake unto me, calling me by name and said, pointing to the other—This is my beloved Son. Hear Him!"

⁴⁷ Jerald and Sandra Tanner, *The Changing World of Mormonism,* (Chicago, IL: Moody Press, 1980, 592 pp), 188. "There are two personages...the Father and the Son: The Father being a personage of spirit, glory and power: possessing all perfection and fullness: The Son, who was in the bosom of the Father... possessing the same mind with the Father, which mind is the Holy Spirit..." *Doctrines and Covenants of the Church, Lectures on Faith,* 1835., 52, 53, 55, 57, 58; (removed from modern editions).

⁴⁸ *Abraham's Grace Covenant,* "From the Hebrew word is 'El Shaddai,' which means...'Shadd' means 'breast' in the Hebrew. Now, He wasn't the 'breast God,' but 'Shaddai,' which the plural, 'breasted God. I am the breasted God, the Strength-giver, the sufficient One, the Life-giver.'...He said, 'I am El Shaddai. I am the breasted, mother God.'"

⁴⁹ WMB, *Workings Of The Holy Ghost,* Aug. 16, 1956, Prince Albert, SK, CAD, "God promised Abraham that...He was what? El Shaddai, the Breast. So in other words He would be the mother...to Abraham. Is God a Mother? Sure He is. We are borned of God. Is that right? So that makes God our Mother. God is our Father. God, in Christ is our brother."

⁵⁰ ———, *Abraham and His Seed After Him,* Apr. 16, 1961, Bloomington, IL, "...Abraham's an old man...And the Lord appeared to him in the Name of El-Shaddai, 'the bosom.'...'El,' comes from the word 'a strong One'; 'Shad' means 'breast.' 'Shaddai" means 'breasted.' God, He said, 'I am Almighty God. 'Now, if you got a 'Scofield Bible...'"

⁵¹ WMB used a Scofield Reference Bible and Dr. Cyrus Scofield's Notes (1917), which state, "The qualifying word Shaddai is formed from the Hebrew word 'shad,' the breast, invariably used in Scripture for a woman's breast...Shaddai therefore means primarily 'the breasted.' God is 'Shaddai'.. It is on every account to be regretted that 'Shaddai' was translated 'Almighty,'" available from http://bible.crosswalk.com/Com mentaries, (accessed March 29, 2008).

⁵² *Theological Dictionary of the Old Testament*, Ed. G. Johannes Botterweck, Helmer Ringgren and Heinz-Josef Fabri, Transl. Douglas W. Scott, Vol.14, (Grand Rapids, MI: Wm. Eerdman's Publishing Company, 2004, 702 pp.), 408, 409, 411. "The word shad represents a common Semitic noun generally assumed to be a primitive noun, possibly originally a children's babbling word...It only occurs 24 times in the OT...the nursing breast and the fertile womb are understood as signs of divine blessing (Gen. 49: 25, "blessings of the breasts")."

⁵³ *Approach To God.*

⁵⁴ *Abraham and His Seed After Him.*

⁵⁵ *Theological Dictionary of the OT.* 421.

⁵⁶ Ibid.

⁵⁷ *Beyond The Curtain Of Time*, Mar. 05, 1961, Jeff., IN.

⁵⁸ *Power of Transformation*, "But the seed of the righteous one, who it was...See, Eve didn't have a seed. You know that. The woman doesn't have a seed, the female. She has an egg, but not a seed. But she... appointed him, a seed, see, appointed by God's appointment, she took the seed. And the great Seed, course, from the woman, was that God gave. See, God appointed her a seed instead of the one that Cain slew; that, the enemy, death, serpent's seed slew God's seed, in perversion there, you see. God appointed, through the woman, a Seed, which is Christ, see, to bring back the original seed again...appointed him, a seed, and then man began to call upon the Name of the Lord, and begin to come back to the Word again."

⁵⁹ *Indictment,* "They crucified, the most shameful death...naked...The crucifix has a...rag wrapped around Him, but they stripped his clothes from Him." [Note: WMB indicated Christ was a man with male sexual organs. Not androgynous like WMB said Adam was. – PMD.

⁶⁰ *Uncertain Sound,* "Man in the beginning, when he was made, a man is a god. He's absolutely a god, for he was made in the image of God, being a son of God, and then he's an heir of all that God is. And man was given a domain, and the domain was the earth."

⁶¹ *Message Of Grace,* "Last year, as all of you know, which is on print and also in testimony and in the tapes, I was setting at a place here in Indiana where the Lord God came down and spoke to me, that my second ministry, that was ready to take place in the near future. And there was spoken into existence three squirrels. All of you know the story; I'm sure."

⁶² WMB, *Father, The Hour Has Come,* Oct. 02, 1956, Aft., Chicago, IL.

⁶³ *Marriage and Divorce,* "And you, some of the women, put on these nasty clothes and get out here to throw yourself before man. Jesus said, "Whosoever looketh upon a woman to lust after her has committed adultery with her already in his heart." Then who is guilty, the man or you? He is a male, made so he could take this act, see; and **you're the female, that ought to refuse.**" [Emphasis mine – PMD]

[64] *Five Definite Identifications Of The True Church Of The Living God*, "Jesus said, 'Whosoever looketh upon a woman to lust after her, has committed adultery with her already in his heart.' Now, when that sinner has to answer for committing adultery, who will be the guilty one? The woman that presented herself."

[65] *Why Are We Not A Denomination.*

[66] *Marriage And Divorce.*

[67] Ibid.

[68] *Q & A On Hebrews # 3.*

[69] Ibid.

[70] *The Serpent's Seed*, "And you women drivers...Listen. Billy Paul and I on this last campaign around the nation, six months, I kept a count of how many scruples on the road. And out of three hundred mishaps on the road, guess how many of them was women drivers? There was only lacking nineteen of them were men, and two hundred and eighty, or I believe two hundred eighty-one of them would be women drivers: women drivers."

[71] ANF01. The Apostolic Fathers with Justin Martyr and Irenaeus, Chapter XXX.—"Doctrines of the Ophites and Sethians," available from http://www.ccel.org/ccel/schaff/anf01.ix.ii.xxxi.html, (accessed June 03, 2004).

Chapter Twenty-One
THE FALL
(SERPENT's SEED)

To what extent is William Branham's Doctrine of the Fall, or his Serpent's Seed teaching, supported by Biblical Revelation?

The Serpent Seed Doctrine

In the early 1950s WMB began teaching the Serpent's Seed, which remained prominent throughout his later teaching career. It was used by WMB, and it is still used by his followers, as the reason why non-disciples of WMB cannot accept his Message. They simply cannot follow, because they are Serpent's Seed.

Even in his day it was no secret that WMB had strange theories and leanings. He had often been warned by his pastors while in the "Full Gospel Missionary Baptist Church" in Jeffersonville, Indiana.[1] Freda, Gordon Lindsay's wife, notes, "At the very beginning Gordon had to act as a liaison between the sponsoring pastors, for it seemed that Branham had some erratic ideas. In fact, at first some of his opinions, because of his lack of sound teaching and background, bordered on the occult."[2] Mrs. Gordon Lindsay was being charitable when she noted these things. The earliest evidence of WMB preaching the Serpent's Seed is found in 1953.[3] WMB started to propagate this in a covert manner before coming out in the open with it:

> God said, "Where are you, Adam?"...And here come Adam the same way, his big manly shoulders and this sheepskin around him. He was...Couldn't stand no more naked. He was in shame. <u>I got my idea of what it was. You can have yours.</u>[4]
> (Underline mine - PMD. This is a definite covert reference to the Serpent's Seed outside of his own church building).

Though he often spoke about Serpent's Seed, WMB did not preach a sermon called by that title until 1958.[5] WMB's belief was that the serpent was a being between a Chimpanzee and man, which could and did, pro-create with Eve. This is contradicted, by WMB's own arguments. According to WMB's own teaching, everything had to bring forth after its kind. That meant that the serpent, being an animal, had to bring forth an animal; God, therefore, brought forth Adam, a god. WMB failed to see that God is not of the created order. God did not birth Adam, but made him from dirt. According to WMB, when two different species breed it produces a non-reproducing hybrid. This WMB illustrated with cross-breeding a horse with a donkey, producing a hybrid mule. Cain, by having children, proved he was not a hybrid. The Bible says Cain was a man (Hebrew = *ish*) and not just *like* a man. WMB's describes the serpent:

> Now, watch the serpent, this serpent which was first…He's a great big fellow. He's between the chimpanzee and the man. And the serpent, the devil, Lucifer, knew that that was the only blood that would mix with this human blood. The only person he could deal with…Great big fellow, prehistoric giant. That's where they find these big bones, and I'll show you this in the Bible…This great big fellow, let's say…he was ten foot tall, great big shoulders, looked just like a man. What did he do? He begin making love to Eve. And he lived with her as a husband. And she saw it was pleasant, so she went and told her husband; but she was already pregnant by Satan. And she brought forth her first son whose name was Cain, the son of Satan…"God had done quit creating for years and years and years, until He made the woman out of a rib out of his side. [6]

WMB introduced sin as occurring completely distanced from God. Perhaps, in order to "protect" God from becoming the author of Evil, Eve was made a by-product in WMB' teaching. Eve was not a part of the original creation of man.[7]

> Adam had been made in the image of God. As a son of God he could not be tempted and fall. That would be impossible. So God took a by-product of man to cause the fall. Woman never stepped fresh from the hand of God as a true product of God. She was produced from man. And when God caused her to be brought forth from man she was vastly different from the other females He had created. She was able to be seduced. No other female in creation can be immoral; but the human female may be touched at almost any time. And that weakness in her allowed Satan to seduce her by way of the serpent…She is the type of all things vulgar, foul and loathsome on the one hand and on the other hand she is the type of all things clean and beautiful, and holy as the receptacle of the Spirit and blessings of God.[8]

God turned Eve over to Satan, who became her designer.[9] As stated, *designer* is a synonym for creator. WMB used the words *create* and *made* interchangeably when he spoke about God. This serpent was not a reptile[10] according to WMB, but a man who, due to the curse, lost his legs and became a snake.[11] WMB said, "The Word says that Eve was,…actually seduced by the serpent."[12] Eve committed adultery with the serpent and that union produced Cain,[13] a bastard child.[14] Eve became an immoral woman, she was designed to commit adultery.[15]

WMB 'revealed' this mystery[16] of the Serpent's Seed that had been hidden from the foundation of the earth,[17] prior to his 1965 *Marriage and Divorce* message, which became key within the WMB community. It covered the serpent's seed teaching in great detail. As addressed earlier, Eve supposedly had relations with the serpent and afterwards she had relations with Adam,[18] which brought forth twins.[19] There are a number of proof texts used by WMB and his followers to establish the Serpent's Seed doctrine to be true. One is the word "beguiled," found in Gen. 3: 13. WMB translated that to mean seduced or defiled.[20] Eve had not sinned, because she was deceived and did not know any better, said WMB. Adam, however, was not deceived, but walked into it with his eyes open. He did this because he wanted to redeem Eve, and Adam became a type of Christ redeeming His Bride.[21] However, Scripture states Adam sinned and did not simply take upon himself Eve's sin, as WMB argued.[22] This was also contradicted by WMB's own words. He stated that Eve was deceived,[23] but did not sin.[24] If so, why was Eve punished? The sin regarded blood and off-spring said WMB; thus God had to shed animal blood to atone for their sin:

> Adam put his arm around Eve, and there they go walking out of Eden condemned. I can just hear that old bloody sheepskin around the beautiful figure of those two people, slapping against their legs as they were going, walking out of Eden…And that same Saviour, with His own Blood around His garments flapping against His legs, walked up Golgotha's hill and was crucified to redeem the man.[25]

Did God atone for Adam and Eve's sin by slaying animals? Short answer, "No explicit scriptural evidence is found!" More about this later.

WMB used Prov. 30: 20 to "prove" that Eve committed adultery, "Such is the way of an adulterous woman; she eateth, and wipeth her mouth, and saith, I have done no wickedness." The context lies within

> There be three things which are too wonderful for me, yea, four which I know not: 19 The way of an eagle in the air; the way of a serpent upon a rock; the way of a ship in the midst of the sea; and the way of a man with a maid. 20 Such is the way of an adulterous woman; she eateth, and wipeth her mouth, and saith, I have done no wickedness. Prov. 30: 18, 19.

These are the words of Agur, son of Jakeh (V. 1, 18, 19). He states that there are three things he cannot understand and four of which he does not know the way:

1. an eagle in the air;
2. a serpent upon a rock;
3. a ship in the midst of the sea;
4. a man with a maid.

CHAPTER TWENTY-ONE

Agur continues and says that in the same way he does not understand those four things, he does not understand how, "An adulterous wife eats and wipes her mouth and says, 'I've done nothing wrong.'" Agur does not reference Eve, nor does he reference the woman eating fruit. WMB linked the two without any Scriptural warrant. To make his point, he connected this with what Paul says,

> Would to God ye could bear with me a little in my folly: and indeed bear with me. 2 For I am jealous over you with godly jealousy: for I have espoused you to one husband, that I may present you as a chaste virgin to Christ. 3 But I fear, lest by any means, as the serpent beguiled Eve through his subtilty, so your minds should be corrupted from the simplicity that is in Christ (2 Cor. 11: 1-3).

These verses, quoted by WMB, must be seen in the context of Paul's exhortation regarding his Apostolic authority and his fear of other, so called teachers, creeping in and corrupting his converts,

> 12 For we dare not make ourselves of the number, or compare ourselves with some that commend themselves: but they measuring themselves by themselves, and comparing themselves among themselves, are not wise. 13 But we will not boast of things without *our* measure, but according to the measure of the rule which God hath distributed to us, a measure to reach even unto you. 14 For we stretch not ourselves beyond *our measure*, as though we reached not unto you: for we are come as far as to you also in *preaching* the gospel of Christ: 15 Not boasting of things without *our* measure, *that is*, of other men's labours; but having hope, when your faith is increased, that we shall be enlarged by you according to our rule abundantly, 16 To preach the gospel in the *regions* beyond you, *and* not to boast in another man's line of things made ready to our hand. 17 But he that glorieth, let him glory in the Lord. 18 For not he that commendeth himself is approved, but whom the Lord commendeth (2 Cor. 10: 12-18).
>
> Would to God …etc., (2 Cor. 11: 1-3).
>
> 4 For if he that cometh preacheth another Jesus, whom we have not preached, or *if* ye receive another spirit, which ye have not received, or another gospel, which ye have not accepted, ye might well bear with *him*. 5 For I suppose I was not a whit behind the very chiefest apostles. 6 But though *I be* rude in speech, yet not in knowledge; but we have been throughly made manifest among you in all things(2 Cor. 11:4).

Thus, there is nothing in Paul to suggest that he is speaking about any physical disloyalty, but a mind loyalty. WMB engaged, as do many teachers of novelty, in what is called *Eisegesis*, or reading *into* the text, rather than Exegesis, where the information comes out of the text itself.

WMB's personal view

WMB throughout his entire career stressed the fact that the Bible cannot be understood by learned people, theologians[26] and seminarians.[27] Of course, the biblical context showed that was true of the majority of the religious leaders of Jesus' day. They were not the spiritual leaders that were seeking after God. They sought after power and recognition. Sadly enough, it is often the same today. It must never be assumed, however, that educated persons cannot grasp the meaning of God's Word; they may especially so, when possessing the spirit of God. Within WMB's experience, education was, and still is, eyed suspiciously.

Yet, WMB was very conscious of the fact he had no more than a grade seven education,[28] and often stated his disdain for education. Had WMB been more open-minded and perhaps better educated, he might have realized that without learned educated people there would have been neither Bible, nor Bible translations. He based his misunderstanding of the value of biblical education on the remarks made by leaders of Israel who observed that these men had not been educated by *their* schools.[29] Acts 4 records their amazement about "unlearned men" being so well educated by Jesus. They acknowledged that they could not refute their teaching, and therefore forbade them (Acts 4: 18). WMB did not understand this, and he misapplied this misunderstanding throughout his career. This error, coupled with his background which did not encourage education,[30] would suit WMB.

WMB initially taught his doctrine of Serpent's Seed covertly.[31] Later he stated that the serpent was a pre-historic[32] giant, some ten feet tall[33] who was possessed by Satan. This serpent approached Eve and she fell for his beauty, because he was "fairer than her husband." This man[34] had intercourse with Eve and she conceived[35] and "brought forth her first son, Cain, the son of Satan.[36] Eve, immediately after the act with the serpent, went to Adam and, "She persuaded Adam to do the same thing, telling him what it was,"[37] and *this* union produced Abel. WMB said that Eve was not yet Adam's wife,[38] which would have made Adam guilty of fornication. However, prior to the Fall, God had said in Gen. 2: 23-25, that Eve was Adam's wife,

> And Adam said, This is now bone of my bones, and flesh of my flesh: she shall be called Woman, because she was taken out of Man. 24 Therefore shall a man leave his father and his mother, and shall cleave unto his wife: and they shall be one flesh. 25 And they were both naked, the man and his wife, and were not ashamed.

WMB stated that Eve was an adulterous woman who, after having sex with the serpent, slept with Adam, conceived and produced Abel, Cain's twin. WMB stated the serpent was a beast, which would have implicated Eve in committing Bestiality.

CHAPTER TWENTY-ONE

This is an utterly despicable teaching regarding the mother of all mankind. Nothing in the Bible suggests anything like that. These two supposed impregnations are the basis upon which WMB built his Serpent's Seed doctrine. These two seeds became two races: God's Seed and Serpent's Seed. However there is no record of Abel having any off-spring. WMB "solved" that problem by saying that Seth[39] replaced Abel, as per Gen. 4: 25, which reads,

> And Adam knew his wife again; and she bare a son, and called his name Seth: For God, said she, hath appointed me another seed instead of Abel, whom Cain slew.

This verse WMB read naturally, without the mental gymnastics displayed in his interpretation of Gen. 4: 1- 2a,

> And Adam knew Eve his wife; and she conceived, and bare Cain...

Yet this verse is of identical sentence structure. When read naturally, it simply states Adam had intercourse with Eve and produced Cain - there is no mention of a serpent. This kind of the natural reading is seen in Gen. 4: 17

> And Cain knew his wife; and she conceived, and bare Enoch...

No one would think something else was going on behind the scenes, as WMB suggested regarding Gen. 4: 1, 2.

WMB interpreted the King James word "subtil" to mean to be smart, to be crafty, having a true knowledge of the principles of life,[40] beautiful, handsome, fair, great, masculine,[41] walking upright like a man,[42] subtleness or beauty.[43] These varying meanings are not warranted by the text. The Hebrew word for *subtil* is translated: cunning, crafty, subtil. The English translation of the LXX (Septuagint) translates *subtil* to mean crafty.

After their sin, Adam and Eve became ashamed and discovered they were naked. WMB interpreted shame, nakedness and eating fruit to be the sexual act,[44] but the text in Genesis 3 says nothing, nor does it hint, about intercourse. It only notes their self-awareness of their naked condition and how they acted to deal with it. WMB was reading into the text things which are not there. The word Eve used, to explain what happened, is transliterated as *Nasha*, which means beguiled or deceived. There is no sexual connotation in the text whatsoever.

According to WMB, this mingling of the seeds (blood) required a blood sacrifice, which God performed by slaying a lamb.[45] Nothing in the text suggests this act of disobedience was atoned for by the shedding of blood, it simply states, "Unto Adam also and to his wife did the LORD God make coats of skins, and clothed them" (Gen. 3: 21). Commentators may note this was a sacrificial event, Scripture is not explicit. Scripture does not state these garments were made from lambskins, nor does it mention the shedding of blood. Even IF it were a sacrifice for their sin, nowhere does the Bible make it a *sexual* sin. What is seen from what is written is that Adam and Eve disobeyed God and brought all subsequent off-spring under condemnation.

Later, Abel, by revelation killed a lamb and was accepted by God for making the right sacrifice, said WMB. The text does not say that Abel did this by "revelation" nor does it hint Abel was accepted because he offered a lamb. Neither was Cain rejected because he brought fruit. That it was a matter of Cain's heart is seen when fruit and grain offerings were later instituted in the Law. WMB fabricated, or borrowed these ideas. They do not originate in Scripture and they are speculative and unwarranted.

The law of God dictates that everything should bring forth after its kind, noted WMB. Thus, when Cain did not show forth God's nature, but rather a lying and murdering nature, which was shown in the killing of his brother Abel, WMB concluded Cain was Satan's off-spring.[46] His reasoning was flawed, because Adam too, did not display God's characteristics when he disobeyed God's Word. Yet Adam was created free of sin and Cain was not. WMB countered the orthodox understanding of, "Eve conceived and brought forth Cain and said 'I have begotten a man from the Lord,'" by stating, "All life has to come from God…Adolf Hitler come from God…<u>Every person come from God</u>.[47] (Underlining this author's -PMD)

WMB taught it was Eve just speaking her mind when she attributed Cain to God, she simply did not understand that all life came from God.[48] God is a spirit WMB said, and as a Spirit he could not have given Eve the son called Cain.[49] In other words, WMB implied that, as a Spirit, God *could* give Eve the son called Abel, without Adam being involved? That is a contradiction which makes WMB's teaching invalid. WMB failed to see Adam being Cain's father[50] in Gen. 4: 1- 2a, "And Adam knew Eve his wife; and she conceived, and bare Cain…"

It cannot be said any plainer as in, "A man got in his car and his car crashed." This really needs no interpretation, but in WMB's scheme he would have another man get behind the wheel, because the first man was a regular Mario Andretti and could not have crashed the car. No one would believe that story! The biblical passage simply states that Adam had intercourse with Eve and Eve conceived and Eve brought forth a son called Cain. WMB also argued that after Eve bore Cain she brought forth Abel, without another conception being mentioned; which to him meant Eve bore twins. Even if they were twins, nothing in the text suggests that they had different fathers, as WMB alleged. WMB "forgot" that conception by a serpent was not mentioned either.

When Eve brought forth Seth, she exclaimed God had appointed her another seed instead of Abel whom Cain slew (Gen. 4:25). Of course, Eve did not mention Cain as being her seed in this context, because she spoke about the replacement for Abel. It would have been redundant since Cain was still alive and needed no replacement. However, WMB misinterpreted that to mean Adam was not Cain's father.[51] The fact that Cain is not mentioned in Luke's genealogy of Jesus was proof for WMB that Cain is Serpent's Seed.[52] Again, WMB read into the text and did not see that in the genealogy in Genesis 5:3ff, no mention is made of Cain or Abel as sons of Adam, whereas Seth *is* mentioned. So if both Cain and Abel are not mentioned, WBM's conclusion that this text shows that Adam was not Cain's father proves too much. This same line of reasoning would require the argument that Abel was not Adam's son, something that WMB would not want to argue. In Luke 3:37-38 there is no mention of Abel either. Luke seems to be dependent on the genealogy in Genesis 5 which does not mention either Cain or Abel. Again, WMB's use of this text proves too much. Seth is listed in the generations of Adam found in Gen. 5 and Luke 3, but not Cain. That must be understood in the context of Scripture. Gen. 4: 36 makes it clear that when Seth sired a son called Enoch, then men began to call on the name of the Lord. Cain went off to the land of Nod and out of the presence of the Lord (Gen. 4: 16). He was not of those who called upon the name of the Lord. The aforementioned genealogies deal with Seth's seed and Cain is not in that line. Both lines were sinners, but Seth's line contained the Promise. WMB spoke about Enoch and not Cain being the seventh from Adam (Jude 1: 14). Luke, the physician, shows Enoch to be the fifth from Adam. Jude quotes from the Book of Enoch, a Pseudographia.

> Jude did not intend to refer to the Enoch of Gen 5, but referred entirely, even in the introductory line, to words found in the apocryphal Enoch. While the prophecy has no canonical status, its predictions are paralleled and supported by numerous Biblical passages, such as, Mt. 25: 31-46."[53]

Jude is not using Scripture, but an outside source known to others, as did Paul in Athens.[54] WMB's argument regarding Cain's absence from the genealogy as proof of the truth of the Serpent's Seed teaching, is untenable.

WMB stated that the serpent impregnated Eve and afterwards she was co-habited with Adam. In the beginning, taught WMB, Adam was supposed to multiply by spiritual multiplication,[55] simply speaking the creative word.[56] Strangely enough, perhaps due to the complexity and convoluted, impossible explanations of serpent's seed, one of WMB's interpretations of what constituted Serpent's Seed was the physical act of pro-creation between Adam and Eve. Eve could not wait but played the whore, WMB stated.[57] He gave the example of Noah being given the command to replenish the earth.[58] WMB supported that notion by stating that he himself was a perversion, the result of a sexual union between his father and mother.[59]

To no extent is William Branham's Doctrine of the Fall, or Serpent's Seed teaching supported by Biblical Revelation. The "fall-out" of the Serpent's Seed teaching has been horrendous. It has infected all WMB's other teachings.

Notes - Chapter Twenty-One

[1] *Life Story*, Columbus, "About twenty-one, I was converted, went into the Baptist church, preached for several years. Visions, just as He'd appear to me, and tell me things that was going to happen. The ministers told me it was the devil. Said, 'It's the devil doing that. Don't you think that. You're going to be a fortuneteller.' Well…It scared me to death, brethren. I didn't know what to do."

[2] Mrs. Gordon Lindsay. 87.

[3] *Q & A #3*, "When one of those things like the serpent's seed, when it was presented to me, I couldn't see it, nothing; but I just kept following that, and the first thing you know… and then the Holy Spirit begins to open it up. Now, I want somebody try to condemn it now…Can't do it."

[4] *Show Us The Father And It'll Satisfy Us*, Connersville.

[5] *Serpent's Seed*

[6] Ibid.

[7] *Marriage and Divorce*, "Notice, the reason that she [Eve] did this, she was not… in God's original creation; she is a byproduct. Remember, Adam was both masculine and feminish in the original creation: one. But then he was separated by a rib. But a byproduct… the only one of all God's creation of every animal and anything else, she was the only one designed this way. Every other female was in the original creation…but Eve was not in the original creation, that had to be made that way. ; Notice, in this creation that she was in, not in the original, but a byproduct; and in this creation, there is…nothing designed to be so deceitful as a woman that's deceitful… She was not in the original beginning creation. She was in Adam, but not in a female sex herself at the beginning. She was a byproduct, made."

[8] *Church Age Book*. 215-216.

[9] Ibid., "She is the only specie of female that is made prettier than the male … All other creatures of God is beautiful males, such as in animals, birds, and so forth…Why was it done? To deceive by. Her designer, Satan, is still working on her too in these last days. Now, there's nothing can stoop like her, and she is designed so that she can be deceiving. And Satan is really working on her today (in these last days), because he is her designer…That's her designer…You may question me about Satan being her designer, but that's the truth. Satan designed her."

[10] *Cruelty of Sin*, "And He [God] said then, 'Serpent, because you did this, walked up…' He wasn't a reptile. He was a beast, walked up, more subtle than all the beasts of the field. Bear me record: that's Scripture. Walked up, like a man, and he had deceived her. And He said, 'And because you did this, off comes your legs…'"

[11] *Condemnation by Representation*, "Eve was the mother of hybreeding. She mis-bred the human race. You now, after she had did this evil thing and… had this affair with the serpent, which was not a serpent, a reptile…The serpent was a man."

CHAPTER TWENTY-ONE

[12] *Church Age Book.* 98.

[13] *Marriage and Divorce,* "We know that it was Eve... She committed adultery that brought forth the first child, which was Cain, Satan's own son...."

[14] Ibid.

[15] Ibid.

[16] On Feb. 28, 1963, WMB claimed to have received a commission to preach and open the seven sealed mystery. WMB used a Mystery Cloud that appeared over Arizona as evidence this was his prophecy of his ascension into a pyramid cloud, shaped like seven angels who revealed the Seven Seals to him. He preached them in March, 1963. The problem? He was not in Arizona but in Texas. When this author exposed the error in a pamphlet, history was re-written and spiritualized by WMB's own family members.

[17] *Marriage and Divorce,* "But now that the Seals are opened, the Spirit of Truth directs us to the Word. That explains why all the mistakes has been down through the ages, because the Seals was not open. This was not revealed. It's true."

[18] *The Invisible Union,* "Now, here's where you may disagree, many of you theologians. That's what defiled the whole human race, is that adultery at the beginning. Her bedding ground was marred. She brought forth those twins, Cain and Abel. One act, two children. Search the Scriptures."

[19] WMB, *God's Power To Transform,* Sep. 11, 1965, Phoenix, AZ, "Adam knew his wife, and she bare Cain and also bare Abel - twins. Satan was with her that morning, Adam that afternoon. You see the big fuss in the paper here, I believe, in Tucson now, of that woman bringing forth a colored child and a white child at the same time. She lived with her husband that morning, and the man that afternoon..."

[20] _____, *What Shall I Do With Jesus Called Christ?* Nov. 24, 1963, AM, Jeff., IN, "The woman said, "The serpent beguiled me...He was the one that had the sexual affair with me. He beguiled me. He did this."

[21] _____, *God making His Promise,* Dec. 09, 1956, Aft., Brooklyn, NY, "Look at Adam, what a beautiful type. Adam and Eve was a type of Christ in the church. Now, remember, Eve did not sin Adam sinned. That's right. Not Eve, Adam sinned. Not Eve, she was the one who did the act, but Adam done the sinning. The woman was deceived. The Bible said she was deceived. She thought she was right. But Adam knowed it was wrong. And now, look, when Adam saw Eve had sinned and had done wrong, Adam walked right out not deceived but with both eyes open. But he so loved Eve that he took her place in death with her and walked out with her. You know that?"

[22] *Thirsting For Life,* Chicago, "...Adam, which was a product of sin from listening to his wife, and the wife was a product of sins come from Satan. And Adam followed his wife out, a perfect type of Christ, going with His--the Bride to take her sins, as Adam took the sins of Eve and left the garden of Eden, not deceived, but willingly walked out with her, so was Christ not deceived."

[23] *Show Us The Father,* Connersville, "Eve was deceived."

24 *God Making His Promise*. "Adam and Eve was a type of Christ in the church. Now, remember, Eve did not sin. Adam sinned. That's right. Not Eve, Adam sinned. Not Eve, she was the one who did the act, but Adam done the sinning. The woman was deceived. The Bible said she was deceived. She thought she was right. But Adam knowed it was wrong. And now, look, when Adam saw Eve had sinned and had done wrong, Adam walked right out not deceived but with both eyes open. But he so loved Eve that he took her place in death with her and walked out with her...And that's exactly what Jesus done." See also: *The Invisible Union*, "Eve didn't mean to do wrong. It wasn't willfully. The Bible said, in...First Timothy 3, "She was deceived." And deceived is not when you willfully do it. It's when you're deceived into doing it."

25 *Why I Am A Holy Roller*.

26 WMB, *Why It Had To Be Shepherds*, Dec. 21, 1964, Tucson, AZ, "Why was it revealed to shepherds and not to the theologians of that day; they were the one were trained to hear it? And why did it come and bypass the rich, and come to the poor? Also, why did it bypass the learned and wise and come to the humble and unlearned?"

27 _____, *What Think Ye Of Christ*, Mar. 21, 1954, "When Peter made his first confession, 'Thou art the Christ, the Son of the living God,' He said, 'Blessed art thou, Peter, for flesh and blood has not revealed this to you. You never learned it in the seminary. You never learned it from what somebody else said, but My Father, which is in heaven has revealed this to you."

28 *Angel And The Commission*, "I'm not much of a scholar, because I never got but just a grammar school education, seventh grade at that."

29 *Message Of Grace*, "When He came, He never come to the great theologians. Neither did He go to Caiaphas the high priest; only to be condemned by him... But He took fishermen, men who were poor and walked the common life, and to there He revealed Himself."

30 Gordon J. Melton, *Encyclopedia of American Religions*, 6th Ed., (Detroit: Gale Research, 1999), 524. "...higher learning is not required for ministers for the following reasons: "Elders in the New Testament were primarily self-educated in the Scriptures, Elders in the New Testament learned under the direction of the Holy Spirit and other elders rather than academicians, and the system makes the scriptures themselves to be the curriculum."

31 *Cruelty Of Sin*, "Adam taken Eve as his wife. And then when sin came in...And I have my idea of what that was. I don't express it out in the church, less I just having a little class of some sort, of what the sin was in the beginning."

32 *Serpent's Seed*, "Now, watch the serpent, this serpent which was first. Let's draw a picture of him now... big fellow, prehistoric giant. That's where they find these big bones, and I'll show you this in the Bible... This great big fellow, let's say he was--he was ten foot tall, great big shoulders, looked just like a man...Here he was a great big fellow. And the devil comes down...and got into the serpent, and he found Eve in the garden of Eden naked...What did he do? He begin making

CHAPTER TWENTY-ONE

love to Eve. And he lived with her as a husband. And she saw it was pleasant, so she went and told her husband; but she was already pregnant by Satan. And she brought forth her first son whose name was Cain, the son of Satan."

[33] Throughout WMB's messages references can be found regarding a pre-Adamic creation. No time or space to develop that here. – PMD.

[34] *Condemnation By Representation,* "The serpent was a man." Influences can be seen here that can be traced back to Mormonism and Freemasonry, etc. Joseph Smith had been a Freemason.

[35] *Joseph meeting His Brethren,* "He was the one who beguiled the woman in his beauty. And she conceived…"

[36] *Serpent's Seed,* "What did he do? He begin making love to Eve. And he lived with her as a husband. And she saw it was pleasant, so she went and told her husband; but she was already pregnant by Satan. And she brought forth her first son whose name was Cain, the son of Satan."

[37] *Power Of Transformation,* "This fellow found Eve in the Garden of Eden, this young woman that knowed no sin, knowed not what her nakedness was. And he knew. He was smart, subtile, wise. And he told her, 'The…fruit was pleasant and it was desirable,' and when he lived with her that morning. And then, see, then, the afternoon, she persuaded Adam to do the same thing, telling him what it was. And then Adam deliberately, knowing he ought not to a-done it, walked out with his wife and did this act."

[38] *Third Seal,* "Now, there was a natural bride in the garden of Eden…she was Adam's sweetheart, not yet his wife, 'cause he hadn't knew her yet as a wife… before Adam knew his wife, she was just a bride to him…she fell in the garden of Eden because she failed to hold to God's Word."

[39] It would have caused a break in the continuity because Seth would have been the third set of seed. The Serpent's Seed teaching completely self-destructs right there.

[40] *Serpent's Seed,* "Now, I went and got dictionaries today from everywhere to look up this word, what the word of 'subtil' meant. It means 'to be smart, to be crafty.' And the best interpretation of the--of the Hebrew from 'm-a-h-a-h, mahah' means 'having a true knowledge of the principles of life.'"

[41] *Greatest Battle,* "The battle raged when Eve opened up her mind to listen to her reasonings…that's the channel it run down: her reasoning. She in her soul, she reasoned. Her eyes, with sight she saw the serpent. He was beautiful, handsome, far better than her own husband. He was the most subtil of all the beast of the field. And be was probably a fairer man than her husband; he look like a great masculine beast standing there. How great he was, and he was trying to tell her what a great thing it was. And the first thing she did, she opened up her mind. And when she did, human reasonings caught it. 'Why, wouldn't that be a thrill.'"

⁴² *Israel and the Church # 4*, "God judged the serpent in the garden of Eden, in the 3rd chapter of Genesis and the 14th verse; God already passed judgment upon the serpent. Oh, he was beautiful and walked upright; he was the most subtil of all the beasts of the field. But God judged him, and put him down on his belly for the rest of his days, on his belly, judged."

⁴³ WMB, *He Swore By Himself*, Dec. 12, 1954, Jeff., IN, "The snake to begin with was not a reptile. The Bible said, 'He was a beast, and the most subtil of all the beasts of the field.' He walked like a man and everything, 'the most subtil.' But the curse cursed him, and taken away his--his--his subtleness, or his--his beauty, and throwed him onto the ground, and put him on his belly to crawl."

⁴⁴ *Serpent's Seed*, "And there he was. And when he did, God said, begin to call for Eve and Adam. And he said, 'I was naked.' And He said, 'Who told you you was naked?' Then they begin to--in army fashion, passing the buck. Said, 'Well, the woman You gave me done it. She was the one who persuaded me.' And she said, 'The serpent give me an apple.' All right, preacher, get next to yourself. She said, 'The serpent beguiled me.' Do you know what 'beguile' means? Means 'defiled.'...The devil never gave her an apple. 'The serpent has beguiled me.' And then the curse came."

⁴⁵ WMB, *Law*, Jan. 15, 1955, Chicago, IL, "God in order to get Adam back to Himself again so He could talk to him, God went out and got some skins and made aprons. Is that right? Now, if He got skin, something died to get skin. See, it had to be substitutionary. Something had to substitute the guilty man's place. And that was that lamb that He killed out there was Christ Jesus, speaking in a figure."

⁴⁶ *The Mark of the Beast and The Seal of God # 1*, "Now, we find out that because that Cain listened to the enemy, then what happened? He become the first murderer. He become the first one that had jealousy on earth. Tell me where that pure line from God to Adam... That's the only connection. Adam was the son of God. Bible said so. Then where did that jealousy come from? Where did that murderer come from? Where did all that kind of a spirit come from? Out of Adam? Couldn't have. Come from Satan. It's exactly where it come from."

⁴⁷ WMB, *Q & A*, Jun. 28, 1959, PM.

⁴⁸ Ibid., "Would you please explain your theory that Eve conceived Cain of the devil? I never said that; I said Eve conceived Cain of the serpent. In Genesis 4...1st verse, clearly states that Adam knew his wife Eve, and she conceived, and bare Cain, and said, 'I have gotten a man from God.' Absolutely. All life has to come from God...Adolf Hitler come from God."

⁴⁹ *Q & A on The Seals*, "Eve talked here, if you want to take it in the language that's here which is written so it's hid from the eyes, wise and prudent...Eve, here, the way it's taught, that God was the One that she begotten this son by, and He's a Spirit, and He can't do it."

⁵⁰ *God's Power To Transform*, "...Eve had a pair of twins. And one of them was of Satan, and one of them was of God. Now you say, 'Oh, no! No. Now, Brother Branham!' Just a minute. You find me one Scripture, anywhere, that says that Cain was Adam's son. I'll show you in the Scripture where It says, 'Cain was of that evil one,' not Adam."

CHAPTER TWENTY-ONE 301

⁵¹ *Church Age Book*. 185. "She does not say God had GIVEN her another seed--that would have been Christ, for He is GIVEN. This son, Seth, was APPOINTED instead of Abel. She recognizes her son that came by Adam; she does not now recognize Cain for he came by the serpent. When she says ANOTHER SEED instead of Abel, she is saying that Cain was different from Abel, for if they were of the same father she would have had to say, 'I have been given some MORE SEED.'"

⁵² *Q&A #3*, "Enoch is the seventh from Adam....In the 3rd chapter of Luke we get the same thing. '...which was the son of Enos, which was the son of Seth, which was the son of Adam, which was the son of God.' Where did Cain come in? Where's Cain at, the firstborn? The birthright's to him; where'd he come from? He was the Satan's seed, and not God's. Wasn't Adam's either, 'cause Adam's son's name was Seth. Cain, the serpent's seed, slew his first son...I want to see somebody put him in there now and say it wasn't the serpent's seed. It wasn't recognized in the genealogies of God's, or neither the genealogies of the human race, the genealogies of Adam, any of the rest of them. Is that right? How many believes it, say, "Amen." Sure. He was not; he was the serpent's seed and not Adam's seed. She said that was Adam's son. It was not Adam's son. She said, 'I got it from God.'...it was serpent's seed."

⁵³ *The Wycliffe Bible Commentary*, ed. Charles F. Pfeiffer and Everett F. Harrison, (Chicago, IL: Moody Press, 1977, 1525 pp.).

⁵⁴ *The New Laymen's Bible Commentary*, editors G.C.D. Howley, and others, (Grand Rapids, MI: Zondervan Publishing House, 1979, 1712 pp.), 1673-1674. "May imply that Jude actually believed that the patriarch Enoch had himself written the book bearing his name; but this is not the only possibility. The phrase describing Enoch is not Jude's own. But is again drawn from the pseudepigrapha (cf. 1 Enoch 60: 18), It may be that Jude was arguing from grounds he knew to be acceptable to his hearers or opponents. We might compare Paul using Greek Poetry when addressing an Athenian audience."

⁵⁵ *Does God Ever Change His Mind?* "[I]t was not God's perfect will for children to be born on the earth through sex. No, sir. God created man out of the dust of the earth, breathed the breath of life into him, and he become a living soul. He took from that man a helpmate, and made a wife to him. That was God's first and original will. But when sin come in and did the thing that it did, then He permitted man to marry a wife, legally, and have children by her. 'Multiply and replenish the earth,' then, if that's the way you're going to do it.' But, you see, it never was His perfect will."

⁵⁶ *Marriage and Divorce*, "He [God] said to Adam, before sex was...introduced, 'Multiply, to replenish the earth,' when he was yet in the beginning, when he was yet both male and female in himself. There, shows then that the Bride has got to come from the Word, by spiritual multiplication, multiplications, see, replenishing the earth."

⁵⁷ *Spoken Word*, "Did not God tell her, 'Multiply and replenish the earth?' But she had to walk over here play the part of a whore."

⁵⁸ *Future Home*, "Now, she [Eve] didn't have any seed; she never did have. So she had to receive a seed from some way. God gave her a seed, not by sexual intercourse, but by creation. Can't you blind people see, that's the seed of the serpent...Now, can you see the serpent's seed

there?... After Noah came out of the ark, notice what was said to Noah...He said 'Multiply and replenish the earth'...Notice, was to be fruitful, replenish the earth, as Adam at the first... Adam was to multiply and replenish the earth...Get it? Now, can't you see what the serpent's seed is? What replenished the earth? You get it?"

[59] *Wisdom Versus Faith,* "There's only one Person could be the Word, that was Jesus. He was God's spoken Word by a virgin birth. I'm a perversion ...I'm the results of a union between my father and mother. This has to die, that's me (See?); the body that has to die. It wasn't so with Jesus; He was the Word. He was born, virgin. Brother, there was no woman, man, or nothing else had nothing to do with Him. The woman was the incubator (that's right), and He nursed her breast, and so forth. That might have been true about that, but let me tell you: He was God, that's Who He was! Was no sex about it at all. He had to be free from sex to bring forth Life through that blood…"

Chapter Twenty-Two

THE FALL

Wm. Branham's Hermeneutic

To what extent is William Branham's Hermeneutic supported by Biblical Revelation?

The word "hermeneutics," according to Webster's dictionary, means the science of interpretation, or of finding the meaning of an author's words and phrases, and of explaining it to others. WMB, throughout his entire career, employed "typology" as a system of interpretation. He called himself a "typologist"[1] and said, "Being uneducated, like my brethren are educated, I teach the scriptures from types and shadows."[2] To that system WMB added writing between the lines;[3] divine unction of "Thus saith the Lord;"[4] inspiration[5] and revelation.[6] Thus, it did not really matter what the text actually said. Therefore, in WMB's case, there is no objective way to measure the truth of anything. Therefore the Word of God becomes a sealed book that only a prophet can reveal which, WMB stated emphatically, was his office. WMB did not study the Scriptures but relied on what he called the Holy Spirit, or on his intuition, or on sixth sense.[7]

Were the words typology and shadows synonymous to WMB? WMB said that, because he was not a scholar and uneducated, he used types and shadows, because he could determine from the shadow what something looked like.[8] That this is a very dangerous "hermeneutic," goes without saying. What if one sees the shadow of something one has never seen?

The word "type" is used in Scripture, as is the word "shadow." There is a need to understand the Biblical meaning of both. The word "type" comes from the Greek word "tupos." There are various renderings in Scripture translations for *tupos,* such as: ensample, fashion, figure, form, manner and print and are seen to be representations.[9] The word translated "shadow" (Gk. *skia*), is used of the image or outline cast by an object; of ceremonies under the Law (Col. 2: 16, 17); of the Tabernacle and its appurtenances and offerings, (Heb. 8: 5); of these appointed under the Law (Heb. 10: 1)." The word *type*, in its various forms, is used in Scripture, and certainly Paul makes it clear Adam was a type of Christ in that he was our representative head. Scripture does not say that Eve was a type of the Church, as WMB alleged, that role was reserved for Sarah (and Hagar).

In Scripture, Adam's disobedience is contrasted with the second Adam's obedience and Adam causing death is contrasted with the second Adam bringing life. WMB's focus, in all of his teaching, is Eve's fall. Whereas Paul's focus is on the First Adam's fall, with the subsequent death of the human race, AND the obedience of the Second Adam and the resultant salvation of many.

It is obvious that WMB used both "types" and "shadows" as synonyms, because he used them in the same sentence and context,[10] alluding to Heb. 10: 1.[11] The problem with WMB's use of the word type is his random, inconsistent application. Some samples might be helpful here:

> Friends, let's look at the honey… "The wafer, it tastes like honey," He said, "in the rock." Now, that was a type of the Holy Spirit.[12]
>
> Manna was a type of the Holy Spirit[13]
>
> Water's a type of the Holy Spirit, the smitten rock.[14]
>
> Circumcision, which was a type of the Holy Spirit[15]

Above are listed four types of the Holy Spirit: Honey, Manna, Water and Circumcision. Below are two contradictory types of Moses. Which is which in these instances?

> Moses, a very outstanding character of the Bible: the greatest of all the prophets. He was a type of the Lord Jesus Christ, the Priest, and the King, and the law Giver; a very perfect type."[16]
>
> [Moses]…was a type of the church. And you notice today, the church does what Moses did. Moses glorified himself before the people, and instead of glorifying the Lord.[17]

Space does not permit to list more examples. It is evident that WMB applied his 'typology' in an inconsistent fashion without showing any discernment. It is safe to say he did not really have a system, something that is clearly seen in his methodology of dealing with the Genesis account.

If the story of the Fall of mankind is to be understood typologically, WMB's interpretation should at least have been consistent. Without consistency there is no truth, only error. In Scripture, Eve was approached by Satan in the form of a serpent. He deceived her into partaking of the fruit of the Tree of the Knowledge of Good and Evil. Eve gave Adam (who was with her) of the fruit and he also partook. The simple understanding would be that Eve disobeyed God's command not to partake of the Tree of Knowledge. WMB interpreted it as Eve committing "adultery" with the serpent. However, there are serious inconsistencies.

CHAPTER TWENTY-TWO 305

If Eve's transgression consisted of cohabitation with the Serpent, it logically would have to follow that Adam also would have to have been involved in a sexually deviant act with the Serpent. This whole "Branhamic" interpretation has no type or shadow, in all of Scripture.

A Critique of WMB's Exegetical Interpretation

Genre Issues

When reading, it is important to understand to which particular genre the piece being read belongs. Genesis, by its literary form and structure, indicates that it perhaps should be viewed as a form of historical narrative. Not all would agree with this analysis. From the way the story unfolds regarding the generations and their habitations, etc, a structured selective arrangement of material can be discerned expressing a particular understanding of history. Others believe the book to be historical with the exception of the first few chapters which they take as allegorical. Again, others hold that the early chapters of Genesis are mythological, though not in the same sense as Greek, or other cultural, spiritual mythologies; some state they are symbolic stories, etc., etc. This is not the time, nor place, to develop, and/or refute, other views. In the context of WMB's teaching, the focus must remain on WMB's use of what he called typology. There is not found a New Testament Anti-type, nor a physical reality of a supposed shadow regarding the alleged sexual relations in the Garden of Eden. The scenario in the Garden of Eden, though historical and literal, does have some allegorical dimensions regarding the two trees in the midst of the Garden, the Tree of Life and the Tree of the Knowledge of Good and Evil. Of course, allegory, as presented in Scripture does not do away with the literal historical meaning of the narrative, as can be seen in Paul's allegorical[18] interpretation of Sarah and Hagar. Paul elsewhere regards them as historical figures. As stated above, whichever hermeneutic is used, it must remain consistent. WMB, the proper terminology being unknown to him, actually interpreted the first four chapters of Genesis as a mixture of literal and, for lack of a better word, pseudo-allegorical. Pseudo-allegorical, because what WMB thought to be typological, or foreshadowing, was in reality mythological and without Scriptural warrant. A myth is a belief system that is based on non-historical events, which is employed in a culture in order to make sense of its worldview. The Biblical text discussed presents itself as a historical and allegorical account of the Fall.

Language Issues

There is the issue of language. WMB did not understand biblical languages. He had enough problems with his own native Kentucky tongue, let alone King James

English. Even simple things he did not understand. One example should suffice. WMB said, "God's even without form, the Bible said. No, nothing formal about God."[19] He relied on the explanations of others and he used Bible[20] helps. WMB did not follow any rules of grammar when interpreting Gen. 4: 1. WMB's ignorance of these matters and his almost sole dependence on the Scofield Bible and selected helps, led him to make interpretative leaps that cannot be sustained.

Contextual Issues

The context of Genesis One is the creation. The key player is the Creator, not man, and this Creator God, throughout the entire Bible, remains the main player, not his creation, including humankind. The biblical creation story is not myth, like the accounts of neighboring nations like Egypt. In fact, Genesis One demolishes every single one of Egypt's gods. It establishes the true God and creator of all, but especially of humankind. During their 400+ years of exile there, they had forgotten the God of their fathers (Ex. 3: 13). They had been steeped in the religion of Egypt and never did leave off worshipping their gods. (Acts 7: 39-43).

Genesis Two recaps the creation in more detail and shows how man and woman were actually created. The man and the woman are shown to be created beings and not gods like Egypt's Pharaohs. This is seen by their desire to become as gods. Prior to the Fall they were commanded to be fruitful and multiply, which they did. To teach Adam was androgynous like his Father, is not warranted by the text. WMB's serpent, or snake, was created by God and He pronounced it to be very good. WMB completely ignored the natural reading of the text.

To what extent is William Branham's Hermeneutic supported by biblical Revelation? WMB did not have any system of interpreting the Bible. He did not even have an understanding of the "typology" he used, nor was he consistent in its application. He applied sixth sense, intuition, nature, reading between the lines, and Eisegesis, etc., to a text in order to get the meaning. His interpretation was not, "Thus saith the Lord," as he claimed. To no extent did WMB have a consistent, biblical Hermeneutic for interpreting the Word of God, the Bible.

Notes Chapter Twenty-Two

[1] *I will Restore Unto You*, "It's marvelous to see how our heavenly Father teaches us in parables. And that's about the way that I can understand it, is parables and types. And I'm a typologist myself."

[2] *Seal of the Antichrist*, "Now, being uneducated, like my brethren are educated, I teach the Scriptures from types and shadows. And if I know what the shadow of

anything is, I'll have some understanding of it. If I see what the shadow looks like, I can pretty well tell what it's going to look like."

[3] *Israel And The Church # 2*, "You know, if you read the Word right like this here, it's all right, but you sure miss the meanings of It. The Word is written between the lines. Jesus said, 'I've hid It from the eyes of the wise and prudent and revealed It to babes such as will learn.'" Paul stated that nothing was written between the lines (NLT - 2 Cor. 1: 13, 14a).

[4] *Easter Seal,* "There stood seven angels. And throwed a sword in your hand, said, 'Go home and open these Seven Seals that are given.' And here they are, the true mystery of marriage and divorce, and the serpent's seed and all of these things that's been fussed about. It's, 'Thus saith the Lord.'"

[5] *Q & A On Hebrews # 1*, Sep. 25, 1957, Jeff., IN, "He beguiled this woman, and she brought forth her first son which was Cain after the nature of the serpent, on inspiration, the devil had got in the serpent, that did that."

[6] Ibid., "Today science is looking for a bone of some animal that connects man and monkey together. The closest they got is a chimpanzee. They can't find a bone. They'll never, because it's a serpent. It's a revelation of God."

[7] *Super Sense,* "You're only taking what somebody else said, what you learned by intellectual, what you learned by the natural five senses. But when the sixth sense comes in, the Holy Spirit, It takes away all the reasonings of these six senses--and five senses, and lifts you up into that sixth sense, to make you believe things that you can't see, taste, feel, smell, or hear. It does something to you. Then you can say Jesus is the Christ, because you have witnessed it; not what intellectual teaching has taught you, but what you've experienced."

[8] WMB, *Christ*, Feb. 21, 1955, Phoenix, AZ, "Therefore, not being educated, and I just more as a typologist...I am not a--a scholar. So I, knowing that I have some way of not knowing how to pronounce the big Greek and Hebrew words like the brothers do that knows these things, I just take all the old things as a type or a shadow. And if I see what a shadow of anything looks like, I have a pretty good idea what the real thing's going to look like when it gets there."

[9] W. E. Vine, *Vine's Expository Dictionary of Old and New Testament Words*, Editor F.F. Bruce (Old Tappan, NJ: Fleming H. Revell Company, 1981, 351 pp.). "Figure – 1. Tupos, a type, figure, pattern, is translated 'figures' (i.e., representations of gods) in Acts 7: 43; in the R.V. of ver. 44 (for A.V., 'fashion') and in Roma. 5: 14, of Adam as a 'figure' of Christ. See also Ensample, Fashion, Form, Manner, Print. 2. Antitupos – Antitype, in the NT corresponding to an arch type…3 Parabole - Parable, a casting or placing side by side…with a view to comparison, or resemblance."

[10] *Law*, "For it was only a type or a shadow of good things to come, because the life in the blood cell of the dying animal, the substitute, was only the life of an animal."

[11] Heb. 10: 1, "For the law having a shadow of good things to come, and not the very image of the things, can never with those sacrifices which they offered year by year continually make the comers thereunto perfect"

[12] *Believest Thou This?* Minneapolis.

[13] WMB, *Believest Thou This?* Oct. 03, 1951, New York, NY.

[14] _____, *Separation From Unbelief*, Feb. 28, 1955, Phoenix, AZ.

[15] _____, *God Provided A Lamb*, Jun. 14, 1956, Indianapolis, IN.

[16] *What Think Ye Of Christ*, Chicago.

[17] *Jairus And Divine Healing*.

[18] W. E. Vine, "Allegory – allegoreo, 'came to signify to speak, not according to the primary sense of the word, but so that the facts stated are applied to illustrate principles. The allegorical meaning does not do away with the literal meaning of the narrative. There may be more than one meaning, though, of course, only one literal meaning. Scripture histories represent or embody spiritual principles, and these are ascertained, not by the play of the imagination, but by the rightful application of the doctrines of Scripture.'"

[19] WMB, *Smyrnaean Church Age*, Dec. 06, 1960, Jeff., IN. See also: *From That Time*, May 20, 1961, Dawson Creek, BC, CAD, "And now, I am not very formal, because, you know, God's without form. The Bible said so."

[20] Emphatic Diaglott, ed. Benjamin Wilson, (Brooklyn, NY: International Bible Students Association Watch Tower Bible and Tract Association, 1942).

Chapter Twenty-Three
SALVATION

To what extent is William Branham's
doctrine of Salvation supported
by Biblical Revelation?

WMB's Doctrine of Salvation

All Christian doctrine is interconnected and is part of a larger body found in Scripture. WMB correctly said that one cannot have a church without doctrine.[1] In fact, WMB's teachings on a number of issues were compiled into a two-volume book called, "Conduct, Order and Doctrine." Within WMB circles, this book is typically referred to as COD, or the Church Order book.[2] Harold O. Brown says that without doctrine a religious community cannot call itself Christian.[3] That is a very poignant statement. The "non-denominational" Message groups have fragmented and they have become the very thing they so despise, a denomination with many factions. WMB decried the word "Dogma,"[4] as a negative man-made religious thing;[5] a "theory of some man, or some idea of a creed."[6] Obviously the proper meaning within a religious context was misunderstood and dismissed, by WMB. Yet, WMB's message is very dogmatic. Particularly, the dogma of God, of Creation and of the Fall, differentiate WMB's message from orthodox evangelicalism. Without these there would not even be a distinctive message of WMB.

The Christian faith, like many other things, is based upon a presupposition. In order to do Mathematics, the presupposition, or assumption, is that "One equals One." If that is not accepted as a presupposition, one cannot proceed. It is foundational. Hebrews 1: 1 declares that for Christianity the presupposition is,

He that cometh to God must believe that He is (exists)

When that presupposition is accepted, it becomes the touchstone for everything else in Scripture, against which everything is measured. The Christian faith is a revelatory faith, but not in the sense that WMB understood and taught revelation. It is seen in the Gospels that, of all people mentioned, only Peter received a revelation of who Jesus was. YET, within seconds, he was called Satan, and he was severely rebuked. The other disciples did not "get it" either. They walked with Jesus for three years; they saw the miracles He did; they experienced the dead being raised; they sat under his instruction; they were trained to minister with power; they were told Jesus had to suffer and die; they watched him suffer and die, but they still did not "get it." It was not until Emmaus and Jesus showed them who Christ was from Scripture, that they received the revelation; they "got it." Evidently, WMB never did "get it." He read the Scripture, "between the lines" to get the revelation, but there is nothing written there. As a consequence, WMB built his ministry without a solid Scriptural foundation. As the Emmaus Road travelers found out, it was all about Jesus, from Genesis 1: 1 right through the end of the OT.

WMB's foundational doctrine of the godhead, included other beings, as well as the spirits of humankind, which God had created in eternity. Due to Lucifer's disobedience, one-third of the angels were cast out of heaven, including pre-existent human spirits. Salvation, in WMB's scheme, became a quest to shed this corrupted flesh and to get back home.[7] This is a Gnostic and heretical concept.

The doctrine of Salvation is particularly connected to the doctrine of God, the Creation of Mankind and the Fall. None of these teachings by WMB have been found to have been interpreted scripturally. Therefore, one cannot expect that WMB would have the salvation doctrine correct. WMB believed in a form of Predestination that needs of necessity be looked into in detail. He mentioned the word Predestination 104 times, though the Scriptures never use it as a noun, but always, and only, as a verb, or action word. The Apostle Paul used the verb "predestinate" only a few times, he said it in the context that God predestinated His called out ones to:

- be conformed to the image of his Son (Rom. 8: 29)
- the adoption of children by Jesus Christ to himself (Eph. 1: 5)
- the praise of his glory, who first trusted in Christ (Eph. 1: 12).

Without going into a theological study, it is clear that, however one interprets the Scripture, there is no hint found of a physical election in the Bible. In Jesus' day we see the Pharisees finding comfort and shelter in being Abraham's seed (Jn, 8: 22). Jesus acknowledged they were Abraham's seed (Jn. 8: 37), yet Jesus told them that they were of their father the Devil (Jn. 8: 44). Jesus told them that God could from stones raise up children unto Abraham (Matt. 3: 9; Lu. 3: 8). Therefore, for WMB to teach that his followers were all God's predestined seed, is presumptuous. Abraham was the Father of the faithful and the founder of the Jewish and Ishmaelite race; not a mention here of Adam. There is also no Scriptural warrant that God's off-spring will manifest because that eternal seed, like a divine spark, is resident in them. Scripture states that there is seed involved, but it is not a resident seed. It is a seed that is sown in people's hearts. It brings forth fruit in those who hear, understand and nurture it (Matt. 13: 19-23), "Faith cometh by hearing and hearing by the Word of God" (Rom. 10: 17). A wonderful example of how that works is seen in the conversion of, "Lydia, a seller of purple, of the city of Thyatira, which worshipped God…whose heart the Lord opened …she was baptized…" (Acts 16: 14-15). "And when the Gentiles heard this, they were glad, and glorified the word of the Lord: and as many as were ordained to eternal life believed" (Acts 13: 48). It would be remiss not to list WMB's favorite passage of Scripture, Acts 2: 38-39,

> [38] Then Peter said unto them, Repent, and be baptized every one of you in the name of Jesus Christ for the remission of sins, and ye shall receive the gift of the Holy Ghost. [39] For the promise is unto you, and to your children, and to all that are afar off, even as many as the LORD our God shall call.

For WMB salvation is a three step process,[8] repentance, baptism in water in the name of the Lord Jesus Christ, and baptism with the Holy Spirit. He illustrated it as picking up a glass, cleaning the glass and the filling of said glass.[9] In other words, according to WMB, you are only potentially saved. You are not yet converted until you have received the Holy Spirit.[10] How true is that statement? In the Acts 2 passage, 3,000 people that heard and received Peter's message, were baptized and were saved. There is nothing said that they should expect tongues of fire coming upon them. The Bible says they were saved, not just potentially. A number of the disciples had already received the Holy Spirit when Jesus breathed on them (Jn. 20: 22). They had not as yet been endued with power to witness, which had been promised to them. As seen in the quote below, Jesus said *He* was given ALL authority and He gave His disciples authority. In Mat. 28: 18-20, He promised to be with them as they went forth in that authority,

> [18] And Jesus came and spake unto them, saying, All power is given unto me in heaven and in earth. [19] Go ye therefore, and teach all nations, baptizing them in the name of the Father, and of the Son, and of the Holy Ghost: [20] Teaching them to observe all things whatsoever I have commanded you: and, lo, I am with you always, even unto the end of the world. Amen.

These Scripture verses show that Jesus sent them out and told them that those who believed and were baptized would be saved. He gave them authority (In the Name of…) to cast out demons. Again, Jesus sent the Promise of His Father upon them, but tells the disciples to wait until they receive the power to witness:

46 And said unto them, Thus it is written, and thus it behooved Christ to suffer, and to rise from the dead the third day: 47 And that repentance and remission of sins should be preached in his name among all nations, beginning at Jerusalem. 48 And ye are witnesses of these things. 49 And, behold, I send the promise of my Father upon you: but tarry ye in the city of Jerusalem, until ye be endued with power from on high. 50 And he led them out as far as to Bethany, and he lifted up his hands, and blessed them (Lu. 24: 46-50).

Here Jesus repeats what was already said in other passages. They will receive power to be witnesses:

But ye shall receive power, after that the Holy Ghost is come upon you: and ye shall be witnesses unto me both in Jerusalem, and in all Judaea, and in Samaria, and unto the uttermost part of the earth (Acts 1: 8).

Lastly, the fulfillment of what Jesus promised is seen in the powerful witness of his disciples in a multitude of languages people could understand.

And they were all filled with the Holy Ghost, and began to speak with other tongues, as the Spirit gave them utterance (Acts 2: 4 ff).

Contrary to popular belief, there is nothing in these passages that says there is some kind of magic in the Name of Jesus. People do all sorts of gymnastics and jump six feet up off the platform and shout at the top of their lungs, "In the Name of Jesus," without having any authority. Paul tells the Corinthians, "We are ambassadors for Christ…" (2 Cor. 5: 20). Ambassadors are representatives that have received authority to speak for a King or a Government. When a US ambassador speaks to the government of another nation, it is the President speaking. If that ambassador would yell and jump up in the air he would lose all credibility. His authority is not measured in decibels or performance; it is vested in the President. When the ambassador speaks he really is saying, "I speak by the power vested in me by the President of the United States of America." He could use a shortcut and say, "In the Name of the President," and all would understand. So it was with the disciples Christ authorized. Jesus said that they had the power and authority of the Father, and of the Son and of the Holy Spirit to do what He commanded them. When one reads the history of the church in Acts, Luke shows the disciples using a "shortcut." Perhaps it was Luke using "shorthand." Either Luke, or the baptizers, evidently did not follow any particular protocol. They did *everything* by Jesus' authority, or "In Jesus' Name":

1. For as yet he was fallen upon none of them: only they were baptized in the name of the Lord Jesus.) [17] Then laid they their hands on them, and they received the Holy Ghost. (Acts 8: 16-17).

2. "[Philip]commanded the chariot to stand still: and they went down both into the water, both Philip and the eunuch; and he baptized him." No details as to how and no mention of the Holy Spirit. (Acts 8: 38).
3. Ananias…said, Brother Saul, the Lord, even Jesus, that appeared unto thee in the way as thou camest, hath sent me, that thou mightest receive thy sight, and be filled with the Holy Ghost. [18]And immediately there fell from his eyes as it had been scales: and he received sight forthwith, and arose, and was baptized. (Acts 9: 17).
4. For they heard them [Cornelius & Co.] speak with tongues, and magnify God. Then answered Peter, [47] Can any man forbid water, that these should not be baptized, which have received the Holy Ghost as well as we? [48]And he commanded them to be baptized in the name of the Lord. (Acts 10: 46).
5. [Lydia] was baptized. (Acts 16: 15). No details as to how.
6. Philippian Jailer & Co. were baptized. (Acts 16: 33). No details as to how.
7. Crispus, the chief ruler of the synagogue, believed on the Lord with all his house; and many of the Corinthians hearing believed, and were baptized. (Acts 18: 8).
8. When they heard this, they were baptized in the name of the Lord Jesus. [6] And when Paul had laid his hands upon them, the Holy Ghost came on them; and they spake with tongues, and prophesied. (Acts 19: 5).

The Book of Acts, is not a book of specific doctrinal instruction, nor is it an Apostolic epistle to the Church. It is a history of what the Apostles did in the power of the Holy Spirit. Of all the above listed accounts we see that Luke has none of the Apostles or Evangelists reciting a specific "formula." Luke simply recorded that people were baptized, as Jesus had commanded. When reference to the Lord was made, it was simply: "Baptized in the name of the Lord Jesus," or "in the Name of the Lord." WMB made the argument that, "the name of the Father, and of the Son, and of the Holy Ghost," was not a name. Therefore, one ought to baptize in the name of the "Lord Jesus Christ," WMB said. In reality, if one takes WMB's definition of a name, the words, "Lord," and "Christ," also are not names, they are Titles. Even "Jesus," or Joshua/Jeshua, means, "Jehovah is Savior." What does Scripture teach regarding the meaning "in the name of?"

> And Jonathan said to David, Go in peace, forasmuch as we have sworn both of us in the name of the LORD, saying, The LORD be between me and thee, and between my seed and thy seed for ever. (1 Sam. 20: 42a).

Would WMB's argument make sense had David asked, "What IS the Name of the Lord?" Don't try this at home when the police come to your door and they shout, "Open up, in the Name of the Law!" WMB's folly is seen clearly in the following,

> At that time the LORD separated the tribe of Levi, to bear the ark of the covenant of the LORD, to stand before the LORD to minister unto him, and to bless in his name, unto this day (Deut. 10:8, Cff., Deut, 21: 5a,1 Chron. 23: 13).

The question which may be asked at this time, regarding the name in which the Levites were to bless the Israelites, is answered below:

> Speak unto Aaron and unto his sons, saying, On this wise ye shall bless the children of Israel, saying unto them, 24 The LORD bless thee, and keep thee: 25 The LORD make his face shine upon thee, and be gracious unto thee: 26 The LORD lift up his countenance upon thee, and give thee peace. (Nu. 6: 23-26).

"On this wise," indicates that God is dictating to Moses what needs to be said. This is one of the few, if any other, verses in Scripture where God does not "inspire" to write; He *dictates* exactly what needed to be said in the blessing. Thus we see that in Scripture the use of the words "in His Name," even in blessing involves more than just mentioning the words and indicates that, "in the name" means, "by authority of." This is verified by the clarification of what clearly is, not "in the name of the Lord," which is called presumption, or speaking presumptuously.

> When a prophet speaketh in the name of the LORD, if the thing follow not, nor come to pass, that is the thing which the LORD hath not spoken, but the prophet hath spoken it presumptuously: thou shalt not be afraid of him. (Deut. 18 22).

> Many will say to me in that day, Lord, Lord, have we not prophesied in thy name? and in thy name have cast out devils? and in thy name done many wonderful works? And then will I profess unto them, I never knew you: depart from me, ye that work iniquity. [Matthew 7: 22-23].

If to be *presumptuous* is to presume something WITHOUT authority, clearly the opposite is to speak WITH authority. Therefore, to speak "in the name of the Lord," is to speak by the authority of the Lord. WMB was well aware that baptism in water was not required to be saved,[11] yet he was very dogmatic regarding the "correct" formula. Incidentally, WMB insisted that the Acts "formula" be modified from, "In the Name of the Lord," or "In the Name of the Lord Jesus," to "In the Name of the Lord Jesus Christ," by ADDING one word,[12] "Christ." because there was a need to identify which Jesus was meant.[13] God does not need help protecting His Name,[14] something which Uzzah[15] discovered when God struck him dead for trying to steady the Ark.[16] WMB should have been aware of this truth. Therefore, regarding Baptism, there is no reason to abandon the instructions of Jesus, recorded for us in Matt. 28: 18-20. As Shakespeare

CHAPTER TWENTY-THREE 315

well understood, "A rose by any other name would smell as sweet."[17] The above argument regarding Christian baptism is only mentioned here because of the importance attached to it by WMB, in connection with the receiving of the Holy Spirit. This, for WMB was the third step in conversion.

So, how and when is a person saved? Saved is the state of having received salvation. The word "salvation" according to Merriam-Webster means, "deliverance from the power and effects of sin." How does one receive that deliverance? "Believe on the Lord Jesus Christ, and thou shalt be saved, and thy house" (Acts 16: 31). Rom. 8: 29-30 says,

> Those God foreknew he also predestined to be conformed to the image of his Son, that he might be the firstborn among many brothers and sisters. And those he predestined, he also called; those he called, he also justified; those he justified, he also glorified.

This is not the time and place to go into a theological debate over these verses. They are simply used to demonstrate[18] that in the progression of Paul, from earth to glory, there is nothing said about the Baptism of the Holy Spirit from the stage of, "those he justified" to those he "also glorified." In other words, in Paul's theology of salvation, once a person is justified, that person is saved from that moment on into eternity, without any mention of the Baptism of the Holy Spirit.

Thus, the question must be asked, "What is this Baptism of the Holy Spirit?" This exact phrase is not found in Scripture, though John the Baptist is heard telling his converts that, "I indeed baptize you with water unto repentance. but he that cometh after me…he shall baptize you with the Holy Ghost, and with fire" (Matt 3: 11; Cf. Mk. 1: 18, Lu. 3: 16). John the Baptist preached repentance and he told the people, "I am the voice of one crying in the wilderness, Make straight the way of the Lord, as said the prophet Esaias" (Jn. 1: 23). Regarding the Lord, John said, "Behold the Lamb of God, which taketh away the sin of the world" (Jn. 1: 29) and told the crowd, "And I knew him not: but he that sent me to baptize with water, the same said unto me, Upon whom thou shalt see the Spirit descending, and remaining on him, the same is he which baptizeth with the Holy Ghost" (Jn. 1: 33). In other words, Jesus is the one who baptizes with the Holy Spirit.

What is the Holy Spirit? The Holy Spirit is the Seal believers receive after they repent, believe and are baptized,[19] signifying the down payment of the Promise of God,[20] which is eternal life. The NT accounts indicate that upon baptism in water, believers received the Holy Spirit, a simultaneous occurrence. There is no question that this does not always occur that way today. That, however, is not because the Scripture is not true, nor because the Lord is not true to His Word. When the Gospel is preached and sinners truly repent of their sin and believe, they do receive the Holy Spirit. The sign gifts of the Book of Acts might not manifest as they did then, but that does not nullify the power of God. Today, like then, the evidence of the Holy Spirit is a changed life and a person's surrender to the will and commands of God.

The Apostle Paul asks the question, "Are all apostles? are all prophets? are all teachers? are all workers of miracles? Have all the gifts of healing? do all speak with tongues? do all interpret?" (1 Cor. 12: 29-30). Paul's questions indicate not all did receive these gifts. WMB appeared to preach that,[21] but it was only part of his message. WMB believed that could be faked, because he typically only looked at outward conformity in dress and lifestyle. The true evidence of having received the Holy Spirit in WMB, and in his followers, is the acceptance of what WMB called the Message of the Hour.[22] Scripture states that, "[I]f any man have not the Spirit of Christ, he is none of his" (Rom. 8: 9c). By implication that would mean, in the context of WMB's message, that those who do not follow his message, do not have the evidence of the Holy Spirit. Hence, they do not belong to Christ and therefore they are not saved. However, no man knows another man's ultimate destiny. All any human knows is that those, who do not truly believe in Christ Jesus, the Son of God, are in great peril of the judgment. It is not a question of any man's reception of any message that saves, but rather the reception of Christ, because in Jn. 1: 12) He says,

> As many, as received him, to them gave he power to become the sons of God, even to them that believe on his name...

In fact, Luke records that in (Acts 2: 41, 1 Cor. 12: 13, Gal. 3: 14), resp.,

> Then they that gladly received his word were baptized: and the same day there were added unto them about three thousand souls.
>
> For by one Spirit are we all baptized into one body, whether we be Jews or Gentiles, whether we be bond or free; and have been all made to drink into one Spirit.
>
> That the blessing of Abraham might come on the Gentiles through Jesus Christ; that we might receive the promise of the Spirit through faith.

Through faith in Christ Jesus, the promised Holy Spirit is received, not through any physical manifestation of belief in any message. Does that mean that the Holy Spirit does not play any role in the life of a believer? Of course, He does. Christians are exhorted to be filled with the Holy Spirit (Eph. 5: 18; Col. 1: 9) and to keep in step with the Holy Spirit (Gal. 5: 25) and to endure to the end and be saved (Matt. 10: 22). In contrast to that, WMB taught that the faith that would bring the Church to glory was contained in his message he was sent to bring.[23]

To what extent is William Branham's doctrine of Salvation supported by Biblical Revelation? WMB's teaching of Salvation is quite complex, but it has very little biblical content. In the end, for WMB, what counted was that one received the Holy Spirit. How is that measured or discerned? For WMB and his followers, believing the Message of God for this hour, is the evidence of having the Holy

CHAPTER TWENTY-THREE

Spirit. Therefore, to no extent is William Branham's doctrine of Salvation supported by Biblical Revelation.

Notes - Chapter Twenty-Three

[1] *Palmerworm, Locust, Cankerworm, Caterpillar,* Jeff., IN, "[A] church without a doctrine is just like a jellyfish; it has no backbone…we've got to have backbone in it."

[2] COD is a compilation of 23 of WMB's messages.

[3] Harold O. Brown, *HERESIES, The Image of Christ in the Mirror of Heresy and Orthodoxy from the Apostles to the Present,* (Grand Rapids, MI: Baker Book House, 1984, 486 pp.), 21-22. "Although he may not think of it as 'dogma' or refer to it as 'doctrine,' no one can be a Christian at all unless he accepts the truth of certain fundamental statements we usually call dogmas. Unless a religious community holds certain specific and well-defined teachings, it will gradually dissolve, and in any event cannot be considered a Christian community."

[4] Merriam-Webster's definition of Dogma: 1 *a* : something held as an established opinion; 2 : a doctrine or body of doctrines concerning faith or morals formally stated and authoritatively proclaimed by a church .

[5] *Why?* Bloomington, IL, "[Y]ou people who are making up a bunch of man-made dogma and call it doctrine, call it creeds, church creeds…"

[6] *Christianity Versus Idolatry.*

[7] WMB, *Tell My Disciples,* Apr. 05, 1953, Sunday School class, Jeff., IN, "Then if God is my Father, I've got a right to believe in the supernatural, because I'm born of the supernatural Spirit, that makes a supernatural being out of me. Inward, outwardly, I am a man of clay; you're a man of clay. But inwardly, when you're born of the Spirit of God, you become a supernatural being in there, and that supernatural being hungers and thirsts for its heavenly home, yonder."

[8] *Why?* South Gate, "I only got one step: that's repent, and next is to be baptized in the Name of Jesus Christ for the remission of your sins. Then the next thing God said, 'I'll give you the Holy Ghost.' That's the three steps that I know of to take."

[9] WMB, *Birth Pains,* Jan. 24, 1965, Phoenix, AZ, "It's water: justification by faith, believing on God, receiving Him as your personal Savior, and being baptized; second is sanctification of the Spirit, that God cleanses the spirit from all elements of the world and the desire of the world; and then the Holy Spirit comes in and gives new birth and fills up that sanctified vessel…Now, a glass is laying out in the chicken yard. You don't just pick that up and put it on your table and fill it up with water or milk. No. By picking it up is justification. Cleansing it is sanctification, 'cause the Greek word "sanctify' is a compound word which means 'cleansed and set aside for service (not in service; for service).' Then when you fill it, it is put in service."

[10] *Q & A # 3,* "You're not converted, until you receive the Holy Ghost. Remember that. You're only potentially converted."

¹¹ WMB, *Communion*, Apr. 18, 1957, Jeff., IN, "Water baptism does not save you, as much as people sometimes think it does."

¹² WMB, *Church Choosing Law For Grace*, Mar. 16, 1961, Middletown, OH, "There's where we always make our mistakes, is when we try to add something to what God has done and what God has said. Just let it alone."

¹³ *Palmerworm, Locust, Cankerworm, Caterpillar*, Jeff, "I baptize in the Name of the Lord Jesus Christ. There's many Jesuses, but there's only one Lord Jesus Christ. Not in "Jesus name"; but in the Name of "The Lord Jesus Christ"; that's Father, Son, Holy Ghost."

¹⁴ *Let Your Light So Shine Before Men*, "God will take out of the Book of Life, for that man who will take one Word out of this or add one word to it.'"

¹⁵ 2 Sam. 6: 6-7, "Uzzah put forth his hand to the ark of God, and took hold of it; for the oxen shook it. 7 And the anger of the LORD was kindled against Uzzah; and God smote him there for his error; and there he died by the ark of God"

¹⁶ WMB, *Trying To Do God A Service Without It Being His Will*, Nov. 27, 1965, Brkfst., Shreveport, LA, "[H]e caused the death of sincere man; putting his hand on the ark when he shouldn't have done, it...The oxen stumbled and the cart was being pitched over; and a sincere man, with his heart full of love, put his hand upon the ark to hold it back, and was stricken dead because no man could touch that ark but a Levite."

¹⁷ Wm. Shakespeare, *Romeo and Juliet*.

¹⁸ 2 Tim. 3: 16, "All Scripture is given by inspiration of God, and is profitable for doctrine, for reproof, for correction, for instruction in righteousness"

¹⁹ Eph. 1: 13. "In whom ye also trusted, after that ye heard the word of truth, the gospel of your salvation: in whom also after that ye believed, ye were sealed with that holy Spirit of promise..." (Cf. Mk, 16: 16).

²⁰ 2 Cor. 1: 22, "Who hath also sealed us, and given the earnest of the Spirit in our hearts."

²¹ WMB, *What Think ye Of Christ*, Mar. 21, 1954, "Have you actually felt the power of God that changed your life and you become a new creature?"

²² *Church Age Book*. 169. "The evidence of receiving the Holy Ghost today is just the same as it was back in the day of our Lord. It is receiving the Word of truth for the day in which you live." See also: *Questions And Answers #2*,"There's only one evidence of the Holy Spirit that I know of, and that is a genuine faith in the promised Word of the hour."

²³ *Absolute*, Jeff., "Oh, and I remember when He swept down there in that big Light, standing yonder at the bottom of the river, 1933, in June, when He said, "As--as John the Baptist was sent forth and forerun the first coming of Christ, I send you with a Message to the world to forerun the second coming of Christ."...And now, I believe she's ready to strike that final climax yonder to bring forth a faith that'll rapture the Church into glory (It's the truth.), and She's laying in the Messages. We're really at the end time."

Chapter Twenty-Four

SUMMARY, CONCLUSION AND EPILOGUE

Summary

WMB was born in the hills of Kentucky. His father, a moonshiner and bootlegger, was a fugitive from the law and ran off to Indiana, where his wife and family joined him later. His mother came from Cherokee stock. WMB's parents were married in 1906. WMB stated that he was born about a year after his parents wed. He also said his birth date was not known. However, he always claimed to have been born on April 6, 1909, a date which he received from a Fortune teller. However, this author has obtained WMB's marriage license which lists his birth date as April 8, 1908. This date must be taken as correct, which jeopardizes WMB's integrity.

WMB often spoke about his parents being non-religious, nominal Roman Catholic, party-throwing sinners. However, shortly after his birth his mother took him to a "Baptist" church to be dedicated; indicating some kind of evangelical background. His mother, when young, attended a Methodist church, which building WMB's grandfather had built. He said they never went to church and never took him, except when he was eight days old. Yet, he said he was rocked in a Baptist cradle and was raised as a Baptist. He also played on a church league baseball team. He did not work, trap or fish on Sundays.

At age 14, while hunting, he got shot in his legs. In the hospital he felt his life ebbing away, he called out to "his" God. He saw a great light and a golden cross in the sky. The glory of God fell of the cross into his chest, he said. He claimed to have had visions of heaven and hell and promised the Lord that if he lived, he would serve Him. He attended many different churches, but found they were all wrong (Shades of Joseph Smith?). He believed God to be nature and nature to be God. Contrary to what he often said, they did not, as a family of ten children, live in a two room shack. They had enough to eat and even got treats of candy each week. When he was 8 or 10 years old his father gave him a dime as his weekly spending money. As a teenager he fished and trapped and made enough money to buy guns and ammunition, good clothes and new running shoes. He had money to go out with friends. He went on dates and he bought sandwiches and Cokes. He worked in a grocery store and fished and trapped besides. In 1926 he purchased a brand new 1926 car. A year later, he went off to Arizona to work on a ranch. He returned home for the funeral of his brother Edward and was challenged by the message of the presiding Baptist pastor. He got ill and felt he was dying. He cried out to God and he lived. After he was released from hospital, he knelt in a shed, in a garage, in a black church, in a converted saloon. He saw a great light in the form of a cross and a voice spoke to him in tongues, which to WMB meant his sins were forgiven. He promised he would preach the Gospel. WMB said he started reading the Bible.

His mother had a boarding house to provide for her off-spring, since WMB's father was an absentee husband. He stated he lived a happy life. Throughout his life story accounts, he reminisced about his wonderful childhood and his enjoyment of the great food they ate. He met Hope Brumbach, who convinced him to come to church with her. The date of his acceptance into the Missionary Baptist church is obscure. His ordination as an exhorter supposedly occurred within a year. WMB married Hope.

WMB was a master story teller who maximized his impact upon his hearers. He enthralled his audiences with often sad, and yet humorous tales, of extreme poverty and hardship. He held his audiences spell bound with his home-spun tales in his native Kentucky "corn-cracker" style and accent. WMB's early childhood, though certainly not easy, did not contain the poverty he constantly described in his stories. It appears he exaggerated his circumstances in order to have his audience be very empathetic and bring them into an emotional state, conducive to psychosomatic healing. In reality, these stories were not all that different from many other stories by evangelists of that era. In fact, almost anyone and everyone in rural USA had experienced the same, or at least heard of, similar stories of, poverty from parents and grandparents. WMB's fabricated, or embellished, stories were designed to one end: to create maximum emotional impact upon his hearers.

WMB was widely acclaimed by many religious leaders within Pentecostalism tradition as a true prophet. However, not much, if any, of this information can be verified against any established truth. WMB sources have been trying desperately to spin a better image for WMB.

WMB made much of his angelic commission which he said already happened before his birth, at his birth, at seven years of age, ten commissions in all. Two of these commissions stand out, one, his commission at the Ohio River, in either 1931 or in 1932 or 1933. The other commission occurred in 1946, in his cabin or cave. None of WMB's ten alleged commissions can be substantiated. The last mentioned claim actually had the angel of God visit him in person to give him a divine healing gift. The angel told him that, if he could get people to believe in him, nothing would stand before him, not even cancer. This gift supposedly consisted of two signs like those of Moses. First, he would be able to detect diseases by way of hand vibrations. After he had proven himself to be faithful, he would be able to discern people's thoughts, or read their minds. The angel of God, WMB claimed, gave him a gift of healing that he should bring to the nations. Yet later, WMB was adamant that this did not mean that he could heal. In fact, contrary to Scripture, WMB averred that no one could heal, not even Jesus. Healing came from inside a person; healing could only come through faith. However, Jesus performed the ultimate healing on three dead people, without any faith on their part whatsoever; Jairus' daughter; the young man from Nain and Lazarus. The Divine Gift of healing was his angel, WMB said. This angel would posses WMB; speak through him; discern people's thoughts and read their minds. This was done to build up people's faith, which then would heal them. This method, in WMB's own words, was not scriptural.

A person's faith could be placed in any object, even an idol, because only God could heal. Faith was the sixth sense; a mental capacity that reached inside. After all, WMB said a man fully submitted to God was deity. God is man and man is God, WMB declared. Man is a part of God and that makes man eternal, he said.

WMB taught that Satan caused all sickness and ignored God's hand in it, except to acknowledge that God *sometimes* used Satan to bring sickness upon people. In WMB's scheme of things, faith is a substance, or faith in faith. WMB's Healing campaigns appear to be fraught with fraud. He, supposedly, had an angel on the platform with him. That claim was disqualified by this same "angel," whom WMB claimed was either, the angel of God, the Pillar of Fire, the Holy Spirit, or Christ Himself, because he made mistakes. Often this angel was not able to pronounce people's names and he would spell it out, just like WMB did with difficult words. The angel would not always call out the right name, but confused it with another person's name. WMB's audience consisted, by his own estimation, of 80% neurotics, or hysterics. Neurotics or hysterics have all sorts of psychosomatic illnesses and are healed today and gone tomorrow. WMB's "trophies of healing" are also found to be non-existent.

The question might be asked, "Were there any healings in WMB's meetings?" That is like asking if there is any gold in one's backyard, there might well be. The healing claims would be difficult to check, because most, if not all, of these people are long dead. There are also no prior, or subsequent, medical records that could verify any claims.

WMB made strong claims regarding the healings of some renowned people. There was Congressman William Upshaw, healed through his ministry. A closer look reveals that what WMB said was not what Upshaw claimed had happened. The next thing noted was the miraculous healing of Florence Nightingale Shirlaw. This whole account has been embellished beyond compare. Another was that of the healing of King George VI. WMB never saw the King, nor was he ever inside Buckingham Palace. He did not even know King George's ailments beyond his ulcers, which were common knowledge. After King George died, WMB still proclaimed him healed. Donny Morton is another very sad story. Though he died of his illness, WMB claimed he was healed.

The little boy from Finland who was supposedly raised from the dead through WMB's ministry, is another account that raises serious questions regarding its authenticity. WMB claimed he had in his possession five death certificates of people who were resurrected through his ministry. This author requested to see these death certificates, but he was told by Billy Paul Branham they were lost.

WMB said he believed the Bible to be the infallible Word of God, right down to its punctuation. He said that one should not add to it, or subtract from it. However, WMB had more than one Bible. The written one was for intellectuals, solely constructed to confuse them; written between the lines, so only babes could get it. The other Bibles for WMB were Nature, the Zodiac and the one written in the Great Pyramid. When WMB came across something that he did not understand, he would consult these "bibles," especially nature, to make sense of it. He said, "Grand old mother nature. If you'll just follow that, you won't be too far off the road." Besides the four bibles mentioned, WMB put the utmost stock in the "spoken word," or the divine utterance he received as God's prophet, which he allegedly spoke to his generation.

It is readily apparent that WMB's understanding of Scripture did not come from his study of the written Bible, except perhaps that which he found written between the lines. Rather, he received it from many sources, including, but not limited to, Seventh Day Adventism, Jehovah's Witnesses, Mormonism, Rosicrucians, Freemasonry, British (American) Israelism, Eastern religions, New Thought, Christian Science, E.W. Kenyon, Eastern religions, and many other sources beyond." It must be noted that WMB did not necessarily receive this information firsthand. WMB's claim, "I don't know too much about the Word, the Book; I just know the Author real well, the One Who wrote it, the Holy Spirit." is too horrifying to even contemplate.

WMB's teachings on the several attributes, or perfections, of God, leave a lot to be desired. WMB at first believed in the Trinity doctrine, but embraced a Modalistic view. He was ignorant of the development of the Trinity doctrine, and its purpose, and called it a doctrine of devils. WMB's doctrine of God reflects the Gnostic belief of the Pleroma from which aeons emanate which, in turn, created the Demiurge, the great architect, or Creator. This Fountain includes the pre-existent spirits of predestinated sons of God.

CHAPTER TWENTY-FOUR

WMB stated man is as eternal as God is. The first "man," that was created was God Himself, he said. The second man was created a spirit being, a "theophany." The third man was man created out of the dust of the earth and in him was placed this pre-existent theophany, or soul. Adam and Eve were created male and female, which WMB interpreted to mean "androgynous." If these pre-existent spirit beings are androgynous, how are they separated into male and female today? Does that not destroy WMB's argument for the pre-existent spirits, but most importantly his doctrine of the Serpent's Seed, the linchpin of WMB's message?

The Fall of Adam and Eve was caused by Eve having sexual relations with an upright man-like creature called the Serpent. This union brought forth Cain, the Son of Satan, or the Serpent's Seed. This seed co-mingled with God's off-spring and continues to war against God's people even now. There is not a hint found within the Canon of Scripture of the Serpent being a man-like being. Where were the other serpents which God had blessed to be fruitful and multiply? In Scripture, no one, including Christ, ever mentioned anything about this teaching. Any internal inconsistency or contradiction in a teaching makes that teaching invalid. It is sufficiently clear that there are serious irreconcilable inconsistencies throughout WMB's Serpent's Seed teaching.

For WMB salvation is only available to God's Seed, those that have His Seed from eternity. It is a three step process, repentance, baptism in water in the name of the Lord Jesus Christ, and baptism with the Holy Spirit.

WMB taught that "Rapturing faith" was contained in his message. WMB taught a physical election for those of God's seed. However, there is no Scriptural warrant that God's off-spring will manifest simply because an eternal seed, like a divine spark, is resident in them.

It appears that WMB taught his own system of reincarnation. At first glance he appeared to be abhorred by this teaching, but he actually only reacted to reincarnation to a different species. Humans possess an eternal seed, or divine spark, which will spring to life when God's light strikes it.

WMB taught that Jesus was virgin born. In WMB's theology that meant that God created both sperm and egg in Mary's womb. WMB's teaching, unwittingly perhaps, showed Jesus to be a Cosmic Christ, like an Avatar. Jesus was not human flesh of which John says that these people are Antichrist (1 Jn. 4: 3; 2 Jn. 1: 7). Jesus only seemed to be a man, which is Docetism.

WMB did acknowledge that the Spirit of God was a Person. However, WMB's theology has more to do with the actions of the Holy Spirit, rather than His Person. The Holy Spirit, according to WMB, dwelt in man to replicate what Jesus did on earth. God would operate through this fully yielded person's lips and body. This person (read WMB - PMD), was taken over by the Spirit, and was completely out of control. Of course, a Christian is commanded to not ever lose control. When WMB spoke about the anointing of the Holy Spirit, he equated that with a number of things, though he most often said it was the angel of the covenant, or Christ. WMB, though he denied this, ascribed deity to this angel and prayed to him. To WMB the Holy Spirit was the Sixth Sense, which would never lead one astray.

WMB spoke often about a series of seven visions that he received, regarding the end-times. The dates vary, though in one account he clearly said he was reading it from a paper dated 1932. Later it became 1933. Five of the visions had already been fulfilled during WMB's time, he claimed. The visions included Mussolini invading Ethiopia. His visions contained errors, and were manipulated over time. Ethiopia was called Abyssinia and WMB's vision did not match Mussolini's exploits. The next vision was about the Siegfried line in Germany, though WMB confused it with the Maginot line in France. The Maginot line construction started in 1930. The Siegfried line was built in 1938. Until 1958 there is no mention by WMB of the Maginot, nor did he mention the Siegfried until 1959. This was an after the fact, or rear-view mirror prophecy. The next prophecy had to do with three "isms," Communism, Fascism and Nazism. These three "isms" would all end up into Communism and that Communism would burn the Vatican. In the end there would only remain Catholicism. Of course, Communism as a system is extinct in Europe and thus no longer able to burn the Vatican.

Next was the prophecy of the egg-shaped car that drives without a steering wheel. This type of car was shown in a number of magazines, prior to WMB "predicting" it in 1957.

One of the most controversial "prophecies" was WMB's prediction that by 1977 the United States of America would be destroyed by atomic bombs. This, obviously, has not occurred. By 1977 the Rapture should have taken place and the end of the world should have been ushered in. Before 1977, said WMB, a woman would rise to rule the United States. He did not know if she was an actual woman President, or the Roman Catholic Church, or a possible Pope who would be elected from the USA, or a RC president (JFK). Sadly enough, most of the prophecies had already occurred when he prophesied. Often he updated the prophecies to reflect more current events. Other prophecies, even his, "Thus saith the Lord," pronouncements, failed and never came to pass.

Conclusion

To what extent are the claims of William Branham regarding his life, call and ministry supported by Scripture, or by his own messages, or by reality? This author has invested almost forty years of research into the message of WMB. First as a convert, then as a pastor/evangelist and later as a person who fell into deep despair about what he found within the ministry of WMB's followers. Due to his travel as an Evangelist of WMB's message and his desire to preach only that which was

CHAPTER TWENTY-FOUR

found in God's Word alone, he became convicted to commence independent research into WMB's message. This book is the culmination of that research. This analysis of William Branham's life and teaching has shown that to no extent are the claims of William Branham regarding his life, call and ministry supported by Scripture, neither by his messages, nor by reality.

May many readers make the choice to go with "Sola Scriptura!"

Soli Deo Gloria

Peter M. Duyzer

2014

BIBLIOGRAPHY

Audio Transcripts of Wm. Branham's Messages

Abraham, (Jehovah-Jireh #3) Aug. 03, 1960, Yakima, WA.
Abraham, June 08, 1955, Macon, GA.
Abraham And His Seed After Him, Apr. 16, 1961, Bloomington, IL.
Abraham's Covenant Confirmed, Mar. 18, 1961, Middletown, OH.
Abraham's Grace Covenant, Mar. 17, 1961, Middletown, OH.
Absolute, Dec. 01, 1963, AM, Shreveport, LA.
Absolute, Dec. 30, 1962, AM, Jeff., IN.
Absolute, Jan. 27, 1963, Phoenix, AZ.
Absolute, Mar. 04, 1963, Houston, TX.
Accepting God's Provided Way, Jan. 15, 1963, Phoenix, AZ.
Acts of the Holy Spirit, Dec. 19, 1954, PM, Jeff., IN.
Adoption # 1, May 15, 1960, PM, Jeff., IN.
Adoption # 2, May 18, 1960, Jeff., IN.
Adoption # 4, May 22, 1960, PM, Jeff., IN.
And Thy Seed Shall Possess The Gate Of His Enemy, Jan. 21, 1962, AM, Phoenix, AZ.
Angel and The Commission, Aug. 21, 1950, Cleveland, OH.
Angel Of God, Jul. 20, 1951, Toledo, OH.
Angel Of God, Mar. 04, 1948, Phoenix, AZ.
Angel Of God, Nov. 02, 1947, Phoenix, AZ.
Angel Of The Lord, Jul. 18, 1951, Toledo, OH.
Anointed Ones At The End Time, Jul. 25, 1965, AM, Jeff., IN.
Approach To God, Jan. 23, 1955, Aft., Chicago, IL.
Ark, May 22, 1955, Jeff., IN.
Arrow Of God's Deliverance, Shot From A Bow, Aug. 01, 1956, Shreveport, LA.
As I Was With Moses, May 03, 1951, Los Angeles, CA.
As I Was With Moses, So I Will Be With Thee, Sep. 11, 1960, AM, Jeff., IN.
As The Eagle Stirreth Up Her Nest, Aug. 15, 1959, Chautauqua, OH.
As The Eagle Stirreth, Apr. 03, 1960, Tulsa, OK.
As The Eagle Stirs Her Nest, Jan. 22, 1961, Beaumont, TX.

BIBLIOGRAPHY

Ashamed, (Africa Trip Report), Jul. 11, 1965, Jeff., IN.
At Thy Will, Jun. 08, 1953, PM., Connersville, IN.
At Thy Word, Jul. 14, 1950, Minneapolis, MN.
At Thy Word, Lord, Mar. 05, 1948, Phoenix, AZ.
At Thy Word, May 06, 1951, PM, Los Angeles, CA.
AT Thy Word, Sep. 28, 1951, New York, NY.
Audio Letter To Lee Vayle, May 1964, Tucson, AZ.
Balm In Gilead, Jul. 7, 1959 Cleveland, TN.,
Baptism Of The Holy Spirit, Sep. 28, 1958, AM, Jeff., IN.
Basis Of Fellowship, Feb. 14, 1961, Long Beach, CA.
Be Certain Of God, Jan. 25, 1959, Jeff., IN.
Be Certain Of God, Jul. 8, 1959, PM, Cleveland, TN.
Be Not Afraid, Jul. 17, 1960, Klamath Falls, OR.
Be Not Afraid, It Is I, Apr. 14, 1962, Bloomington, IN.
Be Not Afraid, It Is I, Mar. 5, 1960, Phoenix, AZ.
Beginning And Ending Of The Gentile Dispensation, Jan. 9, 1955, PM, Jeff., IN.
Behold, A Greater Than Solomon Is Here, July 21, 1962, Salem, OR.
Being Led Of The Holy Spirit, Feb. 19, 1956, Minneapolis, MN.
Believe Ye That I Am Able To Do This? Aug. 20, 1950, PM, Cleveland, OH.
Believe Ye That I Can Do This? May 9, 1951, Los Angeles, CA.
Believer's Position In Christ, Jan. 16, 1955, Aft., Chicago, IL.
Believest Thou This? Jul. 16, 1950, Minneapolis, MN.
Believest Thou This? Oct. 3, 1951, New York, NY.
Believest Thou This? Sept. 6, 1953, AM, Chicago, IL.
Believing God, Feb. 24, 1952, Jeff., IN.
Beyond The Curtain Of Time, Mar. 5, 1961, Jeff., IN.
Birth Pains, Jan. 24, 1965, Phoenix, AZ.
Blasphemous Names, Nov. 4, 1962, AM, Jeff., IN.
Blind Bartimaeus, Jan. 24, 1961, Beaumont, TX.
Blind Bartimaeus, Jan. 27, 1957, PM, Lima, OH.
Blind Bartimaeus, Nov. 27, 1959, San Jose, CA.
Breach between the Seven Church Ages and the Seven Seals, Mar. 17, 1963, Jeff., IN.
But From The Beginning It Was Not So, Oct. 2, 1958, Jeff., IN.
But It Wasn't So From The Beginning, Apr. 11, 1961, Bloomington, IL.
By Faith, Moses, Jul. 20, 1958, Jeff., IN.

Calling Jesus On The Scene, Aug. 4, 1963, PM, Chicago, IL.
Children In The Wilderness, Nov. 23, 1947, Phoenix, AZ.
Children Of Israel, Nov. 23, 1947, Phoenix, AZ.
Choosing Of A Bride, Apr. 29, 1965, PM, Los Angeles, CA.
Christ Is The Mystery Of God Revealed, Jul. 28, 1963, Jeff., IN.
Christ, Feb. 21, 1955, Phoenix, AZ.
Christianity Versus Idolatry, Dec. 17, 1961, Jeff., IN.
Church And Its Condition, Aug. 5, 1956, Jeff., IN.
Church Choosing Law For Grace, Mar. 16, 1961, Middletown, OH.
Come Follow Me, Jun 1, 1963, Tucson, AZ.
Come Let Us Reason Together, Oct 4, 1955, Chicago, IL.
Comforter, Oct. 1, 1961, PM, Jeff., IN.
Communion, Apr. 18, 1957, Jeff., IN.
Communion, Dec. 12, 1965, Tucson, AZ.
Condemnation By Representation, Nov. 13, 1960, Jeff., IN.
Conference, Nov. 25, 1960, Shreveport, LA.
Conferences, Apr. 10, 1961, Bloomington, IL.
Conference With God, Dec. 20, 1959, AM, Jeff., IN.
Conference With God, Jan. 8, 1960, Tifton, GA.
Conference With God (Having Conferences), Jun. 8, 1960, Chautauqua, IN.
Confirmation And Evidence, Jun. 21, 1962, PM, South Gate, CA.
Conflict Between God And Satan, May, 31, 1962, Clarksville, IN.
Contending For The Faith, Feb. 00, 1956, Georgetown, IN.
Contending For The Faith, Feb. 20, 1955, PM, Phoenix, AZ.
Convinced And Then Concerned, Nov. 25, AM, 1962, Shreveport, LA.
Corinthians, Book of Correction, Apr. 14, 1957, Jeff., IN.
Countdown, Nov. 25, 1962, PM, Shreveport, LA, "
Cruelty Of Sin, And The Penalty That It Cost To Rid Sin From Our Lives, Apr. 03, 1953, Jeff., IN.
Daniel's Seventieth Week, Aug. 6, 1961, Jeff., IN.
Darkest Hour, Then Jesus Comes Along, Nov. 14, 1955, San Fernando, CA.
Debate On Tongues, Aug. 7, 1960, Yakima, WA.
Dedication Of Building, To The Lord, Jul. 8, 1959, Cleveland, TN.
Deep Calleth Unto The Deep, Nov. 4, 1952, Owensboro, KY.
Deity Of Christ, Dec. 25, 1949, Jeff., IN.
Demonology, Physical Realm, Jun. 8, 1953, Aft., Connersville, IN.

Demonology, Religious Realm, Jun. 9, 1953, Aft., Connersville, IN.
Discerning The Body Of The Lord, Aug. 12, 1959, Chautauqua, OH.
Discernment Of Spirit, Mar. 8, 1960, Phoenix, AZ.
Divine Healing, Dec. 19, 1954, AM, Jeff., IN.
Divine Healing, Jun. 20, 1954, PM, Des Moines, IA.
Do You Now Believe? Aug. 17, 1952, PM, Battle Creek, MI.
Do You Now Believe? Dec. 6, 1953, PM, West Palm Beach, FL.
Do you now Believe? Mar. 7, 1954, PM, Phoenix, AZ.
Do You Now Believe? Nov. 6, 1953, Owensboro, KY.
Does God Ever Change His Mind About His Word? Apr. 18, 1965, PM, Jeff., IN.
Door In A Door, Feb. 23, 1963, Tucson, AZ.
Door Inside The Door, Jul. 11, 1960, Klamath Falls, OR.
Door Of The Door, Dec. 12, 1957, Newark, NJ.
Door To The Heart, Mar. 16, 1958, PM, Harrisonburg, VA.
Doors In Door, Feb. 6, 1965, Flagstaff, AZ.
Eagle Stirring Her Nest, May, 1958, New England Area.
Early Spiritual Experiences, Jul. 13, 1952, Aft., Hammond, IN.
Earnestly Contending For The Faith, Apr. 4, 1954, AM, Louisville, KY.
Easter Seal, Apr. 10, 1965, Phoenix, AZ.
Ensign, Jan. 19, 1962, Phoenix, AZ.
Entombment, Apr. 20, 1957, Jeff., IN.
Ephesian Church Age, Dec. 5, 1960, Jeff., IN.
Evening Messenger, Jan. 16, 1963, Mesa, AZ.
Events Made Clear By Prophecy, Aug. 1, 1965, PM, Jeff., IN.
Ever Present Water From The Rock, Jul. 23, 1961, AM, Jeff., IN.
Exhortation On Healing, May 01, 1951, Los Angeles, CA.
Expectation, Dec. 06, 1954, Binghamton, NY.
Expectation, Feb. 07, 1961, Long Beach, CA.
Expectation, Feb. 20, 1954, Wood River, IL.
Expectation, Sep. 30, 1951, New York, NY.
Expectations And What Love Is, Feb. 28, 1954, Aft., Phoenix, AZ.
Expectations, Apr. 5, 1950, New York, NY.
Expectations, Aug. 10, 1950, Cleveland, OH,
Expectations, May 7, 1953, Jonesboro, AR.
Expectations, May 8, 1958, Burlington, VT.

Expectations, May 7, 1951, Los Angeles, CA.
Experiences, Mar. 2, 1948, Phoenix, AZ.
Faith, Dec. 13, 1953, Chicago, IL.
Faithful Abraham, Apr. 24, 1959, Aft., San Jose, CA.
Faith (Faithful Abraham), Apr. 27, 1956, Charlotte, NC.
Faith - Africa Trip Report, July 25, 1952, Zion, IL.
Faith in the Son of God, Jul. 15, 1952, Hammond, IN.
Faith Is The Sixth Sense, June 11, PM, 1960, Chautauqua, OH.
Faith Is The Substance, Apr. 12, 1947, Oakland, CA.
Faith Is the Substance, May 8, 1951, Los Angeles, CA.
Faith Of Abraham, Nov. 18, 1955, San Fernando, CA.
Faith Once Delivered, Jun. 10, 1957, Indianapolis, IN.
Faith Once Delivered to the Saints, May 1, 1955, PM, Chicago, IL.
Faith That Was Once Delivered To The Saints, Nov. 29, 1953, Aft., West Palm Beach, FL.
Faith Without Works Is Dead, Aug. 22, 1950, Cleveland, OH.
Falling Apart Of The World, Dec. 16, 1962, Jeff., IN.
Feast Of The Trumpets, July 19, 1964, A.M., Jeff., IN.
Fellowship, Jun. 11, 1960, Brkfst., Middletown, OH.
Fifth Seal, Mar. 22, 1963, Jeff., IN.
First Seal, Mar. 18, 1963, Jeff., IN.
Five Definite Identifications Of The True Church Of The Living God, Sept. 11, 1960, PM, Jeff., IN.
Flashing Red Light Of His Coming, Jun 23, 1963, PM, Jeff., IN.
Former And Latter Rain, Mar. 3, 1960, Phoenix, AZ.
Forsaking All, Jan. 23, 1962, Tempe, AZ.
Fourth Seal, March 22, 1963, Jeff., IN.
From That Time, Jul 16, 1960, Klamath Falls, OR.
From That Time, Jul. 13, 1962, Spokane, WA.
From That Time, Mar. 2, 1960, Phoenix, AZ.
From That Time, May 20, 1961, Dawson Creek, BC.
Future Home Of The Heavenly Bridegroom And The Earthly Bride, Aug. 02, 1964, Jeff., IN.
Gabriel's Instructions To Daniel, Jul. 30, 1961, AM, Jeff., IN.
Get The People To Believe, Jul. 17, 1952, Hammond, IN.
Gifts And Callings Are Without Repentance, Mar. 1950, Carlsbad, NM.
Gifts, Dec. 07, 1956, Brooklyn, NY.
Go Awake Jesus, Nov. 30, 1963, PM, Shreveport, LA.

BIBLIOGRAPHY 331

Go Tell My Disciples, Apr. 5, 1953, Sunrise Service, Jeff., IN.
Go, Wake Jesus, Nov. 3, 1963, Tucson, AZ.
God Being Misunderstood, Jul. 23, 1961, PM, Jeff., IN.
God Commissioning Moses, Jun. 03, 1953, Connersville, IN.
God Hath A Provided Way, Jan. 08, 1956, Jeff., IN.
God Hiding Himself In Simplicity, Then Revealing Himself In The Same, Mar. 17, 1963, AM, Jeff., IN.
God Hiding Himself In Simplicity, Apr. 12, 1963, Albuquerque, NM.
God Is His Own Interpreter, Feb. 5, 1964, Bakersfield, CA.
God Keeps His Word, Apr. 7. 1957, AM, Jeff., IN.
God Keeps His Word, Jan. 15, 1957, Sturgis, MI, Op. Cit.
God making His Promise, Dec. 09, 1956, Aft., Brooklyn, NY.
God Perfecting His Church, Dec. 4, 1954, Binghamton, NY.
God Projecting His Love, Aug. 6, 1957, Edmonton, AB, CAD.
God Provided A Lamb, Jun. 14, 1956, Indianapolis, IN.
God Revealing Himself To His People, Aug. 13, 1950, Aft., Cleveland, OH.
God Testifying Of His Gifts, Jul. 13, 1952, PM, Hammond, IN,
God's Chosen Place Of Worship, Feb. 20, 1965, Jeff., IN.
God's Covenant With Abraham, Apr. 28, 1956, Charlotte, NC.
God's Gifts Always Find Their Places, Dec. 22, 1963, Jeff., IN.
God's Provided Way, Jun. 13, 1953, Connersville, IN.
God's Provided Way, May 13, 1953, Jonesboro, AR.
God's Provided Way, May 16, 1961, AM, Grande Prairie, AB.
God's Provided Way For This Day, Feb. 6, 1964, PM, Bakersfield, CA.
God's Provided Way Of Approach To Fellowship, Jul. 9, 1960, Klamath Falls, OR.
God's Provided Way Of Healing, Jul. 19, 1954, Aft., Chicago, IL.
Great Coming Revival And The Outpouring Of The Holy Spirit, Jul. 18, 1954, Aft., Chicago, IL.
Greater Than Solomon Is Here, Jul. 21, 1962, Salem, OR
Greater Than Solomon Is Here, Apr. 12, 1961, Bloomington, IL.
Greater Than Solomon Is Here, Jul. 25, 1962, Port Alberni, BC, CAD.
Greater Than Solomon Is Here, Jun. 28, 1963, PM, Hot Springs, AR.
Greatest Gift In The Bible, Aug. 11, 1957, Aft., Edmonton, AB, CAD.
Guide, Oct. 14, 1962, PM, Jeff., IN.
Hand Of The Lord Came Upon Him, Apr. 3, 1954, Louisville, KY.
Handwriting On The Wall, Jan. 8, 1958, Chicago, IL.

Handwriting On The Wall, Sept. 2, 1956, Jeff., IN.
Harvest Time, Dec. 12, 1964, Phoenix, AZ.
Have I Not Sent Thee, Jan. 24, 1962, Phoenix, AZ.
*Having Conferences, (Conference With God)*Jun. 8, 1960, Chautauqua, IN.
He Swore By Himself, Dec. 12, 1954, Jeff., IN.
He That Is In You, Nov. 10, 1963, PM, Jeff., IN.
Healing Of Jairus' Daughter, Feb. 27, 1955, PM, Phoenix, AZ.
Hear His Voice, Oct. 5, 1958, AM., Jeff., IN.
Hear Ye Him, Jan. 26, 1958, Waterloo, IA.
Hear Ye Him, Jul. 11, 1962, Spokane, WA.
Hear Ye Him, Mar. 10, 1957, PM, Phoenix, AZ.
Hearing, Receiving And Acting, Jun. 7, 1960, Chautauqua, OH.
Hebrews Chapter Five And Six, #1, Sep. 8, 1957, AM, Jeff., IN.
Hebrews Chapter One, Aug. 21, 1957, Jeff., IN.
Hebrews Chapter Seven # 1, Sep. 15, 1957, PM, Jeff., IN.
Hebrews Chapter Seven # 2, Sep. 22, 1957, Jeff., IN.
Hebrews Chapter Six # 2, Sept. 8, 1957, PM, Jeff., IN.
Hebrews Chapter Six And Seven, Sept. 15, 1957, AM, Jeff., IN.
Hebrews Chapter Two #3, Aug. 28, 1957, Jeff., IN.
Here We Have No Continuing City, Feb. 1950, Little Rock, AR.
Hidden Life, Oct. 6, 1955, Aft., Chicago, IL.
His Unfailing Words Of Promise, Jan. 20, 1964, Phoenix, AZ.
Hour Is Come, Apr. 15, 1951, PM, Phoenix, AZ.
How The Angel Came To Me, And His Commission, Jan. 17, 1955, Chicago, IL.
I Am The Resurrection And The Life, Aug. 10, 1952, Aft., Chicago, IL.
I Perceive That Thou Art A Prophet, Jun. 14, 1953, PM, Connersville, IN.
I Was Not Disobedient To The Heavenly Vision, Jul. 18, 1949, Zion, IL.
I Will Restore Unto You, Saith The Lord, Aug. 9, 1954, Aft., Los Angeles, CA.
I Will Restore, June 20, 1954, Aft., Des Moines, IA.
I Will Restore, Mar. 9, 1957, Brkfst., Phoenix, AZ.
Identification, Feb. 16, 1964, Tulare, CA.
Identified Masterpiece Of God, Dec. 5, 1964, Yuma, AZ.
Identified With Christ, Dec. 20, 1959, PM, Jeff., IN.
If God Be With Us, Then Where Is All The Miracles? Dec. 31, 1961, PM, Jeff., IN.
Impersonation Of Christianity, Jan. 20, 1957, AM, Jeff., IN.

BIBLIOGRAPHY 333

In His Presence, Sep. 9, 1962, PM, Jeff., IN.
Indictment, July 7, 1963, Jeff., IN.
Infallibility Of God's Word, Apr. 4, 1956, Chicago, IL.
Infallible Proof Of The Resurrection, Jan. 14, 1957, Sturgis, MI.
Investments, Mar. 14, 1964, Beaumont, TX.
Invisible Union Of The Bride Of Christ, Nov. 25, 1965, Shreveport, LA.
Is There Anything Too hard For The Lord? Mar. 28, 1960, Tulsa, OK.
Is This The Sign Of The End Sir? Dec. 30, 1962, PM, Jeff., IN.
Is Your Life Worthy Of The Gospel, Jun 30, 1963, PM, Jeff., IN.
Israel And The Church # 2, Mar. 26, 1953, Jeff., IN.
Israel And The Church # 3, Mar. 27, 1953, Jeff., IN.
Israel And The Church # 4, Mar. 28, 1953, Jeff., IN.
Israel And The Church # 5, Mar. 29, 1953, Jeff., IN.
It Is I, Be Not Afraid, Aug. 11, 1959, Chautauqua, OH.
It Is I, Nov. 24, 1960, Shreveport, LA.
It Is The Rising Of The Sun, Apr. 18, 1965, AM, Jeff., IN.
Jairus And Divine Healing, Feb. 16, 1954, Wood River, IL.
Jehovah Of Miracles, Nov. 26, 1959, San Jose, CA.
Jehovah Jireh, Jan. 27, 1958, Waterloo, IA.
Jehovah-Jireh #1, Jul. 5, 1962, Grass Valley, CA.
Jehovah-Jireh #2, Apr. 3, 1964, Louisville, MS.
Jehovah-Jireh, Apr 29, 1956, Charlotte, NC.
Jehovah-Jireh, Aug. 10, 1957, Edmonton, AB, CAD.
Jehovah-Jireh, Aug. 17, 1955, Karlsruhe, DEU.
Jehovah-Jireh, Feb. 9, 1961, Long Beach, CA.
Jehovah-Jireh, June 12, 1957, Indianapolis, IN.
Jehovah-Jireh, Mar. 12, 1961, Richmond, VA.
Jesus At The Door, May 29, 1958, New Haven, CT.
Jesus Christ The Same Yesterday And Today And Forever Mar. 23, 1958 Middletown OH
Jesus Christ The Same Yesterday, And Today, And Forever, May 06, 1953, Jonesboro, AR.
Jesus Christ The Same Yesterday, Today And Forever, Feb. 14, 1958, Terra Haute, IN.
Jesus Christ The Same Yesterday, Today And Forever, Jan. 16, 1955, PM, Chicago, IL.
Jesus Christ The Same Yesterday, Today And Forever, Jun., 1955, Macon, GA.
Jesus Christ The Same Yesterday, Today, And Forever, Jun. 27, 1963, Hot Springs, AR.
Jesus Christ, The Same Yesterday, Today And Forever, Aug. 10, 1952, PM, Chicago, IL.

Jesus Christ, The Same Yesterday, Today And Forever, Aug. 6, 1955, Campbellsville, KY.

Jesus Christ, The Same Yesterday, Today And Forever, Feb. 5, 1961, PM, Tucson, AZ

Jesus Christ, The Same Yesterday, Today And Forever, Jul. 18, 1962, Salem, OR.

Jesus Christ, The Same Yesterday, Today And Forever, May 16, 1961, Aft., Grande Prairie, CAD.

Jesus Christ, The Same Yesterday, Today, And Forever, Oct. 27, 1952, Edmonton, CAD.

Jesus Keeps All Of His Appointments, Apr. 18, 1964, PM, Tampa, FL.

Jesus On The Authority Of The Word, Feb. 17, 1954, Wood River, IL.

Jezebel Religion, Mar. 19, 1961, Middleton, OH.

Joseph Meeting His Brethren, Dec. 30, 1956, Jeff., IN.

Just Once More, Lord, Dec. 1, 1963, PM, Shreveport, LA.

Key To The Door, Oct. 10, 1962, Jeff., IN.

Lamb and Dove, Aug. 5, 1960, Yakima, WA.

Lamb's Book Of Life, Jun. 03, 1956, Jeff., IN.

Laodicean Church Age, Dec. 11, 1960, PM, Jeff., IN.

Law, Jan. 15, 1955, Chicago, IL.

Law Having A Shadow, Jun. 21, 1956, Chicago, IL.

Law Or Grace, Oct. 6, 1954, Jeff., IN.

Leadership, Dec. 7, 1965, Covina, CA.

Lean Not Unto Thine Own Understanding, Jan. 20, 1965, Phoenix, AZ.

Led By The Spirit, Apr. 7, 1959, Los Angeles, CA,

Let Us See God, Nov. 29, 1959, San Jose, CA.

Let Your Light So Shine Before Men, Sep. 3, 1961, Jeff., IN.

Letting Off The Pressure, May 18, 1962, Green Lake, WI.

Life Story, Apr. 15, 1951, Aft., Phoenix, AZ.

Life Story, Apr. 19, 1959, Aft., Los Angeles, CA.

Life Story, Feb. 1950, Little Rock, AR.

Life Story, Jul. 20, 1952, Aft., Hammond, IN.

Life Story, Jul. 22, 1951, Aft., Toledo, OH.

Life Story, Jun. 26, 1955, Aft., Zurich, SW.

Life Story, Los Angeles, May 08, 1951, Los Angeles, CA.

Life Story, Mar. 14, 1954, Columbus, OH.

Life Story, Nov. 8, 1953, Aft., Owensboro, KY.

Life, Jun. 2, 1957, Jeff., IN.

Life, May 12, 1958, Everett

Life, May 19, 1958, Bangor, ME.

BIBLIOGRAPHY 335

Living, Dying, Buried, Rising, Coming, Apr. 03, 1959, Los Angeles, CA.
Living, Dying, Buried, Rising, Coming, March 29, 1959, Sunrise, Jeff., IN.
Look Away To Jesus, Dec. 29, 1963, PM, Jeff., IN.
Look, Apr. 28, 1963, Phoenix, AZ.
Looking For Jesus, Feb. 28, 1954, PM, Phoenix, AZ.
Lord, Show Us The Father, And It Sufficeth Us, Sep. 07, 1953, Aft., Chicago, IL.
Make The Valley Full Of Ditches, Jul. 19, 1952, Hammond, IN.
Man Running From The Presence Of The Lord, Feb. 17, 1965, Jeff., IN.
Maniac Of Gadara, Jul. 20, 1954, Aft., Chicago, IL.
Manifestation Of The Spirit, Jul. 17, 1951, Toledo, OH.
Manifestation Of Thy Resurrection to the People of this Day, Aug. 09, 1954, PM, LA CA.
Mark Of The Beast And The Seal Of God # 1, Feb. 16, 1961, Long Beach, CA.
Mark Of The Beast And The Seal Of God # 2, Feb. 17, 1961, Long Beach, CA.
Mark Of The Beast, May 13, 1954, Jeff., IN.
Marriage And Divorce, Feb. 21, 1965, AM, Jeff., IN.
Marriage Of The Lamb, Jan. 21, 1962, PM, Phoenix, AZ.
Mary's Belief, Apr. 09, 1959, Los Angeles, CA.
Mary's Belief, Jan. 21, 1961, Beaumont, TX.
Mary's Belief, Mar. 11, 1960, Phoenix, AZ.
Meanest Man I Know, Jan. 27, 1962, Phoenix, AZ.
Message Of Grace, Aug. 27, 1961, Jeff., IN.
Message To The Laodicean Church, Jun. 9, 1958, Dallas TX.
Messiah, Jan. 17, 1961, Shreveport, LA.
Mighty Conqueror, Aug. 8, 1957, Edmonton, AB, CAD.
Mighty God Unveiled Before Us, Jun. 29, 1964, Philadelphia, PA.
Ministry Explained, Jul. 11, 1950, Minneapolis, MN.
Ministry Of Christ, Jun. 7, 1953, Aft., Connersville, IN.
Missionary Talk, Mar. 30, 1958, Aft., Middletown, OH.
Modern Events Made Clear By prophecy, Dec. 6, 1965, San Bernardino, CA.
Moses' Commission, Jan. 10, 1950, Houston TX.
My Commission, May 5, 1951, Los Angeles, CA.
My Life Story, Aug. 20, 1950, Aft., Cleveland, OH.
Obey The Voice Of The Angel, Jul. 13, 1950, Minneapolis, MN.
On The Wings Of Snow White Dove, Nov 28, 1965, PM, Shreveport, LA.
Oncoming Storm, Feb. 29, 1960, Phoenix, AZ.

Oneness, Feb. 11, 1962, Jeff., IN.

Our Hope Is In God, Sep. 29, 1951, New York, NY.

Painted Face Jezebel, Oct. 5, 1956, Chicago, IL.

Palmerworm, Cankerworm, Locust And Caterpillar, Jun. 12, 1953, Connersville, IN.

Palmerworm, Locust, Cankerworm, Caterpillar, Aug. 23, 1959, Jeff., IN.

Paradox, Apr. 18, 1964, Brkfst., Tampa, FL.

Path Of Life, Jun. 21, 1962, Brkfst., South Gate CA.

Patmos Vision, Dec. 4, 1960, PM, Jeff., IN.

Paul, a Prisoner, Jul. 17, 1963, Jeff., IN.

Perfection, Apr. 19, 1957, Jeff., IN.

Pergamean Church Age, Dec. 7, 1960, Jeff., IN.

Perseverance, Jan. 13, 1963, PM, Jeff., IN.

Perseverant, Aug. 2, 1963, Chicago, IL.

Perseverant, July 29, 1962, Victoria, BC, CAD.

Perseverant, Jun. 23, 1962, South Gate, CA.

Personal Experience With God, Jul. 24, 1954, Chicago, IL.

Pillar Of Fire, May 9, 1953, Jonesboro, AR.

Power Of Decision, Oct. 7, 1955, Chicago, IL.

Power Of God, Oct. 6, 1955, PM, Chicago, IL.

Power Of Transformation, Oct. 31, 1965, AM, Prescott, AZ.

Prayer Line, Nov. 27, 1953, Palm Beach, FL.

Presence Of The Lord Jesus, Jun. 12, 1955, Macon, GA.

Presuming, June 10, 1962, AM, Southern Pines, NC.

Principles Of Divine Healing, Sep. 23, 1951, Jeff., IN.

Prophet Elisha, Jul. 23, 1954, Chicago, IL.

Proving His Word, Aug. 16, 1964, Jeff., IN.

Queen Of Sheba, Feb, 8, 1958, South Bend, IN.

Queen Of Sheba, Feb. 19, 1961, Long Beach, CA.

Queen Of Sheba, Jan. 19, 1961, PM, Beaumont, TX.

Queen Of The South, Jun 20, 1958, Greenville, SC.

Questions And Answers # 1, Jan. 3, 1954, Jeff., IN.

Questions And Answers # 2, Aug. 23, 1964, PM, Jeff., IN.

Questions And Answers # 3, Aug. 30, 1964, AM, Jeff., IN.

Questions And Answers # 4, Aug 30, 1964, PM, Jeff., IN.

Questions And Answers On Genesis, July 29, 1953, Jeff., IN.

BIBLIOGRAPHY 337

Questions And Answers On Hebrews # 1, Sep. 25, 1957, Jeff., IN.
Questions And Answers On Hebrews # 2, Oct. 2, 1957, Jeff., IN.
Questions And Answers On Hebrews # 3, Oct. 6, 1957, Jeff., IN.
Questions And Answers On the Holy Ghost, Dec. 19, 1959, Jeff., IN.
Questions And Answers On the Seals, Mar. 24, 1963, AM, Jeff., IN.
Questions And Answers, Dec. 23, 1959, Jeff., IN.
Questions And Answers (COD), Jan. 12, 1961, Jeff., IN,
Questions And Answers, Jun. 28, 1959, PM, Jeff., IN.
Questions And Answers, (Image of the Beast), May 15, 1954, Jeff., IN.
Questions And Answers, May 27, 1962, Jeff., IN.
Questions And Answers (COD), Oct. 15, 1961, AM, Jeff., IN.
Rapture, Dec. 04, 1965, Yuma, AZ.
Reaction To An Action, Aug, 10, 1959, Chautauqua, OH.
Redeemer, Redemption, Nov. 19, 1955, San Fernando, CA.
Redemption In Completeness, In Joy, Mar. 30, 1954, Louisville, KY.
Reproach For The Cause Of The Word, Dec. 12, 1962, Jeff., IN.
Restoration Of The Bride Tree, Apr.22, 1962, Jeff., IN.
Resurrection Of Jairus' Daughter, Mar. 31, 1954, Louisville, KY.
Resurrection Of Lazarus, Aug. 13, 1950, Aft., Cleveland, OH.
Resurrection Of Lazarus, Jul. 29, 1951, Aft., Erie, PA.
Resurrection, Dec. 5, 1953, West Palm Beach FL.
Revelation, Book Of Symbols, Jun. 17, 1956, Jeff., IN.
Revelation Chapter Five # 2, Jun. 18, 1961, Jeff., IN.
Revelation Chapter Five, # 1, Jun. 11, 1961, Jeff., IN.
Revelation Chapter Four # 2 (24 Elders), Jan. 1, 1961, Jeff., IN.
Revelation Chapter Four # 3, Jan. 8, 1961, Jeff., IN.
Revelation Of Jesus Christ, Dec. 4, 1960, AM, Jeff., IN.
Revelation That Was Given Me, Feb. 10, 1960, San Juan, PR.
Sardisean Church Age, Dec. 9, 1960, Jeff., IN.
Scriptural Signs Of The Time, Apr. 10, 1964, Birmingham, AL.
Seal Of Antichrist, Mar. 11, 1955, Los Angeles, CA.
Second Seal, Mar. 19, 1963, Jeff., IN.
Secondhanded Robe, Nov. 25, 1956, AM, Jeff., IN.
Seed Shall Not Be Heir With The Shuck, Apr. 29, 1965, Brkfst., Los Angeles, CA.
Seeking After Jesus, May 31, 1953, Connersville, IN.

Separation From Unbelief, Feb. 28, 1955, Phoenix, AZ.

Serpent's Seed, Sep. 28, 1958, PM, Jeff., IN.

Seven Church Ages, May 12, 1954, Jeff., IN.

Seventh Seal, Mar. 24, 1963, PM, Jeff., IN.

Seventieth Week Of Daniel, Aug. 06, 1961, Jeff., IN.

Shalom, Jan. 12, 1964, Sierra Vista, AZ.

Shalom, Jan. 19, 1964, Phoenix, AZ.

Show Us The Father And It Suffices, Aug. 19, 1950, Cleveland, OH.

Show Us The Father And It Will Satisfy Us, Jul. 31, 1960, Yakima, WA.

Show Us The Father And It'll Satisfy Us, Jun. 10, 1953, Connersville, IN.

Show Us The Father And It'll Satisfy, Apr. 22, 1956, Spindale, NC.

Show Us The Father, Jun. 25, 1955, Zurich, SW.

Show Us The Father, May 21, 1961, Dawson Creek, BC.

Sirs, Is This The Time? Dec. 30, 1962, PM, Jeff., IN.

Sirs, *We Would See Jesus,* Dec. 11, 1957, Newark, NJ.

Sirs, We Would See Jesus, Jan. 9, 1960, Tifton, GA.

Sirs, We Would See Jesus, May 16, 1957, Saskatoon, SK, CAD.

Sixth Seal, Mar. 23, 1963, Jeff., IN.

Smyrnaean Church Age, Dec, 06, 1960, Jeff., IN.

Souls That Are In Prison Now, Nov. 10, 1963, AM, Jeff., IN.

Speak To This Mountain, Dec. 15, 1957, Brooklyn, NY.

Spirit Of Truth, Jan. 18, 1963, Phoenix, AZ.

Spiritual Food In Due Season, Jul. 18, 1965, PM, Jeff., IN.

Spoken Word is the Original Seed #1, Mar. 18, 1962, AM, Jeff., IN.

Standing In The Gap, Jun. 23, 1963, AM, Jeff., IN.

Super Sense, Dec. 27, 1959, PM, Jeff., IN.

Super Sign, Dec. 27, 1959, AM, Jeff., IN.

Super Sign, Jul. 8, 1962, Grass Valley, CA.

Super Sign, Jun. 24, 1962, South Gate, CA.

Supernatural, Jan 29, 1956, Owensboro, KY.

Take The Rod And Gather The People, Aug. 27, 1950, PM, Cleveland, OH.

Taking Sides With Jesus, Jun. 1, 1962, Jeff., IN.

Teaching On Moses, May 13, 1956, Jeff., IN.

Tell My Disciples, Apr. 05, 1953, Sun. Sch., Jeff., IN.

Ten Virgins And The Hundred And Forty-four Thousand Jews, Dec. 11, 1960, AM, Jeff., IN.

BIBLIOGRAPHY

Testimony (Believe Ye That I Can Do This?), May 09, 1951, Los Angeles, CA.
Testimony of a True Witness, Nov. 5, 1961, Jeff., IN.
Testimony Of Jesus Christ, Aug. 29, 1953, Chicago, IL.
Testimony On The Sea, Mar. 7, 1964, Dallas, TX.
Testimony Upon The Sea, Jul. 26, 1962, Port Alberni, BC, CAD.
Testimony, Nov. 29, 1953, PM, West Palm Beach, FL.
That Day On Calvary, Sep. 25, 1960, Jeff., IN.
There Is Only One Way Provided By God For Anything, Jul. 31, 1963, Chicago, IL.
Thinking Man's Filter, Aug. 22, 1965, PM, Jeff., IN.
Things That Are To Be, Dec. 5, 1965, Rialto, CA.
Third Seal, March 20, 1963, Jeff., IN.,
Thirst, Sep. 19, 1965, Tucson, AZ.
Thirsting For Life, Mar. 4, 1960, Phoenix, AZ.
Thirsting For Life, May 12, 1958, Everett, MA.
Thirsting For Life, Jun. 13, 1957, Indianapolis, IN.
Thirsting For Life, Jul. 28, 1957, Tacoma, WA.
Thirsting For Life, Jun. 30, 1957, Chicago, IL.
This Day This Scripture Is Fulfilled, Jan. 25, 1965, Phoenix, AZ.
Three Witnesses, Jul. 28, 1951, Erie, PA.
Thy House, Aug. 8, 1961, Tifton, GA.
Thy Loving Kindness, Feb. 2, 1958, Chattanooga, TN.
Thyatirean Church Age, Dec. 8, 1960, Jeff., IN.
Time Is At Hand, Apr. 08, 1956, PM, Chicago, IL.
To Take On The Whole Armor Of God, Jul. 01, 1962, Santa Maria, CA.
Token, Mar. 8, 1964, Dallas, TX.
Token, Nov. 28, 1963, PM, Shreveport, LA.
Total Deliverance, Jul. 12, 1959, Jeff., IN.
Trial, Apr. 19, 1964, Tampa, FL.
Trial, Apr. 27, 1964, Tucson, AZ.
Trial, Apr. 5, 1964, Louisville, MS.
True Sign That's Overlooked, Nov. 12, 1961, Jeff., IN.
True Vine And The False Vine, Jun. 07, 1955, Macon, GA.
Trying To Do God A Service Without Being The Will Of God, Jul. 18, 1965, AM, Jeff., IN.
Turning Northward, Jan. 29, 1961, Phoenix, AZ.
Twentieth Century Prophet – Movie, Aug. 1953, Jeff., IN.

Uncertain Sound, Dec. 18, 1960, Jeff., IN.

Uncertain Sound, Mar. 15, 1961, Middletown, OH.

Unchangeable God Working In An Unexpectable Way, Jan. 20, 1962, Phoenix, AZ.

Unconditional Covenant, Mar. 6,1954, Phoenix, AZ.

Unfailing Realities Of The Living God, Jun. 26, 1960, Jeff., IN.

Unpardonable Sin, Oct. 24, 1954, Jeff., IN.

Unwelcomed Christ, Sep. 11, 1955, Jeff., IN.

Victory Day, Apr. 21, 1963, Sierra Vista, AZ.

Visions Of William Branham, Sep. 30, 1960, Jeffersonville, IN.

Voice of the Sign, Feb. 14, 1964, Tulare, CA.

Voice of the Sign, Mar. 21, 1964, PM, Denham Springs, LA.

Watchman, What Of The Night? Jul. 22, 1960, Lakeport, CA.

Water Baptism, Jan. 19, 1961, Aft., Beaumont, TX.

Water Of Separation, Jan. 21, 1955, Chicago, IL.

Way Back, Nov. 23, 1962, Shreveport, LA.

We Would See Jesus, Dec. 05, 1954, Binghamton, NY.

We Would See Jesus, Jul. 04, 1962, Grass Valley, CA.

We Would See Jesus, Jul. 27, 1962, Victoria, BC, CAD.

We Would See Jesus, Jun. 12, 1958, Dallas TX.

What Hearest Thou, Elijah, Jun. 09, 1959, Chicago, IL.

What Is The Attraction On The Mountain? Jul. 25, 1965, PM, Jeff., IN.

What Is The Holy Ghost? Dec. 16, 1959, Jeff., IN.

What Shall I Do With Jesus Called Christ? Nov. 24, 1963, AM, Jeff., IN.

What Think ye Of Christ, Mar. 21, 1954, Chicago, IL.

What Think Ye Of Christ, Dec. 13, 1953, AM, Chicago, IL.

What Was The Holy Ghost Given For? Dec. 17, 1959, Jeff., IN.

When Their Eyes Were Opened, They Knew Him, March 12, 1964, Beaumont, TX.

Who Has Believed Our Report, Jul. 20, 1952, PM, Hammond, IN.

Who Hath Believed Our Report, Jul. 19, 1951, Toledo, OH.

Who Is This Melchisedec? Feb. 21, 1965, PM, Jeff., IN.

Who Is This? May 10, 1959, PM, Jeff., IN.

Who Is This? Oct. 4, 1959, AM, Clarksville, IN.

Why Are People So Tossed About? Jan. 1, 1956, Jeff., IN.

Why Are We Not A Denomination? Sept. 27, 1958, Jeff., IN.

Why Cry, Speak, Jul. 14, 1963, AM, Jeff., IN.

BIBLIOGRAPHY   341

Why I Am A Holy Roller, Aug. 30, 1953, Aft., Chicago, IL.
Why I'm Against Organized Religion, Nov. 11, 1962, PM, Jeff., IN.
Why It Had To Be Shepherds, Dec. 21, 1964, Tucson, AZ.
Why Little Bethlehem? Dec. 14, 1963, Phoenix, AZ.
Why? Apr. 13, 1961, Bloomington, IL.
Why? Jan. 28, 1961, Phoenix, AZ.
Why? Jun. 22, 1962, PM, South Gate, CA.
Wisdom Versus Faith, Apr., 1962, Jeff., IN.
Without Money Or Without Price, Aug. 2, 1959, Jeff., IN.
Witnesses, Mar. 3, 1954, Phoenix, AZ.
Word Became Flesh, India Trip Report, Oct. 3, 1954, AM, Jeff., IN.
Workings Of The Holy Ghost, Aug. 16, 1956, Prince Albert, SK, CAD.
Works is Faith Expressed, Nov. 26, 1965, Shreveport, LA.
Works That I Do Bear Witness Of Me, Apr. 13, 1951, Phoenix, AZ.
Ye Must Be Born Again, Jun. 19, 1958, Brkfst., Greenville, SC.
You Must Be Born Again, Dec. 31, 1961, Jeff., IN.
Zacchaeus, May 17, 1958, Brkfst., Bangor, ME.
Zacchaeus, The Businessman, Jan. 21, 1963, Tucson, AZ.

BOOKS

Allison, Ronald and Riddell, Sarah., *Royal Encyclopedia*, (London: MacMillan Press, 1991).

Augsburger, Myron, ed. Gerald R. Brunk, *Irvin B. Horst, Historian, Bibliophile, Churchman.* in *MENNO SIMONS: A REAPPRAISAL.* Harrbonburg, VA: EMC, 1992.

Blocher, Henri. Translated by David G. Preston. *IN THE BEGINNING, The opening chapters of Genesis.* Downers Grove, IL: IVP, 1984.

Bloch-Hoell, Nils, *The Pentecostal Movement.* New York: Humanities Press, 1964.

Botterweck, G. Johannes, Helmer Ringgren and Heinz-Josef Fabri. Transl. by Douglas W. Scott. *Theological Dictionary of the Old Testament*, Vol.14. Grand Rapids, MI: EPC, 2004, 702.

Branham, William, *Breach Between The Seven Church Ages And The Seven Seals*, Tucson, AZ: Spoken Word Publications, 1967.

Branham, William, *Exposition of the Seven Church Ages*. Dallas, TX: VOH, 1975.

———, *Footprints on the Sands of Time, An Autobiography of William Marrion Branham*, Vol. 1. Jeff. IN.: SWP, 1975.

———, *I was Not Disobedient To The Heavenly Vision*. Jeff. IN.: Branham Campaign, 1945.

———, *Jesus Christ The Same Yesterday, Today And Forever,*. Jeff. IN: Branham Campaign, 1945.

———, *The Revelation of The Seven Seals*. Tucson: SWP, 1945.

Brown, Harold O., *HERESIES, The Image of Christ in the Mirror of Heresy and Orthodoxy from the Apostles to the Present*. Grand Rapids, MI: BBH, 1984.

Burgess, Stanley M. and Gary B., McGee, editors, Patrick H. Alexander, assoc. ed., *Dictionary of Pentecostal and Charismatic Movements*. Grand Rapids, MI: ZPH, 1988, 914 pp.

Calvin, John. Transl. Henry Beveridge, *Institutes Of The Christian Religion*, Vol. 1. EPC 1973.

Carson, D.A. *The Gospel According to John*. Grand Rapids, MI: EPC, 1991, 715 pp.

Cassuto, U. *A Commentary on the Book of Genesis*. Jerusalem: MP, Heb. Univ..

Chastain, Warren. *Muslim Stumbling blocks*, in *Perspectives on the World Christian Movement*, ed. Ralph D. Winter and Stephen C. Hawthorne. Pasadena, CA: WCL, 3rd Ed., July 2000.

Copeland, Kenneth. *John G. Lake, His Life, His Sermons, His Boldness of Faith*. Fort Worth, TX: KCP, 1994, 548 pp.

Crisp, Oliver D. *Divinity and Humanity*, Cambridge, UK: Cambridge University Press, 2007, 187 pp.

Davis, John J. *Paradise to Prison*. Grand Rapids, MI: BBH, 1975.

Durrant, Michael. *Theology and Intelligibility*. London: RKP, 1973.

Duyzer, Peter M., *'Mystery Cloud' - Exposé on Wm. Branham*, (Fort McMurray, AB, Canada: Peter M. Duyzer, 1980, 27 pp.

Dyck, Carl. *WILLIAM BRANHAM, The Man and His Message*. Saskatoon, SK: WTM, 1984, 65.

Feinberg, Paul D. Ed. Steven B. Cowan, *Five Views on Apologetics*. Grand Rapids, MI: ZPH, 2000.

George, Timothy. *GOD, the Holy Trinity, Reflections of Christian Faith and Practice*. Grand Rapids, MI: BA, 2006, 175 pp.

BIBLIOGRAPHY

Gill, John. *An Exposition of the Gospel According to John.* 2003 ed. Springfield, MO: PBP.

Green, Pearry. *The Acts of the Prophet.* First Edition, Tucson, AZ: TTB, n.d.

Guiley, Rosemary Ellen. *Harper's Encyclopedia of Mystical & Paranormal Experience.* New York: HC, 1991.

Hall, Thor. *The Evolution Of Christology.* Nashville, TN: AP, 1982.

Harrell Jr., David Edwin. *All Things Are Possible.* Bloomington, IN: IUP, 1975.

Hartley, John E. *New International Biblical Commentary, Genesis.* Peabody, MA: HP, 2000.

Hinson, Ed and Ergun Caner. *The Popular Encyclopedia Of Apologetics, Surveying the Evidence for the Truth of Christianity.* Eugene, OR: HHP, 2008.

Hollenweger, Walter J. *The Pentecostals.* Peabody: HP, 1988.

Howley, G.C.D., F.F. Bruce, and H.L. Ellison. Editors, *The New Laymen's Bible Commentary.* Grand Rapids, MI: ZPH, 1979, 1712 pp.

Jamieson, Robert, A.R. Fausset and David Brown. *Commentary Practical And Explanatory Of The Whole Bible.* Grand Rapids, MI: ZPH,, 1978, 1591 pp.

Kydd, Ronald. *Healing Through The Centuries: Models for Understanding.* Peabody, MA: HP, Feb. 2010, 272 pp.

Leupold, H.C. *Exposition of Genesis*, Vol. I Chapters 1-19. Grand Rapids, MI: BBH, 1975.

Lindsay, Gordon. *God's 20th Century Barnabas.* Dallas: CFN, 1980.

Lindsay, Gordon. *William Branham, A Man Sent From God.* Jeffersonville, IN: WBP, 1950, 216.

Lippy, Charles H., ed., *Twentieth Century Shapers of American Popular Religion.* New York: GP, 1989. xxv + 494 pp.

Luther, Martin. *Small Catechism*, Saint Louis, MO: Concordia Publishing House, 1943.

Machen, J. Gresham. *The Virgin Birth Of Christ.* London: JCC, 1958.

Mathews, Kenneth A. General Editor E. Ray Clendenen. *The New American Commentary, Genesis 1-11: 26.* Nashville, TN: BHP, 1995.

McElvaine, Robert S. *The Great Depression.* Toronto: FHW, 1984.

Meade, Marion. *Bobbed Hair and Bathtub Gin: Writers Running Wild in the Twenties*. New York, NY: DD, 2004, 340 pp.

Melton, Gordon J. *Encyclopedia of American Religions*, 6th Ed. Detroit: GR, 1999.

Middleton, John, ed. *Theories of Magic"* in *Encyclopedia of Religion Vol. 9*. New York, NY: MCM, 1987.

New Haven, Conn: YUP, 1996, 267 pp.

Mosby's Medical Dictionary, 8th edition. © 2009, Elsevier.

Pelikan, Jaroslav. *Mary Through the Centuries, Her Place in the History of Culture*. New Haven, Conn: YUP, 1996, 267.

Pfeiffer, Charles F. and Everett F., Harrison, Editors, *The Wycliffe Bible Commentary*. Chicago, IL: MP, 1977, 1525 pp.

Philips, Dirk. *The Writings of Dirk Philips*, Translated and edited by Cornelius J. Dyck, William E. Keeney, and Alvin J. Beachy. Scottsdale, PA: HrldP, 1992, 701 pp.

Russell, Bertrand. *History of Western Philosophy*. London: GAU, 1961.

Schaff, Philip and Lenski, R.C.H. *The Interpretation of St. John's Gospel*, Minneapolis, MN: APH, 1961.

Sidlow-Baxter, J. *Divine Healer of the Body*. Grand Rapids, MI: ZPH, 1979, 296 pp.

Sinclair Deckard, Barbara. *The Women's Movement: Political, Socioeconomic and Psychological Issues. Third Edition*. New York: HR, 1983.

Skinner, John. *Genesis, 2nd Ed*. Edinburgh: TTC, 1969.

Smith, Joseph Jr. *Teachings of the Prophet Joseph Smith*, ed. Joseph Fielding Smith, 4th ed. Salt Lake City: DNP, 1943.

Smith, Joseph. *Joseph Smith's History, Doctrines and Covenants of the Church of Jesus Christ and the Latter-Day Saints, and The Pearl of Great Price*. Salt Lake City, Utah: COLDS, 1982.

Smith, Uriah, *Daniel And The Revelation*, Review and Herald Publishing Association, Washington, DC, 1906, 757 pp.

Stadsklev, Julius. *A Prophet Visits South Africa*. Minneapolis, MN: Julius Stadsklev, 1952.

Steinbeck, John, *The Grapes of Wrath*. New York, NY: PB, 1976.

Tanner, Jerald and Sandra Tanner. *The Changing World of Mormonism*. Chicago, IL: MP, 1980.

ten Doornkaat Koolman, Jacobus. *DIRK PHILIPS, Friend and Colleague of Menno Simons, 1504-1568*. Transl. William E. Keeney. Kitchener, ON: PP, 1998, 234 pp.

Urban, Linwood. *A Short History Of Christian Thought*. New York, NY: OUP, 1995.

Vayle, Lee. *Twentieth Century Prophet: The Messenger To The Laodicaen Church Age*. Jeff., IN: SWP, 1965, 73pp.

Vine, W. E.. *Vine's Expository Dictionary of Old and New Testament Words*, Editor F.F. Bruce. Old Tappan, NJ: FHRC, 1981, 351 pp.

Wallender, William H. *Why the Holy Spirit Was Poured Out in 1900: An Insight for the People of God*. Bloomington, IN: AH, 272 pp.

Weaver, C. Douglas. *The Healer-Prophet, William Marrion Branham*. Macon: MUP, 1987.

Wilson, Benjamin. *The Emphatic Diaglott*. Brooklyn, NY: WTBTA, 1942.

Yancey, Philip. *Reaching for the Invisible God*. Grand Rapids, MI: ZPH, 2000.

Zeitz, Joshua. *Flapper: A Madcap Story of Sex, Style, Celebrity, and the Women Who Made America Modern*. New York, NY; CP, 2006, 352pp.

Electronic References

Ancestry, "1920 United States Federal Census," entry for Charles Branham, derived from Roll: T625_425; Page: 11A; Enumeration District: 5; Image: 60, database, (Year 1920, Census Place: Jeffersonville, Clark, Indiana, 2010), accessed 23 February, 2011. http://www.ancestry.com

_____ , Entry for Ellie R. Harvey, or Ella R. Harvey, derived from: Roll T623_ 506; Page 18B; Enumeration District: 4, (Year 1900, Census Place: Gradyville, Adair, Kentucky), accessed 23 February, 2011. http://www.ancestry.com

Apostolic Friends Forum, "Pentecostal History- September," accessed June 6, 2012.

_____ , Military Records," entry for Charles Alton Brumback, derived from: US World War II Draft Registration Cards 1942, U747, database (year 1942, Jeffersonville, Clark, Indiana, 1917), accessed 23 February, 2011. http://www. .apostolicfriendsforum.com/index.php/t-26307.html

Aronowitz, Al., "The Beatles," *The Blacklisted Journalist*, accessed April 19, 2005. http://www.blacklistedjournalist.com/column17.htm

Bible Way Church, "Charles Branham's Death", accessed January 31, 2006. http:/www.biblebelievers.org/bblife.htm

_____ , "William Branham's Conversion at 20," accessed April 1, 2002. http://www.biblebelievers.org

_____ , "Wm. Branham's Ordination," accessed April 1, 2002. http://www.biblebelievers.org

Billy Graham Center, "Ephemera of James Gordon Lindsay – Coll. 121," accessed March 14, 2008. http://www2.wheaton.edu/bgc/archives/GUIDES/121.htm

Bible Believers, St. John's, CAD, Billy Paul Is Born, accessed April 01, 2002. http://www.williambranhamhomepage.org/lbpaul.htm

_____ , "Branham Tabernacle Mortgage," accessed May 6, 2010. http://www.williambranhamhomepage.org/lilypond.htm

_____ , "Charles Branham," accessed October 19, 2008. http://www.williambranhamhomepage.org/lfather.htm

_____ , "Charles Branham Dies," accessed January 31, 2006. http://www.biblebelievers.org/bblife.htm

_____ , "Conversion of William Branham," accessed April 01, 2002. http://www.williambranhamhomepage.org/lconv

_____ , "Laying of the Cornerstone," accessed May 6, 2010. http://www.williambranhamhomepage.org/lcstone.htm#lilypond

_____ , "Goes to Arizona, accessed July 15, 2011. http://www.williambranhamhomepage.org/lwest.htm

_____ , Marries Hope Brumbach, accessed April 1, 2002. http://www.williambranhamhomepage.org/lhope.htm

_____ , "Marries Meda Broy," accessed October 20, 2008. http://www.williambranhamhomepage.org/lmeda.htm

_____ , "Tabernacle Completion," accessed December 16, 2008. http://www.bridemessage.org/lcstone.htm#lilypond

BIBLIOGRAPHY

Bible Believers, St. John's, CAD,, "William Branham, a Man Sent From God", accessed April 01, 2002. http://www.williambranhamhomepage.org/mansent2.htm

Book Of Enoch, Ch. XLVI, "Head of Days and the Son of Man." Ibid, Ch. XLVIII, accessed June 14, 2005. http://www.sacred-texts.com/bib/boe/boe049.htm

Bowen, Dan. "A Tribute to Ern Baxter," *Life on Wings*, accessed November 3, 2011. http://ern-baxter.blogspot.ca/2006_03_01_archive.html

Buckingham Palace, "Buckingham Palace Fact No. 36," accessed June 15, 2010. http://www.londonforfun.com/info-for-Buckingham-palace.htm.

Burkesville, "Area History." accessed November 17, 2008 http://www.burkesville.com/html/area_history.html

Business Journals, "Growing Corn for Whiskey," accessed November 19, 2008. http://www.bizjournals.com/louisville/stories/2007/05/07/story2.html?jst=s_cn_hl

Cain, Paul, Official Website, accessed July19, 2012. http://www.paulcain.org/sandbox/newsite/pagesaboutpaul.html

Catechism of the Catholic Church. Part Two; Section Two; Chapter One; Article One, THE SACRAMENT OF BAPTISM 1284. accessed November 17, 2008. http://www.vatican.va/archive/ccc_css/archive/catechism/p2s2c1a1.htm

Center for History, "Indiana Through Change (1920-1940)," accessed November 10, 2005. http://centerforhistory.org/learn-history/indiana-history/indiana-through-change-1920-1940

Knowledge of Reality, "Christ and the Kundalini, " *KOR*, accessed July 10, 2012. http://www.sol.com.au/kor/8_01.htm

Christian Apologetics & Research Ministry, "Irenaeus, *Against Heresies*," acessed September 18, 2010. http://carm.org/irenaeus-heresies3-15-25

Christian Classics Ethereal Library, "Ante-Nicene Fathers, The Apostolic Fathers with Justin Martyr and Irenaeus, Chapter XXX. - Doctrines of the Ophites and Sethians," accessed June 3, 2004. http://www.ccel.org/ccel/schaff/anf01.ix.ii.xxxi.html

Civil Twilight, accessed April 26, 2010. http://www.planetultra.com/civil.html

Cloverdale Bibleway Church, "Who was William Branham," accessed April 7 2007. http://www.bibleway.org/home.do#path=/missions.

Davis, Roy E., "Pentecostal Holiness," Louisville, KY; 1929, accessed June 9, 2012. http://www.ptc.dcs.edu/teacherpages/tthrasher/listings/Ta.htm

Business Journals, "Distilling Whiskey." accessed November 19, 2008. http://louisville.bizjournals.com/louisville/stories/2007/05/07/story2.html?jst=s_cn_hl

Eleanor Roosevelt Papers Project, "Alfred E. Smith," accessed October 14, 2004. http://www.gwu.edu/~erpapers/teachinger/glossary/smith-al.cfm

Elijah the Restorer, "John Alexander Dowie, History and Times of the Kingdom," accessed September 4, 2002. http://www.fwselijah.com/dowie.htm

Elmoziffle, Paul Cain with Todd Bentley, Pt.1, "I've Been Celibate," accessed June 17, 2008, http://www.youtube.com/watch?v=o25jTVb5Bj8

_____ , Paul Cain with Todd Bentley, Pt.2, "The New Breed," accessed June 17, 2008. http://www.youtube.com/watch?v=oR6JraFDtLk

Ethiopia. accessed 07 April, 2002. http://www.hmml.org/resources/Ethiopia/History.htm

Ethiopian History, "The Italo-Ethiopean Wars," accessed November 17, 2010. http://www.selamta.net/history.htm.

Find A Grave, "Charles C. Branham and Ella R. Harvey," accessed January 02, 2010. http://www.findagrave.com/cgi-bin/fg.cgi?page=gr&GRid=73486882

_____ , William. Branham, accessed June 5, 2012. http://www.findagrave.com/cgi-bin/fg.cgi?page=gr&GRid=73469206

Ford Motorcar, 1926, accessed June 07, 2003. http://www.wiley.com/legacy/products/subject/business/forbes/ford.html

Golden Gloves. accessed January 17, 2005. http://www.goldenglovesofamerica.com/gghistory.htm

Grady, J. Lee., "Prophetic Minister Paul Cain Issues Public Apology for Immoral Life-style," *Charisma*, accessed February 28, 2005. http://www.charismamag.com

Great Architect of the Universe, accessed October 15, 2010. http://www.themasonictrowel.com/Articles/Freemasonry/antifreemasonry_files/the_great architect.htm

Great Depression. "Indiana Through Change" *Northern Indiana Center for History (1920-1940),* accessed November 10, 2005. http://www.centerforhistory.org/indiana_history_main9.html#_ftnref5

Hamburger, H. Wayne. Yoke Of Bondage, *Gospel Assembly*, accessed April, 2010. http://www.gospelassemblyfree.com/gac/yoke8.htm

BIBLIOGRAPHY 349

Hamilton, Frank W. "My Life and Times," Yesterdays of Hamilton County, IL. accessed December 3, 2008. http://www.carolyar.com/Illinois/Family/ArthurHamilton.htm

Harvey, Ella. Wm. Branham Support Forum, accessed January 4, 2010. http://forums.delphiforums.com/kennah/messages?msg=1777.15 EricP73, General "Message" Discussion – Birthdate for Ella Harvey Branham post 2789.1

Hoover, Herbert, " Prosperity," accessed November 29, 2008. http://www.spartacus.schoolnet.co.uk/USAprosperity.htm

Indiana Historic Landmarks, "John Work House," accessed May10, 2010. http:wwwhistoriclandmarks.org/NEWSPHOTOS/10MOST/Pages/JohnWorkHouse.aspx

Interest Rates for 1926, accessed June 07, 2003. http://www.nber.org/databases/macrohistory/rectdata/13/m13031.dat_

Irenaeus, St., "Against Heresies", accessed September18, 2010. http://carm.org/irenaeus-heresies3-15-25

Irenaeus, St., ANF01. The Apostolic Fathers with Justin Martyr and Irenaeus, Chapter XXX.—Doctrines of the Ophites and Sethians, Philip Schaff. access-ed June 3, 2004. http://www.ccel.org/ccel/schaff/anf01.ix.ii.xxxi.html

João Texeira de Faria, "John of God," accessed June 12, 2010. http://www.johnofgod-healing.com/?gclid=CNex94u_m6ICFRmjagod-2L2yw

Jones, James W., "The Open Door," April 1956, accessed March 9, 2012. http://jonestown.sdsu.edu/AboutJonestown/PrimarySources/theopendoor_text.html

Jones, Jim. Jonestown Audiotape Primary Project: Transcripts. Tape Number: Q 612, Jonestown Institute, accessed November 22, 2006. http://jonestown.sdsu.edu/AboutJonestown/Tapes/Tapes/TapeTranscripts/Q612.html

Jorgenson, Owen, Supernatural: The Life of William Branham, Book 5: The Teacher and His Rejection 1955-1960 *Amazon.com*, 2002[on-line]; accessed 10 March 2008. http://www.amazon.com/

Joseph Smith. Joseph Smith-History, Extracts from the History of Joseph Smith the Prophet, accessed April 13, 2010. http://scriptures.lds.org/en/js_h/1/19a

Kennah, John, Cloud Quotes, "William Branham Places Himself at Sunset Peak at the Time Cloud was Photographed"; accessed July16, 2011. http://forums.delphiforums.com/n/mb/display.asp?webtag=kennah&msg=930.2

Kennah, John, Issues & Events in WMB's Life. accessed July16, 2011. http://forums.delphiforums.com/kennah/messages?msg=2132.502

———, "Was Wm. Branham Really Commissioned by an Angel in 1946?" accessed May 9, 2010. http://people.delphiforums.com/johnk63/evetns.htm

King Ben, founder of the House of David, Rearview Mirror, accessed April 22, 2002. http://www.marycityofdavid.org

Lindsay, James Gordon. "Ephemera of James Gordon Lindsay - Collection 121." *Billy Graham Center Archives*, accessed March 13, 2002. http://www.wheaton.edu/bgc/archives/GUIDES/121.htm

McGhee, Fielding M. III, Jonestown Audiotape Primary Project: Transcripts, Tape Number : Q612, "The Jonestown Institute," accessed November 22, 2006. http://jonestown.sdsu.edu/AboutJonestown/Tapes/Tapes/TapeTranscripts/Q612.html

Maginot Line. accessed October 15, 2004. http://www.winterwar.com/M-line/Mline2.htm and http://www.mannerheim.fi/10_ylip/e_mlija.htm

Man Sent From God. accessed April 1 2002. http://www.biblebelievers.org/mansent2.htm

Maryboy, Nancy C., and David H. Begay, PhDs, "Vibrational Diagnosis, Shift Issue #03," Integral Health and Healing, May 2004, accessed May 25, 2010. http://www.shiftinaction.com/node/105

Mason, Wanda, Wiliam Sowders & William Branham, Similarities in Doctrine, accessed July 7, 2003. http://www.gospelassemblyfree.com/facts/sowdersbranhamprint.htm

Mayo Clinic, "Gastritis," accessed December 20, 2008. http://www.mayoclinic.com/health/gastritis

Message of the Hour Forum, accessed October 11, 2010. http://forums.delphiforums.com/branham/messages?msg=3356.325

———, Post # 2000,107, .accessed May 3, 2005, http://forums.delphiforums.com/branham/messages?msg=2000.107

Voice of God Recordings, Inc., "The Life And Ministry Of William Branham," accessed April 7, 2007. http://www.branham.org/BranhamDefault.asp?Home=WilliamBranham&LoadPageDetail=WilliamBranham.htm?

Old Alimony Case Summaries, 12. THOMPSON v. THOMPSON, 226 U.S. 551 (1913), accessed December 5, 2008. https://bulk.resource.org/courts.gov/c/US/226/226.US.551.45.html

BIBLIOGRAPHY 351

Old Landmark, Celebrating Our Pentecostal Heritage, accessed May 29, 2010. http://oldlandmark.wordpress.com/glossary-of-pentecostal-history/

Pencilsmudge, "Pillar of Fire Photo, 1950"; Issues & Events in WMB's Life, Message of William. Branham Support Forum, accessed February 8, 2007. http://forums.delphiforums.com/kennah/messages?msg=2199.64

Public Service Company of Indiana; accessed December 5, 2008. http://www.funduniverse.com/company-histories/PSI-RESOURCES-Company-History.html

Regular Grand Lodge of England, "Great Architect of the Universe," accessed August 11, 2012. http://www.rgle.org.uk/RGLE_Tenet.htm

Rise and Set for the Sun for 1909, Burkesville, KY, Astronomical Applications Dept. U. S. Naval Observatory. Washington, DC 20392-5420, accessed April 26, 2010. http://aa.usno.navy.mil/cgi-bin/aa_rstablew.pl?FFX=1&type=0&st=KY& place =Burkesville&xxy=1909

Rise and Set for the Sun for 1908, Burkesville, KY, Astronomical Applications Dept. U. S. Naval Observatory. Washington, DC 20392-5420, accessed April 26, 2010. http://aa.usno.navy.mil/cgi-bin/aa_rstablew.pl?FFX=1&type=0&st=KY& place=Burkesville&xxy=1908

Scott, Ziba. Family Tree Maker, "Ancestors of Merritt Scott," accessed December 5, 2008. http://webcache.googleusercontent.com/search?q=cache:5G8bpRnh1woJ:familytreemaker.genealogy.com/users/h/e/n/Cynthia-L-E3Henning/P DFGE E3Henning/PDFGE NE3.pdf+1923+trapper+prices

Scofield, Cyrus., "Reference Bible and Notes (1917)," accessed March 29, 2008. http://bible.crosswalk.com/Commentaries

Shannahan, J. N. accessed December 5, 2008. http://www.funduniverse.com/company-histories/PSI-RESOURCES-Company-History.html

Smith, Alfred E., accessed October 14, 2004. http://www.wordiq.com/definition/Alfred_E._Smith

Smythe, Edward J. Ed "Gunboat Smith," accessed December 7, 2008. http://www.cyberboxingzone.com/boxing/gunboat.htm

Spartacus Educational, "American economy-Herbert Hoover," accessed November 29, 2008. http://www.spartacus.schoolnet.co.uk/USAprosperity.htm

Sun or Moon Rise/Set, One Year Table; Sunrise Burkesville, KY, April 6, 1909. accessed April 26, 2010. http://aa.usno.navy.mil/cgi-bin/aa_rstablew.pl

Sunrise Sunset Calendar, accessed December 11, 2012. http://www.sunrisesunset.com/calendar.asp

Thuruthiyil, Scaria., "Reincarnation in Hinduism," *New Age Catholic Website*, accessed October 25, 2010. www.spiritualwholeness.org/faqs/reincgen/hindrein.htm

Vayle, Lee., Godhead 11, July 1, 2000, accessed January 5, 2009. http://www.messagedoctrine.com/LeeVayle/Godheadseries/Godhead11.htm

_____ , "Leo Mercier and Gene Goad," accessed January 3, 2009. http://www.messagedoctrine.com/LeeVayle/Godheadseries/Godhead11.htm

Voice of God Recordings, "A visitation of an Angel," accessed May 10, 2010. http://branham.org/content/AboutUs/williambranham_pg3.aspx

_____ , Life and Ministry of William Branham, accessed April 7 2007. http://www.branham.org/Branham&LoadPageDetail=WilliamBranham.htm?

What Did You Do In The War, Grandma? " Timeline of WWII (1939-1945), accessed May 10, 2010 www.stg.brown.edu/projects/WWII_Women/NewTimeline.html#1945

Western seaboard of the United States from Washington to California, accessed May 3, 2005. http://www.elook.org/dictionary/west-coast.html

What Did You Do In The War, Grandma? Timeline WWII (1939-1945), accessed May 10, 2010. http://www.stg.brown.edu/projects/WWII_Women/NewTimeline.html#1945

WMB Sermons, Public Domain, http://branham.org/MessageSearch.htm

WMB1 Document Portal, , Sarah. Branham de Corado, "Letter to followers of Wm. Branham's mesage," accessed 31 May, 2011. http://wmb1.com/portico/modules.php?name=News&file=article&sid=15

_____ , Jackson, Raymond M., "Letter to Billy Paul Branham, June 25, 1990, " accessed June 3, 2010. http://www.wmb1.com/portico/modules.php?name=News&file=article&sid=66

_____ , William Branham Legacy, accessed January 12, 2006. http://wmb1.com/de/~diego/images/t/ori/wb_family/Photographs_wb_family_01.shtml

Yacker, Heidi G. Daylight Saving Time; Congressional Research Service Library Of Congress, Number: 98-99 C. accessed 26 April 26, 2010. http://www.webexhibits.org/daylightsaving/congressionalResearchService.html;

Yesterdays of Hamilton County, IL, accessed December 3, 2008. http://www.carolyar.com/Illinois/Family/ArthurHamilton.htm

Video Recordings

"Paul Cain and Todd Bentley Pt. 1, " Youtube video, 2:49 [n.d.], June 17, 2008,. Posted by Elmoziffle, http://www.youtube.com/watch?v=o25jTVb5Bj8

"Paul Cain and Todd Bentley Pt. 2, " Youtube video, 2:49 [n.d.], June 17, 2008. Posted by Elmoziffle, www.youtube.com/watch?v=oR6JraFDtLk

Magazines/Periodicals

Branham Smith, Rebekah, "Bread Upon The Waters," *Only Believe,* Vol. 5, No. 1, June 1992, Believers Int'l Inc. Tucson, AZ.

_____, "Free Indeed, Testimony of Rosella Griffith Martin," *Only Believe,* Vol. 6, No. 2, June 1993, Believers Int'l, Inc., Elizabethon, TN. 5-7.

_____, "Road to Sunset," *Only Believe,* Vol. 5, No. 1, June 1992, : Believers Int'l Inc., Tucson, AZ. 5-8.

_____, "Whose Book Is It?" *Only Believe,* Vol. 4, issue 11, June 1991, Believers Int'l Inc. Tucson, AZ: Believers Int'l Inc.

Cain, Paul, "Equipping the Saints," *Vineyard Ministries Int'l,* Anaheim, Vol. 4, No.4/Fall 1990.

Cloud, David, "Pastor Alfred Pohl Interview," *'O TIMOTHY'* magazine. Feb. 21, 1990.

Davies, Dave, "The Cloud," pull-out section in Arizona Republic newspaper, March 26, 1967.

Francis, Gwilam I. "Vindication of William Branham of Attack by 'Prophecy Magazine,'" *Voice Of Healing,* Nov. 1954. 6.

Leggett, Dick, "Interview with Ern Baxter," *New Wine Magazine,* December 1978. 5-7; 22-24.

LIFE Magazine, May 17, 1963, Time Inc., p. 112 Printed with permission.

Lindsay, Gordon, *Voice Of Healing,* April-May, 1951.

_____, "Sketches from the Ministry of William Branham," *Voice of Healing.* February 1966, Vol. XVIII, No. 11, Gordon Lindsay, editor, Dallas, TX: Voice of Healing Publishing.

_____, "Story of the Great Restoration Revival," No. IV. *World Wide Revival,* June 1958

Smith, Alma Edwards. "The Miracle of Donny Morton," *Reader's Digest,* Vol. 61, Nov. 1952.

Vancouver Sun, Thursday, A 4, *"Scientists Create Mice without male's sperm."* April 22, 2004.

Telephone Interviews

Deeks, Ken. D. Phil, D.A.S. phone interview with author March 14, 2008.

Freund. Kevin. Email message to author, February 24, 2011.

Logsdon, Nathaniel, phone interview with author, 15 December, 2010.

Middleton, Vern. Ph. D., interview with author, April 8, 2008.

Miller, Mark, phone interview with author, 12: 45 PM, Jun 13, 2012.

Purlee, Gary D., e-mail message to author, May 19, 2010.

Sekula, Greg, e-mail to author, December 15, 2010.

Wallender, William H., phone interview with author, April 15, 2010.

Death Certificate

Ella Branham, Death Certificate, Indiana State Board Of Health, Division of Vital Records, Medical Certificate of Death. Cause of death (Ella Branham): Cerebral Thrombosis, Arteriosclerosis, Diabetes Myelitis, etc. [Note: Ella, or Ella Rhea, (Ellie R) Harvey, WMB's mother was born June 24, 1887, according to Find A Grave and the 1900 USA Census Records. This means that WMB falsified his mother's death certificate. WMB recorded that his mother was born in 1891 and died on Oct. 30, 1930. – PMD].

INDEX

Numbers

7th grade 241
20th century prophet 256
26 Chevrolet 35, 44, 52
200 pounds 115
1926, Model T Ford 26, 44
1928 12, 20, 26, 40, 41, 80, 101, 116, 207, 208
1929 11, 26, 34, 35, 40, 45, 47, 53, 68, 80, 101, 102, 103, 347
1930 9, 26, 34, 47, 78, 84, 90, 101, 102, 104, 105, 109, 111, 201, 202, 324, 354
1932 v, 12, 26, 36, 69, 84, 90, 101, 102, 109, 201 204, 210, 320, 324
1933 11, 26, 35, 46, 54, 66, 68, 69, 76, 80, 81, 84, 90, 99, 100, 101, 102, 103, 104, 105, 109, 110, 111, 201, 202, 204, 206, 207, 208, 211, 318, 320, 324
1933 Ford 46, 54, 66, 76
1934 9, 12, 20, 26, 27, 46, 53, 66, 68, 69, 70, 100, 101, 102, 103, 113, 201
1937 flood 162
1945 27, 37, 113, 115, 116, 119, 122, 123, 124, 201, 202, 342, 352
1948 14, 27, 84, 88, 94, 146, 159, 208, 234, 271, 326, 327, 330
1951 16, 17, 19, 22, 27, 28, 35, 36, 47, 50, 80, 100, 109, 122, 147, 161, 182, 183, 185, 186, 188, 189, 192, 194, 195, 196, 238, 271, 308, 326, 327, 329, 330, 332, 334, 335, 336, 337, 339, 340, 341, 353
1954 17, 20, 27, 38, 52, 62, 73, 75, 83, 89, 90, 92, 100, 109, 110, 123, 159, 162, 166, 181, 182, 184, 189, 196, 205, 208, 212, 221, 224, 238, 240, 241, 244, 268, 269, 270, 282, 298, 300, 318, 326, 329, 331, 332, 333, 334, 335, 336, 337, 338, 340, 341, 353
1955 17, 20, 28, 33, 34, 35, 48, 71, 75, 76, 81, 82, 94, 100, 101, 107, 109, 148, 159, 160, 184, 197, 243, 245, 247, 248, 263, 272, 300, 307, 308, 326, 327, 328, 330, 332, 333, 334, 336, 337, 338, 339, 340, 349
1959 16, 17, 50, 52, 71, 72, 75, 76, 79, 82, 85, 90, 95, 101, 122, 163, 184, 187, 195, 219, 220, 247, 261, 263, 264, 270, 272, 284, 300, 324, 326, 327, 328, 329, 330, 332, 333, 334, 335, 336, 337, 338, 339, 340, 341
1960 17, 20, 28, 35, 36, 49, 51, 52, 54, 58, 60, 72, 74, 76, 77, 79, 80, 89, 90, 91, 94, 95, 101, 121, 124, 148, 149, 162, 182, 200, 207, 210, 218, 220, 221, 234, 239, 245, 248, 269, 308, 326, 327, 328, 329, 330, 331, 332, 333, 334, 335, 336, 337, 338, 339, 340, 349
1962 1, 16, 34, 35, 49, 51, 52, 53, 71, 72, 73, 74, 76, 78, 80, 90, 93, 101, 107, 108, 109, 110, 128, 132, 136, 138, 139, 181, 183, 200, 218, 219, 220, 221, 235, 239, 246, 247, 259, 260, 326, 327, 328, 329, 330, 331, 332, 333, 334, 335, 336, 337, 338, 339, 340, 341
1963, Feb. 28, 125, 127, 129, 132, 133, 134, 135, 136, 137, 139, 297
1963 March 4, 135
1965 xv, 8, 13, 17, 23, 28, 45, 73, 78, 80, 91, 100, 102, 106, 107,

108, 109, 111, 124, 127, 134, 135, 138, 139, 147, 149, 180, 181, 199, 209, 210, 212, 216, 221, 243, 248, 259, 264, 270, 273, 282, 290, 297, 317, 318, 326, 327, 328, 329, 331, 333, 334, 335, 336, 337, 338, 339, 340, 341, 345
1977   ix, 5, 139, 201, 204, 205, 206, 207, 209, 245, 301, 324, 344

A

Abimelech 151
Abyssinia 201, 202, 324
Acupuncture 145
Adam, the spirit man 234
Adultery 44, 73, 89, 153, 223, 279, 280, 286, 287, 289, 290, 297, 304
Africa 13, 22, 77, 84, 109, 147, 149, 184, 189, 191, 196, 197, 198, 202, 238, 327, 330, 344
Albania 202
Alcoholism 43
Alexander, Patrick H., 22, 342
Allen, A.A. 16
Allen Circuit Court 31, 34
Allison, Ronald 200
Altar calls 62, 75
American Pentecostalism 13
American Pope 209
Anderson, Robert M. 22
Androgynous 252
Anesthesia 61
Anesthetic 45, 58, 61, 62, 63, 64
Angelic commission 10, 12, 27, 37, 68, 84, 85, 96, 100, 101, 102, 113, 115, 118, 119, 121, 173, 320
Angel of God 88, 116, 122, 149, 156, 158, 161, 163, 165, 166, 176, 178, 236, 268, 271, 272, 321
Angel of the Lord 16, 89, 90, 92, 94, 100, 104, 111, 113, 120, 121, 163, 271
Angel spirit 234, 245
Apostolic Friends Forum 20

Apostolic practice 62
Apostolic tradition 144, 177
Appendectomy 61
Appendicitis 45, 61, 64
Arianism 228
Arius 229, 230
Arizona Game and Fish Department 135, 137, 139
Arizona Republic 129, 138, 353
Aronowitz, Al 150
Arteriosclerosis 38, 191, 354
Assemblies of God 21, 82
Astigmatism 61, 67, 77
Astrologist 40, 47
Astronomer 40, 60, 74
Atomic bombs 205, 324
Auditory 10
Augustine 228
Augsburger, Myron 264
Automatic writing 10
Avatar 158, 252, 261, 323
Azusa Street Revival 34, 208

B

Baptism 27, 68, 97, 98, 106, 112, 199, 201, 218, 238, 242, 314, 315, 327, 340
Baptismal service 27, 69, 98, 99, 102, 105, 110
Baptism of the Holy Ghost/Spirit 97, 98, 106, 238, 315
Baptized in the name of Jesus Christ 80, 107, 317
Barefoot 115
Barlow knife 143
Basham, Don 16
Bastard child 289
Bathtub gin 10, 19
Batten, Louis 134
Baxter, Ern 12, 13, 16, 21, 22, 27, 38, 176, 188, 190, 347, 353
Beachy, Alvin J. 264, 344
Bearcat, Stutz 10
Beatles, the 145, 146
Beard 69, 81, 98, 108, 112, 115, 123, 134, 171, 239

INDEX 357

Begay, David H, 181
Bell, E.N. 21
Bentley, Todd 8, 14
Benton Harbor 69, 70, 81, 112
Birth date 25, 31, 32, 34, 39, 40, 45, 69, 87, 101, 102, 319
Birth record 17, 39, 40
Black church 66, 320
Blazing whirling star 99
Blindness 61, 146, 179
Blocher, Henri 283
Bloch-Hoell, Nils 21
Bloody ulcer 78
Boarding house 44, 45, 320
Bobbed hair 19
Bootleg gin 20
Borgmann, Lisbeth 25, 34
Bosworth, F.F. 12, 16
Bowen, Dan 22
Boxing ring 45
Boy Scouts 52, 116, 117
Bracelet 141, 142, 143
Brainon, Charley 25
Branam 9, 17, 40, 41
Branham, Billy Paul 10, 26, 36, 37, 128, 129, 163, 174, 175, 183, 193, 322, 352
Branham, Charles 9, 24, 25, 33, 37, 41, 56, 345, 346
Branham, Charles C. 25, 33, 348
Branham, Charles R. 25, 48
Branham, Dolores R. 26
Branham, Edgar Lee 25
Branham, Edward M. 26, 35, 40
Branham, Ella (Ellie) Harvey 28
Branham, Ella Harvey 56, 349
Branham, Henry Levi 25
Branham, Howard E. 25
Branham, James Donald (Donnie) 26
Branham, Jessie F. (Jesse) 25
Branham, Joseph 28, 37
Branham, Meda Broy 5
Branham, Melvin F. 25
Branham, Rebekah 5, 14, 27, 37, 38, 88, 125, 126, 129, 131, 138, 235, 245, 246
Branham, Sarah 27, 38

Branham, Sharon Rose 27
Branham, Valerie 5
Branham, William 8
Branham, Winferd 25, 26, 34, 40, 47
Branhan, Charles 24, 25
Branhan, Winferd 25, 34, 40
Branham Campaigns Prayer Card 175
Branhamism 5
Branham Tabernacle ix, 26, 68, 69, 85, 102, 103, 110, 128, 136, 346
Breeding, KY 56
British-Israelism 69, 213, 232
Brown, Harold O. 309, 317
Brown bear 209
Broy, Emma Hooper 25
Broy, Frank William 24
Broy, Meda M. 27, 25, 35, 37, 346
Broy, Roger 114
Brumbach, (Amelia) Hope 25, 36, 66, 320, 346
Brumbach, Charles Alton, 33
Brumbach, Charlie 45, 66
Brumback, Hazel Elizabeth Scott 25
Brumback,Charles A. (Alton) 25
Buckingham Palace 192, 197, 198, 200, 322, 347
Bucking horse 44
Bullet 9, 17
Burgess, Stanley M. 22
Burkesville 39, 40, 41, 47, 56, 57, 72, 86, 93, 347, 351
Business Journals 48, 347, 348
Byskal, Ed 2, 3, 4

C

Cabin 39, 40, 46, 47, 85, 86, 106, 115, 116, 117, 118, 122, 173, 320
Cablegram 199
Cadle Tabernacle 11
Cain, Paul 8, 10, 14, 16, 19
Cain the son of Satan 289, 292, 299
California 134, 200, 209, 212, 352
Calvin, John 227, 228, 229, 240, 250, 259, 342
Camera 69, 81, 109, 120, 134
Candy 39, 41, 49, 319

Caner, Ergun 249
Capernaum 209
Car crash 28, 64
Carson, D.A. 283
Cassuto, U. 283
Cave 115, 116, 117, 118, 121, 122, 320
Cayce, Edgar 209
Cerebral Thrombosis 38, 354
Cerinthianism 253
Cerullo, Morris 16
Charismata 153, 164
Charleston 10
Charlestown 116, 122, 123
Chastain, Warren 225, 239
Cherokee 9, 10, 42, 167, 319
Chimpanzee 288
Christ For The Nations 8
Christian fringe 69
Christian Science 118, 144, 149, 187, 195, 230, 232, 322
Civic auditorium 120
Clark County Memorial Hospital 59, 73, 107
Cloud, David 199
Cloud of Mystery (1929) 5, 28, 87, 93, 125, 126, 127, 128, 129, 131, 133, 134, 136, 137, 138, 139, 244, 271, 297, 342
Cloverdale Bible Way 2, 3, 23, 33, 134
Cold Reading 170
Colors of the rainbow 233, 242
Coming of the Lord 106, 108, 205
Constellation of seven angels 28, 125, 129, 132 135, 137
Conversion disorder 146
Copeland, Kenneth 21
Corn cracker 9
Corn dances 10, 18, 167
Cornerstone 66, 67, 77, 78, 80, 81, 103, 109, 111
Creation of man v, 273, 280, 281
Creeds 27, 225, 228, 232
Crisp, Oliver D. 265
Cross of light 63, 64
Crown chakra 120

D

Daugherty, Rev. Robert 119, 123
Davies, Dave 127, 138
Davis, John J. 276, 283
Davis, Roy E. 12, 26, 67, 68, 80
DeArk, George 67, 77
Deckard, Barbara Sinclair 20
deCorado, Sarah Branham 38
Dedication service 103
Deism 217
Deity doctrine 4
Demiurge 232, 241, 323
Denomination 111, 161, 211, 221, 243, 287, 340
Destruction of California 209
Destruction of the USA 205
Detonated rocket 125
Devil-dancers 18
Diabetes myelitis 38, 354
Different species 235, 289, 323
Distillery, R. E. Wathen 41, 48
Divine being 232
Divine healing 47, 67, 77, 80, 92, 140, 147, 153, 155, 156, 159, 164, 173, 180, 196, 198, 199, 219, 282, 308, 329, 333, 336, 344
Divine spark 237, 249, 311, 323
Docetism 232, 253, 255, 263, 323
Double portion 27, 90, 113, 114, 121, 147, 156
Dowie, John Alexander 13, 21
Drunkenness 9
Dublin, Ireland 56, 71
duPlessis, David 16
Durrant, Michael 240
Dyck, Carl 13, 22, 199
Dyck, Cornelius J. 264, 344
Dying, 62, 96

E

Easter 28, 189, 216, 307, 329
Eastern mysticism 98, 124, 232, 233, 237
Eastern religions 120, 322
Edward Branham's funeral 26, 60

INDEX

Egg and sperm 250
Egg-shaped car 204
Eighty cents 103, 111
Eisegesis 275, 291, 306
Electric chair 136
El Shaddai 261, 278, 279, 285
Entertaining angels unawares 118
Epicurus 255
Erickson, Clifton 16
Erratic ideas 10
Eskimos 163
Ethiopia 201, 202, 324, 348
Euphoria 145, 179
Evangelist ii, 8, 11, 14, 21, 36, 325
Eve xv, 5, 14, 28, 142, 152, 214, 216, 237, 255, 275, 276, 277, 278, 280, 283, 286, 288, 289, 290, 291, 292, 293, 294, 295, 296, 297, 298, 299, 300, 302, 304, 305, 323
Eve was a by-product 276
Exhorter 20, 36, 67, 224, 320
Extra-terrestrials 231

F

Faith healing 140, 160
Faith in faith 140
Faith is the sixth sense 141, 147, 148, 149
False teacher 146, 191
FBI 120, 124
Feast of tabernacles 9
Feinberg, Paul D. 265
Fertility religions 279
Find A Grave 25, 33, 38, 348, 354
Finger 225
First Baptist church 62
First Pentecostal Baptist Church 12, 26, 68
First revival 110
fFve death certificates 193
Five hundred 54, 89, 90, 110, 111, 183
Flagstaff 111, 126, 129, 130, 133, 134, 136, 199, 329
Flapper 10, 11, 20
Fletcher, Morris 73

Flood 62
Flynn, Errol 11
Ford 20
Fortune teller 3, 24, 25, 32, 33, 40, 128, 168, 169, 319
Francis, Rev. Gwilam 188
Freeman, William 16, 185
Freemasonry 213, 232, 233, 244, 252, 299, 322, 348
Freund, Kevin 35, 36
Frick, Billy 53
Fuller Seminary 9
Full Gospel Businessmen 16
Full Gospel Men's Voice 7, 14, 23
Fullness 232, 241
Funeral 26, 45, 60, 65, 96, 101, 280, 320

G

Gambling 18, 44
Game warden 46, 55, 62, 114, 136
Garage 64, 76, 97, 320
Gardner, Velmer 16
Gas poisoning 61
Gas rations 37, 119
Gas works 60
Gastritis 67, 78, 350
General Council of the Assemblies of God 21
General revelation 223, 224
George, Timothy 224, 238
George Rogers Clark Memorial Bridge 26
Gibbs, Gertie 114
Gift of discernment 157, 160, 168
Gift of healing 113, 156
Gift of prophecy 157
Gift of revelation 157
Gift of second sight 10
Gift of the Holy Spirit. 163
Gift of visions 157
Gill, John 283
Girlfriend 9
Glory of the Lord 96
Gnostic 98, 232, 237, 240-241, 244, 249, 251, 255, 256, 259, 274, 310, 323

Gnostic heresy 251
God, Immutability (unchangeableness) 216
God is androgynous 237
God is hermaphroditic 252
God is indivisible 218
God is infinite 215
God is without potentiality 157, 217
god of nature 165
God is infinite 215
God, self-sufficiency 215
God was man, man was God 161, 221
Godman 8
Golden cross 57, 58, 59, 73, 96, 107, 319
Golden gloves 26, 53, 348
Graham, Billy 11, 22
Great Architect 233, 241, 348, 351
Great Balls of Fire 115
Great Fountain of Spirit 232, 233
Great golden cross 58, 59, 73, 96, 107
Great Healing Revival 56
Great Pyramid 213, 322
Great Spirit 241, 242
Greece 93, 202
Green, Perry 5, 13, 21, 36, 37, 45, 52, 53, 56, 61, 65, 66, 67, 72, 76, 84, 86, 89, 90, 92, 94, 96, 97, 99, 102, 107, 108, 110, 116, 117, 118, 121, 122, 129, 130, 131, 132, 134, 212, 220, 247, 334, 343
Green Briar Ridge 56, 72
Green's Mill 52, 90, 116, 117, 122
Guiley, Rosemary Ellen 124

H

Haas, Barbara Thatcher 34
Haavik, O.L. 21
Hades 61
Hagen, William 16
Hagin, Kenneth 16
Hall, Franklin 16, 213, 232
Halo 3, 5, 85, 116, 120, 121, 122, 124, 158, 196, 217, 244
Hamburger, Wayne 112
Hamilton, James Arthur 42, 43

Hand trembler 167
Hanson, Dale 16
Harrell, David Edwin 19, 21
Harrell, David Edwin Jr. 19, 21, 33
Harrell 19, 21, 22, 23, 33, 38, 46, 71, 343
Hartley, John E. 283
Harvey, Ella R. 9, 33, 345, 348
Harvey, Ellie R. 25, 33, 345
Harvey 9, 25, 28, 33, 56, 345, 348, 349, 354
Hatched Jesus 251
Haunted 116
Headshakes 61
Healing campaign 114, 119, 173
Healing entity 164
Healing ministry xi, 7, 78, 91, 164-5
Healing revival 12-13, 21, 28, 56, 119, 154
Healing was in the atonement 157
Heart attack 42, 43, 51
Heavenly light 98, 99, 102
Henry, Matthew 257, 265
Heresies 228, 229, 230, 254, 259
Hermeneutic v, 303, 306
Hermeticism 232
Heterodoxy 232
Hicks, Tommy 16
High altitude rocket 134, 139
Hillbilly 10
Hinduism 98, 244, 247, 261, 274, 352
Hinson, Ed 249
Hoffman's, 'Head of Christ,' 134
Hollenweger, Walter 23, 33, 168
Holy Ghost preachers 36
Holy-rollers 65, 82
Homosexuality 8
Hoover, Herbert 41, 48, 207, 351
Horse races 44, 45
Hospital v, 43, 46, 54, 58, 59, 61, 62, 66, 73, 75, 76, 89, 96, 98, 104, 106, 146, 191, 192, 193, 319, 320
Hot Reading 171
House of David 69, 81, 112, 350
Houston, Texas v, 21, 120, 84, 125, 135, 139, 196, 326

INDEX 361

Hoyt, William G. 139
Humbard, Rex 16
Humpy 25, 34, 40, 41, 49
Hungry Thirties 41
Hunting accident 54, 57-59, 64-65, 96
Hybrid 289
Hypnosis 145
Hysteria 9, 45, 145, 178
Hysterical blindness 61
Hysterical child 94, 146, 150

I

Idols 149, 177, 188, 247, 269
Immune system 145
In-breaking of God's reign 154
Incubator 239, 251, 252, 255, 259, 260, 263, 302
Indiana Electric Corporation 53
Indians 18, 163
In Jesus' name 113
Institute of Atmospheric Physics of Utah 134
Insull, Samuel 53
Interpretation 10
Intra-trinity dialogue 276
In-vitro-fertilization 255
Irish-Cherokee descent 9
Irish folklore 10, 232
IRS 28
Italy 202

J

Jackson, Marion T. 110
Jackson, Raymond M. 163
Jacobs, John 19
Jaggers, O.L. 16
Jamieson, Fausset and Brown 181
Javalina 125, 127, 138, 139
Jeffersonville City Directory 37
Jehovah's Witnesses 232, 253, 322
Jesus Christ was reincarnated 235
Jesus-Freak 2
Jesus Only 12, 26, 27, 37, 46, 70, 81, 97, 113, 119, 232
Jesus People 1
Jesus neither Jew nor Gentile 226, 251

Jewish Hospital 58, 73
John of God 187, 195, 349
Jones, James W. 19
Jones, Jim "Jonestown" 10
Jubilee 75, 205, 206

K

Keeney, William E. 264, 345
Kelley, Clarence M. 124
Kennah, John iii, x, 124, 129, 131, 138
Kentucky 9
Kentucky-corn cracker 12
Kentucky mountain magic 232
Kenyon, E. W. 232
Khalah 151
King George VI 190, 191, 192, 194, 322
Kings 200, 221
Kinsman redeemer 157, 251
Ku Klux Klan 232
Knothole 116, 122
Koolman, Jacobus ten Doornkaat 264
Kopp, LeRoy 185, 186
Kundalini 98, 107, 145, 187, 232, 347

L

Lacy, George J. 120
Lake, John G. 13, 21
Lakeland, Florida 8
Laodicean Church Age 80, 206, 211, 334
Las Alderaines 149
Latter Rain 16
Legs 57, 58, 73, 96, 179, 200, 245, 289, 290, 296, 319
Lenski, R.C.H. 284
Leupold, H.C. 283
Liar 146, 173, 248, 280
Life Magazine 126, 133, 134, 136
Light 12, 18, 19, 33, 60, 63-66, 83, 85, 86-87, 90, 92, 93, 96-102, 106, 109, 111, 113, 115-117, 120, 122, 124, 127, 173, 191, 214, 217, 229, 230, 232, 237, 248, 250, 263-265, 319-230, 323
Lincoln Heritage Council of the Boy Scouts of America 116

Lindsay, (James) Gordon 7, 12-16, 19, 21-22, 27, 37-38, 45, 60-62, 66-67, 73, 75, 77, 84-85, 88, 97-98, 102, 114-115, 124, 188-189, 193-194, 235, 288, 296, 350, 353
Lindsay, Mrs. Gordon (Freda) 8, 10, 19, 22, 288, 296
Lineman 46
Lippy, Charles H. 14, 22, 343
Little Renox (Rennick's) Creek 39, 40, 72
Logos 217, 232, 233, 241, 242, 243, 244, 263, 273, 281
Logsdon, Nathaniel 122
Lone Star Meeting House 56
Louisville 18, 41, 47-48, 58-59, 60-61, 68, 69, 73, 75, 80-82, 104, 106, 111, 112, 122-123, 148, 270, 329, 331, 333, 337, 339, 347
Louisville Herald 111
Lucifer 236, 248, 253, 254, 263, 278, 283, 284, 289, 310
Lucretius 255
LXX (Septuagint) 293
Lying iii, 44, 153, 193, 294

M

Madison 114
Magi 34, 40
Magic 10, 142, 143, 150, 152, 154, 217, 344, 346
Magician 169, 170, 173
Maginot Line 202, 203, 350
Making the lame walk 179
Mammon 10
Manifested Sons of God 9, 16
Man is eternal 217, 236
Man is God 157, 321
Manuscript 232, 235, 246
Mark of the beast 12
Marriage 1, 25, 28, 40, 69, 101, 252, 255, 277, 307, 319
Marriage certificate/license 25, 34, 40, 319
Married xiv, 1, 2, 9, 18, 25, 26, 27, 34, 36, 43, 46, 50, 54, 66, 67, 69, 70, 71, 77, 78, 79, 81, 100, 101, 103, 109, 111, 261, 319, 320
Martin, Rosella G. 175, 176, 183, 353
Maryboy, Nancy C. 181
Mary's womb 250, 253, 267, 323
Masonic temple 111
Mathews, Kenneth A. 283
Mayo clinic 67
McDonald, Dr. James 134
McElvaine, Robert S. 19
McGann, Dennis 2
McGee, Gary B. 22
McGhee, Fielding M., III 19
Meade, Marion 19
Meditation 98
Meisner, Chris 44, 51
Melton, Gordon J. 298
Mental breakdown 61, 88
Mental healing 118, 187
Mental illness 61, 178
Mental telepathy 141, 144, 147, 148, 149, 173, 182
Message believers xiii, 129, 130, 208
Message churches 208
Message in tongues 100
Meta-physics 10, 232
Methodist Church League 57
Michael 228, 240, 248, 253, 254, 263, 278, 284, 342
Middleton, John 154
Middleton, Vern 16
Military records 33, 345
Military Registration Card 24, 25
Millennium 205
Miller, Mark 75
Mill Town 114
Milltown Baptist Church 121
Mind-reader 148, 182
Mishawaka 12, 20, 26, 36, 46, 55, 68, 70, 80, 82, 83, 113, 124
Mishawaka, IN 26, 70, 83, 113
Misner, Chris 44, 52
Misogynous 280
Missionary Baptist Church 12, 20, 26, 56, 57, 68, 71, 72, 78, 83,

INDEX 363

224, 288, 320
Mnemonics 172, 175, 176
Modalism 224, 228, 230, 232, 253, 266, 322
Modalities of healing 164
Mohammed 119
Monarchianism 228
Money 36, 40-44, 46, 55, 81-82, 91, 103, 207, 218, 319- 320
Moonshine stills 41, 87
Moore, Jack 13, 16
Mormonism 5, 60, 232, 244, 252, 278, 285, 299, 322, 345
Morris chair 55
Morton, Donny 192, 194, 200, 322, 353
Mother nature 67, 71, 213
Multi-cultural society 118
Multiple sclerosis 191, 199-200
Mumford. Bob 16
Mussolini 201-203, 324
Mysteries of the seven seals 125-129, 132
Mystery Cloud (see Cloud)
Mystic light 127, 217

N

National Recovery Association 12
Nation Wide Ministers Convention 10
Native Indian lore 232
Nature 50, 67, 71, 213, 249, 322
Navajo diagnosticians 167
Nazi 203, 211
Neither Jew nor Gentile 252, 253, 260
Nervous breakdown 146
Nervous debility, 61
Neurosis 149
Neurotic disorder 150
New Age xi, 157, 237, 247, 352
New Albany 25, 34, 35, 36, 39, 41, 48, 60, 124
New Breed 8, 14
New Religious Movement 6
Newspaper 90, 99, 120, 138, 146, 190, 191, 270, 353
New Thought 10, 118, 232, 322
Nicaea Council 196, 225
Nicene Creed 266

Nickle, Thomas R. 38
Norman, Gene 125 - 130, 133
Nunn, David 16

O

Ockam's Razor 178
Ogilvie, Wilbur 185
O'Hara, George 45, 53
Ohio River v, 26, 68-69, 90, 98 - 106, 110, 201, 320
One-dimensional view of God 225
Oneness Pentecostal 12, 106, 112, 225, 226
Only Believe 14, 38, 88, 125, 127, 129, 135-136, 138, 183, 245, 353
Open season 135
Operation 14, 45, 58-62, 64-67, 73, 77, 104, 107, 145, 181
Opossum Kingdom Baptist Church 56
Ordained 7, 12, 20, 26, 36, 67, 71, 77, 78, 81, 83, 91, 97, 108, 224, 237, 245, 311
Order of the Latter Rain 9
Orgy 10
Orthodoxy 224, 233, 317, 342
Osborne, T.L. 8

P

Pagan 27
Pantheism 274
Pantheistic Monism 157
P. A. of J. C. 36
Paranormal 178
Paraplegics 187
Parham, Charles Fox 13, 21
Parker, Reginald 21
Parousia 205
Parsonage 111, 198
Part of God 157, 158, 161, 217, 218, 221, 233, 237, 321
Pathway to bliss 98
Paul the Apostle 64
Pelikan, Jaroslav 265
Pennsylvania Railroad 43, 51, 54
Pentecostal Assemblies of Jesus Christ 36, 82

Pentecostal Evangel 21
Pentecostalism (American) 22
Perfections (Attributes) of God 214
Petacci, Claretta 202
Petting parties 10
Phoenix, AZ, 191
Philips, Dirk 256, 257, 264, 344
Pigalle 190, 199
Pillar of fire 87, 90, 99, 100, 113, 116, 120, 122, 271
Placebo 145
platform 108, 147, 159, 165, 171, 173-174, 176-177, 181, 185, 194, 200, 246, 274, 312, 321
Pleroma 232, 237, 241, 323
pneumonia 27
poachers 136
Pohl, Alfred 199, 353
polytheism 217, 218
Poole, Jim 73
Pope Benedict XVI 209
Pope Francis I 209
Positive confession 67
Post-modern 230
Prayer cards 174
Praying for the sick 157
Predestination 187, 188, 221, 238, 243
Pre-existence of Christ 257
Preexistence of souls/spirits 233, 234, 253, 323, 327
Presumption 216
Price, Anna Jean Moore 235
Primordial awareness 224
Prince, Derek 16
Professional boxer 26, 35, 53
Prunicus 280
Psychic power 149, 170, 187, 195
Pychic readers 182
Psychics 120, 169, 209
Psychological problems 146
Psycho-somatic illness 145, 178
Public Service Company of Indiana 53, 60, 61, 96, 102, 351
Purlee, Dr. Gary D. 117
Purnell, Benjamin (King Ben) 69

Pyramid xi, 67, 79, 126, 130, 132, 134, 213, 297, 322

Q

Quantum physics 230

R

Radical Reformation 256
Rain 72, 97, 98, 100, 101, 107
Ranch 60, 320
Rapture 98, 106, 165, 205, 208, 209, 212, 245, 324, 337
Rare Nacreous Clouds 134
Raven 11
Reader's Digest 192, 200, 353
Re-baptized 70, 82
Reformers 227, 257, 276
Regina, Saskatchewan 168
Regular Grand Lodge of England 241, 351
Reincarnation 234, 247, 352
Reitman, Tim 19
Religious symbol 98
Rheumatic heart failure 26, 35, 47
Richey, Raymond T. 16
Ride this trail again 209
Roaring Twenties 10, 41
Roberts, Oral 11, 16, 21, 167, 185
Rodriguez, Ms. Maria 135, 137, 139
Roosevelt, Franklin D. 35, 36, 202, 211, 212, 348
Rosemary's Baby 2
Davis, Roy 20, 68, 77, 80
Russell, Bertrand 264
Ryan, John 54, 55, 69, 81, 112

S

Sabellianism 228
Sabino Canyon 132, 133, 135, 136, 139
Saint or Ain't 5
Saloon 65, 66, 70, 82, 97, 320
Salt Lake City 5
Salvation v, 223, 309, 310, 316, 317
Santa Monica 186
Sarah 27, 38, 78, 151, 159, 200,

INDEX 365

263, 304, 305, 341, 352
Satan xv, 53, 142-143, 146, 151-153,
   168-169 173, 176, 182, 188,
   199, 236, 250, 253, 263, 275,
   277-278, 283, 284, 289,
   292, 294, 296, 297, 299, 300,
   301, 304, 310, 321, 323, 328
School of the Prophets 69, 81, 104, 112
Scientific Christianity 10
Scofield Reference Bible 115, 122,
   285, 306
Scott, Ziba 43, 51
Scoutmaster 116, 117, 123
Scoutmaster's cabin 116
SDA 60, 233, 241
Sekula, Greg 122
Selassie, Haile 201
Semi-godhood 275
Serpent's Seed 1, v, xv, xvi, 10, 14, 27,
   110, 211, 237, 277, 278, 280,
   287, 288, 290, 292, 293, 295,
   296, 298, 299, 300, 323, 338
Seven angels iii, 125, 128, 129, 131
   , 132, 133, 242, 297, 307
Seven Church Ages xv, xvi, 28, 69,
   86, 92, 106, 139, 234, 235,
   245-247, 260, 327-338, 341, 342
Seven end-time visions 26
Seven rainbow colors 242
Seven spirits 233, 242
Seven Tests of Truth 258
Seventh Angel 133
Seventh Day Adventism 232, 254, 322
Seventh Messenger 69
Seven year cycles 61
Shamanism 232
Shankaracharya 98
Shannahan, J. N. 53
Sharks down-town Los Angeles 210
Shed 63, 76, 79
Shekarian, Demas 16
Shepherding Movement 9
Shirlaw, Florence Nightingale
   188, 189, 190, 194, 322
Siegfried Line 202
Sikhs 98, 108

Simons, Menno 256, 257, 264, 345
Simpson, Charles 16
Six foot tall 115, 197
Six Second Smith 45, 53
Sixth sense 141, 143, 144, 147-149, 268,
   272, 303, 306-307, 321, 324, 330
Skinner, John 276, 283
Smith, Alfred E. 207, 212, 348
Smith, George 53
Smith, Joseph Fielding 161, 284, 344
Smith, Joseph 60, 74, 119, 161, 278,
   284, 285, 299, 319, 344, 349
Smith, Joseph Jr 161, 284, 285
Smith, Rebekah Branham 5, 14,
   27, 37, 38, 88, 125, 131,
   138, 235, 245, 246
Smith-Wigglesworth 13
Snake dances 167
Soininen, Pastor Vilho 192, 193
Sonic boom 127
Sophia 280
Sothmann, Fred 126, 127, 129, 130
Sound barrier 127, 128
Southern Baptist Church 56, 71
Sovereignty of God 216
Sowders, William 69, 104-106
Space age 230, 232
Spain 202
Speaking in tongues 10
Special revelation 223-224
Spinal anesthetic 62
Spirit of a worldly nature 234
Spirit of Beethoven 236
Spirit of Fidel Castro 236
Spirit of John Dillinger 236
Spirit of love 242
Spirit of righteousness 242
Spirit of Shakespeare 236
Spoken Word Publications viii, 17, 20,
   27, 37, 121, 138, 260, 341
Spontaneous remission 145
Spring Street 69, 78, 80, 90,
   99, 101, 110, 111
Stadsklev, Julius 13, 22, 39, 45-46,
   48, 53, 61, 65-67, 76-77,
   84-89, 92, 94, 96-99, 102,
   107-108 115, 121, 189, 344

Staging 173
Stargazer 40, 47
Stealing 44
Steinbeck, John 20
Stevens, John Robert 16
St. Louis 119, 123, 124
Stolee, H.J. 21
Stomach ulcers 191
Strychnine 43, 51
Sunset Peak 127, 129, 130, 349
Super Seed 9
Superstitious 10, 18
Swami 118
Sweet, Richard 21
Sword 134, 307
Systematic theology xi, 213

T

Tabernacle viii, ix, 11, 26, 37, 55, 67, 68, 69, 80, 85, 102-104, 109-111, 123, 128, 129, 131, 132, 134, 136, 220, 246, 247, 303, 346
Technology 204, 232
Ten Commandments 57
Tent ministry 103
The Deseret News Press 161, 284
The Devil 152
The Fable 5
The greatest prophet in the 20th century 8, 119
Theophany 233, 234
Theosophy 118, 232
The "shakes," 146
The Trail of the Serpent 209
The Voice of Healing 14, 185, 186
Third Wave 9, 10, 16
Three Bibles 67, 79
Three-dimensional view of God 225
Three-foot rule 224
Three "isms' Communism, Fascism and Nazism 203
Three step process 97, 311, 323
Three thousand congregation 110
Three unclean spirits like frogs 165, 188, 222

Through a glass darkly 226
Thys saith the Lord
    108, 136, 186, 190, 205
Tongues 10, 18, 63-64, 68-69, 70, 79, 80, 82-83, 100, 108, 109, 159, 181, 311- 313, 316, 320
Transmigration 234, 235
Trapping cabin 116
Trauma 145
Trinitarian 57, 68, 70, 104, 221, 224, 227, 231, 238, 240, 267
Trinity ii, ix, xii, 27, 104, 188, 217, 222, 224-232, 238, 240, 266, 273, 276, 282, 322, 342
Trinity of frogs 222, 225
Trinity of offices 224
Trinity of spirits 225
Tri-theism 218
Trouser leg 136
Tucson Tabernacle
    viii, 129, 131, 132, 134, 247
Tunnel Mill 116, 123
Turban 98, 108, 118
Turtledove 198
Two-dimensional view 224, 225
Two gifts 12
Two hundred pounds in weight 117
Typology 303, 304, 305, 306

U

UN 27, 89
United States Federal Census 24-25, 33, 345
University of Northern Arizona 139
Unscrupulous men 10
UPCI 36
Urban, Linwood 258, 265

V

Valdez, A.C. Jr. 16
Vandenberg AFB, CA 134, 139
Vatican 93, 203, 212, 239, 324
Vayle, Lee 9, 13, 17, 26, 40, 45, 47, 61, 86, 88, 95-97, 102-103, 111

INDEX

123, 234, 235, 246, 251, 253, 327
Vineyard Church 9
Virgin birth 250, 262, 343
Virgin Mary 250, 252, 253
Vision 25, 34, 36, 37, 57-59, 61, 65-66, 73, 77, 79, 81, 85, 89, 91, 96, 98, 107-109, 111, 117, 123, 128, 129, 132-136, 139, 141, 162, 186, 187, 193-195, 202 206, 207, 209, 210, 324
Visionary delusions 10
Voice of God Recordings (VOGR) 8, 27, 37
Volkswagen 204

W

Wagner, C. Peter 9, 16
Walker, David 16
Wallender, William H. 81, 112
Warnock, George 16
Watch Russia 203
Wathen, O. H. 41, 48
WCC 208
WEATHERWISE 134
Weaver, C. Douglas 20
West Coast 209, 212
Wheelchair 149, 187, 195
White garment 98, 108
White robe 108, 115, 118
White wig 134
William Branham Evangelistic Association 37
Wimber, John 9
Winnipeg 26, 190, 199
Wiseman, Prod 114
Wise men 138, 166, 167
Witch 18, 149, 168, 173, 181
Woman ruling the USA 206
Word-Faith Movement 9
Work house 116, 349
Writing, automatic (see Automaic)
WWII ii, 27, 87, 119, 190, 124, 201, 352

Y

Yellow paper 209
Yoga 98, 187

Yogi 98
Yugoslavia 202

Z

Zeitz, Joshua 19
Zodiac 10, 67, 79, 213, 224, 322

LEGEND OF THE FALL
An Evaluation of William Branham and His Message

LEGEND OF THE FALL was originally made available in 2011 as an e-book on my website **WMBranham.net**. It was offered as a free-read and had an option to purchase the notes and bibliography. Now that it is out in a print edition the free option will no longer be available.

As mentioned in LEGEND OF THE FALL, there are a number of websites dedicated to the research of Branham's messages, among them are the following recommended sites:

Believe The Sign
http://www.believethesign.com

Searching for Vindication
http://searchingforvindication.com

Seek Ye The Truth
http://www.seekyethetruth.com

Examining the Message of William Branham
forums.delphiforums.com/n/nav/start.asp?webtag=kennah

The views expressed in the recommended websites are solely those of the individuals providing them and do not necessarily reflect the opinions of the author of Legend of the Fall, or of **WMBranham.net**, or of Canada Apologetics Research Team (CART).

Around the globe many new factions of Wm Branham followers are springing up and this will necessitate constant updating and revision of data. This new information will be available through periodic publications that will some day be rolled into a second edition of LEGEND OF THE FALL. We would, therefore, respectfully, ask our readers to send us any information they deem necessary to be included in the next edition.

WMBranham.net

www.ingramcontent.com/pod-product-compliance
Lightning Source LLC
Chambersburg PA
CBHW030300080526
44584CB00012B/384